A HISTORY OF
THE CRUSADES

VOLUME I (1951)

THE FIRST CRUSADE
AND THE FOUNDATION OF THE
KINGDOM OF JERUSALEM

VOLUME II (1952)

THE KINGDOM OF JERUSALEM
AND THE FRANKISH EAST
1100–1187

THE MINNESINGER FREDERICK OF HAUSEN SETS OUT
FOR THE THIRD CRUSADE

A HISTORY OF
THE CRUSADES

VOLUME III
THE KINGDOM OF ACRE
and the Later Crusades

BY

STEVEN RUNCIMAN

CAMBRIDGE
AT THE UNIVERSITY PRESS
1966

PUBLISHED BY

THE SYNDICS OF THE CAMBRIDGE UNIVERSITY PRESS

Bentley House, 200 Euston Road, London, N.W.1
American Branch, 32 East 57th Street, New York, N.Y. 10022

First Edition 1954
Reprinted with corrections 1955
Reprinted 1966

First Printed in Great Britain at the University Press, Cambridge
Reprinted in Great Britain, by lithography, by Butler & Tanner Ltd, Frome and London

To
KATHARINE FARRER

CONTENTS

Contents

LIST OF PLATES

List of Plates and Maps

LIST OF MAPS

PREFACE

This volume is intended to cover the history of Outremer and the Holy Wars from the revival of the Frankish kingdom at the time of the Third Crusade till its collapse a century later, with an epilogue on the last manifestations of the Crusading spirit. It is a story with several interwoven themes. The decline of Outremer, with its petty but complex tragedies, was periodically interrupted by great Crusades, all of which, after the Third, closed in diversion or disaster. In Europe, though it was still usual for every potentate to pay lip-service to the Crusading movement, not even the fervent piety of Saint Louis could arrest its decline, while the growing enmity between Eastern and Western Christendom reached its climax in the greatest tragedy of the Middle Ages, the destruction of Byzantine civilization in the name of Christ. In the Moslem world the constant stimulus of the Holy War resulted in the replacement of the kindly and cultured Ayubites by the more efficient and less sympathetic Mameluks, whose Sultans were to eliminate Frankish Syria. Finally, there was the arbitrary irruption of the Mongols, whose coming seemed at first likely to rescue Eastern Christendom but whose influence in the end, through the mishandling and misunderstanding of their potential allies, was only destructive in its effects. The whole tale is one of faith and folly, courage and greed, hope and disillusion.

I have included short chapters on the commerce and the arts of Outremer. The treatment is necessarily perfunctory; for neither the commercial nor the artistic history of a colonial state such as Outremer can be detached from the general history of medieval trade and civilization. I have therefore tried to confine myself within limits that are strictly relevant to the understanding of Outremer.

The history of the Crusades is a large subject with undefined frontiers; and the treatment that I have given to it represents my own personal choice. If readers consider that the emphasis that I have given to its various aspects is wrong, I can only plead that an author must write his book in his own way. It is beside the point for critics to complain that he has not written the book that they would have written had they undertaken the theme. But I hope that I have not entirely omitted anything that is essential to its comprehension.

The large debts that I owe to many scholars, dead and living, are, I think, apparent in my footnotes. Sir George Hill's great history of Cyprus and Professor Atiya's meticulous history of the Later Crusades are both essential for the study of the period; and students must be permanently grateful to Professor Claude Cahen for the learned information contained in his works. I must mention with regret the death of M. Grousset, whose broad vision and lively writing did much to elucidate the politics of Outremer and the Asiatic background. I have again been largely dependent on the work of American scholars, such as the late Professor La Monte, and Mr P. A. Throop.

Once again I must thank my friends in the Near East, who have helped me during my travels there, in particular the Iraq Petroleum Company; and the Syndics of the Cambridge University Press for their kindness.

STEVEN RUNCIMAN

LONDON 1954

BOOK I

THE THIRD CRUSADE

CHAPTER I

THE CONSCIENCE OF
THE WEST

*'The kings of the earth, and all the inhabitants of the world, would
not have believed that the adversary and the enemy should have
entered into the gates of Jerusalem.'* LAMENTATIONS IV, 12

Bad news travels fast. The battle of Hattin had hardly been fought
and lost before messengers hurried westward to inform the princes
of Europe; and they were soon followed by others telling of the
fall of Jerusalem. Western Christendom learned of the disasters
with consternation. In spite of all the appeals that had come from
the kingdom of Jerusalem in recent years, no one in the West,
except perhaps at the Papal Court, had realized the urgency of the
danger. The knights and pilgrims that had journeyed eastward had
found in the Frankish states a life more luxurious and gay than any
that they had known at home. They heard tales of military prowess;
they saw commerce flourishing. They could not comprehend how
precarious was all this prosperity. Now, suddenly, they heard that
it was all ended. The Christian army had been destroyed; the Holy
Cross, most sacred of the relics of Christendom, was in the hands
of the infidel; and Jerusalem itself was taken. In the space of a few
months the whole edifice of the Frankish East had collapsed; and
if anything was to be rescued from the ruins, help must be sent,
and sent quickly.

The refugees who had survived the disaster were crowded
together behind the walls of Tyre, their courage maintained by
the ruthless energy of Conrad of Montferrat. The lucky chance of
his arrival had saved the city from surrendering; and one by one
the lords that had escaped from Saladin's clutches joined him there,
gratefully accepting his leadership. But they all knew that without

assistance from the West their chances of holding Tyre were small and their chances of recovering lost land were none. In the lull that followed Saladin's first attack on Tyre, when he passed on to conquer Northern Syria, they had sent the most revered of their colleagues, Josias, Archbishop of the city, to tell the Pope and the kings of the West in person how desperate was their need. About the same time the survivors amongst the Military Orders wrote round to impress upon their western brothers the same anxious story.[1]

The Archbishop set sail from Tyre in the late summer of 1187 and arrived after a swift voyage at the court of King William II of Sicily. He found the King deeply distressed by rumours of the disaster. When he learned of its full extent William dressed himself in sackcloth and went into a retreat for four days. Then he wrote to his fellow-monarchs to urge them to join a Crusade and himself prepared to send as soon as possible an expedition to the East. He had a war with Byzantium on his hands. In 1185 his troops had attempted to capture Thessalonica and had been heavily defeated; but his fleet was still cruising in Cypriot waters, giving help to the usurper lord of Cyprus, Isaac Comnenus, in his revolt against the Emperor Isaac Angelus. Peace was hastily made with the Emperor; and the Sicilian admiral, Margaritus of Brindisi, was summoned home to refit his ships and sail with three hundred knights to Tripoli. Meanwhile Archbishop Josias, escorted by a Sicilian embassy, made his way to Rome.[2]

There, too, the gravity of his news was understood; for the Genoese had already sent a report to the Papal Court.[3] The old Pope, Urban III, was a sick man, and the shock was too much for him. He died of grief on 20 October.[4] But his successor, Gregory VIII, at once sent out a circular letter to all the faithful of the West

---

[1] Ernoul, pp. 247-8, for Josias's journey. The Templar Terence's report to his brethren is given in Benedict of Peterborough, II, pp. 13-14, the Hospitallers in Ansbert, *Expeditio Friderici*, pp. 2-4. Terence also wrote to Henry II; Benedict of Peterborough, II, pp. 40-1. [2] Ernoul, *loc. cit.*

[3] Benedict of Peterborough, II, pp. 11-13.

[4] *Annales Romani* in Watterich, *Pontificum Romanorum Vitae*, II, pp. 682-3.

He told the serious story of the loss of the Holy Land and of the Holy Cross. He reminded his readers that the loss of Edessa forty years before should have been a warning. Great exertions were needed now. Let everyone repent from his sins and lay up treasure in heaven by taking the Cross. He promised a plenary indulgence to all Crusaders. They should enjoy eternal life in heaven, and in the meantime their goods on earth would be under the protection of the Holy See. He finished his letter by ordaining a fast on every Friday for five years to come and abstinence from meat on Wednesdays and Saturdays. His own kinsfolk and those of his Cardinals would fast on Mondays also. Other messages sent from Rome enjoined a truce for seven years on all the princes of Christendom; and it was reported that the Cardinals had all sworn to be among the first to take the Cross. As mendicant preachers they would lead the Christian armies to Palestine.[1]

Pope Gregory did not see the result of his efforts. He died at Pisa on 17 December, after a pontificate of two months, leaving the work to the Bishop of Praeneste, who was elected two days later as Clement III. While Clement hastened to make contact with the greatest potentate of the West, the Emperor Frederick Barbarossa, the Archbishop of Tyre moved on over the Alps to see the Kings of France and England.[2]

The news of his mission had gone before him. The aged Patriarch of Antioch, Aimery, wrote a letter in September to King Henry II to tell him of the tribulations of the East, and sent it by the hand of the Bishop of Banyas;[3] and, before Josias of Tyre arrived in France, Henry's eldest surviving son, Richard, Count of Poitou, had taken the Cross.[4] Henry himself had for many years been carrying on a desultory war with Philip Augustus of France. In

[1] Benedict of Peterborough, II, pp. 15–19, giving the text of the Pope's letters. The Provencal poet Giraut considered, however, that the Pope was insufficiently active (see Throop, *Criticism of the Crusades*, pp. 29–30).
[2] *Annales Romani* in Watterich, *op. cit.* II, p. 692.
[3] Benedict of Peterborough, II, pp. 36–8.
[4] Ambroise, *L'Estoire de la Guerre Sainte*, col. 3; *Itinerarium Regis Ricardi*, p. 32; Rigord, pp. 83–4. Politically the conference at Gisors was a failure.

January 1188, Josias found the two kings at Gisors, on the frontie
between Normandy and the French domain, where they had me
to discuss a truce. His eloquence persuaded them to make peac
and promise to go as soon as possible on the Crusade. Philip
Count of Flanders, ashamed, perhaps, of his abortive Crusade te
years before, hastened to follow their example; and many of the
high nobility of both kingdoms swore to accompany the Kings
It was decided that the armies should march together, the French
troops wearing red crosses, the English white and the Flemish
green. To pay for the expedition both Kings raised special taxes.
At the end of January King Henry's Council assembled at Le Man:
to order the payment of the Saladin Tithe, a ten per cent tax on
revenue and movables to be collected from every lay subject of
the King, in England and in France. Henry then crossed to England
to make further arrangements for the Crusade, which was preached
with fervour by Baldwin, Archbishop of Canterbury. The Archbishop of Tyre started back on his homeward journey full of hope.[2]

Soon after the conference at Gisors Henry wrote an answer to
the Patriarch of Antioch to say that help was coming quickly.[3]
His optimism was not justified. The Saladin Tithe was collected
satisfactorily in spite of the attempt of a Templar knight, Gilbert
of Hoxton, to help himself to the money that he had collected;
while William the Lion, King of the Scots, who was Henry's
vassal, was quite unable to persuade his thrifty barons to contribute
a single penny. Plans were made for the government of the country
while Henry and his heir should be in the East.[4] But, long before
the army could be assembled, war broke out again in France. Some
of Richard's vassals rebelled against him in Poitou, and in June 1188,
he was involved in a quarrel with the Count of Toulouse. The
French King, angry at this attack on his vassal, answered by in-
vading Berry. Henry in his turn invaded Philip's territory; and
war dragged on through the summer and autumn. In January 1189,

[1] Benedict of Peterborough, II, p. 30; Ambroise, cols. 3–4; *Itinerarium*,
pp. 32–3.   [2] Benedict of Peterborough, II, pp. 30–2.
[3] *Ibid*. pp. 38–9.   [4] *Ibid*. pp. 44, 47–8.

Richard, whose filial loyalty was inconstant, joined with Philip in an offensive against Henry. The endless fighting horrified most good Christians. Among Philip's vassals, the Counts of Flanders and Blois refused to bear arms till the Crusade should be launched.[1] In the autumn of 1188 the Pope had sent the Bishop of Albano and, after the bishop's death next spring, Cardinal John of Anagni to order the Kings to make peace, in vain. Nor was Baldwin, Archbishop of Canterbury, more successful. Throughout the early summer Philip and Richard penetrated successfully into Henry's French possessions. On 3 July Philip took the great fortress of Tours; and next day Henry, who was now desperately ill, agreed to humiliating peace terms. Two days later, before they could be ratified, on 6 July he died at Chinon.[2]

The old King's disappearance eased the situation. It is doubtful whether he ever seriously saw himself leaving for the Crusade. But his heir, Richard, had every intention of fulfilling his vow; and, though he inevitably inherited his father's quarrel with King Philip, he was ready to make any settlement that would leave him free to go East, particularly if Philip would join in the Crusade. Philip for his part had less awe of Richard than of Henry, and saw that it was bad policy to postpone the Crusade much longer. A treaty was hastily made; and Richard passed on into England to be crowned and to take over the government.[3]

The coronation took place on 3 September at Westminster, and was followed by a lively persecution of the Jews in London and in York. The citizens were jealous of the favour shown them by the late King; and Crusading fervour always provided an excuse for killing God's enemies. Richard punished the rioters and permitted a Jew, who had turned Christian to avoid death, to return to his faith. The chroniclers were shocked to learn of Archbishop Baldwin's comment that if he would not be God's man he had

[1] *Ibid.* pp. 34–6, 39–40, 44–9; Rigord, pp. 90–3.
[2] Benedict of Peterborough, II, pp. 50–1, 59–61, 66–71; Rigord, pp. 94–7; Roger of Wendover, I, pp. 154–60.
[3] Benedict of Peterborough, II, pp. 74–5; Roger of Wendover, I, pp. 162–3.

better be the devil's. The King stayed on in England over th
autumn, reorganizing his administration. Empty episcopal see
were filled. After some preliminary rearrangement, William
Longchamp, Bishop of Ely, was made chancellor and justiciar fo
the south of England, while Hugh, Bishop of Durham, wa
justiciar for the north but also constable of Windsor. The Queen
mother Eleanor was given vice-regal powers; but she did not in
tend to remain in England. The King's brother John was enfeoffed
with huge estates in the south-west and a prudent ban on his entry
into England for three years was rashly withdrawn. Royal estate
were sold to raise money. The proceeds, together with gifts and
the Saladin Tithe, provided the King with a vast treasure; and
William of Scotland sent ten thousand pounds in return for hi
release from allegiance to the English crown and the restoration
of his towns of Berwick and Roxburgh, which he had lost i
Henry's reign.[1]

In November Rothrud, Count of Perche, arrived from France
to say that King Philip had almost completed his preparations fo
the Crusade and wished to meet Richard at Vézelay on 1 April
when they would discuss their joint departure.[2] A letter had
reached the French court at the end of 1188 from its agents a
Constantinople telling of a prophecy by the holy hermit Danie
that in the year when the Feast of the Annunciation fell on Easte
Sunday the Franks would recover the Holy Land. This conjunction would happen in 1190. The report added that Saladin wa
troubled by quarrels among his family and his allies, even though
the Emperor Isaac was impiously aiding him, and it mentioned
a rumour that Saladin himself had been severely defeated near
Antioch.[3] News reaching France next year was not quite so
optimistic, but it was learnt that, thanks to Sicilian help, the Frank
there were taking the offensive.[4] Moreover, the Western Emperor

---

[1] Benedict of Peterborough, II, pp. 80–8, 97–101; Roger of Wendover
I, pp. 164–7; Ambroise, cols. 6–7.
[2] Benedict of Peterborough, II, pp. 92–3.
[3] *Ibid.* II, pp. 51–3. [4] *Ibid.* II, p. 93.

'rederick Barbarossa, was already on his way to the East.[1] It was ime for the Kings of France and England to set out.

After taking the advice of his Council, King Richard agreed to he meeting at Vézelay. He was back in Normandy by Christmas nd prepared himself to set out for Palestine in the late spring. At he last moment everything had to be postponed, owing to the udden death of the Queen of France, Isabella of Hainault, early in March.[2] It was not till 4 July that the Kings met again at Vézelay, vith their knights and their infantry, ready to set out on their holy nterprise.[3]

It was three years now since the kingdom of Jerusalem had met vith disaster at Hattin; and it was well for the Franks in the East hat other Crusaders had not been so dilatory. The promptness f King William of Sicily's help saved Tyre and Tripoli for Christendom. William died on 18 November 1189; and his uccessor Tancred had troubles to face at home.[4] But already in eptember an armada of Danish and Flemish ships, estimated by he hopeful chroniclers to number five hundred, arrived off the yrian coast; and about the same time came James, lord of Avesnes, he bravest knight of Flanders.[5] Even the English had not all vaited for their King to move. A flotilla manned by Londoners eft the Thames in August and reached Portugal next month. There, like their compatriots some forty years before, they agreed o take temporary service under the Portuguese King; and thanks o their help, King Sancho was able to capture from Islam the ortress of Silves, east of Cape Saint Vincent. On Michaelmas Day the Londoners sailed on through the Straits of Gibraltar.[6]

---

[1] See below, p. 11.
[2] Benedict of Peterborough, II, p. 108; *Itinerarium*, p. 146; Rigord, pp. 97–8.
[3] Benedict of Peterborough, II, p. 111; *Itinerarium*, pp. 147–9; Ambroise, ols. 8–9; Rigord, pp. 98–9.
[4] See Chalandon, *Domination Normande en Italie*, II, pp. 416–18. William's leath is mentioned as a disaster in all the Anglo-Norman and French chronicles.
[5] Benedict of Peterborough, II, p. 94; *Itinerarium*, p. 65; Ambroise, cols. 77–8.
[6] Benedict of Peterborough, II, pp. 116–22; Ralph of Diceto, II, pp. 65–6; *Narratio Itineris Navalis ad Terram Sanctam, passim.*

But the most portentous force that had already started out for th
Holy Land was the army of the Emperor Frederick Barbarossa
Frederick had been deeply moved to hear of the disasters i
Palestine. Ever since he had returned with his uncle Conrad from
the ill-starred Second Crusade, he had longed to do battle agai
with the infidel. He was an old man now, nearly in his seventietl
year, and he had been ruler of Germany for thirty-five years. Ag
had not diminished his gallantry nor his charm, but many bitte
experiences had taught him prudence. He had not had man
personal connections with Palestine. Very few of the settlers ther
were of German origin; and his long controversy with the Papac
had made the Frankish government shy of asking for his help. Bu
the house of Montferrat had always been amongst his supporters
News of Conrad's gallant defence of Tyre may have stirred him
The recent marriage of his heir Henry with the Sicilian Princes
Constance had brought him into close touch with the Norman
of the South. The death of Pope Urban III in the autumn of 118
enabled him to make his peace with Rome. Gregory VIII eagerl
welcomed so valuable an ally for the rescue of Christendom, an
Clement III was equally friendly.[1]

Frederick took the Cross at Mainz on 27 March 1188, from th
hands of the Cardinal of Albano. It was the fourth Sunday i
Lent, known from the introit as *Laetare Hierusalem*.[2] But mor
than a year passed before he was ready to leave for the East. Th
regency over his domains was given to his son, the future Henry VI
His great rival in Germany, Henry the Lion of Saxony, wa
ordered either to cede his rights over part of his lands, or to ac
company the Crusade at his own expense, or to go into exile fo
three years, and chose the last alternative, retiring to the court o
his father-in-law, Henry II of England.[3] Thanks to Papal sympath

[1] The best general life of Frederick I is still Prutz, *Kaiser Friedrich I*. Hi
expedition to the East is fully recorded by Ansbert, *Expeditio Friderici*, and b
Historia Peregrinorum and *Epistola de Morte Friderici Imperatoris*. (All thes
published in Chroust, *Quellen zür Geschichts des Kreuzzüges Kaiser Friedrichs I*.

[2] Hefele-Leclercq, *Histoire des Conciles*, v, 2, pp. 1143–4.

[3] Benedict of Peterborough, II, pp. 55–6.

the German Church was pacified after a long series of quarrels.
The western frontier of Germany was strengthened by the creation
of a new Margravate.[1] While he collected together his army,
Frederick wrote to the potentates through whose lands he would
pass, the King of Hungary, the Emperor Isaac Angelus and the
Seldjuk Sultan Kilij Arslan; and he sent an ambassador, Henry of
Dietz, with a boastful letter to Saladin demanding the restoration
of all Palestine to the Christians and challenging him to battle on
the field of Zoan in November 1189.[2] The King of Hungary and
the Seldjuk Sultan replied with messages promising assistance.
A Byzantine embassy arrived at Nuremberg in the course of 1188
to arrange details for the Crusaders' passage through Isaac's
territory.[3] But Saladin's reply, though courteous, was haughty.
He offered to release his Frankish prisoners and to restore the Latin
abbeys in Palestine to their owners, but no more. Otherwise there
must be war.

Early in May 1189, Frederick set out from Ratisbon. He was
accompanied by his second son, Frederick of Swabia, and many of
his greatest vassals; and his army, the largest single force ever yet
to leave on a Crusade, was well armed and well disciplined.[4] King
Bela gave him a friendly welcome and every facility in his passage
through Hungary. On 23 June he crossed the Danube at Belgrade
and entered Byzantine territory.[5] There misunderstandings began.
The Emperor Isaac Angelus was not the man to deal with a situation that needed tact, patience and courage. He was a clever but
weak-willed courtier who had reached the throne by accident and
who was always conscious that he had many potential rivals in his

---

[1] Hefele-Leclercq, *op. cit.* p. 1144, with references.

[2] Ansbert, *Expeditio Friderici*, p. 16. A version of Frederick's letter to Saladin
is given by Benedict of Peterborough, II, pp. 62–3. It is almost certainly
spurious.

[3] Ansbert, *Expeditio Friderici*, p. 15; Hefele-Leclercq, *loc. cit.*

[4] Arnold of Lübeck estimated that a census was taken when the army
crossed the Save, and that there were 50,000 horsemen and 100,000 foot-soldiers
(pp. 130–1). The German chroniclers give the round figure of 100,000 for the
whole army.   [5] Ansbert, *Expeditio Friderici*, p. 26.

dominions. He was suspicious of all his officials but did not dare to control them strictly. Neither the armed forces of his empire nor its finances had recovered from the strain imposed by the vainglorious reign of Manuel Comnenus. The attempt of the Emperor Andronicus to reform the administration had not survived his fall. It was now more corrupt than ever before. High and unfair taxation was causing trouble in the Balkans. Cyprus was in revolt under Isaac Comnenus. Cilicia was lost to the Armenians. The Turks were encroaching on the Imperial provinces in central and south-western Anatolia; and the Normans had launched a great attack on Epirus and Macedonia. The defeat of the Normans was the only military triumph of Isaac Angelus' reign. For the rest he depended upon diplomacy. He made a close alliance with Saladin, to the horror of the Franks in the East. His motive was not to damage their interests but to curb the power of the Seldjuks; but his incidental achievement in having the Holy Places at Jerusalem returned to the care of the Orthodox was particularly shocking to the West. To improve his hold over the Balkans he made friends with King Bela of Hungary, whose young daughter Margaret he married in 1185. But the extraordinary taxation raised on the occasion of the marriage was the spark that set off the smouldering Serbs and Bulgarians into open rebellion. In spite of a few successes at first, his generals were unable to crush the rebels. When Frederick appeared at Belgrade there was an independent Serbian state already formed in the hills in the north-west of the peninsula; and though Byzantine forces still held the fortresses along the main road to Constantinople, Bulgarian marauders were masters of the country-side.[1]

Hardly had the German army crossed the Danube before there was trouble. Brigands, Serbian and Bulgarian, attacked stragglers and the country-folk were frightened and unfriendly. The Germans at once accused the Byzantines of instigating this hostility, refusing

[1] For Isaac Angelus see Cognasso, 'Un Imperatore Bizantino della Decadenza, Isacco II Angelo', in *Bessarione*, vol. XXXI, pp. 29 ff., 246 ff. Letter of Frederick I to Henry in Bohmer, *Acta Imperii Selecta*, p. 152.

PLATE I

THE EMPEROR FREDERICK BARBAROSSA AND HIS SONS,
HENRY VI, KING OF THE ROMANS AND
FREDERICK, DUKE OF SWABIA

to realize that Isaac was powerless to stop it. Frederick wisely sought the friendship of the rebel chieftains. Stephen Nemanya, Prince of Serbia, came with his brother Sraćimir to Nish to greet the German monarch as he passed through the town in July; and the Vlach brothers, Ivan Asen and Peter, leaders of the Bulgarian revolt, sent him messages promising him assistance. News of these negotiations caused not unnatural concern at the Court of Constantinople. Isaac was already suspicious of Frederick's intentions. His former ambassadors to the German Court, John Ducas and Constantine Cantacuzenus, had been sent to greet Frederick on his entry into Byzantine territory, and, to the horror of their old friend, the historian Nicetas Choniates, they took advantage of their mission to incite Frederick against Isaac; who soon learnt of their intrigues. While Frederick's mistrust of Byzantium, which dated from his experiences during the Second Crusade, was being fanned by the schemes of his Byzantine escort, Isaac's good sense deserted him. Hitherto the discipline of the German army and the adequate arrangements of the Byzantine authorities for its victualling had prevented unpleasant incidents. But when Frederick occupied Philippopolis and from there sent envoys to Constantinople to arrange for the passage of his troops into Asia, Isaac threw them into prison, meaning to hold them as hostages for Frederick's pacific behaviour. He entirely misjudged Frederick; who at once sent his son, Frederick of Swabia, to take the town of Didymotichum in Thrace as a counter-hostage, and wrote home to his son Henry to collect a fleet to use against Byzantium and to secure the Pope's blessing for a Crusade against the Greeks. Unless the Straits were held by the Franks, he said, the Crusading movement would never succeed. Faced with the prospect of the German army, to be joined by a western fleet, attacking Constantinople, Isaac prevaricated for some months and at last climbed down and released the German ambassadors. Peace was patched up at Adrianople. Isaac gave Frederick hostages and promised to provide ships if he would cross the Dardanelles and not the Bosphorus, and to victual him on his passage through Anatolia. Frederick's

13

wish was to proceed to Palestine. He controlled his anger and accepted the terms.

The German army had marched very slowly through the Balkans; and Frederick was too cautious to attempt to cross Anatolia in winter time. He spent the winter months at Adrianople, while the citizens of Constantinople trembled lest he should refuse Isaac's apologies and march on their city. Eventually, in March 1190, his whole expedition moved down to Gallipoli on the Dardanelles, and with the help of Byzantine transports, crossed into Asia, to the relief of Isaac and his subjects.[1]

On leaving the Asiatic shore of the Dardanelles, Frederick roughly kept the road taken by Alexander the Great fifteen centuries before, crossing over the Granicus and the flooded river Angelocomites, till he struck a paved Byzantine high-road between Miletopolis and the modern Balikesir. He followed this road through Calamus to Philadelphia, where the inhabitants were friendly at first but attempted to rob the rearguard of the army and were punished. He reached Laodicea on 27 April, thirty days after his passage across the Dardanelles. From there he struck inland along the road that Manuel had taken on his fatal march to Myriocephalum; and on 3 May, after a skirmish with the Turks, he passed the site of the battlefield, where the bones of the victims still could be seen. He was now in territory controlled by the Seldjuk Sultan. It was clear that Kilij Arslan, in spite of his promises, did not intend to let the Crusaders pass peaceably through his domains. But, awed by the size of their army, he attempted little more than to hang round its skirts, picking off stragglers and interfering with the search for food. It was effective tactics. Hunger and thirst as well as Turkish arrows began to cause casualties. Making his way round the end of the Sultan Dagh mountains on to the old road from Philomelium eastward,

---

[1] Nicetas Choniates, pp. 525–37; Ansbert, *Expeditio Friderici*, pp. 27–66; *Gesta Federici in Expeditione Sacra*, pp. 80–4; Otto of St Blaise, pp. 66–7; *Itinerarium*, pp. 47–9. See Hefele-Leclercq, *op. cit.* pp. 1147–9; Vasiliev, *History of the Byzantine Empire*, pp. 445–7.

Frederick reached Konya on 17 May. The Sultan and his court had retired before him; and, after a sharp battle with the Sultan's son, Qutb ad-Din, he was able next day to force an entry into the town. He did not remain long within the walls, but let his army rest for a while in the gardens of Meram, in its southern suburbs. Six days later he moved on to Karaman, where he arrived on the 30th; and thence he led the army over the passes of the Taurus without opposition, towards the south coast at Seleucia. The port was now held by the Armenians, whose Catholicus hastened to send a message to Saladin. The road lay through difficult country; food was short, and the summer heat intense.[1]

On 10 June the great host descended into the plain of Seleucia, and prepared to cross the river Calycadnus to enter the city. The Emperor rode ahead with his bodyguard, and came down to the waterside. What happened then is uncertain. Either he leapt from his horse to refresh himself in the cool stream and the current was stronger than he thought, or his aged body could not stand the sudden shock; or else his horse slipped and threw him into the water, and the weight of his armour sank him. By the time that the army reached the river his corpse had been rescued and was lying on the bank.[2]

The death of the great Emperor was a bitter blow not only to his own followers but to the whole Frankish world. The news of his coming at the head of a great army had enormously heartened the knights fighting on the Syrian coast. His force alone seemed sufficient to drive back the Moslems: and its combination with the armies of the Kings of France and England, who were known to be setting out soon for the East, would surely recover the Holy

[1] Nicetas Choniates, pp. 538–44; Ansbert, *Expeditio Friderici*, pp. 67–90; *Gesta Federici*, pp. 84–97; *Epistola de Morte Friderici*, pp. 172–7; *Itinerarium*, pp. 49–53. Frederick's route is discussed by Ramsay, *Historical Geography of Asia Minor*, pp. 129–30. The Armenian Catholicus's warning to Saladin is reported by Beha ed-Din (*P.P.T.S.* pp. 185–9).

[2] Nicetas Choniates, p. 545; Ansbert, *Expeditio Friderici*, pp. 90–2; *Epistola de Morte Friderici*, pp. 177–8; *Gesta Federici*, pp. 97–8; Otto of St Blaise, p. 51; *Itinerarium*, pp. 54–5; Ibn al-Athir, ii, p. 5; Beha ed-Din, *P.P.T.S.* pp. 183–4.

Land for Christendom. Saladin himself was afraid that the combination might be too much for him. When he heard that Frederick was on the road to Constantinople he sent his secretary and future biographer, Beha ed-Din, to Baghdad to warn the Caliph Nasr that the faithful must gather to meet the threat; and he summoned all his vassals to join him. He collected information about every stage of the German army's march and wrongly believed that Kilij Arslan was secretly helping the invaders. When they suddenly learned of Frederick's death it seemed to the Moslems that God had wrought a miracle for the Faith. The army that Saladin had gathered to hold the Germans in Northern Syria could safely be reduced and detachments sent to join his forces on the coast of Palestine.[1]

(The danger had been great for Islam; and Saladin was right to see his salvation in the Emperor's death.) Though a number of German soldiers had perished and some equipment been lost in the arduous march across Anatolia, the Emperor's army was still formidable. But the Germans, with their strange longing to worship a leader, are usually demoralized when the leader disappears. Frederick's troops lost their nerve. The Duke of Swabia took over the command; but, though he was gallant enough, he lacked his father's personality. Some of the princes decided to return with their followers to Europe; others took ship from Seleucia or Tarsus for Tyre. The Duke, with the army much reduced, marched on through the damp summer heat of the Cilician plain, carrying with him the Emperor's body preserved in vinegar. After some hesitation the Armenian Prince Leo paid a deferential visit to the German camp. But the German leaders could not make adequate arrangements for the feeding of their men. Bereft of the Emperor's control, the troops lost their discipline. Many were hungry, many were sick, and all were unruly. The Duke himself fell seriously ill and had to linger in Cilicia. His army went on

[1] Ernoul, pp. 250–1; *Estoire d'Eracles*, II, p. 140; *Itinerarium*, pp. 56–7; Ambroise, col. 87; Ibn al-Athir, *loc. cit.*; Abu Shama, pp. 34–5. Beha ed-Din, *P.P.T.S.* pp. 189–91; Bar-Hebraeus, pp. 332–4.

without him, to be attacked with heavy losses as it passed through the Syrian Gates. It was a sorry rabble that arrived on 21 June at Antioch. Frederick followed a few days later, on his recovery.[1]

Prince Bohemond of Antioch gave the Germans a hospitable welcome. It was their undoing. Leaderless, they had lost their enthusiasm, and after the hardships of their journey they were unwilling to abandon the luxuries of Antioch. Nor did the excesses in which they indulged improve their health. Frederick of Swabia, pleased with the homage paid him by Bohemond and encouraged by a visit that his cousin, Conrad of Montferrat, made him from Tyre, was eager to continue the journey. But when he left Antioch at the end of August it was with an army that was still further reduced. Nor was his effort appreciated by many of the Franks whom he had come to help. All Conrad's opponents, knowing Frederick to be his cousin and friend, whispered that Saladin had paid Conrad sixty thousand besants to take him away from Antioch where he would have been more useful to the Christian cause. With apposite symbolism the old Emperor's body had disintegrated. The vinegar had been ineffective, and the decaying remains were hastily buried in the Cathedral of Antioch. But some bones were removed from the corpse and travelled on with the army, in the vain hope that at least a portion of Frederick Barbarossa should await the Judgement Day at Jerusalem.[2]

The grim fiasco of the Emperor's Crusade made it more than ever urgent that the Kings of France and England should arrive in the East, to share in the bitter and fateful contest that was being waged on the coast of northern Palestine.

---

[1] Sicard of Cremona, p. 610; Otto of St Blaise, p. 52; Abu Shama, pp. 458-9; Beha ed-Din, *P.P.T.S.* pp. 207-9.

[2] Abu Shama, pp. 458-60; Beha ed-Din, *P.P.T.S.* pp. 212-14; Ernoul, p. 259.

CHAPTER II

ACRE

'Behold, I will turn back the weapons of war that are in your hands, wherewith ye fight against the king of Baby-lon, and against the Chaldeans, which besiege you without the walls.'
                                        JEREMIAH XXI, 4

In the moment of triumph Saladin had made one grave mistake, when he let himself be daunted by the fortifications of Tyre. Had he marched on Tyre immediately after his capture of Acre in July 1187, it would have been his. But he thought that its sur-render had been arranged, and delayed a few days. When he arrived before Tyre, Conrad of Montferrat was there already and refused to consider capitulation. Saladin was not equipped at that moment to undertake a systematic siege of the town and moved on to easier conquests. It was not till after the fall of Jerusalem in October that he made a second attack on Tyre, with a large army and all his siege-machines. But the walls across the narrow isthmus had been strengthened now by Conrad, who devoted the money that he had brought with him from Constantinople to improve all the defences. After his engines proved ineffectual and his fleet was destroyed in a battle at the harbour entrance, Saladin lifted the siege once more and disbanded most of his troops. Before he came again to complete the conquest of the coast, help had arrived from overseas.[1]

The forces dispatched by William II of Sicily in the late spring of 1188 were not large, but they consisted of a well-armed fleet under the Admiral Margaritus and two hundred trained knights. The presence of these reinforcements caused Saladin to raise the siege of Krak des Chevaliers in July 1188, and deterred him from

---

[1] See above, vol. II, pp. 471–2.

attacking Tripoli.[1] He would have been glad now to negotiate a peace. There was a knight from Spain who had arrived at Tyre in time to share in its defence. His name is unknown, but from the armour that he wore men called him the Green Knight. His valour and prowess greatly impressed Saladin, who interviewed him near Tripoli in the summer of 1188, hoping to persuade him to arrange for a truce and himself take service with the Saracens. But the Green Knight answered that the Franks would consider nothing less than the restoration of their country, especially as help was coming from the West. Let Saladin evacuate Palestine; then he would find the Franks the most loyal of allies.[2]

Though peace was not to be had Saladin showed his friendly intentions by releasing some of his eminent prisoners. It had been his practice to induce the captive Frankish lords to obtain their liberty by ordering the surrender of their castles to him. It was a cheap and easy way of obtaining the fortresses. His chivalry went further. When Stephanie, lady of Oultrejourdain, failed to persuade her garrisons at Kerak and Montreal to give themselves up in order that her son, Humphrey of Toron, might be released, Saladin returned him to her even before the obstinate castles were taken by storm. The price of King Guy's release was to have been Ascalon. But the citizens there, ashamed of their King's selfishness, refused to honour his undertaking. Ascalon now had fallen; and so Queen Sibylla wrote again and again to Saladin, begging him to give her back her husband. In July 1188, Saladin granted her request. After solemnly swearing that he would go back across the sea and never again take arms against the Moslems, King Guy, with ten distinguished followers, including the Constable Amalric, was sent to join the Queen at Tripoli. At the same time the aged Marquis of Montferrat was allowed to go to his son at Tyre.[3]

[1] *Itinerarium*, pp. 27–8; Benedict of Peterborough, II, p. 54; *Estoire d'Eracles*, I, pp. 114, 119–20; Abu Shama, pp. 362–3; Ibn al-Athir, pp. 718, 720–1. *Eracles* and the Moslem authors say that Margaritus had an interview with Saladin at Lattakieh.   [2] Ernoul, pp. 251–2.

[3] For the problem and the exact place and date of Guy's release see above, vol. II, p. 462 n. 4, with references. Ernoul (p. 253), *Eracles* (p. 121) and Beha

Saladin's generosity alarmed his compatriots. Not only did he allow the Frankish citizens in every town that surrendered to him to go and join their fellows at Tyre or Tripoli, but he further swelled the garrisons of these last Christian fortresses by setting free so many of the captive lords. But Saladin knew what he was doing. (The party quarrels that had rent the latter years of the kingdom of Jerusalem had been healed by the tact of Balian of Ibelin only a few weeks before the battle of Hattin, and they had broken out again on the very eve of the battle. The disaster embittered them. The Lusignan and Courtenay supporters blamed it on Raymond of Tripoli, and Raymond's friends, the Ibelins and the Garniers and most of the local nobility, blamed it, with better reason, on King Guy's weakness and the influence of the Templars and Reynald of Châtillon. Raymond and Reynald were dead now, but the bitterness lasted on.) Cooped up behind the walls of Tyre, the dispossessed nobles had little else to do but to hurl recriminations at each other. Balian and his friends who had eluded captivity now accepted Conrad of Montferrat as their leader. They had seen that it was he alone who had saved Tyre. But Guy's supporters, emerging from prison after the worst of the crisis was over, merely saw him as an interloper, a potential rival to their King. Guy's release, so far from strengthening the Franks, brought the quarrel to a head.[1]

Queen Sibylla, probably to escape from an atmosphere hostile to her husband, had retired to Tripoli. On Raymond's death in the autumn of 1187 Tripoli had passed to the young son of his cousin, Bohemond of Antioch; and Bohemond, who was easy-going and, perhaps, grateful to have the garrison at Tripoli reinforced, made no objections when the Lusignan partisans gathered round her there. Guy joined her as soon as he was freed; and at once a cleric was found to release him from his oath to Saladin.

ed-Din (*P.P.T.S.* p. 143) refer to Guy's oath not to take arms against the Moslems. The *Itinerarium* says that he promised to abandon the kingdom (p. 25), and Ambroise (col. 70) that he would go across the sea. Guy subsequently said that he had fulfilled the promise by going from Tortosa to the Island of Ruad (*Estoire d'Eracles*, II, p. 131).

[1] Ibn-al-Athir, pp. 707–11, is strongly critical of Saladin's policy.

It had been made under duress and to an infidel. Therefore, said the Church, it was invalid. Saladin was angry to hear of this but cannot have been much surprised. After visiting Antioch, where Bohemond gave him a vague promise to help, Guy marched with his supporters from Tripoli to Tyre, intending to take over the government of what remained of his former kingdom. Conrad closed the gates in his face. In the opinion of Conrad's party Guy had forfeited the kingdom at Hattin and during his captivity. He had left it without a government, and all would have been lost but for Conrad's intervention. To Guy's demand to be received as king, Conrad answered that he held Tyre in trust for the Crusader monarchs who were coming to rescue the Holy Land. The Emperor Frederick and the Kings of France and England must decide to whom eventually the government should be given. It was a fair enough claim, and it suited Conrad. Richard of England, as overlord of the Lusignans in Guienne, might favour Guy's cause; but the Emperor and Philip of France were Conrad's cousins and friends. Guy returned disconsolate with his party to Tripoli.[1] It was well for the Franks that at this moment Saladin, with his army partly disbanded, was occupied in reducing the castles in the north of Syria, and that in January 1189 he sent further detachments to their homes. He himself, after spending the first months of the year at Jerusalem and Acre, reorganizing the administration of Palestine, went back to his capital at Damascus in March.[2]

In April Guy came again with Sibylla to Tyre and again demanded to be given control of the city. Finding Conrad as obdurate as before, he encamped in front of its walls. About the same time valuable reinforcements arrived from the West. At the time of the fall of Jerusalem the Pisans and the Genoese were enjoying one of their habitual wars; but amongst the triumphs of Pope Gregory VIII in his short pontificate was the negotiation of a truce between them and the promise of a Pisan fleet for the

[1] Ernoul, pp. 256–7; *Estoire d'Eracles*, II, pp. 123–4; Ambroise, cols. 71–3; *Itinerarium*, pp. 59–60.
[2] Abu Shama, pp. 380–1; Beha ed-Din, *P.P.T.S.* pp. 140–1.

Crusade. The Pisans set out before the end of the year but wintered at Messina. Their fifty-two ships arrived off Tyre on 6 April 1189, under the command of their Archbishop, Ubaldo. Soon afterwards Ubaldo seems to have quarrelled with Conrad; and when Guy appeared, the Pisans joined up with him. He also won the support of the Sicilian auxiliaries. During the early summer there was some slight skirmishing between the Franks and the Moslems. But Saladin still wished to rest his armies, and the Christians awaited more help from the West. Suddenly, at the end of August, King Guy broke his camp and set out to march with his followers southward down the coast road to attack Acre, and the Pisan and Sicilian ships sailed to keep him company.

It was a move of desperate foolhardiness, the decision of a brave but very unwise man. Thwarted of his wish to reign in Tyre, Guy urgently needed a city from which to reconstitute his kingdom. Conrad was seriously ill at the time; and it seemed to Guy a fine opportunity to show that he was the active leader of the Franks. But the risk was enormous. The size of the Moslem garrison of Acre was more than twice that of Guy's whole army; and Saladin's regular forces were in the offing. No one could have foreseen that the adventure would succeed. But history has its surprises. If Conrad's ruthless energy had saved the remnant of Palestine for Christendom, it was Guy's gallant folly that turned the tide and began an era of reconquest.[1]

When the news reached him of Guy's expedition, Saladin was in the hills beyond Sidon, laying siege to the castle of Beaufort. The castle, perched on a high cliff above the river Litani, belonged to Reynald of Sidon and had hitherto been preserved by the cunning of its lord. He had gone to Saladin's court and had charmed the Sultan and his entourage by his deep appreciation of Arabic literature and his interest in Islam. He hinted that, given a little time, he would settle as a convert in Damascus. But the months passed and nothing happened except that the fortifications

[1] Ernoul, p. 257; *Estoire d'Eracles*, II, pp. 124–5; Ambroise, cols. 73–4; *Itinerarium*, pp. 60–2; Beha ed-Din, *P.P.T.S.* pp. 143–4.

of Beaufort were strengthened. At last, early in August, Saladin said that the time had come for the surrender of Beaufort as a gage of Reynald's intentions. Reynald was taken under escort to the castle gate where he ordered the garrison-commander in Arabic to yield up the castle and in French to resist. The Arabs saw through the ruse but were powerless to take the castle by storm. While Saladin brought up his forces to blockade it, Reynald was cast into prison at Damascus.[1] Saladin first thought that Guy's march was intended to draw the Saracen army away from Beaufort, but his spies soon told him that its objective was Acre.) He then wished to attack the Franks while they were climbing over the Ladder of Tyre or the headlands of Naqura. But his Council would not agree. It would be better, they said, to let them reach Acre and catch them between the garrison and the Sultan's main army. Saladin, who was not well at the time, weakly gave way.[2]

Guy arrived outside Acre on 28 August and set up his camp on the hill of Turon, the modern Tel el-Fukhkhar, a mile east of the city, by the little river Belus, which supplied his men with water. When his first attempt, three days later, to take the city by assault failed, he settled down to await reinforcements.[3] Acre was built on a small peninsula that jutted southward into the Gulf of Haifa. To the south and west it was protected by the sea and a strong sea-wall. A broken mole ran out south-eastward to a rock crowned with a fort called the Tower of Flies. Behind the mole was a harbour sheltered against all but the off-shore wind. The north and east of the city were protected by great walls, which met at a right angle at a fort called the Cursed Tower, at the north-east corner. The two land-gates were at either end of the walls, by the shore. A large sea-gate opened into the harbour, and a second on to an anchorage exposed to the dominant west wind. Under the Frankish kings Acre had been the richest town in the kingdom and their favourite residence. Saladin had often visited it during the

---

[1] Beha ed-Din, *P.P.T.S.* pp. 140–3, 150–3.
[2] *Ibid.* pp. 154, 175; Ibn al-Athir, II, p. 6; Ambroise, cols. 74–5.
[3] Ernoul, pp. 358–9; *Estoire d'Eracles*, II, pp. 125–6.

last months and had carefully repaired the damage caused by his troops when he captured it. It was a strong fortress now, well garrisoned and well provisioned, capable of a long resistance.[1]

Reinforcements began to arrive from the West early in September. First came a large fleet of Danes and Frisians, un-

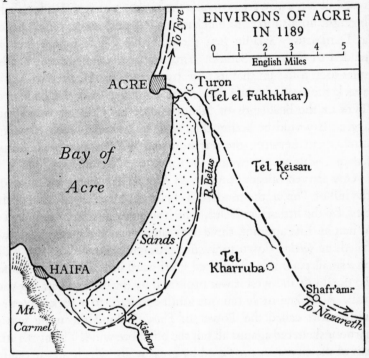

ENVIRONS OF ACRE
IN 1189

0   1   2   3   4   5
English Miles

To Tyre
ACRE
Turon
(Tel el Fukhkhar)
Bay of
Acre
R. Belus
Tel Keisan
Sands
Tel
Kharruba
HAIFA
Shafr'amr
Mt.
Carmel
R. Kishon
To Nazareth

Map 1. Environs of Acre.

disciplined soldiers but excellent sailors, whose galleys were invaluable for blockading the city from the sea, especially when the death of William of Sicily in November led to the withdrawal of the Sicilian squadron.[2] A few days later ships from Italy brought

[1] For account of Acre, see Enlart, *Les Monuments des Croisés*, vol. II, pp. 2–9. *Itinerarium*, pp. 75–6, gives a description of the town.

[2] *Estoire d'Eracles*, II, pp. 127–8; Ambroise, col. 77, mentioning sailors from La Marche and Cornwall; *Itinerarium*, pp. 64–5. See Riant, *Expéditions des Scandinaves*, pp. 277–83.

a Flemish and French contingent, led by the gallant knight, James of Avesnes,[1] the Counts of Bar, Brienne and Dreux, and Philip, Bishop of Beauvais. Before the month was ended a party of Germans arrived, under Louis, Margrave of Thuringia, who preferred to travel with his followers by sea rather than accompany his Emperor. With him were the Count of Guelders and a party of Italians under Gerard, Archbishop of Ravenna, and the Bishop of Verona.

These arrivals alarmed Saladin, who began to gather his vassals again and who came down with part of his army from Beaufort, leaving a smaller detachment to finish the reduction of the castle. His attack on Guy's camp on 15 September failed, but his nephew Taki was able to break round the Frankish lines and establish contact with the north gate of the city. He himself established his camp a little to the east of the Christians'. Soon the Franks felt able to take the offensive. Louis of Thuringia, as he passed through Tyre, was able to persuade Conrad of Montferrat to join the Frankish army, so long as he did not have to serve under Guy's command. On 4 October, after having fortified their camp, which was left under the command of Guy's brother Geoffrey, the Franks launched a great attack on Saladin's lines. It was a bitter battle. Taki, on the Saracen right, retired to lure on the Templars, who were opposite to him; but Saladin himself was deceived by the manœuvre and weakened his centre to rescue him. As a result both his right and his centre were put to flight with heavy losses, some of his troops never reining their horses till they reached Tiberias. The Count of Brienne even penetrated to the Sultan's own tent. But the Saracen left was intact; and when the Christians broke their ranks to pursue the fugitives Saladin charged with it and drove them back in disorder to their camp, which was at the same time assailed by a sortie from the garrison of Acre. Geoffrey of Lusignan held firm there; and soon the greater part of the

---

[1] For James of Avesnes, Ambroise, *loc. cit.*: Benedict of Peterborough, II, pp. 94–5; *Itinerarium*, pp. 67–8, mentioning the Bishop of Beauvais and his companions and the Margrave, and (pp. 73–4) the Italians.

Christian army was safe behind its defences, where Saladin did not venture to attack them. Many Frankish knights fell on the field, including Andrew of Brienne. The German troops panicked and suffered severely; and losses were high amongst the Templars. Their Grand Master, Gerard of Ridfort, who had been King Guy's evil genius in the days before Hattin, was captured and paid for his follies with his death. Conrad himself only escaped capture by the gallant intervention of his rival, King Guy.[1]

The victory had been with the Moslems; but it was not a complete victory. The Christians had not been dislodged; and during the autumn more help came from the West. The Londoners' fleet arrived in November, heartened by their success in Portugal.[2] The chroniclers tell of many other Crusaders drawn from the nobility of France, Flanders and Italy and even from Hungary and Denmark.[3] Many Western knights had refused to wait for their dilatory sovereigns. Thanks to this added strength the Franks were able to complete the blockade of Acre by land. But Saladin too was receiving reinforcements. The news of the Emperor Frederick's journey, while it encouraged the Christians, induced him to summon his vassals from all over Asia; and he even wrote to the Moslems of Morocco and Spain to say that if Western Christendom was sending its knights to fight for the Holy Land Western Islam should do likewise. They answered him with sympathy but very little positive help.[4] Nevertheless his army soon was large enough for him in his turn almost entirely to blockade the Christians. The besiegers were themselves besieged. On 31 October fifty of his galleys broke through the Frankish fleet, though with the loss of

[1] Ambroise, cols. 78–81; *Itinerarium*, pp. 68–72; Ralph of Diceto, II, p. 70; *Estoire d'Eracles*, II, p. 129; Beha ed-Din, *P.P.T.S.* pp. 162–9, a very vivid account as Beha ed-Din was present himself. He does not quite tally with the account in the *Itinerarium*, as he does not mention any sortie by the garrison. He describes the previous skirmishes, pp. 154–62. Abu Shama, pp. 415–22.

[2] *Itinerarium*, p. 65, giving the date as September. But if the dates given by Benedict and Ralph of Diceto are correct (see above, p. 9, n. 6), November is the earliest date at which the ships could reach Syria.

[3] *Itinerarium*, pp. 73–4; Ambroise, col. 84. The date of each arrival is not given.

[4] Beha ed-Din, *P.P.T.S.* pp. 171, 175–8; Abu Shama, pp. 497–506.

some ships, to bring food and munitions into Acre; and on 26 December a larger armada from Egypt reopened communications with the harbour.[1])

Throughout the winter the armies faced each other, neither venturing on a major engagement. There were skirmishes and duels, but at the same time there was growing fraternization. The knights on either side began to know and to respect each other. A fight would be interrupted while the protagonists enjoyed a friendly conversation. Enemy soldiers would be invited to come to the feasts and entertainments arranged in either camp. One day the little boys living in the Saracen camp challenged the Christian boys to a gay mock-combat. Saladin himself was distinguished by the kindness that he showed to Christian prisoners and the courteous messages and gifts that he would send to the Christian princes. The more fanatical of his followers wondered what had happened to the Holy War that he had begged the Caliph to preach; nor did newly-come knights from the West find the atmosphere easy to comprehend. Superficially the bitterness had gone out of the war. But both sides kept a grim determination for victory.[2]

(Despite these pleasant courtesies life in the Christian camp was harsh that winter. Food was short, especially as the Franks had lost command of the sea. As the warmer weather approached, water became a problem and sanitary arrangements broke down. Disease spread through the troops.) Chastened by the difficulties of their men, Guy and Conrad patched up an agreement. Conrad was to hold Tyre, with Beirut and Sidon when they should be recovered, and was to recognize Guy as king. When peace between them was thus made, Conrad left the camp in March and at the end of the month returned from Tyre with ships laden with food and armaments. Saladin's fleet sailed out of the harbour of Acre to intercept him; but after a sharp battle the Saracen ships were driven back, in spite of their use of Greek fire, and Conrad was

[1] *Itinerarium*, pp. 77–9; Ambroise, cols. 84–5; Abu Shama, pp. 430–1.
[2] Abu Shama, pp. 412, 433; Ibn al-Athir, II, pp. 6, 9.

able to land the goods. With the help of the material that he brought, the Franks constructed wooden siege-towers, with which on 5 May they tried to assault the city. But the towers were burnt.[1] Soon famine and sickness reappeared in the Christian camp; and it was little consolation to know that in Acre too there was famine, although from time to time Saracen ships fought their way into the harbour bringing new provisions.[2] Throughout the spring contingents of Moslems joined Saladin's army. On 19 May, Whit Saturday, he began an attack on the camp, which was only beaten off after eight days' fighting.[3] The next full-scale battle was on St James's Day, 25 July, when the Frankish soldiers, led by their sergeants and against the wishes of their leaders, boldly attacked Taki's camp, on Saladin's right. They were terribly defeated and many perished. A distinguished English Crusader, Ralph of Alta Ripa, Archdeacon of Colchester, went to their rescue and was killed.[4]

During the summer other high-born Crusaders arrived in the camp and were made welcome, though every new soldier meant another mouth to feed. Many of the greatest French and Burgundian nobles were among them, hurrying ahead of their King. There were Tibald, Count of Blois, and his brother Stephen of Sancerre, once a reluctant candidate for Queen Sibylla's hand, Ralph, Count of Clermont, John, Count of Fontigny, and Alan of Saint-Valéry, together with the Archbishop of Besançon and the Bishops of Blois and Toul and other prominent ecclesiastics. Their leader was Henry of Troyes, Count of Champagne, a young man of great distinction, for his mother, the daughter of Eleanor of Aquitaine by her French marriage, was half-sister to the Kings of England and France; and both his uncles thought highly of him.

---

[1] *Itinerarium*, pp. 79–85; Ambroise, cols. 85–92; Beha ed-Din, *P.P.T.S.* pp. 178–80; Ibn al-Athir, II, pp. 18–21.

[2] *Itinerarium*, pp. 85–6, 88; Beha ed-Din, *P.P.T.S.* pp. 181–2.

[3] *Itinerarium*, pp. 87–8.

[4] *Itinerarium*, pp. 89–91; Ambroise, cols. 93–4, wrongly dating the battle St John's instead of St James's Day; *Estoire d'Eracles*, II, p. 151; Beha ed-Din, *P.P.T.S.* pp. 193–6.

He was at once given a special position as representative and fore-runner to the Kings. He took command of the actual siege operations, which hitherto James of Avesnes and the Landgrave of Thuringia had directed.[1] The Landgrave, who had been ill for some time, probably with malaria, used his coming as an excuse to return to Europe.[2] Frederick of Swabia, with the remnant of Barbarossa's army, arrived at Acre early in October.[3] A few days later an English contingent landed at Tyre and came down to Acre. At its head was Baldwin, Archbishop of Canterbury.[4]

There was desultory fighting throughout the summer, each side awaiting the reinforcements that would enable it to take the offensive. The fall of Beaufort in July relieved men for Saladin's army, but he had sent troops to the north to intercept Frederick Barbarossa and they did not return till the winter. Meanwhile skirmishes alternated with fraternization. The Christian chroniclers noted with complacency several incidents in which, by the hand of God, Saracens were discomfited and Crusader heroism re-warded; but every attempt to scale the walls of the city failed. Frederick of Swabia launched a fierce attack soon after his arrival and the Archbishop of Besançon soon afterwards tried out some newly constructed battering-ram. Both efforts were in vain.[5] In November the Crusaders managed to dislodge Saladin from his position at Tel Keisan, five miles from the city; but he established himself in a stronger position at Tel Kharruba, a little further away.

[1] *Itinerarium*, pp. 92–4; Ambroise, col. 94; Beha ed-Din, *P.P.T.S.* p. 197. Henry was the son of Henry I, Count of Champagne. Tibald of Blois and Stephen of Sancerre were his father's younger brothers. His father's sister, Alix, was the second wife of King Louis VII and mother of King Philip, who was thus his first cousin as well as his half-uncle.

[2] The Landgrave died on his way home. Ralph of Diceto accuses him of having been in relations with the enemy from whom he accepted money (II, pp. 82–3).

[3] Abu Shama, p. 474, dating it 4 October; Beha ed-Din, *P.P.T.S.* pp. 209, 213; *Itinerarium*, pp. 94–5.   [4] *Itinerarium*, p. 93.

[5] Beha ed-Din, *P.P.T.S.* pp. 214–18; Abu Shama, pp. 480–1; *Itinerarium*, pp. 97–109 (diverse miraculous incidents), pp. 109–11 (attack on the Tower of Flies), pp. 111–13 (Archbishop of Besançon's attack); Ambroise, cols. 98–104.

This enabled them to break through to Haifa on a foraging expedition, which slightly relieved the hunger in the camp. But both in the city and in the two camps there was hunger and illness. Neither side was fitted to make a supreme effort.[1]

Amongst the victims of disease that autumn was Queen Sibylla. The two little daughters that she had borne to King Guy died a few days before her own death.[2] The heiress to the kingdom was now the Princess Isabella; and Guy's crown was in jeopardy. He had won the crown as the Queen's husband. Did his rights survive her death? To the surviving barons of the kingdom, led by Balian of Ibelin, it seemed an opportunity for ridding themselves of his weak unlucky rule. Their candidate for the throne was Conrad of Montferrat. If he could be married to Isabella, his claims would be higher than Guy's. There were difficulties in this solution. Conrad was rumoured to have one wife living at Constantinople and possibly another in Italy, and never to have troubled about any annulment or divorce. But Constantinople and Italy were far away, and if there were deserted ladies there, they could be forgotten. A more pressing problem was the existence of Isabella's husband, Humphrey of Toron, who was not only alive but present in the camp. Humphrey was a charming youth, gallant and cultured; but his beauty was too feminine for him to be respected by the tough soldiers around him; nor had the barons ever forgotten his weak desertion of their cause in 1186, when Guy had secured the crown in defiance of the terms of Baldwin IV's will. They decided that he must be divorced. Humphrey himself was easily persuaded to agree. He was not fitted for married life, and he was terrified of political responsibility. But Isabella was less

[1] *Itinerarium*, pp. 115-19; Ambroise, cols. 105-8; Abu Shama, pp. 513-14.

[2] *Estoire d'Eracles*, II, p. 151 (which gives her daughters' names as Alice and Maria); Ernoul, p. 267 (who says that she had four children); Ambroise, col. 104. Ambroise dates her death the end of August, while one manuscript of Ernoul gives 15 July. She was mentioned as living in a charter given at Acre in September 1190, but as dead in a letter of 21 October (*Epistolae Cantuarenses*, pp. 228-9). Röhricht, *Regesta, Addimentum*, p. 67, says that she died about 1 October 1190.

amenable. Humphrey had always been kind to her, and she had no wish to exchange him for a grim middle-aged warrior. Nor had she ambitions for the throne. The barons left the matter to the capable hands of her mother, Queen Maria Comnena, Balian's wife. She used her maternal authority to make the reluctant princess abandon Humphrey. Then she declared before the assembled bishops that her daughter had been forced into the marriage by her uncle Baldwin IV, and had only been eight years old when the engagement was arranged. In view of her extreme youth and Humphrey's known effeminacy, the marriage should be annulled. The Patriarch Heraclius was too ill to attend the meeting and appointed the Archbishop of Canterbury to represent him; and the Archbishop, knowing that his master King Richard was devoted to the Lusignans, refused to pronounce the annulment. He mentioned Conrad's previous marriage and declared that a marriage between Conrad and Isabella would be doubly adulterous. But the Archbishop of Pisa, who was Papal Legate, had been won over to Conrad's cause, on the promise, it was said, of trade concessions for his countrymen; and the Bishop of Beauvais, who was King Philip's cousin, used the Legate's backing to secure a general agreement for Isabella's divorce, and himself married her to Conrad on 24 November 1190. The Lusignan supporters were furious at a marriage that abolished Guy's right to the throne; and King Richard's vassals from England, Normandy and Guienne gave them full sympathy. But Archbishop Baldwin, their chief spokesman, after hurling excommunications on everyone connected with the affair, had died suddenly on 19 November. The English chroniclers did all that they could to blacken Conrad's memory. Guy himself went so far as to challenge Conrad to single combat; but Conrad, knowing that legitimate right was now on his side, refused to admit that the case could be discussed any more. The Lusignans might call it cowardice. But all that had the future of the kingdom at heart realized that if the royal line was to be continued, Isabella must remarry and have a child; and Conrad, the saviour of Tyre, was the obvious choice for her. The newly wedded pair retired to Tyre, where, next year, Isabella gave birth to a daughter, called Maria after her Byzantine grandmother. Conrad, correctly, would not take the title of king till he and his wife should be crowned, but, as Guy refused to abdicate any of his rights, he would not return from Tyre to the camp.[1]

The tribulations of the Crusaders continued throughout the winter months. Saladin's reinforcements had arrived from the north, and the Frankish camp was now closely invested. No food could come by land, nor, during the winter months, could much be landed on the inhospitable coast, whereas Saracen ships could sometimes fight their way into the shelter of Acre harbour. Amongst the lords that died of sickness in the camp were Tibald of Blois and his brother, Stephen of Sancerre.[2] On 20 January 1191, Frederick of Swabia died, and the German soldiers found themselves leaderless, though his cousin, Leopold of Austria, who arrived from Venice early in the spring, tried to rally them under his banner.[3] Henry of Champagne was for many weeks so ill that

[1] Ernoul, pp. 267–8; *Estoire d'Eracles*, II, pp. 151–4 (the fullest account, dispassionate in tone); Ambroise, cols. 110–12 and *Itinerarium*, pp. 119–24, both accounts bitterly hostile to Conrad, to Balian and to Queen Maria Comnena. The *Itinerarium* says that Isabella consented willingly, whereas *Eracles* makes it clear that she only consented because it was her political duty. Humphrey consented, according to Ernoul, because he was bribed. Isabella restored to him the fief of Toron held by his grandfather and annexed to the crown by Baldwin IV. Conrad's Italian wife was certainly dead before he married the Byzantine Princess Theodora Angelina (Nicetas Choniates, p. 497) and it is probable from the tone of Nicetas's account that his Byzantine wife had also died (*ibid.* pp. 516–17). Guy of Senlis, the butler, who offered to challenge Humphrey to a duel if he opposed the divorce, was captured by the Saracens on the evening of the wedding.

[2] The deaths of Tibald and his brother are reported by Haymar Monachus, *De Expugnatione Acconis*, p. 38. For the tribulations of the Crusaders, *Itinerarium*, pp. 124–34, with a poem cursing Conrad; Ambroise, cols. 112–15, also blaming Conrad. Beha ed-Din, *P.P.T.S.* p. 236, mentions the death of Count 'Baliat' (Tibald).

[3] Frederick of Swabia's death is reported by Beha ed-Din, *P.P.T.S. loc. cit.* Leopold of Austria's arrival with a party of Rhinelanders from Venice is given by Ansbert, *Expeditio Friderici*, pp. 96–7. He had wintered at Zara. He was the son of Frederick Barbarossa's half-brother, Henry of Austria, and of Theodora Comnena.

his life was despaired of.[1] Many of the soldiers, especially the English, blamed Conrad for their misery, because he was dallying at Tyre and refused to come to their aid. But, whatever his motive may have been, it is hard to see what else he could have done; the camp was sufficiently crowded without him.[2] Now and then an attempt was made to scale the walls, notably on 31 December, when the wreck of a Saracen relief-ship at the harbour entrance was distracting the garrison. It failed; nor were the Crusaders able to profit by a collapse of part of the land-wall six days later. There were many deserters to the Moslems. Thanks to their help and to his excellent spy-system, Saladin was able to send a force to break through the Crusader lines on 13 February, with a fresh commander and garrison to relieve the weary defenders of the city. But he hesitated himself to make a final attack on the Christian camp. Many of his troops were weary, and when reinforcements arrived he sent detachments away to rest. The misery amongst the Christians seemed to be doing his work for him.[3]

He was once again unwise in his forbearance. As Lent approached it seemed that the Franks could not long survive. In their camp a silver penny bought only thirteen beans or a single egg, and a sack of corn cost a hundred pieces of gold. Many of the best horses were slaughtered to provide their owners with food. The common soldiers ate grass and chewed bare bones. The prelates in the camp tried to organize some kind of relief but were hampered by the avarice of the Pisan merchants who controlled most of the food supplies. But in March, when everything seemed desperate, a fully laden corn-ship arrived off the coast and was able to land its cargo; and, as the weather improved, others followed. They were doubly welcome, for they brought not only foodstuffs but the news that the Kings of France and England were at last in Eastern waters.[4]

[1] Beha ed-Din, *loc. cit.*   [2] *Itinerarium, loc. cit.*
[3] Abu Shama, pp. 517–18, 520; Ibn al-Athir, II, pp. 32–3.
[4] *Itinerarium*, pp. 136–7; Ambroise, cols. 119–20.

CHAPTER III

CŒUR-DE-LION

'I will bring evil from the north, and a great destruction. The lion is come up from his thicket, and the destroyer of the Gentiles is on his way.' JEREMIAH IV, 6, 7

(King Philip Augustus landed at the camp before Acre on 20 April 1191, the Saturday after Easter, and King Richard seven weeks later, on the Saturday after Whitsun. Nearly four years had passed since the battle of Hattin and the desperate appeal to the West for help. The weary soldiers fighting on the Palestinian coast were so glad to welcome the Kings that they forgave or forgot the long delay.)But to the modern historian there is something frivolous in Richard's leisurely and quarrelsome journey to the battlefield where he was so urgently needed.

That King Philip should not have hurried is easy to understand. He was no idealist, and he went crusading merely from political necessity. It would have lost him the good-will not only of the Church but also of most of his subjects had he abstained from the holy adventure. But his kingdom was vulnerable, and he was rightly suspicious of Angevin ambitions. He could not afford to leave France until he knew that his rival of England was also on his way. Prudence demanded that they should set out together. Nor could either King be blamed for the ultimate delay caused by the death of the Queen of France. Richard, too, had certain excuses. The death of his father obliged him to reorganize his kingdom. Moreover, he, like Philip, intended to travel by sea; and sea travel was impracticable during the winter months. But that so genuinely eager a Crusader should have made so little haste shows a lack of purpose and responsibility.

(There were grave flaws in Richard's character. Physically he was superb, tall, long-limbed and strong, with red-gold hair and

34

handsome features, and he had inherited from his mother not only the good looks of the House of Poitou, but its charm of manner, its courage and its taste for poetry and romance. His friends and servants followed him with devotion and with awe. From both his parents he derived a hot temper and a passionate self-will. But he had neither the political astuteness and administrative competence of his father, nor Queen Eleanor's sound sense. He had been brought up in an atmosphere of family quarrels and family treachery. As his mother's favourite he hated his father, and he distrusted his brothers, though he loved his youngest sister, Joanna. He had learned to be a violent but not a loyal partisan. He was avaricious, though capable of generous gestures, and he liked a lavish display. His energy was unbounded; but in his fervent interest in the task of the moment he would forget other responsibilities. He loved to organize but was bored by administration. It was only the art of warfare that could hold his attention. As a soldier he had real gifts, a sense of strategy and of tactics and the power to command men. He was now aged thirty-three, in the prime of life, a figure of glamour whose reputation had travelled East before him.[1]

King Philip Augustus was very different. He was eight years younger than Richard; but he had been king for over ten years already, and his bitter experience had taught him wisdom. Physically he was no match for Richard. He was well-built, with a shock of untidy hair, but had lost the sight of one eye. He was not personally courageous. Though choleric and self-indulgent, he could cloak his passions. Neither emotionally nor materially did he like ostentation. His court was dull and austere. He did not care for the arts, nor was he well educated, though he knew the value of men of learning and sought their friendship from policy, and kept it by his wit and his pithy conversation. As a politician he was patient and observant, cunning, disloyal and

[1] Richard's person is described in the *Itinerarium*, p. 144. For his character see the discussion in Stubbs's introduction to the *Itinerarium*, also Norgate, *Richard the Lion Heart*, passim.

unscrupulous. (But he had an overriding sense of his duties and responsibilities. For all his meanness to himself and his friends, he was generous to the poor and protected them from their oppressors. He was an unattractive, unlovable man, but a good king. Amongst the Franks of the East he enjoyed a special prestige, for he was overlord of the families from which almost all of them had sprung; and most of the visiting Crusaders were directly or indirectly his vassals. But they were better able to appreciate Richard, with his courage, his knightly prowess and his charm; and to the Saracens Richard seemed the nobler, the richer and the greater of the two.[1]

The Kings had set out together from Vézelay on 4 July 1190. Richard had already sent the English fleet ahead to sail round the coast of Spain and meet him at Marseilles, but almost all the land-forces of his dominions were with him. Philip's army was smaller, as many of his vassals had already left for the East. The French army, followed closely by the English, marched from Vézelay to Lyons. There, after the French had crossed, the bridge over the Rhône broke under the weight of the English crowds. Many lives were lost, and there was some delay before transport could be arranged. Soon after leaving Lyons the Kings parted company. Philip went south-east across the Alpine foot-hills to strike the coast near Nice and then along the coast to Genoa, where ships awaited him. Richard made for Marseilles, where his fleet joined him on 22 August. Its voyage had been uneventful apart from a short delay in Portugal in June, where the sailors had helped King Sancho to repel an invasion by the Emperor of Morocco. From Marseilles some of Richard's followers, under Baldwin of Canterbury, set sail directly for Palestine; but the main army embarked in various convoys for Messina in Sicily, where it was proposed to join up again with the French.[2]

[1] An eulogy of Philip is given in the *Continuation of William the Breton*, p. 323. The *Itinerarium* throughout puts the worst possible interpretation on his character, for which see Cartellieri, *Philipp II August, passim.*

[2] For the King's journey across France, see *Itinerarium*, pp. 149–53; Ambroise, cols. 11–14; Benedict of Peterborough, II, pp. 111–15; Rigord, pp. 98–9; William the Breton, pp. 95–9.

It had been at the suggestion of King William II of Sicily that the Kings of France and England, when their joint Crusade was first planned, decided to assemble their forces in Sicily. But King William had died in November 1189. He had married Richard's sister, Joanna of England; but the marriage was childless, and his heir was his aunt Constance, the wife of Henry of Hohenstaufen, Frederick Barbarossa's eldest son. To many of the Sicilians the idea of a German ruler was repugnant. A short intrigue, backed by Pope Clement III, who was alarmed by the prospect of the Hohenstaufen controlling southern Italy, brought to the throne in place of Constance and Henry a bastard cousin of the late King, Tancred, Count of Lecce. Tancred was an ugly unimpressive little man, who almost at once found himself in difficulties. There was a Moslem revolt in Sicily and a German invasion of his lands on the mainland; and the vassals that had elected him began to change their minds. Tancred was obliged to recall his men and ships from Palestine, and, thanks to them, he defeated his enemies. But, though he was ready to receive the Crusading kings with honour and to assist them with provisions, he was in no position to accompany them on the Crusade.[1]

King Philip left Genoa at the end of August and after an easy voyage down the Italian coast arrived at Messina on 14 September. Hating pomp, he made his way into the town as unobtrusively as possible, but on Tancred's orders he was received with honour and lodged in the royal palace there. King Richard decided to travel by land from Marseilles. He seems to have disliked sea voyages, doubtless because he suffered from sea-sickness. His fleet conveyed his army to Messina and anchored off the harbour to await him, while he with a small escort took the road along the coast through Genoa, Pisa and Ostia to Salerno. He waited until he heard that his fleet had arrived at Messina and then, it seems, sent most of his escort by ship to Messina to prepare for his arrival. He himself continued on horseback, with only one attendant.

[1] For Tancred's position, see Chalandon, *Domination Normande en Italie*, I, pp. 419–24.

D

When he passed near the little Calabrian town of Mileto he trie
to steal a hawk from a peasant's house and was very nearly done t
death by the furious villagers. He was therefore in a bad tempe
when he reached the Straits of Messina a day or two later. H
men met him on the Italian shore and conveyed him in pomp t
Messina, where he landed on 3 September. The lavish grandeur c
his entry was in sharp contrast with Philip's modest arrival.

As he passed through Italy Richard had learned of many thing
that displeased him about Tancred. His sister, the Dowage
Queen Joanna, was being kept in confinement and her dower wa
withheld from her. She had some influence in the kingdom an
Tancred clearly did not trust her. Moreover, William II had le
a large legacy to his father-in-law, Henry II, consisting of gol
plate and gold furniture, a silk tent, two armed galleys and man
sacks of provisions. As Henry was dead, Tancred proposed t
retain them for himself. From Salerno Richard had sent to Tancre
to demand the release of his sister and the cession of her dowry an
the legacy. These demands, followed by news of Richard's be
haviour in Calabria, frightened Tancred. He saw to it that Richar
was lodged in a palace outside the walls of Messina, but, to con
ciliate him, he sent Joanna with a royal escort to join her brothe
and opened negotiations about money payments in lieu of th
dowry and legacy. King Philip, whom Richard had visited tw
days after his arrival, offered his friendly offices; and when Quee
Joanna went to pay her respects to him, he received her so cordiall
that everyone expected to hear of their forthcoming marriag
But Richard was not in a conciliatory mood. First, he sent
detachment across the Straits to occupy the town of Bagnara, o
the Calabrian coast, and installed his sister there. Then he attacke
a small island just off Messina, where there was a Greek conven
The monks were brutally ejected to give place to his troops. Th
treatment given to these holy men horrified the people of Messin
who were mainly Greeks, while the wealthier citizens were en
raged by the conduct of the English soldiers towards their wive
and daughters.

On 3 October a quarrel in a suburb between some English soldiers and a group of citizens led to a riot. A rumour spread through the town that Richard intended to conquer the whole of Sicily; and the gates were closed against his men. An attempt by his ships to force the harbour was repulsed. King Philip hastily summoned the Archbishop of Messina and Tancred's admiral Margaritus and the other Sicilian notables in the town to his palace, and went with them next morning to pacify Richard at his headquarters outside the walls. Just as it seemed that some arrangement would be made, Richard heard some of the citizens, collected on a hill outside the windows, hurl insults against his name. In a fury he left the assembly and ordered his troops to attack once more. This time the citizens were taken by surprise. In a few hours the English had captured Messina and had pillaged every quarter except for the streets by the palace where King Philip was lodged. Margaritus and the other notables barely had time to escape with their families. Their houses were seized by Richard. The Sicilian fleet anchored in the harbour was burnt. By afternoon the standard of the Plantagenets floated over the town.

Richard's truculence did not end there. Though he agreed to let King Philip's standard float next to his own, he forced the citizens to give him hostages against their King's good behaviour, and announced that he was ready to take the whole province. Meanwhile he constructed a great wooden castle just outside the town, to which he gave the scornful name of Mategrifon, the 'curb on the Greeks'.

Philip was disquieted by this example of his rival's temper. He sent his cousin, the Duke of Burgundy, to find King Tancred at Catania, to warn him of Richard's intentions, and to offer him help if worse were to follow. Tancred was in a difficult position. He knew that Henry of Hohenstaufen was about to invade his lands; and he knew that his own vassals were untrustworthy. A rapid calculation decided him that Richard would be a better ally than Philip. Philip was unlikely to attack him now; but the Kings of France were on good terms with the Hohenstaufens, and Philip's future friendship was uncertain. Richard, on the other hand, was the greatest present menace, but was known to dislike the Hohenstaufen, the enemies of his Welf cousins. Tancred rejected the French offer of help and entered into negotiations with the English. He offered Richard twenty thousand ounces of gold in lieu of the legacy due to Henry II, and Joanna the same sum in lieu of her dowry.

Richard's wrath could usually be assuaged by the sight of gold. He accepted the offer on his own and his sister's behalf, and further agreed that his young heir, Arthur Duke of Brittany, should be betrothed to one of Tancred's daughters. When Tancred further revealed the propositions made to him by King Philip, Richard willingly had the terms embodied in a treaty, which the Pope was asked to sponsor. Peace was restored; and, on the advice of the Archbishop of Rouen, Richard grudgingly gave back to Margaritus and the other leading citizens of Messina the goods that he had confiscated.

King Philip was outwitted but made no public objection. On 8 October, while the treaty was being drawn up, he and Richard met once more to discuss the future conduct of the Crusade. Rules were made about the price-control of foodstuffs. Serving men were bound to their masters. A half of every knight's money was to be devoted to the needs of the Crusaders. Gambling was forbidden, except to knights and clerks; and if they gambled excessively they were to be punished. Debts contracted on the pilgrimage must be honoured. The clergy gave sanction to the regulations, promising to excommunicate offenders. It was easy for the Kings to agree on such matters; but there were political questions that were less readily settled. After some discussion it was agreed that future conquests should be held equally between them. A more delicate problem concerned King Philip's sister Alice. This unfortunate princess had been sent as a child, years before, to the English court to marry Richard or another of Henry II's sons. Henry II had detained her, in spite of Richard's unwillingness to agree to the proposed marriage. Soon there had been ugly rumours that Henry was too intimate with her himself. Richard, whose own tastes did not lie in the direction of marriage, refused to carry out his father's arrangement, in spite of Philip's reiterated demand. Nor would his mother, Queen Eleanor, now that Henry's death had freed her from restraint, see her favourite son tied to a member of a family that she hated, and one whom she believed to have been her husband's mistress. With the interests of her native Guienne at heart she had determined to marry him to a princess of Navarre; and he accepted her choice. So, when Philip brought up again the question of Alice's marriage, Richard refused to consider it, giving Alice's reputation as his reason. Philip was quite indifferent to his family's happiness. He never intervened to help his miserable sister Agnes, the widow of Alexius II of Byzantium. But the insult was hard to bear. His relations with Richard grew still chillier, and he planned to leave Messina at once for the East. But the day after he sailed a great tempest drove him back to Sicily. As it was now mid-October he decided that it would be more prudent to winter at Messina. That, it seems, had always been Richard's intention. His treaty with Tancred was not signed till 11 November. In the meantime he sent to ask his mother to bring Berengaria of Navarre to join him in Sicily.

The winter passed quietly enough in Sicily. On Christmas Day Richard gave a sumptuous banquet at Mategrifon, to which he invited the King of France and the Sicilian notables. A few days later he had an interesting interview with the aged Abbot of Corazzo, Joachim, founder of the Order of Fiore. The venerable saint expounded to him the meaning of the Apocalypse. The seven heads of the Dragon were, he said, Herod, Nero, Constantius, Mahomet, Melsemuth (by whom he probably meant Abdul Muneim, founder of the Almohad sect), Saladin, and finally Antichrist himself, who, he declared, had already been born fifteen years ago at Rome and would sit upon the Papal throne. Richard's flippant reply, that in that case Antichrist was probably the actual Pope, Clement III, whom he personally disliked, was not well received; nor would the Saint agree with him that Antichrist would be born of the tribe of Dan in Babylon or Antioch, and reign in Jerusalem. But it was comforting to learn from Joachim that Richard would be victorious in Palestine and that Saladin soon would be slain. In February Richard organized tilting matches, in the course of which he quarrelled with a French knight, William of Barres; but Philip was able to reconcile them. Indeed, Richard behaved very correctly towards Philip, and a few days later even gave him several galleys that had recently arrived from England. About the same time he heard that Queen Eleanor and Berengaria had arrived at Naples and sent to meet them and escort them to Brindisi, as their company was too large for the strained resources of Messina, where the Count of Flanders had just arrived with a considerable following.

(As spring came near, the Kings prepared to resume their journey. Richard went to Catania to visit Tancred, with whom he swore a lasting friendship. Philip was frightened by this alliance and joined them at Taormina. He was ready now to patch up all his disagreements with Richard, and formally declared him free to marry whomsoever he chose. It was in an atmosphere of general good-will that Philip sailed with all his men from Messina on 30 March. As soon as he had left the harbour, Queen Eleanor and Princess Berengaria arrived there.) Eleanor remained only three days with her son, then left for England, travelling by way of Rome, in order to do some business for him at the Papal Court. Berengaria remained, under the chaperonage of Queen Joanna.[1]

Richard at last left Messina on 10 April, after dismantling the tower of Mategrifon. Tancred was sorry to see him go, with good reason. That same day Pope Clement III died at Rome; and

[1] The story of the King's actions in Sicily is given fully in *Itinerarium*, pp. 154–77; Ambroise, cols. 14–32 (both strongly favourable to Richard); Benedict of Peterborough, II, pp. 126–60 (the fullest account and a little more objective); Rigord, pp. 106–9 (implying that Philip was eager to go on with the Crusade while Richard made difficulties). See Chalandon, *op. cit.* II, pp. 435–42. Richard's interview with Joachim of Fiore is given by Benedict (II, pp. 151–5), apparently based on information by someone who was present.

four days later the Cardinal of Santa Maria in Cosmedin was consecrated as Celestine III. Henry of Hohenstaufen was in Rome at the time; and the new Pope's first action, under pressure, was to crown him and Constance of Sicily as Emperor and Empress.

The French fleet made a good passage to Tyre where Philip was gladly welcomed by his cousin, Conrad of Montferrat. He arrived with Conrad at Acre on 20 April. At once the siege of the Moslem fortress was tightened. To Philip's patient and ingenious temperament siege-warfare was attractive. He reorganized the engines of the besiegers and built towers for them. But an attempt to assault the walls was postponed till Richard and his men should arrive.[1]

Richard's voyage was less peaceful. Strong winds soon separated the flotilla. The King himself put in for a day at a Cretan port, from which he had a tempestuous passage to Rhodes, where he stayed for ten days, 22 April to 1 May, recovering from his sea-sickness. Meanwhile one of his ships was lost in a storm, and another three, including the ship carrying Joanna and Berengaria, were swept on to Cyprus. Two of the ships were wrecked on the south coast of the island, but Queen Joanna was able to reach an anchorage off Limassol.

Cyprus had for five years been under the rule of the self-styled Emperor Isaac Ducas Comnenus, who had led a successful revolt against Byzantium at the time of Isaac Angelus's accession, and who had maintained his independence by volatile alliances, now with the Sicilians, now with the Armenians of Cilicia, now with Saladin. He was a truculent man, who hated Latins, and he was not popular on the island owing to the exorbitant taxation that he raised. Many of his subjects still considered him a rebel and an adventurer. The appearance of great Frankish fleets in Cypriot waters alarmed him; and he faced the problem unwisely. When Richard's shipwrecked men made their way ashore he arrested them and confiscated all the goods that could be salvaged. Then he sent a messenger to Queen Joanna's ship, inviting her and Berengaria to land. Joanna, who had learned from experience of

[1] *Estoire d'Eracles*, II, pp. 155–6; Rigord, p. 108; Abu Shama, II, p. 6.

her value as a potential hostage, replied that she could not leave the ship without her brother's permission; but her request to be allowed to send ashore for fresh water was rudely refused. Indeed, Isaac came himself to Limassol and built fortifications along the shore to prevent any landing.

On 8 May, a week after Joanna's arrival off Limassol, Richard and his main fleet hove in sight. It had undergone a ghastly passage from Rhodes; and Richard's own ship had narrowly escaped destruction in the Gulf of Attalia. Sea-sickness had not improved Richard's temper; and when he heard of the treatment given to his sister and his betrothed he vowed vengeance. At once he began to land men near Limassol and marched on the town. Isaac made no resistance but retired to the village of Kilani on the slopes of Troodos. Not only did the Latin merchants settled in Limassol welcome Richard, but the Greeks in their dislike of Isaac showed themselves friendly to the invaders. Isaac therefore said that he was ready to negotiate. On receiving a safe-conduct he came down to Colossi and went on to Richard's camp. There he agreed to pay compensation for the goods that he had stolen, to allow the English troops to buy provisions free of customs dues and to send a token force of a hundred men to the Crusade, though he refused to leave the island himself. He offered to send his daughter to Richard as a hostage.

Isaac's visit to the camp convinced him that Richard was not quite as formidable as he thought. So, as soon as he returned to Colossi, he denounced the agreement and ordered Richard to leave his land. He made a foolish mistake. Richard had already sent a ship to Acre to announce his approaching arrival in Cyprus; and on 11 May, the day that Isaac saw Richard and returned to Colossi, ships put in at Limassol with all the leading Crusaders opposed to Conrad on board. There was King Guy and his brother, Geoffrey, Count of Lusignan, one of Richard's leading vassals in France, there was Bohemond of Antioch with his son Raymond, there was the Roupenian Prince Leo, who had recently succeeded his brother Roupen, there was Humphrey of Toron,

Isabella's divorced husband, and there were many of the leading Templars. As Philip had taken Conrad's side, they had come to secure Richard's support for their party. This accession of strength decided Richard to undertake the conquest of the whole island. His visitors doubtless pointed out to him its strategic value for the defence of the whole Syrian coast and the danger that might follow should Isaac enter into too close an alliance with Saladin. It was an opportunity too good to be missed.

On 12 May Richard ceremoniously married Berengaria in the chapel of Saint George at Limassol, and she was crowned Queen of England by the Bishop of Evreux. Next day the remaining vessels of the English fleet arrived. Isaac, aware of his danger, moved to Famagusta. The English followed him there, some of the army going by land and the rest by sea. The Emperor made no attempt to defend Famagusta but retired to Nicosia. While Richard rested at Famagusta, envoys reached him from Philip and the Palestinian lords, urging him to hurry to Palestine. But he replied angrily that he would not move until he had taken Cyprus, whose importance to them all he emphasized. One of Philip's envoys, Pagan of Haifa, was then supposed to have gone to Isaac, to give him further warning. Isaac sent his wife, a princess of Armenia, and his daughter to the castle of Kyrenia, and then marched down towards Famagusta. Richard's troops met him by the village of Tremithus and defeated him after a sharp skirmish, in which he was said to have used poisoned arrows. He fled from the battlefield to Kantara; and Richard entered Nicosia without opposition. The Cypriot population showed itself indifferent to Isaac's fate and was even prepared to help the invaders.

At Nicosia Richard fell ill; and Isaac hoped that his four great northern castles, Kantara, Buffavento, Saint Hilarion and Kyrenia, could hold out till Richard tired of the war and sailed away. But King Guy, in command of Richard's army, marched on Kyrenia and captured it, taking the Empress and her child prisoner. He then began to blockade Saint Hilarion and Buffavento. Bereft of his family, with his subjects apathetic or hostile, Isaac lost his nerve

and made an unconditional surrender. He was taken before Richard
and loaded with silver chains. By the end of May the entire island
was in Richard's hands.)

The booty that Richard obtained was huge. Isaac had amassed
a vast treasure by his extortions; and many of his notables bought
their new master's good-will by lavish donations. Richard soon
made it clear that his chief interest was money. A fifty per cent
capital levy was taken from every Greek, but in return Richard
confirmed the laws and institutions that had existed in the days of
Manuel Comnenus. Latin garrisons were installed in all the castles
of the island, and two Englishmen, Richard of Camville and Robert
of Turnham, were appointed justiciars and given charge of the
administration, till Richard should decide on its ultimate fate. The
Greeks soon found that their pleasure in Isaac's fall was ill-founded.
They had no more part in their government; and as a symbol of
their new subservience they were ordered to shave off their
beards.[1]

(To Richard himself the conquest of Cyprus seemed of value
because of the unexpected riches that it brought him. But in fact
it was the most far-sighted and the most enduring of all his
achievements on the Crusade. The possession of Cyprus by the

[1] Richard's conquest of Cyprus is recounted very fully in *Itinerarium*, pp. 177–
204, and Ambroise, cols. 35–57, a little less fully in Benedict of Peterborough,
II, pp. 162–8; William of Newbury, II, pp. 59 ff.; Richard of Devizes, pp. 423–6
—all from the English point of view. Richard's own brief despatch is given
in *Epistolae Cantuarenses*, p. 347. Ernoul, pp. 207–13 and *Estoire d'Eracles*, II,
pp. 159–70 (with alternative versions in Mas Latrie, *Documents*, II, pp. 1 ff.;
III, pp. 591 ff.), giving the point of view of Outremer, favourable to Richard.
Rigord, pp. 109–10, and William the Breton, pp. 104–5, justifying Richard
because of the Cypriots' refusal to aid the Crusaders. A full account by a Greek,
Neophytus, very hostile to Isaac but distressed by the conquest, is published in
the preface to Stubbs's edition of the *Itinerarium*, pp. clxxxv–clxxxix (*De
Calamitatibus Cypri*). Nicetas Choniates (p. 547) briefly notices the conquest.
Abu Shama (II, p. 8) and Beha ed-Din (*P.P.T.S.* p. 242) also give a brief
notice. Ibn al-Athir (II, pp. 42–3) says that Richard captured the island by
treachery. Both Abu Shama and Beha ed-Din mention that some Christian
renegades from Lattakieh had raided the island a few months before. See Hill,
History of Cyprus, I, pp. 314–21.

Franks prolonged the life of their lands on the mainland; and their establishments in the island outlasted those in Syria by two centuries. But it boded ill for the Greeks. If Crusaders were ready and able to annex an Orthodox province, would they not be tempted soon to launch the long desired Holy War against Byzantium?

On 5 June the English fleet sailed out from Famagusta for the Syrian coast. The Emperor Isaac was on board, a captive in King Guy's charge; and his little daughter was attached to Queen Joanna's court, to learn there the Western way of life. King Richard's first sight of the Syrian coast was the castle of Marqab. After making the landfall he turned south, past Tortosa, Jebail and Beirut, and landed on the evening of 6 June near Tyre. He was refused admission into the town by the garrison, acting on the orders of Philip and Conrad; so he continued his way by sea to Acre, watching as he went the glad sight of a great Saracen galley being sunk by his ships. He arrived in the camp by Acre on 8 June.[1]

To the weary soldiers besieging Acre, King Richard's arrival with twenty-five galleys brought confidence and hope. Bonfires were kindled to celebrate his coming, and trumpets sounded through the camp. The King of France had built many useful siege-machines, including a great stone catapult which his soldiers called the Evil Neighbour, and a grappling ladder known as the Cat. The Duke of Burgundy and the two Military Orders each had their catapult, and there was one built from the common funds called God's Own Sling.[2] These had been hammering at the walls with some effect; but a leader was needed to spur the besiegers on to a final effort. The King of France was too cautious for such a role, and the other local or Crusader princes were too tired or

---

[1] *Itinerarium*, pp. 204–11; Ambroise, cols. 57–82; Benedict of Peterborough, II, pp. 168–9; Ernoul, p. 273, and *Estoire d'Eracles*, pp. 169–70 (both emphasizing the charming welcome given by Philip to Richard); Abu Shama, II, pp. 42–3; Beha ed-Din, *P.P.T.S.* pp. 242–3, 248, telling of the capture of some of Richard's transports.

[2] *Itinerarium*, p. 218; Haymar Monachus, pp. 44–6.

discredited. Richard brought new vigour to it all. (Almost as soon as he landed, he sent an envoy with a confidential interpreter, a Moroccan captive whom he trusted, to Saladin's camp to suggest an interview. He was curious to see the celebrated infidel, and he hoped that some peaceful settlement could be made if he could only talk with so chivalrous an enemy. But Saladin replied cautiously that it was not wise for enemy kings to meet till they had signed a truce.) He was, however, ready to allow his brother al-Adil, to meet Richard. Three days of respite from fighting was arranged, and it was agreed that the meeting should take place on the plain between the camps, when the Kings of England and France both fell suddenly ill. It was the sickness that the Franks called *arnaldia*, a fever that caused the hair and the nails to fall out. Philip's attack was mild, but Richard was seriously ill for some days. But he directed operations from his sick-bed, instructing where the great catapults that he had brought should be placed, and ordering the construction of a great wooden tower, like the Mategrifon that he had built at Messina. While he was still barely convalescent he insisted on visiting his soldiers' lines.[1]

(Saladin on his side received reinforcements at the end of June. The army of Sinjar arrived on 25 June, closely followed by a fresh Egyptian army and the troops of the lord of Mosul. The lords of Shaizar and of Hama brought companies early in July. In spite of this accession of strength he was unable to drive the Crusaders from their camp. They had used the lull in the winter, when the rain had softened the soil, to surround themselves with earthworks, ramparts protected by ditches which were easy to defend. Throughout June and early July the order of battle remained much the same.) The Frankish engines kept up their bombardment of the walls of Acre; but if they made a slight breach and the Franks rushed in to try to force it, the garrison would signal to Saladin

---

[1] *Ibid.* pp. 213–25; Ambroise, col. 123; Benedict of Peterborough, II, p. 170; 'Arnaldia', which Ambroise calls 'Leonardie', was probably a form of scurvy or trench mouth. See La Monte and Hubert's translation of Ambroise, p. 196, n. 2.

who at once launched an attack on the camp, thus drawing the aggressors away from the walls. There were occasional sea-battles. The coming of the English and French fleets had taken the command of the sea from the Saracens, and it was rare now for their ships to be able to break through with supplies into the harbour. Food and war material were running short in the beleaguered city, and there was talk there of surrender.[1]

Sickness and quarrels continued within the Christian camp. The Patriarch Heraclius died, and there were intrigues over the election of a successor.[2] The dispute over the Crown was continued. Richard had taken up the cause of King Guy, while Philip supported Conrad. The Pisans had joined Richard's party, so when a Genoese flotilla arrived it offered its services to Philip. When Philip planned a fierce assault upon the city, towards the end of June, Richard, probably because he was not yet well enough to fight in person and feared that he might therefore lose the spoils of victory, refused to let his men co-operate. The attack failed because of the absence of his followers and friends; and Saladin's counter-attack on the camp was only repulsed with difficulty.[3] Relations between Richard and Philip had been complicated by the death on 1 June of Philip, Count of Flanders, the reluctant Crusader of 1177. He left no direct heirs; and while the King of France had some claim on the inheritance, the King of England was unwilling to let so rich and strategically placed a province fall into his rival's hands. When Philip, citing the terms made at Messina, demanded half of the island of Cyprus, Richard countered by demanding half Flanders. Neither side pursued the demand, but each was left with a grievance.[4]

On 3 July, after Saladin's nephew Taki had vainly tried to break through into the city, the French made a serious breach in the wall, but were forced to retire. Eight days later the English and Pisans,

---

1 Beha ed-Din, *P.P.T.S.* pp. 224–7.
2 See Mas Latrie's preface to Haymar Monachus, p. xxxvi.
3 Ambroise, col. 123; Rigord, pp. 108–9; Haymar Monachus, p. 35.
4 Rigord, p. 113; Benedict of Peterborough, II, p. 171.

using a moment when the other Crusaders were at dinner, tried their luck with the same initial success but ultimate failure. By this time the garrison had already decided to give up the struggle. They had sent envoys to the Crusader camp on 4 July, but Richard rejected their proposals; though that same day his ambassadors visited Saladin, asking to be allowed to buy fruit and snow, and hinting that they were ready to discuss peace terms. Saladin was shocked to hear that his men inside Acre had given up hope. He promised them immediate help; but he could not stir his army into making the great attack on the Christian camp that he had planned for 5 July. On 7 July a swimmer brought him a last appeal from the city. Without aid the garrison could hold out no longer. The battle on the 11th was the final effort of the besieged. Next day they offered to capitulate; and their terms were accepted. Acre was to be surrendered with all its contents, its ships and its military stores. Two hundred thousand gold pieces were to be paid to the Franks, with an extra four hundred for Conrad in person. Fifteen hundred Christian prisoners, with a hundred prisoners of rank, to be specifically named, were to be liberated and the True Cross was to be restored. If this were done the lives of the defenders would be spared.

A swimmer left the harbour to tell Saladin what was agreed, for it was for him to implement the clauses. He was horrified. As he sat in front of his tent composing an answer forbidding the garrison to submit to such terms, he saw the Frankish banners being unfurled on the city towers. It was too late. His officers had made the treaty in his name, and as a man of honour he abode by it. He moved his camp to Shafr'amr on the road to Sephoria, further from the city, now that he could do nothing more to help it, and he steeled himself to receive the ambassadors of the victorious Franks.[1]

[1] *Itinerarium*, pp. 227–33; Ambroise, cols. 133–9; Benedict of Peterborough, II, pp. 174–9; Rigord, pp. 115–16; Ernoul, p. 274; *Estoire d'Eracles*, II, pp. 173–4; Abu Shama, II, pp. 19–29; Beha ed-Din, *P.P.T.S.* pp. 258–69; Ibn al-Athir, II, pp. 44–6.

No sooner had the capitulation been accepted than the Saracen garrison marched out of Acre. The conquerors were moved to see t pass by into captivity, for they admired its courage and tenacity, worthy of a better cause. When the last Saracen had left the Franks moved in, headed by Conrad, whose standard-bearer carried his personal standard and the standards of the Kings. King Richard took up his residence in the former Royal Palace near the north wall of the city, King Philip in the former establishment of the Templars, on the sea near the tip of the peninsula. Unseemly quarrels marred the assignment of quarters in the city. The Duke of Austria, as head of the German army, claimed a position equal to the Kings of France and England and set his standard up beside Richard's, only to see it taken down by the English and hurled into the fosse below. It was an insult that Leopold of Austria never forgave. When he returned home a few days later, it was with hatred for Richard in his heart. The Frankish merchants and nobles who had previously held property in Acre asked for their possessions to be given back. They were nearly all of them supporters of Conrad, and therefore appealed to King Philip when the visiting Crusaders tried to displace them. He insisted that their claims should be honoured.[1]

The first task to be done was to clean and reconsecrate the churches of Acre. When this was done, under the direction of the Papal Legate, Adelard of Verona, the princes met together to settle finally the question of the kingship. After some debate it was agreed that Guy should remain king till his death, when the crown would pass to Conrad and Isabella and their issue. In the meantime Conrad would be lord of Tyre, Beirut and Sidon, and he and Guy would share the royal revenues. Having secured the future for Conrad, King Philip talked of going home. He had suffered from almost continuous illness since he came to the Holy

[1] *Itinerarium*, p. 234; Ernoul, pp. 274–5; *Estoire d'Eracles*, II, pp. 175–6; *Chronica Regia Coloniensis*, p. 154, for the story of Richard's quarrel with Leopold of Austria. Ansbert, *Expeditio Friderici*, p. 102, says that Leopold resented Richard's attack on Isaac Comnenus of Cyprus, who was his mother's first cousin.

Land; he had done his Christian duty in helping to reconquer
Acre; and he would leave the Duke of Burgundy and the large
portion of the French army behind him. Richard in vain pressed
for a joint declaration that the two Kings would remain for three
years in the East. The most that Philip would promise was that he
would not attack Richard's French territories till Richard came
home, a promise that was not entirely kept. Then on 31 July he
left Acre for Tyre, accompanied by Conrad, who said that he
must see to his lands there, but who in reality did not wish to serve
in an army dominated by King Richard. Three days later King
Philip set sail from Tyre for Brindisi.[1]

Philip's departure was regarded by the English as a cowardly
and traitorous desertion. But it seems that his health was really
bad; and there were problems at home, such as the Flanders inheritance, for whose solution he was personally responsible. He
moreover suspected that Richard was plotting against him and
that his life was in danger. A curious story went round that when
he was lying very ill Richard came to see him and told him falsely
that his only son Louis was dead, either as a piece of heavy
buffoonery or in the sinister hope that the shock would prove too
much for him. There were many in the Christian army ready to
sympathize with Philip in his anxieties. Though Richard commanded the devotion of his own men and the admiration of the
Saracens, to the barons of the Frankish East the King of France
was the monarch whom they respected and whom they felt to
understand their needs.[2]

With Philip gone, Richard took full command of the army and
of the negotiations with Saladin. The Sultan agreed to abide by

[1] *Itinerarium*, pp. 238–9; Ambroise, cols. 142–3; Benedict of Peterborough,
II, pp. 183–5, 192–9, 227–31; *Estoire d'Eracles*, II, pp. 179–81, saying that Philip
was really ill. Ernoul, pp. 277–8; Rigord, pp. 116–17; William the Breton,
pp. 106–9.
[2] *Estoire d'Eracles, loc. cit.* for story of Richard's intrigues. Beha ed-Din,
P.P.T.S. p. 240, says that the King of France's authority was universally
acknowledged, and, later on, p. 242, that the King of England was his inferior in
rank, though he outstripped in wealth, valour and fame.

the treaty made by his officers at Acre. While the Crusaders set about rebuilding and strengthening the walls of Acre, Saladin began to collect the prisoners and the money demanded from him. On 2 August Christian officers visited his camp bearing Richard's consent to his suggestion that the payments should be made and the prisoners returned in three monthly instalments. The Saracen prisoners would be liberated after the first instalment had been paid. The visitors were shown the Holy Cross, which Saladin had kept with him, and paid it reverence. On 11 August the first instalment of men and money was sent down to the Christian camp; and Richard's ambassadors returned to say that the figures were correct, except that the prisoners of rank specially named had not all been handed over. For that reason they would not free the Sultan's soldiers captured at Acre. Saladin requested them either to accept the instalment with hostages for the missing lords, and send him his men, or to accept the instalment and leave hostages with him to guarantee the release of his men. The ambassadors rejected both suggestions. They demanded the instalment and only offered to give a pledge about the Saracen prisoners. Saladin, distrusting their word, refused to give anything unless his men were released.

Richard was now eager to leave Acre and march on Jerusalem. The Saracen prisoners were an embarrassment to him; he was glad of an excuse to rid himself of them. Cold-bloodedly, on 20 August, more than a week after his ambassadors had returned to him, he declared that Saladin had broken his bargain and ordered the massacre of the twenty-seven hundred survivors of the garrison at Acre. His soldiers gave themselves eagerly to the task of butchery, thanking God, so Richard's apologists gleefully tell us, for this opportunity to avenge their comrades who had fallen before the city. The prisoners' wives and children were killed at their side. Only a few notables and a few men strong enough to be of use for slave-labour were spared. The Saracen outposts nearest to Acre saw what was being done and rushed up to save their countrymen, but though they fought till nightfall they

could not penetrate through to them. When the slaughter was ove
the English left the spot with its mutilated and decaying corpses
and the Moslems could come and recognize their martyred friends

(On Thursday, 22 August, Richard led the Crusading army ou
of Acre. Conrad and many of the local barons were absent, an
the French, under the Duke of Burgundy, followed grudgingl
in the rear.) None of the soldiers had wanted to leave the cit
where they had lived so comfortably for the last month, with foo
in plenty and wanton women to gratify their lusts; nor were the
pleased to hear that the only female camp-followers permitted t
march with them were washerwomen. But the force of Richard'
personality overrode them. Saladin was still at Shafr'amr, com
manding the two main roads from the coast, the road to Tiberia
and Damascus and the road through Nazareth to Jerusalem. Bu
Richard moved south along the coast road, where his flank woul
be protected by the sea and his fleet. The Sultan therefore followe
him on a parallel course and encamped at Tel-Kaimun, on th
slopes of Carmel. From there he rode out to inspect the countr
by the shore south of Carmel, to choose a site for a battle.

The Christians journeyed past Haifa which Saladin had dis
mantled shortly before the fall of Acre, and round the spur o
Carmel. Their progress was slow, to let the fleet keep up wit
them; and Richard believed that the soldiers should be allowed t
rest almost every other day. For the wind was in the west, and th
ships had difficulty in rounding the point. (Saracen light horseme
from time to time swooped down from Carmel on the marching
army, cutting off stragglers, who were taken to Saladin, cross
questioned and then slain, in vengeance for the massacre at Acre

[1] *Itinerarium*, pp. 240–3; Ambroise, cols. 144–8 (both justifying Richard owin
to Saladin's truculence and saying that Conrad tried to keep the prisone
entrusted to him. Ambroise praises God for the massacre). Ernoul, pp. 276–7
Estoire d'Eracles, II, pp. 178–9; Beha ed-Din, *P.P.T.S.* pp. 270–4, a more cor
vincing story; Abu Shama, II, pp. 30–3, according to whom Saladin asked th
Templars, whose word he trusted though he hated them, to guarantee th
terms, but they refused, suspecting that Richard would break them. The Hol
Cross was not returned.

Only the washerwomen were spared. Meanwhile Richard led his main army over the ridge of Carmel and encamped inland from Caesarea.[1]

On the 30th the two armies came into closer contact, as the Christians approached Caesarea. Thenceforward there was sharp fighting every day. But Richard led his army doggedly on. He was at his best, usually fighting in the van, but now and then riding down the whole line to encourage the men onward. The heat was intense, and the Westerners, heavily armed and unused to the sun, lost many lives from sunstroke, and many fainted and were killed where they lay. The Duke of Burgundy and the French troops were nearly annihilated as they lagged in the rear, behind the provision-wagons, but they extricated themselves. The whole host trudged steadily on, crying out at intervals the prayer, *Sanctum Sepulchrum adjuva*, 'Help us, Holy Sepulchre'.

A few days later Saladin chose his battle-ground. It was to be just north of Arsuf, where the plain was wide enough for the use of cavalry but well veiled by the forests which came down within two miles of the sea. On 5 September, Richard asked for a parley, and met the Sultan's brother, al-Adil, under a flag of truce. But, weary though he was of fighting, he demanded nothing less than the cession of all Palestine. Al-Adil at once broke off the negotiation.

On Saturday morning, 7 September, it was clear to Richard that the Moslems were going to force a battle, and he drew up his men in preparation. The baggage train was spread out along the coast, with Henry of Champagne and part of the infantry to guard them. The bowmen were in the front line and behind them were the knights. The Templars were on the right, at the southern end of the line. Next were the Bretons and the men of Anjou, and next to them the troops of Guienne, under Guy and his brother, Geoffrey of Lusignan. In the centre was the King himself, with his English and Norman troops, then the Flemish and the native barons, under James of Avesnes, and the French under Hugh of

---

[1] *Itinerarium*, pp. 248–56; Ambroise, cols. 152–60; Beha ed-Din, *P.P.T.S.* p. 275–81; Abu Shama, II, pp. 33–6.

Burgundy, and on the extreme left the Hospitallers. When all was arranged, Richard and the Duke of Burgundy rode along the lines giving words of encouragement.

The Saracen attack began in the middle of the morning. Wave after wave of lightly armed negro and Bedouin foot-soldiers rushed on the Christians, hurling arrows and darts. They flung the first line of infantry into disorder but could make no impression on the knights in their heavy armour. Suddenly they divided their ranks and the Turkish horsemen charged through, flashing sabres and axes. They drove their fiercest attacks against the Hospitallers and the Flemings and native barons next to them, hoping to turn the Christian left flank. The knights held their ground and after each wave the bowmen reformed their line. Despite his soldiers' pleading Richard would not allow any part of his army to attack till all were ready and the Turkish charges showed signs of weariness and till the main Saracen army was closer. Several times the Grand Master of the Hospital sent to beg him to give the signal. His knights, he said, would have to yield unless they could take the offensive. When Richard still ordered patience, two of the knights, the Marshal of the Order and Baldwin Carew, took matters into their own hands and rode out into the enemy, and all their comrades galloped after them. At the sight of the charge the knights all down the line spurred their horses on. There was confusion at first, for the bowmen were unprepared and were in the way. The King himself rode into the midst of the turmoil to restore some order, and took command of the onslaught. Saladin's secretary, watching from a nearby hill, gasped at the splendour of the spectacle as the Christian cavalry thundered towards him. It was too much for the Moslem soldiers. They broke their ranks and fled. Saladin rallied them in time to defend his camp and even to lead another charge against the enemy. But it was in vain. By evening the Christian army was in command of the field and was continuing its southward march.[1]

[1] *Itinerarium*, pp. 256–78; Ambroise, cols. 160–78; Beha ed-Din, *P.P.T.S.* pp. 281–95; Abu Shama, II, pp. 36–40.

The battle of Arsuf was not decisive, but it was a great moral victory for the Christians. Their losses had been surprisingly small, though among the dead was the great knight James of Avesnes, who lay with fifteen Saracen corpses round him. But the Saracen losses had been almost as small. No emir of note had fallen; and by next day Saladin had gathered together all his men and was ready to try another encounter, which Richard refused and which he was not quite strong enough to force. The value of the victory lay in the confidence that it gave to the Christians. It was the first great open battle since Hattin, and it showed that Saladin could be defeated. Coming so soon after the capture of Acre, it seemed to indicate that the tide had turned and that Jerusalem itself could be liberated once more. Richard's repute was at its height. The victorious charge had, it is true, been launched against his orders, but only a few minutes before he was ready; and his patient restraint beforehand and his direction of the charge when it came had shown superb generalship. It promised well for the future of the Crusade.

Saladin, on the other hand, had suffered a personal and a public humiliation. His army had been ineffectual at Acre, and now it had been defeated in open battle. Like his great predecessor Nur ed-Din, Saladin as he grew older lost something of his energy and his command of men. His health was poor; he suffered from recurrent malarial attacks. He was less able than in his younger days to force his decisions on the quarrelsome emirs who were his vassals. Many of them still regarded him as an upstart and a usurper, and were quick to show insubordination if his star seemed to be declining. He could ill afford to be out-generalled by Richard. Above all, he must not lose Jerusalem, whose capture had been his most glorious triumph. He took his army in good order to Ramleh, on the road to Jerusalem, to await Richard's next move.

The Crusading army marched on to Jaffa and set about rebuilding its fortifications. Hitherto Richard had had the fleet on his flank, to keep him in supplies. He was not prepared to march inland to the Holy City without a strong base on the coast. Moreover, after its long march down the coast his army was tired and needed a rest. His caution and delay have puzzled many historians; for had he moved swiftly against Jerusalem he would have found it poorly garrisoned and its walls in bad repair. But Saladin's army had only been defeated, not destroyed. It was still formidable; and even had Richard broken through to Jerusalem, it could have cut him off from the sea. It was prudent to make certain of Jaffa before starting on the greater adventure. Nevertheless the delay was over-long. It enabled Saladin to strengthen the defences of the Holy City. Then, fearful lest Richard should move on Ascalon and establish a base there that would cut off the road to Egypt, his main source of man-power, he took part of his army from Ramleh to Ascalon and methodically demolished the whole city, rich and prosperous though it was.[1] Meanwhile the Christian army enjoyed the comforts of Jaffa. Life was pleasant there. Fruit and vegetables abounded in the gardens round the town, and the ships brought ample provisions. They brought, too, gay ladies from Acre to divert the men. The Saracens kept at a distance. There were only a few chivalrous skirmishes in the plain of Lydda, on the outskirts of the camp. The army grew indolent and soft. Many soldiers found their way back to Acre. Richard sent King Guy to urge them to return to the camp, but they took no notice of him. It needed Richard's own visit to Acre to gather them together again.[2] Richard had his own worries. He was not happy about affairs at Acre and further north, where Conrad's party was powerful. There was trouble in Cyprus, where Richard of Camville had died and Robert of Turnham had difficulty in suppressing a revolt; and he feared what King Philip might do on his return to France. He solved his trouble in Cyprus by selling the island to the Templars.[3] But he was also anxious to start negotiations with

[1] *Itinerarium*, pp. 280–1; Beha ed-Din, *P.P.T.S.* pp. 295–300; Abu Shama, II, pp. 41–4, Ibn al-Athir, II, pp. 50–1, showing that Saladin gave way to his emirs against his wishes over Ascalon.

[2] *Itinerarium*, pp. 283–6; Ambroise, cols. 187–9.

[3] Benedict of Peterborough, II, pp. 172–3; Ernoul, p. 273; *Estoire d'Eracles*, II, pp. 170, 189–90.

Saladin. Saladin was ready to listen to his proposals and empowered his brother, al-Adil, to treat for him.

As soon as he reached Jaffa, Richard sent Humphrey of Toron, who was the best Arabic scholar in his army, and for whom he had a deep affection, to Lydda, where al-Adil was in command, to discuss preliminaries for a truce, but nothing was decided. Al-Adil was a skilled diplomat, and restrained his brother's longing for a settlement. His diplomacy was given a wonderful opportunity when in October envoys came to him from Tyre, asking if he would receive an embassy from Conrad. Richard's first demand was for nothing less than Jerusalem with the whole country west of the Jordan, and the return of the Holy Cross. Saladin sent back a reply that the Holy City was holy to Islam too; and he would not return the Cross without some counter-concession. A few days later, on 20 October, Richard made fresh proposals. Like all the Crusaders, he admired al-Adil, whom they called Saphadin, and suggested that al-Adil should receive the whole of Palestine at present owned by Saladin, and that he should marry the King's sister, Queen Joanna of Sicily, who should be endowed with the coastal cities conquered by Richard, including Ascalon. The married couple should live at Jerusalem, to which the Christians should be given full access. The Cross should be restored. All prisoners on each side should be released, and the Templars and the Hospitallers should be given back their Palestinian properties. Saladin, when his secretary visited him with the offer, treated it as a joke and gaily agreed. But Richard may have been quite serious about it. Queen Joanna, who, with Queen Berengaria, had joined him at Jaffa, was horrified when she heard the suggestion. Nothing, she said, would induce her to marry a Moslem. So Richard next asked al-Adil whether he would consider becoming a Christian. Al-Adil politely refused the honour, but invited Richard to a sumptuous banquet at Lydda on 8 November. It was a happy festivity and they parted with protestations of affection and each with many gifts from the other. But at the same moment Saladin was entertaining in his camp close by the ambassador sent by

Conrad, the charming Reynald of Sidon, whose trickery over Beaufort the Sultan had forgiven.

Next morning Saladin received Richard's envoy, Humphrey of Toron. He brought an offer that al-Adil should be recognized as ruler of all Palestine so long as the Christians might have a share of Jerusalem. It was hoped that the marriage with Joanna might be arranged, though Richard admitted that Christian public opinion was somewhat shocked by the idea. A Papal dispensation might, Richard thought, make Joanna change her mind. If not, al-Adil could have his niece, Eleanor of Brittany, who as the King's ward could be married off without Papal interference. When all this was settled Richard would return to Europe. Conrad's offer was less sensational. In return for Sidon and Beirut he would break with the other Crusaders and even suggested returning Acre to the Moslems. But when asked if he would actually take up arms against Richard, his ambassador prevaricated.

Saladin held a council to decide with which Frankish party talks should continue. Al-Adil and the other emirs voted for Richard's party, less, perhaps, from any liking for the King than because he would soon be leaving Palestine, whereas Conrad, for whom they all felt some awe, meant to stay permanently there. Richard's proposals were accepted in principle; but Humphrey's suite were distressed one day to see Reynald of Sidon out hunting with al-Adil and on obvious terms of intimacy with him. Indeed, al-Adil kept the negotiations spinning out till winter came.[1] Fighting between the armies had meanwhile been desultory and sporadic. One day in late November Richard, when out hawking, fell into a Saracen ambush, and might have been taken had not the valiant knight, William of Preaux, shouted out that he was the King and let himself be taken prisoner. Some other knights fell that day; but apart from that small skirmish there were no engagements of note.[2]

When the November rains began Saladin disbanded half his

---

[1] *Itinerarium*, pp. 295–7; Beha ed-Din, *P.P.T.S.* pp. 302–35, a detailed account of the negotiations; Abu Shama, II, pp. 45–50.
[2] *Itinerarium*, pp. 286–8.

army and retired with the rest to winter-quarters at Jerusalem. Reinforcements were on the way from Egypt. But Richard refused to be discouraged by the weather. In the middle of the month he led his army, increased by fresh detachments from Acre, out of Jaffa as far as Ramleh, which he found deserted and dismantled by the Saracens. He waited there for six weeks, looking for a chance to move on to Jerusalem. There were frequent Saracen raids on his outposts. He himself was nearly captured when reconnoitring near the castle of Blanchegarde. In another skirmish the Earl of Leicester was taken but subsequently released. During the last days of the year the weather was so bad that Saladin withdrew his raiders. Richard spent Christmas at Latrun, on the edge of the Judaean hills; and on 28 December his army moved up into the hills unopposed by the enemy. The rain fell in torrents. The road was deep in mud. A high wind broke down the tent-poles before any tent could be erected. By 3 January the army had reached the fort of Beit-Nuba, only twelve miles from the Holy City. The English and French soldiers were full of enthusiasm. Even the discomforts of the camp on the wet windy height and the ruin by the rain of the stores of biscuit and pork that were their main food, the loss from cold and under-feeding of many of their horses and their own weariness and chills were bearable if they were so soon to attain their goal. But the knights that knew the country, the Hospitallers, the Templars and the native-born barons, took a wiser and a sadder view. They told King Richard that even if he penetrated over the muddy hills through the storms to Jerusalem and even if he could contain Saladin's army there, there was a Saracen army from Egypt encamped on the hills outside. He would be caught between the two. And if he captured Jerusalem, they added, what then? The visiting Crusaders when they had paid their pilgrimage would all return home to Europe; and the native soldiery was not numerous enough to hold it against the forces of united Islam. Richard was convinced. After five days' hesitation he sounded the retreat.[1]

[1] *Ibid.* pp. 303–8; Ambroise, cols. 203–8.

Angrily and dejectedly the army marched back through the sleet to Ramleh. The English bore the disappointment sturdily, but the French, with their mercurial temperament, began to desert. Many of them, including the Duke of Burgundy, retired to Jaffa, some even to Acre. Richard saw that to restore his men's spirits some activity was needed. He held a council on 20 January and with its support gave orders to the army to move from Ramleh through Ibelin to Ascalon. There he set about repairing the great fortress that Saladin had dismantled a few months before. Like Saladin, he well understood its strategic importance. He persuaded the French to rejoin him there.[1]

Apart from a visit to Acre, Richard spent the next four months at Ascalon, making it the strongest castle on all the coast of Palestine. His men worked well, in spite of much discomfort. There was no harbour there, and the food supplies, which came by sea, could often not be landed. The weather that winter was consistently bad. But Saladin did not molest them. Some of Richard's followers thought that he chivalrously refused to attack them when they were so vulnerable, to the discontent of his emirs. But in fact he wished to rest his army and to wait for reinforcements from the Jezireh and Mosul. It may well be that some of his emirs were discontented, though not because of his inaction. While they were in such a mood he would not risk a battle.[2]

Moreover, news from Acre showed him that the Franks were disunited. In February Richard summoned Conrad to help in the work at Ascalon, and Conrad brusquely refused to come. A few days later Hugh of Burgundy and many of the French deserted and went to Acre. King Philip had left the Duke with very little money for his troops, and their pay had hitherto been provided out of loans made by Richard. But even Richard's huge treasury was running low. He would not finance them any longer. At Acre the eternal rivalry between the Pisans and the Genoese, both of whom now had many men and ships quartered there, had blazed

[1] *Itinerarium*, pp. 309–12; Ambroise, cols. 208–11; Abu Shama, II, p. 51.
[2] *Itinerarium*, pp. 313–17; Ambroise, cols. 212–14.

nto open war. The Pisans, claiming to act in King Guy's name, eized the city in the teeth of Hugh of Burgundy who had just rrived. They held it for three days against Hugh, Conrad and the Genoese, and sent to Richard to come to their aid. On 20 February Richard arrived at Acre and tried to make peace. He had an interview with Conrad at Casal Imbert on the road to Tyre; but it was insatisfactory. Conrad still refused to join the army at Ascalon, even when Richard threatened that unless he did so all his lands would be forfeited. It was a threat that could not be carried out. When Richard returned to Ascalon, having patched up a precarious truce, he was more than ever convinced that peace must be made with Saladin.[1]

He was still in touch with al-Adil. An English envoy, Stephen of Turnham, visited Jerusalem to see the Sultan and his brother, and was shocked on his arrival at the gate of the city to see Reynald of Sidon and Balian of Ibelin emerging. Saladin's negotiations with Conrad had not been broken off; and Balian's presence was inister, for he was a knight whom the Sultan greatly esteemed. However, on 20 March al-Adil rode down to Richard's camp with a definite offer. The Christians should keep what they had conquered and have the right of pilgrimage to Jerusalem, where the Latins could maintain priests. The Holy Cross should be restored to them. They might annex Beirut also, if it were dismantled. The embassy was well received by the King. Indeed, as a mark of peculiar honour, one of al-Adil's sons was girded with he belt of knighthood, though doubtless the usual Christian elements in the ceremony were omitted. When al-Adil rejoined his brother early in April it seemed that a settlement had at last been reached.[2]

The need for the settlement was emphasized a few days later, when the Prior of Hereford arrived from England, to tell Richard that things were going ill in England. The King's brother John was usurping more and more authority, and the Chancellor,

[1] *Itinerarium*, pp. 319–24; Ambroise, cols. 218–21.
[2] Beha ed-Din, *P.P.T.S.* pp. 328–9; *Itinerarium*, p. 337.

William, Bishop of Ely, begged Richard to come home at once. Richard had spent Easter, 5 April, in the camp, furious because the remaining Frenchmen had just left him, summoned north by Hugh of Burgundy. Now, more than ever, the quarrels of the Crusaders must be stilled. A Council of all the knights and barons of Palestine was called by the King. He told them that he soon must leave the country, and that the question of the crown of Jerusalem must be decided; and he offered them the choice of King Guy and the Marquis Conrad. To his shocked surprise no one spoke up for Guy. It was Conrad whom everybody wanted.

Richard was wise and magnanimous enough to abide by the decision. He agreed to recognize Conrad as King. A mission, headed by his nephew Henry of Champagne, set out for Tyre to give the good news to the Marquis.

When Henry arrived at Tyre, on about 20 April, there was great rejoicing. It was decided that the coronation should take place within a few days at Acre; and then it was understood that Conrad would at last consent to join the camp at Ascalon. Henry left Tyre for Acre at once, to prepare the city for the ceremony.[1]

On hearing the news Conrad had fallen on his knees and asked God that if he were unworthy of the kingship it should not be granted to him. A few days later, on Tuesday, 28 April 1192, he was kept waiting for his dinner by his wife, the Princess Isabella, who was lingering too late in her bath. He decided to go round and dine with his old friend, the Bishop of Beauvais. He found that the Bishop had finished his meal, so, though he was pressed to stay while food was prepared for him, he walked gaily homeward. As he passed round a sharp corner two men came up, and while one of them gave him a letter to read, the other stabbed him in the body. He was carried dying to his palace.

One of the murderers was struck down on the spot. The other was taken and confessed, before he was executed, that he and his comrade were Assassins sent to do the task by the Old Man of the Mountains, the Sheik, Sinan. The Assassins had preserved a quiet

[1] *Itinerarium*, pp. 329–38; Ambroise, cols. 225–31.

neutrality throughout the Crusade, which had given them an opportunity to strengthen their castles and amass greater wealth. Conrad had offended Sinan by an act of piracy against a merchant ship, laden with a rich cargo that the sect had bought. Despite Sinan's remonstrances, he had not returned the goods or the crew, who, indeed, had all been drowned. It is possible that Sinan also feared that the establishment of a strong Crusader state on the Lebanese coast might eventually endanger his territory. It was said that the two murderers had been for some time in Tyre awaiting their chance, and that they had even accepted baptism, with Conrad and Balian of Ibelin as their sponsors. But public opinion sought deeper causes. Some said that Saladin had bribed Sinan to murder both Richard and Conrad; but Sinan feared that Richard's death might leave Saladin free to march against the Assassins, so would only undertake the latter task. Another theory more generally held was that Richard himself had arranged the assassination. Saladin's connivance is not to be credited; while Richard, much as he disliked Conrad, never made use of such a weapon. But his enemies, headed by the Bishop of Beauvais, refused to believe in his innocence.[1]

The death of Conrad was a blow to the renascent kingdom. Harsh, ambitious and unscrupulous, yet trusted and admired by the native Frankish nobility, he would have been a strong and cunning king. Yet his disappearance had its compensations. The heiress of the kingdom, Isabella, was free to marry and bring the crown to some less controversial candidate. When Henry of Champagne heard of the murder he hurried back from Acre to Tyre. There the widowed Princess had shut herself up in the castle and refused to hand over the keys of her city to any but the representative of the King of France or the King of England. Henry on his arrival was at once acclaimed by the people of Tyre as the man that should marry their princess and inherit the throne. He was

[1] *Itinerarium*, pp. 337–42; Ambroise, cols. 233–8; Ernoul, pp. 288–90; *Estoire d'Eracles*, II, pp. 192–4; Beha ed-Din, *P.P.T.S.* pp. 332–3; Abu Shama, II, pp. 52–4.

young and gallant and popular, and the nephew of two Kings. Isabella yielded to the public clamour. She gave herself and her keys to Henry. Two days after Conrad's assassination their betrothal was announced.)There were some who thought that a longer delay would have been seemly; and it was doubtful whether remarriage within a year could be canonically legal. Henry himself was a little lukewarm. Isabella was a very lovely young woman of twenty-one, but she had been twice married already, and she now had an infant daughter, who would be her heir. It seems that Henry insisted that the engagement should be ratified by Richard. Messengers had brought Richard up to Acre, and there he met his nephew. It was rumoured that Henry told him of his doubts and of his longing to go home to his fair lands in France. But to Richard the solution seemed admirable. He advised Henry to accept election to the throne and promised that some day he would return with fresh help for his kingdom. He refused to give advice about the marriage; but Henry could not become king except as Isabella's husband. On 5 May 1192, after just one week of widowhood, Isabella entered Acre with Henry by her side. The whole population came out to greet them, and the marriage was celebrated with pomp and general delight. The Princess and her husband then took up their residence in the castle of Acre.[1]

It was a happy marriage. Henry soon fell deeply in love with his wife and could not bear her out of his sight; and she found his charm irresistible, after the grimness of the ageing Piedmontese to whom she had been forcibly united.

Richard had already disposed of King Guy. He had understood at last that no one in Palestine had any use for the ineffectual ex-monarch. But there was the future of Cyprus to be considered. He had no desire to maintain officers there when he returned to

---

[1] *Itinerarium*, pp. 342–3; Ambroise, cols. 238–9 (both saying that the people insisted on Henry's election; the French favoured it, but Richard would not commit himself); Ernoul, pp. 290–1; *Estoire d'Eracles*, II, pp. 195–6 (both implying that Richard insisted on it); Abu Shama, *loc. cit.* He says that Isabella was enceinte when she married Henry. Her daughter Maria was, however, probably born before Conrad's death.

Europe; nor were the Templars, to whom he had sold the government, wise in their treatment of the Greek natives. They wished to return it to him; so he permitted Guy to buy the government from them, himself demanding an additional sum, which, in fact, Guy never fully paid him. Early in May, Guy landed in Cyprus with complete authority to govern it as he pleased.[1]

When all this was settled, Richard invited Henry to join him at Ascalon. (There was a rumour that one of Saladin's nephews in Mesopotamia had begun a dangerous revolt against the Sultan. So Richard, whose treaty with the Saracens was not yet ratified, decided on a sudden attack on Daron twenty miles down the coast. But Henry, with the French army, dallied at Acre. Without waiting for them Richard advanced by sea and land on Daron; and on 23 May, after five days' fierce fighting, the lower town was stormed and the garrison in the citadel surrendered. Richard had learned little from Saladin's courtesy. Some of the garrison were killed by the sword or flung over the battlements, or taken away bound into perpetual captivity.[2]

The easy capture of Saladin's last fortress on the Palestinian coast so heartened the Crusaders that they planned once more to march on Jerusalem. Henry and the French arrived at Daron the day after its capture, in time to spend Whitsun there with the King. The army returned to Ascalon immediately afterwards, and the French and English alike urged an immediate attack upon the Holy City.) Richard had just heard more disquieting news from England, and he was doubtful whether the expedition was militarily feasible. He took to his bed in perplexity, and was only aroused by a stirring address given him by one of his Poitevin chaplains. He then vowed to stay in Palestine till the following Easter.[3]

On 7 June the Christian army set out again from Ascalon. Bypassing Ramleh by marching on the road through Blanchegarde,

---

[1] For the sale of Cyprus, see Hill, *History of Cyprus*, II, pp. 36–8, 67–9.

[2] *Itinerarium*, pp. 352–6; Ambroise, cols. 245–51; Beha ed-Din, *P.P.T.S.* p. 337; Abu Shama, II, p. 54.

[3] *Itinerarium*, pp. 356–65; Ambroise, cols. 252–9.

it reached Latrun on the 9th and Beit-Nuba on the 11th. Ther
Richard halted, and there the army remained for a month. Saladin
waited at Jerusalem, where his reinforcements from the Jezireh and
Mosul had just arrived. Without better stores and baggage
animals it would be folly for the Christians to advance further into
the hills. Both sides settled down to skirmishing, with varying
success. One day as he was riding out over the hills above Emmau
King Richard suddenly saw a distant view of the walls and tower
of Jerusalem. Hastily he covered his face with his shield, that he
might not fully behold the City which God had not allowed him
to deliver. But there were compensations. The Syrian Bishop of
Lydda came one day to the camp with a portion of the True Cross
that he had saved. A little later the Abbot of the Greek Conven
of Mar Elias, a venerable man with a long white beard, told the
King of a spot where he had buried another portion of the Cross
to save it from the infidel. It was dug up and given to Richard
These fragments consoled the army for its failure to retrieve the
major part of the relic, which, it seems, Saladin had now restored
to the Holy Sepulchre at Jerusalem.

On 20 June, when the army leaders were hesitating whether to
abandon the attempt on Jerusalem and march instead into Egypt
news came of a great Moslem convoy making its way from the
south towards the Holy City. Three days later Richard fell on it by
the Round Cistern, the wells of Kuwaifa, in the barren country
some twenty miles south-west of Hebron. The Moslems were ill-
prepared for the onslaught. After a short battle the whole caravan
was captured with its rich merchandise, its plentiful supplies of
food and some thousands of horses and camels. The Christian
army returned in triumph to the camp at Beit-Nuba.

Saladin was horrified by the news. Richard would now surely
march on to Jerusalem. He hastily sent men to block up all the
wells between Beit-Nuba and the city, and cut down all the fruit
trees. On 1 July he held an anxious council in Jerusalem, to discuss whether he should retire eastward. He himself wished to stay
there, and his assembled emirs supported his decision, protesting

heir loyalty to him. But the Turkish and Kurdish troops were quarrelling, and he was unsure how well they would stand up to a rigorous attack.

His worries soon were settled. There had been anxious debates n the Christian camp also. The French soldiers were eager to press on now that food and transport were abundant. But Richard's couts had warned him of the lack of water; and there was still he problem how to hold Jerusalem when the Western Crusaders eturned home. To the jeers and insults of the French, Richard once again ordered the army to retreat from Beit-Nuba. On July news reached Saladin that the Christians had broken camp nd were beginning to move down towards the coast. He rode out to a neighbouring hill at the head of his men to watch the distant procession.[1]

As soon as he was back at Jaffa Richard again sought a truce that would leave him free to go home. Henry of Champagne sent Saladin an arrogant message announcing that he was now heir to he kingdom of Jerusalem and that it all should be given to him. Richard's ambassadors, who came to Jerusalem three days later, were more conciliatory. Richard recommended his nephew to Saladin's good graces and urged a friendly arrangement. With he approval of his council, Saladin agreed to treat Henry as a son, o allow Latin priests in the Holy Places, and to cede the coast of Palestine to the Christians, provided only that Ascalon was dismantled. Richard refused to consider the dismantling of Ascalon, even when Saladin offered Lydda in exchange. While the argument was still being carried on by messengers going to and fro, Richard moved to Acre, planning to sail away even if the treaty was not yet signed. His scheme was to march suddenly on Beirut and seize it and embark there for Europe.[2]

His absence gave Saladin an opportunity. Early on 27 July he

---

[1] *Itinerarium*, pp. 365–98; Ambroise, cols. 260–87; Beha ed-Din, *P.P.T.S.* p. 337–52; Abu Shama, ii, pp. 56–62.
[2] *Itinerarium*, pp. 398–9; Ambroise, cols. 287–8; Beha ed-Din, *P.P.T.S.* p. 353–60; Abu Shama, ii, pp. 63–6.

took his army out from Jerusalem and arrived that evening befor
Jaffa, and at once began the assault of the city. After three days o
bombardment his sappers made a breach and the Saracen arm
poured in. The defence was heroic but vain. The garrison wa
forced to capitulate on the understanding that their lives would b
spared. The negotiations were conducted for the Christians by th
new Patriarch, who happened to be in the city. Saladin's troop
were now out of hand. Kurds and Turks rushed through th
streets seeking plunder and slaughtering the citizens who tried t
defend their houses. So Saladin advised the garrison to shut itsel
in the citadel till he could restore order.

A swift message had brought news of the attack on Jaffa t
Richard as soon as Saladin approached the walls. He at once se
out to its rescue, going himself by sea, with Pisan and Genoese help
and sending his army by land. Contrary winds held him up o
the point of Carmel, and his army, reluctant to arrive at Jaffa befor
him, delayed on the road to Caesarea. On the 31st, when Saladi
had pacified his troops sufficiently to allow him to evacuate forty
nine of the knights of the garrison, with their wives and baggag
from the citadel through the town, Richard's fleet of fifty galley
sailed into sight. The garrison at once resumed the battle and in
desperate charge almost drove the disorganized Moslems from th
town. Richard, not knowing what was happening, hesitated t
land till a priest swam out to tell him that the citadel was untaker
He beached his ships at the foot of the citadel and waded ashore a
the head of his men. The garrison in despair had already sent nev
envoys to treat with Saladin, who was talking with them in his ten
when Richard launched his attack. The Saracens, many of then
still scattered about the streets, were taken by surprise. The ferocit
of Richard's onslaught, himself fighting furiously in the fore
combined with another attack from the garrison, drove them int
headlong flight. A secretary came to Saladin's tent and whispere
to him of the rout. As he tried to detain his visitors with pleasan
conversation, the torrent of Moslem fugitives revealed the truth
The Sultan was obliged to order the retreat. He was able t

emain in his camp himself, with a handful of cavalry, but his main army fled to Assir, five miles inland, before it reassembled its ranks. Richard had recaptured Jaffa with some eighty knights and four hundred bowmen, and perhaps two thousand Italian marines. His whole force had only three horses.[1]

The very next morning Saladin sent his chamberlain, Abu-Bakr, to resume the peace talks. He found Richard joking with some captive emirs, both about Saladin's swift capture of Jaffa and about his recapture of it. He said he had been unarmed and not even had time to change his shoes. But he agreed at once with Abu-Bakr that the war must stop. Saladin's message suggested, as a bargaining point, that as Jaffa was now half ruined the Frankish frontier should stop at Caesarea. Richard countered by offering to hold Jaffa and Ascalon as a fief under Saladin, without explaining how the vassaldom would work when the King was in Europe. Saladin's answer was to offer Jaffa, but to insist on keeping Ascalon. Once again Ascalon proved the stumbling-block. Negotiations were broken off.[2]

The Frankish army which Richard had summoned to rescue Jaffa was advancing past Caesarea. Saladin, well aware now how small was Richard's force at Jaffa, determined to strike at his camp outside the walls before the fresh army could arrive. At daybreak on Wednesday, 5 August, a Genoese, wandering about outside the camp, heard the neighing of horses and the tramp of soldiers and saw afar off steel glistening in the light of the rising sun. He roused the camp; and when the Saracens appeared Richard was ready. His men had not had time to arm themselves. Each took what was at hand. There were only fifty-four knights fit for battle and only fifteen horses, and about two thousand infantrymen. Behind a low palisade of tent-pegs, designed to disconcert the enemy horses, Richard set his men in pairs, their shields fixed as a fence

---

[1] *Itinerarium*, pp. 400–11; Ambroise, cols. 289–302; Beha ed-Din, *P.P.T.S.* p. 361–71; Abu Shama, II, pp. 66–71.

[2] These preliminary negotiations are only mentioned by the Moslems, Beha ed-Din (*P.P.T.S.* pp. 371–4) and Abu Shama (II, pp. 71–3).

in front of them and their long spears planted in the ground at a angle to impale the oncoming cavalry. Between each pair a archer was stationed. The Moslem cavalry charged in seven wave of a thousand men each. But they could not pierce the wall c steel. These charges continued till the afternoon. Then, when th enemy horses seemed to be tiring, Richard passed his bowme through to the front line and discharged all his arrows into th oncoming host. The volley checked the enemy. The archer passed back again behind the spearmen, who charged with Richar on horseback at their head. Saladin was lost in angry admiratio at the sight. When Richard's horse fell under him, he gallantl sent a groom through the midst of the turmoil with two fres horses as a gift to the brave King. Some Moslems crept round t attack the town itself, and the marines guarding it fled towards the ships, till Richard rode up and rallied them. By evening Saladi called off the battle and retreated to Jerusalem, adding to the forti fications there lest Richard still might pursue him.[1]

It was a superb victory, won by Richard's tactics and his person; bravery. But it was not followed up. Within a day or two Saladi was back at Ramleh, with a fresh army of levies from Egypt an northern Syria; while Richard, worn by his exertions, lay seriousl ill of a fever in his tent. Richard now longed for peace. Saladi repeated his former offer, still insisting on the cession of Ascalor It was hard for Richard to bear. He wrote to his old friend al-Adi who himself was on a sick-bed near Jerusalem, to beg him to inter cede with Saladin to leave him Ascalon. Saladin held firm. H sent the fevered King peaches and pears and snow from Moun Hermon to cool his drinks. But he would not yield Ascalor Richard was in no position to bargain. His health, as well as h brother's misdeeds in England, demanded his swift return to h home. The other Crusaders were weary. His nephew Henry an the Military Orders showed that they distrusted his politics. C what use would Ascalon be to them if he and his army had left

---

[1] *Itinerarium*, pp. 413–24; Ambroise, cols. 304–11; Beha ed-Din, *P.P.T.* pp. 374-6; Abu Shama, II, p. 74. The Moslem writers minimize the battle.

He had made public too often his determination to leave Palestine. On Friday, 28 August, al-Adil's courier brought him Saladin's final offer. Five days later, on 2 September 1192, he signed a treaty of peace for five years, and the Sultan's ambassadors added their names to his. The ambassadors then took Richard's hand and swore on their master's behalf. Richard as a King refused to take an oath himself, but Henry of Champagne, Balian of Ibelin and the Masters of the Hospital and the Temple swore for him. Saladin himself signed the treaty next day, in the presence of Richard's ambassadors. The war of the Third Crusade was over.

The treaty gave the coastal cities as far south as Jaffa to the Christians. Pilgrims might freely visit the Holy Places. Moslems and Christians might pass through each other's lands. But Ascalon was to be demolished.[1]

As soon as Saladin had made arrangements for their escort and lodging, parties from the Crusading army went up unarmed, with a passport from the King, to pay their homage at the shrines of Jerusalem. Richard himself would not go and refused to give any of the French troops a passport, but many of his own knights made the journey. One party was led by Hubert Walter, Bishop of Salisbury, who was received there with honour and given an audience with the Sultan. They talked of many subjects and in particular of Richard's character. The Bishop declared that he possessed every good quality, but Saladin thought that he lacked wisdom and moderation. When Saladin offered the Bishop a parting present, the prelate asked that two Latin priests and two Latin deacons might be allowed to serve at the Holy Sepulchre, and also at Bethlehem and Nazareth. Saladin consented; and a few months later the priests arrived and were allowed to perform their duties unmolested.[2]

Rumours had reached Constantinople that Richard was pressing for the latinization of the Holy Places. While Saladin was still at

[1] *Itinerarium*, pp. 424–30; Ambroise, cols. 314–17; Beha ed-Din, *P.P.T.S.* pp. 378–87; Abu Shama, II, pp. 75–9.

[2] *Itinerarium*, pp. 431–8; Ambroise, cols. 317–27.

Jerusalem an embassy arrived there from the Emperor Isaac Angelus, asking that the Orthodox might be given back the full control of the Orthodox Church that they had possessed in the days of the Fatimids. Saladin refused the request. He would not allow any one sect to be dominant there, but, like the Ottoman Sultans after him, he would be arbiter of them all. He also refused at once a request made by the Queen of Georgia to purchase the Holy Cross for 200,000 dinars.[1]

When the treaty was signed Richard journeyed to Acre. There he set his affairs in order, paying the debts that he owed and trying to collect those owed to him. On 29 September Queen Berengaria and Queen Joanna sailed out from Acre, to reach France safely before the winter storms. Ten days later, on 9 October, Richard himself left the land where he had fought so valiantly for sixteen bitter months. Fortune was against him. Bad weather forced him to call in at Corfu, in the territory of the Emperor Isaac Angelus. Fearing that he might be taken prisoner, he took passage at once, disguised as a Templar knight, with four attendants, in a pirate boat that was bound for the head of the Adriatic. This boat was wrecked near Aquileia; and Richard and his companions went on by land through Carinthia and Austria, intending to hurry quietly on to the territory of his brother-in-law, Henry of Saxony. But Richard was not a man to wear disguise convincingly. On 11 December he was recognized when he paused at an inn near Vienna. He was at once led before Duke Leopold of Austria, the man whose banner he had thrown down at Acre. Leopold accused him of the murder of Conrad of Montferrat and cast him into prison. Three months later he was handed over to Leopold's suzerain, the Emperor Henry VI. His long friendship with Henry the Lion and his recent alliance with Tancred of Sicily made him odious to the Emperor, who kept him captive for a year and only released him in March 1194, on the payment of a huge ransom and an oath of vassaldom. During the weary months of his captivity

[1] Beha ed-Din, *P.P.T.S.* pp. 334–5. The Emperor's demand for help to reconquer Cyprus was also refused.

his lands had been exposed to the intrigues of his brother John and the open attacks of King Philip. When he returned to them he had far too many tasks to do ever to contemplate another journey to the East. For five years he fought brilliantly in France defending his inheritance against the cunning Capetian, till, on 26 March 1199, a stray arrow shot from a rebel castle in the Limousin brought his life to a close. He was a bad son, a bad husband and a bad king, but a gallant and splendid soldier.[1]

[1] The army's return home is told in *Itinerarium*, pp. 439–40; Ambroise, cols. 327–9. Richard's own voyage and disasters are told briefly in *Itinerarium*, pp. 441–6 (including a spurious letter from the Old Man of the Mountains to Leopold of Austria declaring Richard to be innocent of the murder of Conrad), and in other chronicles. See Norgate, *Richard the Lion Heart*, pp. 264–76.

CHAPTER IV

THE SECOND KINGDOM

*'And the coast shall be for the remnant of the
house of Judah.'* ZEPHANIAH II, 7

The Third Crusade had come to a close. Never again would such a galaxy of princes go eastward for the Holy War. Yet, though all Western Europe had combined in the great effort, the results were exiguous. Tyre had been saved by Conrad before the Crusaders arrived and Tripoli by the Sicilian fleet. Acre and the coastline down to Jaffa were all that the Crusaders had contributed to the rebirth of the Frankish kingdom, apart from the island of Cyprus, filched from its Christian lord. One thing, however, had been achieved. Saladin's career of conquest had been checked. The Moslems were wearied by the long war. They would not yet awhile try again to drive the Christians back into the sea. The kingdom had indeed been reborn, firmly enough to last for another century. It was a very small kingdom; and though its kings were in name Kings of Jerusalem, Jerusalem lay out of their grasp. All that they owned was a strip of land, never as much as ten miles wide, stretching for ninety miles by the sea, from Jaffa to Tyre. Further north Bohemond's judicious neutrality had preserved for him his capital and a little land around, down to the port of Saint Symeon; while his son retained Tripoli itself and the Hospital held Krak des Chevaliers and the Templars Tortosa under him. It was not much to have salvaged from the wreck of the Frankish east; but for the moment it was safe.

Saladin was only fifty-four, but he was tired and ill after all the struggles of the war. He stayed on at Jerusalem till he heard that Richard had set sail from Acre, busying himself over the civil administration for the province of Palestine. He hoped then to revisit Egypt and afterwards to fulfil his pious ambition of a pilgrimage to Mecca. But duty called him to Damascus. After touring for three weeks through the lands that he had conquered and meeting Bohemond at Beirut to sign a definite peace with him, he arrived at Damascus on 4 November. There was a pile of work awaiting him there, an accumulation that had mounted during his four years of life with the army. It was a severe winter and, with so much to be done in his capital, he put off his journey to Egypt and his pilgrimage. When he had time to spare he would listen to the debates of men learned in philosophy, and sometimes he would go hunting. But as the winter months went on, those that knew him best saw that his health was failing. He complained of utter weariness and of forgetfulness. He could scarcely make the effort to hold audiences. On Friday, 19 February 1193, he braced himself to ride out to meet the pilgrimage coming home from Mecca. That evening he complained of fever and of pain. He bore his sickness patiently and calmly, knowing well that the end was coming. On 1 March he fell into a stupor. His son, al-Afdal, hurried off to secure the allegiance of the emirs; and only the Cadi of Damascus and a few faithful servants stayed by the Sultan's bedside. On Wednesday the 3rd, as the Cadi was repeating the words of the Koran over him and came to the passage, 'there is no God but He; in Him do I trust', the dying man opened his eyes and smiled, and went in peace to his Lord.[1]

Of all the great figures of the Crusading era Saladin is the most attractive. He had his faults. In his rise to power he showed a cunning and a ruthlessness that fitted ill with his later reputation. In the interests of policy he never shrank from bloodshed; he slew Reynald of Châtillon, whom he hated, with his own hand. But when he was severe it was for the sake of his people and his faith.

---

[1] Saladin's last days are vividly described by Beha ed-Din (*P.P.T.S.* pp. 392–402), who was at his Court at the time. Abu Shama, II, pp. 93–7, gives various accounts. See also Ibn al-Athir, II, pp. 72–5. Ernoul (p. 304) and *Estoire d'Eracles* (II, p. 217) misdate his death 1197 and *Gestes des Chiprois* (p. 15) 1196. Roger of Hoveden (III, p. 213) dates it correctly.

He was a devout Moslem. However kindly he felt towards his Christian friends, he knew that their souls were doomed to perdition. Yet he respected their ways and thought of them as fellow-men. Unlike the Crusader potentates, he never broke his word when it was pledged to anyone, whatever his religion. For all his fervour, he was always courteous and generous, merciful as a conqueror and a judge, as a master considerate and tolerant. Though some of his emirs might resent him as a Kurdish parvenu and though preachers in the West might call him Antichrist, there were very few of his subjects that did not feel for him respect and devotion, and few of his enemies could withhold admiration from him. In person he was slight of build. His face was melancholy in repose but would readily light up with a charming smile. His manner was always gentle. His tastes were simple. He disliked coarseness and ostentation. He loved the open air and the chase, but he was also well read and delighted in intellectual discussions, though he held free-thinkers in horror. In spite of his power and his victories he was a quiet modest man. Many years later a legend reached the ears of the Frankish writer, Vincent of Beauvais, that when he lay dying he summoned his standard-bearer and bade him go round Damascus with a rag from his shroud set upon a lance calling out that the Monarch of all the East could take nothing with him to the tomb save this cloth.[1]

His achievements had been great. He had completed the work of Nur ed-Din in uniting Islam and he had driven the Western intruders out of the Holy City down to a narrow strip of coast. But he had been unable to expel them altogether. King Richard and the forces of the Third Crusade had been too much for him. Had he been followed by another ruler of his calibre, the small remaining task might soon have been done. But the tragedy of

---

[1] Beha ed-Din gives a convincing eulogy of his character with illustrations and anecdotes (*P.P.T.S.* pp. 4–45). The story of the rag is given by Vincent of Beauvais (Douai edition), p. 1204. All the Christian chronicles mention him with respect. For legendary stories about him see Lane-Poole, *Saladin*, pp. 370–401.

medieval Islam was its lack of permanent institutions, to carry on authority after a leader's death. The Caliphate was the only institution to have an existence transcending that of its holders; and the Caliph was now politically impotent. Nor was Saladin Caliph. He was a Kurd of no great family who commanded the obedience of the Moslem world only by the force of his personality. His sons lacked his personality.

At the time of his death Saladin had seventeen sons and one little daughter. The eldest of them was al-Afdal, an arrogant young man of twenty-two, who had been designed by his father to inherit Damascus and the headship of the Ayubite family. While Saladin was dying al-Afdal had summoned all the emirs at Damascus to swear allegiance to him and to promise to divorce their wives and disinherit their children if ever they broke the oath. The last clause shocked many of them, and others would not swear unless al-Afdal in turn swore to maintain them in their fiefs. But when his father died and was buried in the great Mosque of the Ommayads, his authority in Damascus was accepted. His next brother, al-Aziz, was already governor of Egypt, at the age of twenty-one, and proclaimed himself there as independent Sultan. A third, az-Zahir, ruled in Aleppo and showed no willingness to admit his brother as overlord. Another, Khidr, younger still, held the Hauran but acknowledged al-Afdal's suzerainty. Only two of Saladin's brothers survived, Toghtekin, who had succeeded Turanshah as lord of the Yemen, and al-Adil, whose ambitions Saladin had come to mistrust. He had the former Frankish land of Oultrejourdain as his fief, and lands in the Jezireh, round Edessa. Nephews and cousins possessed lesser fiefs throughout the Sultan's dominions. Princes of the house of Zenghi, Izz ed-Din and Imad ed-Din, held Mosul and Sindjar as vassals: and the Ortoqids were still established at Mardin and Kaifa. Of the other feudatories, most of them successful generals whom Saladin had employed, the most prominent was Bektimur, lord of Akhlat.[1]

[1] Abu Shama, II, pp. 101-9; Ibn al-Athir, II, pp. 75-7; Kemal ad-Din, trans. Blochet, p. 305.

On Saladin's death the unity of Islam began to crumble. Whil
his sons watched each other jealously, a plot was hatched in th
north-east to restore Zengid rule in the person of Izz ed-Din, wit
the support of Bektimur and the Ortoqids. The Ayubites wer
saved by the precautions of al-Adil, and by the sudden deaths o
both Izz ed-Din and Bektimur, in which his agents were though
to have had a hand. Izz ed-Din's son and heir, Nur ed-Din Arslan
and Bektimur's successor Aqsonqor took note of the lesson and fo
the time being were deferential to al-Adil. Further south al-Afda
soon quarrelled with al-Aziz. The former had unwisely dismisse
most of his father's ministers and had given his entire trust to az
Ziya ibn al-Athir, the brother of the historian Ibn al-Athir, whil
he himself spent his days and nights enjoying the pleasures o
music and wine. The ex-ministers fled to Cairo, to al-Aziz, wh
was delighted to welcome them. On their advice al-Aziz invade
Syria in May 1194, and reached the walls of Damascus. Al-Afda
appealed in terror to his uncle al-Adil, who came in force dow
from the Jezireh and interviewed al-Aziz in his camp. A nev
family arrangement was made. Al-Afdal was obliged to ced
Judaea to al-Aziz and Lattakieh and Jabala to his brother az-Zahi
of Aleppo, but both al-Aziz and az-Zahir recognized his supremacy
Al-Adil received nothing from the bargaining except the prestig
of having been arbiter of the family. Peace did not last for long
In less than a year al-Aziz marched again on Damascus, and agai
al-Adil came to his eldest nephew's rescue. Al-Aziz's allies amongs
the emirs began to desert him; and al-Afdal drove him back acros
Judaea into Egypt and planned to march on Cairo. This was mor
than al-Adil wished. He threatened to give his support to al-Aziz
unless al-Afdal returned to Damascus. Once again his wishe
were obeyed.

It was soon clear that al-Afdal was unfit to reign. The govern
ment of Damascus was entirely in the hands of the vizier az-Ziya
who provoked sedition amongst all his master's vassals. Al-Adi
decided that Ayubite interests could not afford so incompetent
head of the family. He changed his policy and allied himself wit

al-Aziz, with whose help he took Damascus in July 1196, and annexed all al-Afdal's lands. Al-Afdal was provided with an honourable retreat in the little town of Salkhad in the Hauran, where he gave up sensual pleasures for a life of piety; and al-Aziz was recognized as supreme Sultan of the dynasty.

This arrangement lasted for two years. In November 1198, al-Aziz, whose authority over his uncle had never been more than nominal, fell from his horse when hunting jackal near the Pyramids. He died from his injuries on 29 November. His eldest son, al-Mansur, was a boy of twelve. His father's ministers, frightened of al-Adil's ambition, summoned al-Afdal from Salkhad to be Regent of Egypt. In January 1199 al-Afdal arrived at Cairo and took over the government. Al-Adil was then in the north, laying siege to Mardin, whose Ortoqid prince, Yuluk-Arslan, was restive at Ayubite control. His temporary embarrassment roused his third nephew, az-Zahir of Aleppo, to plan an alliance against him. Az-Zahir throughout his reign had been troubled by turbulent vassals whom he suspected his uncle of encouraging. While al-Afdal sent an army up from Egypt to attack Damascus, az-Zahir prepared to come down from the north. Other members of the family, such as Shirkuh of Homs, joined them. Al-Adil, hurrying from Mardin, where he left his son al-Kamil in charge of the siege, reached Damascus on 8 June. Six days later the Egyptian army came up and at its first assault penetrated into the city, to be quickly driven out again. Az-Zahir and his army arrived a week later; and for six months the two brothers besieged their uncle in his capital. But al-Adil was a trained and subtle diplomat. Gradually he won over many of his nephew's vassals, including Shirkuh of Homs; and when at last in January 1200, his son al-Kamil appeared with an army that had been victorious in the Jezireh, the brothers, who had begun to quarrel, separated and retired. Al-Adil pursued al-Afdal into Egypt, defeating his troops at Bilbeis. In February al-Afdal, in a new access of piety, yielded to his uncle and returned to his retirement in Salkhad. Al-Adil took over the regency of Egypt. But az-Zahir was undefeated. Next spring, while al-Adil was still in Egypt, he made a sudden march on Damascus and persuaded al-Afdal to join him again. Again al-Adil hastened back to his capital in time to be besieged by his nephews. But he was soon able to foment a quarrel between them. Al-Afdal was bought off by the promise of the cities of Samosata and Mayyafaraqin in the north, in exchange for Salkhad. Az-Zahir's vassals one by one began to desert him; and he was glad to make his peace with al-Adil whose strict suzerainty he admitted. By the end of 1201 al-Adil was master of all Saladin's empire and had taken the title of Sultan. Al-Mansur of Egypt was given only the city of Edessa. Al-Afdal was never allowed to control Mayyafaraqin, which was passed with its neighbouring lands to al-Adil's fourth son al-Muzaffar. The eldest son, al-Kamil, held Egypt under his father, the second, al-Muazzam, was his father's deputy in Damascus, and the third, al-Ashraf, ruled most of the Jezireh from Harran. Younger sons were enfeoffed as they grew old enough; but all of them were closely supervised by their father. The unity of Islam was thus restored under a prince less respected than Saladin, but wilier and more active.[1]

The family squabbles of the Ayubites prevented the Moslems from taking the offensive against the renascent Frankish kingdom. Henry of Champagne had slowly been able to restore some order there. It was not an easy task; nor was Henry's position entirely secure. For some reason that cannot now be explained, he was never crowned king. He may have waited in the fond hope of some day recovering Jerusalem; he may have found public opinion unwilling to accept his royal title; or he may have found the Church unco-operative.[2] The omission limited his authority,

[1] For the confused history of the Ayubites during these years see Abu Shama, pp. 110–49; Ibn al-Athir, II, pp. 78–89. For further references see Cahen, *La Syrie du Nord*, p. 581 n. 3.

[2] See the interesting discussion in Prawer, 'L'Etablissement des Coutumes du Marché à Saint Jean d'Acre', in *Revue Historique de Droit Français et Etranger*, 1951. He suggests (pp. 341–3) that Henry's marriage, concluded a few days after Isabella's widowhood, was not considered legal by the customs of the country and Henry was therefore shy of taking the royal title.

particularly over the Church. On the death of the Patriarch Heraclius there had been some difficulty in finding a successor to his throne. Eventually an obscure cleric called Radulph had been appointed. When he died in 1194, the Canons of the Holy Sepulchre, who were now at Acre, met together and elected as Patriarch Aymar, surnamed the Monk, Archbishop of Caesarea, and sent to Rome to have the election confirmed. Henry, who was displeased at the choice, complained angrily that he had not been consulted and arrested the Canons. His action was severely criticized even by his friends; for he was not the crowned king and therefore had no right to intervene. His chancellor, Josias, Archbishop of Tyre, persuaded him to climb down and to appease the Church by releasing the Canons with an apology and by presenting the new Patriarch's nephew with a rich fief near Acre; and at the same time he received a sharp reproof from the Pope.[1] Though peace was restored the Patriarch may well have been unwilling to oblige Henry now by crowning him. With his lay vassals Henry was more fortunate. He had the support of their leader, Balian of Ibelin, and of the Military Orders. But Guy of Lusignan still looked longingly from Cyprus at his former kingdom, and was encouraged by the Pisans, to whom he had promised rich concessions and who were angry at the favour shown by Henry to the Genoese. In May 1193, Henry discovered that the Pisan colony at Tyre was plotting to seize the city and hand it over to Guy. He at once arrested the ringleaders and ordered that the colony should be reduced to thirty persons. The Pisans retaliated by raiding the coastal villages between Tyre and Acre. Henry therefore expelled them from Acre itself. The Constable of the kingdom was still Guy's brother, Amalric of Lusignan, who had been responsible for Guy's arrival in Palestine many years before but who had managed to establish good relations with the local baronage. His wife was Eschiva of Ibelin, Balian's niece and daughter of Guy's bitterest opponent Baldwin of Ramleh; he had not been a faithful husband in the past but he

[1] *Estoire d'Eracles*, II, pp. 203–5 (manuscript D).

was now reconciled to her. He intervened on behalf of the Pisans only to be arrested himself by Henry for his interference. The Grand Masters of the Hospital and the Temple soon persuaded Henry to release him; but he thought it prudent to retire to Jaffa of which King Richard had appointed his brother Geoffrey a Governor. He did not resign from his office of Constable, but Henry considered that he had forfeited it and in 1194 appointed as his successor John of Ibelin, Balian's son and Isabella's half-brother. Peace was made about the same time with the Pisans whose quarter in Acre was restored to them and who hencefor-ward admitted Henry's government.[1]

A general reconciliation was made possible by the death of King Guy in Cyprus in May 1194. His elimination left Henry secure and deprived the Pisans and other dissidents of a rival candidate. Guy had bequeathed his authority in Cyprus to his eldest brother Geoffrey. But Geoffrey had returned to France; and the Franks in Cyprus had no hesitation in summoning Amalric from Jaffa to take his place. Henry at first demanded as representative of the Kings of Jerusalem to be consulted about the succession, but he could not implement his claim; and both he and Amalric soon saw that they must work together. The Constable of Cyprus, Baldwin, formerly lord of Beisan, came to Acre and induced Henry both to recognize Amalric and to offer to visit him in Cyprus. Their interview was very friendly, and they planned a close alliance, binding it with the betrothal of Amalric's three young sons, Guy, John and Hugh, with Isabella's three daughters, Maria of Mont-ferrat and Alice and Philippa of Champagne. It was thus hoped to unite their possessions in the next generation; but two of the little Cypriot princes died too young. The only one of the marriages to be achieved was that between Hugh and Alice, which bore its dynastic fruit in time to come. Some such arrangement was badly needed; for if the Frankish possession of Cyprus was to benefit the Franks in Palestine and provide them with a secure base, the two countries must co-operate. There was a continuous temptation

[1] *Estoire d'Eracles*, II, pp. 202–3.

not only for immigrants from the West to settle in the pleasant island rather than in the small remnant of the Palestinian kingdom where no fiefs were now to be found, but also for the dispossessed baronage of Palestine itself to cross the narrow sea. If the Cypriot lords were willing to come over the sea to fight for the Cross whenever danger approached, then Cyprus would be an asset to the Frankish east. If there were misunderstandings it might well become a dangerously centrifugal force.[1]

Friendly though he was, Amalric was not prepared to be subservient to Henry. He had already sought for himself the title of king, in order to define clearly to his subjects and colonists, as well as to foreign powers, the nature of his authority. But he felt in need of some higher sanction. It must have been the past history of the Kings of Jerusalem that made him unwilling to apply to the Pope for his crown. The Eastern Emperor would certainly never give it to him. So, unwisely for the future, he sent to the Western Emperor, Henry VI. The Emperor was planning a Crusade; and a client king in the East would suit him well. In October 1195, Amalric's ambassador, Rainier of Jebail, did homage for the kingdom of Cyprus on his master's behalf to the Emperor at Gelnhausen, near Frankfurt. Amalric was sent a royal sceptre by his suzerain; and the coronation took place in September 1197, when the Imperial Chancellor, Conrad, Bishop of Hildesheim, came to Nicosia to take part in the ceremony, and Amalric did homage to him.[2] The government of the country was planned to follow the strictly feudal practices that had been worked out in the kingdom of Jerusalem, with a High Court equivalent to the High Court of Jerusalem; and the laws of Jerusalem, with the emendations made by its kings, were held to operate in the island. For organizing his church, Amalric had recourse to the Pope; who

[1] See Hill, *History of Cyprus*, II, p. 44 and notes, a full discussion of the succession to Cyprus. For Henry's reconciliation with Amalric, *Estoire d'Eracles*, II, pp. 207–8, 212–13 (manuscript D).

[2] *Estoire d'Eracles*, II, pp. 209–12; Ernoul, pp. 302–3; Arnold of Lübeck, p. 204; *Annales Marbacenses*, p. 167.

G

appointed the Archdeacon of Lattakieh and Alan, Archdeacon of Lydda and Chancellor of Cyprus, to establish sees as they thought best. They created an Archbishopric of Nicosia, of which Alan became the holder, and Bishoprics at Paphos, Famagusta and Limassol. The Greek bishops were not immediately expelled, but they lost their tithes and much of their lands to the new Latin incumbents.[1]

Though Henry of Champagne could not obtain control over Cyprus, the barons in his own kingdom were now loyal to him. Indeed, his opponents retired happily to Cyprus, leaving the Palestinian lands to his friends. The former lords of Haifa, Caesarea and Arsuf were reinstated in their former baronies; and Saladin, before he died, presented Balian of Ibelin with the valuable fief of Caymon, or Tel-Kaimun, on the slopes of Carmel.[2] The friendship of the Ibelins, his wife's stepfather and half-brothers, was of value in making Henry's authority generally acceptable. A greater problem was provided by the Principality of Antioch.

Bohemond III of Antioch, ruler also of Tripoli in the name of his young son, had played a rather equivocal part during Saladin's wars of conquest and the Third Crusade. He had made no serious effort to prevent Saladin's capture of his castles in the Orontes valley in 1188, nor to recover Lattakieh and Jabala, which had been betrayed to the Moslems by his Moslem servant, the qadi Mansur ibn Nabil. He had been glad to accept from Saladin a truce that allowed him to keep Antioch itself and its port of Saint Symeon. Tripoli had been saved for his son only by the intervention of the Sicilian fleet. When Frederick of Swabia and the remnants of Barbarossa's army had arrived at Antioch, Bohemond made a mild suggestion that they might fight for him against the Moslems in the north, but when they pressed on southward, he took no active part in the Crusade, beyond paying a deferential visit to King Richard in Cyprus. He had meanwhile changed his position with regard to Palestinian party politics. As soon as his

[1] Mas Latrie, *Documents*, III, pp. 599–605; Makhaeras, pp. 28–9.
[2] Ernoul, p. 293.

ousin Raymond of Tripoli was dead and he had secured his inheritance for his own son, he gave his support to Guy of Lusignan and his friends, probably for fear lest Conrad of Montferrat should have designs on Tripoli. He had no wish for a strong aggressive king on his southern border, for he was fully occupied in a quarrel with his northern neighbour, the Roupenian prince of Armenia, Leo II, brother and heir of Roupen III.

On his accession in 1186 Leo sought an alliance with Bohemond and recognized his suzerainty. The two princes joined to beat off a Turcoman raid in 1187; and soon afterwards Leo married a niece of the Princess Sibylla. About the same time he lent a large sum of money to Bohemond. But there the friendship ended. Bohemond showed no haste to repay the loan; and when Saladin invaded Antiochene territory, Leo remained carefully neutral. In 1191 Saladin dismantled the great fortress of Baghras, which he had captured from the Templars. Hardly had his workmen left before Leo came up and reoccupied the site and rebuilt the fortress. Bohemond demanded its return to the Templars and, when Leo refused, complained to Saladin. Saladin was too busy elsewhere to intervene; and Leo remained in possession of Baghras. But he was furious at Bohemond's appeal to Saladin, and his resentment was fanned by Bohemond's wife, Sibylla, who hoped to use his help in securing the Antiochene inheritance for her own son William, at the expense of her stepsons. In October 1193, Leo invited Bohemond to come to Baghras to discuss the whole question. Bohemond arrived, accompanied by Sibylla and her son, and accepted Leo's offer of hospitality within the castle walls. No sooner had he entered than he was taken prisoner by his host, with all his entourage, and was told that he would be released only if he yielded the suzerainty over Antioch to Leo. Bohemond ruefully accepted the terms, persuaded, perhaps, by Sibylla who hoped that Leo as overlord of Antioch would give the succession there to her son. Bohemond's Marshal, Bartholomew Tirel, and Leo's nephew-in-law, Hethoum of Sassoun, were sent with Armenian troops to Antioch to prepare the city for the new régime.

When the delegation arrived at Antioch, the barons there, wh
had no great liking for Bohemond and many of whom ha
Armenian blood, were ready to accept Leo as overlord, an
allowed Bartholomew to bring the Armenian soldiers into th
city and establish them in the palace. But the bourgeois citizen
Greeks as well as Latins, were horrified. They believed that Le
intended to govern the city himself and that Armenians would b
put over them. When an Armenian soldier spoke disrespectfull
of Saint Hilary, the French bishop to whom the palace chapel wa
dedicated, a cellarer who was present began to throw stones a
him. At once a riot began in the palace and spread through th
city. The Armenians were driven out and prudently retired wit
Hethoum of Sassoun back to Baghras. The citizens then assemble
in the Cathedral of St Peter, with the Patriarch at their head, an
proceeded to set up a Commune to take over the administra
tion of the city. To legalize their position the elected member
hastened to take an oath of allegiance to Bohemond's eldest sor
Raymond, till Bohemond should return. Raymond accepte
their homage and recognized their claims. Meanwhile messenger
were sent to his brother Bohemond of Tripoli and to Henry o
Champagne, begging them to come and preserve Antioch fron
the Armenians.

The episode showed that while the barons of Antioch wer
ready to go even further than their cousins in Jerusalem to identif
themselves with the Christians of the East, opposition to such
merger came from the commercial community. But the circum
stances differed from those in the Kingdom a few years before
Both the Franks and the Greeks in Antioch considered th
Armenians as barbarous mountaineers. The Latin Church, in th
person of the Patriarch, showed its sympathy with the Commune
but it is doubtful whether it played a leading part in its inception
The Patriarch, Radulph II, was a weak and aged man who ha
only recently succeeded the redoubtable Aimery of Limoges. It i
more likely that the chief instigators were the Italian merchants
who feared for their trade under Armenian domination. The ide

of a commune was one which at that time would occur more easily to an Italian than to a Frenchman. But whoever promoted the Commune, the Greeks of Antioch soon played a leading part in it.[1]

Bohemond of Tripoli hurried to Antioch in answer to his brother's summons; and Leo realized that he had missed his chance. He retired with his prisoners to his capital at Sis. Early next spring Henry of Champagne decided to intervene. It was fortunate that the Saracens were in no state after Saladin's death to be aggressive; but so dangerous a situation could not be allowed to continue. As he moved northwards he was met by an embassy from the Assassins. The Old Man of the Mountains, Sinan, had recently died; and his successor was anxious to revive the friendship that had existed between the sect and the Franks. He sent apologies for the murder of Conrad of Montferrat, a crime that Henry found easy to forgive; and he invited Henry to visit his castle at al-Kahf. There, on a rugged crest in the Nosairi mountains, Henry was offered sumptuous entertainment. He was shown, till he begged that the demonstration should stop, how willingly the sectaries would kill themselves at their sheikh's orders. He left laden with costly gifts and the Assassins' friendly promise to assassinate any of his enemies whom he might name.[2]

From al-Kahf Henry marched up the coast to Antioch, where he barely paused before continuing his journey into Armenia. Leo, unwilling to face an open war, met him before Sis, ready to negotiate a settlement. It was agreed that Bohemond should be released without any ransom, that Baghras and the country around should be recognized as Armenian territory and that neither prince should be suzerain of the other. To seal the treaty and ultimately, it was hoped, to unite the principalities, Bohemond's heir Raymond was to marry Leo's niece and heiress-presumptive, Alice, daughter of Roupen III. Alice, it is true, was already married to Hethoum

[1] See Cahen, *La Syrie du Nord*, pp. 582-5, for a fully referenced account of these episodes.
[2] Ernoul, pp. 323-4; *Estoire d'Eracles*, pp. 216, 231 (manuscript D).

of Sassoun. But the difficulty was easily overcome. Hethoum met with a sudden but timely death. The settlement promised peace for the north; and Henry as its architect showed himself a fit successor of the early kings of Jerusalem. He returned southward with his prestige greatly enhanced.[1]

Leo's ambitions were not, however, satisfied. Knowing that Amalric of Cyprus was seeking a royal crown he followed his example. But legal opinion at the time considered that a crown could only be granted by an Emperor or, according to the Franks, by the Pope. Byzantium, cut off now from Cilicia and Syria by Seldjuk conquests, was no longer strong enough for its titles to carry weight with the Franks, whom Leo wished to impress. He therefore sent to the Western Emperor, Henry VI. Henry prevaricated. He hoped to come soon to the East and he would look into the Armenian question then. So Leo approached the Pope, Celestine III. He had already been in touch with Rome in the time of Clement III, hinting at the submission of his Church to the Papacy; for he knew that as chief of a heretic state he would never be an acceptable overlord for Franks. His own clergy, jealous for their independence and their creed, violently opposed the flirtation. But Leo patiently persevered. His bishops were at last grudgingly persuaded that Papal suzerainty would be merely nominal and would change nothing, while Pope Celestine's legates were told that the bishops unanimously welcomed the change. The Pope had ordained forbearance and tact; so the legates asked no questions. Meanwhile the Emperor Henry, who had now promised a crown to Amalric, made the same promise to Leo, in return for a recognition of his suzerain rights over Armenia. The actual coronation would take place on his arrival. He never visited the East; but in January 1198, soon after his death, his Chancellor, Conrad of Hildesheim came with the Papal legate Conrad, Archbishop of Mainz, to Sis and was present at a great coronation ceremony. The Eastern Emperor, Alexius Angelus, hoping to retain some influence in Cilicia, had a few months previously sent Leo a

[1] Cahen, *op. cit.* pp. 585–6.

oyal crown, which was gratefully received. The Armenian
Catholicus, Gregory Abirad, placed the crown on Leo's head,
while Conrad gave him a royal sceptre. The Orthodox Arch-
ishop of Tarsus, the Jacobite Patriarch and ambassadors from the
Caliph all assisted at the rite, as well as many of the nobility from
antioch. Leo could claim that his title was recognized by all his
subjects and his neighbours.[1]

It was a great day for the Armenians, who saw in it a revival of
he ancient kingdom of the Armenians; and it completed the in-
egration of the Roupenian principality into the world of the
Frankish East. But it is doubtful whether Leo's policy was in
he interests of the Armenians as a whole; for it divided off the
armenians of old Great Armenia, the home of the race, from their
outhern brothers. And, after a brief spell of glory, the Cilician
Armenians were to find that in the end occidentalization brought
hem very little profit.

The Archbishop Conrad's presence in the East was due to the
determination of the Emperor Henry to launch a new Crusade.
Owing to his father Frederick's untimely death the German con-
ribution to the Third Crusade had been pitiably ineffective.
Henry was ambitious to make of his empire an international
eality; and his first task, as soon as he was firmly established in
Europe, must be to restore German prestige in the Holy Land.
While he himself laid plans for a great expedition that would
bring the whole Mediterranean under his control, he arranged for
he early dispatch of a German expedition to sail straight to Syria.
Archbishop Conrad of Mainz and Adolf, Count of Holstein, set
out from Bari with a large company of soldiers, derived mainly
from the Rhineland and the Hohenstaufen duchies. The first con-
ingents arrived at Acre in August, but the leaders paused in
Cyprus for Amalric's coronation. Henry, Duke of Brabant, with
a regiment of his companions had preceded them.[2]

---

[1] *Ibid.* pp. 587–90.
[2] *Estoire d'Eracles*, II, pp. 214–16 (manuscript D). Henry's preparations for
he Crusade were made at the Diet of Gelnhausen (*Annales Marbacenses*, p. 167).

Henry of Champagne did not welcome them gladly. He ha
learned from experience of the folly of provoking an unnecessar
war. His chief advisers were the Ibelins, his wife's stepfather an
stepbrothers, and the lords of Tiberias, the stepsons of Raymon
of Tripoli. They, faithful to their family traditions, advised a
understanding with the Moslems and a delicate diplomacy playin
off the sons and brothers of Saladin against each other. The polic
had been successful, and peace, vital for the recovery of th
Christian kingdom, had been maintained, in spite of the provoca
tion caused by the pirate emir of Beirut, Usama, whom neithe
al-Adil at Damascus nor al-Aziz at Cairo could control.[1] Beiru
and Sidon were still in Moslem hands, separating the kingdom fron
the county of Tripoli. Early in 1197 this gap was lessened by th
recovery of Jebail. Its Dowager Lady, Stephanie of Milly, was th
niece of Reynald of Sidon, and had his gifts for dealing wit
Moslems. An intrigue with the Kurdish emir there enabled he
to reoccupy the town without a struggle and to hand it over t
her son.[2]

The Germans had come determined to fight. Without stoppin
to consult the government of Acre, the first arrivals marche
straight into Moslem territory in Galilee. The invasion roused th
Moslems. Al-Adil, to whom the land belonged, summoned hi
relatives to forget their quarrels and join him. Hardly had th
Germans crossed the frontier before there was news of al-Adil'
approach. Rumour exaggerated the size of his army; and, withou
waiting to meet it, the Germans fled in panic towards Acre, th
knights deserting the infantrymen in their haste. It seemed likel
that al-Adil would march on unopposed to Acre. But Henry, o
the advice of Hugh of Tiberias, rushed up his own knights an
such Italian soldiers as he could muster to reinforce the Germa
infantrymen; who, braver than their leaders, were ready now t
stand firm. Al-Adil was not prepared to risk a pitched battle, bu
was unwilling to waste his army. He swerved southward an

[1] Ibn al-Athir, II, p. 85; Ernoul, pp. 315–16.
[2] *Estoire d'Eracles*, II, pp. 217–18; Ernoul, p. 305.

marched on Jaffa. Jaffa was well fortified, but its garrison was small; and Henry could not afford to replenish it. Amalric of Lusignan had governed the town before he went to Cyprus. Henry now offered it back to him if he would defend it. It would be better to have the Cypriots there than that it should pass either to the Moslems or to the irresponsible Germans. As soon as the offer reached him, Amalric sent one of his barons, Reynald Barlais, to take command at Jaffa and to prepare for the coming siege. But Reynald was an easy-going man. News soon came to Acre that he was spending his days in frivolous gaiety and had no intention of putting up any resistance to al-Adil. Henry therefore gathered together what troops he could spare in Acre and asked the Pisan colony there to provide reinforcements.[1]

On 10 September 1197 his troops assembled in the palace court-yard; and Henry reviewed them from the window of an upper gallery. At that moment envoys from the Pisan colony entered the room. Henry turned to greet them, then, forgetting where he was, stepped backward through the open window. His little dwarf, Scarlet, was standing by him and grabbed at his clothes. But Henry was a heavy man and Scarlet very light. They crashed together on to the pavement below and were killed.[2]

The sudden elimination of Henry of Champagne threw the whole kingdom into consternation. He had been very popular. Though a man of no outstanding natural gifts, he had by his tact, his perseverance and his reliance on good advisers proved himself a capable ruler, ready to learn from experience. He had played a useful part in ensuring the continuance of the kingdom. But the barons could not afford to waste time on grief. A new ruler must be found quickly, to deal with the Saracen war and the German Crusade and all the regular problems of government. Henry's widow, Princess Isabella, was too utterly distraught by her bereave-

---

[1] *Estoire d'Eracles*, II, pp. 216–19 (manuscript D); Ernoul, pp. 305–7; Abu Shama, II, pp. 116, 152; Ibn al-Athir, II, pp. 84–6.

[2] *Estoire d'Eracles*, II, p. 220; Ernoul, p. 306; Amadi, pp. 90–1; Ibn al-Athir, II, p. 86.

ment to take charge; but she was the pivotal figure, as heiress of the royal line. Of her children by Henry two little girls, Alice and Philippa, survived. Her daughter by Conrad, Maria of Montferrat, known from her father's rank as La Marquise, was only five years old. It was clear that Isabella must remarry. But the barons, while acknowledging her position as heiress, considered it their business to choose her next husband. Unfortunately they could not agree on a suitable candidate. Hugh of Tiberias and his friends proposed his brother Ralph. His family, the house of Falconberg of St Omer, was one of the most distinguished in the kingdom. But it was poor; it had lost its lands in Galilee to the Moslems; and Ralph was a younger son. It was widely felt that he lacked sufficient wealth and prestige. In particular, the Military Orders opposed him. While the debate went on, news came that Jaffa had fallen without a struggle. The Duke of Brabant had set out for its relief. Now he turned back to Acre and took charge of the government. A few days later, on 20 September, Conrad of Mainz and the German leaders arrived from Cyprus. Conrad, as a prelate of the Western Empire and confidant of the Emperor, and friend, as well, of the new Pope, Innocent III, was a man of immense authority. When he suggested that the throne should be offered to King Amalric of Cyprus, there was no opposition, except from the Patriarch, Aymar the Monk, whose own clergy would not support him. It seemed an excellent choice. Amalric's first wife, Eschiva of Ibelin, had recently died; he was free to marry Isabella. Though many of the Syrian barons could not quite forget that he was a Lusignan, he had ostentatiously abandoned any partisan policy, and he had shown himself a far abler man than his younger brother Guy. His election pleased the Pope, to whom it seemed wise to combine the Latin East under one chief. But the Chancellor Conrad's motive was subtler. Amalric owed his Cypriot crown to the Emperor Henry, whose vassal he had become. As King of Jerusalem would he not therefore bring his new kingdom under imperial suzerainty? Amalric himself hesitated a little. It was not till January 1198 that he came to Acre. On the morrow of his arrival he was married to Princess Isabella; and a few days later the Patriarch crowned them King and Queen of Jerusalem.[1]

The union of the crowns was not to be as complete as the Pope or the Imperialists had hoped. Amalric made it clear from the outset that the two kingdoms were to be administered separately and that no Cypriot money was to be spent on the defence of the mainland. He himself was only a personal link between them. Cyprus was a hereditary kingdom; and his heir there was his son Hugh. In the kingdom of Jerusalem hereditary right was admitted by public sentiment, but the High Court preserved its claim to elect to the throne. There Amalric owed his position to his wife. If he died she might remarry, and the new husband be accepted as king. And her heir was her daughter, Maria of Montferrat. Even if she bore Amalric a son it was doubtful whether the child of a fourth marriage could claim precedence over a child of the second. But in fact their only children were two daughters, Sibylla and Melisende.[2]

Though he regarded himself as little more than regent, Amalric was an able and active ruler. He persuaded the High Court to join him in a revision of the constitution, in order that the royal rights should be clearly defined. In particular he made a point of consulting Ralph of Tiberias, his rival for the throne, whom, we are told, he esteemed but did not like. Ralph was celebrated for his legal knowledge, and it was natural that he should be asked to edit the *Livre au Roi*, as the new edition of the Laws was called. But Amalric feared that Ralph's learning might be used against him. In March 1198, when the Court was riding through the orchards round Tyre, four German horsemen galloped up to the

[1] *Estoire d'Eracles*, II, pp. 221–3; Ernoul, pp. 309–10. Roger of Hoveden, IV, p. 29 (wrongly calling the bride Melisent), says that the pair were married and crowned at Beirut by Conrad of Mainz. This was probably German propaganda as Innocent III wrote to the Patriarch Aymar reproving him for first refusing to allow the marriage because of consanguinity, then performing it and the coronation (letter in *M.P.L.* vol. CCXIV, col. 477). It was usual henceforward for the coronation of the King of Jerusalem to take place in the cathedral at Tyre.

[2] See La Monte, *Feudal Monarchy*, p. 43. For hereditary monarchy in Cyprus, see Hill, *op. cit.* vol. II, p. 50 n. 4.

King and fell on him. He was rescued without serious hurt. His assailants refused to say on whose behalf they were acting; but Amalric announced that Ralph was guilty and sentenced him to banishment. Ralph, as was his right, demanded trial by his peers and John of Ibelin, the Queen's half-brother, persuaded the King that he must submit the case to the High Court; which found that the King had done wrong in banishing Ralph without a hearing. The matter was only resolved when, probably owing to the tactful intervention of John of Ibelin, Ralph himself announced that as he had lost the King's good-will he would go into voluntary exile and retired to Tripoli. The episode had shown the barons that the King could not be opposed with impunity, but it had shown the King that he must abide by the constitution.[1]

His foreign policy was vigorous and flexible. In October 1197 before he had accepted the throne, he had helped Henry of Brabant to take advantage of the Moslem concentration at Jaffa by sending a sudden expedition, composed of Germans and Brabancons under Henry's leadership, to recover Sidon and Beirut. Sidon had already been demolished by the Moslems, who had thought it untenable. When the Christians arrived there, they found the town a mass of ruins. The pirate-emir Usama at Beirut, finding that al-Adil was sending him no aid, decided that he would destroy his town. But he started too late. When Henry and his troops came up, they found the walls dismantled, so that they could easily enter them, but the bulk of the town was intact and soon repaired. Beirut was given as a fief to the Queen's half-brother, John of Ibelin. With Jebail already restored to its Christian lords, the kingdom once again marched with the county of Tripoli. But the coast round Sidon was not yet entirely cleared of the enemy, who remained in possession of half the suburbs.[2]

Encouraged by their success at Beirut, the German Crusaders,

---

[1] *Estoire d'Eracles*, II, pp. 228–30; John of Ibelin, pp. 327–8, 430; Philip of Novara, pp. 522–3, 570.

[2] Ernoul, pp. 311–17; *Estoire d'Eracles*, II, pp. 224–7; Arnold of Lübeck, p. 205; Ibn al-Athir, II, p. 86.

with the Archbishop at their head, planned next to march on
erusalem. The Syrian barons, who had hoped to restore peace with
l-Adil on the basis of ceding Jaffa and keeping Beirut, tried vainly
o dissuade them. In November 1197 the Germans entered
Galilee and laid siege to the great fortress of Toron. So vigorous
was their first assault that the Moslem garrison soon offered to
abandon the castle, with the five hundred Christian prisoners lying
n its dungeons, if the defenders could be assured of their lives and
personal possessions. But the Archbishop Conrad insisted on unconditional surrender; and the Frankish barons, eager to make
friends with al-Adil and fearing that a massacre might provoke a
Moslem *jihad,* sent to warn the Sultan that the Germans were not
wont to spare lives. The defence continued with renewed vigour;
and al-Adil persuaded his nephew al-Aziz to send an army from
Egypt to deal with the invaders. The Germans began to grow
weary and slacken their efforts. Meanwhile news had come to
Acre that the Emperor Henry had died in September. Many of
the leaders were therefore anxious to return home. And when
news followed of a civil war in Germany, Conrad and his colleagues decided to abandon the siege. On 2 February 1198 the
Egyptian army approached from the south. The German rank and
file was ready to do battle, when suddenly a rumour went round
that the Chancellor and the great lords had fled. There was a general
panic. The whole army never paused in its flight till it had reached
the safety of Tyre. A few days later it began to embark on its return
journey to Europe. The whole Crusade had been a fiasco and had
done nothing to restore German prestige. It had, however, helped
to recover Beirut for the Franks; and it left a permanent institution
behind in the organization of the Teutonic Knights.[1]

The older Military Orders, though they were officially international, had recruited few German members. At the time of the

---

[1] Ernoul, p. 316; *Estoire d'Eracles,* II, pp. 221–2; Arnold of Lübeck, pp. 208–
10; *Chronica Regia Coloniensis,* p. 161; Abu Shama, II, p. 117; Ibn al-Athir, II,
pp. 87–8. For John of Ibelin's enfeoffment see *Lignages d'Outremer,* in *R. H. C.
Lois,* II, p. 458.

Third Crusade some merchants of Bremen and Lübeck organized a hospice for Germans at Acre on the lines of the Hospital of St John. It was dedicated to the Virgin, and it saw to the care of German pilgrims. The arrival of the German expeditions in 1197 inevitably increased its importance. When a number of Crusading knights determined not to return at once to Germany, the organization copied the example of the Hospital of St John a century before. It incorporated these knights, and in 1198 received recognition from the King and from the Pope as a Military Order. It is probable that the Chancellor Conrad was aware that a purely German Order might be of value in furthering imperialistic designs and himself was largely responsible for its inception. It was soon endowed with rich estates in Germany and began to acquire castles in Syria. Its first possession was the tower over the Gate of St Nicholas at Acre, granted by Amalric on condition that the knights surrendered it back at the King's command. Soon afterwards they purchased the castle of Montfort, which they renamed Starkenberg, on the hills dominating the Ladder of Tyre. The Order, like those of the Temple and the Hospital, provided soldiers for the defence of the Frankish East but did not facilitate the government of the kingdom.[1]

As soon as the German Crusaders had gone, Amalric opened negotiations with al-Adil. Al-Aziz had returned quickly to Egypt; and al-Adil, eager to secure the whole Ayubite inheritance, had no wish to quarrel with the Franks. On 1 July 1198, a treaty was signed leaving him in possession of Jaffa and the Franks in possession of Jebail and Beirut, and dividing Sidon between them. It was to last for five years and eight months. The settlement proved useful to al-Adil, for it left him free, on al-Aziz's death in November, to intervene in Egypt and annex the late Sultan's lands. His increased power made Amalric all the more determined to keep the peace with him, the more so as there was trouble again at Antioch.[2]

[1] See Röhricht, *Geschichte des Königreichs Jerusalem*, pp. 677–8.
[2] Ernoul, pp. 316–17; *Estoire d'Eracles*, II, p. 228; Roger of Hoveden, IV, p. 28 (saying the truce was to last for six years, six months and six days); Abu Shama, Arabic text (ed. Bairaq), I, pp. 220–1; Ibn al-Athir, II, p. 89.

Bohemond III had attended the siege of Beirut, and on his return had planned to attack Jabala and Lattakieh. But he had to hurry home. The happy arrangement by which Cilicia and Antioch were to be united in the persons of his son Raymond and his Armenian bride broke down when Raymond suddenly died early in 1197. He left an infant son, Raymond-Roupen, who was heir to Antioch by hereditary right. But Bohemond III was already close on sixty, and unlikely to survive till his grandson came of age. There was every danger of a minority and a regency dominated by the boy's Armenian kin. Bohemond sent the widow Alice back with her infant son to Armenia, perhaps because he planned that one of Sibylla's sons should succeed, perhaps because he thought that they would be safer there. It was about the time of Leo's coronation; and Conrad of Mainz, eager to secure the throne of Antioch for one of his master's vassals, thus complementing his work at Acre, hastened from Sis to Antioch, where he obliged Bohemond to summon his barons and make them swear to uphold Raymond-Roupen's succession.[1]

Conrad would have done better to have gone to Tripoli. Bohemond, Count of Tripoli, Bohemond III's second son, was a young man of great ambition and few scruples, well versed in the law and able to find an argument to justify his most outrageous actions. He was no friend of the Church. He had already supported the Pisans, no doubt for money, in a dispute over some lands with the Bishop of Tripoli; and when the Bishop, Peter of Angoulême, was appointed Patriarch of Antioch and appointed a successor to his see of Tripoli with uncanonical haste, the Pope accepted his excuse that with a ruler like Bohemond the Church could not afford the risk of delay. Bohemond was determined to secure the succession to Antioch, and at once refused to acknow-

[1] Arnold of Lübeck, p. 207; *Chronica Regia Coloniensis*, p. 161; Roger of Hoveden, IV, p. 28 (all implying that Bohemond temporarily occupied the towns); Kemal ad-Din (trans. Blochet), pp. 213–15 (saying that he did not actually attack them). Röhricht, *op. cit.* p. 675 n. 2, mistranslates Gibelet (Jebail) in *Eracles*, II, p. 228, as Jabala (Dschebele).

ledge the validity of the oath sworn in favour of Raymond
Roupen. He needed allies. The Templars, furious at Leo's retentio
of Baghras, gladly joined him. The Hospitallers, though neve
very eager to work with the Templars, were won over by judiciou
grants. The Pisans and Genoese were bribed with trade concession
Most important, the Commune of Antioch itself was frightene
of the Armenians and hostile to any action taken by the baron
At the end of 1198 Bohemond of Tripoli appeared suddenly i
Antioch, ejected his father and induced the Commune to take a
oath of allegiance to himself.

But Leo had one formidable ally, Pope Innocent III. Whateve
doubts the Papacy might have felt about the sincerity of the sub
mission of the Armenian Church to Rome, Innocent was un
willing to alienate his new vassals. Cordially dutiful messages an
requests poured into Rome from Leo and his Catholicus; and the
could not be ignored. Owing, probably, to the opposition of th
Church, the young Bohemond allowed his father back to Antioc
and himself returned to Tripoli; but somehow he managed t
reconcile himself with the old Prince, who veered round to hi
side. Meanwhile the Templars brought all their influence to bea
at Rome. But Leo ignored hints from the Church that he shoul
restore Baghras to the Order; for Baghras was strategically essenti
to him if he were ever to control Antioch. He invited old Princ
Bohemond and the Patriarch Peter to discuss the whole question
but his intransigence drove even the Patriarch over to Bohemon
of Tripoli's side. The Church in Antioch joined the Commun
and the Orders in opposing the Armenian succession. Whe
Bohemond III died in April 1201, Bohemond of Tripoli had n
difficulty in establishing himself in the city. But many of th
nobility, mindful of their oath and fearful of Bohemond's auto
cratic tastes, fled to Leo's court at Sis.[1]

For the next quarter of a century the Christians of Norther
Syria were distracted by the Antiochene War of Succession; an

[1] For the complicated story see Cahen, *op. cit.* pp. 590–5, with a discussion c
the conflicting sources.

long before it was settled, the whole situation in the Orient had altered. It was fortunate that neither the Seldjuk princes of Anatolia nor the Ayubites were in a position to embark on a war of conquest there. The death of the Seldjuk Sultan Kilij Arslan II had been followed by a long civil war between his sons. Nearly ten years passed before one of the younger sons, Rukn ad-Din Suleiman of Tokat, succeeded in reuniting the family lands. There had been a Seldjuk raid on Cilicia in 1193, and again in 1201, distracting Leo at the critical moment when Bohemond III lay dying. But when Rukn ad-Din had time to spare from wars with his brothers and the decadent Danishmend princes, he used it to attack Georgia, whose great Queen Thamar seemed a far more dangerous menace to Islam than any Latin potentate.[1] At Aleppo Saladin's son az-Zahir was far too nervous of his uncle al-Adil's ambition to risk any foreign enterprise. The Antiochenes were free to continue their quarrels without any Moslem interference. From Acre King Amalric watched the civil war in the north with growing impatience. His sympathies were with Leo and the young Raymond-Roupen rather than with the truculent Bohemond, but he never attempted any active intervention. His main preoccupation was to prevent the outbreak of war with al-Adil. There were rumours of a huge Crusade gathering in Europe. Till it arrived, peace must be kept. Al-Adil on his side could not count on the loyal support of his nephews and cousins unless serious Christian aggression was to provoke a Holy War.

It was not always easy to keep the peace. At the end of 1202 a Flemish squadron put in at Acre. It had sailed round past Gibraltar under the castellan of Bruges, John of Nesle. A few days later a handful of knights arrived in ships from Marseilles, under Bishop Walter of Autun and the Count of Forez. They were followed by a further group of French knights coming from Venice, including Stephen of Perche, Robert of Montfort and Reynald II, Count of Dampierre. The three parties altogether only numbered

---

[1] Ibn Bibi, ed. Houtsma, IV, pp. 5–22; Ibn al-Athir, II, pp. 69–72; *Georgian Chronicle* (ed. Brosset), I, pp. 292–7.

a few hundred men, a tiny proportion of the great host that was now sailing from Dalmatia; but soon afterwards Reynald of Montmirail, who had left that host at Zara, brought news that it would be some time, if ever, before the whole expedition would appear in Syria. Like all newcomers, the French knights were determined to go out at once to fight for the Cross. They were horrified when King Amalric urged them to wait in patience. Reynald of Dampierre insulted the King to his face as a coward, and, as self-appointed leader, persuaded the knights to take service under Bohemond of Tripoli. They set out to join him at Antioch, and passed safely through the county of Tripoli. But Jabala and Lattakieh were still in Moslem hands. The emir of Jabala was a peaceful man, on excellent terms with his Christian neighbours. He offered the travellers hospitality, but warned them that to pass safely through the territory of Lattakieh they must obtain a safe-conduct from his suzerain, az-Zahir of Aleppo. He offered to write himself to the Sultan; who would have granted the request, for he was interested in exacerbating the civil war at Antioch. But Reynald and his friends would not wait. They pressed on past Lattakieh, whose emir, thinking to do his Moslem duty, lured them into an ambush and captured many of them and massacred the rest.[1]

Amalric himself allowed occasional raids against the Moslems. When an emir established himself near Sidon and began to raid the Christian coasts, and al-Adil offered no redress, Amalric retaliated by sending out ships to intercept and capture a rich Egyptian convoy sailing to Lattakieh, and leading a raid into Galilee. Al-Adil, though he marched as far as Mount Thabor to meet him, refused to do battle. Nor did he react violently when the Christian fleet sailed to the Nile Delta and up the river past Rosetta to sack the little town of Fuwa. About the same time the

[1] Ernoul, p. 341; *Estoire d'Eracles*, II, pp. 247–9; Villehardouin, ed. Faral, pp. 102–4; Kemal ad-Din (trans. Blochet), p. 39. John of Nesle and the few survivors from Lattakieh went on to fight for Leo II against Antioch. For the Fourth Crusade see below, pp. 107 ff. Villehardouin bitterly criticizes the Crusaders who insisted on going to the Holy Land.

Hospitallers from Krak and Marqab carried out raids, without any lasting success, against Hama, the emirate of al-Adil's great-nephew, al-Mansur.[1]

In September 1204 a peace treaty to last for six years was concluded between Amalric and al-Adil. It seems that the initiative came from Amalric. But al-Adil on his side was anxious to end the fighting. He may have been disquieted by the Christians' superiority in sea-power, but he was certainly aware that his empire would gain by the resumption of settled trade with the Syrian coast. He was therefore ready not only to abandon Beirut and Sidon finally to Amalric, but also ceded to him Jaffa and Ramleh and simplified the arrangements for pilgrims going to Jerusalem and to Nazareth. To Amalric, who could not expect now to receive any effective help from the West, the terms were surprisingly good.[2] But he was not able to enjoy his enhanced prestige for long. On 1 April 1205, after a short illness caused by a surfeit of fish, he died at Acre, aged little more than fifty.[3]

Amalric II was not a great king, but, like his predecessor Henry, he learned from experience a political wisdom that was very valuable to this poor and precarious kingdom; and his tidy legal mind not only created a constitution for Cyprus but did much to preserve monarchy on the mainland. As a man he was respected but not greatly liked. In his youth he had been irresponsible and quarrelsome, and he always resented opposition. But it was to his credit that though he would have clearly preferred to remain King of Cyprus alone, he accepted and carried out dutifully the tasks that his second crown laid on him. On his death, the two kingdoms were seperated. Cyprus passed to his son by Eschiva of Ibelin, Hugh I, a child of six. The boy's eldest sister, Burgundia, had

[1] Ernoul, pp. 355–60; *Estoire d'Eracles*, II, pp. 258–63; Abu Shama, II, p. 158; Ibn al-Athir, II, p. 96.

[2] Ernoul, p. 360; *Estoire d'Eracles*, II, p. 263; Ibn al-Athir, *loc. cit.*

[3] Ernoul, p. 407; *Estoire d'Eracles*, II, p. 305; Appendix to Robert de Monte, Bouquet, *R.H.F.* vol. XVIII, p. 342, quoting a letter of the Archbishop of Caesarea, which gives the exact date. His infant son by Queen Isabella had died on 2 February. The fish was white mullet.

recently married Walter of Montbéliard, to whom the High Court of the island entrusted the regency.[1] In the Kingdom of Jerusalem the authority passed automatically to Queen Isabella, who was not too deeply distraught by the death of this latest husband to assume government. But she herself did not long survive. The date of her death, like most of her life, is shrouded in obscurity. Alone of the ladies of the Royal House of Jerusalem she is a shadowy figure of whose personality nothing has survived. Her marriage and her very existence were of high importance. Had she held political ambitions she could have been a power in the land; but she let herself be passed from husband to husband without consideration of her personal wishes. We know that she was beautiful; but we must conclude that she was feckless and weak.[2]

Isabella left five daughters, Maria of Montferrat, Alice and Philippa of Champagne, and Sibylla and Melisende of Lusignan. Maria, who was now thirteen, succeeded to the throne; and John of Ibelin, lord of Beirut, was appointed regent. Whether he was nominated by the dying Queen or elected by the barons is unknown. But he was the obvious candidate. As Isabella's elder half-brother he was the child's nearest male relative. He owned the richest fief in the little kingdom and was the accepted leader of the barons; and he combined his father Balian's gallantry and wisdom with a Greek subtlety inherited from his mother, Maria Comnena. For three years he governed the country tactfully and quietly, undisturbed by Saracen wars or by the embarrassment of a Crusade. Indeed, as Amalric had ruefully foreseen when he made his treaty with al-Adil, no Western knight would trouble now willingly to come to Palestine. The Crusade had found a richer hunting-ground elsewhere.[3]

[1] *Estoire d'Eracles*, II, p. 305.   [2] *Ibid.*   [3] *Ibid.*; Ernoul, p. 407.

BOOK II

MISGUIDED CRUSADES

CHAPTER I

THE CRUSADE AGAINST CHRISTIANS

*'She that was great among the nations, and princess among the provinces,
how is she become tributary!..., all her friends have dealt treacherously
with her, they are become her enemies.'* LAMENTATIONS I, I, 2

In November 1199 Count Tibald of Champagne invited his friends
and neighbours to a tournament at his castle of Ecri on the Aisne.
When the jousts were over, conversation amongst the lords turned
to the need of a new Crusade. It was a matter on which the Count
felt strongly; for he was the nephew of Cœur-de-Lion and Philip
Augustus and brother to Count Henry who had reigned in
Palestine. On his suggestion an itinerant preacher, Fulk of Neuilly,
was called in to talk to the guests. Fired by his eloquence the whole
company vowed to take the Cross; and a messenger was sent to
report the pious decision to the Pope.[1]

Innocent III had been on the Papal throne for rather more than
a year. He was passionately ambitious to establish the trans-
cendental authority of the See, but at the same time he was prudent, far-sighted and clear-headed, a lawyer who liked a legal basis
for his claims and a politician who was ready to use whatever instrument lay nearest to his hand. He was troubled by the situation
in the East. One of his first actions had been to express publicly
his desire for a new Crusade; and in 1199 he wrote to the Patriarch
Aymar of Jerusalem to ask for a detailed report on the Frankish
kingdom.[2] The Kings of Jerusalem were his vassals; and his desire
to succour them was enhanced by the active policy of the Emperor
Henry VI, whose bestowal of crowns to Cyprus and Armenia was
an implicit challenge to Papal authority in those parts. Experience

---

[1] Villehardouin, I, pp. 2–6.   [2] Röhricht, *Regesta*, pp. 202–3.

had shown that kings and emperors were not wholly desirable on Crusading expeditions. The only Crusade to be a complete success was the First, in which no crowned head had taken part. A Crusade of barons, more or less homogeneous in race, would avoid the royal and national rivalries that had so greatly damaged the Second and Third Crusades. Such jealousies as arose would be petty and easily controlled by an able Papal representative. Innocent therefore gave a warm welcome to the news from Champagne. The movement that Tibald had launched not only would bring effective help to the East but also could be used to strengthen the unity of Christendom under Rome.[1]

The moment was well chosen for the Papacy. As at the time of the First Crusade, there was no Emperor in the West in a position to interfere. Henry VI's death in September 1197 had relieved the Church from a very real threat. As son of Frederick Barbarossa and husband of the heiress of Sicily, whose inheritance was firmly in his hands by 1194, Henry was more formidable than any potentate since Charlemagne. He had a high sense of this office and almost succeeded in establishing it on an hereditary basis. His bestowal of crowns in the East and his demand of allegiance from the captive Cœur de Lion showed that he saw himself as 'king of kings'. He made no secret of his hatred of Byzantium, the ancient Empire whose traditions outrivalled his own, nor of his aim to carry on the Norman policy of building a Mediterranean dominion, which in itself involved the destruction of Byzantium. A Crusade was an inevitable part of this policy. Throughout 1197 he laid his careful plans. The German expedition that landed that year at Acre was to be the forerunner of a greater army that he himself would command. Pope Celestine III, a timorous, vacillating man, was embarrassed but made no attempt to dissuade him, though he advised him not to launch an immediate attack against Constantinople, with whose Emperor he was negotiating for Church union. Had Henry not died suddenly at Messina, at the age of

[1] For Innocent III's attitude, see Fliche, *La Chrétienté Romaine* (vol. x of Fliche and Martin, *Histoire de l'Eglise*), pp. 44–60.

thirty-two, just as he was preparing a great armada to conquer the East, he might well have succeeded in making himself master of all Christendom.[1]

Pope Celestine died a few months after the Emperor. Innocent III therefore found himself on his accession without a lay rival. The widowed Empress Constance put her Sicilian Kingdom and her little son Frederick into his care. In Germany, where the Sicilian-born prince was unknown, his uncle, Henry's brother, Philip of Swabia, took over the family lands and claimed the Empire, and found that the enemies of the Hohenstaufen had only been temporarily cowed. The House of Welf put up a rival candidate, Otto of Brunswick. Richard of England was killed in March 1199, and his brother John and his nephew Arthur were disputing the inheritance, with King Philip of France actively taking part in the quarrel. With the Kings of France and England so occupied, with Germany distracted by civil war and Papal authority restored in southern Italy, Innocent could proceed in confidence to preach his Crusade. As a preliminary step he opened negotiations with the Byzantine Emperor Alexius III over the union of the Churches.[2]

In France the Pope's chief agent as preacher was the itinerant Fulk of Neuilly, who had long sought to inspire a crusade. He was famed for his fearlessness before princes, as when he ordered King Richard to abandon his pride and avarice and lust.[3] At the Pope's request he toured the country, persuading the countryfolk to follow their lords to the Holy War. In Germany the sermons of Abbot Martin of Pairis were almost equally inspiring, though there the nobles were too deeply involved in the civil war to pay him much attention.[4] But neither Fulk nor Martin aroused the same enthusiasm as the preachers of the First Crusade. The recruitment

[1] See Foreville and de Pina, *Du Premier Concile du Latran à l'avènement d'Innocent III* (vol. IX of Fliche and Martin, *Histoire de l'Eglise*), pp. 216–26.

[2] Fliche, *op. cit.* pp. 46, 50; *Gesta Innocentii III, M.P.L.* vol. CCXIV, cols. 119–23.

[3] Villehardouin, *loc. cit.*; Roger of Hoveden, IV, pp. 76–7. Richard offered to marry his pride to the Templars, his avarice to the Cistercians and his lust to his bishops.

[4] Gunther, *Historia Constantinopolitana* in Riant, *Exuviae*, I, pp. 60–5.

was more orderly and in the main restricted to the dependants of barons who had taken the Cross and many of these barons were moved less by piety than by a wish to acquire new lands far away from the disciplinary activity of King Philip Augustus. Tibald of Champagne was generally accepted as leader of the movement. With him were Baldwin IX of Hainault, Count of Flanders, and his brother Henry, Louis, Count of Blois, Geoffrey III of Le Perche and Simon IV of Montfort and their brothers, Enguerrand of Boves, Reynald of Dampierre and Geoffrey of Villehardouin, and many lesser lords from northern France and the Low Countries. The Bishop of Autun announced his adhesion with a company of knights from Auvergne. In the Rhineland the Bishop of Halberstadt and the Count of Katznellenbogen took the Cross with many of their neighbours.[1] Their example was followed soon afterwards by various magnates of northern Italy, led by Boniface, Marquis of Montferrat, whose participation aroused in Pope Innocent his first misgivings about the whole venture; for the princes of Montferrat were the faithful friends and allies of the Hohenstaufen.[2]

The expedition could not be organized quickly. The first problem was to find ships to carry it to the East; for with the decline of Byzantium the land-route across the Balkans and Anatolia was no longer practicable. But none of the Crusaders had a fleet at his disposal, except the Count of Flanders; and the Flemish fleet sailed on its own to Palestine, under the command of John of Nesle.[3] Next, there was the question of general strategy. Richard Cœur-de-Lion had given his opinion when he left Palestine that Egypt was the vulnerable point in the Saracen Empire. It was eventually decided that Egypt should be the

[1] Villehardouin, I, pp. 6–14, and Robert of Clary (ed. Lauer), pp. 2–3, give lists of the French Crusaders. Villehardouin, p. 74, mentions names of the German Crusaders.

[2] Villehardouin, I, p. 44, implies that Boniface only took the Cross when he was appointed commander-in-chief; *Gesta Innocentii III, loc. cit.* col. 132, suggesting the Pope's suspicions. Boniface's mother was half-sister to Henry VI's grandfather, and his father half-brother to Philip of France's grandmother.

[3] See above, p. 101.

rusaders' objective. The year 1200 was spent in varied negotia-
ons, over which Innocent tried to keep some control. In March
201 Tibald of Champagne died suddenly; and the Crusade elected
 leader in his place Boniface of Montferrat. It was a natural
 oice. The House of Montferrat had notable connections with
 e East. Boniface's father William had died as a Palestinian baron.
 f his brothers William had married Sibylla of Jerusalem and been
 e father of the child-King Baldwin V; Rainier had married the
 aughter of the Emperor Manuel and had been murdered at Con-
 antinople; and Conrad had been the saviour of Tyre, the ruler
 f the Holy Land and the father of its present heiress. But his
 ppointment to command the Crusaders moved it from Pope
 nocent's influence. Boniface came to France in August 1201
 d met his chief colleagues at Soissons, where they ratified his
 adership. From there he went on to Germany to spend the
 inter months with his old friend Philip of Swabia.[1]

Philip of Swabia was himself interested in Eastern affairs, but in
 yzantium rather than in Syria. He fully shared the dislike that
 is dynasty felt towards the Byzantine Emperors. He expected
 on to become Western Emperor, and he wished to carry out his
 rother Henry's full programme. He had moreover a personal
 onnection with Byzantium. When Henry VI conquered Sicily,
 mongst his prisoners had been the young widow of the dis-
 ossessed Sicilian crown-prince Roger, Irene Angelina, the
 aughter of the Emperor Isaac Angelus; and he gave her as bride
 Philip. It was a love-match; and through his love for her Philip
 ecame involved in the dynastic quarrels of the Angeli.[2]

A few months after Philip's marriage, his father-in-law Isaac
 st his throne. Power had not improved Isaac's capacity. His
 fficials were corrupt and uncontrolled, and he himself far more
 xtravagant than his impoverished Empire could afford. He had
 st half the Balkan peninsula to a vigorous and menacing Vlacho-

[1] Villehardouin, I, pp. 40–6; Robert of Clary, pp. 4–6; *Gesta Innocentii III*,
 c. cit., hinting that Philip of France intervened in Boniface's favour.
[2] *Chronica Regia Coloniensis*, p. 157.

Bulgarian kingdom. The Turks, till the death of Kilij Arslan I in 1192, were steadily encroaching in Anatolia, cutting Byzantium off from the south coast and from Syria. More and more trade concessions were sold for ready cash to the Italians. The lavish and tactless splendour of the Emperor's wedding to Princess Margaret of Hungary enraged his over-taxed subjects. His own family began to desert him; and in 1195 his brother Alexius engineered a successful palace plot. Isaac was blinded and thrown into prison together with his son, the younger Alexius. The new Emperor, Alexius III, was little abler than his brother. He showed some diplomatic activity, wooing the friendship of the Papacy with the offer of talks on ecclesiastical union—a friendship that may have preserved him from an attack by Henry VI—and his intrigue helped to keep the Seldjuk princes disunited. But home affairs were left to his wife Euphrosyne, who was as extravagant and as corruptly served as her dispossessed brother-in-law.[1]

At the end of 1201, the young Alexius, Isaac's son, escaped from his prison in Constantinople and made his way to his sister's court in Germany. Philip received him well and introduced him to Boniface of Montferrat. The three of them took counsel together. Alexius wished to obtain his father's throne. Philip was ready to help him, in order to make the Eastern Empire client to the Western. Boniface had a Crusading army at his disposal. Would it not be of advantage to the Crusade if it paused on its way to enthrone a friendly ruler at Constantinople?[2]

---

[1] See Vasiliev, *History of the Byzantine Empire*, pp. 440–5, 487.

[2] Nicetas Choniates, p. 712; Innocent III, letters, v, 122, *Gesta Innocentii III*, loc. cit., cols. 123–5; *ibid.* cols. 130–2. The whole question whether the diversion of the Fourth Crusade was premeditated has been bitterly argued. See Vasiliev, *op. cit.* pp. 455–8. The truth seems to be that while Philip of Swabia, Boniface and the Venetians all had separate reasons for desiring an attack on Constantinople, it was the accident of Alexius's arrival which made the diversion practicable. The Pope had no such intention, and the average Crusader, who was French, genuinely intended to go to the Holy Land but allowed himself to be swayed by circumstances. For Boniface's attitude, see Grégoire, 'The Question of the Diversion of the Fourth Crusade', *Byzantion*, vol. xv. For Philip of Swabia's deliberate scheme see Winkelmann, *Philipp von Schwaben*, I, pp. 296, 525

The Crusaders had meanwhile been seeking transport for their sea-voyage. Early in 1201, while the Count of Champagne was still alive, they opened negotiations with Venice and sent Geoffrey of Villehardouin there to arrange terms. A treaty was signed between Geoffrey and the Venetians in April. In return for 85,000 silver marks of Cologne, Venice agreed to supply the Crusade by 28 June 1202 with transport and victuals for a year for 4500 knights and their horses, 9000 esquires and 20,000 foot-soldiers. In addition, the Republic would provide fifty galleys to accompany the Crusade, on condition that one-half of its conquests should be given to Venice. As soon as the agreement was made, the Crusaders were summoned to assemble at Venice, ready to sail against Egypt.[1]

A few Crusaders were suspicious of the treaty. The Bishop of Autun took his company direct from Marseilles to Syria. Others, under Reynald of Dampierre, were impatient of the delay at Venice and made their own arrangements to sail to Acre. There was also some dissatisfaction among the humbler Crusaders at the decision to attack Egypt. They had enlisted to rescue the Holy Land and could not understand the point of going elsewhere. Their discontent was encouraged quietly by the Venetians, who had no intention of giving help to an attack on Egypt. Al-Adil was well aware of the advantages that trade with Europe brought to his dominions, and his conquest of Egypt had been followed by the offer of valuable trading concessions to the Italian cities. At the very moment when the Venetian government was bargaining with the Crusaders about the transport of their forces, its ambassadors were in Cairo planning a trade agreement with the Sultan's viceroy, who signed a treaty with them in the spring of 1202, after special envoys sent by al-Adil to Venice had been assured by the Doge that he would countenance no expedition against Egypt.[2]

[1] Villehardouin, II, pp. 18–34. The Pope gave his approval to the treaty, but without enthusiasm as he was clearly suspicious of the Venetians (*Gesta Innocentii III, loc. cit.* col. 131).

[2] The existence of a definite treaty, which Hopf, *Geschichte Griechenlands*, I, p. 118, dated 13 May 1202, has been denied, and indeed Hopf gives no sources. But Ernoul, pp. 345–6, states very positively that negotiations between Venice

It is uncertain whether the Crusaders understood the subtleties of Venetian diplomacy. But, if any of them suspected that they were being duped, there was nothing to be done. Their treaty with Venice placed them entirely in her power: for they could not raise the 85,000 marks that they had promised. By June 1202 the army was assembled; but as the money was not forthcoming the Republic would not provide the ships. Encamped on the little island of San Niccolo di Lido, harassed by Venetian merchants with whom they had run up debts, threatened that their supplies would be entirely cut off unless they produced the money, the Crusaders were ready by September to accept any terms that Venice might offer. Boniface, who joined them that summer, after an unsatisfactory visit to the Pope at Rome, was already prepared to work with the Venetians. For some decades past there had been a desultory war between the Republic and the King of Hungary for the control of Dalmatia, and the key-city of Zara had recently passed into Hungarian possession. The Crusaders were now informed that the expedition could start out and the settlement of the debt be postponed if they would join in a preliminary campaign to recapture Zara. The Pope, hearing of the offer, sent at once to forbid its acceptance. But, whatever they might feel about its morality, they could not but comply with it.[1]

The arrangement had been made behind the scenes between Boniface of Montferrat, who had few Christian scruples, and the Doge of Venice, Enrico Dandolo. Dandolo was a very old man, but age had not quenched his energy or his ambition. Some thirty years before he had been on an embassy to Constantinople, where he had been involved in a brawl and had partially lost his sight. His consequent bitterness against the Byzantines was increased when, soon after his elevation to the Dogeship in 1193, he had some difficulty in securing from the Emperor Alexius III a

and the Sultan were being conducted at the time. There is no need to suppose that he was inventing this story, which he presumably derived from the Venetians in Syria. For defections from the Crusade, Villehardouin, I, pp. 52–4

[1] Villehardouin, I, pp. 58–66; Robert of Clary, pp. 9–11.

renewal of the favourable trading terms given to Venice by the Emperor Isaac. He was therefore ready to discuss with Boniface schemes for an expedition against Constantinople. But for the moment the semblance of the Crusade must be maintained. As soon as the attack on Zara was approved there was a solemn ceremony at St Mark's where the Doge, and his leading counsellors, ostentatiously took the Cross.[1]

The fleet sailed from Venice on 8 November 1202, and arrived off Zara two days later. After a fierce assault, the city capitulated on the 15th and was thoroughly pillaged. Three days later the Venetians and Crusaders came to blows while dividing the spoil, but peace was patched up. The Doge and Boniface then decided that it was too late in the year to venture to the East. The expedition settled down for the winter at Zara, while its leaders planned their future operations.[2]

When the news of the sack of Zara reached Rome, Pope Innocent was aghast. It was intolerable that in defiance of his orders a Crusade should have been used to attack the territory of a faithful son of the Church. He excommunicated the whole expedition. Then, realizing that the Crusaders themselves had been the victims of blackmail, he forgave them but maintained the excommunication of the Venetians.[3] Dandolo was unperturbed. Through Boniface he was already in touch with Philip of Swabia, a fellow-excommunicate. Early in 1203 a messenger came from Germany to Zara from Philip to Boniface with a definite offer from his brother-in-law Alexius. If the Crusade would proceed to Constantinople and place Alexius upon the Imperial throne there, then Alexius would guarantee to pay the Crusaders the money that they still owed the Venetians; he would provide them with the necessary money and supplies for the conquest of Egypt, and would add a contingent of 10,000 men from the Byzantine

[1] Villehardouin, I, pp. 66–70; Robert of Clary, pp. 10–12. For Dandolo see Diehl, *Une République Patricienne, Venise*, pp. 47–8; Vasiliev, *op. cit.* pp. 452–3.
[2] Villehardouin, I, pp. 76–90; Robert of Clary, pp. 12–14.
[3] Innocent III, letters, V, 161, 162, VI, 99–102 (*M.P.L.* vol. CCXIV, cols. 1178, 1182; vol. CCXV, cols. 103–10); Villehardouin, I, pp. 104–8.

army; he would pay for the maintenance of five hundred knights to remain in the Holy Land, and he would ensure the submission of the Church of Constantinople to Rome. Boniface referred the matter to Dandolo, who was delighted. It meant that Venice would receive her money and at the same time would humble the Greeks and would be able to enlarge and strengthen her trading-privileges throughout the Byzantine Empire. The attack against Egypt could easily be thwarted later on.[1]

When the proposal was put before the Crusaders, there were a few dissentients, such as Reynald of Montmirail, who felt that they had taken the Cross to fight against the Moslems and saw no justification for further delay. They left the host and sailed on to Syria. Others remained with the army, protesting; others again were silenced by timely Venetian bribes. But the average Crusader had been taught to believe that Byzantium had consistently been a traitor to Christendom throughout the Holy Wars. It would be a wise and meritorious act to enforce its co-operation now. The pious men in the army were glad to help in a policy that would bring the schismatic Greeks into the fold. The more worldly reflected on the riches of Constantinople and its prosperous provinces and looked forward to the prospects of loot. Some of the barons, including Boniface himself, may have looked forward further still and have calculated that estates on the shores of the Aegean would be far more attractive than any that could be found in the stricken land of Syria. All the resentment that the West had long borne against Eastern Christendom made it easy for Dandolo and Boniface to bring public opinion round to their support.[2]

The Pope's disquiet about the Crusade did not lessen when he heard of the decision that it had taken. A scheme hatched between the Venetians and the friends of Philip of Swabia was unlikely to do credit to the Church. He had moreover met the young Alexius

[1] Villehardouin, I, pp. 90–100. He tells of previous negotiations between Alexius and the Crusaders at Venice, pp. 70–4.

[2] Villehardouin, I, pp. 100–4; Robert of Clary, pp. 14–15. Hugh of Saint Pol, letter in *Chronica Regia Coloniensis*, p. 205, says that nearly all the Crusaders wished to proceed to Palestine but were overpersuaded.

nd summed him up as a worthless youth. But it was too late for
im to make an effective protest; and if the diversion was really
oing to secure active Byzantine aid against the infidel and at the
ame time achieve the union of the Churches, it would be justified.
Ie contented himself by issuing an order that no more Christians
vere to be attacked unless they were actively hindering the Holy
War. It might have been wiser in the long run for him to have
xpressed, however vainly, open and uncompromising disap-
roval. To the Greeks, always suspicious of Papal intentions and
gnorant of the intricacies of Western politics, the half-heartedness
f his condemnation seemed proof that he was the power behind
 he whole intrigue.[1]

On 25 April Alexius arrived at Zara from Germany; and a few
ays later the expedition sailed on, pausing for a time at Durazzo,
vhere Alexius was accepted as Emperor, and then at Corfu. There
Alexius solemnly signed a treaty with his allies. The voyage was
ontinued on 25 May. The fleet rounded the Peloponnese and
urned northward to the island of Andros, refilling its water-tanks
rom the abundant springs there. From Andros it made for the
Dardanelles, which it found undefended. The Thracian harvest was
ipening; so the Crusaders put in at Abydos to gather what they
ould. On 24 June they arrived before the Imperial capital.[2]

The Emperor Alexius III had made no preparation against their

[1] *Gesta Innocentii III, loc. cit.* cols. 130–2: Innocent III, letters, v, 122 (to the
Emperor Alexius, *M.P.L.* vol. CCXIV, cols. 1123–5), and letter to Archbishop
Ebrard of Salzburg, *Registrum de Negotio Romani Imperii*, LXX (*M.P.L.* vol.
CXVI, cols. 1075–7), where he talks of the need for reflection in such matters.
Philip of Swabia probably knew of the project to attack Zara, as Cardinal Peter
of Capua was sent by him jointly with Crusading chiefs to secure the Pope's
upport for Alexius at a time when no answer would have been possible if the
Crusade were going straight to the East. See Bréhier, *Les Croisades*, p. 155.
The *Novgorod Chronicle* (ed. Lasonov, p. 241) declares that the Pope supported
he scheme to attack Constantinople, while *Chronica Regia Coloniensis*, p. 200,
mplies that he raised the excommunication on the Crusaders for having attacked
Zara when they decided to go on to Constantinople.
[2] Villehardouin, I, pp. 110–28; Robert of Clary, pp. 30–40; Anonymous of
Halberstadt, in Riant, *Exuviae*, I, pp. 14–15; *Devastatio Constantinopolitana* (ed.
Hopf), pp. 88–9; Nicetas Choniates, p. 717.

arrival. The Imperial army had never recovered from the disaster
of Manuel's last years. It was almost entirely mercenary. The
Frankish regiments were obviously unreliable at such a moment
the Slav and Petcheneg regiments could be trusted only in so far
as there was ready money to pay them. The Varangian Guard
now mainly English and Danish in composition, had traditions of
loyalty to the Emperor's person; but Alexius III was not a man
who inspired great personal loyalty. He was a usurper who had won
his throne not through any merit as a soldier or a statesman but by
a petty palace plot; and he had shown himself little fitted to govern
He was unsure not only of his army but of the general temper of
his subjects. It seemed safer to do nothing. Constantinople had
weathered many storms before in the nine centuries of her history
Doubtless she could weather another.

After attacking, without success, Chalcedon and Chrysopolis
on the Asiatic shore of the Bosphorus, the Crusaders landed at
Galata, across the Golden Horn. They occupied the town and
were able to break the chain across the entrance to the Golden
Horn and to bring their ships into the harbour. The young Alexius
had led them to believe that all Byzantium would rise to welcome
him. They were surprised to find the city gates closed against them
and soldiers manning the walls. Their first attempts at assault, made
from their ships against the walls along the Golden Horn, were held
but after a fierce struggle on 17 July Dandolo and the Venetians
effected a breach. Alexius III, who was as surprised as the Crusaders to find his city defended, was already meditating flight; he
had read in the Bible how David had fled before Absalom and so had
lived to recover his throne. Taking with him his favourite daughter
and a bag of precious stones, he now slipped through the land-
walls and took refuge at Mosynopolis in Thrace. The government
officials, left without an Emperor, made a quick but subtle decision.
They brought the blind ex-Emperor Isaac out from his prison and
set him on the throne, announcing to Dandolo and the Crusaders
that as the Pretender's father had been restored there was no need
to continue fighting. The young Alexius had chosen hitherto to

PLATE II

CONSTANTINOPLE FROM THE ASIATIC COAST

The sea of Marmora is on the left, the Bosphorus on the right, and the Golden Horn in the centre. The land-walls of the city can be seen stretching from the Marmora to the Golden Horn in the background.

ignore his father's existence, but he could not well repudiate him now. He persuaded his allies to call off the attack. Instead, they sent an embassy into the city to say that they would recognize Isaac if his son was raised to be co-Emperor and if they both honoured the treaty that the latter had made. Isaac promised to carry out their demands. On 1 August, at a solemn service in the Church of St Sophia, in the presence of the leading Crusader barons, Alexius IV was crowned to be his father's colleague.[1]

Alexius IV soon found that an Emperor cannot be as irresponsible as a pretender. His attempt to force the clergy of the city to admit the supremacy of Rome and to introduce Latin usages was met with sullen resistance. Nor was it easy for him to raise all the money that he had promised. He rashly began his reign by making lavish gifts to the Crusader leaders, whose greed was thereby stimulated. But when he had to hand over to the Venetians the money due to them from the Crusaders, the Treasury was found to be insufficiently well supplied. Alexius therefore announced new taxes, and further enraged the Church by confiscating large quantities of ecclesiastical plate, to be melted down for the Venetians. Throughout the autumn and winter of 1203 the atmosphere in the city grew steadily more tense. The sight of the haughty Frankish knights striding through their streets exasperated the citizens. Trade was at a standstill. Parties of drunken Western soldiers constantly pillaged the villages in the suburbs, so that life was no longer safe outside the walls. A disastrous fire swept through a whole quarter of the city when some Frenchmen in an access of piety burned down the mosque built for the use of visiting Moslem merchants. The Crusaders on their side were as dissatisfied as the Byzantines. They came to realize that the Byzantine government was quite unable to carry out the promises made by Alexius IV. Neither the men nor the money that he had offered

[1] Nicetas Choniates, pp. 718–26 (a full account from the Greek point of view); Villehardouin, I, pp. 154–84 (the fullest Crusader account); Robert of Clary, pp. 41–51; Anonymous of Halberstadt, pp. 15–16; *Devastatio Constantinopolitana*, pp. 89–90; letter of Hugh of Saint Pol in *Chronica Regia Coloniensis*, pp. 203–8.

were forthcoming. Alexius himself soon gave up the hopeless task of trying to content his guests. He invited them to an occasional feast at the palace, and with their help he made a brief military excursion against his uncle Alexius III in Thrace, returning home to celebrate a triumph as soon as he had won one little skirmish. The rest of his days and nights were spent in private pleasures. His father Isaac, who was too blind to take part in the government, shut himself up with his favourite astrologers, whose prophecies gave him no re-assurance for the future. An open breach was inevitable; and Dandolo did his best, by making unreasonable demands, to hasten it on.[1]

Only two men in Constantinople seemed fitted to take control, both of them sons-in-law of the ex-Emperor Alexius III. Anna's husband, Theodore Lascaris, was a distinguished soldier who had organized the first defence against the Latins. But after his father-in-law's flight he had gone into retirement. Eudocia's husband, Alexius Murzuphlus, had, on the contrary, sought the favour of Alexius IV and had been given the title of Protovestiarius. He had now made himself the leader of the nationalists. Probably in order to frighten Alexius IV from the throne he organized a riot in January 1204. But its only concrete result was the destruction of the great statue of Athena, the work of Phidias, which stood in the forum facing the west. It was hacked to pieces by a drunken mob, because the goddess seemed to be beckoning to the invaders.[2]

In February a deputation from the Crusaders came to the palace of Blachernae to demand from Alexius IV the immediate fulfil-ment of his promises. He could only confess his impotence; and the delegates were nearly torn to pieces by the angry crowd as they passed out from the imperial audience chamber. The populace then rushed to St Sophia and there they declared Alexius deposed and elected in his place an obscure nobleman called Nicholas Canabus, who happened to be present and who tried to repudiate

[1] Nicetas Choniates, pp. 736–8; Villehardouin, I, pp. 186–206; Robert of Clary, pp. 57–8; *Devastatio Constantinopolitana*, pp. 90–1.
[2] Nicetas Choniates, pp. 738–47; Villehardouin, II, pp. 6–23; Robert of Clary, p. 57; *Devastatio Constantinopolitana*, p. 91.

the honour. Murzuphlus then invaded the palace. No one attempted to defend Alexius IV, who was thrown into a dungeon and strangled there, universally and deservedly unlamented. His father Isaac died of grief and judicious ill-treatment a few days later. The shadowy Canabus was imprisoned; and Murzuphlus ascended the throne as Alexius V.[1]

The palace revolution was a direct challenge to the Crusaders. The Venetians had long been urging on them that the only effective course was to take Constantinople by storm and to instal there a Westerner as Emperor. Their advice seemed now to be justified. But it would not be easy to choose an Emperor. Discussions were carried out throughout the month of March at the camp at Galata. There were some who pressed for the election of Philip of Swabia, to unite the two Empires. But Philip was far away. He had been excommunicated, and the Venetians disliked the idea of one powerful Empire. Boniface of Montferrat was the obvious candidate. But there again, in spite of Dandolo's protestations of affection for him, the Venetians disapproved. Boniface was too ambitious for their tastes. He had, moreover, connections with the Genoese. It was decided at last that a panel of six Franks and six Venetians should elect the Emperor as soon as the city was taken. If, as seemed best, the Emperor was to be a Frank, then a Venetian should be elected as Patriarch. The Emperor should have for himself the great imperial palace and the residential palace of Blachernae, and a quarter of the city and the Empire. The remaining three-quarters should go half to the Venetians and half to the Crusading knights, to be divided into fiefs for them. With the exception of the Doge all the fief-holders should do homage to the Emperor. All things would thus be ordered to 'the honour of God, of the Pope and of the Empire'. The pretence that the expedition was ever to go on to fight the infidel was frankly abandoned.[2]

---

[1] Nicetas Choniates, pp. 738–47; Villehardouin, II, pp. 6–23; Robert of Clary, pp. 58–9; *Devastatio Constantinopolitana*, p. 92.

[2] Villehardouin, II, pp. 34–6; Robert of Clary, p. 68; Andrea Dandolo, *Chronicle* (ed. Pastorello), p. 279.

Alexius V was a vigorous but not a popular ruler. He dismissed any minister whom he thought disloyal to his person, including the historian Nicetas Choniates, who took vengeance on him in his History. There was some attempt to repair the walls and organize the population for the defence of the city. But the city guards had been demoralized by the constant revolutions; and there had never been an opportunity for bringing up troops from the provinces. And there were traitors in Venetian pay inside the city. The first attack by the Crusaders, on 6 April, was driven back with heavy losses. Six days later the Crusaders attacked again. There was a desperate fight on the Golden Horn, where Greek ships vainly tried to keep the Venetian fleet from landing troops below the walls. The main assault was launched against the Blachernae quarter, where the land-walls came down to the Golden Horn. A breach was made in the outer wall there. The defenders were holding in the inner wall when, either by accident or by treachery, a fire broke out in the city behind them and trapped them. Their defence collapsed; and the Franks and the Venetians poured into the city. Murzuphlus fled with his wife along the walls to the Golden Gate, near the Marmora, and out into Thrace, to seek refuge with his father-in-law at Mosynopolis. When it was known that he had fled, the remaining nobles met in St Sophia to offer the crown to Theodore Lascaris. But it was too late to save the city. Theodore refused the empty honour. He came out with the Patriarch to the Golden Milestone in the square between the church and the Great Palace and spoke passionately to the Varangian Guard, telling them that they would gain nothing by surrender now to new masters. But their spirit was broken; they would fight no more. So Theodore and his wife and the Patriarch, with many of the nobility, slipped down to the palace harbour and took ship for Asia.[1]

---

[1] Nicetas Choniates, pp. 748–56; Villehardouin, II, pp. 32–50; Robert of Clary, pp. 60–79; Gunther, pp. 91–4, 100–4; letter of Baldwin, *R.H.F.* vol. XVIII, p. 522; *Devastatio Constantinopolitana*, p. 92; Ernoul, pp. 369–73; *Novgorod Chronicle*, pp. 242–5.

There was a little fighting in the streets as the invaders forced their way through the city. By next morning the Doge and the leading Crusaders were established in the Great Palace, and their soldiers were told that they might spend the next three days in pillage.

The sack of Constantinople is unparalleled in history. For nine centuries the great city had been the capital of Christian civilization. It was filled with works of art that had survived from ancient Greece and with the masterpieces of its own exquisite craftsmen. The Venetians indeed knew the value of such things. Wherever they could they seized treasures and carried them off to adorn the squares and churches and palaces of their town. But the Frenchmen and Flemings were filled with a lust for destruction. They rushed in a howling mob down the streets and through the houses, snatching up everything that glittered and destroying whatever they could not carry, pausing only to murder or to rape, or to break open the wine-cellars for their refreshment. Neither monasteries nor churches nor libraries were spared. In St Sophia itself drunken soldiers could be seen tearing down the silken hangings and pulling the great silver iconostasis to pieces, while sacred books and icons were trampled under foot. While they drank merrily from the altar-vessels a prostitute set herself on the Patriarch's throne and began to sing a ribald French song. Nuns were ravished in their convents. Palaces and hovels alike were entered and wrecked. Wounded women and children lay dying in the streets. For three days the ghastly scenes of pillage and bloodshed continued, till the huge and beautiful city was a shambles. Even the Saracens would have been more merciful, cried the historian Nicetas, and with truth.[1]

[1] Nicetas Choniates, pp. 757–63; Nicholas Mesarites, in Heisenberg, *Neue Quellen zur Geschichte des Lateinischen Kaisertums*, I, pp. 41–8; Letter of Greek clergy in Cotelerius, *Ecclesiae Graecae Monumenta*, III, pp. 510–14; Innocent III, letters, VIII, 126 (*M.P.L.* vol. CCXV, cols. 699–702), an unsparing account of the horrors reported to him; Villehardouin, II, pp. 52–8; Robert of Clary, pp. 68–9, 80–1; Gunther, pp. 104–8; letter of Baldwin, *loc. cit.*; Ernoul, pp. 374–6; *Novgorod Chronicle*, pp. 245–6. The Latin chroniclers were more shocked at the

At last the Latin leaders realized that so much destruction was to nobody's advantage. When the soldiers were exhausted by their licence, order was restored. Anyone who had stolen a precious object was forced to give it up to the Frankish nobles; and unfortunate citizens were tortured to make them reveal the goods that they had contrived to hide. Even after so much had wantonly perished, the amount of booty was staggering. No one, wrote Villehardouin, could possibly count the gold and silver, the plate and the jewels, the samite and silks and garments of fur, vair, silver-grey and ermine; and he added, on his own learned authority, that never since the world was created had so much been taken in a city. It was all divided according to the treaty; three-eighths went to the Crusaders, three-eighths to the Venetians, and a quarter was reserved for the future Emperor.[1]

The next task was to select the Emperor. Boniface of Montferrat still hoped to be chosen. To enhance his position he had rescued the Dowager Empress Margaret, Isaac's Hungarian widow, and had forthwith married her. But the Venetians would have none of him. Under their influence the throne was given to a less controversial prince, Baldwin IX, Count of Flanders and Hainault, a man of high lineage and great wealth, but weaker and more tractable. His title was to be grander than his actual power. He was indeed to be overlord of all the conquered territory, with the ominous exception of the lands allotted to the Doge of Venice. His personal domain was to include Thrace, as far as Chorlu, and Bithynia and Mysia as far as Mount Olympus, and some of the Aegean islands, Samothrace, Lesbos, Chios, Samos and Cos. But his capital was not to be entirely his own; for the Venetians claimed their right to three-eighths of Constantinople, and took the portion that included St Sophia, where a Venetian, Thomas Morosini, was

rapacity than at the cruelty of the Crusaders. Gunther admits that even the worthy Martin of Pairis was determined to have his share of the booty, though out of piety he only robbed churches. Ernoul blames the Venetians as being the most rapacious. Abu Shama (II, p. 154) says that they sold much of their booty to the Moslems.

[1] Villehardouin, II, pp. 59–60; Robert of Clary, pp. 80–1.

installed as Patriarch. In addition, they demanded those parts of the Empire that would aid their maritime supremacy, the western coasts of continental Greece, the whole Peloponnese, Naxos, Andros and Euboea, Gallipoli and the Thracian ports on the Marmora, and Adrianople. To Boniface, as compensation for missing the throne, they offered a vague dominion in Anatolia, the east and centre of continental Greece and the island of Crete. But, having no desire to go out to conquer lands in Asia, he demanded instead Macedonia with Thessalonica. Baldwin demurred, but public opinion supported him, especially when he put forward a hereditary claim derived from his brother Rainier, who had married the Porphyrogennete Maria; and he won over the Venetians by selling them Crete. He became King of Thessalonica under the Emperor. Lesser nobles were assigned fiefs suited to their rank and importance.[1]

On 16 May 1204 Baldwin was ceremoniously crowned in St Sophia. On 1 October, after he had suppressed a bid by Boniface for independence, he held a court at Constantinople, where he enfeoffed some six hundred of his vassals with their lordships. Meanwhile, a constitution was worked out, based partly on the theories of feudal lawyers and partly on what was believed to be the practice of the Kingdom of Jerusalem. A council of tenants-in-chief, assisted by the Venetian *podestà* of Constantinople, advised the Emperor on political matters; it directed military operations and could countermand the Emperor's administrative orders. A High Court, similarly composed, regulated his relations with his vassals. He became little more than the chairman of a house of peers. Few constitutions have been so impracticable as that embodied in the Assizes of Romania.[2]

Romania, as the Latins called their Empire, had little more

---

[1] For a discussion of the division of the Empire see Longnon, *L'Empire Latin de Constantinople*, pp. 49–64. The partition treaty is given in Tafel and Thomas, *Urkunden*, I, pp. 464–8.

[2] Villehardouin, II, pp. 66–8; Robert of Clary, p. 93. See *Assises of Romania* (ed. Recoura), *passim*.

reality than its Emperor's power. Many of its provinces were still unconquered, and never would be conquered. The Venetians, in their realism, took only what they knew that they could hold, Crete and the ports of Modon and Croton in the Peloponnese and for a while Corfu. They set up vassal lords of Venetian origin in their Aegean islands, and in Cephalonia and Euboea accepted the homage of Latin princes who had installed themselves ahead of them. Boniface of Montferrat soon overran most of continental Greece and set up his vassals there, a Burgundian, Otho of La Roche becoming Duke of Athens and Thebes. The Peloponnese fell to two French lords, William of Champlitte and Geoffrey of Villehardouin, nephew of the chronicler, who founded a dynasty of Princes of Achaea.[1]

Nearly all the European provinces of the Empire passed thus into Latin hands. But the Latins were mistaken in their belief that the capture of Constantinople would give them the whole Empire. In times of disaster the Greek spirit shows itself at its most courageous and energetic. The loss of the Imperial capital led at first to chaos. But within two years the independent Greek world was reorganized in three succession-states. Away in the East, two grandsons of the Emperor Andronicus, Alexius and David Comnenus, had with the help of their aunt, the great Queen Thamar of Georgia, occupied Trebizond and established a dominion along the Black Sea shores of Asia Minor. David was killed in 1206 while fighting to extend their power towards the Bosphorus; but Alexius lived on to take the title of Emperor and to found a dynasty that lasted for two and a half centuries, enriched by the trade from Persia and the East that passed through its capital and by the silver-mines in the hills behind, and famed for the beauty of its princesses. Away in the West a bastard of the Angeli made himself Despot of Epirus and founded a dynasty that was to extinguish the Montferrat kingdom of Thessalonica. Most formidable of the three was the Empire set up at Nicaea by Alexius III's daughter Anna and her husband Theodore Lascaris

[1] Longnon, *loc. cit.*; Hopf, *Geschichte Griechenlands*, II, p. 10.

The leading citizens that had escaped from Constantinople gathered there around them. The Greek Patriarch, John Camaterus, who had fled to Thrace, resigned his office in order that a priest already at Nicaea, Michael Autoreanus, might be elected by the clergy exiled from the old Imperial capital; and Michael thereupon performed the coronation of Theodore and Anna. In the eyes of the Greeks Nicaea thus became the seat of the legitimate Empire. Theodore soon extended his rule over most of the lands that had been left to Byzantium in Asia. In little more than fifty years his successors would reign again in Constantinople.[1]

The Latins also forgot the other races of the Balkans. The Vlacho-Bulgarian Empire of the Asen brothers would have willingly allied with them against the hated Greeks. But the Latin Emperor claimed territory that the Tsar Kaloyan had occupied, and the Latin Patriarch claimed authority over the Orthodox Bulgarian Church. Bulgaria was driven into an unnatural alliance with the Greeks; and at the battle of Adrianople in 1205 the army of Romania was almost annihilated and the Emperor Baldwin led off to die a prisoner in a Balkan castle. It seemed for a moment that the next Emperor to rule in Constantinople would be the Bulgarian Tsar. But in Baldwin's brother Henry the Latin East produced its one great ruler. The energy and tolerant wisdom that he showed in his ten years' reign saved the Latin Empire from immediate destruction; and the rivalries of the Greek potentates, their quarrels with each other and with the Bulgarians, and the presence in the background of the Turks kept it alive till 1261.[2]

The exultant conquerors of 1204 could not foresee how empty would be the results of their enterprise, and their contemporaries were equally dazzled by the conquest. There was exultation at first throughout the Latin world. True, the Cluniac satirist Guyot de Provins asked in his poems why the Pope permitted a Crusade

---

[1] Vasiliev, 'Foundation of the Empire of Trebizond', *Speculum*, vol. XI, pp. 3–37; Ostrogorsky, *Geschichte des Byzantinischen Staates*, 2nd ed., pp. 337–46.
[2] Longnon, *op. cit. passim*, esp. pp. 77–186; Ostrogorsky, *op. cit.* pp. 337–59; Zlatarsky, *History of the Bulgarian Empire* (in Bulgarian), III, pp. 211–47.

conducted against Christians, and the Provençal troubadour, Guillem Figuera bitterly accused Rome of perfidy against the Greeks. But when he wrote, Rome was preaching a Crusade against his fellow-countrymen.[1] Such dissidents were rare. Pope Innocent, for all the misgivings that he had felt about the diversion of the Crusade to Constantinople, was at first delighted. In answer to an ecstatic letter from the new Emperor Baldwin boasting of the great and valuable results of the miracle that God had wrought, Innocent wrote that he rejoiced in the Lord and gave his approval without reserve.[2] Throughout the West there were paeans of praise, and the enthusiasm mounted when precious relics began to arrive for the churches of France and Belgium. Hymns were sung to celebrate the fall of the great ungodly city, *Constantinopolitana Civitas diu profana*, whose treasures were now disgorged. The Latins in the East were encouraged by the news.[3] Surely with Constantinople in the hands of their kinsmen the whole strategy of the Crusades would be far more effective. Rumours came that the Moslems were struck with terror; and the Pope congratulated himself on the alarm that the Sultan of Egypt was said to have expressed.[4]

Second thoughts were less encouraging. The Pope's misgivings began to return. The integration of the Eastern Empire and its Church into the world of Roman Christendom was a fine achievement; but had it been done in a way that would bring lasting benefit? He received more information, and learned to his horror of the blasphemous and bloodthirsty scenes at the sack of the city. He was profoundly shocked as a Christian, and he was disquieted

[1] Guyot de Provins, *Œuvres* (ed. Orr), p. 34; Guillem Figuera, 'Dun Servientes Far' in de Bartholomaeis, *Poesie Provenziale Storiche*, II, pp. 98–9. See Throop, *Criticism of the Crusade*, pp. 30–1.

[2] Innocent III, letters, VII, 153, 154, 203, 208 (*M.P.L.* vol. ccxv, cols. 454–61, 512–16, 521–3).

[3] Hymns given in Riant, *Exuviae*, II, pp. 43–50, esp. *Sequentia Andegavensis*.

[4] Innocent III, letters, VIII, 125 (*M.P.L.* vol. ccxv, col. 698). Ibn al-Athir, II, p. 95, remarks that the conquest of Constantinople helped the Crusaders to reach Syria more easily.

a statesman. Such barbarous brutality was not the best policy
or winning the affections of Eastern Christendom. He wrote in
itter fury to Constantinople enumerating and denouncing the
rocities. He learned too that the conquerors had blandly divided
p the State and the Church there without any reference to his
uthority. His rights had been deliberately ignored, and he could
e how incompetent were the arrangements made for the new
mpire and how completely the Crusaders had been outwitted
y the Venetians. Then, to his disgust, he heard that his legate,
eter of Saint-Marcel, had issued a decree absolving all who had
ken the Cross from making the further journey to the Holy
and. The Crusade was revealed as an expedition whose only aim
as to conquer Christian territory. It was to do nothing to help
he Christian soldiers fighting against Islam.[1]

The Franks in Syria had already realized that they could not
ope for any expedition in 1204. The summer passed with the
Crusaders still remaining at Constantinople; and in September King
malric made a truce with al-Adil, knowing that no reinforce-
ents would now come.[2] But soon it became clear that the Latin
stablishments further north would do positive harm to the
stablishments in Syria. The Emperor Baldwin had boasted to
ope Innocent that many knights from Outremer had come to
is coronation; and he did his best to persuade them to stay with
im. When it was discovered that there were rich and pleasant
efs to be had by the Bosphorus or in Greece, other knights who
ad lost their lands in Syria to the Moslems hastened to Con-
antinople to join them. Amongst them was Hugh of Tiberias,
he eldest of Raymond of Tripoli's stepsons and husband of
Margaret of Ibelin, Maria Comnena's daughter. Adventurous
nights from the West now found it pointless to go so far as the
vercrowded kingdom of Jerusalem to look for a lordship or an
eiress. There were better lands to be found in Greece. The con-
uest of Cyprus had already lured aways settlers from the Syrian

[1] Innocent III, letters, VIII, 126 (*M.P.L.* vol. CCXV, cols. 699–702).
[2] See above, p. 103.

mainland. After the conquest of Romania recruits for the Militar
Orders were almost the only knights to come out from Europ
to defend the Holy Land.[1]

There was never a greater crime against humanity than th
Fourth Crusade. Not only did it cause the destruction or di:
persal of all the treasures of the past that Byzantium had devotedl
stored, and the mortal wounding of a civilization that was sti
active and great; but it was also an act of gigantic political folly
It brought no help to the Christians in Palestine. Instead it robbe
them of potential helpers. And it upset the whole defence of
Christendom. Had the Latins been able to take over the whol
Byzantine Empire as it had been in the days of Manuel, then the
could have provided powerful aid to the Crusading movemen
though Byzantium run in the interests of Latin Syria would no
long have prospered. But Byzantium had lost territory in Anatoli
since Manuel's death; and the Latins could not even conquer a
that was left, while their attack on the Greeks gave further strengt
to the Turks. The land route from Europe to Syria became mor
difficult as a result of the Fourth Crusade, with the Greeks of Nicae
suspicious and the Turks hostile to travellers. No armed compan
from the West was ever to attempt the journey across Anatoli
again. Nor was the sea route made easier; for Italian ships now
preferred to carry passengers to the Greek islands and the Bos
phorus rather than to Acre or the Syrian ports.

In the wide sweep of world history the effects were wholly dis
astrous. Since the inception of its Empire Byzantium had bee
the guardian of Europe against the infidel East and the barbaria
North. She had opposed them with her armies and tamed ther
with her civilization. She had passed through many anxious period
when it had seemed that her doom had come, but hitherto sh
had survived them. At the close of the twelfth century she wa
facing a long crisis, as the damage to her man-power and he
economy caused by the Turkish conquests in Anatolia a centur
before began to take full effect, enhanced by the energetic rivalr

[1] Villehardouin, II, p. 124.

of the Italian merchant cities. But she might well have shown her resilience once again and have reconquered the Balkans and much of Anatolia, and her culture could have continued its uninterrupted influence over the countries around. Even the Seldjuk Turks might well have fallen under its sway and in the end been absorbed to refresh the Empire. The story of the Empire of Nicaea shows that the Byzantines had not lost their vigour. But, with Constantinople gone, the unity of the Byzantine world was broken and could never be repaired, even after the capital itself was recovered. It was part of the achievement of the Nicaeans to keep the Seldjuks in check. But when a new, more vigorous Turkish tribe appeared, under the leadership of the brilliant house of Osman, the East Christian world was too deeply divided to make an effective stand. Its leadership was passing elsewhere, away from the Mediterranean birthplace of European culture to the far northeast, to the vast plains of Russia. The Second Rome was giving place to the Third Rome of Muscovy.

Meanwhile hatred had been sown between Eastern and Western Christendom. The bland hopes of Pope Innocent and the complacent boasts of the Crusaders that they had ended the schism and united the Church were never fulfilled. Instead, their barbarity left a memory that would never be forgiven them. Later, East Christian potentates might advocate union with Rome in the fond expectation that union would bring a united front against the Turks. But their people would not follow them. They could not forget the Fourth Crusade. It was perhaps inevitable that the Church of Rome and the great Eastern Churches should drift apart; but the whole Crusading movement had embittered their relations, and henceforward, whatever a few princes might try to achieve, in the hearts of the East Christians the schism was complete, irremediable and final.

CHAPTER II

THE FIFTH CRUSADE

'Can two walk together, except they be agreed?' AMOS III, 3

The failure of the Fourth Crusade to send material help to Palestine was not without its compensations. For over ten years the little kingdom was left in peace. The truce that King Amalric had arranged with the Sultan held good. Without Western aid the Franks could not venture to break it, while al-Adil was sufficiently busy keeping together his own dominions not to trouble himself over the conquest of a state that was harmless, whereas if he were to attack it, he might well provoke a Crusade. For three years John of Ibelin was able to rule undisturbed as regent for his niece Queen Maria.

In 1208 the Queen reached the age of seventeen, and it was time to find a husband. An embassy consisting of Florent, Bishop of Acre, and Aymar, lord of Caesarea, was sent to France to ask King Philip to provide a candidate. It was hoped that the offer of a crown would lure some rich and vigorous prince to come to the rescue of the Frankish East. But it was not so easy to find a bridegroom. At last, in the spring of 1210, Philip announced that a knight from Champagne, called John of Brienne, had accepted the position.[1]

It was a disappointing choice. John was a penniless younger son who had already reached the age of sixty. His elder brother Walter had married King Tancred of Sicily's eldest daughter and had put in an ineffectual claim to the Sicilian throne; but John had spent his life in comparative obscurity as one of the French King's commanders. It was rumoured that he was chosen now because of a love-intrigue with the Countess Blanche of Cham-

[1] Ernoul, pp. 407–8; *Estoire d'Eracles*, II, pp. 305–8; see La Monte, 'John d'Ibelin', in *Byzantion*, vol. XII.

pagne which was scandalizing the Court. But, apart from his poverty, he was not ill-fitted for the post. He had a wide knowledge of international politics, and his age was guarantee that he would not embark on rash adventures. To make him more acceptable King Philip and Pope Innocent each gave him a dower of 40,000 silver pounds.[1]

Meanwhile, till he should arrive, John of Ibelin carried on the government. In July 1210 the truce with al-Adil came to an end, and the Sultan sent to Acre to suggest its renewal. John of Ibelin presided over a Council at which he recommended the acceptance of the offer; and he was supported by the Grand Master of the Hospital, Guerin of Montaigu, and the Grand Master of the Teutonic Knights, Hermann Bardt. But the Grand Master of the Temple, Philip of Le Plessiez, persuaded the bishops to insist on rejecting the suggestion, on the legal ground that the future King could not be bound by any new truce. There was little actual fighting. Al-Adil sent his son, al-Mu'azzam, with a few troops to Mount Thabor and their presence there kept the Franks in check.[2]

John of Brienne landed at Acre on 13 September 1210. Next day the Patriarch Albert of Jerusalem married him to Queen Maria; and on 3 October the royal pair were crowned at Tyre.

The new King soon became popular. He showed tact in the handling of his vassals and the Military Orders and caution in his dealings with the Moslems. While the court was at Tyre for the coronation al-Mu'azzam had raided the suburbs of Acre but had not ventured to attack the city itself. Early next summer John allowed some of his vassals to combine with the Templars on an expedition by sea to the Damietta mouth of the Nile; but it was ineffectual. A few months later he accepted a fresh offer from al-Adil to sign a truce for five years, which came into force in July 1212. In the meantime messages were sent by the King to Rome, to ask that a new Crusade should be ready to come to Palestine as soon as the truce should expire.[3]

---

[1] *Estoire d'Eracles, loc. cit.*   [2] *Ibid.* pp. 310, 316; Abu Shama, II, p. 158.
[3] *Estoire d'Eracles, loc. cit.* and p. 317; Abu Shama, *loc. cit.*

The same year the young Queen died, after giving birth to a daughter called Isabella after her grandmother, but more usually known as Yolanda. Her death made John's judicial position doubtful. He had reigned as the Queen's husband. Now the kingdom had passed to Yolanda; and her father had no legal right. But he was her father, and he was accepted as natural regent of the kingdom, at least until she should marry. He continued to govern the country in peace till the coming of the next Crusade. To console himself in his widowhood he married in 1214 the Princess Stephanie of Armenia, daughter of Leo II. She proved a bad stepmother; and gossip attributed her death in 1219 to the severe beating that John had given her for having tried to poison the child Yolanda.[1]

The neighbouring Latin states were less fortunate than the kingdom of Acre. In Cyprus King Amalric had been succeeded by his ten-year-old son Hugh, and the regency was given to Walter of Montbéliard, a French knight who had been Amalric's constable and had married Hugh's eldest sister Burgundia. He was an unsuccessful regent, who involved the island in an unhappy war with the Turks; and when he handed over the power to his brother-in-law in 1210 he was forcibly exiled on the suspicion of gross peculation during his period of office. King Hugh was now fifteen.[2] Two years previously he had married his stepsister, Alice of Jerusalem, according to the arrangement made by their respective fathers. The negotiations for the actual marriage were conducted by the bride's grandmother, Queen Maria Comnena, and the dowry was provided by Blanche of Navarre, Countess of Champagne, widow of the bride's uncle. She feared that unless Alice and her sister were both safely married in the East, one of them might come and claim the county of Champagne

---

[1] Ernoul, p. 411. See below, p. 165. *Estoire d'Eracles*, II, p. 320. See La Monte, *Feudal Monarchy*, p. 55. The chronicles of Outremer all call the young Queen Isabella, but she is usually called Yolanda in Western chronicles. I employ the latter name to lessen confusion with other Isabellas.

[2] *Estoire d'Eracles*, II, pp. 15–16; Mas Latrie, *Documents*, II, p. 13.

from her own infant son. King Hugh was a youth with a fiery temper, whose relations with his neighbours, his vassals, his Church and the Papacy were consistently stormy. But he provided his kingdom with a firm government.[1]

The situation in the Principality of Antioch was far stormier. Bohemond, Count of Tripoli, had established himself there on his father Bohemond III's death in 1201, in defiance of the rights of his nephew, Raymond-Roupen. Raymond's maternal great-uncle, Leo of Armenia, continued to press his cause. Complications were introduced by Leo's quarrel with the Templars, whose castle of Baghras he refused to return. The Hospitallers therefore sided with him against Bohemond. Bohemond, however, could call on the help of the Seldjuk Turks, with whom Leo was perpetually at war; and az-Zahir of Aleppo was always ready to send him reinforcements. Al-Adil was therefore hostile to Bohemond. The Kings of Jerusalem and Cyprus were inconstant in their sympathies. Religious problems added to the chaos. In the interests of the whole Crusading movement it was essential that the question of the Antiochene succession should be settled; and Pope Innocent felt it his duty to intervene. Two of his legates, Sofred of Saint-Praxedis and Peter of Saint-Marcel, in turn, then together, attempted to hear the case; but while Leo was verbally deferential to Rome, he refused to make peace with the Templars by the cession of Baghras, as the Pope bade him. Bohemond on the other hand denied the Pope's right to take notice of a purely feudal question. Soon after Bohemond III's death the Patriarch Peter of Antioch had joined Leo's party, for which neither Bohemond IV nor the Commune of Antioch, which was strongly anti-Armenian, forgave him. But in 1203 Leo had written to the Pope to ask that the Armenian Church should be put directly under the jurisdiction of Rome; and in 1205 the Patriarch quarrelled with the Papal Legate Peter of Saint-Marcel over the appointment of the Arch-

[1] Mas Latrie, *Histoire de l'Ile de Chypre*, I, pp. 175–7; *Documents*, II, p. 34; Innocent III, letters, IX, 28 (*M.P.L.* vol. ccxv, cols. 829–30); Hill, *History of Cyprus*, II, pp. 72–83.

deacon of Antioch. The Patriarch found himself without friends; and Bohemond could take vengeance on him.[1]

Bohemond himself had his troubles. Though he held Antioch and had the support of the Commune, his power in the country-side was restricted. His county of Tripoli was disturbed at the end of 1204 by the revolt of Renoart, lord of Nephin, who had married the heiress of Akkar without Bohemond's leave. Several lords joined him, including Ralph of Tiberias, whose brother Otto was now at Leo's court; and the rebels had the sympathy of King Amalric. While Bohemond sought to suppress the revolt, Leo laid siege to Antioch and only retired when an army sent by az-Zahir of Aleppo came to Bohemond's help. After Amalric's death John of Ibelin withdrew any support for the rebels, whom Bohemond defeated at the end of the year, after losing an eye during the campaign. Meanwhile, to show that Antioch as a lay state was outside of the Pope's jurisdiction, he announced that its overlord had always been the Emperor of Constantinople. When Maria of Champagne, wife of the new Latin Emperor Baldwin, visited Palestine in 1204 on her way to join her husband, he journeyed to Acre to pay her homage.[2]

In 1206, irritated now both with the Pope and with his Patriarch, Bohemond deposed the latter, and summoned the titular Greek Patriarch, Symeon II, to take his place. It is probable that Symeon was already living in Antioch; and it is certain that Bohemond's move was supported if not suggested by the Commune. Despite a century of Frankish rule the Greek element in Antioch was still large and prosperous, and, in the course of time, many of the Latin merchant families must have intermarried with Greeks. They all hated the Armenians; and the Pope's flirtation with Leo

[1] For Antiochene history during this period, see Cahen, *La Syrie du Nord*, pp. 600–15, with full references.
[2] Alberic of Trois Fontaines, *Chronicon, R.H.F.* vol. xviii, p. 884. The assumption amongst the Franks was that the Latin Empire of Constantinople had inherited all the rights of the Byzantines. Leo of Armenia, however, at once negotiated with the Nicaean Emperor, who equally claimed to be heir of the Byzantines. See Cahen, *loc. cit.* esp. p. 606.

turned them against Rome. Bohemond for his part, now that Byzantium could no longer menace him, was very ready to favour a Church whose traditions enjoined deference to the secular prince. It was ironical that the restoration of the Greek Patriarchate, for which the Byzantine Emperors of the last century had fought so hard, should have been achieved after the destruction of Byzantium by the Latins. The Latin Patriarch Peter at once made up his quarrel with the Legate, who restored to him his power of excommunication which had been questioned. With the full approval of Rome he excommunicated the Prince and the Commune. They answered by crowding to the Greek churches in the city. The Latin Patriarch then resorted to plots. Towards the end of the next year, 1207, he introduced some knights that were faithful to him into the city by night. They managed to capture the lower city but Bohemond collected his forces in the citadel and soon drove them out. The Patriarch Peter, whose complicity was patent, was tried for treason and thrown into prison. No food nor water was given to him there. In despair he swallowed the oil from his lamp and died in agony.[1]

Pope Innocent began to weary of the interminable struggle, and handed the responsibility of settling it to the Patriarch of Jerusalem. In 1208 Leo angrily devastated the country round Antioch while Tripoli was invaded by al-Adil's forces, who had come, unfairly, to avenge an attack by some Cypriots on Moslem merchants, and an aggressive raid by the Hospitallers. Bohemond saved himself by calling in the Seldjuks against Leo, while the Pope appealed to az-Zahir of Aleppo to save Antioch from the Greeks. There followed a diplomatic revolution. The Patriarch of Jerusalem, Albert, was a friend of Bohemond's allies, the Templars. He offended Leo by insisting that the first preliminary to any settlement must be the return of Baghras to the Order. Meanwhile Bohemond agreed to accept a new Latin Patriarch, Peter of

[1] Cahen, *loc. cit.* esp. pp. 612–13. The episode shows that the Greek element in the Commune must have been strong. There was presumably a large amount of intermarriage in bourgeois circles.

Locedio, in Antioch. Leo therefore forgot his obedience to Rome. He ostentatiously made an alliance with the Greek Emperor at Nicaea; he welcomed the Greek Patriarch of Antioch, Symeon, to Cilicia, and he gave much of the Latin church lands there to the Greeks. But at the same time he sought the friendship of Hugh of Cyprus, whose sister Helvis was married to Raymond-Roupen, and he gave castles in Cilicia to the Teutonic Order. The struggle went on.[1]

In 1213 Bohemond's eldest son, Raymond, who was aged eighteen, was murdered by a band of Assassins in the cathedral of Tortosa. It seems that the murderers were instigated by the Hospitallers, to whom the Assassins now paid tribute. The Patriarch Albert of Jerusalem, another enemy of the Hospitallers, was murdered by Assassins the following year. Bohemond sought vengeance, and with a Templar reinforcement attacked the Assassin castle of Khawabi. The Assassins appealed to az-Zahir, who in his turn appealed to al-Adil. The siege of Khawabi was lifted, and Bohemond apologized to az-Zahir. But az-Zahir was less ready now to support him. Moreover, rumours of a new Crusade brought the Moslem world together. Az-Zahir began to woo the friendship of his uncle al-Adil.[2]

Leo profited by the situation to make his peace once more with Rome. The new Patriarch of Jerusalem, Ralph, former Bishop of Sidon, was amenable, and the Pope was ready to forgive Leo if he would help in the coming Crusade. John of Brienne's marriage with Leo's daughter Stephanie sealed an alliance between Armenia and Acre. In 1216 Leo managed by a successful intrigue, in which the Patriarch Peter undoubtedly helped, to smuggle troops into Antioch and to occupy the city without a blow. Bohemond was away at Tripoli, and his troops in the citadel soon yielded to Leo. Raymond-Roupen was consecrated as Prince. In his joy at the successful outcome of the long war, Leo at last gave back Baghras to the Templars and restored the Latin church lands in Cilicia.

[1] Cahen, *op. cit.* pp. 615–19.
[2] *Ibid.* pp. 619–21.

But he paid for his victory by losing fortresses in the west and across the Taurus to the Seldjuk Prince Kaikhaûs of Konya.[1]

The question of Antioch had been settled just in time for the new Crusade. Ever since his disillusion over the Fourth Crusade Innocent had been preparing for a more meritorious effort to save the East. He had been troubled by many distractions. There had been the difficult problem of the heretics in southern France to solve; and the fierce solution of the Albigensian Crusade, though he had instigated it and given the Crusaders indulgences similar to those earned by a war against the infidel, had raised difficulties in its turn. In 1211, in answer to an invasion of Castile by the Almohad vizier, an-Nasir, he had preached the Crusade in Spain; and his efforts were justified by the magnificent victory of Las Navas de Tolosa, in July 1212, when the African army was routed and a new phase of Christian reconquest began. But there were few knights ready to make the journey to the Holy Land. The only response to the prayers for the rescue of Jerusalem came from a very different class.[2]

One day in May 1212 there appeared at Saint-Denis, where King Philip of France was holding his court, a shepherd-boy of about twelve years old called Stephen, from the small town of Cloyes in the Orléannais. He brought with him a letter for the King, which, he said, had been given to him by Christ in person, who had appeared to him as he was tending his sheep and who had bidden him go and preach the Crusade. King Philip was not impressed by the child and told him to go home. But Stephen, whose enthusiasm had been fired by his mysterious visitor, saw himself now as an inspired leader who would succeed where his elders had failed. For the past fifteen years preachers had been going round the country-side urging a Crusade against the Moslems of the East or of Spain or against the heretics of Languedoc. It was easy for an hysterical boy to be infected with the idea that he too could

[1] *Ibid.* pp. 621–3.
[2] For Innocent's policy in Languedoc and Spain see Fliche, *La Chrétienté Romaine*, pp. 107–8, 112–37.

be a preacher and could emulate Peter the Hermit, whose prowess had during the past century reached a legendary grandeur. Undismayed by the King's indifference, he began to preach at the very entrance to the abbey of Saint-Denis and to announce that he would lead a band of children to the rescue of Christendom. The seas would dry up before them, and they would pass, like Moses through the Red Sea, safe to the Holy Land. He was gifted with an extraordinary eloquence. Older folk were impressed, and children came flocking to his call. After his first success he set out to journey round France summoning the children; and many of his converts went further afield to work on his behalf. They were all to meet together at Vendôme in about a month's time and start out from there to the East.

Towards the end of June the children massed at Vendôme. Awed contemporaries spoke of thirty thousand, not one over twelve years of age. There were certainly several thousand of them, collected from all parts of the country, some of them simple peasants, whose parents in many cases had willingly let them go on their great mission. But there were also boys of noble birth who had slipped away from home to join Stephen and his following of 'minor prophets' as the chroniclers called them. There were also girls amongst them, a few young priests, and a few older pilgrims, some drawn by piety, others, perhaps, from pity, and others, certainly, to share in the gifts that were showered upon them all. The bands came crowding into the town, each with a leader carrying a copy of the Oriflamme, which Stephen took as the device of the Crusade. The town could not contain them all, and they encamped in the fields outside.

When the blessing of friendly priests had been given, and when the last sorrowing parents had been pushed aside, the expedition started out southward. Nearly all of them went on foot. But Stephen, as befitted the leader, insisted on having a gaily decorated cart for himself, with a canopy to shade him from the sun. At his side rode boys of noble birth, each rich enough to possess a horse. No one resented the inspired prophet travelling in comfort. On the contrary, he was treated as a saint, and locks of his hair and pieces of his garments were collected as precious relics. They took the road past Tours and Lyons, making for Marseilles. It was a painful journey. The summer was unusually hot. They depended on charity for their food, and the drought left little to spare in the country, and water was scarce. Many of the children died by the wayside. Others dropped out and tried to wander home. But at last the little Crusade reached Marseilles.

The citizens of Marseilles greeted the children kindly. Many found houses in which to lodge. Others encamped in the streets. Next morning the whole expedition rushed down to the harbour to see the sea divide before them. When the miracle did not take place, there was bitter disappointment. Some of the children turned against Stephen, crying that he had betrayed them, and began to retrace their steps. But most of them stayed on by the sea-side, expecting each morning that God would relent. After a few days two merchants of Marseilles, called, according to tradition, Hugh the Iron and William the Pig, offered to put ships at their disposal and to carry them free of charge, for the glory of God, to Palestine. Stephen eagerly accepted the kindly offer. Seven vessels were hired by the merchants, and the children were taken aboard and set out to sea. Eighteen years passed before there was any further news of them.

Meanwhile tales of Stephen's preaching had reached the Rhineland. The children of Germany were not to be outdone. A few weeks after Stephen had started on his mission, a boy called Nicholas, from a Rhineland village, began to preach the same message before the shrine of the Three Kings at Cologne. Like Stephen, he declared that children could do better than grown men, and that the sea would open to give them a path. But, while the French children were to conquer the Holy Land by force, the Germans were to achieve their aim by the conversion of the infidel. Nicholas, like Peter, had a natural eloquence and was able to find eloquent disciples to carry his preaching further, up and down the Rhineland. Within a few weeks an army of children had gathered at Cologne, ready to start out for Italy and the sea. It seems that the Germans were on an average slightly older than the French and that there were more girls with them. There was also a larger contingent of boys of the nobility, and a number of disreputable vagabonds and prostitutes.

The expedition split into two parties. The first, numbering according to the chroniclers, twenty thousand, was led by Nicholas himself. It set out up the Rhine to Basle and through western Switzerland, past Geneva, to cross the Alps by the Mont Cenis pass. It was an arduous journey for the children, and their losses were heavy. Less than a third of the company that left Cologne appeared before the walls of Genoa, at the end of August, and demanded a night's shelter within its walls. The Genoese authorities were ready at first to welcome the pilgrims, but on second thoughts they suspected a German plot. They would allow them to stay for one night only; but any who wished to settle permanently in Genoa were invited to do so. The children, expecting the sea to divide before them next morning, were content. But next morning the sea was as impervious to their prayers as it had been to the French at Marseilles. In their disillusion many of the children at once accepted the Genoese offer and became Genoese citizens, forgetting their pilgrimage. Several great families of Genoa later claimed to be descended from this alien immigration. But Nicholas and the greater number moved on. The sea would open for them elsewhere. A few days later they reached Pisa. There two ships bound for Palestine agreed to take several of the children, who embarked and who perhaps reached Palestine; but nothing is known of their fate. Nicholas, however, still awaited a miracle, and trudged on with his faithful followers to Rome. At Rome Pope Innocent received them. He was moved by their piety but embarrassed by their folly. With kindly firmness he told them that they must now go home. When they grew up they should then fulfil their vows and go to fight for the Cross.

Little is known of the return journey. Many of the children, especially the girls, could not face again the ardours of the road and stayed behind in some Italian town or village. Only a few stragglers found their way back next spring to the Rhineland. Nicholas was probably not amongst them. But the angry parents whose children had perished insisted on the arrest of his father, who had, it seems, encouraged the boy out of vainglory. He was taken and hanged.

The second company of German pilgrims was no more fortunate. It had travelled to Italy through central Switzerland and over the Saint Gotthard and after great hardships reached the sea at Ancona. When the sea failed to divide for them they moved slowly down the east coast as far as Brindisi. There a few of them found ships sailing to Palestine and were given passages; but the others returned and began to wander slowly back again. Only a tiny number returned at last to their homes.

Despite their miseries, they were perhaps luckier than the French. In the year 1230 a priest arrived in France from the East with a curious tale to tell. He had been, he said, one of the young priests who had accompanied Stephen to Marseilles and had embarked with them on the ships provided by the merchants. A few days out they had run into bad weather, and two of the ships were wrecked on the island of San Pietro, off the south-west corner of Sardinia, and all the passengers were drowned. The five ships that survived the storm found themselves soon afterwards surrounded by a Saracen squadron from Africa; and the passengers learned that they had been brought there by arrangement, to be sold into captivity. They were all taken to Bougie, on the Algerian coast. Many of them were bought on their arrival and spent the rest of their lives in captivity there. Others, the young priest among them, were shipped on to Egypt, where Frankish slaves fetched a better price. When they arrived at Alexandria the greater part of the consignment was bought by the governor, to work on his estates. According to the priest there were still about seven hundred of them living. A small company was taken to the slave-markets of Baghdad; and there eighteen of them were martyred for refusing to accept Islam. More fortunate were the young priests and the few others that were literate. The governor of Egypt, al-Adil's son al-Kamil, was interested in Western languages and letters. He bought them and kept them with him as interpreters, teachers and secretaries, and made no attempt to convert them to his faith. They stayed on in Cairo in a comfortable captivity; and eventually this one priest was released and allowed to return to France. He told the questioning parents of his comrades all that he knew, then disappeared into obscurity. A later story identified the two wicked merchants of Marseilles with two merchants who were hanged a few years afterwards for attempting to kidnap the Emperor Frederick on behalf of the Saracens, thus making them in the end pay the penalty for their crimes.[1]

It was not the little children that would rescue Jerusalem. Pope Innocent had larger and more realistic views. He decided to hold a great Council of the Church at Rome in 1215, where all the religious affairs of Christendom should be regulated and above all the Greek Church should be integrated. He wished to have a Crusade already launched by then. Throughout 1213 his legate, Robert of Courçon, toured France with orders, so great was the emergency, not to examine over-carefully the suitability of those that took the Cross. The Legate carried out his master's instructions with a zeal that was excessive. Very soon the French nobles began to write to their King that their vassals were being excused their vows by the Legate's preachers, and that an absurd collection of old men and children, lepers, cripples and women of ill fame had been gathered together to conduct the Holy War. The Pope was obliged to restrain Robert; and when the Lateran Council of 1215 opened, there was still no Crusade ready to embark. At the first session the Pope himself spoke on the plight of Jerusalem, and the Patriarch of Jerusalem rose to plead for aid. The Council hastened

[1] For the story of the Children's Crusade see Röhricht, 'Die Kinderkreuzzug' in *Historische Zeitschrift*, vol. XXXVI; Alphandéry, 'Les Croisades d'Enfants' in *Revue de l'Histoire des Religions*, vol. LXXIII; Munro, 'The Children's Crusade' in *American Historical Review*, vol. XIX; Winkelmann, *Geschichte Kaiser Friedrichs des Zweiten*, I, pp. 221–2. The German participation is given in *Annales Stadenses* (*M.G.H. Scriptores*, vol. XVI, p. 355).

to reaffirm the privileges and indulgences to be accorded to Crusaders and to arrange for the financing of the expedition, which was to assemble in Sicily or Apulia and set sail for the East on 1 June 1217.[1]

The Council stirred the Church into activity. Throughout the spring of 1216 preachers set out all over Western Christendom, as far afield as Ireland and Scandinavia. The doctors of the University of Paris declared that anyone who took the Cross and then tried to avoid the fulfilment of his vow committed mortal sin. Popular visions were reported of crosses floating in the air and were given full advertisement. Innocent was hopeful. He had already noticed that the 666 years allotted in Revelation to the Beast were nearly spent. It was, indeed, six and a half centuries since the birth of Mahomet. He had written to the Sultan al-Adil warning him of the wrath to come and urging him to cede Jerusalem peaceably while there was still time. But his optimism was a little premature. Gervase, Abbot of Prémontré, wrote to him confidentially to say that the nobles of France were ignoring the views of the doctors at Paris, and that something drastic must be done to keep the Dukes of Burgundy and Lorraine to their vows. He also wisely advised that there should be no combined French and German expedition. The two nations did not work together harmoniously. But the poorer people were taking the Cross with enthusiasm. They must not be discouraged by delay.[2]

In May 1216 Pope Innocent went to Perugia to try to settle the long feud between Genoa and Pisa, that both might contribute to the transport of the Crusaders. There, after a short illness, he died on 16 July. Few Papal reigns have been more splendid or more outwardly triumphant. Yet his dearest ambition, to recover

---

[1] Fliche, *op. cit.* pp. 156–216. For the whole history of the Fifth Crusade see Donovan, *Pelagius and the Fifth Crusade*, a careful and well-documented account, slightly biased in favour of Pelagius.

[2] See Luchaire, *Innocent III, La Question d'Orient*, pp. 281–9, a full account of the negotiations. Miraculous events are reported by Oliver of Paderborn, *Historia Damiatana*, pp. 174–5, 285–6, 287–8; also Innocent III, letters, XVI, 28, 37 (*M.P.L.* vol. CCXVI, cols. 817–22, 831–2).

Jerusalem, was never realized. Two days after his death the aged Cardinal Savelli was elected Pope, as Honorius III.[1]

Honorius eagerly took over his great predecessor's programme. A few days after his accession he wrote to King John at Acre to tell him that the Crusade was coming.[2] John was growing anxious; for his truce with al-Adil was due to expire next year. Honorius also wrote round to the Kings of Europe. Few of them responded. In the far north King Ingi II of Norway took the Cross, only to die next spring; and when the Scandinavian expedition started out it was a paltry affair.[3] King Andrew II of Hungary had already taken the Cross, but had been excused by Innocent from fulfilling his vow earlier because of civil war in his country. He now showed zeal, but he had another motive. His Queen was the niece, through her mother, of the Latin Emperor Henry of Constantinople, who was childless, and he had hopes of the inheritance. But when Henry died in June 1216, her father, Peter of Courtenay, was chosen in his place. King Andrew's ardour began to fade; but he agreed at last to have his army ready by the following summer.[4] In the lower Rhineland there was a good response to the preaching; and the Pope hoped for a large fleet manned by Frisians.[5] But here again there were delays. Nor was the news from Palestine very encouraging. James of Vitry, who had recently been sent there as Bishop of Acre, with instructions to rouse the local Latins, gave a bitter report of what he found. The native Christians hated the Latins and would prefer Moslem rule, while the Latins themselves led indolent, luxurious and immoral lives and were completely Oriental. Their clergy was corrupt, avaricious and intriguing. Only the Military Orders were worthy of commendation, though the Italian colonists, who were wise enough to lead frugal lives, kept some energy and enter-

[1] Fliche, *op. cit.* p. 212.
[2] *Regesta Honorii Papae III* (ed. Pressutti), nos. 1, 673, I, pp. 1, 1178–80.
[3] *Regesta Honorii Papae III*, no. 399, I, p. 71.
[4] Innocent III, letters, xv, 224 (*M.P.L.* vol. ccxvi, col. 757); Theiner, *Vetera Monumenta*, I, pp. 5–6.
[5] *Regesta Honorii Papae III*, no. 885, I, pp. 149–50.

prise; but the mutual jealousy of the great Italian cities, Venice, Genoa and Pisa, made them unable ever to work together. In fact, as Bishop James discovered, the Franks of Outremer had no desire for a Crusade. Two decades of peace had added to their material prosperity. Since Saladin's death the Moslems showed no tendency to aggression, for they too were profiting by the increased commerce. Merchandise from the interior filled the quays of Acre and Tyre. The palace that John of Ibelin had built at Beirut bore witness to revived prosperity. There were Italian colonies happily established in Egypt. With the purchasing power of Western Europe steadily growing, there was a fine future for the Mediterranean trade. But it all depended precariously on the maintenance of peace.[1]

Pope Honorius thought otherwise. He hoped that a great expedition would be sailing from Sicily in the summer of 1217. But when the summer came, though various companies of French knights had reached the Italian ports, there were no ships. The King of Hungary's army reached Spalato in Dalmatia in August, and was joined there by Duke Leopold VI of Austria and his army.[2] The Frisian fleet only reached Portugal in July, and part of it remained at Lisbon. It was in October that the rest sailed in to Gaeta, too late to proceed to Palestine till the winter was over.[3] At the end of July the Pope ordered the Crusaders assembled in Italy and Sicily to proceed to Cyprus; but still no transport was provided. At last in early September Duke Leopold found a ship at Spalato to take his small company to Acre. His voyage took only sixteen days. King Andrew followed him about a fortnight later; but the Spalatans could not let him have more than two ships; so the bulk of his army was left behind.[4] About the same time King

---

[1] James of Vitry, *History of Jerusalem* (trans. Stewart), *P.P.T.S.* vol. XI, pp. 56–91.

[2] Thomas Spalatensis, *Historia Salonitana* (*Scriptores Rerum Hungaricarum*, III, p. 573).

[3] *Gesta Crucigerorum Rhenanorum*, pp. 29–34; *De Itinere Frisonum*, pp. 59–68 (both in Röhricht, *Quinti Belli Sacri Scriptores Minores*).

[4] *Regesta Honorii Papae III*, no. 672, I, p. 117; Thomas Spalatensis, p. 574; *Annales Claustroneoburgenses* (*M.G.H. Scriptores*, vol. IX, p. 622).

Hugh of Cyprus landed at Acre with the troops that he could raise.[1]

The harvest had been poor that year in Syria, and it was difficult to feed an idle army. When the Kings arrived, John of Brienne recommended an immediate campaign. On Friday, 3 November, the Crusaders set out from Acre and marched up the plain of Esdraelon. Their numbers, though not great, were larger than any that had been seen in Palestine since the Third Crusade. Al-Adil, when he heard that the Christians were assembling, had come with some troops to Palestine, but he had not expected so early an invasion. He was outnumbered; so, when the Crusade advanced towards Beisan, he retired, sending his son al-Mu'azzam to cover Jerusalem, while he waited at Ajlun, ready to intercept any attack on Damascus. His fears were scarcely justified. The Christian army lacked discipline. King John considered himself as being in command, but the Austro-Hungarian troops looked only to King Andrew and the Cypriots to King Hugh, while the Military Orders obeyed their own leaders. Beisan was occupied and sacked. Then the Christians wandered aimlessly across the Jordan and up the eastern shore of the Sea of Galilee, round past Capernaum and back through Galilee to Acre. Their chief occupation had been the capture of relics. King Andrew was delighted to obtain one of the water-jugs used at the marriage feast at Cana.[2]

King John was dissatisfied and planned an expedition of his own to destroy the fort that the Moslems had erected on Mount Thabor. Neither Hugh nor Andrew joined him, nor would he wait for the Military Orders. His first attack on the fort, on 3 December, failed, though in fact the garrison was ready to surrender. When the Orders arrived two days later a second assault was attempted, but in vain. Once more the army retreated to Acre.[3]

About the New Year a small band of Hungarians, against local

[1] *Estoire d'Eracles*, II, p. 322.

[2] *Ibid.* pp. 323-4; Oliver, *Historia Damiatana*, p. 165; Johannes Thwrocz, *Chronica Hungarorum* (*Scriptores Rerum Hungaricarum*, vol. I, p. 149).

[3] *Estoire d'Eracles*, II, pp. 324-5; Oliver, *Historia Damiatana*, pp. 165-7; James of Vitry, *History of Jerusalem*, p. 119; Abu Shama, II, pp. 163-4.

advice and without their King's approval, planned a foray into the Bekaa and was almost annihilated in a snowstorm when crossing the Lebanon.[1] Meanwhile King Andrew rode off with King Hugh to Tripoli, where Bohemond IV, ex-Prince of Antioch, recently widowed of his first wife, Plaisance of Jebail, celebrated his marriage to Hugh's half-sister, Melisende. There Hugh suddenly died, on 10 January, leaving the throne of Cyprus to an eight-month-old boy, Henry, under the regency of his widow, Alice of Jerusalem.[2] King Andrew returned to Acre and announced his departure for Europe. He had fulfilled his vow. He had recently added to his relic-collection the head of St Stephen. It was time to go home. The Patriarch of Jerusalem pleaded with him and threatened him in vain. He took his troops northward, through Tripoli and Antioch, to Armenia, and thence, with a safe-conduct from the Seldjuk Sultan, to Constantinople. His Crusade had achieved nothing.[3]

Leopold of Austria remained behind. He was short of money and had to borrow 50,000 besants from Guy Embriaco of Jebail, but he was ready to work further for the Cross. King John used his help for the refortification of Caesarea, while the Templars and Teutonic knights set about the construction of a great castle at Athlit, just south of Carmel, the Castle of the Pilgrims. Al-Adil meanwhile dismantled his fort on Mount Thabor. It was too vulnerable and not worth its upkeep.[4]

On 26 April 1218 the first half of the Frisian fleet arrived at Acre, and a fortnight later the half that had wintered at Lisbon. There was news that the French Crusaders massed in Italy were soon to follow. King John at once took counsel about the best

---

[1] *Ibid.* pp. 164–5; Oliver, *Historia Damiatana*, pp. 167–8.

[2] Ernoul, p. 412; *Estoire d'Eracles*, II, pp. 325, 360; *Gestes des Chiprois*, p. 98.

[3] Oliver, *Historia Damiatana*, p. 168; James of Vitry, *Epistola*, III (ed. Röhricht), *Zeitschrift für Kirchengeschichte* (Z.K.G.), vol. xv, pp. 568–70; Johannes Thwrocz, *loc. cit.* Andrew had also obtained the head of St Margaret, the right hands of St Thomas and St Bartholomew and part of Aaron's rod.

[4] *Estoire d'Eracles*, II, pp. 325–6; Oliver, *Historia Damiatana*, p. 169; Abu Shama, II, pp. 164–6.

L

use to be made of the newcomers. It had never been forgotten that King Richard had advised an attack on Egypt; and the Lateran Council had also mentioned Egypt as the chief objective for a Crusade. If the Moslems could be driven out of the Nile valley, not only would they lose their richest province, but they would be unable to keep a fleet in the Eastern Mediterranean; nor could they hold Jerusalem long against a pincer attack coming from Acre and from Suez. With the Frisian ships at their disposal the Crusaders now had the means for a great attack on the Delta. Without hesitation it was decided that the first objective should be the port of Damietta, the key to the Nile.[1]

The Sultan al-Adil was an old man now and had hoped to spend his latter years in peace. He had his worries in the north. His nephew, az-Zahir of Aleppo, died in 1216, leaving as his successor a child called al-Aziz, for whom a eunuch, Toghril, acted as regent. Az-Zahir's brother, Saladin's eldest son, al-Afdal, emerged from his retirement at Samosata to make a bid for the inheritance and summoned to his help the Seldjuk Sultan of Konya, Kaikhaûs. The Anatolian Seldjuks were now at the height of their power. Byzantium was no more; and the Emperor of Nicaea was too busy fighting the Franks to disturb them. The Danishmends had faded out. Their Turcoman subjects were settled now and orderly, and prosperity was returning to the peninsula. Early in 1218 Kaikhaûs and al-Afdal swept into the territory of Aleppo and advanced on the capital. The Regent Toghril, knowing al-Adil to be threatened by the Crusade, appealed to his young master's cousin, al-Ashraf of Iraq, al-Adil's third son. Al-Ashraf routed the Seldjuk army near Buza'a; al-Afdal retired back to Samosata; and the Prince of Aleppo had to acknowledge al-Ashraf as his overlord. But the Seldjuks remained a menace until the death of Kaikhaûs next year, when he was planning to intervene in a disputed succession at Mosul. This enabled al-Ashraf to con-

[1] *Gesta Crucigerorum Rhenanorum*, pp. 37–8; *De Itineri Frisonum*, pp. 69–70; Ernoul, pp. 414–15; James of Vitry, *loc. cit.*; Oliver, *Historia Damiatana*, p. 175. See Donovan, *op. cit.* pp. 36 n., 54.

solidate his power, and to become a serious rival to his brothers further south.[1]

Up to the last al-Adil seems to have hoped that the Franks would not be so foolish as to break the peace. His son, al-Malik al-Kamil, viceroy of Egypt, shared his hopes. Al-Kamil was on excellent terms with the Venetians, with whom he had signed a commercial treaty in 1208. In 1215 there were no fewer than 3000 European merchants in Egypt. The sudden arrival that year at Alexandria of two Western lords with an armed company had frightened the authorities, who had put the whole European colony under temporary arrest. But good relations had been restored. In 1217 a new Venetian embassy was cordially received by the viceroy. The ineffectual meanderings of the Crusade of 1217 had not impressed the Moslems. They could not believe that there was any danger now.

On Ascension Day, 24 May 1218, the Crusading army, with King John in command, embarked at Acre in the Frisian ships, and sailed down to Athlit to pick up further supplies. After a few hours the ships lifted anchor, but the wind dropped. Only a few of them managed to leave the anchorage and sail on to Egypt. They arrived off the Damietta mouth of the Nile on the 27th, and anchored there to await their comrades. The soldiers did not venture at first to try to land, as there was no senior officer amongst them. But on the 29th, when still no fleet appeared, the Archbishop of Nicosia, Eustorgius, persuaded them to accept Count Simon II of Sarrebruck as their leader and to force a landing on the west bank of the river mouth. There was very little opposition; and the operation was nearly complete when the sails of the main Crusader fleet appeared over the horizon. Soon the ships came in across the bar and King John, the Duke of Austria and the Grand Masters of the three Military Orders stepped ashore.[2]

[1] See Cahen, *La Syrie du Nord*, pp. 624–8.
[2] James of Vitry, *History of Jerusalem*, pp. 118–19; Oliver, *Historia Damiatana*, pp. 175–7; *Gesta Crucigerorum Rhenanorum*, pp. 38–9; *Estoire d'Eracles*, II, pp. 326–7.

Damietta lay two miles up the river, on the east bank, with its rear protected by Lake Manzaleh. As the Franks' experience in 1169 had shown, it could not be efficiently attacked except by water as well as by land. As in 1169 a chain had been stretched across the river a little below the town, from the east bank to a tower on an island close to the west bank, blocking the only navigable channel; and a bridge of boats lay behind the chain. The Crusaders made this tower their first objective.

When the Moslems realized that the Crusade was directed against Egypt, al-Adil hastily recruited an army in Syria, while al-Kamil marched the main Egyptian army northward from Cairo and encamped at al-Adiliya, a few miles south of Damietta. But he had insufficient men and ships to attack the Christian positions, though he reinforced the tower. The first serious assault on the fort, at the end of June, failed. Oliver of Paderborn, the future historian of the campaign, then suggested the making of a new device, for which he and one of his fellow-citizens paid. It was a tower built on two ships that were lashed together, covered with leather and fitted with scaling-ladders. The fort could now be attacked from the river as well as from the shore.[1]

On Friday, 17 August, the Christian army held a solemn service of intercession. A week later, on the afternoon of the 24th, the assault began. About twenty-four hours later, after a fierce struggle, the Crusaders managed to establish themselves on the ramparts and poured into the fort. The garrison fought on till only a hundred survivors remained; then it surrendered. The booty found in the fort was immense, and the victors made a small bridge of boats to carry it to the west bank. They then hacked down the chain and bridge of boats across the main channel, and their ships could sail through, up to the walls of Damietta.[2]

---

[1] Abu Shama, II, p. 165; *Histoire des Patriarches d'Alexandrie*, trans. Blochet pp. 240–1; Oliver, *Historia Damiatana*, pp. 179–82.

[2] Oliver, *Historia Damiatana*, pp. 182–4; *Gesta Crucigerorum Rhenanorum* p. 40; John of Tulbia, *De Domino Johanne*, in Röhricht, *loc. cit.* p. 120; *Histoir des Patriarches*, p. 243.

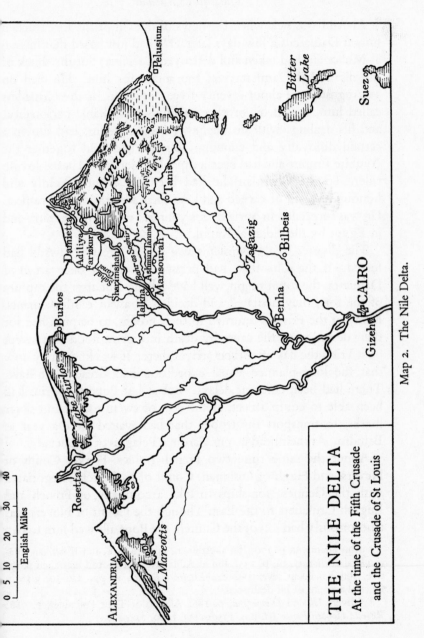

Map 2. The Nile Delta.

Al-Adil was sick when the news of the fall of the fort reached him at Damascus a few days later. He had just heard that his son al-Mu'azzam had taken and destroyed Caesarea; but the shock of the disaster at Damietta was too much for him. He died on 31 August, aged about seventy-five. Saphadin, as the Crusaders called him, lacked his brother Saladin's remarkable personality; and his dealings with his nephews, Saladin's sons, had shown a certain disloyalty and cunning. But he had held together the Ayubite Empire and had been a capable, tolerant and peace-loving ruler. To the Christians he had been consistently kindly and honourable, and he earned and kept their admiration and respect. He was succeeded in Syria by his younger son, al-Mu'azzam, and in Egypt by the elder, al-Kamil.[1]

The disaster to the Moslems was not so great as al-Adil had feared. If the Christians had pressed on and at once attacked Damietta, the town might well have fallen. But after the capture of the fort, they hesitated and decided to await reinforcements. Many of the Frisians returned to their homes, to be punished for their desertion of the cause by death in a great flood that swept over Frisia the day after their arrival there. It was known by now that the long-planned Papal expedition had already left Italy. There had been constant delays. But at last Pope Honorius had been able to equip a fleet, at the cost of twenty thousand silver marks, to transport the troops that had waited over a year at Brindisi. At their head he put Cardinal Pelagius of St Lucia.[2]

About the same time two French nobles, Hervé, Count of Nevers, and Hugh of Lusignan, Count of La Marche, negotiated with the Genoese for ships to take a company of French and English Crusaders to the East. Though the Count of Nevers was a notoriously bad son of the Church, the Pope allowed him to pay

[1] Abu Shama, II, p. 170; Ibn al-Athir, II, pp. 116, 148; Ibn Khallikan, *Biographical Dictionary*, III, p. 235. Ibn al-Athir says that al-Adil was aged sixty-five, Ibn Khallikan seventy-three. *Estoire d'Eracles*, II, pp. 229–30, gives a fanciful account of his death-bed.

[2] Oliver, *Historia Damiatana*, p. 186; Alberic of Trois Fontaines, p. 788; *Regesta Honorii Papae III*, nos. 1350, 1433, I, pp. 224, 237.

for the transport with a tax of a twentieth of their income taken from the ecclesiastics of France. The two Counts were joined at Genoa by the Archbishop of Bordeaux, William II, and the Bishops of Paris, Laon and Angers, and other lesser potentates, and by the Earls of Chester, Arundel, Derby and Winchester. The Pope sent Robert, Cardinal Courçon, to be spiritual director of the fleet, but without any legatine powers.[1]

Cardinal Pelagius and his expedition arrived at the Christian camp in the middle of September. Pelagius was a Spaniard, a man of great industry and administrative experience, but singularly lacking in tact. He had been already employed to settle the question of the Greek Churches in the Latin Empire of Constantinople, and had only succeeded in making them more passionately hostile to Rome. His coming to Damietta at once caused trouble. John of Brienne had been accepted as leader of the Crusade. His leadership had been disputed the previous years by the Kings of Hungary and Cyprus; but the one had departed and the other was dead. Pelagius considered that as Legate he alone was in charge. The rivalry of the various participant nations was all too clearly visible. Only the Pope's representative could keep them in order. He brought news that the young Western Emperor, Frederick II, had promised to follow with an Imperial army. When he came he would certainly be given supreme military command. But Pelagius was not going to take any order from King John, who was, after all, King only through his dead wife.[2]

In October al-Malik al-Kamil had sufficient reinforcements to attempt an attack on the Crusaders' camp by a flotilla that he sent down the river. It was driven off, chiefly through King John's energy. A few days later the Moslems built a bridge across the Nile a little above the town. Pelagius organized an unsuccessful

---

[1] *Regesta Honorii Papae III*, nos. 1498, 1543, 1558, I, pp. 248, 256, 260. For a correct list of these Crusaders see Greven, 'Frankreich und der fünfte Kreuzzug', *Historische Jahrbuch*, vol. XLII. Matthew of Westminster gives the names of the English Crusaders (*Flores Historiarum*, II, p. 167).

[2] See Donovan, *op. cit.* pp. 46–9 and notes.

raid on the works; but al-Kamil did not follow up the construction by moving his army across the river. Instead, he made another attack from the water. It was a fierce onslaught; but it was too late. The first contingent of French Crusaders had arrived and led the defence. A second attack reached the edge of the camp itself, but was driven back into the river, where many of the Moslem troops were drowned.[1]

After the whole French and English army arrived, late in October, there was a lull in the fighting. Al-Adil's death had delayed the help that al-Kamil expected from Syria. He now awaited an army that his brother al-Mu'azzam promised him. The Christians had their own difficulties. They dug a canal from the sea to the river above the Moslem bridge, but they could not fill it. On the night of 29 November a northerly gale blew the sea in over the low land on which their camp stood. Every tent was flooded and the stores 'were soaked. Several boats were wrecked and others driven across to the Moslem camp. Horses were drowned. When the flood subsided, there were fishes lying about everywhere, a delicacy, says the chronicler Oliver of Paderborn, that everyone would gladly have foregone. To prevent a recurrence Pelagius ordered a dyke to be quickly constructed. All the wreckage, even torn sails and horses' carcasses were used to raise it higher. The only good result of the flood was that the canal now was filled, and Christian boats could penetrate up the river.[2]

Hardly was the camp repaired before a serious epidemic struck the army. The victims suffered from a high fever, and their skins turned black. At least a sixth of the soldiers died of it, including the Cardinal Robert Courcon. The survivors were left enfeebled and depressed. There followed a winter that was unusually severe.

[1] Oliver, *Historia Damiatana*, pp. 190–2; *Histoire des Patriarches*, p. 394; *Gesta Obsidionis Damiate* (in Röhricht, *op. cit.* pp. 79–80); John of Tulbia, p. 123.

[2] Oliver, *Historia Damiatana*, pp. 131–2, 196–7; *Gesta Obsidionis Damiate*, p. 82; John of Tulbia, p. 124; *Liber Duellii Christiani in Obsidione Damiate Exacti* (in Röhricht, *op. cit.*), pp. 148–9; James of Vitry, *Epistola* v (*Z.K.G.* vol. xv, pp. 582–3); *Histoire des Patriarches*, pp. 245–6.

It was well for the Christians that the Moslems also suffered from illness and the cold.[1]

Early in February 1219, Pelagius considered that the morale of the army could only be restored by activity. On Saturday, 2 February, he persuaded the army to set out to attack the Moslems. But a blinding rainstorm forced it back. The following Tuesday news reached the camp that the Sultan and his army were retreating. The Crusaders hurried across to al-Adiliya and found the site deserted. After driving back a sortie from the garrison of Damietta they occupied al-Adiliya, and thus cut the town off completely.[2]

Al-Kamil's sudden flight had been caused by his discovery of a conspiracy in his entourage. One of his emirs, Imad ad-Din Ahmed Ibn al-Mashtub, was planning to murder him and replace him by his brother al-Faiz. In his despair, not knowing how many of his staff were implicated, the Sultan thought of fleeing to Yemen, where his son al-Masud was governor, when he heard that his brother al-Mu'azzam was at last coming to his help. He moved with his troops south-eastward to Ashmun, where the two brother Sultans met on 7 February. Al-Mu'azzam's presence with a large army cowed the conspirators. Ibn al-Mashtub was arrested and sent to prison at Kerak, while the Prince al-Faiz was banished to Sinjar and died mysteriously on the way there. Al-Kamil had saved his throne, but at the price of losing Damietta.[3]

Even with al-Mu'azzam's help al-Kamil could not now dislodge the Christians. The river, the lagoons and the canals made it impossible for the Moslems to take advantage of their superior numbers. Attacks on the two camps, on the west bank and at al-Adiliya, failed. The Sultan then set up his camp at Fariskur, some six miles south of Damietta, ready to attack the Crusaders

[1] Oliver, *Historia Damiatana*, pp. 192–3; James of Vitry, *loc. cit.*; John of Tulbia, p. 125; *Gesta Obsidionis Damiate*, p. 83; *Histoire des Patriarches*, p. 249.

[2] Oliver, *Historia Damiatana*, pp. 194–201; *Gesta Obsidionis Damiate*, pp. 83–4; *Estoire d'Eracles*, II, p. 337; John of Tulbia, *loc. cit.*

[3] Ibn al-Athir, II, pp. 116–17; Ibn Khallikan, III, p. 240; *Histoire des Patriarches*, pp. 246–7.

in the rear should they try to assault Damietta. Throughout the spring the stalemate continued. There were fierce battles on Palm Sunday and again on Whit-Sunday, when the Moslems vainly tried to force their way into al-Adiliya. In Damietta itself, though food was still plentiful, the garrison had been greatly reduced by disease; but still the Christians did not dare to make an assault.[1]

In the meantime the Sultan al-Mu'azzam decided to dismantle Jerusalem. It might be necessary to offer the Christians Jerusalem to terminate the war. If so, it would be handed over in a ruined and untenable condition. The demolition of the walls was begun on 19 March. It caused panic in the city. The Moslem citizens believed that the Franks were coming, and many of them fled in terror across the Jordan. The tenantless houses were then pillaged by the soldiers. Some fanatics wished to destroy the Holy Sepulchre; but the Sultan would not allow it. After Jerusalem the fortresses of Galilee, Toron, Safed and Banyas, were all dismantled. At the same time the two Sultans appealed for help throughout the Moslem world, addressing their prayers in particular to the Caliph at Baghdad; who promised to send a vast army, which never came.[2]

The icy winter was followed by a burning summer; and the morale of the Crusaders fell again. Again Pelagius insisted on action. After a vigorous Moslem attack on the camp had been driven back on 20 July, with heavy losses on both sides, the Crusaders concentrated on the bombardment of the town walls. While they were so engaged, vainly, as the Greek fire used by their defenders did great damage to their engines and could not be quenched by wine and acid, another Moslem attack very nearly destroyed the whole Christian army, which was only saved by the sudden fall of darkness. A second assault on the walls on 6 August was equally ineffectual.[3]

[1] Oliver, *Historia Damiatana*, pp. 202-6; *Liber Duellii*, pp. 151-2; *Gesta Obsidionis Damiate*, pp. 87-90.

[2] Abu Shama, II, pp. 173-4; Ibn al-Athir, II, p. 119; *Histoire des Patriarches*, p. 52; *Estoire d'Eracles*, II, p. 339; Oliver, *Historia Damiatana*, p. 203.

[3] Oliver, *Historia Damiatana*, pp. 208-10; *Gesta Obsidionis Damiate*, pp. 87, 90-7; John of Tulbia, pp. 127-8.

The reverses roused the common soldiers of the Crusade to action. They blamed their leaders for sloth and bad generalship. Many of the more distinguished nobles had been killed, including the Counts of La Marche and Bar-sur-Seine and William of Chartres, Grand Master of the Templars. Others had returned to Europe. Leopold of Austria left the army in May. He had been the most energetic of the princes; but he had served for two years in the East, and no one could reproach him for returning to his own country. His gallantry had erased the ill-repute that his father had won by his quarrels with Cœur-de-Lion on the Third Crusade. He took home with him a fragment of the True Cross. But the convoy that took him to Europe carried others whose departure seemed a desertion of the cause.[1] Towards the end of August, while King John and Pelagius wrangled over strategy, the one advocating a tightening of the siege, the other an attack on the Sultan's camp, the soldiers took matters into their own hands and on the 29th poured out in a disorderly mass against the Moslem lines. The Moslems feigned retreat, then counter-attacked. Pelagius had tried to assume command; but despite his exhortations the Italian regiments turned round and fled, and soon there was general panic. It was only the skill of King John and the French and English nobles and the Military Orders that rescued the survivors and held the camp.[2]

The battle had been watched with a sad dismay by a distinguished visitor to the camp, Brother Francis of Assisi. He had come to the East believing, as many other good and unwise persons before and after him have believed, that a peace-mission can bring about peace. He now asked permission of Pelagius to go to see the Sultan. After some hesitation Pelagius agreed, and sent

[1] Oliver, *Historia Damiatana*, pp. 188, 207–8; *Gesta Obsidionis Damiate*, p. 90; *Liber Duellii*, p. 258. For the relics that Leopold acquired, see Riant, *Exuviae Sacrae Constantinopolitanae*, II, p. 283. The Count of Bar-sur-Seine was Milo III of Le Puiset.

[2] Oliver, *Historia Damiatana*, pp. 213–19; *Fragmentum Provinciale de Captione Damiatae* (in Röhricht, *op. cit.*), pp. 185–92; *Gesta Obsidionis Damiate*, pp. 101–4; John of Tulbia, pp. 132–3; *Estoire d'Eracles*, II, pp. 340–1.

him under a flag of truce to Fariskur. The Moslem guards were suspicious at first but soon decided that anyone so simple, so gentle and so dirty must be mad, and treated him with the respect due to a man who had been touched by God. He was taken to the Sultan al-Kamil who was charmed by him and listened patiently to his appeal, but who was too kind and too highly civilized to allow him to give witness to his faith in an ordeal by fire; nor would he risk the acrimony that a public discussion on religion would now arouse. Francis was offered many gifts, which he refused, and was sent back with an honourable escort to the Christians.[1]

The Saint's intervention was not in fact needed, for al-Kamil himself inclined towards peace. The Nile had risen very little that summer, and Egypt was threatened with famine. The government needed all its resources to rush in food from neighbouring lands. Al-Mu'azzam was anxious to return with his army to Syria; and neither Sultan was happy about the activities of their brother al-Ashraf further north. At Baghdad the Caliph Nasr was in the power of the Khwarismian Shah, Jelal ad-Din, whose father Mohammed had destroyed the Seldjuk dominion in Iran and founded an empire stretching from the Indus to the Tigris. Jelal ad-Din could be used against al-Ashraf, but in view of his known ambitions it would be dangerous to encourage him too far. Al-Mu'azzam was ready therefore to support al-Kamil in any friendly overture to the Franks. Some time in September a Frankish prisoner came from the Sultan offering a short truce and suggesting that the Moslems would be prepared to cede Jerusalem. The truce was accepted; but the Christians refused to discuss further peace terms.[2]

The truce was spent by both sides in repairing their defences. Many of the Crusaders found it also a suitable opportunity for returning home. Some had already left at the beginning of the month, and on 14 September twelve more shiploads sailed away.

---

[1] *Acta Sanctorum*, October 4, pp. 611 ff. See van Ortroy 'Saint François et son Voyage en Orient' in *Analecta Bollandiana*, vol. XXXI. The story in Ernoul, p. 431, about the unnamed clerics, seems to refer to the Saint's visit to the Sultan.

[2] Oliver, *Historia Damiatana*, p. 218; *Gesta Obsidionis Damiate*, p. 105.

The loss was recovered a week later when the French lord Sauvary of Mauléon arrived with a company transported in ten Genoese galleys.[1] When al-Kamil broke the truce and attacked the Franks on the 26th, the newcomers successfully led the defence.[2]

Al-Kamil still hoped for peace. He knew that Damietta could not be held. The garrison was too much thinned by disease to man the walls, and his attempts to throw in reinforcements had failed. Nor were the traitors in the Christian camp whose services he had bought successful in any of their projects. At the end of October he sent two captive knights to give the Franks his definite terms. If they would evacuate Egypt, he would return them the True Cross, and they could have Jerusalem, all central Palestine and Galilee. The Moslems would only retain the castles of Oultrejourdain, but would pay a tribute for them.[3]

It was a startling offer. With no more fighting the Holy City, with Bethlehem, Nazareth and the True Cross, could be restored to Christendom. King John advised its acceptance, and his own barons and the barons from England, France and Germany supported him. But Pelagius would have none of it, nor would the Patriarch of Jerusalem. They thought it wrong to come to terms with the infidel. The Military Orders agreed with them for strategic reasons. Jerusalem and the Galilean castles had been dismantled; and it would anyhow be impossible to hold Jerusalem without the command of Oultrejourdain. The Italians were equally opposed to the terms. However little the Italian maritime cities had liked the breach with Egypt, now that it had come they wished to secure Damietta as a trading centre. The annexation of inland territory was of no interest to them. The dispute between the two parties grew so bitter that Bishop James of Acre believed

---

[1] Oliver, *Historia Damiatana, loc. cit.; Gesta Obsidionis Damiate,* p. 104; John of Tulbia, p. 133; James of Vitry, *loc. cit.*

[2] Oliver, *Historia Damiatana,* p. 219; *Fragmentum Provinciale,* pp. 193–4; *Gesta Obsidionis Damiate,* p. 106; *Liber Duellii,* p. 160.

[3] Oliver, *Historia Damiatana,* p. 222; *Estoire d'Eracles,* II, pp. 341–2; Ernoul, p. 435; Maqrisi (trans. Blochet), IX, p. 490; *Histoire des Patriarches,* p. 253; *Gesta Obsidionis Damiate,* pp. 109–10; Ibn al-Athir, II, p. 122.

the Sultan to have made his offer merely to cause dissension. At Pelagius's insistence it was refused.[1]

A few days later a scouting party sent by Pelagius reported that the outer wall of Damietta was unmanned. Next day, Tuesday, 5 November 1219, the Crusaders advanced in force and swept over it and over the inner wall, hardly opposed. Within the town they found almost the whole garrison sick. Only three thousand citizens were living, many of them too feeble even to bury the dead. Food and treasure were there in plenty, but disease had done the Christians' work for them. As soon as the town was fully taken over, three hundred of the leading citizens were set aside as hostages; the young children were handed to the clergy to be baptized and used for the service of the Church, and the remainder were sold as slaves. The treasure was to be divided amongst the Crusaders, according to each man's rank; but not all the Legate's anathemas could prevent thieving and concealment of precious objects by the troops.[2]

The future government of Damietta had next to be decided. King John at once claimed that it should be part of the kingdom of Jerusalem; and the Military Orders as well as the lay nobility were on his side. Pelagius maintained that the conquered city belonged to all Christendom, that is, to the Church. But, with public opinion against him, and with John threatening to sail back to Acre, he compromised. The King could govern it till Frederick of Germany joined the Crusade.[3] Meanwhile part of the army had been sent to attack Tanis, on the Tanitic mouth of the Nile, a few miles to the east. The town was deserted by its frightened garrison; and the Crusaders returned with further booty, which only led

---

[1] James of Vitry, *Epistola*, VI (*Z.K.G.* vol. XVI, pp. 74-5); Oliver, *Historia Damiatana*, p. 223, and *Epistola Regi Babilonis*, p. 305; *Estoire d'Eracles*, II, p. 342; letter of French lords to Honorius in Röhricht, *Studien zur Geschichte des fünften Kreuzzüges*, p. 46; Maqrisi, *loc. cit.*

[2] Oliver, *Historia Damiatana*, pp. 236-40; *Gesta Obsidionis Damiate*, pp. 111-14; *Fragmentum Provinciale*, pp. 196-200; Ibn Khallikan, IV, p. 143; Ibn al-Athir, II, p. 119; Abu Shama, pp. 176-7.

[3] *Gesta Obsidionis Damiate*, p. 115; John of Tulbia, p. 139; Ernoul, p. 426.

to further quarrels. The Italians in particular believed that they had been cheated and, when Pelagius would not support them, broke into active revolt. The Military Orders had to drive them from the city. When winter came the whole victorious army was smouldering with discontent.[1]

Pelagius in his first elation foresaw the final destruction of Islam. The Crusade would conquer all Egypt. Help would no doubt come from that gallant Christian potentate, the King of Georgia. Then there was Prester John, who was waiting, rumour said, to strike a new blow for Christendom. He had believed at first that Prester John was the Negus of Ethiopia, who, however, had never replied to a letter from the Pope written forty years before.[2] But now there was a new candidate for the role, an Eastern potentate whose name was Jenghiz Khan. Unfortunately the intended allies did not work together. In 1220 King George of Georgia's army was routed by Jenghiz Khan's Mongols on the borders of Azerbaijan, and the great military power built up by Queen Thamar was destroyed. The victors showed no interest in attacking the Ayubite empire.[3] More serious co-operation was expected from the greatest potentate of Western Europe, Frederick, King of Germany and Sicily.

Frederick had taken the Cross in 1215; but Pope Innocent granted him leave to postpone the Crusade till he had put the affairs of Germany in order. Frederick still delayed. He had promised the Papacy to hand over the throne of Sicily, to which he had succeeded as a boy, to his young son Henry. But he soon

[1] Oliver, *Historia Damiatana*, pp. 240–1; John of Tulbia, p. 139; *Liber Duellii*, p. 166.

[2] Oliver, *Historia Damiatana*, pp. 231–5. Pelagius was also impressed by a hopeful Moslem prophecy. For Prester John see above, vol. II, pp. 422–3.

[3] See below, p. 247. Pelagius wrote to Honorius III about his hopes of Georgian help (Röhricht, *Studien*, p. 52). Innocent III had already asked for Georgian co-operation (Oliver, *Historia Damiatana*, pp. 232–3). James of Vitry showed his interest in Mongol intervention by translating from the Arabic, with the help of experts, a book called *Excerpta de Historia David regis Indiorum qui Presbyter Johannes a vulgo appellatur* (ed. Röhricht, *Z.K.G.* vol. XVI, pp. 93 ff.). His facts are completely inaccurate.

discovered that by reiterating his determination to go Crusading, he could defer the division of his kingdoms and could bargain for his imperial coronation by the Pope. His desire to go to the East was genuine, though ambition rather than piety was its motive. He had inherited his father Henry VI's Eastern aspirations, but he would not try to realize them except as Emperor, with his European kingdoms secure in his grasp. His intentions should have been clear to the Pope. But Honorius, who had once been his tutor, was a simple man who regarded his promises as genuine and continued to send messages to the Crusaders in Egypt telling them to expect the Hohenstaufen army.[1]

The Crusade therefore stood still; and during its inaction the quarrels between Pelagius, King John, the Italians and the Military Orders intensified. A march on Cairo immediately after the fall of Damietta might have succeeded. Al-Kamil was in a desperate position. His army was discouraged. His subjects were starving. Al-Mu'azzam insisted on taking his forces back to Syria, fearing trouble in the north and believing that Islam could best be helped now by an attack on Acre itself. Expecting every day to hear of a Christian advance, al-Kamil established his camp at Talkha, a few miles up the Damietta branch of the Nile, and threw up fortifications on either side of the river to await an offensive that never came.[2]

Leo II, King of Armenia, died in the early summer of 1219, leaving only two daughters. The elder, Stephanie, was the wife of John of Brienne; the younger, Isabella, daughter of Princess Sibylla of Cyprus and Jerusalem, was four years old. Leo had promised the succession to his nephew Raymond-Roupen of Antioch, but on his death-bed he named Isabella as his heir. John at once put in a claim on behalf of his wife and their infant son, and in February 1220 he received the Pope's permission to leave the Crusade and visit Armenia. He was on such bad terms with

---

[1] See Donovan, *op. cit.* pp. 75–9 for a summary, with references, of Frederick's dealings with the Pope.

[2] *Histoire des Patriarches*, p. 254; Abu'l Fida, p. 91.

Pelagius that there was little point in his remaining with the army, over which the Pope now unequivocally gave Pelagius full command. John left for Acre. As he prepared to sail for Cilicia his Armenian wife died, it was rumoured through his own ill-treatment. When their small son died a few weeks later, John had no further claim on the Armenian throne. But he did not return to Egypt.[1] In March al-Mu'azzam invaded the kingdom, attacking the castle of Caesarea, which had just been rebuilt, then moving to lay siege to the Templar stronghold of Athlit. Templar knights were rushed back from Damietta, and King John kept his army in the offing. The siege lasted till November when al-Mu'azzam retired to Damascus.[2]

Meanwhile the Crusade remained stationary at Damietta. There was some attempt to rebuild the town. On the Feast of the Purification in February the chief mosque was rededicated as the Cathedral of the Virgin. In March a company of Italian prelates arrived, led by the Archbishop of Milan, and accompanied by two envoys from Frederick II. They brought considerable forces and at once agreed with Pelagius that an offensive should be launched. But the knights would not agree. King John, they said, was the only leader whom all the nations would obey; and he was absent.[3] When in July Matthew, Count of Apulia, brought eight galleys sent by Frederick Pelagius again vainly urged action. Even his own Italian mercenaries turned against him when he suggested a separate expedition. The only enterprise to be undertaken was a raid by the Military Knights on the town of Burlos, twenty miles west of Damietta. The town was pillaged, but the knights were ambushed on their return and several Hospitallers, including their Marshal, captured.[4]

Al-Kamil had by now recovered confidence. Though he was still short of land-forces, he repaired his navy, and in the summer

[1] Ernoul, p. 427; *Estoire d'Eracles*, II, p. 349; Oliver, *Historia Damiatana*, p. 248.
[2] Oliver, *Historia Damiatana*, pp. 244–5, 255–6; Ernoul, pp. 421–4.
[3] Oliver, *Historia Damiatana*, p. 248; Roger of Wendover, II, pp. 260–1.
[4] Oliver, *Historia Damiatana*, p. 252.

M

of 1220 sent out a squadron down the Rosetta branch of the Nile. It sailed to Cyprus, where it found a Crusader fleet lying off Limassol and by a sudden attack sank or captured all the ships, taking many thousands of prisoners. It was said that Pelagius had been warned of the preparations made by the Egyptian sailors but had ignored the warning. When it was too late he sent a Venetian squadron to intercept the enemy and attack the harbours of Rosetta and Alexandria, but to no effect. Lack of money prevented him from maintaining a sufficient number of ships of his own; and the Papal treasury could not spare him any more.[1]

In September more of the Crusaders returned home. But at the end of the year Pope Honorius sent good news. Frederick had come to Rome in November 1220, and the Pope had crowned him and his wife Constance Emperor and Empress. In return Frederick definitely promised to set out for the East next spring. Honorius had been growing distrustful of Frederick's promises, and even advised Pelagius not to turn down any peace proposition from the Sultan without referring it to Rome. But the new Emperor seemed now to be serious. He actively encouraged his subjects to take the Cross, and he dispatched a large contingent under Louis, Duke of Bavaria, which set sail from Italy early in the spring.[2]

The news of the Duke's approach so greatly elated Pelagius that when the Sultan offered peace terms in June, he forgot the Pope's instruction and refused them, only then reporting them to Rome. Al-Kamil once again had proposed the cession of Jerusalem and all Palestine apart from Oultrejourdain, together with a thirty years' truce and money compensation for the dismantling of Jerusalem. Soon after the terms were rejected, Louis of Bavaria arrived.[3]

Frederick had ordered Louis not to launch any major offensive till he should follow himself. But Louis was eager to attack the infidel; and when after five weeks there was no news of Frederick

[1] Ernoul, pp. 429–30; Oliver, *Historia Damiatana*, p. 253.
[2] Oliver, *Historia Damiatana*, p. 257. See Hefele-Leclercq, *Histoire des Conciles*, v, II, pp. 1420–1.
[3] Oliver, *loc. cit.*; James of Vitry, *op. cit.* pp. 106–9; Ernoul, p. 442.

leaving Europe, he fell in with Pelagius's wishes. When the Duke argued that if the reinforced army was to advance into Egypt it must do so at once, for the time of the Nile floods was near, and when the Legate declared that the army's finances necessitated speedy action, the leading Crusaders were convinced. They only insisted that King John be summoned to play his part. There were a few dissentients. The Queen-Regent of Cyprus wrote to Pelagius that a great Moslem army was being formed in Syria by al-Mu'azzam and his brother al-Ashraf; and the Military knights had the news confirmed by their brothers in Palestine. But Pelagius found in it another argument for an immediate advance. He had heard prophecies that the Sultan's domination was soon to be ended.[1]

On 4 July 1221, the Legate ordered a three days' fast in the camp. On the 6th King John arrived back with the knights of his kingdom, full of pessimism but unwilling to be accused of cowardice. On the 12th the Crusading force moved towards Fariskur, and there Pelagius drew it up in battle formation. It was an impressive host. Contemporaries told of 630 ships of various sizes, 5000 knights, 4000 archers and 40,000 infantrymen. A horde of pilgrims marched with the army. They were ordered to keep close to the river bank, to supply the soldiers with water. A large garrison was left at Damietta.

The Moslem army advanced as far as Sharimshah to meet them, but, seeing their numbers, retired behind the Bahr as-Saghir, running from the river to Lake Manzaleh, and waited in prepared positions at Talkha and at the site of the later Mansourah, on either side of the river. By 20 July the Crusaders were in occupation of Sharimshah. King John begged them to remain there. The Nile floods were due, and the Syrian army was approaching. But Pelagius insisted on further advance, backed by the common soldiers, who had heard a rumour that the Sultan had fled from

---

[1] Oliver, *Historia Damiatana*, pp. 257–8; Roger of Wendover, II, p. 264; James of Vitry, *Epistola* VII (*Z.K.G.* vol. XVI, p. 86); Ernoul, pp. 441–3. For the prophecies, Oliver, *Historia Damiatana*, pp. 258–9; James of Vitry, *Excerpta* (*Z.K.G.* vol. XVI, pp. 106–13); *Annales de Dunstaplia* (*Annales Monastici*, vol. III, p. 62); Alberic of Trois Fontaines, p. 790.

Cairo. Just south of Sharimshah a canal came into the river from another branch. The Crusaders, as they pressed on, left no ships to guard its mouth, perhaps because they thought it not to be navigable. By Saturday, 24 July, the whole Christian army lay along the Bahr as-Saghir, facing the enemy.

The Nile had risen now, and the canal was full and easy to defend. But before it had filled too deeply the armies of al-Kamil's brothers had crossed it near to Lake Manzaleh and established themselves between the Crusaders and Damietta. As soon as there was enough water in the canal by Sharimshah, al-Kamil's ships sailed down it and cut the retreat of the Christian fleet. By the middle of August Pelagius realized that his army was outnumbered and completely surrounded, with food that would only last for twenty days. After some argument the Bavarians persuaded the command that the only chance of escape lay in an immediate retreat. On the night of Thursday, 26 August, the retreat began. It was ill-organized. Many of the soldiers could not bear to abandon their stores of wine and drank them all rather than leave them. They were in a stupor when the order came to move. The Teutonic knights foolishly set fire to the stores that they could not carry, thus informing the Moslems that they were abandoning their positions. The Nile was still rising; and the Sultan or one of his lieutenants gave orders that the sluices along the right bank should be opened. The water poured in over the low-lying lands that the Christians had to cross. They floundered through the muddy pools and ditches, closely pursued by the Sultan's Turkish cavalry and Nubian foot-guards. King John and his knights beat off the former and the Military Knights drove back the Nubians, but only after thousands of the infantrymen and pilgrims had perished. Pelagius on his ship was carried by the floodwaters swiftly past the blockading Egyptian fleet; but as he had with him the medical supplies of the army and much of its food, his escape was a disaster. A few other ships escaped, but many were captured.[1]

[1] Oliver, *Historia Damiatana*, pp. 257–73 (the fullest eye-witness account); Roger of Wendover, II, pp. 263–4; Ernoul, pp. 439–44; *Histoire des Patriarches*,

On Saturday the 28th Pelagius gave up hope, and sent an envoy to the Sultan to treat for peace. He still had some bargaining assets. Damietta had been refortified and was well garrisoned and supplied with arms; and a strong naval squadron was in the offing under Henry, Count of Malta, and Walter of Palear, Chancellor of Sicily, sent by the Emperor Frederick. But al-Kamil knew that he had the main Crusading army at his mercy. He was firm but generous. After wrangling over the week-end, on the Monday Pelagius accepted his terms. The Christians would abandon Damietta and observe an eight years' truce, to be confirmed by the Emperor. There would be an exchange of all prisoners on either side. The Sultan for his part would give back the True Cross. Till Damietta should be surrendered the Crusade must hand over its leaders as hostages. Al-Kamil named Pelagius, King John, the Duke of Bavaria, the Masters of the Orders and eighteen others, Counts and Bishops. He sent in return one of his sons, one of his brothers and a number of young emirs.[1]

When the Masters of the Templars and the Teutonic knights were dispatched to Damietta to announce its surrender, the garrison at first rebelled against the decree, and attacked the houses of King John and the Orders. Henry, Count of Malta, had just arrived with forty ships; and they felt strong enough to defy the enemy. But winter was coming and food was short; their leaders were hostages and the Moslems were threatening to march on Acre. The rebels soon gave way. After al-Kamil had entertained King John at a splendid feast and had freely revictualled the Christian army the hostages were exchanged back; and on Wednesday, 8 September, the whole Crusade embarked on its ships and the Sultan entered Damietta.[2]

The Fifth Crusade had ended. It had come very close to success.

pp. 257–8; Abu Shama, II, pp. 180, 182–3, 185; Ibn al-Athir, II, pp. 122–4, 158; Ibn Khallikan, III, p. 241.

[1] Oliver, *Historia Damiatana*, pp. 274–6; Ernoul, pp. 444–7; *Histoire des Patriarches*, pp. 257–8; Abu Shama, II, pp. 183–5.

[2] Oliver, *Historia Damiatana*, pp. 274–6; Ernoul, pp. 444–7; *Histoire des Patriarches*, p. 258.

Had there been one wise and respected leader in the Christian army Cairo might have been occupied and the Ayubite rule in Egypt destroyed. With a friendlier government set up there—for the Franks could never have hoped to govern all Egypt themselves —it would not have been impossible to recover all Palestine. But the Emperor who alone could have filled the role, never came, despite all his promises. Pelagius was a haughty, tactless and unpopular man whose faults as a general were revealed by the last disastrous offensive, while King John, for all his gallantry, had neither the personality nor the prestige to command an international army. Almost every stage of the campaign had been wrecked by personal or national jealousies. It would have been wiser to accept the terms twice offered by the Sultan and have taken back Jerusalem. But the strategists were probably right when they said that without the castles of Oultrejourdain Jerusalem itself could never be held, at least so long as the Moslems in Egypt and Syria worked in alliance. As it was, nothing had been gained and much lost, men, resources and reputations. And the unhappiest victims were the most guiltless. Fear of the Christians from the West raised a new wave of fanaticism in Islam. In Egypt, despite al-Kamil's personal tolerance, fresh disabilities were put upon the local Christians, both Melkites and Copts. Exorbitant taxes were levied, churches were closed, and many of them pillaged by the angry Moslem soldiery. Nor could the Italian merchants quite recover their former position in Alexandria. Their compatriots had encouraged the Crusade. Though they returned to their counters they could not be trusted so well. It was with a shame that was bitter and well-earned that the soldiers of the Cross sailed back to their own countries. They did not even bring back with them the True Cross itself. When the time came for its surrender it could not be found.[1]

[1] For contemporary explanations of the failure of the Crusade see Donovan, *op. cit.* pp. 94–7 and notes, also Throop, *Criticism of the Crusades*, pp. 31–4.

CHAPTER III

THE EMPEROR FREDERICK

'And now, I have sent a cunning man, endued with understanding.'   II CHRONICLES II, 13

When the Crusade sailed away despondent from Damietta, King John returned straight to Acre, but the Cardinal Pelagius went further north, to carry out the Pope's instructions at Antioch and in the Armenian kingdom of Cilicia. On King Leo's death Honorius had recognized John of Brienne's claim that his wife or her son should succeed. On their death he transferred the support of the Church to Raymond-Roupen of Antioch who had come in person to Damietta in the summer of 1220 to consult with Pelagius. A few months previously Bohemond of Tripoli had recaptured Antioch, though the Hospitallers held the citadel. Raymond-Roupen had then invaded Cilicia, together with his Armenian mother, Alice, and established himself at Tarsus, awaiting help from the Hospitallers, with whom he was on good terms; for he had given the citadel of Antioch into their care. But the Armenian nobles carried out the late King's wishes and accepted his young daughter Isabella as the Queen, under the regency of Adam of Baghras. Adam was murdered after a few months' power by the Assassins, doubtless at the instigation of the Hospital. His successor as regent was Constantine, head of the Hethoumian family. The Hethoumians had in the past represented the pro-Byzantine party in Armenia. Now they came forward as the champions of nationalism against the latinizing tendencies of the ruling dynasty. Early in 1221 Constantine marched on Tarsus and captured it, together with the Prince and his mother. Raymond-Roupen died in prison soon afterwards. His elimination left Isabella secure on the Armenian throne and Bohemond of Tripoli at Antioch.[1]

[1] See Cahen, *La Syrie du Nord*, pp. 628-32, for details and sources.

Pelagius was warned by the Pope to act carefully. It was useless to put forward the claims of Raymond-Roupen's infant daughters, who retired with their Lusignan mother to Cyprus. But Bohemond was a bad son of the Church. He managed to wrest the citadel of Antioch from the Hospitallers, and he also deprived them of the promise of Jabala, which Raymond-Roupen had offered to them if they would conquer it, and handed the right to it over to the Templars. There was danger now of open war between the Orders. Pelagius managed to persuade each to accept half of the town; but Bohemond not only refused to readmit the Hospital to Antioch, but annexed its possessions there, even though Pelagius threatened him with excommunication and carried out the sentence. The Templars remained in communion with him, and the Regent of Armenia sought his alliance. The Seldjuk Sultan Kaikobad was now the greatest potentate in Asia Minor. He had occupied the western Taurus mountains and made his winter capital on the coast of Alaya, and he was menacing the whole Armenian frontier. The Armenians needed the good-will of Antioch; so the Regent suggested that Bohemond should send his fourth son, Philip, to marry the young Armenian Queen, insisting only that the bridegroom should join the separated Armenian Church. Bohemond, rankling under his excommunication by the Legate, readily allowed his son to lapse into heresy. The alliance between Armenia and Antioch served its immediate purpose. Kaikobad turned his attention away from them to his Moslem neighbours on the East.

The Armenians had hoped that Philip, who had no expectations of ever inheriting Antioch, would himself become a good Armenian. But his tastes were incorrigibly Latin, and he spent as much time as possible at Antioch. The Hethoumians and their friends were exasperated. At last, at the end of 1224, they arrested him one night as he was journeying to Antioch and imprisoned him at Sis, where he was poisoned a few months later. Bohemond was furious but could do little. The Pope had confirmed his excommunication and had warned the Templars to have nothing to do with him. The Hospitallers openly sided with the heretic Armenians. When the young Queen, Philip's widow, fled broken-heartedly to their protection at Seleucia, they handed the whole town over to the regent Constantine, to avoid the shame of surrendering her in person. Bohemond summoned Kaikobad to his aid, and the Seldjuks invaded Cilicia. Constantine then urged Bohemond to call them off by telling him to come to Cilicia and receive his son back, then arranged for the regent of Aleppo, Toghril, to advance on Antioch. When Bohemond was already in Cilicia he was told that his son was dead, and he had to hurry back to defend his capital from Toghril. Meanwhile the unhappy young Queen Isabella was forced to marry Constantine's son Hethoum. For many years she refused to live with him, but in the end she relented. She and Hethoum were crowned together in 1226. Constantine, for all his nationalism, now thought it wise to reconcile Armenia with the Papacy. Loyal messages were sent in the name of the young couple to the Pope and to the Emperor Frederick.[1]

It was well for the Christians of the north that their two chief Moslem neighbours, the Seldjuks and the Ayubites of Aleppo and Mosul, were continuously fighting together; for the eight years' truce guaranteed by al-Kamil did not apply to them. Further south John of Brienne made eager use of it to rest his weary kingdom and in particular to restore the trade with the Moslem interior that provided its main source of revenue. In the autumn of 1222 he decided to visit the West. He wished to consult the Pope about future aid for his kingdom; and he must find a husband for his daughter, the young Queen. She was only aged eleven, but he was now in his seventies. The succession must be secured. After appointing Odo of Montbéliard as viceroy he embarked from Acre with Pelagius, who had just finished a legatine tour in Cyprus, with the Patriarch of Jerusalem, Ralph

---

[1] Cahen, *op. cit.* pp. 632–5. The Armenian historians write from the point of view of the Hethoumians. The best objective account is given by Ibn al-Athir (II, pp. 168–70).

of Merencourt and with the Grand Master of the Hospital. The Grand Master of the Teutonic Knights, Hermann of Salza, was already at Rome. The party landed at Brindisi at the end of October.[1]

John went straight to Rome, where he claimed that in future any territory conquered by a Crusade must be given to the kingdom of Jerusalem. Pelagius may have demurred, but the Pope agreed with John, and the Emperor sent to say that he also approved. John then went on to France to visit once more his old friend King Philip Augustus. Meanwhile Hermann of Salza put forward the suggestion that Queen Yolanda should marry the Emperor Frederick himself, whose Empress had died four months before. It would be a splendid match. John was flattered by the idea, but hesitated till Hermann promised him that he should retain the regency till his death. The Pope was enthusiastic. If Frederick were Consort of Jerusalem he would surely no longer prevaricate and postpone his Crusade. When John arrived at Paris the negotiations were almost complete. King Philip was not pleased with the news and reproached John. It had been hitherto the King of France who was asked to find a husband for the heiress of Outremer. John himself had been nominated by Philip. But, for old time's sake, Philip welcomed John kindly, and John was present when Philip died at Mantes, on 14 July 1223. In his will Philip left to John the sum of 50,000 marks for the benefit of the kingdom of Jerusalem, with similar legacies to the Hospital and the Temple. John attended the King's funeral and the coronation of his son, Louis VIII, then went on a pilgrimage to Santiago de Compostella in Spain. He stayed some months in Castile, where he married King Ferdinand III's sister, Berengaria, and returned to Italy some time in 1224.[2]

[1] Oliver, *Historia Damiatana*, p. 280; *Estoire d'Eracles*, II, p. 355; Ernoul, pp. 448–9; *Annales de Terre Sainte*, p. 437.
[2] Ernoul, pp. 449–50; *Estoire d'Eracles*, II, pp. 355–6; Richard of San Germano, *M.G.H.* vol. XIX, pp. 342–3; *Historia Diplomatica Friderici Secundi* (ed. Huillard-Bréholles), II, p. 375. As Frederick and Yolanda were third cousins, the Pope gave a dispensation for the marriage (Raynaldus, Anno 1223, no. 7, I, pp. 465–6).

In August next year Count Henry of Malta arrived at Acre with fourteen imperial galleys, to fetch the young Queen, now aged fourteen, to Italy for her wedding. On board was James, Archbishop-elect of Capua, who as soon as he landed, married Yolanda as Frederick's proxy in the Church of the Holy Cross. She was then taken to Tyre and there, being now held to be of age, she was crowned Queen of Jerusalem by the Patriarch Ralph, in the presence of all the nobility of Outremer. There was rejoicing for a fortnight; then the Queen embarked, accompanied by the Archbishop of Tyre, Simon of Maugastel, and by her cousin, Balian of Sidon. She paused for a few days in Cyprus, to see her aunt, Queen Alice. When the time came to part, both Queens and all their ladies were in tears; and they heard Yolanda murmur a sad farewell to the sweet land of Syria, which she would never see again.[1]

The Emperor, with King John, awaited his bride at Brindisi. She was welcomed with imperial pomp, and a second marriage ceremony took place on 9 November 1225, in the Cathedral at Brindisi.[2]

Frederick was in his thirty-first year. He was a handsome man, not tall but well-built, though already inclined to fatness. His hair, the red hair of the Hohenstaufen, was receding slightly. His features were regular, with a full, rather sensual mouth and an expression that seemed kindly till you noticed his cold green eyes, whose piercing glance disguised their short-sightedness. His intellectual brilliance was obvious. He was fluent in six languages, French, German, Italian, Latin, Greek and Arabic. He was well versed in philosophy, in the sciences, in medicine and natural history, and well informed about other countries. His conversation, when he chose, was fascinating. But, for all his brilliance, he was not likeable. He was cruel, selfish, and sly, unreliable as a friend and unforgiving as an enemy. His indulgence in erotic pleasures of every sort shocked even the easy standards of Outremer. He loved to outrage contemporaries by scandalous

---

[1] *Estoire d'Eracles*, II, pp. 357–8; *Gestes des Chiprois*, pp. 22–3.
[2] *Estoire d'Eracles, loc. cit.*

comments on religion and morals. In fact he was not irreligious; but his Christianity was rather that of some Byzantine Emperor. He considered himself to be God's anointed viceroy on earth. He knew himself to be a competent student of theology; he was not going to submit to the dictation of any bishop were it even the Bishop of Rome. He saw no harm in taking an interest in other religions, especially Islam, with which he had been in touch all his life. He would not consider the Greeks to be schismatic because they rejected the authority of the Pope. Yet no ruler persecuted more savagely such Christian heretics as the Cathars and their kin. To the average Westerner he was almost incomprehensible. Though he was by blood half-German, half-Norman, he was essentially a Sicilian by upbringing, the child of an island that was half-Greek and half-Arab. As a ruler in Constantinople or in Cairo he would have been eminent but not eccentric. As King of Germany and Western Emperor he was a terrifying marvel. And yet, for all his understanding of the East in general, he never understood Outremer.[1]

He showed his calibre on the morrow of his wedding. He left Brindisi with the Empress without warning his father-in-law, and when the old King hurried after him, he received him coldly. An open quarrel followed when John learned from his weeping daughter that her husband had seduced one of her cousins. Frederick then coldly announced that he had never promised that John should continue as regent. There was no written agreement, and the King had no legal claim once his daughter was married. John found himself shorn of his position, and Frederick's soldiers even took from him the sum of money that King Philip had bequeathed to him for Jerusalem.[2] He fled in despair to the Papal

---

[1] For Frederick's appearance see Kantorowicz, *Frederick II*, pp. 366–8. This book somewhat idealizes and romanticizes him. See also below, p. 190.

[2] Ernoul, pp. 451–2; *Estoire d'Eracles*, II, pp. 358–60 (also p. 356, where John is said to have counted on keeping the regency till 1227, when Yolanda would be sixteen); Richard of San Germano, p. 345; *Historia Diplomatica Friderici Secundi*, II, p. 392. Frederick already called himself King of Jerusalem in December 1225 (*ibid.* II, p. 526). The seduced cousin was the daughter of Walter of Brienne.

Court. Pope Honorius, who was obstinately loth to think ill of his former pupil, was once again disillusioned and shocked; but he could do nothing for John except give him the government of the Tuscan patrimony. But the old warrior's career was not ended. He had already been suggested for the throne of England. In 1228 the Latin Empire of Constantinople was in need of a regent for the child-Emperor Baldwin II. John, though nearly eighty, gladly took on the job. Baldwin was married to his four-year-old daughter Maria; and John saw to it carefully that he himself was given the title of Emperor to bear till his death in 1237.[1]

The Empress-Queen Yolanda was less fortunate than her father. Frederick sent her to the harem that he kept at Palermo; and there she lived in seclusion, pining for the bright life of Outremer. On 25 April 1228 she gave birth to a son, Conrad, and having done her duty, she died six days later. She was not yet seventeen.[2]

Frederick had promised the Pope first that he would marry his bride in Syria, but at his request, made through King John and the Master of the Teutonic Knights he was granted two years' delay. On 25 July 1225, he met two Papal Legates at San Germano, and took an oath that he would start out for the East in August 1227, that he would send a thousand knights at once, and that he would deposit 100,000 ounces of gold at Rome, to be forfeit to the Church should he break his vow. Had advice from Outremer been taken, the Emperor's departure would have been postponed till 1229, when the truce with al-Kamil would end.[3]

The promised knights were sent in the convoy that was to bring back the future Empress. Frederick himself used his two years of grace in an attempt to establish his rule in northern Italy and so link up his German and south Italian lands. The determined enmity of the Lombard League thwarted him; and he was only

[1] For John's subsequent career see Longnon, *L'Empire Latin*, pp. 169–74.
[2] Ernoul, p. 454; *Estoire d'Eracles*, II, p. 366; Richard of San Germano, p. 447; *Historia Diplomatica Friderici Secundi*, I, p. 858.
[3] *Historia Diplomatica Friderici Secundi*, III, pp. 36–48; *Regesta Honorii Papae II*, no. 5566, II, p. 352.

able to secure a working compromise with the Lombards by wooing the Papacy with a fresh demonstration of enthusiasm for the Crusade. But his old tutor, Pope Honorius, died in March 1227. The new Pope, Gregory IX, was cast in a grimmer mould. He was a cousin of Innocent III, and like Innocent was a man with a clear legalistic mind and a proud unyielding faith in the divine authority of the Papacy. Stern and ascetic himself, he disliked Frederick as a man, and he saw that there could be no truce between the Caesaropapism desired by the Emperor and his own conception of his authority. Policy as well as piety demanded that Frederick should depart for the East.[1]

Frederick seemed ready to go. A party of English and French Crusaders under the Bishops of Exeter and Winchester had already sailed for the East. Throughout the summer of 1227 the Emperor mustered a great army in Apulia. An epidemic of malaria enfeebled the army; but several thousand soldiers sailed from Brindisi in August, under Henry IV, Duke of Limburg. Frederick joined the army a few days later, and embarked on 8 September. They had hardly weighed anchor before one of his companions, Louis, Landgrave of Thuringia, fell desperately ill. Their ship put in at Otranto, where the Landgrave died and Frederick himself took the sickness. He left the fleet, which he sent off to Acre under the Patriarch of Jerusalem, Gerold of Lausanne, and went to recover his health at the spa of Pozzuoli. An envoy was despatched to Pope Gregory at Anagni to explain the unavoidable delay.[2] But Gregory was unconvinced by the tale. The Emperor, he thought, was prevaricating again. He excommunicated him at once, and repeated the sentence solemnly at St Peter's in November.[3]

---

[1] Hefele-Leclercq, *Histoire des Conciles*, v, ii, pp. 1467–8.

[2] *Historia Diplomatica Friderici Secundi*, iii, p. 44, v, p. 329; *Annales Marbacenses*, p. 175; Alberic of Trois Fontaines, p. 920; Richard of San Germano, p. 348. Louis of Thuringia was the husband of Saint Elizabeth of Hungary. See Hefele-Leclercq, *op. cit.* pp. 1469–70. Ernoul, pp. 458–9, mentions the arrival of the first crusading expedition, in which he noted the great number of English.

[3] Hefele-Leclercq, *op. cit.* pp. 1471–2.

Frederick, after issuing a dignified manifesto to the princes of Europe denouncing Papal pretensions, went on with his preparations for the Crusade. Though the Pope warned him that he could not lawfully set out for the Holy War while he was under the ban of the Church, he gathered a small company and embarked from Brindisi on 28 June 1228.[1] The delay had, however, altered his status; for the Empress Yolanda was dead. Frederick was no longer King and the Queen's husband, but guardian of the infant King Conrad, his son. The barons of the kingdom would be entitled, if they so chose, to refuse him the regency.[2]

It was not with unmixed pleasure that the rulers of the Frankish East awaited the Emperor's coming. Bohemond of Antioch and Tripoli was the least disquieted; for he acknowledged no overlord except, perhaps, the Latin Emperor at Constantinople. But Frederick could claim a suzerain's rights over Cyprus; for it was from the Emperor Henry VI that King Amalric had obtained his crown; and, until the death of the Empress, which was not known in the East until about the time of his arrival, he was certainly King of Jerusalem.[3] He had already intervened in the affairs of the kingdom of Jerusalem. In 1226 he sent out Thomas of Aquino, Count of Acerra, to replace Odo of Montbéliard as regent; and Thomas showed a vigour and decision in his dealings with the High Court that was not quite to the barons' liking.[4]

In Cyprus the official regent for the child King, Henry I, was his mother, Alice of Jerusalem. She had entrusted the government to her uncle Philip of Ibelin, the second son of Queen Maria Comnena. The relations between the Queen and her *bailli* were not happy. She complained that her wishes were always disregarded; and an open breach came in 1223 when Philip refused to allow the Orthodox clergy to be robbed of their tithes for the

[1] *Historia Diplomatica Friderici Secundi*, III, pp. 37–48, for the text of Frederick's manifesto.
[2] *Ibid.* I, p. 898; Richard of San Germano, p. 350; *Estoire d'Eracles*, II, pp. 366–7; Hefele-Leclercq, *op. cit.* p. 1477.
[3] For Frederick's legal position see La Monte, *Feudal Monarchy*, p. 59.
[4] *Estoire d'Eracles*, II, p. 364.

benefit of the Latins, as Cardinal Pelagius had recommended at a Council held at Limassol. The Queen had agreed with the Cardinal; and when she failed to have her way, she retired in a rage to Tripoli, where she married Prince Bohemond's eldest surviving son, the future Bohemond V.[1] In 1225, when it was certain that the Emperor seriously intended to come to the East, Philip ordered the coronation of the eight-year-old King Henry, so that at least when Henry came of age at fifteen a regency could not be prolonged on the ground that he was not yet crowned. Queen Alice, though in voluntary exile, still regarded herself as regent. Her attempt to appoint her new husband as *bailli* came to nothing because none of the barons would accept him. She then offered it to one of the leading barons, Amalric Barlais, who, though he had opposed Bohemond's candidature, accepted for himself, largely because he hated the Ibelins. But the barons, with one dissentient, declared that a *bailli* could only be appointed with the consent of the High Court, which demanded that Philip should continue in his post. After an open quarrel with Ibelin adherents, Barlais retired to Tripoli to await the coming of Frederick, while one of his friends, Gavin of Chenichy, went to join the Emperor in Italy.[2] Philip of Ibelin died in 1227; and the High Court invited his elder brother John, lord of Beirut, to take his place as *bailli*. Queen Alice appears to have confirmed his appointment.[3]

John of Ibelin was now the greatest person in Outremer. He was the nearest male relative in the East both of the King of Cyprus and of the Empress-Queen Yolanda. He was rich; he owned the city of Beirut, and his wife was heiress of Arsuf. His personal qualities won him general respect. His birth, wealth and integrity had made him for some decades already the accepted leader of the

---

[1] Hill, *History of Cyprus*, II, pp. 87–8, with references and a discussion of the dates.

[2] *Gestes des Chiprois*, pp. 30–3; *Estoire d'Eracles*, II, pp. 361–2.

[3] *Gestes des Chiprois*, p. 37; *Annales de Terre Sainte*, p. 438; *Estoire d'Eracles*, II, p. 365, misdating Philip's death 1228. It is nowhere definitely stated that John was appointed *bailli*, but he was acting as *bailli* when the Emperor arrived.

baronage of Outremer. Half Levantine-French and half-Greek, he understood the East and its peoples and he was equally versed in the history and the laws of the Frankish kingdom.[1] The Emperor Frederick at once sensed him to be the chief danger to his policy. Frederick too understood the East and its peoples, from his training in Sicily. His dealings with the Moslems were of a sort that the established barons of Outremer could follow with sympathy. But Frederick's conception of monarchy was not theirs. The King of Jerusalem was by tradition a king bound by a constitution, little more than president of the High Court and commander-in-chief. But Frederick saw himself as an autocrat in the Roman-Byzantine manner, the repository of power and law, God's supreme viceroy on earth, with all the advantages that hereditary right could give him thrown in. The Emperor of the Romans was not going to be controlled by a few petty Frankish barons.

Barlais and his party were already in touch with Frederick before he arrived off Limassol on 21 July 1228. On their advice he at once summoned John of Ibelin to come with his sons and the young King of Cyprus to meet him. John's friends warned him of Frederick's reputation for perfidy; but John was courageous and correct. He would not refuse an invitation from the suzerain of Cyprus. On his arrival with his sons and the King, Frederick received him with honour, calling him uncle and offering him rich gifts. He was told to lay aside the mourning that he wore for his brother Philip, and to attend a feast given in his honour. But at the feast Frederick's soldiers crept in and stood behind each of the guests, with their swords drawn. Then Frederick demanded of John that he surrender his fief of Beirut and hand over all the revenues of Cyprus that had come in since the death of King Hugh. John replied that Beirut had been given to him by his sister Queen Isabella, and he would defend his right to it before the High Court of the kingdom of Jerusalem. As for the revenues, both Philip and he had given them, as was right, to the Regent, Queen Alice. Frederick broke into open threats, but John stood firm. He would

[1] See La Monte, 'John of Ibelin', in *Byzantion*, vol. XII.

not have it said, he declared, that he refused to aid the Emperor on his Crusade, but even should he be slain for it he would not break the laws of the land. Frederick, who had only three or four thousand troops with him, dared not risk an open breach. He demanded that twenty nobles, including John's two sons, should be left with him as hostages, that the King should remain with him and that John should come with him to Palestine. In return John and the Cypriot nobles recognized, as was correct, Frederick as suzerain of Cyprus, but not as Regent,—for Queen Alice was the lawful Regent—and as Regent but not as King of Jerusalem; for they knew now that Yolanda was dead and the King was her infant son, Conrad.[1]

The Emperor had meanwhile summoned the leading potentates of Outremer to Cyprus. In August, Balian, Lord of Sidon, arrived with a contingent of troops from the mainland, and soon afterwards Guy Embriaco of Jebail, who disliked the Ibelins, and from whom, like Leopold VI of Austria a few years previously, Frederick borrowed a large sum of money. With these reinforcements the Emperor marched on Nicosia. On the way there he was joined by Bohemond IV of Antioch. John of Ibelin cautiously retired to the castle that the Greeks called the Twin Peaks, Didymi, and the Franks Dieu d'Amour and today we call Saint Hilarion. He had already sent the ladies and the children of his household there, with ample stores of provisions. Feudal law laid down that, during a regency, the barons could not be ejected from castles entrusted to them by the late monarch. Frederick did not attempt now to flout the law. He was anxious to move on to Palestine. Balian of Sidon, who was John's nephew, seems to have acted as mediator. It was arranged that the King should pay homage to the Emperor, and that all the Cypriots should swear fealty to him as overlord. Though Alice alone was recognized as Regent, Frederick would appoint *baillis* to govern the country, and John should come to Palestine, to defend his right to Beirut before the High Court.

[1] *Gestes des Chiprois*, pp. 37–45, a vivid account by Philip of Novara, who was probably present himself; *Estoire d'Eracles*, II, pp. 367–8.

All the hostages would be released. On these terms, after oaths had been sworn to preserve the peace, the Emperor sailed from Famagusta on 3 September, accompanied by the King, the Ibelins and most of the barons of Cyprus. Amalric Barlais was left as *bailli*, aided by Gavin of Chenichy and his other friends.[1]

Frederick had also suggested that Bohemond should pay him homage for Tripoli and Antioch. Bohemond at once feigned a nervous breakdown and slipped off secretly home, where he made a remarkable recovery.[2]

When the Emperor and his companions arrived at Acre, John of Ibelin hurried at once to Beirut, to be sure that it could resist an attack from the Emperor. He then returned to Acre, to defend himself before the High Court. But Frederick did not hasten to take action. News had reached Palestine that the Pope had excommunicated him again, for setting out for the Crusade before he had obtained absolution from his previous excommunication. There was some doubt therefore whether oaths of fealty sworn to him held good; and many pious folk, including the Patriarch Gerold, refused to co-operate with him. The Templars and the Hospitallers would have nothing to do with an excommunicate. He could only rely on the Teutonic Knights, whose Master, Hermann of Salza, was his friend. His own army was not large. Of the troops that had gone out with the Duke of Limburg in 1227, many had already returned home, from impatience or from fear of offending the Church. A few more had sailed East with the Patriarch a month later; and Frederick had sent out in the spring of 1228 five hundred knights under his loyal servant, the Marshal Richard Filangieri. Even with the whole army of Outremer he could not muster an impressive force capable of striking a decisive blow against the Moslems. To add to his disquiet word came from

---

[1] *Gestes des Chiprois*, pp. 45–8; *Estoire d'Eracles*, II, pp. 368–9. According to German law, a King did not reach his majority till the age of twenty-five, but in Jerusalem and Cyprus it was at fifteen. Frederick probably intended Henry to be considered a minor till he was twenty-five. See Hill, *op. cit.* II, p. 98 n. 4.

[2] *Gestes des Chiprois*, p. 48.

Italy that his lieutenant, Duke Reynald of Spoleto, had failed in an attack on the March of Ancona, and that the Pope was massing forces to invade his own kingdom. Frederick could not afford to embark on a large campaign in the East. His Crusade should be a crusade of diplomacy.[1]

Fortunately for the Emperor, the Sultan al-Kamil held similar views. The alliance of the three Ayubite brothers, al-Kamil, al-Mu'azzam of Syria and al-Ashraf of the Jezireh had not long survived their triumph over the Fifth Crusade. Al-Mu'azzam had always been jealous of al-Kamil, and now he rightly suspected that al-Kamil and al-Ashraf were planning to divide his lands. To the east of the Ayubites, the great Khwarismian Empire of Jelal ad-Din was reaching its apogee. Jelal ad-Din had driven off a Mongol invasion and now ruled from Azerbaijan to the Indus, dominating the Caliph at Baghdad. Though the presence of the Mongols in his rear kept him from adventuring too far into the West, he was a potential danger to the Ayubites; and when al-Mu'azzam, to spite his brothers, called on him for help and in 1226 recognized his suzerainty, al-Kamil was genuinely frightened. Al-Ashraf was on the defensive, enduring a siege in his capital of Akhlat. The Mongols at this moment were busy in China, and an appeal to them, were it indeed a wise idea, would go unheeded. So, in the autumn of 1226, al-Kamil had sent one of his most trusted emirs, Fakhr ad-Din ibn as-Shaikh, to Sicily, to ask help from the Emperor Frederick. Frederick was sympathetic but made no promises. He was then still contemplating an active Crusade. But, to keep the negotiations open, he sent Thomas of Acerra, who was already in Palestine, together with the Bishop of Palermo, to Cairo, with gifts and friendly messages for the Sultan. Al-Kamil suggested, as he had done during the Fifth Crusade, that he was ready to restore Jerusalem to the Christians. Unfortunately, it belonged to his brother al-Mu'azzam; and when the Bishop

---

[1] Röhricht, *Geschichte des Königreichs Jerusalem*, pp. 776–7, discusses the numerical strength of Frederick's army. It was never more than 11,000 strong and many soldiers returned quickly home.

of Palermo went to Damascus to clinch the arrangement, al-Mu'azzam angrily replied that he was no pacifist; he still used his sword. Meanwhile Fakhr ad-Din revisited Sicily, where he became an intimate friend of the Emperor and received knighthood from him. Frederick's departure for the East, so eagerly pressed by the Pope, was equally urged by the Sultan.[1]

But, before Frederick set out, the situation was altered. Al-Mu'azzam died on 11 November 1227, leaving his dominions to a youth of twenty-one, his son an-Nasir Dawud. As the new ruler was weak and inexperienced, al-Kamil at once prepared to annex his territory. He marched into Palestine and captured Jerusalem and Nablus. An-Nasir appealed to his uncle al-Ashraf, who hastened to his rescue, announcing that he had come to see that the Franks did not take advantage of the situation to annex Palestine. Al-Kamil was loudly making the same claim, which sounded plausible, as Frederick was now on his way to the East. Eventually the two brothers met at Tel-Ajul, near Gaza, and decided to divide their nephew's lands between them, still protesting that they were acting altruistically in the interests of Islam. An-Nasir was encamped at Beisan, where al-Ashraf planned to capture him. But the boy heard of the plot and fled to Damascus. His uncles' armies followed him and laid siege to the city about the end of the year 1228.[2]

Under these circumstances al-Kamil regretted Frederick's coming. He had every prospect of obtaining Palestine permanently for himself; for the Khwarismians showed no sign of coming to an-Nasir's help. But the presence of a Crusading army at Acre meant that he could not concentrate all his forces on the siege of Damascus. Frederick was not entirely to be trusted; he might decide to intervene on an-Nasir's behalf. When Frederick sent

---

[1] For a general account of al-Kamil's policy, Ibn al-Athir, II, pp. 162–8; Abu'l Feda, pp. 99–102; al-Aïni, pp. 183–6; Maqrisi, trans. Blochet, IX, pp. 470–511; *Histoire des Patriarches d'Alexandrie*, p. 518.

[2] Ibn Khallikan, II, p. 429; Maqrisi, IX, pp. 516–18; Abu Shama, II, pp. 187–91; Ibn al-Athir, II, pp. 173–4; *Histoire des Patriarches*, p. 519.

Thomas of Acerra and Balian of Sidon to al-Kamil to announce his arrival, al-Kamil told Fakhr ad-Din to visit the Emperor once more, to open negotiations and keep them open as long as possible, till Damascus should fall or Frederick go home. There followed several months of bargaining, in an atmosphere partly of mutual bluff and partly of mutual admiration. Neither Emperor nor Sultan was fanatically devoted to his religion. Each was interested in the other's way of life. Neither was prepared to go to war if it could be avoided; but each had, for the sake of his prestige with his own people, to drive as hard a bargain as possible. Frederick was pressed for time and his army not large enough for a major campaign; but al-Kamil was alarmed by any show of force while Damascus was still untaken, and he was ready to make concessions to the Christians if it would help him to pursue his greater policy, which was to reunite and dominate the Ayubite world. But the concessions must not go too far. When Frederick demanded the retrocession of all Palestine, Fakhr ad-Din, on al-Kamil's instructions, told him that his master could not afford to offend Moslem opinion to such a degree.

At the end of November 1228, the Emperor tried to hasten matters by a military display. He assembled all the troops that would follow him and marched down the coast to Jaffa, which he proceeded to refortify. At the same moment an-Nasir, who was not yet closely invested in Damascus, led an army to Nablus, to intercept his uncle's supply lines. But al-Kamil refused to be bluffed. He broke off negotiations, saying that Frederick's men had pillaged Moslem villages, and only resumed them again when Frederick paid out compensation to the victims.[1]

In the end Frederick proved the better bargainer. When February came an-Nasir was still unscathed in Damascus, and Jelal ad-Din the Khwarismian was turning his attention westward again. Frederick had completed the fortifications of Jaffa, and, on Fakhr ad-Din's advice, he sent Thomas of Acerra and Balian of Sidon once more to al-Kamil. On 11 February they brought back

[1] *Estoire d'Eracles*, II, pp. 369–72; Ernoul, pp. 460–3; al-Aïni, pp. 186–8.

the Sultan's final terms. Frederick agreed to them, and a week later, on the 18th, he signed a peace treaty, together with al-Kamil's representatives, Fakhr ad-Din and Salah ad-Din of Arbela. The Grand Master of the Teutonic Order and the Bishops of Exeter and Winchester were witnesses. By this treaty the kingdom of Jerusalem was to receive Jerusalem itself and Bethlehem, with a corridor running through Lydda to the sea at Jaffa, Nazareth and western Galilee, including Montfort and Toron, and the remaining Moslem districts round Sidon. But in Jerusalem itself the Temple area, with the Dome of the Rock and the Mosque al-Aqsa, was to remain in Moslem hands, and Moslems were to be allowed the right of entry and freedom of worship. Frederick might rebuild the walls of Jerusalem, but the concession was made to him personally. All prisoners on both sides were to be released. The peace was to last ten years by the Christian calendar and ten years and five months by the Moslem. But it did not apply to Bohemond's principality of Antioch-Tripoli.[1]

Thus, without striking a blow, the excommunicate Emperor won back the Holy Places for Christendom. But seldom has a treaty met with such immediate and universal disapproval. The Moslem world was horrified. At Damascus an-Nasir, not without relish, ordered public mourning for the betrayal of Islam. Even al-Kamil's own imams abused him to his face; and his lame reply that he had only ceded ruined houses and churches, while the Moslem shrines were intact and saved for the Faith, was little consolation; nor did his comment that the Moslems were still strategic masters of the province seem an adequate excuse.[2] The Christians, on the other hand, were well aware of the strategic position. The more intransigent of them lamented that Jerusalem had not been won back by the sword, and were disgusted that the

---

[1] *Historia Diplomatica Friderici Secundi*, III, pp. 90–1, 93–5, 102 (letter of Hermann of Salza to the Pope, manifesto of Frederick and letter of Patriarch Gerold, announcing the peace terms); *Ibid.* pp. 86–7 (a partial text of the treaty with the Patriarch's comments); Ernoul, p. 465; *Estoire d'Eracles*, II, p. 374; al-Aïni, pp. 188–90; Maqrisi, IX, p. 525.

[2] Al-Aïni, pp. 190–1; Abu'l Feda, p. 104; Maqrisi, X, pp. 248–9.

infidel should retain their shrines; and all of them remembered the negotiations of the Fifth Crusade, when al-Kamil's offer of all Palestine was rejected because the strategists pointed out that without Oultrejourdain Jerusalem could not be held. How then could it be held when only one narrow strip of land connected it with the coast? There was none of the rejoicing that Frederick had expected. No one suggested that excommunication should be lifted from the man who had done such a great service to Christendom. The Patriarch Gerold proclaimed his displeasure and hurled an interdict against the Holy City if it should receive the Emperor. The Templars, furious at the Temple remaining with the Moslems, made their protest. Neither they nor the Hospitallers would have dealings with the enemy of the Pope. The local barons, already resentful of Frederick's absolutism, were alarmed by the impracticability of the new frontier; and their dislike of the Emperor was enhanced when he announced that he would go up to Jerusalem and be crowned King. For, in fact, he was not their King, but only the regent and father of the King.[1]

On Saturday, 17 March 1229, Frederick made his ceremonious entry into Jerusalem. His German and Italian troops escorted him, but very few of the local baronage. Of the Military Orders only the Teutonic Knights were represented; and of the clergy there were only Frederick's Sicilian Bishops and his English friends, Peter of Winchester and William of Exeter. The Emperor was met at the gate by the Qadi Shams ad-Din of Nablus, who handed him the keys of the city in the name of the Sultan. The short procession then passed through empty streets to the old building of the Hospital, where Frederick took up his residence. There was no sign of enthusiasm. The Moslems had deserted the city except for their shrines. The native Christians held aloof, fearing with reason that a Latin restoration would do them no good. Frederick's own companions were embarrassed by his excommunication; and

[1] *Historia Diplomatica Friderici Secundi*, III, pp. 101, 138–9 (letters of Hermann and of Gerold); Matthew Paris, III, p. 177.

when it was known that the Archbishop of Caesarea was on his way with orders from the Patriarch to put the city under an interdict, there was constraint and hesitation at the Court. Next morning, Sunday the 18th, Frederick went to attend Mass in the Church of the Holy Sepulchre. Not a priest was there, only his own soldiery and the Teutonic Knights. Undeterred, he had a royal crown laid on the altar of Calvary, then took it up himself and placed it on his head. Thereupon the Master of the Teutonic Knights read out, first in German, then in French, an encomium of the Emperor-King, describing his achievements and justifying his policy. The Court then moved back to the Hospital; and Frederick held a council to discuss the defence of Jerusalem. The Grand Master of the Hospital and the Preceptor of the Temple, who at a discreet distance had followed the Emperor to Jerusalem, consented to be present, along with the English bishops and Hermann of Salza. Frederick ordered that the Tower of David and the Gate of St Stephen were to be repaired at once, and he handed over the royal residence attached to the Tower of David to the Teutonic Order. Except from the Teutons he met with little co-operation.[1]

It was with relief that Frederick turned aside from his work to visit the Moslem shrines. The Sultan had tactfully ordered the Muezzin at al-Aqsa not to make the call to prayer while the Christian sovereign was in the city. But Frederick protested. The Moslems must not change their customs because of him. Besides, he said, he had come to Jerusalem in order to hear the Muezzins' call through the night. As he entered the holy area of the Haram as-Sharif he noticed a Christian cleric following behind. He at once himself rudely ejected him, and gave orders that any Christian priest that crossed its threshold without permission from the Moslems should be put to death. As he walked round the

---

[1] *Historia Diplomatica Friderici Secundi, loc. cit.* Hermann discouraged Frederick from holding a religious service in the Church of the Holy Sepulchre. Frederick made his own speech in Italian. *Estoire d'Eracles*, II, pp. 375, 385; Ernoul, p. 465.

Dome of the Rock he noticed the inscription that Saladin had erected in mosaic round the cupola, to record the building's purification from the polytheists. 'Who', asked the Emperor with a smile, 'might the polytheists be?' He remarked on the gratings over the windows and was told that they were put up to keep out the sparrows. 'God has now sent you the pigs', he said, using the vulgar Moslem term for the Christians. It was noted that he had Moslems in his suite, amongst them his teacher of philosophy, an Arab from Sicily.

The Moslems were interested by the Emperor but not deeply impressed. His appearance disappointed them. They said that he would not be worth two hundred dirhems in the slave-market, with his smooth red face and his myopic eyes. They were disquieted by his remarks against his own faith. They could respect an honest Christian; but a Frank who disparaged Christianity and paid crude compliments to Islam roused their suspicions. It may be that they had heard the remark universally attributed to him that Moses, Christ and Mahomet were all three impostors. In any case he seemed a man without religion. The enlightened Fakhr ad-Din, with whom he had often discussed philosophy in the palace at Acre, fell victim to his fascination; and the Sultan al-Kamil, whose speculative outlook was akin to his own, regarded him with affectionate admiration, particularly when Fakhr ad-Din reported his confidence that he would never have insisted on the cession of Jerusalem had not his whole prestige been at stake. But pious Moslems and pious Christians alike looked askance at the whole episode. Obvious cynicism never wins the hearts of the people.[1]

On Monday the 19th, Peter of Caesarea arrived, to hurl the Patriarch's interdict on Jerusalem. In his rage at the insult, Frederick at once abandoned further work on the defence of the city and, gathering together all his men, hastened down to Jaffa. He paused for a day there, then moved up the coast to Acre, where he arrived on the 23rd. He found Acre seething with discontent.

[1] Al-Aïni, pp. 192–3; Maqrisi, IX, pp. 525–6.

The barons could not forgive him for flouting the constitution; though only Regent he had made a treaty without their consent and had crowned himself King. There were riots between local men at arms and the Emperor's garrison. The Genoese and Venetian colonists resented favours shown to the Pisans, whose mother-city was one of Frederick's few constant allies in Italy. The Emperor's return only intensified the bitterness in the atmosphere.[1]

On the following morning Frederick summoned representatives of all the realm to meet him and gave them an account of his actions. His words were met with angry disapproval. He then had recourse to force. He threw a cordon of police round the Patriarch's palace and round the headquarters of the Templars; and he put guards at the city gates so that no one unauthorized could leave or enter the city. It was rumoured that he intended to confiscate the great Templar fortress at Athlit, but he learned that it was too strongly garrisoned. He contemplated kidnapping John of Ibelin and the Grand Master of the Temple and sending them to Apulia; but they each kept themselves well guarded, and he did not attempt the venture. But meanwhile he received serious news from Italy, where his father-in-law, John of Brienne, had invaded his states at the head of a Papal army. He could not defer his departure from the East much longer. Without more troops than he possessed in Syria he could not crush his opponents. So he compromised. He announced his forthcoming departure and appointed as *baillis* for the kingdom Balian of Sidon and Garnier the German. Balian was known for his moderate views and his mother was an Ibelin. Garnier, despite his German origin, had been a lieutenant of King John of Brienne. Odo of Montbéliard was left as Constable of the kingdom, in charge of the army.

These appointments in fact represented a defeat for the Emperor. He knew that he had lost and, to avoid humiliating scenes, he planned to embark on 1 May at sunrise, when no one would be about. But the secret was not kept. As he and his suite passed

[1] *Historia Diplomatica Friderici Secundi*, III, p. 101; *Estoire d'Eracles*, II, p. 374.

down the Street of the Butchers to the harbour, the people crowded out of the doors and pelted him with entrails and dung. John of Ibelin and Odo of Montbéliard heard the riot and rode up to restore order. But when they bade a courteous good-bye to the Emperor on his galley, he answered with muttered curses.[1]

From Acre Frederick sailed to Limassol. He remained some ten days in Cyprus, where he confirmed that the *baillis* should be Amalric Barlais and his four friends, Gavin of Chenichy, Amalric of Beisan, Hugh of Jebail and William of Rivet. He entrusted the King's person to them. At the same time he arranged a marriage between the young King and Alice of Montferrat, whose father was one of his staunch supporters in Italy. On 10 June 1229, he landed at Brindisi.[2]

Of all the great Crusaders the Emperor Frederick II is the most disappointing. He was a man of great brilliance, who knew the mentality of the Moslems and could appreciate the intricacies of their diplomacy; and he saw that there must be some understanding between them and the Christians, if Frankish Outremer was to endure. But he failed to comprehend the nature of Frankish Outremer. The experience and achievements of his Norman ancestors and his own temperament and conception of Empire led him to seek to build a centralized autocracy. He found it too hard a task in Europe, outside of his Italian lands. In Cyprus he might have achieved it, had he chosen his instruments better. But in the diminished kingdom of Jerusalem the experiment was bound to fail. The kingdom was little more than a group of towns and castles, strung precariously together without a defensible frontier. A centralized government was no longer possible. The local authorities, wearisome though their mutual quarrels and jealousies might be, had to be trusted with the government under a tactful and respected leader. These authorities were the lay barons and the Military Orders. Frederick alienated the lay barons by trampling upon the rights and traditions of which they were

[1] *Estoire d'Eracles*, II, p. 375; Ernoul, p. 466; *Gestes des Chiprois*, p. 50.
[2] *Gestes des Chiprois*, pp. 50-1.

proud. The Military Orders were even more important, for they alone, now that lay knights preferred to seek their fortunes in Frankish Greece, could provide recruits to fight and settle in the East. But they, though their masters sat on the King's council and though they might obey him as commander-in-chief on the battle-field, owed allegiance only to the Pope. They could not be expected to aid a ruler whom the Pope had excommunicated and branded as an enemy to Christendom. Only the Teutonic Knights, whose Order was the least important of the three, were prepared, because of their master's friendship with the Emperor, to defy the Papal ban. It was remarkable that with so few assets and with such hatred roused against him Frederick was able to win a diplomatic success as startling as the recovery of Jerusalem itself.[1]

In fact the recovery of Jerusalem was of little profit to the kingdom. Owing to Frederick's hurried departure it remained an open city. It was impossible to police the road up from the coast; and Moslem bandits continually robbed and even killed the pilgrims. A few weeks after Frederick had left the country fanatical Moslem imams in Hebron and Nablus organized a raid on Jerusalem itself. The Christians of all rites fled for safety to the Tower of David, while the governor, Reynald of Haifa, sent to Acre for help. The arrival of the two *baillis*, Balian of Sidon and Garnier, with an army, obliged the raiders to retire. The Moslem rulers repudiated any connection with the raid; and when a larger garrison was left in the city and some minor fortifications were built, there was a little more security. The Patriarch lifted his interdict and came to reside there for part of the year. But the situation was precarious. The Sultan could have recaptured Jerusalem at any time that he chose. In Galilee, where the castles of Montfort and Toron were rebuilt, the Christian hold was stronger. But, with the Moslems in Safed and Banyas, there was no guarantee of permanence.[2]

---

[1] For opposing views of Frederick's achievements in Palestine, see Kanto-rowicz, *op. cit.* pp. 193 ff. and Grousset, *Histoire des Croisades*, III, pp. 322–3.
[2] *Estoire d'Eracles*, II, pp. 303–5.

Frederick's main legacy, both in Cyprus and in the kingdom of Jerusalem, was a bitter civil war. In Cyprus it started at once. The five *baillis* there had been instructed to exile all the friends of the Ibelins from the island. They had agreed also to pay a sum of 10,000 marks to Frederick, and the castles, still garrisoned by Imperial troops, were not to be handed over to them till they paid a first instalment. They raised the money by levying heavy taxes and by confiscating the property of the Ibelin party. It chanced that one of John of Beirut's most devoted supporters, the historian poet Philip of Novara, was in the island, and the *baillis* offered him a safe-conduct to come to Nicosia and discuss some sort of truce between themselves and the Ibelins. But when Philip arrived they changed their minds and arrested him. After an angry scene in front of the boy-King, who knew Philip well but was unable to intervene, the *baillis* granted him bail; and he fled to the House of the Hospital, wisely, for armed men broke into his own house that night. He sent off an appeal, written in doggerel, to John of Ibelin at Acre, to come and rescue him and save the property of all his friends. John at once fitted out an expedition at his own expense and managed to force a landing at Gastria, north of Famagusta. He then moved cautiously to Nicosia, where he met the *baillis'* army. It was much larger than his own, but less enthusiastic. After some parleys the Ibelins gave battle on 14 July. A spirited attack by John's knights, led by his son Balian, combined with a sortie from the Hospital organized by Philip of Novara, decided the day. The *baillis* fled with their troops to the three castles of Dieu d'Amour, Kantara and Kyrenia. John followed and laid siege to all three. Kyrenia was soon captured, but Dieu d'Amour, where Barlais had taken the young King and his sisters, and Kantara were almost impregnable. They only surrendered in the summer of 1230, from starvation. John's peace terms were generous. Of the five *baillis*, Gavin of Chenichy had been killed at Kantara, and William of Rivet, who was his half-brother, had fled from Kyrenia to seek help in Cilicia and had died there. The other three were unpunished, to the annoyance of many of John's friends. John would not even allow Philip of Novara to make a satirical poem about them. A messenger was sent in the King's name to the potentates of Europe to justify the steps that had been taken against the Emperor. John himself took over the government, till King Henry should come of age in 1232.[1]

Meanwhile the kingdom of Jerusalem was peacefully governed by Balian of Sidon and Garnier the German. In the autumn of 1229 Queen Alice of Cyprus had come to Acre to put in a claim to the crown. The regency of Cyprus, which she still nominally held, offered nothing but trouble. She had divorced young Bohemond of Antioch on the grounds of consanguinity; for they were cousins in the third degree. Now she declared that, though the Emperor's son Conrad was legally King of Jerusalem, he had forfeited his right by failing to come to his kingdom. The High Court should therefore hand the Crown on to the next legitimate heir, which was herself. The Court rejected her claim. Conrad was a minor and his presence therefore not essential; but it was agreed to send an embassy to Italy to ask that Conrad be sent out within a year to the East in order that homage might be paid to him in person. Frederick replied that he would do what he thought best.[2]

On 23 July 1230, Frederick made his peace with the Pope by the Treaty of San Germano. He had been on the whole victorious in Italy, and he was ready now to make concessions over the control of the Church in Sicily in order to be absolved from his excommunication. His reconciliation with the Papacy strengthened his hand in the East. The Patriarch Gerold was told to lift the interdict from Jerusalem, and was reproved for having laid it without reference to Rome. The Military Orders no longer felt obliged to stand aloof; and the barons could no longer count on ecclesiastical support.[3] The Emperor waited his time. In the autumn of 1231,

---

[1] *Gestes des Chiprois*, pp. 50–76 (Philip of Novara's own account); *Estoire d'Eracles*, II, pp. 375–7. See Hill, *op. cit.* II, pp. 100–7.
[2] *Estoire d'Eracles*, II, p. 380. See La Monte, *Feudal Monarchy*, p. 64 n 1.
[3] Hefele-Leclercq, *op. cit.* pp. 1489–90.

telling the Pope that he must send out an army for the defence of Jerusalem, he collected some 600 knights, 100 sergeants, 700 armed infantrymen and 3000 marines, and dispatched them under his Marshal, the Neapolitan Richard Filangieri, in thirty-two galleys Filangieri was given the title of Imperial Legate.[1]

John of Ibelin was at Acre when an agent of his, who had come from Italy in a ship belonging to the Teutonic Knights, warned him of the approaching armada. He guessed that its first objective would be Cyprus and hastened to collect all his men from Beirut leaving only a small garrison in the castle, and set sail for Cyprus When the Imperial fleet arrived off the coast of Cyprus Filangier learned that John was with King Henry at Kiti and Balian o Ibelin held Limassol. He sent an ambassador to see the King with a message from Frederick telling him to banish the Ibelins and confiscate their lands. Henry replied that John was his uncle and tha in any case he would not dispossess his own vassals. Barlais, who was present and spoke up for Frederick, would have been lynched by the crowd had John not rescued him.

On his ambassador's return Filangieri sailed straight for Beirut The town, which was ungarrisoned, was handed over to him by it timorous bishop; and he began to lay siege to the castle. Leaving it closely invested, he occupied Sidon and Tyre and appeared a Acre. There he summoned a meeting of the High Court and showed it letters from Frederick appointing him as *bailli*. The barons confirmed the appointment, whereupon Filangieri proclaimed the forfeiture of the Ibelin lands. At this all the baron protested. Estates could not be confiscated unless the High Cour to decided, after the owner had had the chance of defending hi case. Filangieri haughtily replied that he was the Emperor's *bailli* and would carry out the Emperor's instructions. So gross a violation of the constitution shocked even such moderates as Balian o

[1] Pope Gregory wrote to Frederick saying that Filangieri must not cal himself Imperial Legate, only Legate for the Emperor in Jerusalem. He recommended Filangieri to the Syrian bishops on those terms (letter of Gregory IX 12 August 1231 in *M.G.H. Epistolae Saeculares*, XIII, 1, p. 363).

Sidon and Odo of Montbéliard, who hitherto had been ready to support the Emperor. The whole of the baronage moved over to John of Ibelin's party. The merchants of Acre, with whom John was popular and who resented Filangieri's high-handed methods, added their support. Most of them, together with a few of the nobles, belonged to a religious fraternity dedicated to St Andrew. Using that as a basis they set up a commune to represent the whole of the local bourgeoisie, under twelve consuls, and they invited John of Ibelin to be their first mayor. But Filangieri was formidable. He had a good army, mainly of Lombards, that he had brought with him. The Teutonic Knights and the Pisan community were his faithful friends. The Patriarch and the Hospital and the Temple held aloof. They none of them cared for Frederick, but since his reconciliation with the Pope they were uncertain where their duty lay.

When news of the attack on Beirut reached Cyprus, John of Ibelin begged King Henry to come with the island's forces to its rescue. The young King agreed and ordered the whole army of the kingdom to set sail. Meanwhile John heard of his election as Mayor of Acre. Though it was risky to leave Cyprus unguarded, John believed that the mainland must first be saved; and, as a precaution, Barlais and his friends were obliged to accompany the expedition. John had hoped to leave Cyprus at Christmas 1231; but, owing to stormy weather, it was not till 25 February that the army could sail from Famagusta. The ships made a swift passage through a great rain-storm and anchored off the little port of Puy du Connétable, just south of Tripoli. There Barlais and his friends, eighty knights in all, secretly landed and went to Tripoli, leaving their equipment behind. Filangieri sent a ship to take them to Beirut. John followed them ashore with most of his men while the Cypriot fleet sailed southward but ran into bad weather off Botrun. A few ships were wrecked and others damaged, and much material lost. When John passed through Jebail, some of the infantry deserted. At last he reached Beirut and fought his way into the castle. Thence he appealed to the barons to rescue him.

Many came, led by his nephew, John of Caesarea. But Balian of Sidon still hoped for a compromise. He hurried to Beirut with his former co-*bailli*, Garnier, with the Patriarch and the Grand Masters of the Hospital and the Temple. But Filangieri refused to consider terms that would leave the Ibelins in possession of their lands, and the negotiators would agree to nothing less.

Having reinforced his garrison at Beirut, John moved to Tyre where he was well received and won many recruits, particularly from the Genoese. He also sent an embassy under his son Balian to Tripoli to arrange for the marriage of King Henry's younger sister Isabella with Bohemond's second son, Henry. But Bohemond had not much faith in the Ibelin cause and treated the embassy with scant courtesy. Filangieri, however, was nervous. He had made his headquarters at Tyre, leaving the command at Beirut to his brother Lothair. He now ordered Lothair to raise the siege and join him at Tyre.

In the meantime Barlais, reinforced by Lombard troops, crossed back to Cyprus and began to overrun the island. One by one the castles fell to him, except for Dieu d'Amour, where the King's sisters took refuge, and Buffavento, the most impregnable of all, to which the lady Eschiva of Montbéliard, King Henry's cousin and Odo's niece, fled disguised as a monk, with ample provisions, and which she held for the King. Her first husband, Walter of Montaigu, had been killed by Barlais's men at the battle of Nicosia, and she had recently married Balian of Ibelin; but as they were cousins the marriage had been kept secret. Balian heard of the invasion when he was at Tripoli from two Genoese sea-captains, who offered help but whose ships were impounded by Bohemond.

At the end of April the Genoese agreed, in return for concessions in Cyprus, to aid the Ibelins in an attack on Filangieri at Tyre. The army moved northwards to Casal Imbert, some twelve miles away. But there John met the Patriarch of Antioch, Albert of Rezzato, who had recently been appointed Papal Legate in the East and had come south to mediate. He had just visited Tyre and heard Filangieri's new terms. John said correctly that they must be given to the High Court, and he rode back to Acre with the Patriarch, taking an escort that seriously depleted his army. Late in the night of 2 May Filangieri, who knew of John's departure and had perhaps even arranged it with the Patriarch, came out with all his forces from Tyre and fell upon the unsuspecting and ill-guarded Ibelin camp. Anselm of Brie, who was in command with the young Ibelin lords, fought with supreme bravery; but the camp was captured. The young King of Cyprus was hurried half-dressed to the safety of Acre. The other survivors took refuge on a hill-top.

Filangieri did not attempt to follow up his victory, but retired with all his booty to Tyre, leaving a contingent to guard the pass of the Ladder of Tyre. John of Ibelin, hearing of the disaster, hastened up from Acre and rescued his sons, but when he tried to catch up with the heavily laden enemy he was held at the pass. He returned to Acre. Meanwhile Filangieri crossed to Cyprus with reinforcements for Barlais. John thereupon confiscated all the ships in the harbour of Acre, while King Henry offered fiefs in Cyprus to local knights and even to Syrian merchants if they would join him, and arranged that the Genoese should give help in return for freedom from tolls and the right to have their own quarters and courts in Nicosia, Famagusta and Paphos. Money was short; but John of Caesarea and the younger John of Ibelin, Philip's son, sold property in Caesarea and Acre to the Templars and the Hospitallers and loaned the 31,000 besants that they raised to the King.

Thus equipped, John and King Henry set sail from Acre on 30 May. They called at Sidon to pick up Balian of Ibelin, on his way from his embassy at Tripoli, and crossed to Famagusta. Filangieri's Lombards were in the town, with over 2000 horsemen, while the Ibelins had only 233. Nevertheless John risked landing his main troops after dark on a rocky islet, just to the south of the harbour. It was unguarded as no one thought that horses could be put ashore there. Then a small detachment in boats forced its way into the harbour, with such loud cries that the Lombards thought a great army to be upon them. They fired their own ships and hastily left the town. In the morning, when the Ibelin army crossed the rocks to the mainland, Famagusta was deserted.

John stayed there long enough for the King to fulfil his promise to the Genoese by signing a treaty with them which allotted them a quarter. Then the army set out for Nicosia. The Lombards had made themselves unpopular on the island by brutal behaviour, and they feared that the peasants would rise against them. As they retired before the Ibelins they burnt all the granaries where the new harvest had just been stored. They decided not to hold Nicosia but moved along the road that goes over the hills to Kyrenia, where they would be in touch with Filangieri himself, who was besieging Dieu d'Amour, and where they would have their rear protected by Kyrenia, which they held. The garrison of Dieu d'Amour was known to be starving and on the point of surrender. If Filangieri could hold his enemies till the castle was in his power, together with the King's two sisters who were within it, he would be in a strong position for bargaining with the King.

The Ibelins moved slowly to Nicosia, suffering from lack of food; but in Nicosia itself they found large stores, overlooked by the Lombards. John was so suspicious of this that he would not camp within the city but led his army on at once on 15 June towards Kyrenia, intending to camp at Agridi, just below the pass. Fearing an attack at any moment it marched in battle array. John's son Balian should have led the vanguard, but he had been excommunicated for marrying his cousin Eschiva, the gallant lady who watched the whole campaign from her eyrie at Buffavento, and his father would not allow him a high command. The first company was therefore commanded by his brother Hugh, with Anselm of Brie. John's third son, Baldwin, commanded the second company, John of Caesarea the third, and John of Ibelin himself the rearguard, with his other sons and the King. They were a small army, so short of horses that the knights' squires had to fight on foot. To the Lombards, looking down from the top of the pass, where the track from Dieu d'Amour joins the road, they seemed contemptible. The order was given to attack them without delay.

The first troop of Lombard horses came thundering down the hill under the command of Walter, Count of Manupello. It passed along the flank of the Ibelin army but could not break its lines, and then it was carried on by the momentum of the charge into the plain below. John forbade his men to pursue them; and the Lombards did not venture to turn and ride up the steep slope, but galloped on eastward, never stopping till they reached Gastria. The second Lombard troop, under Walter's brother Berard, charged straight into the lines commanded by Hugh of Ibelin and Anselm of Brie. But the rough rocky hillside was difficult for the horses. Many stumbled and threw their riders, who were too heavily armed to regain their feet. The Ibelin knights fought mainly on foot, and though outnumbered soon mastered the enemy. Berard of Manupello was killed by Anselm himself. Filangieri, waiting at the head of the pass, had intended to come down to Berard's rescue; but suddenly Balian of Ibelin appeared with a handful of knights, who had ridden up from the rear of the Ibelin army by a mountainous track to the west of the road, and charged into Filangieri's camp. Here again the Lombards had the superiority in numbers, and Balian was hard pressed. His father refused to detach troops for his assistance; but soon Filangieri lost his nerve, finding that Manupello's divisions were not returning, and led his men off in disorder down to Kyrenia.

Dieu d'Amour was relieved, its besiegers fleeing south-westward into the plain, where, when darkness fell, they were surprised and captured by Philip of Novara. Walter of Manupello reached Gastria, but the Templars, who held the castle, refused to admit him, and he was captured, hiding in the fosse, by John, son of Philip of Ibelin. Meanwhile John of Beirut marched on to besiege Filangieri in Kyrenia.

The siege of Kyrenia lasted for ten months. The Ibelins lacked ships at first, whereas Filangieri had a squadron that kept in touch with Tyre. It was not until the Genoese could be induced to help once more that it was possible to blockade the fortress from the sea. Before the blockade was complete, Filangieri fled with

Amalric Barlais, Amalric of Beisan and Hugh of Jebail, going first
to Armenia to try, vainly, to secure aid from King Hethoum, then
to Tyre, and eventually to Italy, to report to the Emperor. The
Lombards in Kyrenia, under Philip Chenart, put up a vigorous
defence. In the course of the fighting the young Ibelin lords were
all of them wounded, and the staunch warrior, Anselm of Brie,
whom John of Beirut nicknamed his 'red lion', was struck by an
iron shaft and died after six months of agony. Amongst the refugees
within Kyrenia was Alice of Montferrat, the Italian princess whom
Frederick had chosen to be the bride of King Henry. She had
been married by proxy and it is doubtful if she had ever seen
her husband, having arrived in Cyprus escorted by the imperialists
after the King had joined the Ibelins. During the siege she was
taken ill and died; and the fighting was interrupted while her corpse,
dressed as became a Queen, was ceremoniously handed over and
borne to Nicosia for a royal burial by the husband who had never
known her living.

Kyrenia surrendered in April 1233. The defenders, with their personal belongings, were allowed to retire to Tyre, and the prisoners
captured by the Ibelins were exchanged for those held by Filangieri
at Tyre. Cyprus was now wholly restored to the rule of Henry and
his Ibelin cousins. The King's loyal vassals were rewarded, and
loans that they had made were repaid.[1] The island entered into
an era of peace, marred only by the attempts of the Latin Church
hierarchy, in spite of the opposition of the lay barons, to suppress
any of the Greek clergy who would not admit their authority or
who would not conform with their usages. The more obstinately
disobedient of the Greek monks were even burnt at the stake.[2]

[1] The long story of the Lombard War is told in detail by Philip of Novara
from a passionately Ibelin standpoint (*Gestes des Chiprois*, pp. 77–117) and at
some length in *Estoire d'Eracles*, pp. 386–402, again from an anti-imperial standpoint. Amadi (pp. 147–82) and Bustron (pp. 80–104) only vary in minor
details. Frederick's chroniclers pay no attention to the episode.

[2] For the ecclesiastical history of Cyprus at this period, see Hill, *op. cit.* III,
pp. 1043–5. There is a narrative account of the martyrdom of thirteen Greeks
at the hands of the Latins in 1231, published in Sathas, Μεσαιωνικὴ Βιβλιοθήκη,
vol. II, pp. 20–39.

Though Cyprus was pacified, Filangieri still held Tyre on the mainland, and Frederick was still legal ruler of Jerusalem for his young son. When Frederick learned, possibly from Filangieri himself, of the failure of his policy, he sent letters to Acre, by the hand of the Bishop of Sidon, who had been visiting Rome, cancelling Filangieri's appointment as *bailli* and appointing in his stead a Syrian noble, Philip of Maugastel. If he had hoped to appease the barons by naming a local lord, he was disappointed; for Maugastel was an effeminate young man whose intimacy with Filangieri had given rise to scandal. And Filangieri was left in possession of Tyre. Kyrenia had not yet been captured when the news of the appointment reached John of Beirut. He at once hurried across to Acre. There Balian of Sidon and Odo of Montbéliard had been prepared to accept Maugastel, and had arranged that oaths should be taken to him in the Church of the Holy Cross, but John of Caesarea rose when the ceremony opened and declared the proceedings illegal. The Emperor could not cancel by his own whim arrangements made before the High Court. An angry dispute began; and John sounded the tocsin of the Commune of Acre, summoning its members to his aid. A furious crowd rushed into the church. It was only John's personal intervention that saved Balian and Odo from death at its hands, while Maugastel fled in terror to Tyre. John was re-elected mayor of the Commune and became in fact the ruler of the kingdom, except for Tyre, which Filangieri ruled in the Emperor's name, and Jerusalem itself, which seems to have been under a direct representative of the Emperor. It is probable that Balian of Sidon remained nominal *bailli*, but in fact the High Court accepted John's leadership till some new legal arrangement should be made. Two envoys, Philip of Troyes and Henry of Nazareth, were sent to Rome to explain the barons' and the Commune's actions; but Hermann of Salza, the Grand Master of the Teutonic Order, who was there, saw that they were not given a fair hearing. The Pope was still on good terms with Frederick and was anxious to restore his authority in the East. In 1235 he sent the Archbishop of Ravenna as his Legate to Acre, but the Archbishop only recommended that Filangieri's authority should be obeyed; which was unacceptable. The barons in return sent a jurist, Geoffrey Le Tor, to Rome. Pope Gregory was beginning to quarrel with the Emperor again, but was determined to act correctly. In February 1236, he wrote to Frederick and to the barons, saying that Filangieri must be accepted as *bailli*, but that Odo of Montbéliard should assist him till September, when Bohemond of Antioch should be appointed *bailli*. As Frederick and Conrad were legal rulers, the barons had acted wrongly, but all should be forgiven except the Ibelins, who must stand trial before the High Court. The Commune of Acre must be dissolved.[1]

These terms were unacceptable to the barons and the Commune, who ignored them. At this juncture John of Ibelin died, as the result of a riding accident. The Old Lord of Beirut, as his contemporaries called him, had been the dominant figure of the Frankish East. Of his high personal qualities no one could have any doubt. He was courageous, honourable and correct, and his blameless character did much to strengthen the barons' cause.[2] But for him Frederick might well have succeeded in establishing an autocracy in both Cyprus and the Syrian kingdom; and, though the barons' government tended to be haphazard, it is hard to see how autocratic rule would have been an improvement. Frederick himself was too far away to control it; and he was a bad judge of men. Absolutist government in the hands of a man such as Richard Filangieri would have soon brought disaster. The better solution was what the Pope himself recommended, the union of the mainland government with Cyprus.[3] But the legalism of the barons which made them oppose the autocracy of Frederick would not allow them to have any king other than their lawful sovereign, his son Conrad. Union with Cyprus must wait till it should be authorized by the hand of God. The barons' attitude was consistent and correct. But in the meantime it legalized anarchy.

[1] *Estoire d'Eracles*, II, pp. 406–7; *Gestes des Chiprois*, pp. 112–13.
[2] See above, p. 181 and note 1.
[3] The Pope suggested to Geoffrey Le Tor that the mainland should accept the authority of the Cypriot King (*Estoire d'Eracles*, II, p. 407).

CHAPTER IV

LEGALIZED ANARCHY

'The law made nothing perfect.'   HEBREWS VII, 19

The death of the Old Lord of Beirut deprived Outremer of its natural leader. No other Frankish baron was ever to enjoy again such a high prestige. But he had fulfilled his rôle. He had founded an alliance between the baronage and the Commune of Acre, and he had given them a common policy based on their legal rights. Of his four sons two remained on the Syrian mainland, Balian, who succeeded to Beirut, and John, who inherited his mother's fief of Arsuf, and two took over the family estates in Cyprus, both making politic marriages that reunited the nobility of the kingdom; Baldwin, who became Seneschal, married the sister of Amalric of Beisan, and Guy, who became Constable, the daughter and heiress of the arch-rebel, Amalric Barlais. The Old Lord's nephew, another John, later to become Count of Jaffa, and the author of the *Assizes of Jerusalem*, was the leading lawyer in the kingdom. Their cousin, Balian of Sidon, still acted as *bailli*, together with Odo of Mont-béliard, but the failure of his policy of compromise had lessened his authority. The most vigorous among the barons was another cousin, Philip of Montfort, son of Helvis of Ibelin and her second husband, Guy of Montfort, brother of that Simon who led the Albigensian Crusade. Philip had recently married the Armenian Princess Maria, daughter of Raymond-Roupen, who was heiress of Toron through her great-grandmother, sister of its last lord. Yet another cousin, John of Caesarea, son of Margaret of Ibelin, completed the family party that now dominated Outremer. It was a tribute to the Old Lord's posthumous reputation that his sons and nephews were ready to work together in amity; and they were further united by their hatred of Filangieri, who still held Tyre for the Emperor.[1]

Even so, the position of Outremer was precarious. Bohemond IV, Prince of Antioch and Count of Tripoli, had died in March 1233, reconciled at last with the Church. During the wars between the Imperialists and the barons of Outremer he had shown a remarkable suppleness. He had at first welcomed Frederick, chiefly from his dislike of the Ibelins, who had opposed the appointment of his son Bohemond, the husband of Queen Alice, to the regency of Cyprus. Then, fearing Frederick's ambition, he had changed his policy, and, when Alice and the young Bohemond were divorced for consanguinity, willingly agreed to a suggestion by John of Ibelin that his youngest son, Henry, should marry Isabella of Cyprus, King Henry's eldest sister, a marriage that was eventually to put a Prince of Antioch on the Cypriot throne. But at that moment Filangieri won the battle of Casal Imbert; so Bohemond prevaricated, wishing to be on the victor's side. It was only after the Imperialists' defeat in Cyprus that the marriage took place.[2] About the same time Bohemond reconciled himself with the Hospitallers. Their common dislike of the Emperor Frederick had made the Temple and the Hospital co-operate for a while, and he could not play off the one against the other. He therefore made his own submission to the Church and asked Gerold, Patriarch of Jerusalem, to negotiate with the Hospital for him. In return for large rents on property in the cites of Antioch and Tripoli, the Order agreed to abandon its claim to the privileges promised it by Raymond-Roupen and to recognize Bohemond's feudal rights. At the same time Gerold lifted the sentence of excommunication against him, and sent to Rome to have the settlement confirmed; the Pope's approval came a few weeks after Bohemond's death.[3]

[1] For the Ibelin family and its cousins, see genealogical tree, Appendix III below, based on *Lignages d'Outremer*.

[2] Amadi, pp. 123–4 (for Alice's divorce) and *Gestes des Chiprois*, pp. 86–7; *Estoire d'Eracles*, II, p. 360 (for Isabella's marriage).

[3] Röhricht, *Regesta Regni Hierosolymitani*, pp. 269–70. See Cahen, *La Syrie du Nord*, pp. 642–3.

For all his faults, Bohemond IV had been a vigorous ruler; and even his enemies admired his culture and his learning as a lawyer. His son, Bohemond V, was a feebler man. He was a good son of the Church, and allowed the Pope, Gregory IX, to choose him his second wife, Lucienne of Segni, who was of the Pope's family.[1] A few years later, in 1244, profiting from his father's experience, he obtained from Rome a guarantee that he could only be excommunicated by the Pope in person.[2] But he was not master in his own principality. Antioch itself was governed by its Commune, with which he did not enjoy his father's popularity, probably because his friendship with Rome displeased the strong Greek element there. He preferred therefore to reside at his second capital, Tripoli. He had no control over the Military Orders. Armenia, under the Hethoumians, was unfriendly. The Moslem enclave of Lattakieh cut his dominions in two. His reign marks a rapid decline.[3]

Frederick, who was annoyed at the time with Bohemond IV, had excluded Antioch and Tripoli from his peace treaty with al-Kamil. Bohemond had, however, kept the peace with his Moslem neighbours, apart from some desultory attacks on the Assassins, whom he disliked as the allies of the Hospital. Much to his disapproval, the Military Orders were more incautious. The Hospitallers had provoked al-Kamil to make a raid against Krak when he was attacking Damascus in 1228. In 1229 they made a counterraid on Barin; and in 1230 they combined with the Templars of Tortosa to make an attack on Hama, where they were caught in ambush and severely defeated. Next year the Orders made a sudden swoop on Jabala, only to hold it for a few weeks. A truce was at last made in the spring of 1231, which lasted for two years.[4]

[1] Estoire d'Eracles, II, p. 408. Lucienne was Innocent III's great-niece and therefore a cousin of Gregory IX.

[2] Innocent IV, Registres, 418 (ed. Berger), I, p. 75.

[3] See Cahen, op. cit. pp. 650–2, 664–6; Rey, Histoire des Princes d'Antioche, p. 400.

[4] Ibn al-Athir, II, p. 180. See Cahen, op. cit. p. 642 nn. 6, 7 for manuscript sources.

Soon after his accession, Bohemond V sent his brother Henry, together with contingents from Acre and Cyprus, to help the Orders in another attack on Barin, which was bought off by the promise of a tribute to be paid by Hama to the Hospital. The renewed truce lasted till 1237, when the Templars of Baghras fell upon the unsuspecting Turcoman tribes settled east of the Lake of Antioch. In revenge the army of Aleppo moved in force to besiege Baghras, which was only rescued by the arrival of Bohemond himself, who arranged to renew the truce. The Preceptor of the Temple at Antioch, William of Montferrat, resented this humiliation, and, against Bohemond's expressed wishes, decided to break the truce almost as soon as it was made. In June that year he induced his own knights, together with the lord of Jebail and a few other lay barons, to attack the castle of Darbsaq, to the north of Baghras. The garrison there was taken by surprise, but put up a strong resistance, while messengers hastened to Aleppo whose governor at once dispatched a powerful army. Some Christian captives in Darbsaq, hearing of the relieving force, managed to send a message to William to urge him to retire. He arrogantly ignored the warning, only to find the Moslem cavalry upon him. His small force was routed, he himself slain and most of his comrades captured. On the news of the disaster both the Temple and the Hospital wrote anxiously to the West for succour; but the Moslems did not follow up their victory. After receiving the promise of ample sums of money for the ransom of their prisoners they agreed to renew the truce. The Orders were abashed, and they kept the peace for ten years, with the approval of the Pope, who had been obliged to provide most of the ransom money.[1]

The lack of aggressive spirit fortunately shown by the Moslems was largely due to the personality of the great Sultan al-Kamil. Al-Kamil was a man of peace and honour. He was ready to fight and to indulge in unscrupulous intrigue in order to unite the Ayubite dominions under his rule; for the family quarrels and

---

[1] *Estoire d'Eracles*, II, pp. 403–5; *Annales de Terre Sainte*, p. 436; Kemal ad-Din, trans. Blochet, pp. 85, 95–6; Abu'l Feda, pp. 110–12.

divisions were to no one's advantage; and he was ready to ward off attacks from the Seldjuk or the Khwarismian Turks. But so long as the Christians caused no trouble, he would leave them in quiet. All the Moslem princes were well aware of the commercial advantages of having the Frankish sea-ports close to their borders. They were unwilling to risk the dislocation of the great trade between the East and West by imprudent hostilities. Al-Kamil in particular was anxious to secure his subjects' material prosperity. He was moreover, like his friend Frederick II, a man of wide intellectual interests and curiosity; and he was more genuinely tolerant and far more kindly than the Hohenstaufen. Though he lacked the heroic grandeur of his uncle Saladin and the brilliant subtlety of his father al-Adil, he had more human warmth than either. And he was an able King. Moslem contemporaries might deplore his liking for the 'blond men', but they respected the justice and good order of his government.[1]

Al-Kamil succeeded in his ambition to restore unity to the Ayubite world. In June 1229, his brother al-Ashraf at last managed to oust their nephew, an-Nasir, from Damascus. An-Nasir was given as compensation a kingdom in the Jordan valley and Transjordan, with Kerak as its capital, to hold under al-Kamil's effective suzerainty. Al-Ashraf kept Damascus, but acknowledged al-Kamil's hegemony and ceded to him lands in the Jezireh and along the middle Euphrates. These were the provinces of the Ayubite Empire that were most open to attack; and al-Kamil wished to have a more direct control of them. Jelal ad-Din the Khwarismian was a very positive menace; and behind him to the east was the unknown strength of the Mongols, while the great Seldjuk Sultan Kaikobad was pressing eastward from Anatolia. In 1230, when al-Ashraf was at Damascus, Jelal ad-Din captured his great fortress of Akhlat, near Lake Van, and moved on to attack the Seldjuks. Al-Ashraf hastened northward and made an alliance with Kaikobad. The allies decisively beat Jelal ad-Din near

[1] For al-Kamil, see Abu'l Feda's eulogy, p. 114, and Ibn Khallikan, III, pp. 241–2.

Erzinjan. Attacked at the same time in the rear by the Mongols, the Khwarismian Empire began to disintegrate. Next year Jelal ad-Din was defeated in person by the Moslems. During his flight from the battle he was murdered on 15 August 1231 by a Kurdish peasant, whose brother he had long ago slain.[1]

His elimination upset once more the balance of power. The Seldjuks were left without a rival in eastern Anatolia, and the Mongols could advance freely westward. Meanwhile the Abbasid Caliphate of Baghdad enjoyed a few, rare, precarious months of independence. It was not long before Kaikobad cast his eye on al-Kamil's lands on the middle Euphrates. From 1233 to 1235 there was continual war while Edessa, Saruj and other towns of the province passed from one master to the other, till at last al-Kamil re-established his position. Al-Kamil's successes roused his relatives' jealousy. Al-Ashraf disliked his subservient position. At Aleppo the young King al-Aziz, az-Zahir's son, suddenly died in 1236, and his mother Dhaifa, al-Kamil's sister, who took over the regency for her young grandson, az-Zahir II, feared her brother's ambition. A number of minor Ayubite princes shared her fears. During the early months of 1237 al-Ashraf assembled his allies and secured the active help of Kaikobad. A civil war seemed inevitable when, early in the summer, Kaikobad died, and al-Ashraf fell dangerously ill. His death on 27 August dissolved the conspiracy. A younger brother, as-Salih Ismail, took over Damascus and tried to reunite the conspirators, in vain. With the aid of an-Nasir of Kerak, al-Kamil marched on Damascus in January 1238, and annexed it. As-Salih Ismail was compensated with an appanage at Baalbek. But al-Kamil did not long survive his triumph. Two months later, on 8 March, he died at Damascus, aged sixty.[2]

His death let loose civil war. His elder son, as-Salih Ayub, whose mother was a Sudanese slave, was in the north, but marched at

---

[1] Ibn Khallikan, III, pp. 242, 488–9; Ibn al-Athir, II, pp. 176–8; Maqrisi, X, pp. 250–2. See Cahen, *op. cit.* pp. 644–6 and notes (for manuscript references).
[2] Ibn Khallikan, III, pp. 242–4; Kemal ad-Din, trans. Blochet, pp. 88–99. See Cahen, *op. cit.* pp. 645–6.

once on Damascus, where one of al-Kamil's nephews, al-Jawad, had seized power. With the help of Khwarismian freebooters he dislodged his cousin. Meanwhile his younger brother, al-Adil II, was installed as Sultan in Egypt. Ayub was determined to have his father's richest province, but when he set out to invade Egypt a sudden *coup d'état* in Damascus dethroned him in favour of his uncle as-Salih Ismail. As Ayub fled southward he fell into the hands of an-Nasir of Kerak, who, however, joined his cause and lent his troops for the invasion of Egypt. It was an easy task; for al-Adil offended his ministers by entrusting the government to a young negro whom he adored. A successful plot deposed him in June 1240; and Ayub was invited to take over the Egyptian throne. An-Nasir was rewarded with the post of military governor of Palestine. But Ismail remained master of Damascus; and for the next decade the Ayubite world was torn by the rivalry between uncle and nephew. The north was soon in chaos. Leaderless Khwarismians roamed ravaging through northern Syria, nominally under the orders of Ayub. In the Jezireh the Ayubite prince of Mayyafaraqin, al-Muzaffar, kept small authority. Ayub's son, Turanshah, attempted to hold his grandfather's lands together, but many of the towns fell into the hands of the Seldjuk Sultan, Kaikhosrau II. In Aleppo an-Nasir Yusuf, who had succeeded his brother in 1236, remained on the defensive, while the princes of Hama and Homs were fully occupied in warding off the Khwarismians.[1]

It was in the midst of these convulsions that the treaty made between Frederick II and al-Kamil came to an end. In preparation for this, Pope Gregory IX had sent out in the summer of 1239 agents to preach the Crusade in France and England. Neither the French nor the English King felt ready to respond in person to his appeal, but they gave every encouragement to the preachers. By the early summer a distinguished company of French nobles was

[1] For this confused history see Ibn Khallikan, II, pp. 445–6, III, pp. 245–6; Maqrisi, x, pp. 297–330; Kemal ad-Din (trans. Blochet), *loc. cit.* See Cahen, *op. cit.* pp. 646–9.

ready to sail for the East. At their head was Tibald of Champagne, King of Navarre, the nephew of Henry of Champagne and cousin therefore to the Kings of France, England and Cyprus. With him were the Duke of Burgundy, Hugh IV, Peter Mauclerc, Count of Brittany, the Counts of Bar, Nevers, Montfort, Joigny and Sancerre, and many lesser lords. The number of infantrymen was less than might have been expected, considering the eminence of the leaders; but the whole expedition was formidable.[1]

Tibald had hoped to embark with his comrades at Brindisi; but wars between the Emperor and the Pope made travel through Italy difficult; and the Emperor, in whose dominions Brindisi lay, was not pleased by the Crusade. He considered himself ruler of Palestine for his young son, and an expedition to help his kingdom should have been organized under his authority. He could not approve of French nobles whose instinct would certainly be to support the barons of Outremer against him. Moreover, aware of the position in the Moslem world, he hoped to drive a good bargain for the kingdom by diplomacy. The coming of these rash impatient knights would ruin any such negotiations. But, owing to his troubles in Italy he could not afford to send men himself to control them. He secured a promise that nothing would be done till the truce came to an end in August, then dissociated himself from the whole affair. The Crusaders were therefore obliged to embark from Aigues-Mortes and Marseilles.[2]

The Crusade had a stormy voyage through the Mediterranean, some of its ships being driven to Cyprus and some even back to Sicily. But Tibald himself arrived at Acre on 1 September; and during the next few days an army of about a thousand knights had assembled there. A Council was held at once to decide how best this army could be used. Besides the visiting princes the chief local barons were present, with representatives from the Military Orders,

[1] *Estoire d'Eracles*, II, pp. 413–14; *Gestes des Chiprois*, p. 118; Gregory IX letter, in Potthast, *Regesta*, I, p. 906.

[2] *Estoire d'Eracles*, II, *loc. cit.*; *MS. of Rothelin*, p. 528; Gregory IX, letter, in Potthast, *op. cit.* I, p. 910.

while the Archbishop of Tyre, Peter of Sargines, deputized for the Patriarch of Jerusalem. It was a moment for diplomatic enterprise. The quarrels between al-Kamil's heirs offered to the Christians the opportunity of using their new strength as a bargaining point and to obtain handsome concessions from one or other of the warring factions. But the Crusaders had come to fight; they would not follow Frederick II's disgraceful example. The local barons therefore recommended an expedition against Egypt. This would not only cause no offence to their immediate Moslem neighbours in Syria, but in view of the Sultan al-Adil's known unpopularity promised a good chance of success. Others maintained that Damascus was the enemy; the army should fortify the Galilean castles, then march on against the Syrian capital. But Tibald desired a plurality of victories. He decided that the army would first attack the Egyptian outposts of Ascalon and Gaza, probably on the suggestion of the Count of Jaffa, Walter of Brienne, who did not belong to the Ibelin family faction; then, when the southern frontier was secure, he would attack Damascus. On the news of his decision messengers hurried round the Ayubite Courts, to arrange a temporary armistice between the Moslem princes.[1]

The expedition set out from Acre for the Egyptian frontier on 2 November, detachments from the Orders and several local barons accompanying the Crusaders. As they were marching to Jaffa a spy told Peter of Brittany that a rich Moslem caravan was moving up the Jordan valley towards Damascus. Peter at once rode out with Ralph of Soissons and two hundred knights and laid an ambush for it. The caravan was well armed, and in the ensuing battle Peter was nearly killed; but in the end the Moslem soldiers fled, leaving a great herd of cattle and sheep in the Christians' hands. Peter drove his booty back in triumph to Jaffa, where his colleagues had now arrived. As food for the army was running short, his victory was very welcome. But it made an enemy of an-Nasir of Kerak.[2]

---

[1] *MS. of Rothelin*, pp. 531–2; *Estoire d'Eracles*, II, pp. 413–14.
[2] *MS. of Rothelin*, pp. 533–6.

P

An Egyptian army, under the Mameluk Rukn ad-Din, had hastily been sent from the Delta to Gaza. The first news that reached the Christians of its arrival told of only a thousand men. Henry of Bar, who was jealous of the Count of Brittany's success, determined at once to attack it and secure all the credit and the loot. He kept his plan secret from all but a few friends, such as the Duke of Burgundy and various lords from eastern France. Then the two *baillis* of the kingdom, Balian of Sidon and Odo of Montbéliard, who were resentful of Tibald's command, together with Walter of Jaffa and one of the Ibelins, John of Arsuf, were admitted into the company. At nightfall on 12 November, the whole party, five hundred horsemen and over a thousand foot, prepared to march out against Gaza. But the news leaked out; and as they were mounting their horses King Tibald, with the three Grand Masters of the Orders and the Count of Brittany, came up and first begged, then ordered them to go back to the camp. But Henry of Bar refused to be deflected. Accusing the King and his friends of cowardice, he defied his command; and the cavalcade set out into the moonlit night. Tibald, who suspected the true strength of the enemy, was powerless to prevent it. Next morning he moved his camp up to the walls of Ascalon, to be at hand, should help be needed.

The Count of Bar was so confident of success that when he drew near to Gaza about dawn, he halted his men in a hollow in the dunes of the seashore and told them to rest awhile. But the Egyptian army was far larger than he knew, and its spies were all around. The emir Rukn ad-Din could scarcely believe that his foes could be so foolish. He sent bowmen to creep round sandhills till the Franks were almost encircled. Walter of Jaffa was the first to realize what was happening. He advised a swift retreat, for the horses could not be manoeuvred in the deep sand. He himself rode away to the north, along with the Duke of Burgundy; and the other knights from Outremer followed him as soon as they could. But Henry of Bar would not leave the infantry whom he had led into the trap; and his closest friends stayed with him. The battle was soon over. With their horses and their heavy infantry floundering in the dunes, the Franks were impotent. More than a thousand were slain, including Count Henry himself. Six hundred more were captured and carried off to Egypt. Among them was the Count of Montfort and the poet, Philip of Nanteuil, who spent his days in prison writing rhymed maledictions on the Orders, whom, with more passion than logic, he blamed for the failure of the senseless expedition.

When the fugitives reached Ascalon, Tibald forgot his caution and wished to march on Gaza at once to rescue his comrades. But the knights of Outremer would not agree. It would be folly to risk the army, and certainly the Moslems would slay what captives they had taken rather than lose them again. Tibald was angry and never quite forgave his hosts. But there was nothing to be done. The diminished army moved slowly back to Acre.[1]

Meanwhile an-Nasir of Kerak replied to the Breton attack on the Moslem caravan by marching on Jerusalem. The Holy City was undefended except for the section of wall by St Stephen's Gate, which Frederick had begun, and a citadel incorporating the Tower of David, which had recently been strengthened. It owed allegiance not to the government at Acre but to Filangieri at Tyre; and he had neglected to supply an adequate garrison. An-Nasir occupied the city without difficulty, but the soldiers in the citadel held out for twenty-seven days, till their supplies were exhausted. They surrendered on 7 December in return for a safe-conduct to the coast. When he had destroyed the fortifications, including the Tower of David, an-Nasir retired to Kerak.[2]

---

[1] *MS. of Rothelin*, pp. 537–50 (a full and vivid account); *Gestes des Chiprois*, pp. 118–20; *Estoire d'Eracles*, II, pp. 414–15; Abu Shama, II, p. 193; Maqrisi, X, p. 324 (a textual error over the date). Philip's poems are quoted in Rothelin, pp. 548–9.

[2] *MS. of Rothelin*, pp. 529–31, placing it before the battle of Gaza, but only giving the date of the year; Maqrisi, X, pp. 323–4, giving 7 December as date of surrender, i.e. after the battle of Gaza; Abu'l Feda, giving the same date; al-Aïni, pp. 196–7, giving only the date of the year. We may accept Maqrisi's date.

After the disaster at Gaza, Tibald moved his forces northward to Tripoli. An envoy had come from the emir of Hama, al-Muzaffar II, who had quarrelled with all his Ayubite relatives and was threatened by a coalition between the Regent of Aleppo and the Prince of Homs. In return for Frankish help he offered to cede one or two fortresses and held out hopes of his conversion to Christianity. Tibald accepted the offer with alacrity; but his advance to Tripoli was enough to deter al-Muzaffar's enemies, and the emir sent politely to say that his services would not be required after all.[1]

It was while the Crusade lingered at Tripoli that Ayub made himself master of Egypt, and war broke out between him and Ismail of Damascus. It was obvious that the Franks could now make a good bargain. Tibald hastily returned to the south and encamped his army in Galilee by the fountains of Sephoria. He had not long to wait. Early in the summer of 1240 Ismail, terrified of an invasion by Ayub and an-Nasir in conjunction, proposed a defensive alliance with the Franks. If they would guarantee to guard the Egyptian frontier by the coast and supply him with armaments, he would cede to them the great fortresses of Beaufort and Safed, and the hills that lay between them. The Templars, who now had financial connections in Damascus, conducted the negotiations and were rewarded with the possession of Safed. But Ismail's subjects were shocked. The garrison of Beaufort refused to hand over their trust to Balian of Sidon, son of its last Christian lord, and Ismail was obliged to go himself to blockade the castle into submission. Two of the leading Damascene theologians, including the chief preacher at the Great Mosque, left the city in disgust and sought refuge at Cairo.[2]

A common distrust of the Emperor Frederick had kept the

---

[1] Abu'l Feda, pp. 115–19 (he was a grandson of al-Muzaffar II); Kemal ad-Din, trans. Blochet, pp. 98, 100, 104; *Estoire d'Eracles*, II, p. 416; *Gestes des Chiprois*, pp. 120–1.

[2] *Estoire d'Eracles*, II, pp. 417–18; *MS. of Rothelin*, pp. 551–3; *Gestes des Chiprois*, p. 12; Abu'l Feda, *loc. cit.*; Maqrisi, x, p. 340; Abu Shama, II, p. 193.

Hospital and the Temple in an uneasy alliance for the last twelve years. But the Templars' acquisition of Safed was more than the Hospitallers could endure. While Tibald took his army to join up with Ismail's forces, between Jaffa and Ascalon, they opened negotiations with Ayub. Their argument was strengthened when half of Ismail's men, disliking to have to work with Christians, deserted to the Egyptian camp, and the allies were obliged to retreat. Ayub, whose first objective was the defeat of Ismail, was delighted to have an opportunity of breaking the alliance. He offered the Franks the release of the prisoners made at Gaza and the right to occupy and fortify Ascalon in return for their neutrality. The Grand Master of the Hospital then signed the agreement at Ascalon with the Sultan's representative. It was a diplomatic triumph for Ayub, who at small cost to himself had broken an alliance which Ismail had humiliated himself to achieve. Tibald, delighted to secure the release of Amalric of Montfort and his other friends, had given his support to the Hospitallers; but public opinion in Outremer was shocked by the shameless abandonment of the pact with Damascus, which, till Saladin's day, had been the traditional ally of the Christians. So unpopular did Tibald become that he decided to return to Europe. After paying a hurried pilgrimage to Jerusalem he sailed from Acre at the end of September 1240. Most of his comrades followed him, except for the Duke of Burgundy who swore to await the completion of the fortifications of Ascalon, and the Count of Nevers who joined the party of the Templars and the local barons, with whom he encamped near Jaffa, vowing to maintain the treaty with Damascus and to oppose any Egyptian invasion.

Tibald's Crusade had not been entirely valueless. Beaufort, Safed and Ascalon had all been recovered for the Christians. But the Moslems had noted one more example of the perfidy of the Franks.[1]

On 11 October, a few days after Tibald's departure, a still more

---

[1] *Estoire d'Eracles*, II, pp. 419–20; *MS. of Rothelin*, pp. 553–5; *Gestes des Chiprois*, pp. 121–2; Maqrisi, X, p. 342.

distinguished pilgrim arrived at Acre. Richard, Earl of Cornwall, was the brother of Henry III of England, and his sister was the wife of the Emperor Frederick. He was aged thirty-one and was considered to be one of the ablest princes of his time. His pilgrimage had the full approval of the Emperor, who gave him powers to make what arrangements he thought best for the kingdom.[1] He was horrified at the anarchy that he found on his arrival. The Temple and the Hospital were almost at open warfare with each other. The local barons, except for Walter of Jaffa, supported the Templars; therefore the Hospitallers were beginning to seek the friendship of Filangieri and the Imperialists. The Teutonic Order kept itself apart. It garrisoned its Syrian castles but devoted its main attention to Cilicia, where the Armenian King entrusted it with large estates. Filangieri himself still held Tyre and was responsible for the administration of Jerusalem.[2]

On his arrival Richard hurried to Ascalon. There he was met by ambassadors from the Egyptian Sultan, who asked him to confirm the treaty made by the Hospitallers. Richard agreed, but, to placate the barons of Outremer, he insisted that the Egyptians should confirm the cessions of territory made by Ismail of Damascus and should add to it the remainder of Galilee, including Belvoir, Mount Thabor and Tiberias. Ismail, who had lost control of Eastern Galilee to an-Nasir, could not prevent this further cession. Meanwhile the Frankish prisoners captured at Gaza were returned, in exchange for the few Moslems that were in Christian hands. The kingdom thus recovered all its ancient lands west of the Jordan, as far south as the outskirts of Gaza, with the ominous

[1] For Richard and his Crusade see Powicke, *King Henry III and the Lord Edward*, I, pp. 197–200. The Pope had urged Richard to abandon his Crusade and give the money instead to the protection of the Latin Empire of Constantinople (see *ibid.* p. 197 n. 2).

[2] Richard's letter in Matthew Paris, *Chronica Majora*, IV, p. 139. Richard himself stayed at the Hospital at Acre (*Gestes des Chiprois*, p. 123). For the Teutonic Order in Cilicia see Strehlke, *Tabulae Ordinis Theutonici*, pp. 37–40, 65–6, 126–7. *Gestes des Chiprois*, loc. cit. for Frederick's control of Jerusalem through his appointed agent Pennenpié.

exception of Nablus and the province of Samaria. Jerusalem remained unfortified; but Odo of Montbéliard, whose wife was the heiress of the Princes of Galilee, began to rebuild the castle of Tiberias; and the work on Ascalon was completed. As governor of Ascalon, Richard appointed Walter Pennenpié, who had been Filangieri's representative at Jerusalem. Probably on Richard's suggestion, the Emperor Frederick sent a congratulatory embassy to the Sultan Ayub. His two ambassadors were received with great honour and pomp at Cairo and remained there till the early spring.

Richard himself stayed in Palestine till May 1241. He had behaved with great wisdom and tact and had made himself generally accepted as temporary viceroy of the kingdom. The Emperor was well satisfied with him, and everyone in Outremer regretted his going. He returned to Europe, to a career of high hopes and small fulfilment.[1]

The order established by Richard of Cornwall did not long survive his departure. The local barons hoped to continue it by petitioning the Emperor to appoint one of his companions, Simon of Montfort, as *bailli*. Simon, whose wife was Richard's sister, and who himself was the cousin of the lord of Toron, had made an excellent impression. But Frederick ignored their request; and Simon returned to a great and stormy career in England.[2] In the Holy Land quarrels soon began again. The Templars refused to be bound by his treaty with Ayub and in the spring of 1242 raided the Moslem city of Hebron. An-Nasir of Kerak retorted by sending troops to cut off the road to Jerusalem and to levy tolls on the pilgrims and merchants that passed by. This roused the Templars

---

[1] Richard's letter in Matthew Paris, IV, pp. 139–45; *Estoire d'Eracles*, II, pp. 421–2; *MS. of Rothelin*, pp. 555–6; *Gestes des Chiprois*, pp. 123–4. It is not clear whether Tibald had already made a treaty with Egypt, which Richard confirmed (as *Gestes* implies, but the passage may be an interpolation) or whether Richard completed negotiations started by Tibald. See also *Histoire des Patriarches d'Alexandrie*, pp. 342–6.

[2] Röhricht, *Regesta*, p. 286. The letter is dated 7 May 1241. Simon's brother Amalric was one of the prisoners recently released from Egypt.

to set out from Jaffa and to fall on Nablus on 30 October and sack it, burning its great mosque and massacring many of the inhabitants, including large numbers of native Christians. Ayub was not yet ready for a war. He contented himself by sending a strong army to blockade Jaffa for a while, as a warning for the future.[1] Within the kingdom there was no overriding authority. The Orders behaved as independent republics. Acre was ruled by the Commune, which, however, could not prevent the Templars and Hospitallers from fighting with each other in the streets. The barons kept to their fiefs, ruling them as they pleased.

To Filangieri in Tyre the chaos seemed full of promise. He was privately in touch with the Hospital in Acre and he won over two of the leading bourgeois, John Valin and William of Conches. One night, in the spring of 1243, he came from Tyre and was admitted secretly into Acre, ready to organize a *coup d'état*. But his presence was noticed, and Philip of Montfort, lord of Toron, who happened to be in Acre, was informed. Philip at once warned the Commune and the Genoese and Venetian colonies. Their officials arrested John Valin and William of Conches, and policed the streets. A message was sent to bring Balian of Ibelin from Beirut and Odo of Montbéliard from Caesarea. Filangieri realized that he had missed his chance, and slipped quietly back to Tyre. The complicity of the Hospitallers was obvious. Balian, when he arrived, blockaded their headquarters in Acre. The blockade lasted for six months. The Grand Master, Peter of Vieille Bride, was at Marqab, conducting a desultory campaign against his Moslem neighbours. He could not afford men to try to rescue his knights at Acre. In the end he made his peace with Balian, offering apologies and swearing that he had no hand in the plot.[2]

On 5 April 1243, Conrad of Hohenstaufen, son of the Emperor

---

[1] *Histoire des Patriarches*, pp. 350–1; Matthew Paris, IV, p. 197. There may also have been a battle near Gaza in 1242 to which Maqrisi (X, pp. 342, 348) twice refers. See Stevenson, *Crusaders in the East*, p. 321 n. 1.

[2] *Gestes des Chiprois*, pp. 124–7; *Estoire d'Eracles*, II, p. 422; *Annales de Terre Sainte*, p. 441, misdating the episode 1243; Richard of San Germano, p. 382, talks of a 'rebellion' in Acre against the Emperor in October 1241.

Frederick and Queen Yolanda, was fifteen years old and officially came of age. It was his duty to appear at Acre and personally take possession of the kingdom. His father had no longer any right to the regency. But, though the young King at once sent Thomas of Acerra as his deputy, he showed no signs of coming himself to the East. The barons therefore considered it their legal obligation to nominate as his regent the next available heir. This was Alice, Queen-Dowager of Cyprus, his great-aunt. After her divorce from Bohemond V, Alice had reconciled herself with her Ibelin cousins, and in 1240, with their approval, she had married Ralph, Count of Soissons, a young man about half her age, who had come to the East with King Tibald. A parliament was summoned by Balian of Ibelin and Philip of Montfort to meet at Acre, in the Patriarch's palace, on 5 June 1243. The barons were all present. The Church was represented by Peter of Sargines, Archbishop of Tyre, and the bishops of the kingdom. The Commune sent its officials, and the Genoese and the Venetian colonies their presidents. Philip of Novara expounded the juridical situation and recommended that no homage should be paid to King Conrad till he came in person to receive it, and that, till he came, Alice and her husband should be entrusted with the regency. Odo of Montbéliard suggested that Conrad should be officially requested to visit his kingdom and nothing be done till he replied. But the Ibelins saw no point in that. Their view prevailed. The assembly swore oaths of allegiance to Alice and Ralph, saving King Conrad's rights.[1]

The decision removed from Filangieri the vestige of authority that had made the barons hesitate to attack him in Tyre. On the appointment of Thomas of Acerra, he himself had just been summoned back to Italy by the Emperor; and he had left his city under

---

[1] *Gestes des Chiprois*, pp. 128–30 (account by Philip of Novara, who claimed to have organized the affair); *Estoire d'Eracles*, II, p. 240; Amadi, pp. 190–1; *Assises*, II, p. 399; Tafel-Thomas, *Urkunden*, II, pp. 351–89 (an account written by a Venetian eyewitness, Marsiglio Giorgio). Philip says that the Pisans were represented, which is improbable in view of their friendship with the Emperor and is not mentioned elsewhere. See La Monte, *Feudal Monarchy*, pp. 71–3.

the command of his brother Lothair. On 9 June Lothair was ordered by the parliament at Acre to surrender Tyre to the Regents. On his refusal Balian of Ibelin and Philip of Montfort, with contingents from the Venetians and the Genoese, marched on the city. Lothair put his faith in the great walls, which had successfully defied Saladin himself. But the local citizens were weary of Filangieri, and offered to open the postern of the Butchers, close by the sea. On the night of 12 June Balian and his men crept round over the rocks to the postern and were let in. They then opened the main gates to their allies. Once they had occupied the houses of the Hospitallers and the Teutonic Knights, the city was theirs, except for the citadel, on the south, to which Lothair retired. It was a formidable fortress; and for four weeks the Imperialists held out. But by an unlucky chance the ship that was carrying Richard Filangieri to Italy was forced by bad weather to turn back. Richard landed unsuspecting at the port of Tyre and fell straight into his enemies' hands. They carried him bound to the gate of the citadel and threatened to hang him unless the garrison surrendered. Lothair refused till he saw the rope tightening round his brother's neck; then he accepted the easy terms offered by the victors. The brothers were allowed to go free with their households and their possessions. Lothair retired to Tripoli, where Bohemond V received him well. He was joined there by Thomas of Acerra. Richard conscientiously returned to his Imperial master, who promptly threw him into gaol. With the Filangieri gone, Jerusalem and Ascalon passed officially with Tyre into the Regents' hands.

Ralph of Soissons had confidently expected that the control of the captured city would be given to the Regents. But Philip of Montfort desired Tyre for himself, to round off his fief of Toron; and the Ibelins gave him their support. When Ralph angrily demanded the city, the barons with cynical amusement replied that they would hold it in trust themselves till it was certain to whom it should belong. Ralph suddenly realized that he was intended to be a mere figurehead. In his humiliation and disgust he promptly left the Holy Land and returned to France. Queen Alice,

PLATE III

VIEW OF TYRE, 1839

The sandy spit joining the city to the mainland was much narrower in medieval times.

whose fifty years of life had taught her patience, remained as titular regent till she died in 1246.[1]

The triumph of the barons meant the triumph of Templar over Hospitaller foreign policy. Negotiations were reopened with the Court of Damascus. Ayub of Egypt had recently quarrelled with an-Nasir of Kerak and was alarmed at the Frankish defection. When Ismail of Damascus, with the approval of an-Nasir, offered the Franks to withdraw from the Temple area at Jerusalem the Moslem priests whose presence there had been guaranteed by Frederick II, Ayub at once made the same offer. By skilfully playing off the Moslem princes against each other, the Templars, who were managing the transaction, secured the approval of them all to the restoration of the area to the Christian cult. The Grand Master, Armand of Périgord, wrote enthusiastically to Europe at the end of 1243 to relate the happy result and to announce that the Order was now busily refortifying the Holy City. It was the last diplomatic triumph of Outremer.[2]

The Emperor Frederick wrote rather acidly to Richard of Cornwall to comment on the Order's readiness to seek a Moslem alliance, when it had denounced him for so doing.[3]

The success encouraged the Templars. When war broke out between Ayub and Ismail in the spring of 1244, they persuaded the barons to intervene actively on the latter's behalf. An-Nasir of Kerak and the young Prince of Homs, al-Mansur Ibrahim, had both joined Ismail; and al-Mansur Ibrahim came in person to Acre to seal the alliance and to offer on the allies' behalf a share of Egypt to the Franks, when Ayub should be defeated. The Moslem prince was received with great honour. The Templars provided most of the entertainment.[4]

But Ayub was not to be so easily defeated. He had found allies

---

[1] *Gestes des Chiprois*, pp. 130–6; *Estoire d'Eracles*, II, p. 420; Tafel-Thomas, *loc. cit.* (the Venetians were not given rewards due to them); *Assises*, II, p. 401. A regent had legally no right over a fortress.

[2] Abu'l Feda, p. 122; Maqrisi, X, pp. 355–7; al-Aïni, p. 197; Matthew Paris, IV, pp. 289–98.   [3] Matthew Paris, IV, p. 419.

[4] Joinville (ed. de Wailly), p. 290.

that were more effective than the Franks. The Khwarismian Turks, ever since the death of Jelal ad-Din, their king, had been wandering through the Jezireh and northern Syria, raiding and pillaging as they went. A coalition of the Ayubite princes of Syria had attempted to control them in 1241 and had severely beaten them in a battle not far from Edessa. But the Khwarismians then established their headquarters in the countryside between Edessa and Harran, and were still prepared to sell their services.[1] Ayub had been in touch with them for some time, and now he invited them to invade the territory of Damascus and Palestine.[2]

In June 1244 the Khwarismian horsemen, ten thousand strong, swept down into Damascene territory, ravaging the land and burning the villages. Damascus itself was too strong for them to attack, so they rode on into Galilee, past the town of Tiberias, which they captured, and southward through Nablus towards Jerusalem. The Franks suddenly realized the danger. The newly elected Patriarch, Robert, hastened to the city with the Grand Masters of the Temple and the Hospital, and reinforced the garrison in the fortifications that the Templars had just rebuilt, but they did not themselves dare to remain there. On 11 July the Khwarismians broke into the city. There was fighting in the streets, but they forced their way to the Armenian convent of St James and massacred the monks and nuns. The Frankish governor was killed in making a sortie from the citadel, together with the Preceptor of the Hospital. But the garrison held out. No help came from the Franks; so they appealed to their nearest Moslem ally, an-Nasir of Kerak. An-Nasir had no liking for the Christians and had resented the necessity of their alliance. So, after sending some troops which cowed the Khwarismians into offering the garrison a safe-conduct to the coast if they would surrender the citadel, he then dissociated himself from its fate. On 23 August some

[1] Abu'l Feda, p. 119; Kemal ad-Din (trans. Blochet), vi, pp. 3–6, 13. See Cahen, *La Syrie du Nord*, pp. 648–9; Grousset, *Histoire des Croisades*, iii, pp. 410–11.

[2] Maqrisi, x, p. 358. Frederick II, letter in Matthew Paris, iv, p. 301, blames the barons of Outremer for provoking this alliance.

six thousand Christian men, women and children marched out of the city, leaving it to the Khwarismians. As they moved along the road towards Jaffa, some of them looked back and saw Frankish flags waving on the towers. Thinking that somehow rescue had arrived, many insisted on returning towards the city, only to fall into an ambush under the walls. Some two thousand perished. The remainder, as they journeyed down to the sea, were attacked by Arab bandits. Only three hundred reached Jaffa.

Thus Jerusalem passed finally from the Franks. Nearly seven centuries passed before a Christian army would once again enter its gates. The Khwarismians showed little mercy to the city. They broke into the Church of the Holy Sepulchre. A few old Latin priests had refused to leave the city and were celebrating Mass there. These were slain, as well as the priests of the native denominations that were there. The bones of the Kings of Jerusalem were torn up from their tombs, and the church itself set on fire. Houses and shops throughout the city were pillaged, and churches burned. Then, when the whole place was desolate, the Khwarismians swept on, to join the Egyptian army at Gaza.[1]

While the Khwarismians sacked Jerusalem, the knights of Outremer had been gathering outside Acre. There the armies of Homs and Damascus joined them, under the command of al-Mansur Ibrahim of Homs; and an-Nasir brought up the army of Kerak. On 4 October 1244, the allied forces began to march southward, along the coast road. Though an-Nasir and his Bedouins kept themselves apart, there was perfect comradeship between the Franks and al-Mansur Ibrahim and his men. The Christian army was the largest that Outremer had put into the field since the fatal day of Hattin. There were six hundred lay horsemen, led by Philip of Montfort, lord of Toron and Tyre, and Walter of Brienne, Count of Jaffa. The Temple and the Hospital both sent over three hundred of their Orders, under the two Grand Masters, Armand of Périgord and William of Châteauneuf. There was a contingent

---

[1] *Chronicle of Mailros* (Melrose), pp. 159–60; Matthew Paris, IV, pp. 308, 338–40; *MS. of Rothelin*, pp. 563–5; Maqrisi, X, pp. 358–9; al-Aïni, p. 198.

from the Teutonic Order. Bohemond of Antioch sent his cousins, John and William of Botrun, and John of Ham, Constable of Tripoli. The Patriarch Robert himself accompanied the army, with the Archbishop of Tyre and Ralph, Bishop of Ramleh. There was a proportionate number of sergeants and foot-soldiers. The troops under al-Mansur Ibrahim's command were probably more numerous, but lighter armed. An-Nasir seems to have provided Bedouin cavalry.

The Egyptian army lay before Gaza, under the command of a young Mameluk emir, Rukn ad-Din Baibars. It consisted of five thousand picked Egyptian soldiers and the Khwarismian horde. The opposing armies made contact on 17 October at the village of Herbiya, or La Forbie, on the sandy plain a few miles north-east of Gaza. The allies hastily held a council of war. Al-Mansur Ibrahim recommended that they should stay where they were, fortifying their camp against any Khwarismian attack. He calculated that the Khwarismians would soon grow impatient. They disliked attacking a strong position; and the Egyptian army could not attack without them. With good luck, the whole Egyptian army might soon retire to Egypt. Many of the Christians agreed with him; but Walter of Jaffa eagerly urged an immediate attack. Their forces were superior in number; it was a glorious opportunity for destroying the Khwarismian menace and humiliating Ayub. He had his way; and the whole army moved out to the attack. The Franks were on the right flank, then came the Damascenes and the men of Homs in the centre, and an-Nazir on the left.

While the Egyptian troops held the Frankish attack, the Khwarismians charged down upon their Moslem allies. Al-Mansur Ibrahim and his men from Homs stood their ground, but the Damascene troops could not withstand the shock. They turned and fled, and with them an-Nasir and his army. While al-Mansur Ibrahim fought his way out, the Khwarismians turned and swooped on to the flank of the Christians, driving them against the Egyptian regiments. The Franks fought bravely but in vain. Within a few hours their whole army was destroyed. Amongst the dead were the Grand Master of the Temple, and its Marshal, the Archbishop of Tyre, the Bishop of Ramleh and the two young lords of Botrun. The Count of Jaffa, the Grand Master of the Hospital and the Constable of Tripoli were taken prisoner. Philip of Montfort escaped with the Patriarch back to Ascalon, where they were joined by the survivors of the Orders, thirty-three Templars, twenty-six Hospitallers and three Teutonic Knights. They went on by sea to Jaffa. The number of the dead was estimated as being not less than 5000 and probably far more. Eight hundred prisoners were taken back to Egypt.[1]

The victorious army marched at once on Ascalon, which was now garrisoned by the Hospital. Its fortifications proved their value. The Egyptians' assaults failed, and they settled down to blockade it, bringing up ships from Egypt to watch the coast. Meanwhile the Khwarismians hurried to Jaffa with its captive Count, whom they threatened to hang unless the garrison surrendered. But he shouted to his men to hold firm. The fortifications were too formidable for the Khwarismians. They retired with their prisoner whose life they spared. He died later in captivity, after a brawl with an Egyptian emir, with whom he was playing chess.[2]

The disaster at Gaza robbed the Franks of all the precarious gains that diplomacy had won for them during the last decades. It is unlikely that Jerusalem and Galilee could have been held against any serious Moslem attack, but the loss of manpower left Outremer quite unable to defend more than the coastal districts and a few of the strongest inland castles. Only at Hattin had the losses been greater. There was, however, a difference between Hattin and Gaza. The victor of the earlier battle, Saladin, was already master of all Syria and Egypt. Ayub of Egypt still had to overcome his rival of Damascus before he could venture to finish with the Christians. This delay saved Outremer.

[1] *Estoire d'Eracles*, II, pp. 427–31; *MS. of Rothelin*, pp. 562–6; *Gestes des Chiprois*, pp. 145–6; *Chronicle of Mailros*, pp. 159–60; Joinville, pp. 293–5; Matthew Paris, IV, pp. 301, 307–11; Maqrisi, X, p. 360; Abu Shama, II, p. 193.
[2] Joinville, *loc. cit.*; Amadi, pp. 201–2.

The Khwarismians had hoped that as a reward for their help Ayub would settle them in rich lands in Egypt. But he refused to allow them across the frontier and posted troops there to see that they remained in Syria. They turned back to raid Palestine, as far as the suburbs of Acre, then moved inland to join the Egyptians at the siege of Damascus. The Egyptian army, under the emir Mu'in ad-Din, marched up through central Palestine, depriving an-Nasir of Kerak of all of his lands west of the Jordan and eventually arrived before Damascus in April 1245. The siege lasted for six months. Ismail of Damascus cut out the dykes that held in the river Barada and the land outside the walls was an impenetrable marsh. But the tight blockade organized by the Egyptians soon caused unrest amongst the merchants and shopkeepers. Early in October Ismail came to terms. He yielded up Damascus in return for a vassal-principality consisting of Baalbek and the Hauran. But the Khwarismians were still left unrewarded. They therefore decided to abandon Ayub's cause and early in 1246 offered their services to Ismail. With their help he returned towards Damascus and laid siege to the city. He had hoped that other Ayubite princes would join him against Ayub; but they disliked the Khwarismians more. The Regent of Aleppo and the Prince of Homs, subsidized by Ayub, sent an army to the relief of Damascus. Ismail and his allies raised the siege and came northward, and met the relieving force early in May, somewhere on the road from Baalbek to Homs. He was severely defeated and the Khwarismians almost annihilated. Those that survived found their way to the East, to join up with the Mongols, while the head of their leader was carried in triumph through the streets of Aleppo. The whole Arab world rejoiced at their disappearance. Ayub's possession of Damascus was confirmed. Ismail was restricted once more back to Baalbek, and the Ayubites of the north recognized Ayub's seniority. He could give his attention again to the Franks.[1]

On 17 June 1247, an Egyptian army captured Tiberias and its

[1] Ibn Khallikan, III, p. 246; Maqrisi, X, pp. 361–5; Abu Shama, II, p. 432; *Estoire d'Eracles*, II, p. 432.

castle, which Odo of Montbéliard had recently rebuilt. Mount Thabor and the castle of Belvoir were occupied soon afterwards. The army moved next to the siege of Ascalon. The fortifications which Hugh of Burgundy had constructed were in good condition, and there was a strong garrison of Hospitallers. Further help was summoned from Acre and from Cyprus. King Henry of Cyprus at once sent a squadron of eight galleys with a hundred knights under his Seneschal, Baldwin of Ibelin, to Acre, where the Commune, with the aid of the Italian colonists, had fitted out seven more galleys and fifty lighter vessels. The Egyptians had brought up a fleet of twenty-one galleys which was blockading the town and which now sailed out to meet the Christians. But before contact was made it ran into a sudden Mediterranean storm. Many of the ships were driven ashore and wrecked; the survivors sailed back to Egypt. The Christian fleet was able to sail on unmolested to Ascalon and revictual the garrison and land the knights. But the bad weather continued, and the ships could not remain in the unprotected anchorage off the town. They returned to Acre and left Ascalon to its fate. The besieging army had been handicapped by a lack of wood for siege-engines; but the wreckage of their ships scattered along the shore provided them with all the material that they needed. A great battering-ram forced a passage-way under the walls right into the citadel; and on 15 October the Egyptian army poured through. The defenders were taken by surprise. Most of them were killed outright, and the remainder taken prisoner. By the Sultan's orders the fortress was dismantled and left desolate.[1] Ayub did not follow up his victory. He paid a visit to Jerusalem, whose walls he ordered to be reconstructed, and then passed on to hold court in Damascus. He was in residence there over the winter of 1248 and the spring of 1249, and all the Moslem princes of Syria came to do him homage.[2]

In the diminished kingdom of Outremer, despite its losses and

---

[1] *Estoire d'Eracles*, II, pp. 432–5; *Gestes des Chiprois*, p. 146; *Annales de Terre Sainte*, p. 442; al-Aïni, p. 200; Maqrisi, X, p. 315.

[2] Ibn Khallikan, *loc. cit.*

its lack of a central authority, there was internal tranquillity. Queen Alice died in 1246; and the regency passed to the next heir, her son King Henry of Cyprus, after a protest from her half-sister, the Dowager Princess Melisende of Antioch. King Henry, whose chief distinction was his enormous corpulence, was not the man to assert his powers.¹ He appointed Balian of Ibelin as his *bailli* and confirmed Philip of Montfort in the possession of Tyre. When Balian died in September 1247, he was succeeded as *bailli* by his brother, John of Arsuf, and as lord of Beirut by his son, another John.²

Further north, Bohemond V of Antioch and Tripoli tried to keep himself apart as far as possible from the concerns of his neighbours. The influence of his Italian wife, Lucienne of Segni, kept him on good terms with the Papacy; but the number of her Roman relatives and friends whom she invited to the East irritated his barons and was to cause him trouble later. It was probably at the Pope's request that he sent a contingent to the disastrous battle of Gaza. But at the same time he kept up friendly relations with Frederick II, and gave Lothair Filangieri and Thomas of Acerra asylum at Tripoli, to the Pope's annoyance, though he refused them active aid. His quarrel with the Armenian Kingdom lasted for some years. He vainly attempted to persuade the Pope to arrange a divorce between the young Roupenian heiress Isabella and the new King Hethoum, in order to deprive Hethoum of his right to the throne. But both he and Henry of Cyprus were specifically forbidden by Rome to attack the Armenians, while Hethoum for his part was too busily engaged in warding off the attacks of the great Seldjuk Sultan, Kaikhosrau, to be aggressive. The marriage of Hethoum's sister Stephanie to Henry of Cyprus in 1237 gradually paved the way to a general reconciliation.³

¹ *Gestes des Chiprois*, p. 146—a rather garbled summary of the solution; Röhricht, *Regesta*, pp. 315–16; Innocent IV, *Registres* (ed. Berger), no. 4427, II, p. 60. Melisende's claim was given by the Pope to Odo of Châteauroux to investigate and was later dropped. See Röhricht, *Geschichte des Königreichs Jerusalem*, p. 873 n. 3.
² *Annales de Terre Sainte*, p. 442; Amadi, p. 198.
³ See Cahen, *La Syrie du Nord*, pp. 650–2.

Bohemond had little control over the Military Orders settled in his dominions; but they had grown more cautious. In an attempt to reconcile the Commune of Antioch, with its strong Greek element, the Papacy, it seems with Bohemond's approval, changed its policy towards the Orthodox Church there. It was clearly impossible now to integrate the Greeks and Latins into one Church. So Honorius III offered the Greeks an autonomous Church with its own hierarchy and ritual, so long as the Greek Patriarch would recognize the supreme authority of Rome. The Greek clergy refused the offer, possibly with the secret encouragement of Bohemond, who considered that an independent Greek hierarchy would be more tractable; and the Patriarch Symeon bustled off to the anti-Latin Council summoned by the Nicaean Emperor at Nymphaeum, where the Pope was solemnly excommunicated. But when Symeon died, about the year 1240, his successor David, in whose appointment it may be that the Princess Lucienne had some part, was willing to enter into negotiations. In 1245 Pope Innocent IV sent the Franciscan, Lorenzo of Orta, to the East with instructions that the Greeks who acknowledged Papal ecclesiastical suzerainty were to be put everywhere on the same footing as the Latins. They need only obey Latin superiors where there was a good historical precedent for it. The Patriarch was invited to dispatch a mission to Rome, at the Pope's expense, to discuss disputed points. David accepted these terms. About the same time the Latin Patriarch, Albert, who was not entirely pleased with the arrangements, went off to France to attend a Council at Lyons, where he died. The next Latin Patriarch, Opizon Fieschi, the Pope's nephew, was not appointed till 1247 and came to Antioch the following year. In the meantime David was the only Patriarch resident at Antioch. But on David's death, the date of which is unknown, his successor Euthymius rejected Papal authority, for which he was excommunicated by Opizon and banished from the city.[1]

[1] *Ibid.* pp. 684–5; *Regesta Honorii Papae III*, nos. 5567, 5570, II, p. 352. The evidence all comes from Papal sources, though Bar Hebraeus (trans. Budge,

A large party in the Jacobite Church had already made its sub-mission to Rome. In 1237 the Jacobite Patriarch, Ignatius of Antioch, while visiting Jerusalem, took part in a Latin procession and was given a Dominican habit, after making an Orthodox declaration of faith. On his return to Antioch he carried many of his clergy with him, and Latins were officially told that they might confess to Jacobite priests, when Latin confessors were not available. In 1245 a Papal emissary, Andrew of Longjumeau, visited Ignatius at Mardin, where he had his main residence; and the terms for union were negotiated. Ignatius was prepared to accept a verbal formula about doctrine and administrative autonomy under the direct suzerainty of Rome. But unfortunately Ignatius spoke only for one party of the Jacobite Church. There was already a feud between the Jacobites of northern Syria and those of the eastern and southern provinces; and the latter disregarded the union. So long as Ignatius lived, his followers remained loyal to the Latins. But after his death in 1252 there was a dispute over the succession. The pro-Latin candidate, John of Aleppo, triumphed for a time, but considered that his Latin friends had given him insufficient support, while his rival, Denys, who eventually displaced him, was consistently opposed to them. Only a small portion of the Church, based on Tripoli, maintained the union.[1]

The work to achieve union had been carried out mainly by the preaching friars, Dominicans and Franciscans, who had begun operations in the East soon after the foundation of their Orders. In the restricted kingdom of Jerusalem they did not find much scope; but they were particularly active in the Patriarchate of Antioch, the Patriarch Albert being their devoted patron. They tended more and more to replace the secular clergy in the scattered dioceses of the Patriarchate. The relations of the Patriarchs with the new monastic order of the Cistercians were less happy.

p. 445) tells of Euthymius's journey to the Mongol Court. See also 'Lettre des Chrétiens de Terre Sainte à Charles d'Anjou' in *Revue de l'Orient Latin*, II, p. 213.

[1] Cahen, *op. cit.* pp. 681–4, with references.

Peter II, himself a former Cistercian abbot, had installed them in two monasteries, Saint George of Jubin, near Antioch, and Belmont near Tripoli. But various scandals arose during the Patriarchate of Albert; and a series of appeals to Rome had to be made before order was reintroduced into the monasteries and the Patriarch's authority made good.[1]

Bohemond V himself took little interest in these proceedings. He seldom visited Antioch, but held his Court at Tripoli. As in the kingdom, the various elements in his dominions drifted apart, saved from extinction by the quarrels of the Ayubites and by a newer and tremendous force that was beginning to agitate the Moslem world, the Empire of the Mongols.

[1] *Ibid.* pp. 668–71, 680–1.

BOOK III

THE MONGOLS AND THE MAMELUKS

CHAPTER I

THE COMING OF THE MONGOLS

'His chariots shall be as a whirlwind! his horses are swifter than eagles. Woe unto us; for we are spoiled.' JEREMIAH IV, 13

In the year 1167, twenty years before Saladin reconquered Jerusalem for Islam, a boy was born far away on the banks of the river Onon in north-eastern Asia to a Mongol chieftain named Yesugai and his wife Höelün. The child was called Temujin, but he is better known in history by his later name of Jenghiz-Khan.[1] The Mongols were a group of tribes living on the upper Amur river, and perpetually at war with their eastern neighbours, the Tartars. Yesugai's grandfather Qabul-Khan had welded them together into a loose confederacy; but after his death his kingdom had disintegrated, and the Chin Emperor of Northern China had established his suzerainty over the whole district. Yesugai inherited only a small portion of the old confederacy, but he increased his power and his reputation by defeating and conquering some of the

---

[1] For the whole career of Jenghiz-Khan see Howorth, *History of the Mongols*, I, pp. 27–115; Grousset, *L'Empire Mongol, 1ère phase*, pp. 35–242 and *L'Empire des Steppes*, pp. 243–315; Martin, *Chingis Khan and his Conquest of Northern China, passim*. The main original sources are the *Yüan Ch'ao Pi Shih* (the Official History of the Mongols) and the *Yüan Shing Wu Ch'in Cheng Lu*, both originally written in Mongol and translated into Chinese. The Mongol text of the former has been reconstituted and published (in Latin letters) and partly translated into French by Pelliot (*L'Histoire Secrète des Mongols*)—and Rashid ad-Din, *Jami at-Tarâwîkh*, written in Persian (part published with translation by Quatremère; whole text published in a Russian translation by Berezin). Various Mongol and Chinese texts dealing with him are published, translated into German by Haenisch ('Die Letzten Feldzüge Cingis Hans und Sein Tod' in *Asia Major*, vol. IX). For the date of Jenghiz's birth, see Grousset, *L'Empire Mongol*, p. 53 n. 3.

Tartar tribes and by interfering in the affairs of the most civilized of his immediate neighbours, the Khan of the Keraits.

The Keraits, who were a semi-nomadic people of Turkish origin, inhabited the country round the Orkhon river in modern Outer Mongolia. Early in the eleventh century their ruler had been converted to Nestorian Christianity, together with most of his subjects; and the conversion brought the Keraits into touch with the Uighur Turks, amongst whom were many Nestorians. The Uighurs had developed a settled culture in their home in the Tarim valley and the Turfan depression and had evolved an alphabet for the Turkish language, based on Syriac letters. In earlier times Manichaeism had been their dominant religion. Now the Manichaeans tended under Chinese influence to become Buddhist. The power of the Uighur was waning, but their civilization had spread over the Keraits and over the Naiman Turks whose country lay between.[1]

About the year 1170 the Kerait Khan Qurjakuz, son of Merghus-Khan, died, and his son Toghrul had some difficulty in securing the inheritance against the opposition of his brothers and uncles. In the course of his fratricidal wars he secured the help of Yesugai, who became his sworn brother. This friendship gave Yesugai a superior position amongst the Mongol chieftains; but before he could establish himself as the chief Mongol Khan he died, poisoned by some Tartar nomads, whose evening meal he was sharing. His eldest son, Temujin, was then nine years old.[2]

The energy of Yesugai's widow, Höelün, preserved for the young chieftain some authority over his father's tribes. But Temujin's childhood was stormy. He showed himself to be a leader while still a boy, and he was ruthless towards his rivals, even amongst his own family. In the course of the wars by which

---

[1] For the various Turco-Mongol tribes, see Howorth, *op. cit.* I, pp. 19–26; Grousset, *L'Empire Mongol*, pp. 1–32; Martin, *op. cit.* pp. 48–58; Pelliot, 'Chrétiens d'Asie Centrale et d'Extrême Orient', in *T'oung Pao*, vol. XI. For the Uighurs, Bretschneider, *Mediaeval Researches from Eastern Asiatic Sources*, I, pp. 236–63.

[2] *Yüan Ch'ao*, Mongol text, pp. 10–14; Grousset, *L'Empire Mongol*, pp. 48–54.

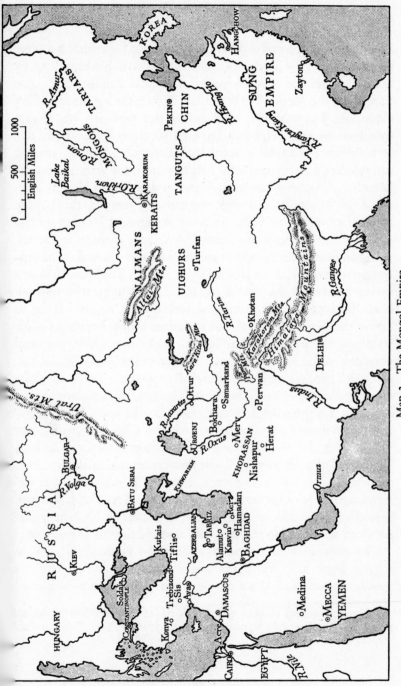

Map 3. The Mongol Empire.

he won a hegemony over the Mongols, he was for a while a captive in the hands of the Tayichiut tribe, and his wife Börke, whom he married when he was seventeen, was held prisoner for some months by the Merkit Turks of Lake Baikal; the legitimacy of her eldest son, Juji, who was born during this captivity, was always therefore suspect. Temujin's growing successes were largely due to his alliance with the Kerait Khan, Toghrul, whom he affected to regard as a father and who helped him in his wars against the Merkits. About the year 1194 Temujin was elected king or khan of all the Mongols, and took the name of Jenghiz, the Strong. Soon afterwards, the Chin Emperor recognized Jenghiz as chief prince of the Mongols and secured his alliance against the Tartars, who had been threatening China. A swift war resulted in the subjection of the Tartars to Jenghiz's rule. When Toghrul-Khan was driven from the Kerait throne in 1197, it was Jenghiz who restored him. In 1199 Jenghiz combined forces with Toghrul-Khan to defeat the Naiman Turks; but it was not long before he grew jealous of the power of the Keraits. Toghrul was now the chief potentate in the Eastern Steppes. He had the title of Wang-Khan, or Ong-Khan, which filtered through to western Asia in the more familiar and euphonious form of Johannes, thus making him a candidate for the role of Prester John. But he was a bloodthirsty and treacherous man, singularly lacking in Christian virtues; nor was he ever able to bring help to his fellow-Christians. In 1203 he quarrelled with Jenghiz. Their first battle, at Khalakhaljit Elet, was indecisive; but a few weeks later the Kerait army was exterminated at Jejer Undur, in the heart of the Kerait land. Toghrul was killed as he fled for refuge. The members of his family that survived submitted to Jenghiz, who annexed the whole country.[1]

The Naiman were the next nation to be subdued, in 1204, at a great battle at Chakirmaut where the whole fate of Jenghiz's power was at stake. Wars during the next two years established

[1] The best modern account of Jenghiz's rise to power is Martin, *op. cit.* pp. 60-84. For Toghrul's reputation as Prester John see Yule, *Cathay and the Way Thither*, III, pp. 15-22.

Jenghiz as supreme over all the tribes between the Tarim basin, the river Amur and the Great Wall of China. In 1206 a Kuriltay, or assembly, of all his subject-tribes held on the banks of the river Onon confirmed his kingly title; and he proclaimed that his people should be known collectively as the Mongols.

Jenghiz-Khan's Empire was basically a conglomeration of clans. He made no attempt to interfere with the old organization of the tribes as clans under hereditary chieftains. He merely super-imposed his own family, the Altin Uruk or Golden Clan, and set up a central government controlled by his own household and familiars, and he placed under the free clans large numbers of slaves taken from the tribes that had resisted him and been con-quered. Serfs in thousands were given to his relations and friends. At the Kuriltay of 1206 his mother Höelün and his brother Temughe Otichin were each given ten thousand families as chattels and his young sons five or six thousand each. Tribes and even cities that submitted to him peaceably were left without interference, so long as they respected his overriding laws and paid to his tax-collectors the heavy tribute that he demanded. To bind his countries together he promulgated a code of laws, the Yasa, which was to supersede the customary laws of the Steppes. The Yasa, which was issued in instalments throughout his reign, laid down specifically the rights and privileges of the clan-chieftains, the conditions of military and other services due to the Khan, the principles of taxation, as well as of criminal, civil and commercial law. Supreme autocrat though he was, Jenghiz intended that he and his successors should be bound by the law.[1]

As soon as the administration of his empire was arranged, Jenghiz set about its expansion. He had now a large army, to whose organization he had also given careful attention. Every tribesman between the ages of fourteen and sixty was by Mongol and Turkish tradition liable to military service; and the great

---

[1] *Ibid.* pp. 85–101. The *Yüan Ch'ao* devotes three chapters (§§ 194–6, pp. 68–72, Mongol text) to the battle of Chakirmaut, which is more than it gives to any other of Jenghiz's battles.

annual winter hunting expeditions, necessary for providing meat for the army and the Court, served as manœuvres to keep the soldiers in training. By temperament the tribesmen were used to give to their leaders an unquestioning obedience; and the leaders, from bitter experience, knew that they must now obey the Khan. His subjects had also, like all nomadic tribes, a yearning to move beyond the horizon, and a fear lest their pasture-lands and forests should be exhausted. The Khan offered them new countries and great booty and hordes of slaves. It was an army of cavalry, archers and lancers mounted on swift ponies, men and beasts accustomed from birth to hard living and to making long journeys across deserts with very little food and drink. Such a combination of speed of movement, discipline and vast numbers had never before been known.[1]

The three great states that now bordered the Mongols were the Chin Empire on the east, with its capital at Pekin; then the Tangut kingdom of Hsia Hsi, along the upper reaches of the Yellow River, where a dynasty of Tibetan origin ruled over a mixed sedentary population of Mongols, Turks and Chinese; and, to the south-west, the kingdom of the Kara Khitai, Buddhist nomads from Manchuria who had been displaced by the Chin Emperors early in the twelfth century and had fought their way westward, to found an empire at the expense of the Uighurs of the Tarim basin and the Moslem Turks of Yarkand and Khotan. Their monarch, the Gur-Khan, was already a formidable factor in eastern Moslem politics; and the Uighurs of Turfan were his clients. The weakest of the three was Hsia Hsi, which, therefore, Jenghiz attacked the first. By 1212 its King had accepted his suzerainty. Invasions of the Chin Empire followed. A series of tremendous battles put the whole countryside as far as the Yellow Sea and Shantung into his power; but the Mongols were unused to attack fortified places, and the great walled cities held out against him. It was only when a Chin engineer, Liu Po-Lin, entered Jenghiz's service that his armies began to learn the art of siege warfare. But by 1226 the

[1] *Ibid.* pp. 11–47, a full discussion of the Mongol army.

Chin Emperor was reduced to vassalage. Already by 1221 the Chin province of Manchuria had been annexed, and Korea had acknowledged Mongol suzerainty. When the last Chin Emperor died in 1223, his remaining provinces were incorporated into the Mongol Empire.[1]

Meanwhile, Jenghiz had extended his power south-westward. At this time the Khwarismian Empire of Mohammed-Shah was at its height. Mohammed was master of all Asia from Kurdistan and the Persian Gulf to the Aral Sea, the Pamirs and the Indus. The Gur-Khan of the Kara Khitai found him a disquieting neighbour and sought to embarrass him by inciting his vassals in Transoxiana against him. The resultant wars seriously weakened the Kara Khitai; and while Mohammed-Shah annexed their southern territory, the throne of the Gur-Khan was usurped by a Naiman refugee prince, Kuchluk. Kuchluk, a Nestorian by birth, had become a Buddhist on his marriage to a Kara Khitai princess; but unlike the Gur-Khans, he was intolerant towards his Christian and Moslem subjects. His unpopularity gave Jenghiz his chance to intervene. When a Mongol army swept down into the Turfan basin, it was welcomed as a force of liberators. The Uighurs gladly submitted to Mongol rule; and Kuchluk was restricted to a small principality in the Tarim valley.[2]

This expansion brought Jenghiz into direct connection with the territory of the Khwarismians. Mohammed-Shah was not the man to tolerate a rival as ambitious as himself. Embassies were exchanged between the two potentates; but Mohammed was affronted when Jenghiz demanded that, as Khan of the Turco-Mongol nations, he should be regarded as suzerain by the Khwarismian prince. In 1218 a great caravan of Moslem merchants travelled from Mongolia, and with them were a hundred Mongols, sent on a special mission to the Khwarismian court. When the caravan reached Otrur, on the Jaxartes river, in Mohammed's

---

[1] *Ibid.* chs. V–VII, IX–X *passim*, for the conquest of the Chin.
[2] For Mohammed-Shah, see Barthold, article 'Khwaresm' in *Encyclopaedia of Islam*; for Kuchluk, Martin, *op. cit.* pp. 103–4, 109–11, 220, 224.

dominions, the local governor massacred the travellers and stole their goods, half of which were sent to the Shah. It was a provocation that Jenghiz could not ignore. Seeing that war was about to break out, Kuchluk made a bid to revive the Kara Khitai kingdom. In a brilliant campaign the Mongol general Jebe pursued Kuchluk and his army through the length of his dominions and finally slew him in a valley high in the Pamirs.[1]

With Kuchluk gone, Jenghiz was ready to set out against the Khwarismians. It was a formidable undertaking. Mohammed-Shah was said to be able to put half a million men into the field; and Jenghiz would be operating a thousand miles from his home. In the late summer of 1219 the Mongol army of two hundred thousand men left its camp by the river Irtysh. The Khan's vassal kings, such as the prince of the Uighurs, joined him on his westward march. Mohammed-Shah, uncertain where the Mongols would strike, divided his troops between the line of the Jaxartes and the passes of Ferghana, with his main body waiting by the great Transoxianan cities of Bokhara and Samarkand. The Mongol army made straight for the middle Jaxartes, and crossed the river by Otrur. Part of the army was left to besiege the town, a slow task, for the Mongols were still unpractised at siege warfare; part moved down the river to attack the Khwarismian army on its banks; part moved up the river to cut off the army in Ferghana; and Jenghiz and his main troops marched straight on Bokhara. He arrived there in February 1220. Almost at once the civilians opened the gates of the city to him. The Turks in the citadel resisted for a few days, then were slaughtered to a man, together with the Moslem imams who had encouraged them to fight on. From Bokhara Jenghiz moved to Samarkand, while Mohammed-Shah, unable to trust his troops, retired to his capital at Urgenj, on the Oxus, near Khiva. At Samarkand, where Jenghiz was joined by his sons, who had captured Otrur, the Turkish garrison at once surrendered, hoping to be enlisted into the conqueror's army. But he distrusted such unreliable soldiers and put them all

[1] Barthold, *op. cit.* pp. 397–9; Martin, *op. cit.* pp. 230–3.

to death. A few civilians tried to organize resistance, but in vain. They too were slain. Jenghiz next sent his sons to lay siege to Urgenj. There the defence was more formidable; and quarrels between the Khan's sons delayed its capture for a few months. Meanwhile Mohammed-Shah fled to Khorassan, pursued by an army under Jenghiz's most trusted generals, Subotai and Jebe. He escaped from his pursuers, only to die, broken and deserted, in December 1220, in a little island in the Caspian Sea.

A better fight was put up by Mohammed's son, Jelal ad-Din, who joined the Khwarismian army in Ferghana, and retreated into Afghanistan. At Parvan, just north of the Hindu Kush, he severely defeated the Mongol army sent to suppress him. Jenghiz himself had moved across the Oxus, past Balkh, which submitted to him and was spared, to Bamian, in the central Hindu Kush. The fortress held out against him and in the course of the siege his favourite grandson, Mutugen, was slain. When therefore the city was taken by assault, not a living creature was left alive in it. Meanwhile his son Tului and his son-in-law Toghutshar campaigned further to the west, capturing Merv, out of whose male population only four hundred trained artisans were spared, and Nishapur, where Toghutshar was killed, and which suffered exactly a similar fate. Toghutshar's widow presided in person over the massacre. The artisans from both cities were sent to Mongolia. In the autumn of 1221 Jenghiz advanced through Afghanistan to attack Jelal ad-Din and caught up with him on the banks of the Indus. In a desperate battle on 24 November the Khwarismian army was destroyed. Jelal ad-Din himself fled across the river and took refuge with the King of Delhi. His children fell into the victor's hands and were massacred.

Jenghiz spent about a year in Afghanistan. The huge city of Herat, which had at first submitted quietly to the Mongols, had revolted after Jelal ad-Din's victory at Parvan. A Mongol army besieged it for several months. On its capture, in June 1222, its whole population, amounting to hundreds of thousands, was put to death. The slaughter lasted for a week. The ruined cities and wasted lands were provided with Mongol administrators, supported by enough troops to keep the cowed inhabitants in order. Jenghiz then returned to Transoxiana, which was less desolate. There he installed a Khwarismian governor, Mas'ud Yalawach, with Mongol advisers to watch and control him. Mas'ud's father, Mahmud Yalawach, was sent eastward to govern Pekin, an honorific method of further ensuring Mas'ud's loyalty. Jenghiz recrossed the Jaxartes in the spring of 1223 and journeyed slowly back across the steppes, reaching the Irtysh in the summer of 1224 and his home on the Tula river next spring.[1]

The fantastic conquests of Jenghiz-Khan did not pass unnoticed by the Christians in Syria. It was known that he was attacking the greatest Moslem power in Central Asia; and the Nestorians, with their churches spreading all across Asia, could testify that he was not ill-disposed towards the Christians. The Khan himself was a Shamanist, but he liked to consult Christian and Moslem priests, with a preference for the former. His sons were married to Christian princesses, Keraits, who had considerable influence at his court. It might well be that he would serve as an ally for Christendom.[2]

These hopes were somewhat shaken in the course of 1221. The army sent by Jenghiz under Subotai and Jebe to capture Mohammed-Shah failed in its immediate purpose. The Shah eluded them and doubled back to the Caspian. But the Mongol generals moved on to the west. In the summer of 1220 they captured and pillaged Reiy, near the modern Teheran, but spared most of the inhabitants. Next, Qum was taken and its inhabitants all massacred. A similar fate befell Kasvin and Zenjan, but Hamadan submitted in time and escaped after paying an exorbitant ransom. The Emir of Azerbaijan bought off an attack on Tabriz; and the Mongols passed by, in February 1221, to attack Georgia.

[1] Browne, *Literary History of Persia*, II, pp. 426–40; Grousset, *L'Empire Mongol*, pp. 31–46; Bretschneider, *op. cit.* I, pp. 276–94; *Yüan Ch'ao*, pp. 105–8 (a brief account); Rashid ad-Din (trans. Berezin), II, pp. 42–85.

[2] *Regesta Honorii Papae III*, no. 1478, I, p. 565. His letter, dated 20 June 1221, talks of forces coming from the Far East to rescue the Holy Land. For Jenghiz's own religion, see Martin, *op. cit.* pp. 310–11, 316–17.

King George IV, son of Queen Thamar, led out the Georgian chivalry to oppose their advance, and was routed at Khunani, just south of Tiflis. It was a disaster from which the Georgian army never quite recovered. But the conquerors turned back south-ward. Hamadan had revolted and must be punished; and on their way to sack and destroy the city they only paused to pillage Maragha, in Azerbaijan. They spent the remainder of the year in north-west Persia. Early in 1222 they turned north again, and after ravaging the eastern Georgian provinces and defeating the troops sent to restrain them, they passed on along the Caspian coast, through the Caspian Gates, towards the territory of the Kipchaks, between the Volga and the Don. The Kipchaks hastily allied themselves with the tribes of the northern Caucasus, the Alans and the Lesghians; but when Subotai and Jebe offered them a share of the booty, they did not intervene while the Mongols crushed the Caucasians. Inevitably, the Mongols next turned on them. They hoped to save themselves by bribing the Russians to come to their help; but on 31 May 1222, a great Russian army, led by the Princes of Kiev, Galich, Chernigov and Smolensk, was destroyed on the banks of the Kalka river, near the Sea of Azov. The Mongol generals did not follow up their victory. They entered the Crimea and pillaged the Genoese trading station at Soldaia, then swept away to the east, only pausing to destroy an army of the Kama Bulgars and ravage their country. They re-joined Jenghiz-Khan by the river Jaxartes, early in 1223.

The Western victims of this vast raid hopefully regarded it as an isolated phenomenon, a ghastly cataclysm that would not recur. But Jenghiz was delighted with his generals. They had not only done some valuable reconnoitring and had discovered that there was no army in western Asia that could stand up to them; but also they had so terri-fied the nations there by their ruthlessness that when the time should come for serious invasion, no one would dare to oppose them.[1]

---

[1] Bretschneider, *op. cit.* I, pp. 294–9. The Russian accounts of the campaign are rather confused. See Karamzin, *History of the Russian Empire* (in Russian), III, p. 545; Vernadsky, *Kievan Russia*, pp. 236–9. The *Novgorod Chronicle* (ed.

When Jenghiz-Khan died in 1227, his dominions stretched from Korea to Persia and from the Indian Ocean to the frozen plains of Siberia. No other man has ever created so vast an empire. It is impossible to explain his success by some theory that the Mongols had any economic urge for expansion; it can only be said that they were a suitable instrument for an expansionist leader. Jenghiz was the architect of his destiny. But he himself remains mysterious. In appearance, we are told, he was tall and vigorous, with eyes like a cat's. It is certain that his physical endurance was great. It is certain too, that his personality profoundly impressed everyone who had dealings with him. His skill as an organizer was superb; and he knew how to choose men and how to handle them. He had a genuine respect for learning, and was always ready to spare a scholar's life; but unfortunately few of his victims were given time to prove their scholarship. He adopted the Uighur alphabet for the Mongols and founded Mongol literature. In religious matters he was tolerant and ready to give aid to any sect that did not oppose him politically. He insisted on a just and orderly government. The roads were cleared of brigands; a postal service was introduced; and under his patronage commerce flourished and great caravans would pass in safety every year across the breadth of Asia. But he was completely ruthless. He had no regard for human life and no sympathy for human suffering. Millions of innocent townsfolk perished in the course of his wars; millions of innocent peasants saw their fields and orchards destroyed. His Empire was founded on human misery.[1]

The death of the great conqueror gave the outside world a respite. Nearly two years passed before the succession to his empire was settled. By Mongol custom, the eldest son and his descendants had the right to succeed to the empire, but the youngest had the right to retain the homelands and the duty to call the assembly that would confirm the succession. Jenghiz had broken

Nasonov), p. 63, remarks that only God knows where the Tartars came from or whither they went.

[1] There is a good summary of Jenghiz's character in Martin, *op. cit.* pp. 1–10.

with custom and had named his third son, Ogodai, as heir to the supreme power, passing over his eldest son, Juji whose legitimacy was questioned and whose military and administrative record was unsatisfactory. His second son, Jagatai, was a brilliant soldier, but too hot-tempered and impulsive to make a good ruler. Ogodai, though less spectacularly gifted, had, so Jenghiz thought, the patience and tact to handle his brothers and vassals. The youngest, Tului, was perhaps the ablest of the brothers but was handicapped by his self-indulgent habits. As the prince responsible for summoning the Kuriltay, Tului was the pivotal figure in deciding the succession; and he persuaded the chieftains of the clan to carry out Jenghiz's wishes. Ogodai became supreme Khan, and great appanages were allotted to his relatives. Jenghiz's brothers took over the eastern provinces, round the Amur river and in Manchuria. Tului kept the 'hearth-lands' by the Onon. Ogodai's personal patrimony was the old Kerait and Naiman territory. Jagatai inherited the former Uighur and Kara Khitai kingdoms. Juji had already died, but his sons, Batu, Orda, Berke and Shiban, were given the western provinces, as far as the Volga. But, while the princes were allowed autocratic rights over their subjects, they had to obey the imperial law of the Mongols and accept the decisions of the supreme Khan's government, which Ogodai set up at Karakorum. The unity of the Mongol Empire was unimpaired.[1]

When Jenghiz-Khan and his armies returned to Mongolia, Jelal ad-Din the Khwarismian left his exile in India and collected round him the considerable remains of his father's armies. He was welcomed in Persia as a liberator from the Mongols. By 1225 he was master of the Persian plateau and Azerbaijan, and by 1226 he was overlord of Baghdad. His kingdom, by threatening the Ayubites, was a useful factor in the policy of the Franks of Syria; but the Christians further north found him a worse neighbour even than the Mongols. In 1225 he invaded Georgia. The Georgian sovereign, George IV's sister Russudan, an unmarried but not a virgin Queen, sent an army to meet him. But the flower of

[1] See Grousset, *L'Empire Mongol*, pp. 284–91.

Georgian chivalry had fallen four years before at Khunani. Her troops were easily defeated at Garnhi, on her southern frontier. While the Queen fled herself to Kutais, Jelal ad-Din occupied and sacked her capital of Tiflis, and annexed the whole valley of the Kur river. An attempt by the Georgians to recover their lost provinces in 1228 ended in disaster. The Georgian kingdom was reduced to its lands by the Black Sea. It was no longer of value as the north-east outpost of Christendom, nor as a power that could challenge the Moslem hold on Asia Minor.[1]

It was not long before the Mongols returned to the west. A Chin revolt had first to be suppressed in northern China. But early in 1231 a huge Mongol army under the general Chormaqan appeared in Persia. The memory of the previous Mongol invasion served him well. As he marched from Khorassan to Azerbaijan, there was no resistance. Jelal ad-Din fled before him, to die obscurely in Kurdistan. His Khwarismian soldiers followed him in his flight, and regrouped themselves in the Jezireh, out of reach, for the moment, of the Mongol hordes. Thence they hired themselves out to the quarrelling Ayubites, till their final destruction near Homs in 1246. Chormaqan annexed all northern Persia and Azerbaijan to the Mongol Empire, and governed the province, from 1231 to 1241, from a camp in Mughan, near the Caspian Sea. In 1236 he invaded Georgia. Queen Russudan had reoccupied Tiflis after the fall of Jelal ad-Din; but she fled once more to Kutais, and the Mongols took over eastern Georgia. The Georgians, once the atrocities of the conquest were over, much preferred them to the Khwarismians because of the efficiency of their administration. In 1243 the Queen herself became their vassal on the understanding that the whole Georgian kingdom was to be given to her son to rule under Mongol suzerainty.[2]

[1] See Jelal ad-Din's biography by an-Nasair, his secretary (ed. Houdas), *passim*; Browne, *op. cit.* II, pp. 447–50. See d'Ohsson, *Histoire des Mongols*, I, pp. 255–9, 306. For the collapse of Georgia, see *Georgian Chronicle* (ed. Brosset), I, pp. 324–31.

[2] Browne, *op. cit.* II, pp. 449–50; d'Ohsson, III, pp. 65–6; *Georgian Chronicle*, I, p. 343.

The Christians further to the north were less well satisfied. In the spring of 1236 a huge Mongol army assembled north of the Aral Sea, under the command of Batu, son of Juji, whose appanage included those steppes. With Batu were his brothers and four of his cousins, Guyuk and Qadan, sons of Ogodai, Baidar, son of Jagatai, and Mongka, son of Tului. The aged general Subotai was sent as chief of staff. After suppressing the Turkish tribes by the Volga, the Mongol army marched into Russian territory in the autumn of 1237. Riazan was taken by assault on 21 December, and its prince and all its citizens massacred. Kolomna fell a few days later; and early in the new year the Mongols attacked the great city of Vladimir. It held out for only six days, and its fall, on 8 February 1238, was marked by another wholesale massacre. Suzdal was sacked about the same time, and there followed the capture and destruction of the secondary cities of central Russia, Moscow, Yuriev, Galich, Pereslav, Rostov and Yaroslavl. On 4 March the Grand Prince Yuri of Vladimir, was defeated and killed on the banks of the river Sitti. Tver and Torzhok fell soon after the battle, and the conquerors advanced over the Valdai hills towards Novgorod. Fortunately for that city, the spring rains flooded the marshes all around. Batu retired, to spend the rest of the year stamping out the last resistance of the Kipchaks, while his cousin Mongka conquered the Alans and the north Caucasian tribes, then made a raid of reconnaissance as far as Kiev.

In the autumn of 1240 Batu led the main Mongol army into the Ukraine. Chernigov and Pereislavl were sacked and Kiev, after a valiant defence, was taken by assault on 6 December. Many of its greatest treasures were destroyed, and most of its population slain, though the commander of the garrison, Dmitri, was spared because of his courage, which Batu admired. From Kiev a branch of the army, under Baidar, son of Jagatai, moved northwards into Poland, sacking Sandomir and Cracow. The Polish King summoned the Teutonic Knights settled on the Baltic coast to his aid; but their joint armies, under Duke Henry of Silesia, were routed after a fierce battle at Wahlstadt, near Liegnitz, on 9 April 1241. But Baidar did not venture to penetrate further westward. He devastated Silesia, then turned south, through Moravia into Hungary.

Batu and Subotai had meanwhile crossed into Galicia, driving before them a horde of terrified fugitives from every nation of the steppes. In February 1241, they passed over the Carpathians into the Hungarian plain. King Bela led his army out to meet them and was disastrously defeated on 11 April by the bridge of Mohi, on the river Sajo. The Mongols poured over Hungary, into Croatia and as far as the shores of the Adriatic. Batu remained himself for some months in Hungary, which he seems to have wished to annex to the Mongol Empire. But early in 1242 messengers arrived with the news that the Great Khan Ogodai had died at Karakorum on 11 December 1241.[1]

Batu could not afford to be away from Mongolia while the succession was decided. During the Russian campaign he had quarrelled bitterly with his cousins, Guyuk, son of Ogodai, and Buri, grandson of Jagatai. Both had retired angrily home. Ogodai supported Batu against his own son, whom he sent disgraced into exile. But Guyuk, as the Khan's eldest son, was still powerful. Ogodai named as his successor his grandson, Shiremon, whose father, Kuchu, had been killed fighting against the Chinese. Shiremon was, however, young and untried. Ogodai's widow, the Khatun Toragina, born a Naiman princess, took over the regency, determined that Guyuk should have the throne. She summoned a Kuriltay, but, though her authority was recognized till a new Great Khan should be appointed, five years passed before she could induce the princes of the blood and the clan-chieftains to accept Guyuk. During these years she administered the government. She was energetic but avaricious. Though a Christian by

[1] Bretschneider, *op. cit.* I, pp. 308–34, from Eastern sources. *Novgorod Chronicle*, pp. 74–6, 285–8. For a complete account see Strakosch-Grossman, *Der Einfall den Mongolen in Mitteleuropa in den Jahren 1241 und 1242*, also Sacerdoteanu, *Marea Invazie Tatara si Sud-estul European.*

birth, she chose as her favourite a Moslem, Abd ar-Rahman, whom gossip accused of having hurried Ogodai's death. His corruption and greed made him universally disliked; but no one had sufficient power to upset the regency.[1]

Till the succession was certain, Batu was unprepared to indulge in western adventures. He maintained garrisons in Russia, but central Europe was given a respite. It was only in western Asia, where the Regent sent as governor an able and active general, called Baichu, that the Mongol advance continued.

Late in 1242, Baichu invaded the lands of the Seldjuk Sultan, Kaikhosrau, who was at that moment in the Jezireh seeking to annex lands left masterless after Jelal ad-Din's collapse. Erzerum fell to the Mongols in the early spring. On 26 June 1243, the Sultan's army was routed at Sadagh, near Erzinjan; and Baichu advanced to Caesarea-Mazacha. Kaikhosrau then made his submission and accepted Mongol suzerainty. His neighbour, King Hethoum the Armenian, hastened to follow his example.[2]

It might have been expected that the princes of Western Christendom would have planned concerted action against so terrible a menace. Already in 1232, when Chormaqan had destroyed the Khwarismian power in Persia, the Assassin Order, whose headquarters at Alamut, in the Persian mountains, was threatened, had sent envoys to Europe to warn the Christians and to ask for help.[3] In 1241, when it seemed that central Europe was doomed, Pope Gregory IX urged a great alliance for its rescue. But the Emperor Frederick, now busily engaged in conquering the Papal States in Italy, refused to be deflected. He ordered his son Conrad, as ruler of Germany, to mobilize the German army, and he appealed for assistance from the Kings of France and

---

[1] For Toragina's regency, Grousset, *op. cit.* pp. 303–6. See Bar-Hebraeus (trans. Budge), pp. 410–11.

[2] Ibn Bibi (ed. Houtsma), IV, pp. 234–47; Bar-Hebraeus (trans. Budge), pp. 406–9; Vincent of Beauvais, *Speculum Historiale* (Douai edition), XXX, pp. 147, 150. See Cahen, *La Syrie du Nord*, pp. 694–6.

[3] See Pelliot, 'Les Mongols et la Papauté', in *Revue de l'Orient Chrétien*, vol. XXIII, pp. 238 ff.

England.[1] When, next year, the Mongols retired into Russia, Western Christendom returned to its illusions. The legend of Prester John spread an almost apocalyptic belief that salvation was coming from the East, which left too strong a mark. No one paused to reflect that if Wang-Khan the Kerait had really been the mysterious Johannes, his destroyer was unlikely to fulfil the same role. Everyone preferred to remember that the Mongols had fought against the Moslems and that Christian princesses had married into the Imperial family. The Great Khan of the Mongols might not be a Christian himself; he might not actually be Prester John; but it was hopefully assumed that he would be eager to champion Christian ideology against the forces of Islam. The presence in the Eastern background of so mighty a potential ally made the moment seem ripe for a new Crusade; and a willing Crusader was at hand.[2]

[1] *Historia Diplomatica Friderici Secundi*, v, pp. 360–841, 921–85 (a series of letters about the Tartar peril).

[2] Pelliot, *loc. cit.*; Marinescu, 'Le Prêtre Jean' in *Bulletin de la Section Historique de l'Académie Roumaine*, vol. x *passim*; Langlois, *La Vie en France au Moyen Age*, vol. III, pp. 44–56.

CHAPTER II

SAINT LOUIS

*'It profiteth a man nothing that he should delight
himself with God.'*　　　　　JOB XXXIV, 9

In December 1244, Louis IX, King of France, fell desperately ill
of a malarial infection. As he lay near to death he vowed that if
he recovered he would set out for a Crusade. His life was spared;
and as soon as his health permitted him, he began to make his
preparations. The King was now thirty, a tall, slightly built man,
fair-haired and fair-skinned, perpetually suffering from erysipelas
and anaemia; but his character never lacked strength. Few human
beings have ever been so consciously and sincerely virtuous. As
King, he felt that he was responsible before God for the welfare
of his people; and no prelate, not even the Pope himself, was
allowed to come between him and this duty. It was his task to
provide a just government. Though he was no innovator and
scrupulously regarded the feudal rights of his vassals, he expected
them to play their part, and if they failed, their powers were
curtailed. This stern devotion won him admiration even from his
enemies; and their admiration was enhanced by his personal piety,
his humility and his spectacular austerity. His standard of honour
was high; he never broke his pledged word. Towards malefactors
he was merciless; and he was harsh, even cruel, in his dealings with
heretics and with the infidel. His intimates found his conversation
full of charm and gentle humour, but he kept aloof from his
ministers and his vassals; and to his own children he was an autocratic master. His Queen, Margaret of Provence, had been a gay
and proud-spirited girl, but he tamed her into a demeanour more
suited to the wife of a saint.[1]

[1] Louis's character comes out very clearly in the lives written about him by
Joinville, by William of Nangis and by William of Saint-Pathus, Queen

In that age, when virtue was so much admired and so seldom achieved, King Louis stood out far above his fellow-potentates. It was natural that he should wish to go Crusading; and his actual adherence to the movement was greeted with delight. A Crusade was desperately needed. On 27 November 1244, just after the disaster at Gaza, Galeran, Bishop of Beirut, sailed from Acre to tell the princes of the West, on behalf of the Patriarch Robert of Jerusalem, that reinforcements must be sent if the whole kingdom were not to perish. In June 1245, Pope Innocent IV, driven from Italy by the forces of the Emperor, held a Council in the Imperial city of Lyons, to discuss how Frederick should be restrained. Bishop Galeran joined him there, together with Albert, Patriarch of Antioch. Innocent was somewhat offended with Louis, who scrupulously refused to condone all his actions against the Emperor, but hearing the sombre report brought by Galeran from the East, he gladly confirmed the King's Crusading vows, and sent Odo, Cardinal-Bishop of Frascati, to preach the Crusade throughout France.[1]

The King's preparations lasted for three years. Extraordinary taxes were levied to pay for the expedition, and the clergy, to their fury, were not exempted from paying them. The government of the country had to be settled. The Queen-Mother Blanche, whose ability as a ruler had been proved during her son's stormy minority, was entrusted once more with the regency. There were foreign problems to solve. The King of England must be persuaded to keep the peace.[2] Relations with the Emperor Frederick were particularly delicate. Louis had won Frederick's gratitude by his strict neutrality in the quarrel between Papacy and Empire; but in 1247 he had to threaten intervention when Frederick proposed

Margaret's confessor. The last was written to provide evidence to justify his canonization.

[1] Hefele-Leclercq, *Histoire des Conciles*, v, 2, pp. 1635, 1651–3, 1655–61; *MS. of Rothelin*, pp. 566–7; Joinville, ed. Wailly, p. 37; William of Saint-Pathus, pp. 21–2; William of Nangis, *R.H.F.* vol. xx, p. 352.

[2] Joinville, pp. 41–2; William of Nangis, *loc. cit.*; Powicke, *King Henry III and the Lord Edward*, 1, p. 239.

to his allies an attack on the Pope's person at Lyons. Moreover, Frederick was the father of the legal King of Jerusalem. Without King Conrad's permission Louis had no right to enter his country. It seems that French envoys kept Frederick fully informed of the intended Crusade, and that Frederick, while expressing his sympathy, passed the information on to the Court of Egypt. Then ships had to be found to carry the Crusade to the East. After some negotiations Genoa and Marseilles agreed to supply what was needed. The Venetians, who were already annoyed at a scheme that might interrupt their good commercial arrangements with Egypt, were thereby made still more hostile.[1]

At last, on 12 August 1248, King Louis left Paris and on the 25th he set sail from Aigues-Mortes for Cyprus. With him were the Queen and two of his brothers, Robert, Count of Artois, and Charles, Count of Anjou. He was followed by his cousins, Hugh, Duke of Burgundy, and Peter, Count of Brittany, both of whom had been Crusaders in 1239, by Hugh X of Lusignan, Count of La Marche, King Henry III's stepfather, who had been as a young man on the Fifth Crusade, by William of Dampierre, Count of Flanders, by Guy III, Count of Saint-Pol, whose father had been on the Third and Fourth Crusades, by John, Count of Sarrebruck, and his cousin John of Joinville, Seneschal of Champagne, the historian, and by many lesser folk. Some of them embarked at Aigues-Mortes, others at Marseilles. Joinville and his cousin, who had nine knights each, chartered a boat from the latter port.[2]

An English detachment under William, Earl of Salisbury, grandson of Henry II and Fair Rosamond, followed close behind. Other English lords had planned to join the Crusade, but Henry III had no wish to lose their services and arranged for the Pope to block their passage. From Scotland came Patrick, Earl of Dunbar, who died on his journey at Marseilles.[3]

[1] Hefele-Leclercq, *op. cit.* v, 2, pp. 1681–3. Al-Aïni, p. 201, says that Frederick warned the Sultan.

[2] Joinville, pp. 39–40, 43–6; Matthew Paris, v, pp. 23–5.

[3] Matthew Paris, IV, pp. 628–9, v, pp. 41, 76. Many English Crusaders were released from their vows by a money payment (*ibid.* v, pp. 73–4). Simon of

The royal squadron reached Limassol on 17 September; and the King and Queen landed there next morning. During the next few days the troops for the Crusade gathered in Cyprus. In addition to the nobles from France, there arrived from Acre the Acting Grand Master of the Hospital, John of Ronay, and the Grand Master of the Temple, and many of the Syrian barons. King Henry of Cyprus received them all with cordial hospitality.[1]

When the plan of campaign was discussed, everyone agreed that Egypt should be the objective. It was the richest and most vulnerable province of the Ayubite Empire; and men remembered how during the Fifth Crusade the Sultan had been willing to exchange Jerusalem itself for Damietta. When the decision was made, Louis wished to start operations at once. The Grand Masters and the Syrian barons dissuaded him. The winter storms would soon begin, and the coast of the Delta, with its treacherous sandbanks and rare harbours, would be dangerous to approach. Besides, they hoped to persuade the King to intervene in the family squabbles of the Ayubites. In the summer of 1248 the Prince of Aleppo, an-Nasir Yusuf, had driven his cousin al-Ashraf Musa out of Homs, and the dispossessed prince appealed for help from Sultan Ayub, who came up from Egypt and sent an army to recover Homs. The Templars had already entered into negotiations with the Sultan suggesting that territorial concessions would win him Frankish auxiliaries. But King Louis would have nothing to do with such a scheme. Like the visiting Crusaders of the previous century, he had come to fight the infidel, not to indulge in diplomacy. He ordered the Templars to break off their negotiations.[2]

The scruples that forbade the King to come to terms with any Moslem did not apply to the pagan Mongols. He had a good

Montfort had wished to go but was restrained by Henry III. See Powicke, *op. cit.* I, p. 214. It had been hoped that King Haakon of Norway would bring a contingent (Matthew Paris, IV, pp. 650–2). Patrick of Dunbar's death is noted in *Estoire d'Eracles*, II, p. 436.

[1] Joinville, pp. 46–7; *Gestes des Chiprois*, p. 147.

[2] Joinville, pp. 47, 51, 52; William of Nangis, pp. 367–9; Abu'l Feda, p. 125; Maqrisi, X, pp. 198–9.

precedent. In 1245 Pope Innocent IV had supplemented his efforts to save Christendom in the Nearer East by sending two embassies to Mongolia to the Court of the Great Khan. One, led by the Franciscan John of Pian del Carpine, left Lyons that April and, after travelling for fifteen months across Russia and the steppes of Central Asia, reached the Imperial camp at Sira Ordu, close to Karakorum, in August 1246, in time to witness the Kuriltay that elected Guyuk to supreme power. Guyuk, who had many Nestorians among his advisers, received the Papal envoy kindly; but when he read the Pope's letter requiring him to accept Christianity, he wrote an answer ordering the Pope to acknowledge his suzerainty and to come with all princes of the West to do him homage. John of Pian del Carpine on his return to the Papal Curia at the end of 1247 gave Innocent, together with this discouraging letter, a detailed report in which he showed that the Mongols were only out for conquest.[1] But Innocent would not allow his illusions to be entirely shattered. His second embassy, under the Dominican Ascelin of Lombardy, had set out a little later and travelled across Syria, and met the Mongol general Baichu in May 1247, at Tabriz. Baichu, whom Ascelin found personally offensive and disagreeable, was ready to discuss the possibility of an alliance against the Ayubites. He planned to attack Baghdad, and it would suit him to have the Syrian Moslems distracted by a Crusade. He sent two envoys, Aïbeg and Serkis, the latter of whom was certainly a Nestorian, back with Ascelin to Rome; and, though they had no plenipotentiary powers, the hopes of the West rose again. They stayed about a year with the Pope. In November 1248 they were told to return to Baichu with complaints that nothing further was happening about the alliance.[2]

While King Louis was in Cyprus, in December 1248, two Nestorians, called Mark and David, arrived at Nicosia, saying that

[1] See Pian del Carpine, *Historia Mongolorum* (ed. Pulle), for a full account of this embassy, esp. pp. 115 ff. Guyuk's letter is given *ibid.* pp. 125–6.

[2] See Pelliot, 'Les Mongols et la Papauté', *Revue de l'Orient Chrétien*, vol. XXVIII, pp. 112, 131.

they were sent by a Mongol general, Aljighidai, who was the Great Khan's commissioner at Mosul. They brought a letter talking in fulsome terms of the Mongols' sympathy for Christianity. Louis was delighted and at once dispatched a mission of Dominicans under Andrew of Longjumeau and his brother, who both spoke Arabic. Andrew had indeed been the Pope's chief agent in recent negotiations with the Monophysites. They carried with them a portable chapel, as a suitable gift for a nomad convert Khan, and relics for its altar and other worldlier presents. They left Cyprus in January 1249, for Aljighidai's camp, and were sent on by him to Mongolia. On their arrival at Karakorum they found that Guyuk had died and his widow Oghul Qaimish was acting as Regent. She was gracious to the mission, but regarded the King's gifts as the tribute from a vassal to a sovereign, while dynastic difficulties at home prevented her, even had she so intended, from sending any large expedition to the West. Andrew returned three years later with nothing more than a patronizing letter in which the Regent thanked her vassal for his attentions, and requested that similar gifts should be sent every year. Louis was shocked by this response, but still hoped some day to achieve a Mongol alliance.[1]

The sojourn of the Crusade in Cyprus was thus wasted diplomatically. Almost a year previously King Louis had sent agents to collect food and armaments for the army. The latter task was usefully performed, but the commissariat had not expected to have to feed so many mouths for more than a month or two. It was, however, not till May 1249, that it was practicable for the expedition to sail against Egypt. When spring came Louis applied to the local Italian merchant colonies to provide him with ships. The Venetians disapproved of the whole Crusade and would not help. In March there began an open war between the Genoese and Pisans along the Syrian coast, and the Genoese, on whom Louis

[1] Pian del Carpine, *op. cit.* pp. 174–95. It is doubtful whether Aljighidai was authorized to send his embassy. Its arrival and Louis's embassy is noted by Joinville, pp. 47–8, and *MS. of Rothelin*, p. 469. Matthew Paris (v, pp. 80, 87) calls the rumours of the Tartar King's conversion most cheerful ('jocundissimi').

principally relied, had the worst of it. John of Ibelin, lord of Arsuf, managed after some three weeks to make the colonies in Acre sign a truce for three years. By the end of May it was possible to find the ships that the Crusade required.[1] Meanwhile Louis received visitors and embassies at Nicosia. Hethoum of Armenia sent him rich gifts; Bohemond of Antioch asked for and obtained a company of six hundred archers to protect his principality from Turcoman brigands. The Latin Empress of Constantinople, Maria of Brienne, made the journey there to beg for help against the Greek Emperor of Nicaea. Louis was sympathetic, but told her that the Crusade against the infidel must take precedence. Finally, in May, William of Villehardouin, Prince of Achaea, arrived with twenty-four ships and a regiment of Franks from the Morea. The Duke of Burgundy had spent the winter with him at Sparta and had persuaded him to join the King. The army assembled in Cyprus was reaching formidable proportions. But the pleasures of the gracious island softened its morale; and the stocks of food that were to have sufficed for the Egyptian campaign were almost exhausted.[2]

On 13 May 1249, a fleet of one hundred and twenty large transports and many smaller vessels lay off Limassol, and the army began to embark. Unfortunately a storm scattered the ships a few days later. When the King himself set sail on 30 May, only a quarter of his army sailed with him. The others made their way independently to the Egyptian coast. The royal squadron arrived off Damietta on 4 June.[3]

Sultan Ayub had spent the winter at Damascus, hoping that his troops would finish the conquest of Homs before the Frankish invasions began. He had first expected Louis to land in Syria, but when he realized that an attack was to be made on Egypt, he lifted

[1] Joinville, pp. 46–7; *Estoire d'Eracles*, II, pp. 436–7; Matthew Paris, V, p. 70; William of Nangis, p. 368.

[2] Joinville, pp. 48–51; Vincent of Beauvais, pp. 1315 ff.

[3] Joinville, pp. 52–3; William of Nangis, pp. 370–1; *MS. of Rothelin*, p. 589; Abu'l Feda, p. 126, estimating the King's army at 59,000 strong; letter of Guy of Melun in Matthew Paris, V, pp. 155–6.

S

the siege of Homs and himself hurried back to Cairo, ordering his Syrian armies to follow him. He was an ill man, in an advanced stage of tuberculosis, and could no longer lead his men in person. He ordered his aged vizier, Fakhr ad-Din, the friend of Frederick II, to take command of the army that was to oppose the Frankish landing, and he sent stores of munitions to Damietta and garrisoned it with the tribesmen of the Banū Kinana, Bedouins famed for their courage. He installed himself at Ashmun-Tannah, to the east of the main branch of the River Nile.[1]

On board the royal flagship, the *Montjoie*, the King's advisers begged him to wait till the rest of his transports arrived before attempting to disembark. But he refused to delay. At dawn of 5 June the landing began in the teeth of the enemy, on the sands to the west of the river mouth. There was a fierce battle on the very edge of the sea; but the fearless discipline of the French soldiers, with the King at their head, and the gallantry of the knights of Outremer under John of Ibelin, Count of Jaffa, forced the Moslems back with heavy losses. At nightfall Fakhr ad-Din drew off his men and retired over the bridge of boats to Damietta. Finding the population there in panic and the garrison wavering, he decided to evacuate the city. All the Moslem civilians fled with him, and the Banū Kinana followed them, after setting fire to the bazaars but neglecting his orders to destroy the bridge of boats. Next morning the Crusaders learned from Christians who had remained in their homes that Damietta was undefended. They marched triumphantly over the bridge into the city.[2]

Their easy capture of Damietta astounded and delighted the Franks. But, for the moment, they could not follow it up. The Nile floods were soon due to begin; and Louis, profiting from the bitter experience of the Fifth Crusade, refused to advance

[1] Maqrisi, x, pp. 200–1; Abu'l Feda, p. 126; Al-Aïni, p. 201.
[2] Joinville, pp. 53–8; William of Nangis, p. 371; *MS. of Rothelin* (letter of John Sarrasin), pp. 589–91; *Gestes des Chiprois*, pp. 147–8; Matthew Paris, v, p. 81, vi, pp. 152–4 (letter of Robert of Artois to Queen Blanche); vi, pp. 155–62 (letter of Guy of Melun); Maqrisi, xiii, pp. 203–4; Abu'l Feda, p. 126; al-Aïni, pp. 201–23; Abu Shama, ii, p. 195.

further till the river should go down. Besides he was waiting for the arrival from France of reinforcements under his brother, Alfonso, Count of Poitou. In the meantime Damietta was transformed into a Frankish city. Once again, as in 1219, the Great Mosque became a cathedral and a bishop was installed. Buildings were allotted to the three Military Orders and money benefices to the leading lords of Outremer. The Genoese and Pisans were rewarded for their services by a market and a street apiece, and the Venetians, repenting their hostility, begged successfully for a similar gift. The native Christians, Coptic Monophysites, were treated with scrupulous justice by King Louis and welcomed his rule. The Queen, who had been sent to Acre with the other ladies of the Crusade when the army left Cyprus, was summoned to join the King. Louis also welcomed another distinguished if impoverished friend, Baldwin II, Emperor of Constantinople, whom he had known in Paris where the Emperor had visited him in order to raise money by selling him relics of the Passion that had survived the Crusaders' sack of the Imperial capital. Throughout the summer months Damietta was the capital of Outremer. But to the soldiers this inaction in the humid heat of the Delta brought demoralization. Food began to run short, and there was disease in the camp.[1]

The loss of Damietta had shocked the Moslem world. But, while the Franks hesitated, the dying Sultan took action. Like his father thirty years before, he offered to buy back Damietta with the cession of Jerusalem. The offer was rejected; King Louis still refused to treat with an infidel. Meanwhile Ayub punished the generals responsible for the loss of the city. The emirs of the Banū Kinana were executed, and Fakhr ad-Din was disgraced, along with the chief Mameluk commanders. The Mameluks wished to carry out a palace-revolution. But Fakhr ad-Din dissuaded them; and his loyalty restored him to the Sultan's favour. Troops were rushed

---

[1] *MS. of Rothelin*, pp. 592–4; Matthew Paris, VI, pp. 160–1; *ibid.* IV, p. 626 (Emperor Baldwin's visit). Louis's report on the Church of Damietta is printed in Baluze, *Collectio Veterum Scriptorum*, IV, pp. 491–5.

up to Mansourah, the town whose name means 'victorious', built by Sultan al-Kamil on the site of his triumph over the Fifth Crusade. Ayub himself was carried there in his litter to organize the army. Bedouin guerrilla-fighters were let loose on the country-side and would creep right up to the walls of Damietta, killing any Frank that strayed outside. Louis was obliged to erect dykes and dig ditches to protect his camp.[1]

The Nile waters went down at the end of October. About the same time, on 24 October, Louis's second brother, Alfonso of Poitou, arrived with the reinforcements from France. It was time to advance on Cairo. Peter of Brittany, supported by the barons of Outremer, then suggested that it would be wiser to attack Alexandria. The Egyptians would be surprised by such a move. The Crusaders had enough ships to cross the branches of the Nile; and once they had taken Alexandria they would control the whole Mediterranean littoral of Egypt. The Sultan would be forced to make terms. But the King's brother, Robert of Artois, pas-sionately opposed such a project, and the King took his part. On 20 November the Frankish army set out from Damietta, along the southern road to Mansourah. A strong garrison was left behind in the city with the Queen and the Patriarch of Jerusalem.[2]

Fortune seemed to favour King Louis; for Sultan Ayub was now on his deathbed. He died at Mansourah three days later, on the 23rd. He had been a grim, solitary man, with nothing of the affability, the liberality or the love of learning of most of his kin. His health was consistently poor; and it may be that his Sudanese blood set him consciously apart from the rest of his family, whose Kurdish descent was unimpaired. But he was an able ruler and the last great member of the great Ayubite dynasty. His death

[1] Al-Aïni, pp. 202–6. Hugh of la Marche was killed during these skirmishes (Matthew Paris, v, p. 89).
[2] Joinville, pp. 64–5; Matthew Paris, vi, p. 161 (letter of Guy of Melun); *ibid*. v, pp. 105–7, misdating the events of the winter in February, and p. 130; Maqrisi, xiii, p. 215.

threatened the Moslems with disaster; for his only son, Turan-shah, was far away, acting as Viceroy in the Jezireh. Egypt was saved by the widowed Sultana, the Armenian-born Shajar ad-Durr. Confiding in the eunuch Jamal ad-Din Mohsen, who controlled the palace, and in Fakhr ad-Din, she concealed her husband's death and forged a document under his signature which appointed Turanshah as heir and Fakhr ad-Din as generalissimo and viceroy during the Sultan's illness. When the news of Ayub's death eventually leaked out, the Sultana and Fakhr ad-Din were firmly in power, and Turanshah was on his way to Egypt. But the Franks were encouraged to hear of it. It seemed to them that this government of a woman and an aged general would soon collapse. They pressed on their march towards Cairo.[1]

The road from Damietta was cut by numberless canals and branches of the Nile, of which the largest was the Bahr as-Saghir, which left the main river just below Mansourah and ran past Ashmun-Tannah to Lake Manzaleh, thus cutting off the so-called Island of Damietta. Fakhr ad-Din kept the bulk of his forces behind the Bahr as-Saghir, but sent cavalry to harass the Franks as they crossed each canal. None of these skirmishes was successful in holding up the Frankish advance. King Louis proceeded slowly and cautiously. There was a battle near Fariskur on 7 December, where the Egyptian cavalry was repulsed, and the Templars, in defiance of the King's orders, insisted on pursuing the fugitives too far and had some difficulty in rejoining their comrades. On 14 December the King reached Baramun, and on the 21st his army encamped on the banks of the Bahr as-Saghir, opposite to Mansourah.[2]

For six weeks the armies faced each other across the wide canal. An attempt by the Egyptian cavalry to cross into the island of Damietta lower down and attack the Franks in the rear was beaten

---

[1] Maqrisi, XIII, pp. 208–15; Abu'l Feda, p. 127; al-Aïni, p. 207; *MS. of Rothelin*, p. 599; Matthew Paris, V, pp. 107–8.

[2] Joinville, pp. 69–70; *MS. of Rothelin*, pp. 597–8; Maqrisi, XIII, pp. 215–16; al-Aïni, p. 207.

off near the camp by Charles of Anjou. Meanwhile Louis ordered the construction of a dyke to bridge the stream; but, though he built covered galleries to protect the workmen, the Egyptian bombardment from the other bank, and in particular the use of Greek fire, was so formidable that the work was abandoned. Early in February 1250, a Copt from Salamun came to the King's camp and offered to reveal for 500 besants the whereabouts of a ford across the Bahr as-Saghir. On 8 February, at dawn, the Crusaders set out across the ford. The Duke of Burgundy was left with strong forces to maintain the camp; while King Louis travelled with the advancing army. His brother, Robert of Artois, led the van, with the Templars and the English contingent. He was given stern orders not to attack the Egyptians till the King gave permission. The difficult passage was successfully achieved, but it was slow. Once he was himself across the river with his men, the Count of Artois feared that unless he attacked the enemy at once, the element of surprise would be lost. The Templars vainly reminded him of his instructions; but when he insisted on advancing, they agreed to accompany the charge. His rashness was justified. The Egyptian camp, some two miles out of Mansourah, was beginning its daily round quite unsuspecting, when suddenly the Frankish cavalry thundered into its midst. Many of the Egyptians were slaughtered as they hurried to find their arms. Others fled half-clad to the safety of Mansourah. The generalissimo Fakhr ad-Din had just left his bath and a valet was dyeing his beard with henna when he heard the uproar. Without waiting to don his armour he leapt on to his horse and rode out into the battle. He found himself in the midst of some Templar knights, who hacked him down.

Robert of Artois was now master of the Egyptian camp. Once again the Grand Master of the Temple begged him to wait till the King and the main army were over the ford and had joined him, and William of Salisbury too advised caution. But Robert was determined to capture Mansourah and finish off the Egyptian army. After denouncing the Templars and the English as cowards, he rallied his men and charged once more into the fleeing Egyptians; and once more the Templars and William felt obliged to follow him. Though Fakhr ad-Din was dead, the Mameluk commanders managed to restore discipline among their troops; and the ablest of them, Rukn ad-Din Baibars, surnamed Bundukdari, 'the arbalestier', took control. He stationed his men at crucial points within the town itself, then let the Frankish cavalry come pouring in through the open gate. When the French knights, with the Templars close behind them, swept up to the very walls of the citadel, the Mameluks rushed out on them from the side-streets. The Frankish horses could not easily turn in the narrow space and at once were thrown into confusion. A few knights escaped on foot to the banks of the Nile, only to drown in its waters. A few others managed to extricate themselves from the town. The Templars fell fighting in the streets; only five out of their two hundred and ninety knights survived. Robert of Artois barricaded himself and his bodyguard in a house, but the Egyptians soon burst in and massacred them all. Amongst the knights that fell in the battle were the Earl of Salisbury and almost all his English followers, the Lord of Coucy and the Count of Brienne. Peter of Brittany had been with them in the vanguard, and was severely wounded on the head. But he succeeded in riding back out of the town and hurried to warn the King.

The Crusading army had almost entirely crossed the Bahr as-Saghir. On hearing of the disaster Louis at once drew up his front line to meet an attack, and meanwhile sent his engineers to make a bridge over the stream. The corps of crossbowmen had been left on the far side, in order that they could if necessary cover the crossing; and he was anxious for them to join him. As he expected, the victorious Mameluks soon charged out of the town into his lines. Louis firmly held back his men while the enemy poured arrows into their ranks; then, as soon as the Mameluks' ammunition began to run short, he ordered a counter-charge. His cavalry swept the Saracens back; but they soon re-formed and charged again, while detachments tried to hinder the building of the pontoon. The King himself was almost forced back into the canal, but another counter-charge saved him. At last, towards sundown, the pontoon was finished and the bowmen crossed over. Their coming gave the King the victory. The Egyptians retired again into Mansourah; and Louis set up his camp on the spot where they had camped the night before. It was only then that he learned from the Acting Grand-Master of the Hospital that his brother had been killed. He broke down in tears.[1]

The Crusaders were victorious, but it had been a costly victory. Had Robert of Artois not led his wild foray into Mansourah, they might have felt strong enough to attempt to attack the town later, though they would have been opposed by war-engines better than their own. As it was, there was nothing to be done. The situation was ominously reminiscent of the Fifth Crusade, when the Christian army that had captured Damietta was held up close to the same spot and at last forced to retreat. Louis could not hope now for a better fate, unless troubles at the Egyptian Court might induce the government at Cairo to offer him acceptable terms. In the meantime he fortified his camp and strengthened the pontoon. It was wise; for three days later, on 11 February, the Egyptians attacked again. Reinforcements had arrived from the south, and they were stronger than before. It was one of the fiercest battles that the men of Outremer could remember. Again and again the Mameluks charged, firing a cloud of arrows as they came; again and again Louis restrained his men till it was time to counter-charge. Charles of Anjou on the left wing and the Syrian and Cypriot barons in the left centre held their ground firmly, but the remnants of the Templars and the French nobles in the right centre were wavering and the King himself had to rescue them in order not to lose contact with the left. The Grand Master William, who had lost an eye at Mansourah, lost the other and died from it. At one moment Alfonso of Poitou, who was guarding the camp, on the right wing, was encircled and was rescued by

[1] Joinville, pp. 71–93; *MS. of Rothelin*, pp. 599–608; Matthew Paris, v, pp. 147–54, vi, pp. 191–3; al-Aïni, p. 208.

the cooks and the women camp-followers. At last the Moslems wearied and retired in good order back to the town.[1]

For eight weeks King Louis waited in the camp before Mansourah. The hoped-for Egyptian revolution never occurred. Instead, on 28 February, Turanshah, son of the late Sultan, arrived at the Egyptian camp. As soon as he heard from his stepmother of his father's death, he had left his capital at Diarbekir and rode swiftly south. He spent three weeks at Damascus, where he was proclaimed Sultan, and reached Cairo towards the end of February. His arrival at Mansourah was the signal for new activity by the Egyptians. He caused a squadron of light boats to be made, which were transported on camel-back to the lower reaches of the Nile. There they were launched and began to intercept the vessels that brought food to the Crusader camp from Damietta. More than eighty Frankish ships were captured one after the other and on 16 March a convoy of thirty-two were lost at one swoop. The Franks were quickly threatened by famine. Famine was followed by disease, dysentery and typhoid.[2]

At the beginning of April King Louis understood that he must extricate the army as best he could from the miasmas of the camp and retreat to Damietta. Now, at last, he brought himself to open negotiations with the infidel, and sent to offer Turanshah the exchange of Damietta for Jerusalem.[3] It was too late. The Egyptians knew now how precarious was his position. When his offer was rejected, Louis called his officers together to discuss the retreat. They begged him to slip ahead himself with his bodyguard to Damietta. But he proudly refused to leave his men. It was decided that the sick should be sent by boat down the Nile and the able-bodied should march along the road by which they had come.

---

[1] Joinville, pp. 93–5; *MS. of Rothelin*, pp. 608–9.

[2] Abu Shama, II, p. 195; al-Aïni, p. 209; Maqrisi, XIII, pp. 220–4; Matthew Paris, VI, pp. 193–4; Joinville, pp. 102–4; *MS. of Rothelin*, pp. 609–12.

[3] Matthew Paris talks of early peace offers made by the Sultan and rejected on the advice of Robert of Artois (V, pp. 87–8, 105) or of the Legate (V, p. 143). Louis's offer is reported by Joinville, pp. 106–7. A rumour reached Europe that Louis had taken Cairo (*ibid.* p. 118, VI, p. 117).

The camp was struck on the morning of 5 April 1250, and the painful journey began, with the King in the rearguard to encourage the stragglers. The Mameluks in Mansourah saw the movement and set out in pursuit. They found that the Franks were all across the Bahr as-Saghir, but the engineers had forgotten to destroy the pontoon. They hurried across and soon were harassing the Franks from all sides. Throughout that day their attacks were beaten off, as the Franks moved slowly on. The King's own gallantry was beyond all praise. But that night he fell ill, and next morning he could scarcely keep himself on his horse. As the day dragged on, the Moslems closed in round the army and attacked in full force. The sick and weary soldiers scarcely tried to resist them. It was clear that the end had come. Geoffrey of Sargines, who commanded the royal bodyguard, took the King into a cottage in the village of Munyat al-Khols Abdallah, just north of Sharimshah, in the centre of the fighting. The French knights could not bear to admit defeat; but the barons of Outremer took control and sent Philip of Montfort to negotiate with the enemy. Philip had almost succeeded in persuading the Egyptian generals to allow the free departure of the army in return for the surrender of Damietta, when suddenly a sergeant called Marcel, bribed, it was thought, by the Egyptians, rode through the Christian ranks telling the commanders in the King's name to surrender without conditions. They obeyed this order, of which Louis himself knew nothing, and they laid down their arms; and the whole army was rounded up and led into captivity. About the same hour the ships conveying the sick to Damietta were surrounded and captured.[1]

The Egyptians were at first embarrassed by the numbers of their prisoners. Finding it impossible to guard them all, those that were too feeble to march were executed at once, and on every evening for a week three hundred were taken out and decapitated, by the

[1] Joinville, pp. 107–10; *MS. of Rothelin*, pp. 612–16; William of Nangis, p. 376; William of Saint-Pathus, pp. 74–5; Matthew Paris, V, pp. 157–9, 165–8, VI, pp. 193–7; al-Aïni, pp. 209–13; Maqrisi, XIII, p. 227; Abu'l Feda, p. 128.

Sultan's own orders. King Louis was moved from his sick-bed and lodged, in chains, in a private house in Mansourah. The leading barons were kept together in a larger prison. Their captors would constantly threaten them with death, but had in fact no intention of slaying anyone who might bring in a good ransom. Joinville, who was on board one of the captured ships, saved his own and his comrades' lives by letting it be understood that he was the King's cousin; and when the Egyptian admiral questioned him about it and learned that it was untrue but that in fact he was a cousin of the Emperor Frederick, his reputation was greatly enhanced.

Indeed, the prestige of the infidel Emperor did much to ease the situation of the Crusaders. When Louis in his prison was ordered by the Sultan to cede not only Damietta but all the Frankish lands in Syria, he replied that they belonged not to him but to King Conrad, the Emperor's son, and only the Emperor could give them away. The Moslems at once dropped the suggestion. But the terms that they exacted from the King were harsh enough. He was to ransom himself by the cession of Damietta, and his army by the payment of 500,000 pounds *tournois*, that is to say, a million besants. It was a vast sum; but the prisoners to be released were very numerous. As soon as the terms were agreed, the King and the chief barons were taken on board galleys, which sailed down the river to Fariskur, where the Sultan took up his residence. It was arranged that they should go on to Damietta and the city be handed over two days later, on 30 April.[1]

It was only through the fortitude of Queen Margaret that the bargain could be made at all. When the King left her to march on Mansourah she had been about to bear a child; and the child was born, with an octogenarian knight as midwife, three days after the news came of the surrender of the army. She called her little son John Tristan, the child of sorrow. That same day she heard

---

[1] Joinville, pp. 110–22; *MS. of Rothelin*, pp. 616–18; Matthew Paris, v, pp. 1604, vi, pp. 196–7 (the writer of this letter, a Hospitaller, says that 'our only hope lies in Frederick'); al-Aïni, pp. 213–14.

that the Pisans and Genoese were planning to evacuate Damietta, as there was insufficient food left to feed the inhabitants. She knew that she could not hold Damietta without the aid of the Italians and she summoned their leaders to her bedside to plead with them; for if Damietta were abandoned there would be nothing to offer in return for the release of the King. When she proposed herself buying up all the food in the city and seeing to its distribution, they agreed to stay. The purchase cost her more than 360,000 pounds, but it saved the morale of the city. As soon as she was well enough to travel, her staff insisted on moving her by sea to Acre, while the Patriarch Robert went with a safe-conduct to the Sultan, to Fariskur, to complete the arrangements for the ransom.[1]

He arrived there to find the Sultan dead. There had been some delay over the final negotiations; and on Monday, 2 May, Turanshah and his captives were still at Fariskur. That day he gave a banquet to his emirs. But he had lost the support of the Mameluks. This great army corps of Turkish and Circassian slaves had grown in importance and power during the reign of Ayub, whose favour had been rewarded by their loyalty; and their support of the Sultana Shajar ad-Durr had preserved the throne for Turanshah. But now, as victor over the Franks, he felt himself strong enough to fill the government with favourites from the Jezireh; and when the Mameluks protested he answered with drunken threats. At the same time he offended his stepmother by claiming from her property that had belonged to his father. She wrote at once to the Mameluk commanders to protect her.

As Turanshah rose to leave his banquet on 2 May, soldiers of the Bahrid regiment of Mameluks, with Baibars Bundukdari at their head, burst in and began, Baibars first of all, to slash at the Sultan with their swords. He fled wounded to a wooden tower beside the river. When the soldiers followed and set it alight, he leapt into the Nile and there, standing in the water, he begged for mercy, offering to abdicate and go back to the Jezireh. No one

[1] Joinville, pp. 142–4.

answered his appeal. After a volley of arrows had failed to kill him, Baibars leapt down the bank and finished him off with his sabre. For three days the mutilated body lay unburied. Eventually the ambassador of the Caliph of Baghdad obtained leave to commit it to a simple tomb. The triumphant conspirators appointed the senior Mameluk commander, Izz ad-Din Aibek, as generalissimo and regent; and he married the Dowager Sultana, Shajar ad-Durr, who represented legitimacy. An infant cousin of the late Sultan, al-Ashraf Musa, was later produced and proclaimed co-Sultan, only to be deposed four years later. His ultimate fate is unknown.[1]

When the aged Patriarch arrived from Damietta with a safe-conduct signed by Turanshah, the new government feigned to regard it as valueless and treated him as a prisoner. Some Mameluks appeared before King Louis with blood still on their swords, claiming money from him for having slain his enemy. Others with a grim sense of fun brandished their swords in the faces of the captive barons. Joinville was frankly terrified. But the Mameluks had no intention of forgoing the huge ransom. They confirmed the previous terms. When Damietta was surrendered, the King and the nobles would be released, but the ordinary soldiers, some of whom had been taken to Cairo, would have to await the payment of the money, which was reduced to 400,000 pounds *tournois*, half to be paid at Damietta and half when the King arrived at Acre. When the King was asked to swear that if he failed in his bargain he would renounce Christ, he firmly refused. Throughout his captivity his dignity and integrity deeply impressed his captors, some of whom jestingly proposed that he should be their next Sultan.[2]

On Friday, 6 May 1250, Geoffrey of Sargines went to Damietta and handed the fortress over to the Moslem vanguard. The King and the nobles were brought there that afternoon; and Louis set

---

[1] Maqrisi, XIII, pp. 230–2; Abu'l Feda, p. 129; Abu Shama, pp. 198–209; Ibn Khallikan, III, p. 248. For Ashraf Musa, see below, p. 310.

[2] Joinville, pp. 123–32; William of Nangis, p. 381; William of Saint-Pathus, pp. 23, 58, 75–6; *MS. of Rothelin*, pp. 618–19; al-Aïni, p. 213.

about finding money for the first instalment of the ransom. But the money in his own coffers came only to 170,000 pounds. Till the remainder was found, the Egyptians held back the King's brother, Alfonso of Poitou. The Templars were known to have large stocks of money in their chief galley; but it was only when they were threatened with violence that they agreed to disgorge what was required. When the whole sum was handed over to the Egyptians the Count of Poitou was set free. That evening the King and the barons set sail for Acre, where they arrived six days later, after a stormy voyage. Neither clothes nor bedding had been made ready for the King on his ship. He was obliged to wear the robes and sleep on the mattress that he had used in prison.[1]

Many wounded soldiers had been left behind at Damietta. Contrary to their promise the Moslems massacred them all.[2]

Soon after his arrival at Acre Louis took counsel of his vassals about his future plans. His mother had written to him from France to urge his speedy return. King Henry of England was said to be on the war-path, and there were many other urgent problems. But he felt that he himself was needed in Outremer. The disaster of the Egyptian campaign had not only destroyed a French army, but it had robbed Outremer of almost all its troops. Moreover it was his duty to remain at hand till the last of the prisoners in Egypt was released. The King's brothers and the Count of Flanders advised him to return to France. But in fact his mind was made up. On 3 July he publicly announced his decision. His brothers and any who wished should go home, but he would stay, and would take into his personal service all those, such as Joinville, who were willing to stay with him. A letter was sent to the barons of France explaining his decision and begging for reinforcements for the Crusade. He had felt bitterly the failure of his great effort. It was all very well for him to declare that the catastrophe was a sign of God's grace, sent to teach him humility, but he must have

---

[1] Joinville, pp. 135–8; *MS. of Rothelin*, pp. 619–20.
[2] *MS. of Rothelin*, p. 620.

reflected that he had paid for the privilege of that lesson with the loss of many thousands of innocent lives.[1]

The King's brothers, together with the leading nobles of the Crusade, sailed from Acre about the middle of July. They left behind all the money that they could spare but only about 1400 men.[2] The Queen remained with the King. He was at once accepted as *de facto* ruler of the kingdom. The throne still belonged legitimately to Conrad of Germany; but it was obvious that Conrad would never now come to the East. On Alice's death the regency passed to her son, King Henry of Cyprus, who had nominated his cousin, John of Arsuf, as *bailli*. He gladly handed over the government to Louis.[3]

The departure of his French vassals permitted Louis to listen more readily to advice. His experience had broadened his mind, and his lack of armed force taught him the need for diplomatic relations with the infidel. Some of his friends found him too ready to follow a 'poulain' policy; but he was wise to do so and the moment was favourable for diplomacy. The Mameluk revolution in Egypt had not been well received in Moslem Syria, where loyalty to the Ayubites persisted. When the news came of Turan-shah's death, an-Nasir Yusuf of Aleppo marched down from Homs and on 9 July 1250, occupied Damascus, where he was enthusiastically welcomed as the great-grandson of Saladin. Once more there was bitter rivalry between Cairo and Damascus, and both courts were eager to buy Frankish aid. Hardly had Louis arrived at Acre before an embassy came there from an-Nasir Yusuf. But Louis would not commit himself. The Damascene alliance might be strategically preferable, but he had to think of the Frankish prisoners still in Egypt.[4]

[1] Joinville, pp. 145–57; William of Nangis, p. 383; William of Saint-Pathus, pp. 91–2; Matthew Paris, v, pp. 173–4.
[2] Joinville, p. 157.
[3] Louis's legal position was never defined, but he was clearly accepted as supreme authority in Conrad's absence.
[4] Abu Shama, ii, p. 200; Abu'l Feda, p. 131; Ibn Khallikan, ii, p. 446; Joinville, p. 158.

In the winter of 1250 the army of Damascus began an invasion of Egypt. On 2 February 1251, it met the Egyptian army under Aibek at Abbasa, in the Delta, twelve miles east of the modern Zagazig. The Syrians were at first successful, though Aibek's own regiment held firm; but a regiment of Mameluks in an-Nasir Yusuf's army deserted his cause in the midst of the battle. The Sultan, whose courage was not remarkable, thereupon turned and fled. The Mameluk power in Egypt was saved. But the Ayubites still held Palestine and Syria. When an-Nasir Yusuf next sent to Acre hinting that he might cede Jerusalem in return for Frankish help, Louis sent an embassy to Cairo to warn Aibek that unless the question of the Frankish prisoners was soon settled he would ally himself with Damascus. His ambassador, John of Valenciennes, succeeded in the course of two visits in securing first the release of the knights, including the Grand Master of the Hospital, taken in 1244 at Gaza, and then some 3000 of the more recent captives, in return for 300 Moslem captives in Frankish hands. Aibek showed his growing anxiety to make friends with the King by sending him, with the second batch, the gift of an elephant and a zebra. Louis was then emboldened to demand the release of all the prisoners remaining in Mameluk hands without any further payment. When Aibek realized that an envoy from Louis, the Arabic-speaking Yves the Breton, was visiting the Court of Damascus, he consented to the King's request, in return for a military alliance against an-Nasir Yusuf. He further promised that when the Mameluks had occupied Palestine and Damascus, they would return the whole of the old Kingdom of Jerusalem as far east as the Jordan to the Christians. Louis agreed; and the prisoners were all released at the end of March 1252. The treaty had nearly been wrecked by the Templars' refusal to break off relations with Damascus. The King was obliged to rebuke them publicly and demand a humble apology.[1]

The Franco-Mameluk alliance came to nothing. As soon as he

[1] Abu Shama, *loc. cit.*; Abu'l Feda, *loc. cit.*; Joinville, pp. 158–60; *MS. of Rothelin*, pp. 624–7; Matthew Paris, v, p. 342.

PLATE IV

SIDON

The Castle of the Sea is on the right, and the castle repaired by Saint Louis on the left.

heard of it, an-Nasir Yusuf sent troops to Gaza, to intercept a junction between the allies. Louis moved down to Jaffa; but the Mameluks failed to advance out of Egypt. For about a year the Syrians and the Franks remained stationary, neither wishing to provoke a battle. Meanwhile Louis repaired the fortifications of Jaffa. He had already strengthened those of Acre, Haifa and Caesarea.[1] Early in 1253 an-Nasir Yusuf appealed to Baghdad to mediate between him and the Mameluks. The Caliph, al-Mustasim, was anxious to unite the Moslem world against the Mongols. He induced Aibek, who recognized his nominal suzerainty, to accept an-Nasir Yusuf's terms. Aibek should be accepted as ruler of Egypt and should be allowed to annex Palestine up to Galilee on the north and the Jordan on the east. The peace was signed in April 1253; and Aibek's arrangement with the Franks was forgotten.[2]

The Damascene army travelled home from Gaza through Frankish territory, raiding as it came. The cities were too strong to be attacked, except for Sidon, whose walls were being reconstructed. Though they made no attempt against the castle on its little island, they sacked the town and retired laden with booty and prisoners. King Louis retaliated by sending an expedition to raid Banyas, but with no success. Fortunately for Outremer, neither Aibek nor an-Nasir Yusuf showed any more serious desire for war.[3]

Their restraint was largely due to the presence of the King of France in the East. Though his military record had been disastrous, his personality made a definite impression. It was as well; for in December 1250, the Emperor Frederick, whose name still carried weight in Moslem circles, died in Italy. His son Conrad inherited none of his prestige.[4] Louis was, moreover, far more successful in handling the inhabitants of Outremer than Frederick had been, for he was tactful and disinterested. His value was shown by his

[1] Joinville, pp. 167–8, 184–5; *MS. of Rothelin*, pp. 627–8; Matthew Paris, VI, p. 206; al-Aïni, p. 215.
[2] Maqrisi, *Sultans*, I, i, pp. 39, 54; Abu'l Feda, p. 132.
[3] Joinville, pp. 197–8; *Estoire d'Eracles*, II, pp. 440–1.
[4] Frederick died on 13 December at Fiorentino. See Hefele-Leclercq, V, I, p. 1693.

T

intervention in the Principality of Antioch. Bohemond V died in January 1252, leaving two children, a daughter, Plaisance, who had married a few months before, as his third wife, the childless King Henry of Cyprus, and a son, Bohemond, aged fifteen, who succeeded under the regency of the Dowager Princess, the Italian Lucienne. Lucienne was a feckless woman, who never left Tripoli and handed the government of the Principality to her Roman relatives. Bohemond VI was soon conscious that his mother was unpopular, and, with Louis's approval, obtained permission from the Pope to come of age a few months before the legal date. When Innocent IV agreed, Bohemond came to Acre where he was knighted by the King. Lucienne was removed from power, and compensated with a handsome income. At the same time Louis completed the reconciliation of the Court of Antioch with that of Armenia. Bohemond V in his later years had entered into relations with King Hethoum; but for him the past was too full of bitter memories. Bohemond VI bore no such rancour. In 1254, on Louis's suggestion, he married Hethoum's daughter Sibylla; and he became to some degree his father-in-law's vassal. The Armenians agreed to share in the responsibility for the protection of Antioch.[1]

King Henry of Cyprus died on 18 January 1253. As his son, Hugh II, was only a few months old, Queen Plaisance claimed the regency of Cyprus and the titular regency of Jerusalem. The High Courts of Cyprus confirmed her position there, but the mainland barons required her attendance in person before they would recognize her. John of Ibelin, lord of Arsuf, remained meanwhile as *bailli*, and Plaisance contemplated marrying his youthful son Balian. In fact, King Louis continued to administer the government.[2]

---

[1] *Estoire d'Eracles*, II, pp. 439, 441–2; *MS. of Rothelin*, p. 624; Joinville, pp. 186–7; Vincent of Beauvais, p. 96.

[2] *Estoire d'Eracles, loc. cit.*; *Assises*, II, p. 420. See La Monte, *Feudal Monarchy*, pp. 74–5; Hill, *History of Cyprus*, II, p. 149. It is unlikely that Plaisance was more than affianced to Balian, as she proposed herself as a bride for Edmund of Lancaster a few years later (Rymer, *Foedera*, I, p. 341). She was not recognized formally as Regent of Jerusalem till her visit to Acre in 1258.

There was no hope of a new Crusade from Europe. Henry III of England, who had taken the Cross with many of his subjects in the spring of 1250, induced the Pope to allow him to postpone any expedition. Louis's brothers refused to send help from France. There public opinion was indignant but disillusioned. When news first arrived of the disaster at Mansourah, a hysterical mass-movement of peasants and labourers, who called themselves the Pastouraux and were led by a mysterious 'Master of Hungary', swept through the country, holding meetings to denounce the Pope and his clergy and vowing themselves to rescue the Christian King. The Queen-Regent Blanche gave them her approval at first; but they became so disorderly that they had to be suppressed. The French nobles contented themselves with bitter comments against a Pope who preferred to preach a Crusade against the Christian Imperialists rather than to send help to those who were struggling against the infidel. Blanche went so far as to confiscate the property of any Royal vassal who responded to the appeal of Innocent IV for a Crusade against King Conrad in 1251. But neither she nor her advisers ventured to send reinforcements to the East.[1]

In his search for foreign allies, King Louis entered into the friendliest relations with the Assassins. Immediately after the disaster at Damietta, their chief in Syria had sent to Acre to demand to be paid for their neutrality, but was deterred by the firm answer that the King gave to his envoys in the presence of the Grand Masters of the Orders. The sect had particularly asked to be released from the obligation of paying a tribute to the Hospital. Its next embassy was far humbler. It brought handsome gifts for the King, with the request for a close alliance. Louis, who had learned of the hostility of the Ismailian Assassins towards the orthodox Sunni Moslems, encouraged their advances and sent Yves the Breton to arrange a treaty. Yves was fascinated by the library kept by the sect at Masyad. He found there an apocryphal

[1] Matthew Paris, *Chronica Majora*, v, pp. 172–3, 259–61; Throop, *Criticism of the Crusades*, pp. 57–9.

sermon addressed by Christ to Saint Peter, who, the sectaries told him, was the reincarnation of Abel, Noah and Abraham. A pact of mutual defence was signed.[1]

Louis's main diplomatic ambition, however, was to secure the friendship of the Assassin's fiercest enemy, the Mongols. Early in 1253 a report reached Acre that one of the Mongol princes, Sartaq, son of Batu, had been converted to Christianity. Louis hastened to send two Dominicans, William of Rubruck and Bartholomew of Cremona, to urge the Prince to come to the aid of his fellow-Christians in Syria. But it was not within the power of a junior Mongol prince to conclude so momentous an alliance.[2] While the Dominicans journeyed further into Asia to the Court of the Great Khan himself, King Louis was obliged to leave Outremer. His mother, the Queen-Regent Blanche, had died in November 1252; and her death was quickly followed by disorders. The King of England began to make trouble, in spite of an oath to go on the Crusade; nor would he support his bishops whom the Pope had charged to preach the Crusade. Civil war broke out over the inheritance to the county of Flanders, and all the great vassals of France were growing restive. Louis's first duty was to his own kingdom. Reluctantly he prepared to go home. He set sail from Acre on 24 April 1254. His boat was nearly wrecked off the coast of Cyprus; but the Queen promised a silver ship to the shrine of Saint Nicholas at Varangéville, and the storm abated. A few days later the Queen's presence of mind saved the boat from destruction by fire. In July the royal party landed at Hyères, in the territory of the King's brother, Charles of Anjou.[3]

Saint Louis's Crusade had involved the Christian East in a

[1] Joinville, pp. 160–5.

[2] Pelliot, 'Les Mongols et la Papauté', *loc. cit.* p. 220. Rubruck's *Itinerarium* is translated and edited by Rockhill. He was doubtful about Sartaq's conversion when he met him (*ibid.* pp. 107, 116). But the Armenians believed it to be genuine (Kirakos, trans. Brosset, p. 173).

[3] Joinville, pp. 218–34; William of Saint-Pathus, pp. 29–30; *MS. of Rothelin*, pp. 629–30; Matthew Paris, v, pp. 434, 452–4. For Blanche's death, on 1 December 1252, see Matthew Paris, v, p. 354.

terrible military catastrophe, and, though his four years' sojourn at Acre did much to repair the damage, the loss of man-power could never quite be recovered. He had the noblest character of all the great Crusaders; but it might have been better for Outremer had he never left France. And his failure struck deeper. He had been a good and God-fearing man, and yet God had led him into disaster. In earlier days the misadventures of the Crusaders could be explained as due punishment for their crimes and their vices, but so facile a theory was now no longer tenable. Was it possible that the whole movement was frowned upon by God?[1]

Though the French King's coming to the East had been unfortunate, his departure brought the risk of immediate harm. He left behind him as his representative Geoffrey of Sargines, who was given the official post of Seneschal to the kingdom. The *bailli* was now John of Ibelin, Count of Jaffa, who succeeded his cousin John of Arsuf in the office in 1254 but returned it to him in 1256. It is possible that John of Arsuf was absent in Cyprus during these years, advising Queen Plaisance, who continued as legal regent of both kingdoms.[2] The death of Conrad of Germany in Italy in May 1254, gave the title of King of Jerusalem to his two-year-old son Conradin, whose nominal rights were scrupulously remembered by the lawyers of Outremer.[3] Just before his departure King Louis had arranged a truce with Damascus, to last from 21 February 1254, for two years, six months and forty days. An-Nasir Yusuf of Damascus was well aware now of the Mongol peril and had no wish for war with the Franks. Aibek of Egypt equally wished to avoid a large war, and in 1255 made a ten years' truce with the Franks. But he expressly excluded Jaffa from the truce, as he hoped to secure it as a port for his Palestinian province.[4] There were raids and counter-raids across the frontier. In January 1256,

[1] Salimbene, *Chronica*, pp. 235–7, says that such doubts were expressed. The Mendicant Friars who had preached the Crusade were publicly insulted after its failure.   [2] La Monte, *loc. cit.* n. 1.

[3] Matthew Paris, v, pp. 459–60. For Conradin's rights, see below pp. 284–5.

[4] Matthew Paris, v, p. 522; *MS. of Rothelin*, p. 630; *Annales de Terre Sainte* p. 446.

Geoffrey of Sargines and John of Jaffa captured a huge caravan of beasts. When the Mameluk governor of Jerusalem led an expedition in March to punish the raiders, he was defeated and killed. Aibek, who had been having difficulties with his generals, including Baibars, made a new treaty with Damascus, again on the Caliph's mediation, and retroceded Palestine; but both Moslem powers renewed their truces with the Franks, to last ten years and to cover the territory of Jaffa.[1]

This forbearance shown by Cairo and Damascus, dictated to them by their growing fear of the Mongols, saved the Franks from the deserved results of a civil war that began soon after King Louis's departure. The most active elements now in the cities of Outremer were the various Italian merchants. The three great republics of Genoa, Venice and Pisa, with their colonies in every Levantine seaport, dominated Mediterranean trade. Apart from the banking enterprises of the Templars, their commerce provided for Outremer most of its revenues and was almost as beneficial to the Moslem princes, whose periodical willingness to sign a truce was largely induced by the fear of interrupting this source of profit. But the republics were bitter rivals. Trouble between Pisa and Genoa had delayed Louis's embarkation from Cyprus in 1249. In 1250, after the murder of a Genoese merchant by a Venetian, there was fighting in the streets of Acre.[2] When Louis had left for Europe trouble broke out again. The Venetian and Genoese quarters in Acre were separated by the hill of Montjoie, which belonged to the Genoese except for its highest spur, crowned by the ancient monastery of Saint Sabas. Both colonies claimed the monastery; and one morning early in 1256, while lawyers still disputed the case, the Genoese took possession of it and, on the Venetians protesting, rushed armed men down the hill into the Venetian quarter. The Pisans, with whom they had some preconcerted arrangement, hurried to join them; and the Venetians,

---

[1] *MS. of Rothelin*, pp. 631–3; *Annales de Terre Sainte, loc. cit.*; Abu'l Feda, pp. 133–4.
[2] *Annales Januenses*, p. 238. See above, p. 260.

taken by surprise, saw their houses sacked, together with their ships that were tied up at the quay. It was only with difficulty that they drove the invaders out again. The monastery and many of their ships were lost to them.[1]

At that moment, Philip of Montfort, lord of Toron and Tyre, who had long contested the title of the Venetians to certain villages near Tyre, thought it opportune to turn them out of the third of Tyre that was theirs by the treaty made when Tyre was captured in 1124, and of their possessions in the suburbs. With the Genoese dispute on their hands, they could not prevent him; but when the government of Genoa, which did not wish to start a war with Venice, offered to mediate, they were too angry to accept the offer. The Venetian Consul at Acre, Marco Giustiniani, was a skilful diplomat. Philip's high-handed action shocked his Ibelin cousins, who were all sticklers for legal correctitude. The *bailli*, John of Arsuf, suspected that the Montforts intended to declare Tyre independent of the government at Acre. Though he had been on cold terms with the Venetians, chiefly because of their chilly attitude towards Louis's Crusade, he was won by Giustiniani over to their side. John of Jaffa was already on bad terms with the Genoese, one of whom had tried to assassinate him. The Fraternities of Acre, alarmed lest Philip should make Tyre a successful commercial rival to their own city, added their sympathy and help to Giustiniani, who next persuaded the Pisans that the Genoese were selfish and untrustworthy allies and secured their support. The Marseillais merchants, who were always jealous of the Genoese, also joined him; whereat the Catalan merchants, who were jealous of the Marseillais, took the other part. The Temple and the Teutonic Knights supported the Venetians, and the Hospital the Genoese. Further north, the Embriaco family, who reigned at Jebail, remembered its Genoese origin. Its head, Henry, defying the specific prohibition of his suzerain, Bohemond VI of Antioch-

---

[1] *Estoire d'Eracles*, II, p. 443; *Annales Januenses*, p. 239; Dandolo, p. 365. See Heyd, *Histoire du Commerce du Levant*, I, pp. 344–54, for the whole history of the 'War of Saint Sabas'.

Tripoli, with whom he had quarrelled, sent troops to help the Genoese in Acre. Bohemond himself tried to maintain neutrality, but his sympathies were with the Venetians and his feud with the Embriaco clan forced him into the conflict. His sister, the Queen-Regent Plaisance, could do nothing. The only man in Outremer that she could trust was Geoffrey of Sargines; and he, as a stranger, had little influence and no material power. The civil war began to involve the whole society of Outremer. It was no longer a case of the native barons combining against an alien master, as in the days of Frederick II. Petty family disputes exacerbated the struggle. Philip of Montfort's mother and Henry of Jebail's wife had been born Ibelins. Bohemond VI's grandmother had been an Embriaco. But ties of kinship meant nothing now.[1]

The Venetian government had been swift to take action. As soon as the Genoese learned that the Pisans had deserted them, they overran the Pisan quarter in Acre, which gave them command of the inner port. But they barely had time to stretch a chain across the entrance before a large fleet under the Venetian admiral Lorenzo Tiepolo sailed up. His ships burst through the chain and landed men on the quay. There was a bloodthirsty battle in the streets. The Genoese were at last driven back into their quarter, protected by the Hospitallers' quarter just to the north. The monastery of Saint Sabas was occupied by the Venetians, but they could not dislodge the Genoese or the Hospitallers from their own buildings.[2]

In February 1258, Plaisance made an attempt to assert her authority. She crossed from Cyprus with her five-year-old son, King Hugh, to Tripoli to her brother Bohemond, who escorted her to Acre. The High Court of the kingdom was summoned; and Bohemond asked it to confirm the claim of the King of Cyprus, as next heir after the absentee Conradin, to be recognized as depository of the royal power, and of his mother and guardian as regent. But Bohemond's hope that his sister's authority and

---

[1] *Estoire d'Eracles*, II, p. 445; Dandolo, pp. 366–7; *Annales Januenses, loc. cit.*
[2] Dandolo, *loc. cit.*; *Annales Januenses*, p. 240; *Estoire d'Eracles*, II, p. 447.

presence would still the civil war was disappointed. As soon as the Ibelins admitted Hugh's and Plaisance's claims, always excepting the rights of King Conradin, and the Templars and Teutonic Knights concurred, the Hospitallers at once declared that nothing could be decided in Conradin's absence, using the argument that had been overruled in 1243. The royal family were thus drawn into the civil war, the Venetian party supporting Plaisance and her son, and, by the cynical irony of history, Genoa, the Hospital and Philip of Montfort, all of them in the past bitter opponents of Frederick II, becoming the advocates of the Hohenstaufen. A majority vote acknowledged Plaisance as regent. John of Arsuf formally resigned his office of *bailli* into her hands and was reappointed by her. She then returned with her brother to Tripoli and thence to Cyprus, after instructing her *bailli* to act sternly against the rebels.[1]

The Patriarch of Jerusalem was James Pantaleon, the son of a shoemaker of Troyes. He had been appointed in December 1255, and only reached Acre in the summer of 1260, when the civil war had begun. Though he had recently shown great ability in dealing with the heathen in Baltic lands, the situation in Outremer was beyond him. He correctly gave his support to Queen Plaisance, and appealed to the Pope to take action in Italy. Pope Alexander IV summoned delegates from the three republics to his court at Viterbo and ordered an immediate armistice. Two Venetian and two Pisan plenipotentiaries were to go to Syria on a Genoese ship, and two Genoese on a Venetian ship, and the whole affair was to be settled. The envoys set out in July 1258, only to hear on the journey that they were too late. The Republic of Genoa had already sent out a fleet under the admiral Rosso della Turca, which arrived off Tyre in June and there joined the Genoese squadrons in the Levant. On 23 June the combined fleet of some forty-eight galleys set sail from Tyre, while a regiment of Philip of Montfort's soldiers marched down the coast. The Venetians and their Pisan allies had

[1] *Assises*, II, p. 401; *Estoire d'Eracles*, II, p. 443; *MS. of Rothelin*, p. 643; *Gestes des Chiprois*, pp. 149, 152.

about thirty-eight galleys, under Tiepolo. The decisive battle took place off Acre on 24 June. Tiepolo proved himself the better tactician. After a fierce struggle the Genoese lost twenty-four ships and 1700 men and retired in disorder. Only a sudden breeze from the south enabled the survivors to return safely to Tyre. Meanwhile the militia of Acre halted Philip's advance, and the Genoese quarter within the city was overrun. As a result of their defeat the Genoese decided to abandon Acre altogether and establish their headquarters at Tyre.[1]

In April 1259, the Pope sent a legate to the East, Thomas Agni of Lentino, titular Bishop of Bethlehem, with orders to resolve the quarrel. About the same time the *bailli*, John of Arsuf, died; and Queen Plaisance came again to Acre and on 1 May appointed Geoffrey of Sargines as *bailli*. He was a respected and a more uncontroversial figure, and he worked with the legate to secure an armistice. In January 1261, a meeting of the High Court, attended by delegates from the Italian colonies, came to an agreement. The Genoese were to have their establishment at Tyre and the Venetians and Pisans theirs at Acre; and the warring nobles and Military Orders were officially reconciled. But the Italians never regarded the arrangement as final. Their war soon began again and dragged on, to the detriment of all the commerce and the shipping along the Syrian coast.[2]

It was to the detriment, too, of the Franks on the east, far beyond the border of Syria. The tottering Latin Empire of Constantinople had survived chiefly through the help of the Italians, who feared to lose their trading concessions. Venice, with her property in Constantinople itself and in the Aegean islands, had a particular interest in its preservation. Genoa therefore gave active support to the vigorous Greek Emperor of Nicaea, Michael Palaeologus. Michael had already laid the foundations for the Byzantine recovery

---

[1] Dandolo, p. 367; *Annales Januenses*, p. 240; *Gestes des Chiprois*, pp. 153–6; Raynald, XXII, pp. 30 ff.; *Estoire d'Eracles*, II, p. 445.

[2] Tafel-Thomas, *Urkunden*, III, pp. 39–44; *Gestes des Chiprois*, p. 156; *Annales de Terre Sainte*, pp. 448–9.

of the Peloponnese in 1259 by his great victory at Pelagonia, in Macedonia, where William of Villehardouin, Prince of Achaea, was captured with all his barons and obliged to cede the fortresses, Maina, Mistra and Monemvasia, that dominated the eastern half of the peninsula. In March 1261, Michael signed a treaty with the Genoese, giving them preferential treatment throughout his dominions, present and future. On 25 July, with the help of the Genoese, his troops entered Constantinople. The Empire of Romania, the child of the Fourth Crusade, was ended. It had done nothing but harm to the Christian East.[1]

The Byzantine recovery of Constantinople and the collapse of the Latin Empire were thus the outcome of a war started round an ancient monastery in Acre. It was a tremendous blow to Latin and to Papal prestige, and a triumph for the Greeks. But Byzantium, even with its capital restored, was no longer the oecumenical Empire that it had been in the twelfth century. It was now only one state amongst many. Besides the remaining Latin principalities, there were now powerful Bulgarian and Serbian kingdoms in the Balkans; and in Anatolia, though the Seldjuk Sultanate had been crippled by the Mongols, there could never be any hope of dislodging the Turks. Indeed, the possession of their ancient home added to the problems rather than to the strength of the Emperors. The chief beneficiaries were the Genoese. They had been beaten in Syria; but their alliance with Byzantium gave them control of the Black Sea trade, a trade which was growing in volume and importance as the Mongol conquests developed the caravan-routes across central Asia.[2]

In Outremer Geoffrey of Sargines, with the prestige of Saint Louis's memory behind him, restored some semblance of order between the barons of the kingdom. Though Italian sailors might continue to fight, active hostilities died down on shore; but there was no return to the old friendship between the Montforts and

---

[1] For the recapture of Constantinople see Vasiliev, *History of the Byzantine Empire*, pp. 538–9. The chief Byzantine sources are Pachymer, pp. 140 ff., and George Acropolita, I, pp. 182 ff.   [2] See Heyd, I, pp. 427 ff.

the Ibelins. The Temple and the Hospital would not mitigate their traditional enmity; while the Teutonic Order, despairing of the future of Syria, began to devote its main attention to the distant shores of the Baltic, where, from 1226 onwards, it had been given lands and castles in return for its help in taming and converting the heathen Prussians and Livonians.[1]

Geoffrey's authority did not extend into the county of Tripoli. There the dislike of Bohemond for his vassal, Henry of Jebail, had blazed up into war. Not only did Henry repudiate Bohemond's suzerainty and maintain himself, with the help of the Genoese, in perfect independence, but his cousin Bertrand, head of the younger branch of the Embriaco family, attacked Bohemond in Tripoli itself. The Dowager Princess Lucienne, when she was removed from the regency, had managed to keep many of her Roman favourites in important posts in the county, to the fury of the native barons. They found their leaders in Bertrand Embriaco, who owned large estates in and around Jebail, and his son-in-law, John of Antioch, lord of Botrun, Bohemond's second cousin. In 1258 the barons marched on Tripoli, where Bohemond was in residence, and laid siege to the city. Bohemond made a sortie but was defeated and wounded on the shoulder by Bertrand himself. He was forced to stay beleaguered in his second capital till the Templars sent men to rescue him. He burned for revenge. One day as Bertrand was riding through one of his villages some armed peasants suddenly attacked him and slew him. His head was cut off and sent as a gift to Bohemond. No one doubted that Bohemond had inspired the murder. For the moment it served his purpose. The rebels were cowed and retired to Jebail. But there was now a blood-feud between the Houses of Antioch and Embriaco.[2]

Geoffrey of Sargines's government came to an end in 1263. Queen Plaisance of Cyprus died in September 1261, deeply

---

[1] For the Teutonic Order, see Strehlke, *Tabulae Ordinis Teutonici.*

[2] *Gestes des Chiprois*, pp. 157–60. See Rey, 'Les Seigneurs de Giblet', in *Revue de l'Orient Latin*, III, pp. 399–404. The lord of Botrun was John, not William (as in the index to Mas Latrie's edition of the *Gestes*). William, his father, had been killed at La Forbie in 1244.

mourned; for she was a lady of high integrity. Her son, Hugh II, was eight years old; and a new regent was required for Cyprus and Jerusalem. Hugh II's father, Henry I, had had two sisters. The elder, Maria, had married Walter of Brienne and had died young, leaving a son, Hugh. The younger, Isabella, was married to Henry of Antioch, brother of Bohemond V, and was still living. Her son, also called Hugh, was older than his cousin of Brienne, whom Isabella had brought up along with her own son. Hugh of Brienne, though next heir to the throne, was unwilling to compete against his aunt and her son for the regency. After deliberation the High Court of Cyprus, considering that a man made a better regent than a woman, passed over Isabella's claim in favour of her son, who was appointed as being the eldest prince of the blood royal. The High Court of Jerusalem was given more time for reflection. It was not till the spring of 1263 that Isabella came with her husband, Henry of Antioch, to Acre. The nobles there accepted her as Regent *de facto*, but, showing scruples that had hitherto been ignored, they refused to give her an oath of allegiance. That could only be done if King Conradin were present. Geoffrey of Sargines resigned the office of *bailli*, which the Regent then gave to her husband. She herself returned happily without him to Cyprus.

She died in Cyprus next year; and the regency of Jerusalem again was vacant. Hugh of Antioch, Regent of Cyprus, claimed it as her son and heir; but a counter-claim was now put in by Hugh of Brienne. He declared that, by the custom of France which was followed in Outremer, the son of an elder sister preceded the son of a younger, no matter which cousin was the senior in age. But the jurists of Outremer considered that the decisive factor was kinship to the last holder of the office. As Isabella had been accepted as the last Regent, her son Hugh took precedence over her nephew. The nobles and high officers of state unanimously accepted him and gave him the homage that they had denied to his mother. The communes and foreign colonies offered him fealty and Grand Masters both of the Temple and Hospital gave him recognition. Though the Italians still fought each other on the seas, there was a general if superficial atmosphere of reconciliation in the kingdom, due in the main to Hugh's energy. He did not appoint a *bailli* to act for him on the mainland, but travelled to and fro between Cyprus and Acre. While he was in Cyprus, the mainland government was entrusted to Geoffrey of Sargines, who was Seneschal once more. It was as well that the administration was in respected hands; for there were great and increasing dangers ahead.[1]

King Louis of France never forgot the Holy Land. Every year he sent a sum of money to maintain the small company of troops that he had left behind at Acre under Geoffrey of Sargines; and the practice was continued even after Geoffrey's death and his own. He always hoped one day to set out again on a Crusade, but the needs of his own country gave him no respite. It was only in 1267, when he was weary and ill, that he felt able to prepare for his second Crusade and began slowly making the necessary arrangements and collecting the necessary money. In 1270 he was ready to embark for Palestine.[2]

The pious project was twisted out of shape and ruined by the King's brother Charles. In 1258 the child Conradin, titular King of Sicily and of Jerusalem, had been displaced by his uncle, Frederick II's bastard son Manfred. Manfred had much of his father's arrogant brilliance; and he received the same measure of hatred from the Papacy. The Popes began to search for a prince to put in his stead upon the Sicilian throne which traditionally was under their suzerainty. After considering Edmund of Lancaster, Henry of England's son, they found their candidate in Charles of Anjou. Charles bore little resemblance to his saintly brother. He was cold and cruel and inordinately ambitious; and his wife, the Countess Beatrice, heiress of Provence and sister of three queens, yearned to wear a crown herself. In 1261 James Pantaleon, Patriarch of Jerusalem, became Pope as Urban IV. He soon persuaded

---

[1] See La Monte, *op. cit.* pp. 75–7, and Hill, *op. cit.* II, pp. 151–4, for discussion of legal points and references.   [2] Joinville, pp. 210–12.

Louis that the elimination of the Hohenstaufen from Sicily was a needful preliminary for the success of any future Crusade.

Louis gave his approval to his brother's candidature and even raised taxes in France on his behalf. Urban died in 1264, but his successor, Clement IV, another Frenchman, completed the arrangements with Charles; who in 1265 marched into Italy and defeated and slew Manfred at the battle of Benevento. The victory put southern Italy and Sicily into his power, and his wife received the crown that she desired. Three years later Conradin made a valiant effort to recover his Italian heritage. It met with disaster near Tagliacozzo; and the sixteen-year-old boy, the last of the Hohenstaufen, was taken prisoner and beheaded. Charles's ambitions now rose higher. He would dominate Italy; Constantinople should be recovered from the schismatic Greeks; he would found a Mediterranean Empire, such as his Norman predecessors had dreamed of in vain. Pope Clement began to fear the monster that he had raised; but he died in 1268. For three years Charles, by intrigues with the Cardinals, blocked the election of a new Pope. There was no one to curb him. But the thought of his brother's intended Crusade disquieted him. Frenchmen and French money should be used to his advantage, not to prop up a distant kingdom in which he was not yet ready to be interested. He had hoped for help for an attack on Byzantium. If that was not forthcoming, at least the Crusade must be diverted into some channel that would bring him profit.[1]

Mustansir, Emir of Tunis, who dominated the African coast opposite to Sicily, was known to be well disposed towards the Christians, but he had offended Charles by giving refuge to rebels from Sicily. Charles persuaded Louis, whose optimism for the Faith had not been dimmed by experience, that the Emir was ready for conversion. A slight show of force would bring him to the fold, and a new province would be added to Christianity in

[1] See Jordan, *Les Origines de la Domination Angevine en Italie, passim*; Hefele-Leclercq, *op. cit.* VI, I, pp. 47–60, 63–6; Powicke, *op. cit.* II, pp. 598–9 (a discussion of Charles of Anjou's policy).

a spot of vast strategic importance for any new Crusade. It may be that Louis's judgement was warped by illness. Wise friends, such as Joinville, made no secret of their dislike of the project. But Louis believed in his brother. On 1 July he set sail from Aigues-Mortes at the head of a formidable expedition. With him were his three surviving sons, his son-in-law, King Tibald of Navarre, his nephew, Robert of Artois, the Counts of Brittany and La Marche and the heir to Flanders, all sons of comrades of his earlier Crusade, and the Count of Saint Pol, a survivor of that Crusade, and the Count of Soissons. The armada arrived off Carthage on 18 July, in the full heat of the African summer. The Emir of Tunis showed no desire to become a Christian convert. Instead, he refortified and regarrisoned his capital. But he did not need to fight. The climate did his work for him. Disease spread quickly through the French camp. Princes, knights and soldiers fell ill in thousands. The King was among the first to be struck down. When Charles of Anjou arrived on 25 August with his army, he learned that his brother had died a few hours before. The heir of France, Philip, was dangerously ill; John Tristan, the prince born at Damietta, was dying. Charles's vigour preserved the expedition from disaster till the autumn, when the Emir paid him a large indemnity to go back to Italy; but the Crusade as a whole had been wasted.[1]

When the news of the tragedy at Tunis reached the East, the Moslems were deeply relieved, and the Christians were plunged into mourning. Their grief was well justified. Never again would a royal army set out from their motherland to rescue the Franks of Outremer. King Louis had been a great and good King of France, but to Palestine, which he had loved even more dearly, he had brought little but disappointment and sorrow. As he lay dying he thought of the Holy City which he had never seen and for whose deliverance his labours had been fruitless. His last words were 'Jerusalem, Jerusalem'.[2]

---

[1] Joinville, pp. 262–3. See Sternfeld, *Ludwigs des Heiligen Kreuzzug nach Tunis, passim.*   [2] William of Saint-Pathus, pp. 153–5.

CHAPTER III

THE MONGOLS IN SYRIA

*'Wilt thou trust him, because his strength is great? or wilt
thou leave thy labour to him?'* JOB XXXIX, 11

When William of Rubruck arrived at the Court of the Great
Khan, in the last days of 1253, he found a government very
different from that which had entertained King Louis's previous
envoy, Andrew of Longjumeau. When Guyuk, son of Ogodai,
died in 1248, his widow, Oghul Qaimish, acted as regent for her
young sons, Qucha, Naqu and Qughu. But she was an inept
ruler, given to avarice and to sorcery; and none of her sons showed
promise of greater ability. Their cousin, Shiremon, whom his
grandfather Ogodai had destined for the succession, continually
plotted against them. But more formidable opposition came from
an alliance between Batu, the viceroy of the West and the Princess
Sorghaqtani, the widow of Jenghiz's youngest son, Tului.
Sorghaqtani, a Kerait by birth and, like all her race, a devout
Nestorian Christian, was highly respected for her wisdom and her
incorruptibility. Ogodai had wished to marry her after her
husband's death to his son Guyuk; but she tactfully refused, preferring to devote herself to the education of her four remarkable
sons, Mongka, Kubilai, Hulagu and Ariqboga. When Guyuk
carried out an inspection of the finances of the Imperial family, she
and her sons alone were proved to have acted always with perfect
scrupulousness. Batu, whose feud with Guyuk had never been
healed, had a great admiration for her. Knowing that his own
title to the throne would always be weakened by doubts about his
father Juji's legitimacy, he joined her in advocating the claims of
Mongka. He came to Mongolia and, as senior prince of the
House, summoned a Kariltay, which, on 1 July 1251, elected

Mongka as supreme Khan. Despite Sorghaqtani's genuine attempts to placate them, Ogodai's grandsons refused to attend the Kuriltay, but plotted to attack its members when they would be inebriated at the feasts that followed the inauguration ceremony. The plot miscarried; and after a year of desultory civil war Mongka triumphed over all his rivals and was installed as Supreme Khan at Karakorum. The Regent Oghul Qaimish and the mother of Shiremon were convicted of sorcery and drowned. The princes of the House of Ogodai were sent into exile.[1]

With Mongka's accession the Mongols revived their policy of expansion. The great princes returned to their governments. The eastern provinces were entrusted to Mongka's second brother, Kubilai, who set energetically and methodically about the conquest of all China. He became a convert of Buddhism; and his wars and his treatment of the conquered were remarkable for their humanity and forbearance. Mongka and his youngest brother, Ariqboga, remained in Mongolia, keeping watchful control of the whole vast empire. The heirs of Jagatai, in Turkestan, began tentative efforts to extend their power across the Pamirs into India. Batu moved his headquarters to the lower reaches of the Volga, so as to dominate his vassal princes in Russia, and founded there the Khanate called Kipchak by Moslem writers, and by the Mongols and the Russians the Golden Horde. The government of Persia passed to Mongka's third brother, Hulagu; and it was to his frontier and to Kubilai's in the east that the main efforts of the Mongols were now directed.[2]

Of the states that bordered the Mediterranean, it was the Armenian kingdom in Cilicia that first realized the importance of the Mongol advance. The Armenians had witnessed with interest the collapse of the Seldjuk army in 1243 before a Mongol expedition led by a provincial governor. They could estimate how

[1] William of Rubruck (ed. Rockhill), pp. 163–4; Howorth, *History of the Mongols*, I, pp. 170–86; Grousset, *L'Empire Mongol*, pp. 306–11.
[2] Grousset, *op. cit.* pp. 312–13, 364–6; Iakoubovski and Grekov, *La Horde d'Or*, pp. 98–120.

irresistible the Imperial army would be. King Hethoum had wisely sent a deferential message to Baichu in 1243. But the Mongols had then retired; and Kaikhosrau recovered his lost Anatolian territory and began once more to press upon Armenia, aided by a rebel Armenian prince, Constantine of Lampron.[1] Hethoum calculated that the Mongols would come back and that they could be of value to all Asiatic Christendom, and in particular to himself. In 1247 he sent his brother, the Constable Sempad, on an embassy to the Court of the Great Khan. Sempad arrived at Karakorum in 1248, not long before Guyuk's death. Guyuk received him with cordiality and, on hearing that Hethoum was ready to regard himself as a vassal, promised to send help for the Armenians to recapture towns taken from them by the Seldjuks. Sempad returned home with a diploma from the Great Khan guaranteeing the integrity of Hethoum's dominions.[2] But Guyuk's death held up any immediate action. In 1254, hearing of the accession of a new vigorous Khan, King Hethoum set out for Karakorum.[3]

Karakorum was now the diplomatic centre of the world. When Louis IX's ambassador, William of Rubruck, arrived there in 1254, he found embassies from the Greek Emperor, from the Caliph, from the King of Delhi and from the Seldjuk Sultan, as well as emirs from the Jezireh and from Kurdistan and princes from Russia, all waiting upon the Khan. There were several Europeans settled there, including a jeweller from Paris with a Hungarian wife and an Alsatian woman married to a Russian architect.[4] There was neither racial nor religious discrimination

[1] Ibn Bibi (ed. Houtsma), pp. 243, 249–50; Sempad, pp. 649–51; Kirakos, trans. Brosset, p. 142; Vincent of Beauvais, pp. 1295–6.

[2] Sempad, letter to Henry of Cyprus, in William of Nangis, pp. 361–3.

[3] Ibn Sheddad, *Geography* (ed. Cahen), in *Revue des Etudes Islamiques* (1936), p. 121; Bar-Hebraeus (trans. Budge), pp. 418–19.

[4] William of Rubruck (trans. Rockhill), pp. 165 ff., 176–7. There was also an Englishman born in Hungary, called Basil, who lived at Karakorum (*ibid.* p. 211). Bar-Hebraeus, p. 411, describes Hethoum as well as the two Kings of Georgia being at Karakorum, together with embassies from Aleppo, from the Franks and from the Assassins at a Kuriltay following Ogodai's death.

at the Court. The supreme posts in the army and the government were reserved to members of the Imperial family, but there were ministers and provincial governors from almost every Asiatic nation. Mongka himself followed the faith of his fathers, Shamanism, but he attended Christian, Buddhist and Moslem ceremonies indiscriminately. He held that there was one God, who could be worshipped as anyone pleased. The chief religious influence was that of the Nestorian Christians, to whom Mongka showed especial favour in memory of his mother Sorghaqtani, who had always remained loyal to her faith, though she was broad-minded enough to endow a Moslem theological college at Bokhara. His principal Empress, Kutuktai, and many other of his wives also were Nestorians.[1] William of Rubruck professed himself much shocked by the ignorance and debauchery of the Nestorian ecclesiastics and considered their services to be little more than drunken orgies. One Sunday he saw the Empress return reeling from High Mass. When his affairs went badly he was inclined to lay the blame upon the rivalry of this heretic hierarchy.[2]

His embassy, indeed, was not an entire success. He had travelled by way of Batu's capital on the Volga, where he found that Batu's son, Sartaq, though probably not actually a Christian, was particularly well disposed towards the Christians. Batu sent him on to Mongolia. He travelled at the government's expense along the great trade-road, in comfort and security, though occasionally whole days passed without a single house being seen. He arrived at the end of December 1253, at the Great Khan's encampment, a few miles south of Karakorum. Mongka received him in audience on 4 January; and soon afterwards he moved with the Court to Karakorum itself. He found the Mongol government already determined to attack the Moslems of western Asia, and

[1] Howorth, *op. cit.* I, pp. 188–91. Sorghaqtani died in February 1252. Bar-Hebraeus (p. 417) calls her 'the all-wise and believing Queen'; William of Rubruck (trans. Rockhill), pp. 184–6; Pelliot, 'Les Mongols et la Papauté', *loc. cit.* p. 198. Hulagu told the Armenian historian Vartan that his mother was a devout Christian (Vartan, Armenian text, ed. Emin, p. 205).

[2] William of Rubruck, *loc. cit.*

ready to discuss common action. But there was one impassable difficulty. The Supreme Khan could not admit the existence of any sovereign prince in the world other than himself. His foreign policy was fundamentally simple. His friends were already his vassals; his enemies were to be eliminated or reduced to vassaldom. All that William could obtain was the quite sincere promise that the Christians should receive ample aid so long as their rulers came to pay homage to the suzerain of the world. The King of France could not treat on such terms. William left Karakorum in August 1254, having learned, like many subsequent ambassadors to the Courts of further Asia, that Oriental monarchs understand neither the usages nor the principles of Western diplomacy. He travelled back through central Asia to the Court of Batu, and thence over the Caucasus and Seldjuk Anatolia to Armenia and so to Acre. Everywhere he was treated with the respect due to an envoy accredited to the Supreme Khan.[1]

King Hethoum arrived at Karakorum shortly after William's departure. He had come of his own accord as a vassal; and as the other foreign visitors were either vassals who had been summoned against their wills or representatives of kings who arrogantly claimed independence, he was shown especial favour. At his formal reception by Mongka on 13 September 1254, he was given a document confirming that his person and his kingdom should be inviolate, and he was treated as the Khan's chief Christian adviser on matters concerning western Asia. Mongka promised him to free all Christian churches and monasteries from taxation. He announced that his brother Hulagu, who was already established in Persia, had been ordered to capture Baghdad and to destroy the power of the Caliphate, and he undertook that if all the Christian Powers would co-operate with him he would recover Jerusalem itself for the Christians. Hethoum left Karakorum on 1 November, laden with gifts and delighted by the success of his efforts. He journeyed home by way of Turkestan and Persia,

---

[1] *Ibid.* pp. 165 ff.

where he paid his respects to Hulagu, and was back in Armenia the following July.[1]

Hethoum's optimism was natural, but a little excessive. The Mongols were certainly eager to control or else to destroy the Caliphate. They had already so many Moslem subjects that it was essential for them to dominate the chief religious institution in the Moslem world. They had no particular animosity against Islam as a religion. Similarly, though they favoured Christianity more than any other faith, they had no intention of permitting any independent Christian state. If Jerusalem was to be restored to the Christians, it would be restored under the Mongol Empire. It is interesting to speculate what might have happened had the Mongol ambitions for western Asia been realized. It is possible that a great Christian Khanate might have been formed and might have in time devolved from the central power in Mongolia. But Saint Louis's dream that the Mongols would become dutiful sons of the Roman Church was unthinkable; nor would the Christian establishments in western Asia have kept any independence. A Mongol triumph might have served the interests of Christendom as a whole; but the Franks of Outremer, who were aware of the Great Khan's attitude towards Christian princes, cannot be entirely blamed for preferring the Moslems, whom they knew, to this strange, fierce and arrogant people from the distant deserts, whose record in eastern Europe had not been encouraging.[2] Hethoum's attempt to build up a great Christian alliance to aid the Mongols was well received by the native Christians; and Bohemond of

[1] Kirakos, pp. 279 ff.; Vahram, *Rhymed Chronicle*, p. 519; Bar-Hebraeus, pp. 418–19; Hayton, *Flor des Estoires*, pp. 164–6; Bretschneider, *Mediaeval Researches*, I, pp. 164–72.

[2] For a defence of the Frankish attitude, see Cahen, *La Syrie du Nord*, pp. 708–9. Grousset in his *Histoire des Croisades* continuously and rightly refers to the chances missed by the Franks in rejecting the Mongol alliance, but, in spite of his knowledge of Mongol history, he seems to have ignored the impossibility of the Great Khan treating the Franks as independent and not as vassals. The Mongols did not recognize that independent foreign states could exist.

Antioch, who was under his father-in-law's influence, gave his adhesion. But the Franks of Asia held aloof.[1]

In January 1256, a huge Mongol army crossed the river Oxus, under the command of the Great Khan's brother Hulagu. Like his brother Kubilai, Hulagu was better educated than most of the Mongol princes. He had a taste for learned men and himself dabbled in philosophy and alchemy. Like Kubilai, he was attracted by Buddhism, but he never himself gave up his ancestral Shamanism, and he lacked Kubilai's humanitarianism. He suffered from epileptic fits, and they may have affected his temper, which was unreliable. He was as savage towards the conquered as any of his predecessors. But the Christians had no reason to complain of him; for the most powerful influence at his Court was that of his principal wife, Dokuz Khatun. This remarkable lady was a Kerait princess, the granddaughter of Toghrul Khan and cousin, therefore, of Hulagu's mother. She was a passionate Nestorian, who made no secret of her dislike of Islam and her eagerness to help Christians of every sect.[2]

Hulagu's first objective was the Assassin headquarters in Persia. Till the sect was destroyed an orderly government would be impossible; and the sectaries had especially offended the Mongols by murdering Jagatai, the second son of Jenghiz Khan. The next objective was Baghdad; then the Mongol army would proceed to Syria. Everything was planned with care. The roads across Turkestan and Persia were repaired and bridges built. Carts were requisitioned to bring siege-machines from China. Pastures were cleared of their herds so that the grass might be plentiful for the Mongol horses. With Hulagu were Dokuz Khatun and two of his other wives, and his two elder sons. The house of Jagatai was represented by his grandson, Nigudar. From the Golden Horde

---

[1] See below, pp. 307–8, 311–12.
[2] Rashid ad-Din (trans. Quatremère), pp. 94–5, 145. He tells of Dokuz Khatun's influence. Mongka admired her and told Hulagu always to take her advice. Like Sorghaqtani she was born a Kerait princess. For Hulagu, see Howorth, *op. cit.* III, pp. 90 ff. and Grousset, *Histoire des Croisades*, III, pp. 563–6.

Batu sent three of his nephews, who travelled down the west shore of the Caspian and joined the army in Persia. Every tribe of the Mongol confederacy provided one-fifth of its fighting men, and there were a thousand Chinese archers, skilled at hurling fire-laden arrows from their cross-bows. An army had been sent nearly three years before to prepare the way, under Hulagu's most trusted general, the Nestorian Kitbuqa, a Naiman by race, who was said to be descended from one of the Three Wise Men from the East. Kitbuqa re-established Mongol authority over the main towns of the Iranian plateau and had captured some of the lesser Assassin strongholds before Hulagu's arrival.[1]

The Grand Master of the Assassins, Rukn ad-Din Khurshah, vainly tried to avert the danger by diplomatic intrigues and diversions. Hulagu entered Persia and moved slowly and relentlessly through Demavend and Abbassabad into the valleys of the Assassins. When the huge army appeared before Alamut and began the close investment of the citadel, Rukn ad-Din yielded. In December he came in person to Hulagu's tent and made his submission. The governor of the castle refused to obey his orders to surrender it, but it was taken by storm a few days later. Rukn ad-Din was promised his life by Hulagu, but he asked to be sent to Karakorum hoping to obtain better terms from the Great Khan Mongka. When he arrived there, Mongka refused to see him, saying that it had been wrong to tire out good horses on such a fruitless mission. Two Assassin fortresses still held out against the Mongols, Girdkuh and Lembeser. Rukn ad-Din was told to go home and arrange for their surrender. On the way he was put to death with his suite. Orders were sent at the same time to Hulagu that the whole sect must be exterminated. A number of the Grand Master's kin were sent to Jagatai's daughter, Salghan Khatun, that she might herself avenge her father's death. Others were collected on the excuse of a census and massacred in their thousands. By the end of 1257 only a few refugees were left in

[1] Bretschneider, *op. cit.* pp. 114–15, from original sources. For Kitbuqa's ancestry, see Hayton, *Flor des Estoires*, p. 173.

the Persian mountains. The Assassins in Syria were as yet out of the Mongols' reach; but they foresaw their fate.[1]

At Alamut the Assassins kept a great library full of works on philosophy and the occult sciences. Hulagu sent his Moslem Chamberlain, Ata al-Mulk Juveni to inspect it. Juveni set aside the Korans that he found, as well as books of scientific and historical value. The heretical works were burnt. By a strange coincidence there was about the same time a great fire, caused by lightning, in the city of Medina, and its library, which had the greatest collection of works on orthodox Moslem philosophy, was totally destroyed.[2]

After the Assassins had been wiped out in Persia, Hulagu and the Mongol host moved against the headquarters of orthodox Islam at Baghdad. The Caliph al-Mustasim, the thirty-seventh ruler of the Abbasid dynasty and son of the Caliph al-Mustansir by an Ethiopian slave, had hoped to revive the power and prestige of his throne. Since the collapse of the Khwarismians the Caliphate had been its own master, and the rivalry between Cairo and Damascus enabled the Caliph to behave as the arbiter of Islam. But, though he surrounded himself with pomp and ceremony, al-Mustasim was a weak and foolish man, whose main interest was his personal amusement. His court was torn by a feud between his vizier, the Shia Muwaiyad ad-Din, and his secretary, the Sunni Aibeg, who had the support of the heir to the throne. Baghdad was strongly fortified, and the Caliph could call upon a large army. His cavalry alone numbered 120,000. But it depended on military benefices; and al-Mustasim did not trust his vassals. He therefore followed his vizier's advice to reduce the army and spend the money thus economized on a voluntary tribute to the Mongols which would keep them away. Such a policy of appeasement was hardly likely to succeed, even were it consistently carried out. But when Hulagu replied by demanding suzerain rights over the Caliphate, Aibeg's influence was in the ascendant; and the suggestion was haughtily refused.[3]

[1] *Ibid.* pp. 116–18; Browne, *Literary History of Persia*, II, pp. 458–60.
[2] Browne, *loc. cit.*   [3] D'Ohsson, *Histoire des Mongols*, III, pp. 215–25.

Hulagu approached the campaign with some trepidation. His astrologers were not all of them encouraging; and he feared treachery from his own Moslem vassals and the intervention of the rulers of Damascus and Egypt. But his precautions against treason were effective; and no one came to the rescue of Baghdad. Meanwhile his own army was strengthened by the arrival of the contingent from the Golden Horde and the army that Baichu had kept for the last decade on the borders of Anatolia, and by a regiment of Georgian cavalry, eager to strike against the infidel capital.

At the end of 1257 the Mongol army moved down from its base at Hamadan. Baichu with his troops crossed the Tigris at Mosul and marched down the west bank. Kitbuqa and the left wing entered the plain of Iraq due east of the capital while Hulagu and the centre advanced through Kermanshah. The Caliph's main army started out under Aibeg to meet Hulagu, when it heard of Baichu's approach from the north-west. Aibeg recrossed the Tigris, and, on 11 January 1258, he came upon the Mongols near Anbar, about thirty miles from Baghdad. Baichu feigned to retreat and so lured the Arabs into a low marshy terrain. He sent engineers to cut the dykes of the Euphrates behind them. Next day the battle was renewed. Aibeg's army was driven back into the flooded fields. Only Aibeg himself and his bodyguard managed to escape through the waters to Baghdad. The bulk of his troops perished on the battlefield. The survivors fled into the desert and dispersed.[1]

On 18 January Hulagu appeared before the east walls of Baghdad, and by the 22nd the city was completely invested, with bridges of boats constructed across the Tigris just above and just below the city walls. Baghdad lay on both sides of the river. The western city, which had contained the palace of the earlier Caliphs, was now less important than the eastern, where the government buildings were concentrated. It was against the eastern walls that the Mongols made their heaviest attacks. Al-Mustasim began to

[1] Browne, *op. cit.* II, pp. 461–2.

lose hope. At the end of January he sent the vizier, who had always advocated peace with the Mongols, together with the Nestorian Patriarch, who, he hoped, might intercede with Dokuz Khatun, to try to treat with Hulagu. They were sent back without obtaining an audience. After a terrible bombardment during the first week of February, the eastern wall began to collapse. On 10 February when Mongol troops were already swarming into the city, the Caliph emerged and surrendered himself to Hulagu, together with all the chief officers of the army and officials of the state. They were ordered to lay down their arms and then were massacred. Only the Caliph's life was spared until Hulagu entered the city and the palace on 15 February. After he had revealed to his conqueror the hiding-place of all his treasure, he too was put to death. Meanwhile massacres continued throughout the whole city. Those that surrendered quickly and those that fought on were alike slain. Women and children perished with their men. One Mongol found in a side-street forty new-born babies whose mothers were dead. As an act of mercy he slaughtered them, knowing that they could not survive with no one to suckle them. The Georgian troops, who had been the first to break through the walls, were particularly fierce in their destruction. In forty days some eighty thousand citizens of Baghdad were slain. The only survivors were a few lucky folk whose hiding-places in cellars were not discovered, and a number of attractive girls and boys who were kept to be slaves, and the Christian community, which took refuge in the churches and was left undisturbed, by the special orders of Dokuz Khatun.[1]

By the end of March the stench of decaying corpses in the city was such that Hulagu withdrew his troops for fear of pestilence. Many of them left with regret, believing that there were still objects of value to be found there. But Hulagu now possessed the vast treasure accumulated by the Abbasid Caliphs through five

---

[1] *Ibid.* pp. 462–6; Bretschneider, *op. cit.* I, pp. 119–20; Abu'l Feda, pp. 136–7; Bar-Hebraeus, pp. 429–31; Kirakos, pp. 184–6; Vartan (Armenian text, ed. Emin), p. 197; Hayton, *Flor des Estoires*, pp. 169–70.

centuries. After sending a handsome proportion to his brother Mongka, he retired by easy stages back to Hamadan, and thence into Azerbaijan, where he built a strong castle at Shaha, on the shore of Lake Urmiah, as a storehouse for all his gold and precious metals and jewels. He left as governor of Baghdad the former vizier, Muwaiyad, who was closely supervised by Mongol officials. The Nestorian Patriarch, Makika, was given rich endowments and a former royal palace as his residence and church. The city was gradually cleaned and tidied, and forty years later it was a prosperous provincial town, a tenth of its former size.[1]

News of the destruction of Baghdad made a deep impression throughout Asia. The Asiatic Christians everywhere rejoiced. They wrote in triumph of the fall of the Second Babylon and hailed Hulagu and Dokuz Khatun as the new Constantine and Helena, God's instruments for vengeance on the enemies of Christ.[2] To the Moslems it was a ghastly shock and a challenge. The Abbasid Caliphate had for centuries been shorn of much material power, but its moral prestige was still great. The elimination of the dynasty and the capital left the leadership of Islam vacant, for any ambitious Moslem leader to seize. The Christian satisfaction was short-lived. It was not long before Islam conquered its conquerors. But the unity of the Moslem world had suffered a blow from which it could never recover. The fall of Baghdad, following half a century after the fall of Constantinople in 1204, put an end for ever to that old balanced dyarchy between Byzantium and the Caliphate under which Near Eastern humanity had flourished for so long. The Near East was never again to dominate civilization.

After the destruction of Baghdad Hulagu turned his attention to Syria. The first step was to strengthen the Mongol hold over the Jezireh and in particular to repress the Ayubite prince of Mayya-

---

[1] Bretschneider, *op. cit.* pp. 120–1; D'Ohsson, *op. cit.* III, p. 257; Levy, *A Baghdad Chronicle*, pp. 259–60.

[2] Stephen Orbelian, *History of Siunia* (Armenian text), pp. 234–5, calls Hulagu and Dokuz Khatun 'the new Constantine and Helena'.

PLATE V

THE ILKHAN HULAGU

faraqin, al-Kamil, who refused to accept Mongol suzerainty and had gone so far as to crucify a Jacobite priest who had visited him as Hulagu's envoy.[1] Before he left his encampment near Maragha Hulagu received envoys from many states. The old Atabeg of Mosul, Badr ad-Din Lulu, came to apologize for past misdeeds. The two Seldjuk Sultans, sons of Kaikhosrau, Kaikaûs II and Kilij Arslan IV, arrived soon afterwards. The former, who had opposed Baichu in 1256, vainly tried to placate Hulagu by fulsome flattery which shocked the Mongols. Finally an-Nasir Yusuf, ruler of Aleppo and Damascus, sent his own son, al-Aziz, to pay humble duty to the conqueror. Mayyafaraqin was besieged and captured early in 1260, largely thanks to the help of Hulagu's Georgian and Armenian allies. The Moslems were massacred and the Christians spared. Al-Kamil was tortured by being forced to eat his own flesh till he died.[2]

In September 1259, Hulagu led the Mongol army out for the conquest of north-west Syria. Kitbuqa led the van, Baichu the right wing, another favourite general, Sunjak, the left, while Hulagu himself commanded the centre. He advanced through Nisibin, Harran and Edessa to Birejik, where he crossed the Euphrates. Saruj attempted to resist him, and was sacked. Early in the new year the Mongol army closed in round Aleppo. As its garrison refused to surrender, the city was invested on 18 January. The Sultan an-Nasir Yusuf was at Damascus when the storm broke. He had hoped that the presence of his son at Hulagu's camp would avert the danger. When he found that he was wrong, he made the still more humiliating move of offering to accept the suzerainty of the Mameluks of Egypt. They promised him help, but were in no hurry to provide it. In the meantime he gathered an army outside Damascus, and summoned his cousins of Hama and Kerak to his aid. But while he waited there some of his Turkish officers began to plot against him. He discovered their

---

[1] D'Ohsson, III, p. 307.
[2] Kirakos, pp. 177–9; Vartan, p. 199; Rashid ad-Din (trans. Quatremère), pp. 330–1; D'Ohsson, III, p. 356.

plans in time; and they fled to Egypt, taking with them one of his brothers. Their defection so weakened his army that he gave up all hope of going to the rescue of Aleppo.

Aleppo was bravely defended by an-Nasir Yusuf's uncle, Turanshah; but after six days of bombardment the walls crumbled and the Mongols poured into the town. As elsewhere, the Moslem citizens were given over to be massacred and the Christians spared, apart from some of the Orthodox whose church had not been recognized in the heat of the carnage. The citadel held out for four more weeks under Turanshah. When at last it fell Hulagu showed himself to be unexpectedly clement. Turanshah was spared because of his age and his bravery, and his suite was untouched. A vast horde of treasure fell into the conqueror's hands. Hulagu allotted Aleppo to the former Emir of Homs, al-Ashraf, who had had the foresight to come as a client to the Mongol camp a few months before. Mongol advisers and a Mongol garrison were provided to keep him in control.[1]

The fortress of Harenc, on the road from Aleppo to Antioch, next had to be punished for refusing to surrender unless Hulagu's word was guaranteed by a Moslem. When it had been captured with the usual massacre, Hulagu came to the frontier of Antioch. The King of Armenia and his son-in-law the Prince of Antioch visited his camp to pay him homage. Hethoum had already provided him with auxiliaries and had been rewarded with some of the spoil from Aleppo, while the Seldjuk princes had been ordered to retrocede to him their father's conquests in Cilicia. Bohemond was also rewarded for his deference. Various towns and forts that had belonged to the Moslems since Saladin's day, including Lattakieh, were given back to the Principality. In return, Bohemond was required to instal the Greek Patriarch, Euthymius, in his capital in place of the Latin. Though King Hethoum was not well disposed towards the Greeks, Hulagu understood the importance of their element at Antioch. It is

[1] Maqrisi, *Sultans*, 1, i, pp. 90, 97; Abu'l Feda, pp. 140-1; Rashid ad-Din (trans. Quatremère), pp. 327-41; Bar-Hebraeus, pp. 435-6.

possible that his friendly relations with the Emperor at Nicaea gave him a further inducement.[1]

To the Latins at Acre Bohemond's subservience seemed disgraceful, especially as it involved the humiliation of the Latin Church at Antioch. Venetian influence was still paramount in the kingdom, and the Venetians were on good commercial terms again with Egypt. Their interest depended on the trade from the Far East travelling by the southern route, up the Persian Gulf or the Red Sea. They watched with growing concern the Mongol caravan routes across central Asia to the Black Sea, where the Genoese, with their alliance with the Greeks, were strengthening their control. The government at Acre looked round for a lay protector. It was known that Charles of Anjou, the French King's brother, had Mediterranean ambitions and was already intriguing for the Sicilian throne. An anxious letter was sent in May 1260, to describe the dangers of the Mongol advance and to beg him to intervene.[2]

By the time that the letter was written, the Mongols were masters of Damascus. The Sultan an-Nasir Yusuf made no attempt to defend his capital. On the news of the fall of Aleppo and the approach of a Mongol army he fled to Egypt, to take refuge with the Mameluks, then changed his mind and was captured by the Mongols as he rode northward again. Hama sent a delegation to Hulagu in February 1260, offering him the keys of the city. A few days later the notables of Damascus followed suit. On 1 March Kitbuqa entered Damascus at the head of a Mongol army. With him were the King of Armenia and the Prince of Antioch. The citizens of the ancient capital of the Caliphate saw for the first time for six centuries three Christian potentates ride in triumph through their streets. The citadel held out against the invaders for a few weeks, but was reduced on 6 April.

[1] *Gestes des Chiprois*, p. 161; letter to Charles of Anjou, *Revue de l'Orient Latin*, vol. II, p. 213; Bar-Hebraeus, p. 436; Hayton, *Flor des Estoires*, p. 171. Bohemond was excommunicated by the Pope for this alliance (Urban IV, *Registres*, 26 May 1263). The cession of Lattakieh is never stated, but it was in Frankish hands when next mentioned. See below, pp. 343-4.

[2] 'Lettre à Charles d'Anjou', in *Revue de l'Orient Latin*, vol. II, pp. 213-14.

With the three great cities of Baghdad, Aleppo, and Damascus fallen it seemed that the end of Islam in Asia had arrived. In Damascus, as everywhere else in western Asia, the Mongol conquest meant the resurgence of the local Christians. Kitbuqa, as a Christian himself, made no secret of his sympathies. For the first time since the seventh century the Moslems of inner Syria found themselves a repressed minority. They burned for revenge.[1]

During the spring of 1260 Kitbuqa sent detachments to occupy Nablus and Gaza, though they never reached Jerusalem itself. The Franks were thus completely surrounded by Mongols. The Mongol authorities had no intention of attacking the Frankish kingdom, provided that it showed them sufficient deference. The wiser Franks were ready to avoid provocation, but they could not control their hotheads. The most irresponsible of the barons was Julian, Lord of Sidon and Beaufort, a large, handsome man, but self-indulgent and foolish, with nothing of the subtle intelligence of his grandfather, Reynald. His extravagance had already forced him to pledge Sidon to the Templars, from whom he had borrowed vast sums; and his bad temper had involved him in a quarrel with Philip of Tyre, who was his half-uncle. He had married one of King Hethoum's daughters; but his father-in-law had no influence over him. The wars between the Mongols and the Moslems seemed to him to offer a good opportunity for a raid from Beaufort into the fertile Bekaa. But Kitbuqa was not going to have the newly established Mongol order upset by raiders. He sent a small troop under a nephew of his to punish the Franks. Julian then summoned his neighbours to his aid, and they ambushed and slew the nephew. Kitbuqa then angrily sent a larger army, which penetrated into Sidon and ravaged the town, though the Castle of the Sea was saved by Genoese ships from Tyre. King Hethoum when he heard of it was furious, and blamed the Templars, who had taken advantage of Julian's losses to foreclose on Sidon and Beaufort. A raid conducted shortly afterwards by John II of Beirut and the

[1] Abu'l Feda, pp. 141–3; *Gestes des Chiprois, loc. cit.*; Hayton, *Flor des Estoires*, pp. 171–2. For MS. references see Cahen, *op. cit.* p. 707 nn. 19, 20.

Templars into Galilee met with equally severe treatment at the hands of Mongol auxiliaries.[1]

Kitbuqa, however, was unable to embark on greater enterprises. On 11 August 1259, the Great Khan Mongka had died while campaigning with his brother Kubilai in China. His sons were young and untried. The army in China therefore pressed for the succession of Kubilai. But Mongka's youngest brother, Ariqboga, controlled the homeland, including Karakorum and the central treasury of the Empire, and he desired the throne for himself. After several months of manœuvring and discovering who was his friend, each of the two brothers held a Kuriltay in the spring. of 1260 which elected him as supreme Khan. Ariqboga was supported by most of his imperial relatives who were in Mongolia, while Kubilai had the stronger support amongst the generals. Neither Kuriltay was strictly legal as all the branches of the family were not represented. Neither side was prepared to wait until Hulagu and the princes of the Golden Horde or even of the house of Jagatai were informed and sent their delegations. Hulagu himself favoured Kubilai, although his son Chomughar was of Ariqboga's party, while Berke, Khan of the Golden Horde, sympathized with Ariqboga. It was only at the end of 1261 that Kubilai finally crushed Ariqboga. In the meantime Hulagu cautiously remained close to his eastern frontier, ready to move into Mongolia should it become necessary. He had reasons for anxiety. Ariqboga intervened autocratically in affairs of the Turkestan Khanate, displacing the regent Orghana by her husband's cousin, Alghu, whose later defection and marriage with Orghana contributed largely to Kubilai's victory. Hulagu feared a similar intervention into his own dominions. He was moreover on worsening terms with his cousins of the Golden Horde. While his Court showed strong Christian sympathies, the Khan Berke was definitely moving into the Moslem camp and disapproved of Hulagu's anti-Moslem

---

[1] *Gestes des Chiprois*, pp. 162–4; Hayton, *Flor des Estoires*, p. 174; *Annales de Terre Sainte*, p. 449, placing these events, probably wrongly, after the battle of Ain Jalud.

X

policy. There was friction in the Caucasus, which was the frontier between Berke's and Hulagu's spheres of influence. Berke and his generals continually persecuted the Christian tribes; but Hulagu's attempt to establish his authority on the north side of the mountains was thwarted when one of his armies was severely defeated by Berke's grand-nephew Nogai near the river Terek in 1269.[1]

With these preoccupations, Hulagu was obliged to withdraw many of his troops from Syria as soon as Damascus was taken. Kitbuqa was left to govern the country with a greatly reduced command. Unfortunately for the Mongols their advance into Palestine provoked the one great unbeaten Moslem power, the Mameluks of Egypt; and the Mameluks were now in a fit state to take up the challenge.

The first Mameluk Sultan, Aibek, had been unsure of his position. To legitimize himself he had not only married the Dowager Sultana Shajar ad-Dur but had appointed an infant Ayubite prince as co-Sultan. But the little al-Ashraf Musa counted for nothing and soon was found to be a useless expense; and in 1257 Aibek quarrelled with the Sultana. She was not prepared to be insulted by an upstart; and on 15 April she arranged for his murder by his eunuchs as he was taking his bath. His death almost provoked a civil war, some of the Mameluks crying for vengeance against the Dowager, others supporting her as the symbol of legitimacy. Eventually her enemies won. On 2 May 1257, she was beaten to death, while Aibek's fifteen-year-old son, Nur ad-Din Ali, was made Sultan. But the youth neither represented a respected dynasty nor had himself the personality of a leader. In December 1259, he was deposed by one of his father's former comrades, Saif ad-Din Qutuz, who became Sultan in his place. On his accession various Mameluks such as Baibars, who had fled to Damascus from dislike of Aibek, returned to Egypt.[2]

[1] Rashad ad-Din, pp. 341 ff., 391 ff.; Bar-Hebraeus, p. 439; Kirakos, pp. 192–4; Hayton, *Flor des Estoires*, p. 173. See Grousset, *L'Empire Mongol*, pp. 317–24; Howorth, *op. cit.* III, p. 151; D'Ohsson, *op. cit.* III, p. 377. Nogai seems to have been connected with the imperial family in the female line.

[2] Abu'l Feda, p. 135.

Early in 1260 Hulagu sent an embassy to Egypt to demand the Sultan's submission. Qutuz put the ambassador to death and prepared to meet the Mongols in Syria. It was at this moment that news of Mongka's death and of the civil war in Mongolia obliged Hulagu to remove the greater part of his army away to the east. The troops left with Kitbuqa were considerably fewer than those which Qutuz now collected. Besides the Egyptians themselves there were the remnants of the Khwarismian forces and troops from the Ayubite Prince of Kerak. On 26 July the Egyptian army crossed the frontier and marched on Gaza, with Baibars leading the van. There was a small Mongol force at Gaza, under the general Baidar. He sent to warn Kitbuqa of the invasion, but before help could arrive, his men were overwhelmed by the Egyptians.[1]

Kitbuqa was at Baalbek. He prepared at once to march down past the Sea of Galilee into the Jordan valley, but he was held up by a rising of the Moslems in Damascus. Christian houses and churches were destroyed, and Mongol troops were needed to restore order.[2] Meanwhile Qutuz decided to march up the Palestinian coast and strike inland further north, to threaten Kitbuqa's communications if he advanced into Palestine. An Egyptian embassy was sent therefore to Acre to ask for permission to pass through Frankish territory and to obtain provisions on the march, if not active military aid.

The barons met together at Acre to discuss the request. They were feeling bitter against the Mongols owing to the recent sack of Sidon, and they were distrustful of this Oriental power with its record for wholesale massacre. Islamic civilization was familiar to them; and most of them much preferred the Moslems to the native Christians to whom the Mongols showed such favour. They were at first inclined to offer the Sultan some armed auxiliaries. But the Grand Master of the Teutonic Order, Anno of Sangerhausen, warned them that it would be unwise to trust the Moslems very far, especially if they were to become elated by victory over

[1] Rashid ad-Din (trans. Quatremère), p. 347; D'Ohsson, *op. cit.* III, pp. 333–5.
[2] Abu'l Feda, p. 143.

the Mongols. The Teutonic Order had many possessions in the Armenian kingdom; and Anno probably appreciated King Hethoum's policy. His prudent words had some effect. The military alliance was rejected, but the Sultan was promised free passage and victualling facilities for his army.[1]

During August the Sultan led his army up the coast road and encamped for several days in the orchards outside Acre. Several of the emirs were invited to visit the city as honoured guests, and amongst them was Baibars, who on his return to the camp suggested to Qutuz that it would be easy to take the place by surprise. But Qutuz was not ready to be so perfidious, nor to risk Christian reprisals while the Mongols were still unbeaten. The Franks grew somewhat embarrassed by the number of their visitors, but were consoled by a promise that they should be allowed to buy at reduced prices the horses that would be captured from the Mongols.[2]

While he was at Acre Qutuz learned that Kitbuqa had crossed the Jordan and had entered eastern Galilee. He at once led his army south-eastward, through Nazareth, and on 2 September he reached Ain Jalud, the Pools of Goliath, where the Christian army had defied Saladin in 1183. Next morning the Mongol army came up. The Mongol cavalry was accompanied by Georgian and Armenian contingents; but Kitbuqa lacked scouts, and the local population was unfriendly. He did not know that the whole Mameluk army was close by. Qutuz was well aware of his own superiority in numbers. He therefore hid his main forces in the hills nearby, and only exposed the vanguard led by Baibars. Kitbuqa fell into the trap. He charged at the head of all his men into the enemy that he saw before him. Baibars retreated precipitately into the hills, hotly pursued, and suddenly the whole Mongol army found itself surrounded. Kitbuqa fought superbly. The Egyptians began to waver, and Qutuz entered the battle himself to rally them. But after a few hours the superior numbers of the Moslems made their

[1] *MS. of Rothelin*, p. 637.
[2] William of Tripoli, *De Statu Saracenorum*, in Du Chesne, v, p. 443; *Gestes des Chiprois*, pp. 164–5.

effect. Some of Kitbuqa's men were able to cut their way out, but he refused to survive his defeat. He was almost alone when his horse was killed and he himself was taken prisoner. His capture ended the battle. He was taken bound before the Sultan, who mocked at his fall. He answered defiantly, prophesying a fearful vengeance on his victors and boasting that he, unlike the Mameluk emirs, had always been loyal to his master. They struck off his head.[1]

The battle of Ain Jalud was one of the most decisive in history. It is true that owing to events that had occurred four thousand miles away the Mongol army in Syria was too small to be able, without great good fortune, to undertake the subjection of the Mameluks, and it is true that had a greater army been quickly sent after the disaster, the defeat might have been retrieved. But the contingencies of history forbade the reversal of the decision made at Ain Jalud. The Mameluk victory saved Islam from the most dangerous threat that it has ever had to face. Had the Mongols penetrated into Egypt there would have been no great Moslem state left in the world east of Morocco. The Moslems in Asia were far too numerous ever to be eliminated but they would no longer have been the ruling race. Had Kitbuqa, the Christian, triumphed, the Christian sympathies of the Mongols would have been encouraged, and the Asiatic Christians would have come into power for the first time since the great heresies of the pre-Moslem era. It is idle to speculate about the things that might have happened then. The historian can only relate what did in fact occur. Ain Jalud made the Mameluk Sultanate of Egypt the chief power in the Near East for the next two centuries, till the rise of the Ottoman Empire. It completed the ruin of the native Christians of Asia. By strengthening the Moslem and weakening the Christian element it was soon to induce the Mongols that remained in western Asia to embrace Islam. And it hastened the extinction of the Crusade States; for, as the Teutonic Grand Master foresaw, the victorious Moslems would be eager now to finish with the enemies of the Faith.

[1] Rashid ad-Din, pp. 349–52; Maqrisi, I, i, *Sultans*, pp. 104–6; Abu'l Feda, pp. 143–4.

Five days after his victory the Sultan entered Damascus. The Ayubite al-Ashraf, who had deserted the Mongol cause, was reinstated in Homs. The Ayubite emir of Hama, who had fled to Egypt, returned to his emirate. Aleppo was recovered within a month. Hulagu, angry as he was at the loss of Syria, could do nothing till order was restored in the heart of the Mongol Empire. He sent troops to recover Aleppo in December, but after a fortnight they were forced to retire, having massacred a large number of Moslems in reprisal for the death of Kitbuqa. But that was all that Hulagu could achieve to avenge his faithful friend.[1]

The Sultan Qutuz set out on the return journey to Egypt covered with glory. But, though Kitbuqa's prophecy of vengeance was never wholly fulfilled, his taunt of the disloyalty of the Mameluks very soon was justified. Qutuz had grown suspicious of his most active lieutenant, Baibars; and when Baibars demanded to be made governor of Aleppo, the request was brusquely refused. Baibars did not wait long to take action. On 23 October 1260, when the victorious army reached the edge of the Delta, Qutuz took a day's holiday to go hunting hares. He set out with a few of his emirs, including Baibars and some of his friends. As soon as they were well away from the camp, one of them came up as though to make a request of the Sultan, and while he firmly held him by the hand as though he was going to kiss it, Baibars rushed up from behind and dug his sword into his master's back. The conspirators then galloped back to the camp and announced the murder. The Sultan's chief of staff, Aqtai, was in the royal tent when they arrived and at once asked which of them had committed the murder. When Baibars admitted that it was he, Aqtai bade him sit on the Sultan's throne and was the first to pay him homage; and all the generals in the army followed his example. It was as Sultan that Baibars returned to Cairo.[2]

[1] Abu'l Feda, p. 144; Bar-Hebraeus, pp. 439–40. See Cahen, *op. cit.* pp. 710–11.

[2] Abu'l Feda, *loc. cit.*; Maqrisi, *Sultans*, I, i, pp. 110–13; Bar-Hebraeus, *loc. cit.*; *Gestes des Chiprois*, pp. 165–6.

CHAPTER IV

SULTAN BAIBARS

'And the Egyptians will I give over into the hand of a cruel lord;
and a fierce king shall rule over them.'   ISAIAH XIX, 4

Rukn ad-Din Baibars Bundukdari was now approaching his fiftieth year. He was a Kipchak Turk by birth, a huge man with a brown skin, blue eyes and a loud resonant voice. When he came first to Syria as a young slave, he was offered for sale to the emir of Hama, who examined him and thought him too coarse a lout. But a Mameluk emir, Bundukdar, noticed him in the market and sensed his intelligence. He was bought for the Sultan's Mameluk Guard. Thenceforward he had risen rapidly, and since his victory over the Franks in 1244 he had been marked as the ablest of the Mameluk soldiers. He now showed that he was a statesman of the highest calibre, unimpeded by any scruple of honour, gratitude or mercy.[1]

His first task was to establish himself as Sultan. In Egypt he was accepted without demur, but at Damascus another Mameluk emir, Sinjar al-Halabi, seized the power. Sinjar was popular in Damascus; and the simultaneous attack of the Mongols on Aleppo threatened Baibars's control of Syria. But the Ayubite princes of Homs and Hama defeated the Mongols, while Baibars marched on Damascus and routed Sinjar's troops outside the city on 17 January 1261. The citizens of Damascus fought on for Sinjar, but their resistance was stamped out. Baibars went on to deal with the Ayubites. The Prince of Kerak was induced by pleasant promises to put himself into the Sultan's power and was quietly eliminated. Al-Ashraf of Homs was allowed to retain his city till his death in

[1] Abu'l Feda, p. 156. See Sobernheim, article 'Baibars' in *Encyclopaedia of Islam*.

1263, when it was annexed. It was only at Hama that a branch of the family was able to last on, closely supervised, for another three generations.[1] Baibars also wished to give his government a religious sanction. Some Bedouins brought to Cairo a dark-skinned man called Ahmet whom they declared to be the uncle of the late Caliph. Baibars pretended to verify his genealogy and saluted him as Caliph and religious leader of Islam, but deprived him of any material power. Ahmet, who was renamed al-Hakim, was soon sent to recover Baghdad from the Mongols. When he was killed during his attempt, to which Baibars gave very little support, a son of his was raised to the nominal Caliphate. This shadowy line of doubtful Abbasids was preserved in Cairo so long as the rule of the Mameluks lasted.[2]

The Sultan's next task was to punish the Christians who had helped the Mongols. His particular resentment was reserved for King Hethoum of Armenia and Prince Bohemond of Antioch. In the late autumn of 1261 he sent an army to take control of Aleppo, whose Mameluk governor had been insubordinate, and to carry out extensive raids in Antiochene territory. Further raids were made next summer, and the port of Saint Symeon was sacked. Antioch itself was threatened; but Hethoum appealed to Hulagu and arrived with a force of Mongols and Armenians in time to save it.[3] The Mongol power in north-east Syria was still strong enough to deter Baibars; so he had recourse to diplomacy. The Khan Berke of the Golden Horde had by now come out openly as a Moslem and was ready to ally himself with Baibars. One of the two Seldjuk Sultans of Anatolia, Kaikaûs, who had been deprived of his lands by an alliance between the Mongols, the Byzantines and his own brother Kilij Arslan, had fled to Berke's Court and had been sent back with aid from the Golden Horde and from Baibars, while a Turcoman chief called Karaman, now

[1] Maqrisi, *Sultans*, I, i, p. 116; Abu'l Feda, pp. 145–50; Bar-Hebraeus, p. 439.
[2] Abu'l Feda, p. 148; Maqrisi, *Sultans*, I, i, pp. 148–64; Bar-Hebraeus, p. 442.
[3] *Gestes des Chiprois*, p. 167; *Estoire d'Eracles*, II, p. 466.

established south-east of Konya, could be used to put permanent pressure on the Armenians.[1]

The Franks of Acre had hoped that their friendliness to the Mameluks at the time of the Ain Jalud campaign would preserve them from hostile attentions. But when John of Jaffa and John of Beirut went to his camp late in 1261 to attempt to negotiate for the return of Frankish prisoners made during recent years and for the fulfilment of a promise made by Sultan Aibek to restore Zirin in Galilee, or else pay an indemnity for it, Baibars, though he seems to have liked John of Jaffa, refused to listen to them and instead sent off all the prisoners to labour-camps.[2] In February 1263, John of Jaffa paid a second visit to the Sultan, who was then encamped by Mount Thabor, and obtained the promise of a truce and an exchange of prisoners. But neither the Temple nor the Hospital would then agree to give up the Moslems in their possession, as they were all trained craftsmen and of material value to the Orders. Baibars himself was shocked by such mercenary greed. He broke off negotiations and marched into Frankish territory. After sacking Nazareth and destroying the Church of the Virgin he made a sudden swoop on Acre, on 4 April 1263. There was severe fighting outside the walls, in which the Seneschal, Geoffrey of Sargines, was badly wounded. But Baibars was not yet ready to besiege the city. He retired after sacking the suburbs. It was suspected that he had arranged to have the co-operation of Philip of Montfort and the Genoese from Tyre, but at the last moment their Christian consciences held them back.[3]

Raids and counter-raids continued on the frontier. The Frankish towns in the maritime plain were constantly threatened. As early as April 1261, Balian of Ibelin, lord of Arsuf, leased his lordship to the Hospital, knowing that he could not afford its defence.

[1] Cahen, *La Syrie du Nord*, p. 711. See also Cahen, 'Turcomans de Roum' in *Byzantion*, vol. XIV.

[2] *Annales de Terre Sainte*, p. 450. Al-Aïni, pp. 216–17, mentions a truce made by the two Johns with the Sultan that year.

[3] *Gestes des Chiprois*, pp. 167–8; *Annales de Terre Sainte*, *loc. cit.*; Maqrisi, *Sultans*, I, i, pp. 194–7; al-Aïni, pp. 218–19.

Early in 1264 the Temple and the Hospital consented to unite forces to capture the little fortress of Lizon, the ancient Megiddo, and a few months later they made a joint raid down to Ascalon, while in the autumn the French troops, paid for by Saint Louis, penetrated very profitably as far as the suburbs of Beisan. But in return the Moslems so ravaged the Frankish countryside south of Carmel that life was no longer safe there.[1]

At the beginning of 1265 Baibars set out from Egypt at the head of a formidable army. The Mongols had shown signs of aggression in northern Syria that winter; and his first intention was to counter-attack. But he learned that his troops in the north had held them. He could therefore use his army to attack the Franks in the south. After feigning to amuse himself with a great hunting expedition in the hills behind Arsuf, he suddenly appeared before Caesarea. The town fell at once, on 27 February, but the citadel held out for a week. The garrison capitulated on 5 March and was allowed to go free; but the town and castle alike were razed to the ground. A few days later his troops appeared at Haifa. Those of the inhabitants that were warned in time fled to boats in the anchorage, abandoning both the town and the citadel, which were destroyed; and the inhabitants that had remained there were massacred. Baibars himself meanwhile attacked the great Templar castle at Athlit. The village outside the walls was burned, but the castle itself resisted him successfully. On 21 March he gave up its siege and marched on Arsuf. The Hospitallers had garrisoned and provisioned it well. There were 270 knights within the castle, who fought with superb courage. But the lower town fell on 26 April, after its walls had been broken down by the Sultan's siege-engines; and three days later the commander of the citadel, who had lost a third of his knights, capitulated in return for a promise that the survivors should go free. Baibars broke his word and took them all into captivity. The loss of the two great fortresses horrified the Franks, and inspired the Templar troubadour, Ricaut Bonomel, to write a bitter poem complaining

[1] *Estoire d'Eracles*, II, pp. 444, 449; *Annales de Terre Sainte*, p. 451.

that Christ seemed now to be pleased by the humiliation of the Christians.[1]

It was now the turn of Acre. But the regent, Hugh of Antioch, who had been in Cyprus, had already hurried across the sea with the men that he could raise in the island. When Baibars moved north again from Arsuf he found that Hugh had landed at Acre on 25 April. The Egyptian army returned home, after leaving troops to control the newly conquered territory. The frontier now was within sight of Acre itself.[2] Baibars hastened to write news of his victories to Manfred, King of Sicily, with whom the Egyptian Court kept up the friendship forged with his father Frederick II.[3]

It had been a good year for Baibars. On 8 February 1265, Hulagu died in Azerbaijan. His brother Kubilai had given him the title of Ilkhan and the hereditary government of the Mongol possessions in south-western Asia; and, though his difficulties with the Golden Horde and with the Mongols of Turkestan, who also were converts to Islam, had kept him from resuming a serious offensive against the Mameluks, yet he was still formidable enough to deter the Mameluks from attacking his allies. In July 1264 he held his last Kuriltay at his encampment near Tabriz. His vassals were all present, including King David of Georgia, King Hethoum of Armenia and Prince Bohemond of Antioch. Hethoum and Bohemond were both in disgrace with Hulagu for having, the previous year, kidnapped Euthymius, the Orthodox Patriarch of Antioch, on whose installation Hulagu had insisted in 1260, and carried him off to Armenia. The Latin Opizon had then been introduced into Antioch. To Hulagu the alliance of the Byzantines was important as a means for keeping the Turks of Anatolia in

---

[1] *Gestes des Chiprois*, p. 171; *Estoire d'Eracles*, II, p. 450; *Annales de Terre Sainte*, pp. 451–2; al-Aïni, pp. 219–21; Abu'l Feda, p. 150; Maqrisi, *Sultans*, I, ii, pp. 7–8. Bonomel's poem is given in Bartholemaeis, *Poesie Provenziale*, II, pp. 222–4.

[2] *Gestes des Chiprois, loc. cit.; Estoire d'Eracles, loc. cit.*

[3] Maqrisi, *Sultans*, I, ii, p. 16. Al-Aïni reports an embassy to Baibars in 1264 from Charles of Anjou, who was planning to attack Manfred (p. 219).

control. He was negotiating for a lady of the imperial family of Constantinople to be added to the number of his wives; and when the Emperor Michael selected for the honour his bastard daughter, Maria, she was escorted to Tabriz by the Patriarch Euthymius, who found refuge at Constantinople and who returned to the east no doubt at Hulagu's express invitation. But the Mongols remained broad-minded and would not allow sectarian quarrels amongst the Christians to interfere with their general policy. It seems that Bohemond was able to excuse himself and that Euthymius was not received back in Antioch.[1]

Hulagu's death inevitably weakened the Mongols at a critical moment. The influence of his widow, Dokuz Khatun, secured the succession for his favourite son, Abaga, who was governor of Turkestan. But it was not till June, four months after his father's death, that Abaga was formally installed as Ilkhan; and several more months passed before the redistribution of fiefs and governor-ships was completed. Dokuz Khatun herself died during the summer, deeply mourned by the Christians. Meanwhile Abaga was continually threatened by his cousins of the Golden Horde, who actually invaded his territory next spring. It was impossible for the Mongol government to intervene for the time being in western Syria. Baibars, to whose diplomacy the Ilkhan's troubles with his northern neighbours were mainly due, could resume his campaigns against the Christians without fear of interference.[2]

In the early summer of 1266, while Abaga's armies were occupied in beating off the Khan Berke's invasion of Persia, two Mameluk armies set out from Egypt. One, under the Sultan himself, appeared before Acre on 1 June. But the regiment maintained there by Saint Louis had recently been reinforced from France. Finding the city so strongly garrisoned, Baibars turned aside to

---

[1] Rashid ad-Din (trans. Quatremère), pp. 417–23; see Howorth, *op. cit.* III, pp. 206–10. Vartan (ed. Emin), pp. 205–6, 211; Bar-Hebraeus, pp. 444–5. 'Lettre à Charles d'Anjou', in *Revue de l'Orient Latin*, vol. II, p. 213. Dokuz Khatun consulted Vartan about the propriety of having a Mass said for Hulagu's soul. He discouraged her (Vartan, ed. Emin, p. 211).

[2] Howorth, *op. cit.* III, pp. 218–25.

make a demonstration before the Teutonic fortress of Montfort, then marched suddenly on Safed, from whose huge castle the Templars dominated the Galilean uplands. The fortifications had been entirely reconstructed some twenty-five years before, and the garrison was numerous, though many of the soldiers were native Christians or half-breeds. The Sultan's first assault, on 7 July, was beaten back, nor was he more successful with his next attempts, on 13 and 19 July. He then announced through heralds that he offered a complete amnesty to any of the native soldiers that would surrender to him. It is doubtful how many of them would have trusted his word; but the Templar knights at once grew suspicious. There were recriminations, which came to blows; and the Syrians began to desert. The Templars soon found it impossible to hold the castle. At the end of the month they sent a Syrian sergeant whom they believed to be loyal down to Baibars's camp to offer surrender. The Syrian, whose name was Leo, returned with the promise that the garrison should be allowed to retire without hurt to Acre. But when the Templars handed over the castle to Baibars on these terms, he had them all decapitated. Whether Leo had been a conscious traitor was uncertain; but his prompt conversion to Islam was evidence against him.[1]

The capture of Safed gave Baibars control of Galilee. He next attacked Toron, which fell to him with hardly a struggle. From Toron he sent a troop to destroy the Christian village of Qara, between Homs and Damascus, which he suspected of being in touch with the Franks. The adult inhabitants were massacred and the children enslaved. When the Christians from Acre sent a deputation to ask to be allowed to bury the dead, he roughly refused, saying that if they wished for martyrs' corpses they would find them at home. To carry out his threat he marched down to the coast and slaughtered every Christian that fell into his hands. But, once again, he did not venture to attack Acre itself, where the Regent Hugh had just arrived from Cyprus. When the Mameluks

---

[1] *Gestes des Chiprois*, pp. 179–81; *Estoire d'Eracles*, II, pp. 484–5; Maqrisi, *Sultans*, I, ii, pp. 28–30; Abu'l Feda, p. 151; al-Aïni, pp. 222–3.

retired in the autumn, Hugh assembled the knights of the Orders and the French regiment under Geoffrey of Sargines and made a counter-raid through Galilee. But on 28 October the vanguard was ambushed by the garrison of Safed, while local Arabs attacked the Frankish camp. Hugh was obliged to retire with heavy losses.[1]

While Baibars campaigned in Galilee, the second Mameluk army, under the ablest of his emirs, Qalawun, assembled at Homs. After a lightning raid towards Tripoli, during which he captured the forts of Qulaiat and Halba and the town of Arqa, which controlled the approach to Tripoli from the Buqaia, Qalawun hurried northward to join with the army of al-Mansur of Hama. Their combined troops then marched to Aleppo and turned westward into Cilicia.[2] King Hethoum had expected a Mameluk attack. In 1263, on the news of Hulagu's death, he had attempted to come to terms with Baibars. The Egyptian navy depended for its shipbuilding on wood from southern Anatolia and the Lebanon. Hethoum and his son-in-law Bohemond controlled these forests and hoped to use their control as a bargaining point. But the attempted blockade only made Baibars the more determined on war.[3] In the spring of 1266, knowing that a Mameluk attack was imminent, Hethoum set out for the Court of the Ilkhan at Tabriz. While he was there, pleading for Mongol help, the storm burst on Cilicia. The Armenian army, led by Hethoum's two sons, Leo and Thoros, waited by the Syrian Gates, with the Templars at Baghras guarding its flanks; but the Mameluks turned northward to cross the Amanus mountains near Sarventikar. The Armenians hastened to intercept them as they descended into the Cilician plain. A decisive battle took place on 24 August. The Armenians were outnumbered and were routed. Of their two princes Thoros was slain and Leo taken prisoner. The victorious Moslems swept through Cilicia. While Qalawun and his Mameluks sacked Ayas, Adana and Tarsus, al-Mansur led his army past Mamistra to the

[1] *Gestes des Chiprois*, pp. 180–1; *Estoire d'Eracles, loc. cit.*
[2] Abu'l Feda, *loc. cit.*; al-Aïni, p. 222.
[3] Mas Latrie, *Histoire de Chypre*, 1, p. 412.

Armenian capital at Sis, where he plundered the palace, burned down the cathedral and slaughtered some thousands of the inhabitants. At the end of September the victors retired to Aleppo with nearly forty thousand captives and great caravans of booty. King Hethoum hurried back from the Ilkhan's Court, with a small company of Mongols, to find his heir a captive, his capital in ruins and his whole country devastated. The Cilician kingdom never recovered from the disaster. It was no longer able to play more than a passive part in the politics of Asia.[1]

After eliminating the Armenians, Baibars sent troops in the autumn of 1266 to attack Antioch. But his generals were sated with loot and were unenthusiastic. Bribes from Bohemond and the Commune induced them to abandon the attempt.[2]

Baibars was furious at his deputies' weakness. He himself allowed the Franks no respite. In May 1267, he appeared once more before Acre. By displaying banners that he had captured from the Templars and the Hospitallers he was able to approach right up to the walls before the ruse was discovered. But his assault on the walls was repulsed, and he contented himself with ravaging the countryside. The headless bodies were left in the gardens round Acre till the citizens ventured out to bury them. When the Franks sent ambassadors to ask for a truce he received them at Safed, where the whole castle was encircled with the skulls of murdered Christian prisoners.[3]

Life at Acre was not made easier by a renewal of the war between the Venetians and the Genoese for the control of the harbour. On 16 August 1267, the Genoese admiral Luccheto Grimaldi forced his way into the port with twenty-eight galleys, after capturing the Tower of Flies, which stood at the end of the

---

[1] Vartan (ed. Emin), pp. 213-15; Hethoum, p. 407; Vahram, *Rhymed Chronicle*, pp. 522-3; King Hethoum, poem, *R.H.C. Arm.* I, pp. 551-2; Ballad on Prince Leo's Captivity, *ibid.* pp. 539-40; Hayton, *Flor des Estoires*, pp. 177-8; Bar-Hebraeus, pp. 445-6; Maqrisi, *Sultans*, I, ii, p. 34; Abu'l Feda, p. 151; *Gestes des Chiprois*, p. 181; *Estoire d'Eracles*, II, p. 455.

[2] Cahen, *op. cit.* p. 716, citing MS. of Ibn Abdarrahîm (Muhi ad-Din).

[3] *Gestes des Chiprois*, pp. 181-3; *Estoire d'Eracles*, II, p. 455; al-Aïni, p. 225.

breakwater. But after twelve days he took fifteen of his ships to Tyre for repairs. During his absence a Venetian fleet of twenty-six galleys appeared and attacked the remaining Genoese. Five Genoese ships were lost in the battle. The others fought their way through to Tyre.[1]

Early in 1268 Baibars set out once more from Egypt. The only Christian possessions south of Acre itself were the Templar castle of Athlit and the lawyer John of Ibelin's town of Jaffa. John, who had always been treated with respect by the Moslems, died in the spring of 1266. His son Guy had not the same prestige. He had hoped that the Sultan would honour the truce that his father had made. In consequence, when the Egyptian army appeared before the town on 7 March, it was in no state to defend itself. After twelve hours of fighting it fell into the Sultan's hands. Many of the inhabitants were slaughtered, but the garrison was allowed to retire unharmed to Acre. The castle was destroyed, and its wood and marble were sent to Cairo for the great new mosque that Baibars was building there.[2]

The Sultan's next objective was the castle of Beaufort, which the Temple had recently taken over from Julian of Sidon. After ten days of heavy bombardment the garrison surrendered on 15 April. The women and children were sent free to Tyre, but the men were all kept as slaves. The castle itself was repaired by Baibars and strongly garrisoned.[3] On 1 May the Mameluk army appeared suddenly outside Tripoli, but, finding it well garrisoned, turned equally suddenly towards the north. The Templars from Tortosa and Safita sent hastily to beg the Sultan that their territory might be spared.[4] Baibars respected their wishes and marched swiftly down the Orontes valley. On 14 May he was before Antioch. There he divided his forces into three parts. One army

---

[1] *Gestes des Chiprois*, p. 186; *Estoire d'Eracles*, II, pp. 455–6; Heyd, *Histoire du Commerce du Levant*, I, p. 354.

[2] *Gestes des Chiprois*, p. 190; *Estoire d'Eracles*, II, p. 456; Abu'l Feda, p. 152; Maqrisi, *Sultans*, I, ii, pp. 50–1; al-Aïni, pp. 226–7.

[3] *Gestes des Chiprois*, *loc. cit.*; *Estoire d'Eracles*, *loc. cit.*; al-Aïni, pp. 227–8.

[4] Al-Aïni, p. 228.

went to capture Saint Symeon, thus cutting off Antioch from the sea. The second army moved up to the Syrian Gates, to prevent any help reaching the city from Cilicia. The main force, under Baibars himself, drew closely round the city.

Prince Bohemond was at Tripoli; and Antioch was under the command of its Constable, Simon Mansel, whose wife was an Armenian, related to Bohemond's Princess. Its walls were in good repair, but the garrison was hardly large enough to man their long extent. The Constable had rashly led out some troops to try to dispute the investment of the city, and had been captured by the Mameluks. He was ordered by his captors to arrange for the capitulation of the garrison; but his lieutenants within the walls refused to listen to him. The first assault on the city took place next day. It was beaten back, and negotiations were opened once again, with no greater success. On 18 May the Mameluk army made a general attack on all sections of the walls. After fierce fighting a breach was made where the defences ran up the slope of Mount Silpius; and the Moslems poured into the city.

Even the Moslem chroniclers were shocked by the carnage that followed. By order of the Sultan's emirs, the city gates were closed, that none of the inhabitants might escape. Those that were found in the streets were slaughtered at once. Others, cowering in their houses, were spared only to end their days in captivity. Several thousands of the citizens had fled with their families to the shelter of the huge citadel on the mountain top. Their lives were spared, but their persons were divided amongst the emirs. On 19 May the Sultan ordered the collection and distribution of the booty. Though its prosperity had been declining for some decades Antioch had long been the richest of the Frankish cities, and its accumulated treasures were stupendous. There were great mounds of gold and silver ornaments, and coins were so plentiful that they were handed out in bowlfuls. The number of captives was enormous. There was not a soldier in the Sultan's army that did not acquire a slave, and the surplus was such that the price of a boy fell to twelve dirhems and a girl to only five. A few of the richer citizens were allowed to ransom themselves. Simon Mansel was set free and retired to Armenia. But many of the leading dignitaries of the government and of the Church were killed or were never heard of again.[1]

The principality of Antioch, the first of the states that the Franks founded in Outremer, had lasted for 171 years. Its destruction was a terrible blow to Christian prestige, and it brought the rapid decline of Christianity in northern Syria. The Franks were gone, and the native Christians fared little better. It was their punishment for their support, not of the Franks but of those more dangerous foes to Islam, the Mongols. The city itself never recovered. It had already lost its commercial importance, for, with the frontier between the Mongol and Mameluk Empires running along the Euphrates, trade from Iraq and the Far East no longer came through Aleppo but kept to Mongol territory and debouched to the sea at Ayas in Cilicia. The Moslem conquerors had therefore no interest in repopulating Antioch. Its importance now was only as a frontier fortress. Many of the houses within its great walls were not rebuilt. The hierarchs of the local churches moved to more lively centres. It was not long before the headquarters both of the Orthodox and of the Jacobite churches in Syria were established at Damascus.[2]

With Armenia weakened and Antioch destroyed, the Templars decided that it was impossible to hold their castles in the Amanus mountains. Baghras and the lesser castle of La Roche de Russole were abandoned without a struggle. All that was left of the Principality was the city of Lattakieh which had been restored to

[1] *Gestes des Chiprois*, pp. 190–1; *Estoire d'Eracles*, II, pp. 456–7; Bar-Hebraeus, p. 448; Maqrisi, *Sultans*, I, ii, pp. 52–3; al-Aïni, pp. 229–34; Abu'l Feda, p. 152.
[2] Antioch still had a considerable population when Ibn Battutah visited it in 1355 (Ibn Battutah, *Voyages*, ed. Defrémery, I, p. 162), but Baibars had destroyed its fortifications. Bertrandon de la Broquière, who visited it in 1432 says that the walls were still entire but that there were only about 300 inhabited houses within them and the inhabitants were mostly Turcoman (*Voyage d'Outremer*, ed. Schefer, pp. 84–5).

Bohemond by the Mongols and was now an isolated enclave, and the Castle of Qusair, whose lord had made friends with the Moslems of the neighbourhood and was allowed to remain on there for seven more years as vassal to the Sultan.[1]

After his triumph at Antioch Baibars rested awhile. There were signs that the Mongols were ready to play a more active role, and there were rumours that Saint Louis was preparing a great Crusade. When the Regent Hugh sent to ask for a truce, the Sultan replied with an embassy to Acre to offer a temporary cessation of hostilities. Hugh had hoped for some concessions and tried to threaten the ambassador, Muhi ad-Din, by showing his troops in battle-array; but Muhi ad-Din merely replied that the whole army was not so numerous as the host of Christian captives at Cairo. Prince Bohemond asked to be included in the truce. He was offended when the Sultan's reply addressed him merely as Count, because he had lost his principality; but he gladly accepted the respite offered to him. There were minor Mameluk raids into Christian lands in the spring of 1269, but on the whole the truce was observed for a year.[2]

Meanwhile the Franks tried to set their house in order. In December 1267, King Hugh II of Cyprus died at the age of fourteen, and the Regent Hugh of Antioch-Lusignan succeeded to the throne as Hugh III. He was crowned on Christmas Day. His accession gave him a surer authority over his vassals, for there was no danger now that his government would abruptly end when his ward came of age. But he was unable to overcome their claim that they were not obliged to serve in his army outside the limits of the kingdom. Whenever he wished to take troops to the mainland he was dependent on men from the royal estates and on volunteers. On 29 October 1268, Conradin of Hohenstaufen was beheaded at Naples by the orders of Charles of Anjou, from whom he had vainly tried to wrest back his Italian inheritance. His death

---

[1] *Gestes des Chiprois*, p. 191; *Estoire d'Eracles*, II, p. 457; Cahen, *La Syrie du Nord*, p. 717 n. 17.

[2] Muhi ad-Din, in Reinaud, *Bibliothèque des Croisades*, pp. 513–15.

meant the extinction of the elder line of the royal house of Jerusalem, which descended from Queen Maria, La Marquise. Next in the line came the house of Cyprus, descended from Maria's half-sister, Alice of Champagne. King Hugh III's claim to be heir had been tacitly acknowledged by his appointment as regent, when his cousin, Hugh of Brienne, whose hereditary rights were legally better than his own, had been passed over. Hugh of Brienne had gone to seek his fortune in the Frankish duchy of Athens, whose heiress he married. He did not now challenge his cousin. But before King Hugh could receive his second crown there was another competitor to be considered. Queen Maria's second half-sister, Melisende of Lusignan, had married as his second wife Prince Bohemond IV of Antioch, and their daughter Maria was still alive. While Hugh could claim to be descended from an earlier marriage of Queen Isabella than Maria, Maria was one generation closer to Queen Isabella. She appeared before the High Court, maintaining that the succession should be decided by the degree of kinship with Queen Isabella, who was the common ancestress of Conradin, Hugh and herself. A granddaughter, she argued, took precedence over a great-grandson. Hugh replied that his grandmother, Queen Alice, had been accepted as regent because she was the next heir, and that her son, King Henry of Cyprus, had been accepted as regent on her death, and after Henry his widow and then Hugh himself as guardians of the young Hugh II. He now represented Alice's line. Maria countered by saying that there had been a mistake; her mother, Melisende, should have succeeded Alice as regent. After some argument, in which Maria was upheld by the Templars, the lawyers of Outremer supported Hugh's claims. Had they refused, they would have been forced to admit that they had been previously in error. Public opinion was on their side; for the vigorous young King of Cyprus was obviously a more desirable candidate than a middle-aged spinster. Maria would not accept the verdict. She issued a formal protest on the day of Hugh's coronation, then bustled off to Italy to lay her case before the Papal Curia. She arrived at Rome during an interregnum; but Gregory X, who was elected in 1271, showed her sympathy and allowed her to bring up the question at the Council of Lyons in 1274. Representatives from Acre appeared and argued that the High Court of Jerusalem alone had jurisdiction over the succession to the kingdom, and the matter was dropped. Before he died in 1276, Gregory arranged for Maria to sell her claim to Charles of Anjou. The transaction was completed in March 1277. The Princess received a thousand gold pounds and an annuity of four thousand pounds *tournois*. The annuity was confirmed by Charles II of Naples; but it is doubtful how much money Maria, who was still living in 1307, actually received.[1]

Hugh was crowned on 24 September 1269, by the Bishop of Lydda, acting for the Patriarch. His first task was to try to restore some unity to his new kingdom. Already before his coronation he managed to compose the old quarrel between Philip of Montfort and the government at Acre. Philip's pride had been humbled by the loss of Toron; he was no longer so anxious to play a lone hand. When Hugh proposed that his own sister, Margaret of Antioch-Lusignan, the loveliest girl of her generation, should marry Philip's elder son, John, Philip was glad to accept the offer. Hugh was thus able to go to Tyre to be crowned in its cathedral, which had been since the fall of Jerusalem the traditional crowning-place of the Kings. Soon afterwards Philip's younger son, Humphrey, married Eschiva of Ibelin, younger daughter of John II of Beirut. This reconciliation between the Montforts and the Ibelins was easier as the older generation of Ibelins was extinct. John of Beirut had died in 1264, John of Jaffa in 1266 and John of Arsuf in 1268. After Baibars's recent campaigns the only Ibelin fief left on the mainland, and, indeed, the only lay fief in the kingdom other than Tyre, was Beirut, which had passed to John's elder daughter, Isabella. She had been married as a child to the child-king of Cyprus, Hugh II, who died before the marriage was consummated. Hugh III hoped to use her as an eligible heiress to attract some

[1] *Gestes des Chiprois*, pp. 190–3; *Assises*, II, pp. 415–19. See La Monte, *Feudal Monarchy*, pp. 77–9, and Hill, *History of Cyprus*, II, pp. 161–5.

distinguished knight to the East. In Cyprus the Ibelins were still the most powerful family. The King soon afterwards won their loyalty by marrying another Isabella of Ibelin, daughter of the Constable Guy.[1]

Though he managed to make peace between his few remaining lay vassals, it was less easy to secure the co-operation of the Military Orders, the Commune of Acre, or the Italians. Venice and Genoa were not going to give up their quarrels at any monarch's bidding. The Templars and the Teutonic Knights resented Hugh's reconciliation with Philip of Montfort. The Commune of Acre was equally jealous of any favour shown to Tyre and disliked to see the end of the absentee monarchy under which their own power had increased. Nor could Hugh call in his Cypriot vassals to enhance his authority. His attempt to make his rule effective was doomed to failure.[2]

Foreign affairs were hardly more encouraging. The shadow of Charles of Anjou lay darkly across the Mediterranean world. Great hopes had been built in the East on Saint Louis's forthcoming Crusade; but in 1270 Charles diverted it to suit his own interests. Louis's death at Tunis that year released Charles from the one altruistic influence that he respected. He was on friendly terms with the Sultan Baibars, but he was personally hostile to King Hugh, against whom he encouraged the claims of Hugh of Brienne to the throne of Cyprus and of Maria of Antioch to that of Jerusalem. It was, indeed, fortunate for Outremer that Charles's main ambitions were directed against Byzantium; for it was clear that any Crusade that he assisted would be turned to suit his own selfish ends.[3]

The Crusading spirit was not, however, entirely dead in Europe. On 1 September 1269, King James I of Aragon sailed

[1] *Gestes des Chiprois*, pp. 192–3. The Princess Margaret grew extremely corpulent later on and lost her looks. She was already aged twenty-four when she married. See also *Lignages*, p. 462, and genealogical tree below, Appendix III.

[2] See Grousset, *Histoire des Croisades*, III, pp. 645–6, overrating Hugh's abilities in the light of what ensued, and Hill, *op. cit.* p. 178.

[3] See above, p. 292.

from Barcelona with a powerful squadron to rescue the East. Unfortunately it ran almost at once into a storm, which caused such havoc that the King and the greater part of his fleet returned home. Only a small squadron, under the King's two bastards, the Infants Fernando Sanchez and Pedro Fernandez, continued the journey. They arrived at Acre at the end of December, eager to fight the infidel. Early in December Baibars broke his truce with Hugh and appeared with three thousand men in the fields before Acre, leaving others concealed in the hills. The Infants wished to hurry out at once to attack the enemy; and it needed all the tact of the Military Knights to restrain them. An ambush was suspected. Moreover the Christians' numbers were depleted, as the French regiment, which the Seneschal Geoffrey of Sargines had commanded till his death that spring, had gone with its new commander, Oliver of Termes, and the new Seneschal, Robert of Crésèques, on a raid beyond Montfort. These raiders caught sight of the Moslem forces as they were returning. Oliver of Termes wished to slip unobserved through the orchards back into Acre; but the Seneschal Robert insisted on attacking the enemy. The Frenchmen fell straight into the ambush laid for them by Baibars. Very few of them survived. When the troops inside Acre clamoured to go to their rescue, the Infants of Aragon, who had learned their lesson, restrained them. Soon afterwards they returned to Aragon, having achieved nothing.[1]

Though help from the West was inadequate, there was still hope from the East. The Ilkhan of Persia, Abaga, like his father Hulagu, was an eclectic Shamanist with strong Christian sympathies. The death of his Christian stepmother, Dokuz Khatun, had robbed her co-religionists of every sect of their chief friend; but they found a new protector in the Byzantine Princess Maria. She had arrived at the Ilkhan's Court to find Hulagu dead, but was married at once to Abaga, who soon conceived a deep respect for her; and all his subjects, to whom she was known as Despina

---

[1] *Gestes des Chiprois*, pp. 183–5 (wrongly dating the campaign in 1267); *Estoire d'Eracles*, II, pp. 457–8; *Annales de Terre Sainte*, p. 454.

Khatun, revered her for her goodness and her sagacity. News of the Ilkhan's good-will induced the King of Aragon, in conjunction with Pope Clement IV, to send James Alaric of Perpignan on a mission to him in 1267, to announce the forthcoming Crusade of the Aragonese and of King Louis and to suggest a military alliance. But Abaga, who was fully occupied by his war against the Golden Horde, would only make vague promises.[1] His inability to do more was shown by his failure to rescue Antioch from the Mameluks next year. He was soon faced with a new war, with his cousins of the House of Jagatai, who invaded his eastern dominions in 1270 and were only driven back after a tremendous battle near Herat. For the next two years Abaga's main task was to reopen communications with his uncle and overlord, the Great Khan Kubilai in China.[2] But in 1270, after his victory at Herat, he wrote to King Louis undertaking to grant military aid as soon as the Crusade appeared in Palestine.[3] King Louis went instead to Tunis, where the Mongols could not help him. The only practical assistance that the Ilkhan was able to give to the Christians was to provide Hethoum of Armenia with a distinguished Mameluk captive, Shams ad-Din Sonqor al-Ashkar, the Red Falcon, whom the Mongols had captured at Aleppo. In return for his release Baibars agreed to free Hethoum's heir, Leo, and to make a truce with Hethoum on condition that the Armenians ceded the fortresses of the Amanus, Darbsaq, Behesni, and Raban. The treaty was signed in August 1268. Early next year Leo, who had been permitted to make a pilgrimage to Jerusalem, returned to Armenia. His father at once abdicated in his favour and retired to a monastery, where he died the following year. Leo's title as King was confirmed by Abaga, to whom he went personally to pay homage.[4]

Throughout the summer of 1270 Baibars remained quiet,

---

[1] D'Ohsson, *Histoire des Mongols*, III, pp. 539–42; Howorth, *op. cit.* III, pp. 278–80. For Maria's reputation, Bar-Hebraeus, p. 505.

[2] D'Ohsson, *op. cit.* pp. 442 ff.   [3] *Ibid.* pp. 458–9.

[4] *Gestes des Chiprois*, p. 191; *Estoire d'Eracles*, pp. 457, 463; Bar-Hebraeus, pp. 446–9; Vahram, *Rhymed Chronicle*, pp. 523–4; Hayton, *Flor des Estoires*, p. 178. See Cahen, *op. cit.* p. 718.

fearing that he might have to defend Egypt against the King of France. But, in order to weaken the Franks, he arranged for the assassination of their one leading baron, Philip of Montfort. The Assassins of Syria were grateful to the Sultan, whose conquests freed them from the necessity of paying tribute to the Hospital, and they strongly resented the Frankish negotiations with the Mongols, who had destroyed their headquarters in Persia. On Baibars's request they sent one of their fanatics to Tyre. There, pretending to be a Christian convert, he penetrated on Sunday, 17 August 1270, into a chapel where Philip and his son John were praying, and suddenly fell upon them. Before help could arrive Philip was mortally wounded, surviving just long enough to learn that his murderer was captured and his heir was safe. His death was a heavy blow to Outremer; for John, though he remained devoted to King Hugh, his brother-in-law, lacked his father's experience and prestige.[1]

King Louis's death before Tunis greatly relieved the Sultan, who had been ready to march to the assistance of the Tunisian emir. He knew that he had nothing to fear from Charles of Anjou. In 1271 he marched again into Frankish territory. In February he appeared before Safita, the White Castle of the Templars. After a spirited defence the small garrison was advised by the Grand Master to surrender. The survivors were allowed to retire to Tortosa. The Sultan then marched on the huge Hospitaller fortress of Krak des Chevaliers, Qalat al-Hosn. He arrived there on 3 March. Next day contingents joined him from the Assassins, as well as al-Mansur of Hama and his army. Heavy rain for some days prevented him from bringing up his siege-engines; but on 15 March, after a brief but heavy bombardment, the Moslems forced an entry into the gate-tower of the outer enceinte. A fortnight later they broke their way into the inner enceinte, slaughtering the knights that they met there and taking the native soldiers prisoner. Many of the defenders held out for ten more

---

[1] *Gestes des Chiprois*, pp. 194–8; *Annales de Terre Sainte*, p. 454; Maqrisi, *Sultans*, I, ii, pp. 80–3.

days in the great tower at the south of the enceinte. On 8 April they capitulated and were sent under a safe-conduct to Tripoli. The capture of Krak, which had defied even Saladin, gave Baibars control of the approaches to Tripoli. He followed it up with the capture of Akkar, the Hospitaller castle on the south of the Buqaia, which fell on 1 May, after a fortnight's siege.[1]

Prince Bohemond was at Tripoli. Fearful that it was to share the fate of his other capital, Antioch, he sent to Baibars to beg for a truce. The Sultan mocked at his lack of courage, and demanded that he should pay all the expenses of the recent Mameluk campaign. Bohemond had enough spirit left to refuse the insulting terms. Baibars had meanwhile made an unsuccessful attack on the little fort of Maraclea, built on a rock off the coast between Buluniyas and Tortosa. Its lord, Bartholomew, had gone to seek help from the Mongol Court. Baibars was so furious at his failure that he tried to induce the Assassins to murder Bartholomew on his journey.[2]

At the end of May Baibars suddenly offered Bohemond a truce for ten years, with no other terms than the retention of his recent conquests. On its acceptance he set out to return to Egypt, pausing only to besiege the Teutonic fortress of Montfort, which surrendered on 12 June, after one week's siege.[3] There were now no inland castles left to the Franks. About the same time he sent a squadron of seventeen ships to attack Cyprus, having heard that King Hugh had left the island for Acre. His fleet appeared unexpectedly off Limassol, but owing to bad seamanship eleven ships ran aground and the crews fell into the hands of the Cypriots.[4]

The Sultan's forbearance towards Bohemond was due to the

[1] Maqrisi, *Sultans*, I, ii, pp. 84–5; al-Aïni, pp. 237–9; Abu'l Feda, p. 154; *Gestes des Chiprois*, p. 199; *Estoire d'Eracles*, II, p. 460.

[2] Maqrizi, *Sultans*, I, ii, pp. 86, 100; *Annales de Terre Sainte*, p. 455; Röhricht, 'Derniers Temps' in *Archives d'Orient Latin*, II, pp. 400–3.

[3] *Gestes des Chiprois*, pp. 199–200; *Estoire d'Eracles*, *loc. cit.*

[4] Maqrisi, *Sultans*, I, ii, p. 88; Abu'l Feda, p. 154; al-Aïni, pp. 239–40; *Gestes des Chiprois*, p. 199; *Estoire d'Eracles*, *loc. cit.*; *Annales de Terre Sainte*, *loc. cit.*

arrival of a new Crusade. Henry III of England had long ago taken the Cross, but he was now an old man, worn out by civil wars. In his stead, he encouraged his son and heir, Prince Edward, to set out for the East. Edward was in his early thirties, an able, vigorous and cold-blooded man who had already shown his gifts as a statesman in dealing with his father's rebels. He decided on his Crusade after he heard of the fall of Antioch; but he planned it carefully and methodically. Unfortunately, though many of the English nobles had agreed to accompany him, one by one they made their excuses. It was with only about a thousand men that the Prince eventually left England in the summer of 1271, together with his wife, Eleanor of Castile. His brother Edmund of Lancaster, one time candidate for the Sicilian throne, followed him with reinforcements a few months later. He was also accompanied by a small contingent of Bretons, under their Count, and one from the Low Countries, under Tedaldo Visconti, Archbishop of Liége. Edward's intention had been to join King Louis at Tunis and sail on with him to the Holy Land, but he arrived in Africa to find the King dead and the French troops about to return home. He wintered in Sicily with King Charles, whose first wife had been his aunt, and sailed on next spring to Cyprus and then to Acre, where he landed on 9 May 1271. He was ioined there soon afterwards by King Hugh and Prince Bohemond.[1]

Edward was horrified by the state of affairs in Outremer. He knew that his own army was small, but he hoped to unite the Christians of the East into a formidable body and then to use the help of the Mongols in making an effective attack on Baibars. His first shock was to find that the Venetians maintained a flourishing trade with the Sultan, supplying him with all the timber and metal that he needed for his armaments, while the Genoese were doing their best to force their way into this profitable business and already controlled the slave-trade of Egypt. But when he reproved the merchants for thus endangering the future

---

[1] *Gestes des Chiprois*, pp. 199–200; *Estoire d'Eracles*, pp. 460–1. For Edward's Crusade, see Powicke, *King Henry III and the Lord Edward*, II, pp. 597 ff.

of the Christian East they showed him the licences that they had received from the High Court at Acre for this purpose. He could do nothing to stop them.[1] Next, he hoped that the whole chivalry of Cyprus would follow its King to the mainland. But, though some feudatories had come, they insisted that they were volunteers; and when King Hugh demanded that they should stay in Syria as long as he was there, their spokesman, his wife's cousin, James of Ibelin, declared firmly that they were only obliged to serve in the defence of the island. He arrogantly added that the King could not count it as a precedent that Cypriot nobles had gone to fight on the mainland, for they had done so more often at the bidding of the Ibelins than at any King's bidding. But he hinted that if Hugh had made his request more tactfully it might have been granted. The argument was carried on till 1273, when, in a rare spirit of compromise, the Cypriots agreed to spend four months on the mainland, if the King or his heir in person were present with the army. It was by then too late for Edward's purpose.[2]

The English Prince was not much more successful with the Mongols. As soon as he arrived at Acre he sent an embassy to the Ilkhan, consisting of three Englishmen, Reginald Russell, Godfrey Welles and John Parker. Abaga, whose main armies were fighting in Turkestan, agreed to send what aid he could. In the meantime Edward contented himself with a few minor raids just across the frontier. In mid-October 1271, Abaga fulfilled his promise by detaching ten thousand horsemen from his garrisons in Anatolia. They swept down past Aintab into Syria, defeating the Turcoman troops that protected Aleppo. The Mameluk garrisons of Aleppo fled before them to Hama. They continued their course past Aleppo to Maarrat an-Numan and Apamea. There was panic amongst the local Moslems. But Baibars, who was at Damascus, was not unduly alarmed. He had a large army with him, and he

---

[1] Dandolo, p. 380; Röhricht, 'Derniers Temps', p. 622; Powicke, *op. cit.* II, pp. 604–5.

[2] *Assises*, I, pp. 347, 626, II, pp. 427–34; *Estoire d'Eracles*, II, pp. 462–4. See Hill, *History of Cyprus*, II, pp. 168–70.

summoned reinforcements from Egypt. When he began to move northwards, on 12 November, the Mongols turned back. They were not strong enough to face the full Mameluk army, and their Turkish vassals in Anatolia were restive. They retired behind the Euphrates, laden with booty.[1]

While Baibars was distracted by the Mongols, Edward led the Franks across Mount Carmel to raid the Plain of Sharon. But his troops were too few for him even to attempt to storm the little Mameluk fortress of Qaqun which guarded the road across the hills. A more effective Mongol invasion and a larger Crusade were needed if any territory was to be reconquered.[2]

By the spring of 1272 Prince Edward realized that he was wasting his time. All that he could do without greater man-power and more allies was to arrange a truce that would preserve Outremer for the time being. Baibars on his side was ready for a truce. The pathetic remnant of the Frankish kingdom lay at his mercy so long as he was not hampered by external complications. His army's first task was to ward off the Mongols, who must further be restrained by diplomatic action in Anatolia and on the Steppes. Till he felt secure on that front it was not worth while to make the effort necessary for the reduction of the last Frankish fortresses. In the meantime he must prevent intervention from the West, and for that purpose he must maintain good relations with Charles of Anjou, the only potentate who might have brought effective help to Acre. But Charles's main ambition was the conquest of Constantinople. Syria was for the moment of secondary interest to him. He already had vague thoughts of adding Outremer to his Empire. He therefore wished to preserve its existence but to do nothing that would enhance the power of King Hugh, whom he hoped some day to displace. He was willing to mediate between Baibars and Edward. On 22 May 1272, a peace was signed at Caesarea between the Sultan and the government of Acre. The

---

[1] *Estoire d'Eracles*, II, p. 461; Abu'l Feda, p. 154; D'Ohsson, *op. cit.* III, pp. 459–60; Powicke, *op. cit.* II, pp. 601–2.
[2] *Gestes des Chiprois*, pp. 200–1; *Estoire d'Eracles*, II, p. 461.

kingdom was guaranteed for ten years and ten months the possession of its present lands, which consisted mainly of the narrow coastal plain from Acre to Sidon, together with the right to use without hindrance the pilgrim-road to Nazareth. The county of Tripoli was safeguarded by the truce of 1271.[1]

Prince Edward was known to wish to come back to the East at the head of a greater Crusade. So, despite the truce, Baibars decided to eliminate him. On 16 June 1272, an Assassin disguised as a native Christian penetrated into the Prince's chamber and stabbed him with a poisoned dagger. The wound was not fatal, but Edward was seriously ill for some months. The Sultan hastened to dissociate himself from the deed by sending his congratulations on the Prince's escape. As soon as he had recovered, Edward prepared to sail for home. Most of his comrades had already left. His father was dying. His own health was bad; and there was nothing more that he could do. He embarked from Acre on 22 September 1272,[2] and returned to England to find himself its king.

The Archbishop of Liége, who had accompanied Edward to Palestine, had left the previous winter on the unexpected news that he had been elected Pope. As Gregory X he never lost his interest in Palestine; and he made it his chief task to see how the Crusading spirit could be revived. His appeals for men to take the Cross and fight in the East were circulated throughout Europe, as far as Finland and Iceland. It is possible that they even reached Greenland and the coast of North America.[3] But there was no response. Meanwhile he collected reports that would explain the hostility of public opinion. These reports were tactful. None of them touched on the essential trouble, that the Crusade itself had

[1] *Estoire d'Eracles*, II, pp. 461–2; *Annales de Terre Sainte*, p. 455; Maqrisi, *Sultans*, I, ii, p. 102; al-Aïni, p. 247. See Delaville le Roulx, *Hospitaliers en Terre Sainte*, p. 225.

[2] *Gestes des Chiprois*, p. 201; *Estoire d'Eracles*, II, p. 462; Sanuto, p. 225. The legend of Edward's wife Eleanor sucking the poison from his wound is first told by Ptolemy of Lucca a century later. See Powicke, *op. cit.* p. 603.

[3] A. Riant, *Les Scandinaves en Terre Sainte*, pp. 361–4.

become debased. Now that spiritual rewards had been promised to men who would fight against the Greeks, the Albigensians and the Hohenstaufen, the Holy War had merely become an instrument of a narrow and aggressive Papal policy; and even loyal supporters of the Papacy saw no reason for making an uncomfortable journey to the East when there were so many opportunities of gaining holy merit in less exacting campaigns.

Though the reports sent in to the Pope were discreet in their criticism of Papal policy, they were frank enough in pointing out the faults of the Church. Four of these reports deserve consideration. First, the *Collectio de Scandalis Ecclesiae*, probably written by a Franciscan, Gilbert of Tournay, while it mentioned the harm done to the Crusades by the quarrels of the kings and nobles, made its main themes the corruption of the clergy and the abuse of indulgences. While prelates spent their money on fine horses and pet monkeys, their agents raised money by the wholesale redemption of Crusading vows. None of the clergy would contribute to the taxes levied to pay for the Crusades, though Saint Louis, to their rage, had refused them exemption. Meanwhile the general public was taxed again and again for Crusades that never took place.[1]

The report sent in by Bruno, Bishop of Olmütz, took a different line. Bruno also spoke of scandals in the Church; but he was a politician. There must, he said, be peace in Europe and a general reform; but this could only be achieved by a strong Emperor. He implied that his master, King Ottocar of Bohemia, was the proper candidate for the post. Crusades in the East, he maintained, were now pointless and outmoded. Crusades should be directed against the heathens on the eastern frontiers of the Empire. The Teutonic Knights were mishandling this work by their greed and lust for power; but were it properly directed by a suitable potentate, it would provide financial as well as religious advantages.[2]

[1] The *Collectio* is published, edited by Stroick, in *Archivum Franciscanum Historicum*, vol. XXIV. See Throop, *op. cit.* pp. 69–104.
[2] Bruno's memoir is published by Hofler in the *Proceedings of the Bavarian Academy of Science*, 1846. See Throop, *op. cit.* pp. 105–14.

William of Tripoli, a Dominican living at Acre, submitted a more disinterested and constructive memoir. He had little hopes for a Holy War in the East conducted from Europe, but he was impressed by prophecies that the end of Islam was near at hand and believed that the Mongols would be its destroyers. The time had come for missionary activity. As a member of a preaching Order he had faith in the power of sermons. It was his conviction that the East would be won by missions, not by the sword. In this opinion he was supported by a far greater thinker, Roger Bacon.[1]

The fullest report came from another Dominican, the ex-Master-General of the Order, Humbert of Romans. His *Opus Tripartitum* was written in anticipation of a General Council, which should discuss the Crusade, the Greek Schism and Church reform. He had no faith in the possibility of converting the Moslems, though the conversion of the Jews was divinely promised and that of the East European pagans should be feasible. He held that another Crusade in the Orient was essential. He mentioned the vices that kept men from sailing eastward, their laziness, their avarice and their cowardice. He deplored the love of the home-land that kept them from travelling and the feminine influences that tried to anchor them at home. Worst of all, few now believed in the spiritual merit that was promised to the Crusader. This incredulity which Humbert sadly reports was certainly widespread. Numerous popular poems made it their theme; and there were many among the troubadours who frankly declared that God had no more use for the Crusades. Humbert's suggestions for combating it and rousing fresh enthusiasm were not very helpful. It was useless to go on maintaining that defeats and humiliations were good for the soul, as Saint Louis believed. It was too late to try to persuade men that the Crusade was the best penance for their sins. The reform of the clergy, which Humbert strenuously advocated, might be of some help. But as a practical guide for the

---

[1] See William of Tripoli, *De Statu Saracenorum, passim*; also Roger Bacon, *Opus Majus*, III, pp. 120–2. He blames the Westerners for not taking the trouble to learn foreign languages for their missionary work.

reform of public sentiment, Humbert's advice was of little value. In consequence his recommendations for the running of the Crusade were premature. There should be a programme of prayers, fasts and ceremonies; history must be studied; there should be a panel of godly and experienced counsellors; and there ought to be a permanent standing army of Crusaders. As for finance, Humbert hinted that Papal methods of extortion had not always been popular. He believed that if the Church were to sell some of its vast treasure and superfluous ornaments, it would have a good psychological as well as material result. But the princes as well as the Church must play their part.[1]

Armed with all this advice, which cannot much have reassured him, Gregory X summoned a Council to meet at Lyons. Its sessions opened in May 1274. There was good attendance from the East, led by Paul of Segni, Bishop of Tripoli. William of Beaujeu, newly elected Grand Master of the Temple, was there. But the pressing invitations sent to the kings of Christendom were ignored. Philip III of France declined to attend, and even Edward I, on whom Gregory specially relied, pleaded business at home. Only James I of Aragon appeared, a garrulous old man whose first attempt at an Eastern Crusade had come to nothing but who was genuinely eager in a swashbuckling way to set out on another adventure, but who was soon bored by the discussions and hurried back to the arms of his mistress, the Lady Berengaria. Delegates from the Byzantine Emperor Michael promised the submission of the Church of Constantinople; for Michael was terrified of the ambition of Charles of Anjou. But it was a promise that could not be fulfilled; the Emperor's subjects would have none of it. The abortive Union of the Churches was the only success of the Council. Nothing of any value was achieved for the reform of the Church; and while everyone was ready to talk about the Crusade, no one came forward with the offers of practical help that would be necessary to launch it.

[1] For the question of the texts of the *Opus Tripartitum* see Throop, *op. cit.* p. 147 n. 1. Throop gives a very full summary of the contents, *ibid.* pp. 147–213.

Nevertheless Gregory persevered, seeking to make the rulers of Europe carry out the pious resolutions passed by the Council. In 1275 Philip III took the Cross. Later that year Rudolph of Hapsburg followed his example, in return for the promise of a coronation by the Pope at Rome. In the meantime Gregory tried to prepare the Holy Land for the arrival of the Crusade. He ordered that fortresses should be repaired and more and better mercenaries sent out. From his personal experience in the East it seems that he had concluded that there was nothing to be hoped from King Hugh's government. He therefore was sympathetic to the claims of Maria of Antioch and encouraged her to sell those claims to Charles of Anjou, whom he wished to take a more active interest in Outremer, not only for its own welfare but also to divert him from his Byzantine ambitions.[1] But all Pope Gregory's plans came to nothing. When he died, on 10 January 1276, no Crusade had left for the East, and none was likely to leave.

King Hugh in Cyprus had a more realistic vision. He neither expected nor desired a Crusade, but merely wished to preserve the truce with Baibars. Yet the truce did little to ease his position. In 1273 he lost control of his chief mainland fief, Beirut. Its lordship had passed on John II of Ibelin's death to his elder daughter Isabella, Dowager-Queen of Cyprus, who had been left a virgin widow in 1267. Her virginity was of short duration. Her notorious lack of chastity and, in particular, her liaison with Julian of Sidon, provoked a Papal Bull, which strongly urged her to remarry. In 1272 she gave herself and her lordship to an Englishman, Hamo L'Estrange, or the Foreigner, who seems to have been one of Prince Edward's companions. He distrusted King Hugh and on his deathbed next year he put his wife and her fief under the protection of Baibars. When Hugh tried to carry off the widow to Cyprus, to remarry her to a candidate of his choice, the Sultan at once cited the pact that Hamo had made and demanded her return. The High Court gave the King no support. He was obliged to send Isabella back to Beirut, where a Mameluk guard was in

[1] See Hefele-Leclercq, *op. cit.* VI, i, pp. 67–8, 153 ff.; Throop, *op. cit.* pp. 262–82.

stalled to protect her.[1] It was only long after Baibars's death that Hugh resumed control of the fief. Isabella married two more husbands before her death, in about 1282, when Beirut passed to her sister Eschiva, the wife of Humphrey of Montfort, who was a loyal friend of the King.[2]

Hugh's next rebuff was over the county of Tripoli. Bohemond VI, last Prince of Antioch, died in 1275, leaving a son, Bohemond, aged about fourteen, and a younger daughter, Lucia. King Hugh, as the next adult heir of the House of Antioch, claimed the regency of Tripoli. But the Princess-Dowager, Sibylla of Armenia, at once assumed the office, as the custom of the family entitled her to do. When Hugh arrived at Tripoli to maintain his claim, he found that the young Bohemond VII had been sent to the Court of his uncle, King Leo III of Armenia, and that the city was administered in Sibylla's name by Bartholomew, Bishop of Tortosa, who seems to have belonged to the great Antiochene family of Mansel. No one in Tripoli supported Hugh, for Bishop Bartholomew was for the moment highly popular. He was a bitter enemy of the Bishop of Tripoli, Paul of Segni, Bohemond VI's maternal uncle, and of all the Romans that he and Lucienne had installed in the county. With the support of the local nobility, Sibylla and Bartholomew put some of the Romans to death and exiled others. Unfortunately, Bishop Paul had the support of the Temple, whose Master he had met at the Council of Lyons. When Bohemond VII came from Armenia in 1277 to take over the government, he was faced by the implacable hostility of the Order.[3]

It was only further north, at Lattakieh, that Hugh's prestige

[1] *Estoire d'Eracles*, II, p. 462; Ibn al-Furat, in Reinaud, *Chroniqueurs Arabes*, p. 532. Powicke, *op. cit.* p. 606 n. 1, shows that Isabella's husband's name was Hamo, not Edmund. Hill, *op. cit.* p. 137 n. 2, accepts the view that her liaison was with John of Jaffa. But that raises difficulties over dating, as John of Jaffa died in 1266. Moreover John was highly respectable, whereas Julian was notoriously loose-living. John's wife was the sister of King Hethoum who died in 1269, while Julian's was the sister of Hethoum's successor. The Bull may well have mistaken the generation of the Princess.

[2] *Lignages*, p. 462; Ducange-Rey, *Familles d'Outremer*, pp. 235–6.

[3] *Estoire d'Eracles*, II, pp. 466–7, 481; *Gestes des Chiprois*, p. 202.

won a minor victory. Lattakieh was all that remained of the Principality of Antioch, and Baibars did not consider it to be covered by his treaties with Tripoli or with Acre. His armies were closing round it, when its citizens made a direct appeal to King Hugh. He was able to negotiate a truce with the Sultan, who called off his troops in return for an annual tribute of twenty thousand dinars and the release of twenty Moslem prisoners.[1]

It was not long before Hugh's difficulties extended to Acre itself. The Commune of Acre had always resented his direct rule, while the Order of the Temple, which had disliked his reconciliation with the Montforts and had opposed his accession to the throne, grew steadily more unfriendly to him. The Hospital, on whose good-will he might have counted, had declined in importance after the loss of its headquarters at Krak. Its only remaining great castle was Marqab, on its high hill overlooking Buluniyas. Already in 1268 the Grand Master, Hugh of Revel, wrote that the Order could now only maintain 300 knights in Outremer, instead of 10,000 as in the old days. But the Temple still possessed its headquarters at Tortosa, as well as Sidon and the huge castle of Athlit, while its banking connections with the whole Levantine world increased its strength. Thomas Berard, who was Grand Master from 1256 to 1273, had in his earlier days been loyal to the Cypriot regents, and, although he had grown to dislike Hugh, he had never openly challenged him. But his successor, William of Beaujeu, was of a different calibre. He was related to the Royal House of France and was proud, ambitious and energetic. When he was elected he was in Apulia, in the territory of his cousin, Charles of Anjou. He came to the East two years later, determined to further Charles's projects and opposed, therefore, from the outset to King Hugh.

In October 1276, the Order of the Temple purchased a village called La Fauconnerie, a few miles south of Acre, from its landlord, Thomas of Saint-Bertin, and deliberately omitted to secure

[1] Maqrisi, *Sultans*, I, ii, p. 125; Muhi ad-Din in Michaud, *Bibliothèque des Croisades*, II, p. 685.

the King's consent to the transaction. Hugh's complaints were ignored. In his exasperation with the Orders, with the Commune and with the merchant-colonies, he determined to leave the thankless kingdom. He suddenly packed up his belongings and retired to Tyre, intending to sail from there to Cyprus. He left Acre without appointing a *bailli*. The Templars and the Venetians, who were their close allies, were delighted. But the Patriarch, Thomas of Lentino, the Hospitallers and the Teutonic Knights, as well as the Commune and the Genoese, were shocked, and sent delegates to Tyre to beg him at least to appoint a deputy. He was too angry at first to listen to them, but at last, probably on the pleading of John of Montfort, he nominated as *bailli* Balian of Ibelin, son of John of Arsuf, and he appointed judges for the Courts of the kingdom. Immediately afterwards he embarked for Cyprus, by night, taking leave of no one. From Cyprus he wrote to the Pope to justify his action.[1]

Balian had a difficult task. There were riots in the streets of Acre between Moslem merchants from Bethlehem, under the Templars' protection, and Nestorian merchants from Mosul, whose patrons were the Hospitallers. Hostilities flared up again between the Venetians and the Genoese. It was only with the help of the Patriarch and of the Hospital that any government was maintained.[2]

In 1277 Maria of Antioch completed the sale of her rights to Charles of Anjou. Charles at once assumed the title of King of Jerusalem and sent out Roger of San Severino, Count of Marsico, with an armed force, to be his *bailli* at Acre. Thanks to the help of the Temple and the Venetians, Roger was able to land at Acre, where he produced credentials signed by Charles, by Maria and by the Pope, John XXI. Balian of Ibelin was acutely embarrassed. He had no instructions from King Hugh, and he knew that the Templars and the Venetians were ready to take up arms on behalf of Roger, while neither the Patriarch nor the Hospital would

[1] *Estoire d'Eracles*, II, pp. 474–5; *Gestes des Chiprois*, p. 206 (post-dating the episode). See Delaville le Roulx, *op. cit.* pp. 210–29.
[2] *Estoire d'Eracles*, *loc. cit.*; *Gestes des Chiprois*, *loc. cit.*

promise to intervene. To avoid bloodshed he delivered the citadel
to the Angevins. Roger hoisted Charles's banner and proclaimed
him King of Jerusalem and Sicily, and then ordered the barons of
the kingdom to do homage to himself as the King's *bailli*. The
barons hesitated, less for love of Hugh than for dislike of an admission that the throne could be transferred without a decision of
the High Court. To preserve some legality they sent delegates to
Cyprus to ask if Hugh would release them from their allegiance
to him. Hugh refused to give an answer. At last Roger, who was
firmly in the saddle, threatened to confiscate the estates of anyone
who did not pay him homage, but he allowed time for one more
appeal to Hugh. It was equally fruitless; so the barons submitted
to Roger. Soon afterwards Bohemond VII acknowledged him as
lawful *bailli*. Roger appointed various Frenchmen from Charles's
Court as his chief officers. Odo Poilechien became Seneschal,
Richard of Neublans Constable and James Vidal Marshal.[1]

These arrangements were very much to the liking of Baibars.
He could trust Charles's representative neither to provoke a new
Crusade nor to intrigue with the Mongols. With this sense of
security he was ready to allow Outremer a few more years of
existence. In the meantime he could take the offensive against
the Ilkhan. Abaga was conscious of the danger and was eager to
build up an alliance with the West. In 1273 he sent a letter to Acre,
addressed to Edward of England, asking when his next Crusade
would take place. It was conveyed to Europe by a Dominican,
David, who was chaplain to the Patriarch, Thomas of Lentino.
Edward sent a cordial answer, but regretted that neither he nor
the Pope had decided when there could be another expedition to
the East. Mongol envoys appeared next year at the Council of
Lyons, and two of them received Catholic baptism from the
Cardinal of Ostia, the future Innocent V. The replies that they
received from the Pope and his Curia were again friendly but

---

[1] *Estoire d'Eracles*, pp. 478–9; *Gestes des Chiprois*, pp. 206–7; Amadi, p. 214;
Sanudo, pp. 227–8; John of Ypres in Martène and Durand, *Thesaurus Novus
Anecdotorum*, vol. III, col. 755.

vague. In the autumn of 1276 the Ilkhan tried again. Two Georgians, the brothers John and James Vaseli, landed in Italy to visit the Pope, with orders to go on to the Courts of France and England. They bore a personal letter from Abaga to Edward I, in which he apologized that his help had not been more effective in 1271. None of this diplomatic activity produced any result. King Edward sincerely hoped to go on another Crusade, but neither he nor Philip III of France was ready yet to do so. The Papal Curia was under the sinister influence of Charles of Anjou, who disliked the Mongols as the friends of his enemies, the Byzantines and the Genoese, and whose whole policy was based on an entente with Baibars. The Popes optimistically hoped to welcome the Mongols into the fold of the Church but would not realize that the promise of rewards in Heaven were an insufficient inducement for the Ilkhan. Even the pleas of Leo III of Armenia, who was at the same time the Ilkhan's faithful vassal and in communion with Rome, could not produce any practical help from the Papacy.[1]

Baibars was able to pursue his schemes without the threat of Western intervention. In the spring of 1275 he led a raid in person into Cilicia, in which he sacked the cities of the plain, but was unable to penetrate to Sis. Two years later he decided to invade Anatolia. The Seldjuk Sultan was now a child, Kaikhosrau III. His minister, Suleiman the Pervana, or Keeper of the Seals, was the chief power in the land but was quite unable to control the local emirates that were arising, of which the most important was the Karamanian. The Ilkhan maintained a loose protectorate over the Sultanate, enforced by the presence of a considerable Mongol garrison. On 18 April 1277, this garrison was routed by the Mameluks at Albistan. Five days later Baibars entered Caesarea-Mazacha. The Sultan's minister, Suleiman, and the Karamanian emir both hastened to congratulate the victor; but Abaga was roused and himself led a Mongol army by forced marches into

[1] William of Nangis, pp. 540, 564; D'Ohsson, *op. cit.* III, pp. 543–9; Powicke, *op. cit.* p. 602 n. 1; Howorth, *op. cit.* III, pp. 280–1.

Anatolia. Baibars did not wait for its arrival, but retired to Syria. Abaga quickly recovered control of the Seldjuk Sultanate. The treacherous Suleiman was captured and executed; and rumour said that his flesh was served in a stew at the Ilkhan's next state banquet.[1]

Baibars did not long survive his Anatolian adventure. Various stories were told of his death. According to some chroniclers he died as a result of wounds received in the recent campaign; according to others he drank too much kumiz, the fermented mare's milk loved by the Turks and the Mongols. But the dominant rumour was that he had prepared poisoned kumiz for the Ayubite Prince of Kerak, al-Qahir, son of an-Nasir Dawud, who was with his army and who had offended him, and then carelessly drank from the same cup before it was cleaned. He died on 1 July 1277.[2]

His death removed the greatest enemy to Christendom since Saladin. When Baibars became Sultan the Frankish dominions stretched along the coast from Gaza to Cilicia, with great inland fortresses to protect them from the East. In a reign of seventeen years he had restricted the Franks to a few cities along the coast, Acre, Tyre, Sidon, Tripoli, Jebail and Tortosa, with the isolated town of Lattakieh and the castles of Athlit and Marqab. He did not survive to see their entire elimination, but he had made it inevitable. Personally he had few of the qualities that won Saladin respect even from his foes. He was cruel, disloyal and treacherous, rough in his manners and harsh in his speech. His subjects could not love him, but they gave him their admiration, with reason, for he was a brilliant soldier, a subtle politician and a wise administrator, swift and secret in his decisions and clear-sighted in his aims. Despite his slave origins he was a patron of the arts and an active builder, who did much to beautify his cities and to reconstruct his fortresses. As a man he was evil, but as a ruler he was amongst the greatest of his time.

[1] Abu'l Feda, p. 165; Maqrisi, *Sultans*, I, ii, pp. 144–5; Bar-Hebraeus, pp. 456–9; D'Ohsson, *op. cit.* pp. 486–9. See Howorth, *op. cit.* III, pp. 252–6.
[2] Maqrisi, *Sultans*, I, ii, p. 150; Abu'l Feda, pp. 165–6; *Gestes des Chiprois*, pp. 208–9; Hayton, *Flor des Estoires*, p. 193; Bar-Hebraeus, p. 458.

BOOK IV

THE END OF OUTREMER

CHAPTER I

THE COMMERCE OF
OUTREMER

*'By the multitude of thy merchandise they have filled the midst of
thee with violence.'*   EZEKIEL XXVIII, 16

Throughout the history of Outremer the straightforward issue
between Christianity and Islam was often obscured or deflected
by questions of economic advantage. The Frankish colonies lay
in an area that was reputedly rich and that certainly controlled
some of the greatest trade-routes in the world. The financial and
commercial ambitions of the colonists and their allies sometimes
ran counter to religious patriotism, and there were occasions when
their basic human needs demanded friendship with their Moslem
neighbours.

There was no commercial motive force behind the launching
of the First Crusade. The Italian maritime cities, whose merchants
were the shrewdest money-makers of the time, had at first been
alarmed by a movement that might well ruin the trading relations
that had been built up with the Moslems of the Levant. It was
only when the Crusade was successful and Frankish settlements
were founded in Syria that the Italians offered their help, realizing
that they could use the new colonies to their own advantage. The
economic urge that impelled the Crusaders was, rather, land-
hunger among the lesser nobles of France and the Low Countries
and the desire of the peasants there to escape from their grim,
impoverished homes and the floods and famines of recent years
and to migrate to lands of legendary wealth. To many of the
simple folk the distinction between this world and the next was
vague. They confused the earthly with the heavenly Jerusalem
and expected to find a city paved with gold and flowing with

milk and honey. Their hopes deceived them; but disillusion came slowly. The urban civilization of the East and its higher standard of living gave an appearance of opulence which returning pilgrims reported to their friends. But as time went on the reports were less favourable. After the Second Crusade there was no mass-movement amongst the peasants of the West to find new homes in the Holy Land. Adventurous noblemen still went East to make their fortunes, but one of the difficulties in organizing the later Crusades was the lack of economic inducement.[1]

In fact, the Frankish provinces of Outremer were not naturally rich. There were fertile districts, such as the plains of Esdraelon, of Sharon and of Jericho, the narrow coastal strip between the Lebanon mountains and the sea, the valley of the Buqaia and the plain of Antioch. But, in comparison with the country beyond the Jordan and the Hauran and the Bekaa, Palestine was barren and unproductive. The value of Oultrejourdain to the Franks had lain as much in the corn that it grew as in its command of the road from Damascus to Egypt.[2] Without the help of Oultrejourdain it was not always easy for the kingdom of Jerusalem to feed itself. If the harvest were bad, corn had to be imported from Moslem Syria.[3] During the last decades of Outremer, when the Franks were reduced to the towns of the coastal strip, corn must always have been imported.

Other foodstuffs were in adequate supply. The hills supported large numbers of sheep, goats and pigs. There were orchards and vegetable gardens surrounding all the towns, and there were plentiful olive-groves. Indeed, it is possible that olive oil was

[1] The essential work for the commercial history of the Crusades is Heyd, *Histoire du Commerce du Moyen Age*. The whole question has recently been discussed in an important article by Cahen, 'Notes sur l'histoire des Croisades et de l'Orient Latin, III', in *Bulletin de la Faculté des Lettres de Strasbourg*, May–June 1951. Cahen gives reasons for minimizing the commercial importance of the Crusader states.

[2] See above, vol. II, pp. 5–6. Though not as fertile as the Hauran, Moab had, since the days of Naomi and Ruth, provided food for Palestine in times of famine.

[3] E.g. in 1185. See above, vol. II, pp. 444–5.

exported in small quantities to the West, while rare Palestinian fruits, such as the sweet-lemon or the grenadine, were sometimes seen on the dinner-tables of the wealthy in Italy.[1]

There were, however, few products that Outremer could export on a big enough scale to bring any appreciable revenue into the country. The most important of these was sugar. When the Crusaders arrived in Syria they found that sugar-cane was cultivated in many coastal areas and in the Jordan valley. They continued the cultivation and learned from the natives the process of extracting sugar from the cane. There was a great sugar factory at Acre, and factories in most of the coastal cities. The main centre of the industry was Tyre. Almost all the sugar consumed in Europe during the twelfth and thirteenth centuries came from Outremer.[2] The second chief export was cloth of various sorts. The silk-worm had been cultivated round Beirut and Tripoli since the end of the sixth century, while flax was grown in the plains of Palestine. Silken stuffs were sold for export. Samite was made up at Acre, Beirut and Lattakieh; and Tyre was famed for the fabric known as zendado or cendal. The linen of Nablus had an international reputation. The purple dye from Tyre was still fashionable for clothes. But the Italians could also buy silks and linens in the markets of Syria and Egypt, where supplies were larger and prices often lower.[3] It was the same with glass. The Jews in various cities, especially Tyre and Antioch, produced glass

---

[1] The Archbishop of Tyre possessed 2040 olive trees in one village alone (Tafel-Thomas, *Urkunder*, p. 299). See Cahen, 'Notes sur l'Histoire des Croisades et de l'Orient Latin, II', in *Bulletin de la Faculté des Lettres de Strasbourg* (April, 1951), p. 293. Rey, *Les Colonies Franques*, p. 245; Heyd, *op. cit.* pp. 177–8. Burchard of Mount Sion, *Description of the Holy Land*, says that the orchards round Tripoli brought their owners a yearly revenue of 300,000 gold besants (ed. *P.P.T.S.* p. 16).

[2] Heyd, *op. cit.* I, p. 179, II, pp. 680–6; Cahen, *op. cit.* II, p. 293; Rey, *op. cit.* pp. 248–9.

[3] Heyd, *op. cit.* I, pp. 178–9, II, pp. 612, 696, 699, 705. The linen of Nablus was coarse compared to that of Egypt (*ibid.* p. 632 n. 1). Rey, *op. cit.* pp. 214–21. Idrisi, *Geography* (Arabic text, ed. Guildermeister, p. 11), says that a particular sort of white cloth was made at Tyre.

for export; but they had to face the competition of glass from Egypt. Tanneries probably only supplied local needs, but pottery was occasionally exported.[1]

There was always a market in Egypt for wood. From the earliest ages the Egyptian fleet had been built with timber that came from the forests of Lebanon and the hills south of Antioch, and the Egyptians also required large quantities of timber for architectural purposes. Wars between Egypt and the Crusading states seldom interrupted this traffic for long.[2] There were iron mines near Beirut, but their production probably was insufficient for export.[3]

A certain number of herbs and spices were exported. The most important was balm. As it was mainly used in Europe for the services of the Church, balm from the Holy Land was particularly popular. In the twelfth century it was grown in large quantities near Jerusalem. But the crop was not easy to grow, as it needed expensive irrigation. After the Moslem reconquest at the end of the century its cultivation declined and was soon abandoned.[4]

Far greater revenues were obtained by the rulers of Outremer from merchandize that passed through the country. There was an increasing demand in medieval Europe for Eastern goods, spices, dyes, scented woods, and silk and porcelain, as well as for goods from the Moslem countries just over the borders of Outremer. But this trade inevitably depended on political circumstances in Asia. When the Crusades began the bulk of the Far Eastern trade travelled by sea across the Indian Ocean and up the Red Sea to Egypt, attracted by the wealth of the Egyptian cities and the security of Fatimid rule away from its earlier route up the Persian Gulf to Baghdad. The Syrian ports only served for the export of

---

[1] Heyd, *op. cit.* I, p. 179; Rey, *op. cit.* pp. 211–12 (quoting *Assises*, II, p. 179), 224–5. See above, vol. II, pp. 295–6.

[2] See Rey, *op. cit.* pp. 234–40, for the forests in Outremer.

[3] Idrisi, p. 16, says that iron from Beirut was sent throughout Syria.

[4] Heyd, *op. cit.* II, pp. 577–8.

more local goods, such as indigo from Iraq or Damascene metal-work, and for any spices from southern Arabia that were carried by caravan rather than by boats. The petty wars that followed the Turkish invasions at the end of the eleventh century did not encourage either commerce or industry in the Syrian hinterland. It was only when Nur ed-Din and, after him, Saladin made an ordered unit of Moslem Syria and Egypt that prosperity in Syria revived. Local products increased, and goods from Iraq and Persia could safely travel across to Aleppo or Homs or Damascus, and thence to the sea. The ports used by the merchants of Aleppo were Saint Symeon, which they reached through Antioch, and Latta-kieh; Tortosa and Tripoli served as the ports of Homs, and Acre for Damascus.[1]

Though the Italians had helped the Crusaders in the conquest of each of these ports, their main business interest remained in Egypt. Acts concerned with commerce published in Venice during the twelfth century mention Alexandria far more often than they mention Acre, particularly after the Venetians had been ejected from Constantinople. The records of the Genoese international lawyer Scriba during the years 1156 to 1164 show that nearly twice as many of his clients were interested in Alexandria as in the Frankish East. It is also remarkable that during the first half of the twelfth century most travellers bound from Europe to Palestine either went first in Venetian or Genoese ships to Con-stantinople and thence by land or in Greek coastal ships to Syria or else sailed direct from southern Italy in ships of the kingdom of Sicily. It seems, therefore, that there were not many ships from the Italian merchant-ports that made regular voyages to Syria till the later years of the century.[2] Till then the amount of goods that passed through the Syrian ports cannot have been very large; and as the customs duties on these transitory goods were only about 10 per cent of their value, it is easy to understand why the ex-chequer of Outremer was seldom full and why the Kings were so

[1] Heyd, *op. cit.* I, pp. 168–77.
[2] Cahen, *op. cit.* III, pp. 330–3, giving statistics.

often tempted to go raiding at times when it would have been more honourable and more diplomatic to keep the peace.[1]

It is also easy to understand why the Italian maritime cities were shy of supporting the Crusade too readily. It might be their Christian duty to aid the Franks against the Moslems. But their whole prosperity depended upon the maintenance of good terms with the Moslems. Whenever they gave help to a Christian enterprise they ran the risk of losing their trading rights with Alexandria. Yet without their co-operation the Crusaders could never have conquered the coastal cities; and the fact of their co-operation shows that their problem was not so simple after all. The Genoese sent help while the First Crusade was still at Antioch. A Pisan squadron set out before the news of the capture of Jerusalem reached the West; and their later coldness towards the kingdom of Jerusalem was due more to Baldwin I's quarrel with Daimbert, who had been their Archbishop, than to any commercial calculation. Even the Venetians, who had the closest connection with Egypt, had offered assistance to Godfrey of Lorraine just before his death. This policy was not quite as risky as it seemed at first sight. Trade cannot exist unless it is to the benefit of both parties. The Moslem authorities in Egypt had no more wish than the Italians to break off commercial relations for long. Though they might in an access of rage close Alexandria to Christian ships, they themselves suffered from the interruption of business. Their reprisals were never therefore enforced too strictly. In addition the Italians found many advantages in securing a share of the newly conquered ports. In Moslem cities and even in Constantinople they could never feel secure. A popular riot might destroy their establishments, or the caprices of alien rulers might interfere with their business. Though the actual volume of trade to be conducted through the Christian Syrian ports might be less than through Constantinople or Alexandria they could count on uninterrupted business. Their only difficulties arose out of the

[1] Cahen, *op. cit.* III, pp. 330–3. Raids such as Baldwin III's in 1157, were conducted entirely to raise cash (see above, vol. II, p. 342).

rivalry of fellow Italians, not from the hostility of local rulers. There was also another advantage of growing importance to be derived from the Frankish ports. The main difficulty of the Italians was to find goods in Europe whose sale would pay for the Oriental goods that they wished to buy. Till the early years of the tenth century the main Venetian export had been slaves from central Europe, but the conversion of the Slavs and the Hungarians had ended this traffic. In the later half of the thirteenth century the Genoese revived the slave-trade, carrying Turkish and Tartar slaves from the Black Sea ports to sell to the Mameluks in Egypt; but during the intervening years there were few slaves available. The only important exports from the West were metal and wood. As the main use for these materials was for armaments, the ecclesiastical authorities in Europe naturally disapproved of their sale to the Moslems. But the Italians gradually learned that the Crusading movement and the existence of Outremer drew a large number of soldiers, diplomats, and above all, pilgrims to the East. If the Italians carried them, the money that they paid for their fares and for their expenses on board gave the shipowners cash that they could spend in the Syrian ports on goods imported from further to the east. Finally, hard-headed though the Italian merchants were, religious scruples were not entirely ignored. Many men, even in Genoa or Venice, preferred to do business in a Christian rather than in a Moslem port; and there was the practical consideration that the Church strongly disapproved of trade with the infidel, and the Church was politically powerful in Italy. Its enmity could cause serious embarrassment.[1]

The heyday of the commerce at Outremer was during the decade just before Saladin's reconquest of Jerusalem and during the first decades of the thirteenth century. The Moslem world was united and prosperous, and the Italians had discovered the advantages of trade through the Christian ports. Meanwhile the

---

[1] *Ibid.* and pp. 340–4. It is possible that Cahen slightly minimizes the general importance of Outremer to the Italians. The evidence of history suggests that they were far less indifferent to its fate than his argument implies.

Frankish colonists had learned how to make friends with their infidel neighbours. The Moslem pilgrim, Ibn Jubayr, who in 1184 travelled with a caravan of Moslem traders from Damascus to Acre, makes it clear that such caravans were of frequent occurrence. He was impressed by the smooth arrangements for the collection of customs-dues.[1] Acre was the busiest port of the coast. It was the natural port of Damascus and therefore not only was used for the products of Damascene factories and of the rich countryside of the Hauran, but also served the merchants from the Yemen who came up the pilgrims' road along the edge of the Arabian coast. It also possessed the only safe harbour in all Palestine. Voyagers to the Holy Places preferred to land there rather than at Jaffa with its open roadstead, where so many accidents had occurred before Acre had been captured by the Crusaders. The one disadvantage of Acre was that the inner harbour was too small to take the larger vessels of the time, which had either to lie off the breakwater, where they were exposed to the south-west wind, or else go up the coast to the larger and more secure harbour of Tyre.[2] In northern Syria the best all-weather harbour was at Lattakieh, though Saint Symeon, at the mouth of the river Orontes, was more convenient for Antioch and Aleppo and was used for smaller vessels.[3]

The Assizes of Jerusalem mention a number of eastern goods that passed through the custom-houses of Outremer. Besides silk and other fabrics, there were various spices, such as cinnamon, cardamum, cloves, mace, musk, galangale and nutmeg, as well as indigo, madder and aloe-wood and ivory.[4] The Franks themselves

[1] Ibn Jubayr (ed. Wright), pp. 306–7.

[2] Ibn Jubayr, pp. 307–8. He remarks that Tyre is a better harbour than Acre for large ships.

[3] The Moslem geographers all praise the harbour of Lattakieh as being especially good (e.g. Idrisi, p. 23; Yakut, *Geographical Dictionary*, ed. Wustenfeld, IV, p. 338; Dimashki, ed. Mehren, p. 209). Saint Symeon (as-Suwaidiyyah) seems to have been used far less, except for commerce to Antioch itself. It is possible that the harbour was already beginning to silt up. Yakut, III p. 385, writing before Baibars's conquest, alluded to it as the port for Antioch used by the Franks.

[4] *Assises*, II, pp. 174–6. See Heyd, *op. cit.* pp. 563 ff. The *Assises* mention 111 dutiable articles.

took very little part in this traffic. The goods were brought to the coast by merchants from the interior, Moslems or native Christians, and in northern Syria by Greeks and Armenians from Antioch also. The visiting merchants were treated with courtesy. The Moslems were allowed to carry out their worship in the Christian cities. Indeed, in Acre itself a portion of the Great Mosque, which had been converted into a church, was put aside for Moslem rites. There were khans at which they could stay, and there were Christian households that took in Moslem lodgers. The Italian merchants bought directly from the Moslem importers. Besides the Italians it seems that a certain number of Moslems came by sea to Acre to buy goods from the interior, in particular Moghrabis from north-west Africa, who would journey themselves as far as Damascus or other inland Moslem cities.[1]

The expansion of the Mongol Empire in the thirteenth century altered the main trade-routes from the Far East. Once the Mongols had conquered the interior of Asia they encouraged merchants to take the overland route from China, through Turkestan and either to the north of the Caspian to the ports on the north coast of the Black Sea, such as Caffa, or south of the Caspian and through Iran to Trebizond, on the south coast of the Black Sea, or to Ayas, in the Cilician kingdom of Armenia. The perfect order kept by the Mongols made this route preferable to the hazardous sea-route across the Indian Ocean.[2] In the twelfth century Chinese junks had frequently sailed west of Ceylon to the Arabian ports. Now it was seldom worth their while to go further than the east coast of India.[3] The Mongol conquest of Iraq resulted in some of the Indian trade reaching the West by sea up the Persian Gulf, and a proportion of it passed through Damascus or Aleppo to the Frankish ports. But most of the merchants preferred to stay within the

---

[1] Ibn Jubayr, pp. 307-9.   [2] Heyd, *op. cit.* II, pp. 70-3.
[3] Idrisi says that in the twelfth century Chinese junks went as far as Daybal at the mouth of the Indus, but in the thirteenth they did not go beyond Sumatra. Arab ships then took over the Indian Ocean trade, which was still prosperous. See Heyd, *op. cit.* I, pp. 164-5.

Mongol dominions and thence cut across to the Mediterranean at Ayas, while most of the Indian trade was carried by land through Afghanistan and Persia.[1] Egypt was still a rich market for Oriental goods, but it was no longer on the cheapest route from the Far East to Europe.[2]

Meanwhile both Venice and Genoa, with Pisa lagging behind, were steadily increasing their trade; and their rivalry with each other grew intense. The shifting of the trade-routes enhanced their competition. Venice at first controlled the Black Sea, owing to her domination over the Latin Empire at Constantinople. She therefore did not object to the rise of Mongol power. But when the Byzantines recaptured their capital in 1261, with the active help of Genoa, the Genoese were able to exclude the Venetians from the Black Sea and to keep the monopoly of the central Asiatic trade and, as a profitable side-line, the slave-trade between the Russian steppes and Egypt. As the Mameluk government was dependent on a steady supply of slaves from the Kipchak and neighbouring Turkish tribes, it was impossible for the Venetians to exclude Genoa from Alexandria. Though the Venetians were allowed by the Armenian King to share in the Mongol trade that came to Ayas, it was essential for Venice to try to drive the Genoese out of the Frankish ports. As far as Acre was concerned, they were successful. Tyre, to which the Genoese had to retire, was less well placed. It became the general policy of Venice, in her hatred of Genoa, to oppose the Mongols, out of whose empire Genoa was reaping such large profits. In consequence, the Venetians used their influence at Acre to induce the government there to support the Mameluks against the Mongols.[3]

The development of Ayas as the main Mediterranean outlet for Mongol trade naturally lessened the importance of the Frankish ports. But the general increase of Asiatic trade under the Mongols

[1] Heyd, *op. cit.* pp. 73 ff.
[2] *Ibid.* The Egyptians also charged higher customs duty (*ibid.* p. 78).
[3] See above, pp. 282 ff.; also Bratianu, *Commerce Génois dans la Mer Noire,* esp. pp. 79 ff.

was such that there was always a surplus that followed the older routes. Merchants from Mosul regularly visited Acre during the second half of the thirteenth century. The wars between the Mameluks and the Mongols did not much inconvenience the passage of caravans from Iraq and Iran to Palestine. Right up to its last years as the Christian capital Acre was full of commercial activity, while, further north, Lattakieh was handling so much trade from Aleppo that the merchants of Aleppo especially begged the Mameluk Sultan to capture the port because so valuable a place should not be in infidel hands.[1]

All this flourishing commerce was, however, of little profit to the Franks themselves. By making the seaports a battleground between rival Italian colonies it was a source of positive political weakness; and even if the Italians kept the peace, not much money came through to the governments of Outremer. The King was officially entitled to about 10 per cent of the custom-tolls, but in fact he had sold huge shares of that percentage to his vassals or to the Church or to the Military Orders. Not much was left for himself. The Princes of Antioch and Counts of Tripoli were slightly better off, for they had created fewer money-fiefs. But great fortunes were not to be made in Outremer. There were lords who were wealthy enough to live in luxury, such as the Ibelins of Beirut, who owned the local iron-mines, or the Montforts of Tyre, with their sugar factories. To the untrained eyes of Western travellers the citizens of Outremer seemed fantastically prosperous; but it was a superficial appearance. The towns were cleaner and better built. Their inhabitants could buy silken garments and employ scents and spices at prices that only the very rich could afford in western Europe. But such things were local products and therefore comparatively cheap.[2]

[1] For Ayas, called by the Italians Lajazzo, see Bratianu, *op. cit.* pp. 158–62. For Syria, Heyd, *op. cit.* II, pp. 62–4. For Lattakieh, see below, p. 403.

[2] Amadi reckoned that the value of Philip of Montfort's fief of Toron in 1241 was 60,000 saracenate besants (p. 186). But Guy of Jebail was able to lend 50,000 saracenate besants to Leopold of Austria and 30,000 to Frederick II (see above, pp. 149, 182). See also La Monte, *Feudal Monarchy*, pp. 171–4.

We have very little information about the activities of the *bourgeois* classes in Outremer. They seem to have taken no part in international trade but to have confined themselves to shop-keeping and the manufacture of goods for local consumption. Politically they had some power. The Commune of Acre, which was composed of the Frankish *bourgeoisie*, was an important element in the state. But it seems to have kept itself apart from the native communities, even from the Orthodox, who were treated as a separate entity.[1] In Antioch, where the Commune was even more influential, the Frankish and Greek *bourgeoisie* worked together. There was probably more intermarriage there, and the Franks had never been as numerous as in Acre, or in Tripoli, which seems to have followed the pattern of Acre.[2] The labouring classes were mostly of native or of half-caste origin; and there were usually considerable numbers of slaves, Moslems captured in the war, to work in the mines or on the construction of public buildings or on royal or noble estates.[3]

The government was always short of money. Even in times of peace the country had to be ready for a sudden outbreak of war; and war usually resulted in the devastation of large areas of the countryside. The revenue from tolls and taxes was inadequate; and a sudden emergency, such as the capture of the King or of whole sections of the army, could not be met without outside help. Fortunately, outside help was often forthcoming. Quite apart from the money obtained, usually unwisely, by raids for plunder into Moslem territory, continual gifts were sent from Europe. Palestine was the Holy Land, and the Crusaders and colonists were generally regarded as the soldiers of Christ. Visitors paid a tax on arrival; and not only did pilgrims bring money with them into the country, to spend there or to give in alms, but many

---

[1] See Cahen, *op. cit.* III, pp. 335–7; also Prawer, 'L'Etablissement des Coutumes du Marché à Saint-Jean d'Acre', in *Revue Historique de Droit Français*, 1951.

[2] For Antioch, Cahen, *La Syrie du Nord*, pp. 549 ff., 153 ff. For Tripoli, Richard, *Le Comté de Tripoli*, pp. 71 ff.

[3] Rey, *Les Colonies Franques*, pp. 105–8.

of the shrines and abbeys there were given lands in the West, whose revenues were sent out to them. The Military Orders derived most of their income from their endowments in the West, to such an extent that they were still enormously wealthy even after the loss of all their Syrian possessions. Individual citizens of Outremer, from the King downwards, would receive occasional gifts from Western relatives or sympathizers. These subsidies helped largely to balance the finances of Outremer; and thus the luxuries that visitors from the West admired in the Syrian cities were paid for in part by their compatriots at home.[1]

Another source of economic strength, whose effect is more difficult to evaluate, was the coinage of Outremer. When the Crusades began, there was no gold coinage in western Europe, except in Sicily and Moslem Spain. Silver was the most precious metal employed. Nor at that time were the Moslem states in Syria issuing gold coins, though the rival Caliphs at Baghdad and Cairo both kept up the practice. Yet almost as soon as the Crusading states were established, the King of Jerusalem, the Prince of Antioch and the Count of Tripoli all began to mint *dinars* of gold, which were known by the name of *Saracenate Besants* and which were imitated from the *dinars* of the Fatimids but contained only about two-thirds of their gold content. These coins, particularly the coins of the kingdom of Jerusalem, which were known to the Moslems as *souri*, the dinars of Tyre, soon circulated widely through the Near East. It is difficult to understand where the Franks obtained the gold. Plunder and ransom can only have produced a small and irregular amount. The main source of gold at the time was the Sudan, and it is possible that some gold was brought to the Frankish ports by the Moghrabi merchants that came to trade there. But to explain the appearance of the coinage there must have been a general movement of gold from the Moslem countries to the Christian. The European settlers must have bought gold, no doubt at a very high price, from the Moslems in return for

[1] La Monte, *op. cit.* pp. 174 ff.

silver, which was plentiful in Europe; and the issues of this debased gold coinage must have helped in the whole movement. Large quantities of gold must have passed on further to the West; for it is remarkable that during the thirteenth century gold coinage of an excellent alloy began to appear in western Europe.[1]

The right to issue gold coins was kept firmly in the hands of the rulers of Outremer. Neither the Italian colonies there nor the Military Orders were allowed to infringe on this monopoly. The tenants-in-chief could only mint bronze coins for local needs.[2]

The Military Orders had an additional source of wealth, derived from their banking activities. With their vast possessions all over Christendom they were admirably placed to finance Crusading expeditions. The French participation in the Second Crusade was only made possible by the help of the Templars, who paid out enormous sums to Louis VII in the East, and were repaid in France. By the end of the twelfth century the Templars made a regular practice of money-lending. They charged a high interest, but, however unreliable they might be politically, their financial reputation was so high that even the Moslems had confidence in them and made use of their services. The Hospitallers and the Teutonic Knights conducted similar operations, but on a lesser scale. The governments of Outremer gained nothing directly from these activities, which increased the power and insubordination of the Orders; but they were for the financial benefit of the country as a whole.[3]

---

[1] Cahen, *Notes sur l'Histoire des Croisades*, III, pp. 337–8 (a very important discussion of the problem). See also Schlumberger, *Les Principautés Franques du Levant*, pp. 8–45. The Saracenate besant of Jerusalem had a gold value of slightly more than one-third of a gold sovereign. That of Antioch was slightly less valuable.　　　　　[2] La Monte, *op. cit.* pp. 174–5.

[3] *The Assises of Jerusalem* ignore banking, though those of Antioch admit it (see Cahen, *op. cit.* p. 339). See Piquet, *Les Banquiers du Moyen Age*, *passim*; also Melville, *La Vie des Templiers*, pp. 75–83. Louis IX's Crusade, like Louis VII's, was largely financed by the Order (Piquet, *op. cit.* pp. 71–8).

The economic history of the Crusades is still very obscure. Information is inadequate, and there are many details that cannot now be explained. But it is impossible to understand their political history without taking into account the commercial and financial needs of the settlers and of the Italian merchants. These needs usually ran counter to the ideological impulse that started and maintained the Crusading movement. Outremer was permanently poised on the horns of a dilemma. It was founded by a blend of religious fervour and adventurous land-hunger. But if it was to endure healthily, it could not remain dependent upon a steady supply of men and money from the West. It must justify its existence economically. This could only be done if it came to terms with its neighbours. If they were friendly and prosperous, it too would prosper. But to seek amity with the Moslems seemed a complete betrayal of Crusader ideals; and the Moslems for their part could never quite reconcile themselves to the presence of an alien and intrusive state in lands that they regarded as their own. Their dilemma was less painful, for the presence of the Christian colonists was not necessary for their trade with Europe, however convenient it might be at times. Good relations were therefore always precarious. The second great problem that Outremer had to face was its relations with the Italian merchant-cities. They were an indispensable element in its existence. Without them communications with the West would have been almost impossible to maintain, and it would have been quite impossible to export the products of the country or to have captured any of the through-trade from the further East. But the Italians, with their arrogance, their rivalries and the cynicism of their policy, caused irremediable harm. They would hold aloof from vital campaigns and openly parade the disunity of Christendom. They supplied the Moslems with essential war-material. They would riot and fight against each other in the streets of the cities. The rulers of Outremer must often have regretted the rich commerce that brought such dangerous and unruly allies to their shores; and yet without this commerce the story of Outremer would have been shorter and grimmer. It is never easy to decide between the hostile claims of material prosperity and ideological faith. Nor can any government hope to satisfy either claim completely. Man cannot live on ideology alone, while prosperity depends on wider issues than can be contained in one narrow strip of land. The Crusaders made many mistakes. Their policy was often hesitant and changeable. But they cannot be entirely blamed for failing to solve a problem for which, in fact there was no solution.

CHAPTER II

ARCHITECTURE AND THE ARTS IN OUTREMER

*'Deck thyself now with majesty and excellency; and array
thyself with glory and beauty.'*   JOB XL, 10

The Franks of Outremer allowed the commerce that should have
established their country to slip out of their grasp. But in some of
the arts they kept control of their productions. Their achievements
here were remarkable; for the colonists were not numerous and
only few of them can have been artists. Moreover they had come
to a land whose artistic traditions were far older than their own;
nor could they find there the materials to which they were used.
Yet they began to develop a style which answered satisfactorily
to their needs.

Most of their smaller works of art have perished. The turbulent
history of Syria and Palestine has not permitted the survival of
things that are delicate and fragile. Their architecture was more
durable, though there, as in most medieval countries, there is little
left except for military and ecclesiastical monuments. Even in
these change and decay have altered the original form. Apart
from the holiest shrines of Christendom, which the Moslems were
too scrupulous to touch, but which later Christians have repaired,
the churches that still stand were preserved because they were
adapted to become mosques. Others have fallen into ruin. The
Frankish castles and fortifications were all so severely damaged in
the course of the wars that the Moslem conquerors were obliged,
if they wished to use them, to reconstruct much of them, especially
the outside walls and the gates. What man left alone, nature helped
to ruin, in that earthquake-stricken land. Even where modern
archaeologists have brought their scholarship to the work of

restoration, as at Krak des Chevaliers, it is not always possible to distinguish clearly between what is Crusader and what is Mameluk.

The first buildings that the Crusaders needed to construct were for their defence. Churches and palaces must wait till the country was securely held. The walls of the towns had to be repaired, and castles built to guard the frontiers and to serve as safe administrative centres for the country districts. The fortifications of the main cities only required to be patched here and there, except in the few cases where the Crusaders had only forced an entry by breaching the walls. At Antioch the great defence system constructed by the Byzantines towards the close of the tenth century had suffered very little damage. The Latin princes had no need to add to them. Similarly little repair work was required on the Fatimid walls of Jerusalem, though the Crusaders seem almost at once to have made alterations and improvements to the Tower of David. But soon they began to build castles in towns where the fortifications were already adequate. These castles were all built on the edge of the town and could be defended independently. Their lords wished not only to be able to carry on resistance even if the town fell to the enemy, but also to be in a position to awe the town, should it prove unruly. The first castle that can be dated with certainty is Count Raymond's at Mount Pilgrim, built in 1104 to provide him with headquarters while he besieged Tripoli. It was outside the town, though Moslem Tripoli was later built at its base. But of Raymond's own work little more than the west wall now survives. The castles of the Princes of Galilee at Tiberias and Toron must have been built about the same time. But the first great age of castle-building began in the second decade of the twelfth century, under Baldwin II, and was continued under Fulk, when such magnificent fortresses as Kerak of Moab, Beaufort and, further north, Sahyun, were constructed, as well as the smaller forts of Judaea, such as Blanchegarde and Ibelin.[1]

The Crusaders found military architecture far more highly

---

[1] See above, vol. II, pp. 60-1, 96, 229-31. See Deschamps, *La Défense du Royaume de Jérusalem*, pp. 5-19, and *Le Crac des Chevaliers*, pp. 43-4.

developed in the East than in the West, where the stone-built castle was only now beginning to appear. The Romans had studied military defence as a science. The Byzantines, stimulated by the endless foreign invasions that they had to face, had evolved it to suit their needs, and the Arabs had learned from them. But the Byzantines' problems were not the same as the Crusaders'. The Byzantines assumed that man-power was always available; they could afford large garrisons. They took immense trouble to defend their cities well. The walls of Constantinople were still able, a thousand years after they were built, to defy the up-to-date cannon of the Ottomans, and the walls of Antioch struck the Crusaders with admiration. But the Byzantine castle was not much more than a fortified camp. It was designed to deal with an enemy whose armaments were less formidable than the Byzantines'; for the Arabs, who were their most dangerous rivals, were less advanced in siege-machinery. Its walls did not have to be solid; for a system of outworks, of which the main feature was at least one ditch of considerable width, prevented the enemy from bringing his battering-rams or grappling-ladders close up against them. Towers were built with a slight salient at regular intervals along the walls, less to defend the walls themselves than to give the archers and pitch-throwers of the garrison a longer range into the enemy lines. The keep in the centre of the enceinte was designed not to be an ultimate point of defence, but, rather, to be a storehouse for armaments and provisions. Except for a few examples on the Armenian frontier where semi-independent border barons lived, the Byzantine castle was not intended to be a residence. The commander was a professional soldier who left his wife and children at home. Finally, though advantage was taken of natural defences, the inaccessibility of the site was not the first consideration. The main use of the castle was as barracks. It was inconvenient to force the soldiers to toil up and down a mountain every time that they moved.[1]

[1] Deschamps, *Le Crac*, pp. 45–57; Ebersolt, *Monuments d'Architecture Byzantine*, pp. 101–6; Fedden, *Crusader Castles*, pp. 22–6.

The Arabs tended to follow the Byzantine models, though, as their armies were essentially mobile and aggressive, they were less interested in problems of defence.[1]

The Crusaders studied the military architecture that they found on their journey eastward, and learned much from it. But their essential needs were different. They were always short of man-power and could not maintain large garrisons. Their castles there-fore had to be far stronger and easier to defend. The site must be chosen for its defensive qualities. Every slope and hillock must be used to the fullest advantage, and, as scouts to carry messages could seldom be spared, each stronghold should be able to see and signal to its neighbour. Walls had to be far thicker and taller, to be able to stand up to a direct attack; for the defence of outworks involved too many men. At the same time the castle must serve as a residence for the lord and an office for his administration. The Franks brought their feudal methods with them and they were governing an alien people. The castle was the seat of local govern-ment. Its enceinte should also be large enough to give protection to flocks and herds during the frequent enemy raids. The castle, in fact, played a far more important part amongst the Franks than ever amongst the Byzantines or the Arabs.[2]

In the West the castle was as yet no more than the solid square keep or donjon, of a type perfected by the Normans. It was in-adequate for the requirements of Outremer. The Crusaders were obliged to be pioneers. They borrowed many ideas from the Byzantines. It was from them that they learned the use of machico-lation, and the value of placing towers along the curtain wall; though there they soon made an amendment, as they discovered that a rounded tower gave a wider range than the rectangular towers that the Byzantines preferred. Their smaller castles built in the earlier twelfth century, such as Belvoir, were built on the

---

[1] Deschamps, *Le Crac*, p. 51; Fedden, *op. cit.* p. 26.
[2] Deschamps, *Le Crac*, pp. 89–103; Smail, 'Crusaders' Castles of the Twelfth Century', in *Cambridge Historical Journal*, vol. x, 2, an excellent discussion of the functions of a castle.

usual Byzantine design, with a more or less rectangular outer wall, studded with towers, enclosing a central space which contained the keep. But the sites were chosen so as to dispense with elaborate outworks, and the whole construction was far more solid. Byzantine work was often incorporated. At Sahyun the wide Byzantine fosses were completed by a narrow channel, ninety feet deep, cut through the solid rock.[1] The Franks also added the portcullis, which had not been used in the East since Roman times, and the bent entrance, which the Arabs were beginning to favour but which the Byzantines seldom employed, probably because it was inconvenient for the heavy engines that they kept within the castles.[2]

The larger castles were naturally more complicated. A fortress such as Kerak had to house not only the lord and his family but also the soldiers and clerks required for the administration of a province. In such a castle in the twelfth century the keep, with the residential quarters, was usually at the furthest and most easily defensible corner of the enceinte. Store rooms and the chapel were usually placed in the central space, while other towers round the enceinte were large enough to contain barrack-rooms and offices. The plan varied according to the terrain of the assiette, the area on which the castle was situated. The keep was still a simple rectangular tower, on the Norman model, usually with only one entrance. The masonry was solid and plain, but some attempt was made to decorate the residential quarters and the chapel. Unfortunately none of the twelfth-century decoration in the castles has survived. Those castles that remained Christian after Saladin's time were redecorated in the next century. The Saracens altered those that they occupied themselves; and the remainder fell into ruin.[3]

[1] For a plan of Belvoir see Deschamps, *La Défense*, p. 121, and for the even simpler plan of Chastel Rouge, *Le Crac*, p. 57. The twin castles of Shoghr-Bakas were strengthened by artificial fosses, as Sahyun (*Le Crac*, pp. 80–1).

[2] Deschamps, 'Les Entrées des Châteaux des Croisés', in *Syria*, vol. XIII.

[3] See, for example, the detailed description and plans of the Castle of Kerak in Moab and Subeibah at Banyas in Deschamps, *La Défense*, pp. 80–93, 167–75, and plates.

As the twelfth century advanced, there were certain changes in the plan of castles. It became to be considered more logical to put the keep, which was the strongest portion of the castle, at the weakest section of the enceinte; and the keep itself was usually rounded rather than rectangular, as a rounded surface resisted bombardment more effectively. More doors and posterns were provided. The size of castles tended to increase, particularly when the Military Orders built castles for themselves or took over castles from the lay nobility. In the castles of the Orders there were no ladies to be accommodated; and though high officials might be provided with elegant quarters, every resident was there for a military purpose. The larger fortresses, such as Krak or Athlit, were military towns capable of housing several thousand fighting men and the servants necessary for such a community. But they were seldom filled to capacity. The defences were now usually strengthened by the use of a double, concentric enceinte. The great Hospitaller castles, such as Krak and Marqab, had a double girdle. The Templars followed the same system at Safita, but as a rule they preferred the single enceinte; their chief thirteenth-century castles, Tortosa and Athlit, kept to the earlier pattern, but in both cases the longer sections of the walls rose straight from the sea. Across the peninsula which joined Athlit to the land there was a complicated double line. The Teutonic castle at Montfort also kept to a single enceinte. The idea of the double enceinte was not new. The land-walls of Constantinople were built with a double line in the fifth century, and in the eighth the Caliph al-Mansur surrounded his circular city of Baghdad with a double line. But the Hospitallers were the first to apply it to a single castle, though it could only be used for a castle of considerable size.[1]

Other thirteenth-century improvements were the carefully smooth facing of the curtain walls, to give less hold to grappling-

---

[1] Rey, *Architecture Militaire des Croisés*, pp. 70 ff. (exaggerating the difference between Templar and Hospitaller styles); Fedden, *op. cit.* pp. 28–9. See Deschamps, *Le Crac*, pp. 279 ff., for the stages and changes in style. See also Melvin, *La Vie des Templiers*, pp. 136–42.

PLATE VI

KRAK DES CHEVALIERS

ladders, the wider use of machicolation and of loopholes for archers, which were now usually given a downward slant and sometimes a stirrup-shaped base, and greater complication in the entrance gates. At Krak there was a long covered approach, commanded by loopholes in the side-walls, then three right-angled corners, a portcullis and four separate gates. Posterns were provided at unexpected corners, a device first introduced by the Byzantines.[1]

These huge fortresses, with their solid masonry, superbly situated on crags and mountain-tops, seemed impregnable in the days before gunpowder was known. The terrain usually made the use of ladders impracticable, nor could siege-towers to dominate the walls be brought up unless there was some flat ground outside and no fosse. It was often hard enough for the besiegers to find a close enough site on which to place mangonels or balistas for hurling rocks. The chief technical danger was the mine. Engineers would dig a tunnel under the walls, propping it up as they went with wooden posts, which were eventually set alight with brushwood, causing the tunnel-chamber, and with it the masonry above to collapse. But mining was impossible if the castle was built, like Krak, on solid rock. When a castle fell it was usually for other reasons. In spite of store-rooms and cisterns, famine and thirst were real dangers. The lack of man-power often meant that the defences could not be properly maintained. The kingdom often could not afford to send a relieving force, and that knowledge induced pessimism amongst the garrison. In the full flush of Saladin's triumphs the great castle of Sahyun, which was reputed to be the strongest of its time, only resisted the Moslems for three days.[2]

The importance of the Crusader castles lies in the sphere of military rather than of aesthetic history. Returning Crusaders brought back to Europe the ideas that had found expression there;

[1] Fedden, *op. cit.* pp. 29–30.
[2] Oman, *History of the Art of War in the Middle Ages*, II, pp. 29 ff.; Fedden, *op. cit.* pp. 34–40.

2B

and such castles as Richard Cœur-de-Lion's Château Gaillard introduced them to the Western world. But the castles in the East had their aesthetic value. Their chapels are amongst the best examples of the ecclesiastical architecture of Outremer. Their Great Halls, of which the loveliest is at Krak, are comparable with the best early Gothic halls of western Europe. Their residential quarters, which survive to give us some idea of the palaces of the nobility of Outremer, show delicacy and taste. The chamber of the Grand Master at Krak, high up in the south-west tower of the inner enceinte, with its ribbed vaulting, its slender pilasters and its simple but well carved decorative ornamental frieze of five-petalled flowers, was perhaps more elegant than most rooms in the great fortresses, but it must have been paralleled in the richer castles and palaces in the towns. Its style is the thirteenth-century Gothic of northern France, while the Great Hall has stone tracery that is akin to work at Rheims, in the contemporary Church of Saint Nicholas.[1]

The castles were mainly the work of engineers. The churches were intended to be works of art. When the Crusaders arrived in the East they found an old tradition of building there, suited to the country. Wood was a rare commodity. All that the forests produced was used for shipbuilding and for armaments. The architects therefore had to build without beams. Their roofs were of stone, and were usually flat, so as to provide a terrace in the cool of the evening. Vaulting was generally used to support the roof, and the pointed arch, with its ability to carry heavy weights, was already fashionable. The Syrian builder's native style was the Byzantine-Arab, which had been perfected under the Ommayad Caliphs, but he was in touch with later Abbasid developments and with Fatimid architecture and its North African influences. He had recently seen Byzantines working on the Holy Places and in Antioch, and there had been an influx of Armenians, skilled craftsmen with their own styles.

[1] Deschamps, *Le Crac*, pp. 197–224; Enlart, *Les Monuments des Croisés*, II, pp. 96–9.

The first church that the Crusaders built in the East was the Cathedral of Saint Paul at Tarsus, which was finished before 1102. It is a coarse inelegant building, in the style of the Romanesque churches of northern France, but with its arches pointed. It is rectangular, with two aisles and a nave lined with alternate piers and columns. The columns come from some ancient building. Their capitals are simple blocks with triangles cut out of the corners, a form of decoration to be found in the Rhineland, but also in Armenia, and here probably made by Armenian workmen. In its crude way it gives a foretaste of later Crusader architecture.[1]

As soon as the colonists were safely settled, their first care was to repair the Holy Places and then to provide their main towns with suitable churches. Of the most sacred shrines the Church of the Nativity at Bethlehem, built by Constantine and repaired by Justinian, was still in good order. The only architectural additions made by the Crusaders were a simple Gothic cloister, erected probably about 1240, and a north and south doorway to the Grotto of the Nativity, built about 1180 in a late Romanesque style with a pointed arch and acanthus-decoration on the capitals which is probably Syrian work. They also built monastic buildings round the church, which have now been destroyed.[2] But the most venerated church of all, that of the Holy Sepulchre at Jerusalem, seemed to them inadequate. After its destruction by the Caliph Hakim, the Byzantines had rebuilt the Rotunda surrounding the tomb itself, but they had flattened the east end and built three apses there. The chapel of St Mary the Virgin had been attached to the north of the Rotunda and the three chapels of Saint John, the Trinity and Saint James to the south. Golgotha had been rebuilt as a separate chapel, as had Saint Helena's chapel with the grotto of the Invention of the Cross. The buildings were all sumptuously decorated with marbles and mosaics. The Crusaders decided to bring all the buildings together under one roof. The main work was apparently carried out after an earthquake in 1114 and before 1130, though parts were unfinished at the time of

[1] Enlart, *op. cit.* II, pp. 378–9.   [2] Enlart, *op. cit.* II, pp. 66–8.

Baldwin II's death in 1131; and the whole new edifice was not consecrated till 15 July 1149, the fiftieth anniversary of the capture of the city. The belfry was added about the year 1175.

The plan of the new building was inevitably affected by the site, which was limited on the south by the rock of Golgotha and on the east by the drop to the Chapel of Saint Helena, which lay several feet lower than the Rotunda. The Crusaders therefore broke down the east wall of the Byzantine Rotunda, destroying its apses, and replacing the central one by a large arch leading into a new church. This consisted of a choir with a dome on pendentives near the west end, with an aisle and an ambulatory going all round it, and with a curved east end, with three apses. Between the central and the southern apse a stairway led straight down into Saint Helena's chapel. The south aisle lay against the chapel of Golgotha, which was rebuilt, though the Byzantine mosaics were retained together with the entrance columns. West of Golgotha and between it, the Rotunda and the chapel of Saint John, a new atrium was built, to include the Stone of Anointing and the tombs of Godfrey and King Baldwin I. A doorway, the present main entrance, led from the atrium into a courtyard. Along the north aisle there was an outer aisle, mainly of Byzantine construction, opening on to another courtyard, from which a passage led past the chapel of Saint Mary into the Street of the Patriarch. A third courtyard surrounded the chapel of Saint Helena and was itself surrounded by new buildings erected to house the Augustinian Priors to whom the church was now entrusted.

Such of the Crusaders' work as has survived the sack by the Khwarismians in 1244, the passage of time and the disastrous fire of 1808 shows a kinship to the great Cluniac pilgrimage churches, in particular that of Saint Sernin of Toulouse, which Pope Urban II consecrated immediately after the Council of Clermont. The ambulatory is strongly reminiscent of those of Cluny itself and Saint Sernin. The difference lies in the proportions. The architects of the Holy Sepulchre kept their columns lower and sturdier, to keep them in harmony with those of the Byzantine Rotunda, whose design was probably intended to resist earthquake shocks. The decorative details, except where Byzantine mosaics and capitals were retained, can be compared to many in southern and south-western France. The carvings, particularly the figure-carvings on the lintels, seem mostly to be the work of the school of Toulouse, though they were probably carved locally. In general it seems that the architects and artists of the whole monument were Frenchmen, probably from south-west France, brought up in the Cluniac tradition. The architect of the belfry is known to have been called Jordan, a name usually given to children baptized in the holy river. He was probably born in Palestine.[1]

The Church of the Holy Sepulchre was the only older shrine to which the Crusaders made extensive alterations. They repaired several small chapels, such as that of the Ascension on the Mount of Olives and the tomb of the Virgin at Gethsemane. To the Dome of the Rock, when it became the church of the Templars, they only added decorative marble and iron-work, and the Mosque al-Aqsa was equally untouched, though the foundations were reconditioned to provide stables and store-rooms, and buildings were set up round the mosque to house the Order, while a wing added on the south-west became the favourite residence of the Kings. In most of the towns that they colonized they found churches too badly ruined to be worth repair or else they left them to the indigenous sects that were already in possession. They took over some older monasteries, but on the whole preferred to erect their own buildings. Sometimes they used previous sites and foundations, as with the basilica of Mount Sion; sometimes they slightly changed the orientation of the older site, as with the church at Gethsemane. More often they chose their own sites, or completely rebuilt churches on traditional sites.[2]

Apart from the Templars' churches, which were circular in shape, the invariable design for a small chapel was a rectangle,

[1] Enlart, *op. cit.* II, pp. 144–80; Duckworth, *The Church of the Holy Sepulchre*, pp. 203–58; Harvey, *Church of the Holy Sepulchre*, pp. ix–x.
[2] Enlart, *op. cit.* II, pp. 207–11, 214–21, 233–6, 243–5, 247–9.

with an apse, sometimes included in the outer wall, at the east end. The masonry was solid. A single vault, pointed and cross-ribbed, supported a flat stone roof. Such chapels were built in every castle, even in such desolate fortresses as that on the hill of the Wueira, by the ruins of ancient Petra.[1] Larger churches also were rectangular, with side-aisles running the length of the building, separated from the nave by pillars or piers. There were almost always three apses, usually hidden from the outside in the thickness of the wall. The great Cathedral at Tyre and one or two other churches had short transepts, which made the floor-plan cruciform but had no structural significance. The Cathedral at Tortosa has a diaconicon and a prothesis built out at the south-east and north-east corners. A few churches, such as Saint Anne's at Jerusalem, and, apparently, the Cathedral at Caesarea, had domes on pendentives over the space before the sanctuary; but the roof was usually flat or barrel-shaped. The side aisles were almost invariably covered by groined vaults. The nave had either a groined vault or one long pointed and ribbed barrel-vault. When the aisles were lower than the rest of the church, there would be windows along the clerestory. Windows, even those at the east end, were small, to keep out the fierce Syrian sunlight. With very few exceptions arches were pointed. Towers were rare. The abbey-church on Mount Thabor had two towers, one on either side of the west entrance, each containing a small apsed chapel at ground level. Belfry towers were sometimes attached to the church, but never as an integral part.[2]

The decoration of the twelfth-century churches was simple.

---

[1] The chapel at Wueira has little more than its apse left. There is a faintly moulded cornice but no other sign of decoration. The stones used for its construction seem smaller than is usual in Crusader buildings. It seems to have had a small narthex as well as a crypt. The chapel at Kerak was considerably larger, with four windows. It is said to have had frescoes, but none now exists. The Templar chapel at Athlit was not circular but dodecagonal; it belongs to the thirteenth century.

[2] See Enlart, *op. cit. passim*. I have largely drawn on personal knowledge of the buildings.

Columns from ancient buildings were often used. The capitals varied. Some were ancient, some copied from the Byzantine and Arab styles of Corinthian and basket-work, made perhaps by native masons or by Franks who had noticed local designs, and some in the Western Romanesque style.[1] Some churches, such as that at Qariat el-Enab, had frescoes in the Byzantine style,[2] and there were mosaics in the Cenacle on Mount Sion and in the chapel of the Dormition next to it.[3] Byzantine artists may have worked there, as they certainly did at the Nativity at Bethlehem, sent there by the Emperor Manuel along with their materials.[4] But pictorial ornament was rare. Carved decorations round the arches were usually chevron or dog-tooth. Very little figure sculpture has survived. The voussoirs of the arches were often cushioned. Another favourite decoration was a simple rosette.[5]

The general effect of the twelfth-century churches was somewhat heavy, almost squat in comparison with contemporary work in the West. This was due to the need to avoid the use of wood and to guard against earthquake; but the result was usually well-proportioned. The Crusaders undoubtedly brought with them their architects, who were imbued in the styles of France, particularly of Provence and the Toulousain, but they clearly took the advice of local builders. Their use of pointed arches was learned in the East. The first known examples in the West are in two churches built about the year 1115 by Ida of Lorraine, the mother of the first two Frankish rulers of Jerusalem. Her eldest son, Eustace of Boulogne, had recently returned from Palestine. It is difficult not to believe that returning architects popularized the new

---

[1] See Enlart, *op. cit.* 1, pp. 70–3.

[2] See below, p. 381.

[3] Daniel the Higumene (in Khitrowo, *Itinéraires Russes*, p. 36) saw mosaics in the Cenacle in 1106; and about 1160 John of Würzburg describes mosaic portraits of the Apostles there, with an inscription in Latin describing the descent of the Holy Ghost, as well as a mosaic in the Chapel of the Dormition of the Dormition itself with an inscription, written in Latin but using Greek terms (*P.P.T.S.* pp. 42–3).

[4] See below, p. 381.   [5] Enlart, *op. cit.* 1, pp. 93 ff.

device in the West, where it was developed to suit local structural needs.[1]

It is impossible to make generalizations about the origins of the various architectural and ornamental detail. The dome of Saint Anne's at Jerusalem closely resembles the domes that French architects built in Périgord; but the same type of dome, built on pendentives without a drum, could be found in the East.[2] Romanesque carving is so often akin to Byzantine and Armenian carving that clear distinctions cannot easily be made. It is probable that figure-carvings and the more fantastic capitals were the work of Frankish artists, but the traditional designs of the acanthus or the vine-leaf were provided locally. The chevron pattern seems to have travelled southward, even in Europe, from the north; but the dog-tooth was already known in the East. It appears, as does the cushioned voussoir, on the great Fatimid gate, the Bab al-Futuh, at Cairo, which was itself built by Armenian architects from Edessa, a city where the Byzantines had a few decades previously been responsible for much new building.[3]

In the pictorial arts the surviving examples show so strong a Byzantine influence that it seems doubtful whether any Frankish artist worked in the East. The mosaics at Bethlehem were certainly designed and erected by artists from Constantinople, whose names were Basil and Ephrem, though they worked in co-operation with

[1] Enlart, *op. cit.* I, pp. 3–4, 67–8. Some of the ornamentation in Ida's churches at Wast and Saint Wlmer at Boulogne is distinctly reminiscent of Arabic work. Pointed arches are found of almost the same date at Cluny. The part played by Armenian architects in the diffusion of the pointed arch and ogival vaulting (which the exaggerated claims of Strzygowski brought into disrepute) needs consideration. See Baltrusaitis, *Le Problème de l'Ogive et l'Arménie*, pp. 45 ff., esp. pp. 68–70. More might still be said about the work of Armenians in Outremer itself. See also Clapham, *Romanesque Architecture*, pp. 107–12.

[2] Clapham, *loc. cit.* The dome of Saint Sophia at Constantinople is without a drum. Drums were rare in Persian architecture.

[3] Clapham, *op. cit.* pp. 110, 112–13. He is unwilling to accept Armenian comparisons as relevant because of doubts of dating. But the ornamentation of churches in Greater Armenia can be dated with some certainty. See Der Nersessian, *Armenia and the Byzantine Empire*, pp. 84–109 (which incidentally shows the difficulty of tracing the origins of decorative patterns).

the local Latin authorities. Western as well as Eastern saints are depicted and the inscriptions are in Latin as well as in Greek. The mosaic Christ in the Latin chapel at Calvary is probably their work.[1] The rapidly perishing frescoes at Qariat el-Enab are Byzantine in style, but while the choice of subjects is Eastern, the inscriptions are Latin.[2] There were certainly Greek artists working in Palestine in about 1170 under the Emperor Manuel's patronage, who were responsible for frescoes at the Orthodox monasteries of Calamon and St Euthymius. No doubt the Latin fathers at Qariat engaged them to decorate their church.[3] The little church at Amioun, not far from Tripoli, is sometimes taken from its architecture to be a Crusader monument; but its dedication to a Greek saint, Phocas, its Greek inscriptions and its Byzantine frescoes show it to have always been an Orthodox shrine. It illustrates the difficulty of a sharp differentiation between local and Frankish styles.[4] Many Frankish churches profited from gifts obtained by their prelates from the Emperor at Constantinople. The great Archbishop William of Tyre tells us that he was given sumptuous presents for his Cathedral by the Emperor Manuel;[5] and the corpse of Bishop Achard of Nazareth, who visited the Imperial city to negotiate Baldwin III's marriage and died there, came back equally well laden.[6] Throughout the twelfth century, particularly in the time of Manuel, there was frequent intercourse between Outremer and Byzantium, and the Byzantine artistic influence must have been great. It lingered on into the next century. The description given by Wilbrand of Oldenburg of the palace of the Ibelins at Beirut, with its mosaic and its marbles,

[1] *Church of the Nativity at Bethlehem* (ed. Schultz), pp. 31–7, 65–6 (John Phocas's description); Enlart, *op. cit.* I, p. 159, II, pp. 65–6; Dalton, *Byzantine Art and Archaeology*, pp. 414–15. See above, vol. II, pp. 391–2 and n. 1. The mosaic Christ in Glory from the vault of the Latin Chapel of Calvary is reproduced as the frontispiece of Harvey, *op. cit.* Very little has been written about it. It may be Byzantine work of the previous century.

[2] Enlart, *op. cit.* II, pp. 323–4. [3] See above, vol. II, p. 392 n. 1.
[4] Enlart, *op. cit.* II, pp. 35–7. [5] William of Tyre, XXII, 4, p. 1068.
[6] *Ibid.* XVIII, 22, p. 857.

suggests Byzantine work. The Old Lord, John of Ibelin, who built it, was the son of a Byzantine Princess.[1]

The palace at Beirut was an exception. The thirteenth-century architecture in Outremer kept closer than the twelfth-century to French traditions. With the restriction of Frankish territory to little more than the coastal cities, native workmen and native traditions seem to have played a smaller part. The last important church to be finished before Saladin's conquests was the Cathedral of the Annunciation at Nazareth. The building was destroyed by Baibars, but the remarkable figure-sculpture that remains is purely French. The great doorway that most of them adorned appears to have closely resembled those of many of the French cathedrals of the time, and the whole building was probably nearer to the French than the previous local style.[2] The chief church to be built in the thirteenth century, that of Saint Andrew at Acre, was a tall and graceful Gothic building. Few traces of it now remain, but the descriptions and drawings of earlier travellers all emphasize its height. Its side-aisles were tall and lit by long, narrow, acutely pointed windows, with a delicate blind arcade running round the outside walls beneath them. We cannot tell how the clerestory or the east end were lit, but over the west door there were three larger windows, and above them three in the form of an *œil de bœuf*. All that now survives of the church is a porch, probably from the west end, which was carried on camel-back to Cairo after the conquest of Acre and set up as an entry to the mosque built in memory of the conquering Sultan, al-Ashraf. Its proportions are tall and delicate. A series of three slender pilasters alternating with two even more slender carries the curve of the arch on each side, and the moulding of the curve corresponds to the pilasters. In the space of the arch there is a trefoil arch, pierced by an *œil de bœuf*. The style is the early Gothic of the south of France.[3]

The thirteenth-century work at Krak des Chevaliers shows the

---

[1] Wilbrand of Oldenburg in Laurent, *Peregrinatores Medii Aevi Quattuor*, pp. 166 ff. See above, vol. II, p. 316.

[2] Enlart, *op. cit.* pp. 298–310. [3] Enlart, *op. cit.* II, pp. 15–23.

same taste for greater height. The Grand Master's airy chamber and the great banqueting hall are both entirely Western in spirit. The latter has a porch whose proportions are very similar to that of Saint Andrew at Acre, though its pilasters are less delicate; but it had an elaborate rose-window in the centre of the arch, where Saint Andrew had an *œil de bœuf*.[1]

There are unfortunately very few monuments of the thirteenth century left; but in general the style of Outremer was coming close to the contemporary French Gothic style of Lusignan Cyprus and had moved away from the more indigenous style of the previous century. The surviving work at Nazareth suggests that Crusader art was keeping in touch with the Gothic movement in the West. Saladin's conquests induced many native craftsmen to throw in their lot with the Moslems. The collapse of Byzantium at the turn of the century inevitably diminished Byzantine influences; and the Third Crusade brought many more Western artists and workmen to the East. At the same time the growing hostility between the Latin and Orthodox churches probably inspired a sharper distinction between their styles.

Only one twelfth-century illuminated manuscript exists which is known to come from Outremer. This is the Psalter known as that of Queen Melisende. It certainly belonged to a woman, and as it mentions the deaths of Baldwin II and of Queen Morphia, but not that of King Fulk, it has been assumed to have belonged to Melisende and to have been written before Fulk's death. It might, however, equally well have been made for Melisende's sister, Joveta, Abbess of Bethany; and in that case, as any mention of Fulk would have been irrelevant, it could date from any year during Joveta's lifetime, that is to say, till about 1180. The text was written by an accomplished Latin scribe and the decorative headpieces seem Latin rather than Byzantine, but the full-page illustrations are Byzantine, in the style of the eastern provinces of the Empire. The signature of a painter called Basil appears; and it is possible that this was the same Basil who was responsible for

[1] Enlart, *op. cit.* I, pp. 134–7.

some of the mosaics at Bethlehem in 1169. The pictures have some resemblance to those in a lectionary in Syria decorated by Joseph of Melitene in the time of a Bishop John, who has been identified with the Bishop that reigned there from 1193 to 1220. It is possible therefore that the artist of the Melisende Psalter was a Syrian trained in a Byzantine school, and it is probable that the work was made for the Abbess Joveta towards the end of her long life.[1]

There is an interesting series of manuscripts, usually considered to be Sicilian work, which modern research proves to have been written at Acre about the time of Saint Louis's sojourn there, from 1250 to 1254. They are markedly Byzantine in style. Louis had made extensive purchases from the Emperor Baldwin II of Constantinople, and it may be that amongst the objects that he acquired were manuscripts which were sent to him at Acre and inspired the artists working there. It is impossible to say whether the school outlasted the King's return to France.[2]

Of the minor arts very little has been preserved; and it is impossible to tell what was made locally and what was imported from the East or from the West. Furniture and objects of daily use came no doubt from workshops on the spot, but most ornamental goods probably came from abroad, from Constantinople or the great Moslem cities, or were brought by visitors from France or Italy. A collection of objects found in the nineteenth century in the foundations of the monastic buildings at Bethlehem included two brass basins which seem to belong to the Mosane school of the twelfth century and which are engraved with a series of pictures

[1] Boase, 'The Arts in the Latin Kingdom of Jerusalem', in *Journal of the Warburg Institute*, vol. II, pp. 14–15. Dalton, *Byzantine Art and Archaeology*, pp. 471–3, believes the full-page illustrations to be provincial Byzantine and made for another work. The headpieces are by another artist; they may be Western Romanesque but with Eastern influences (e.g. Saint John the Evangelist is bearded). The second artist is a more delicate craftsman than the first, but his colours are weaker. In *East Christian Art*, p. 309, he suggests that the first artist may be Armenian. See Buchthal, 'The Painting of Syrian Jacobites', in *Syria*, vol. XX, pp. 136 ff., esp. p. 138.

[2] Any judgement on this group of manuscripts must await the publication of a forthcoming work by Dr H. Buchthal.

PLATE VII

THE CHOIR OF THE CHURCH OF THE HOLY SEPULCHRE IN 1681

This is one of the few drawings that show the Church
as it was before the fire of 1808.

PLATE VIII

THE CATHEDRAL OF TORTOSA

PLATE IX

MOSAIC PANEL OF CHRIST IN GLORY

From the vault of the Latin Chapel of Calvary. The mosaic seems to have been made by Byzantine artists employed by the Latin authorities.

PLATE X

THE CHURCH OF ST ANDREW AT ACRE IN 1681

PLATE XI

THE TEMPTATION

From Queen Melisende's Psalter

PLATE XII

THE TRANSFIGURATION

From Queen Melisende's Psalter

PLATE XIII

ORATIO AD SCAM MARIAM.
SCA MARIA succurre miseris.
iuua pusillanimes. refoue fle
biles. ora pro pplo. interueni
pro clero. intercede pro deuoto femi-

VIRGIN AND CHILD ENTHRONED

From Queen Melisende's Psalter, showing Latin work

illustrating the life of Saint Thomas the Apostle, a pair of silver candlesticks which seem to be Byzantine work of the late twelfth century, another pair of candlesticks of Limoges enamel of the late twelfth century, and a larger candlestick and a crozier-head of Limoges enamel of the thirteenth century.[1] The iron grill set up by the Crusaders in the Dome of the Rock may be local work but strongly resembles the Romanesque iron work of France.[2]

The iron candelabra used in the churches were probably made on the spot but follow the usual designs of western Europe.[3] No identifiable pottery or glass has survived. Coins and seals were made locally. The former were intended for use in the East and therefore followed local Moslem patterns, even having inscriptions in Arabic. The seals of the twelfth century are simple and crude, but those of the thirteenth century are more graceful and elaborate.[4] A reliquary of crystal set in a stirrup-shaped and jewel-encrusted piece of silver and containing an inner case of carved wood, now preserved at Jerusalem, may be indigenous, though the crystal and silver work probably came from Central Europe.[5] Of ivory-work there are the two delicately carved plaques that serve as covers for the Psalter of Queen Melisende. The one has medallions giving the story of David, with the Psychomachia in the corners, the other the Works of Mercy, with fantastic animals in the corners. The iconography is Western rather than Byzantine, though the royal costumes are Byzantine, the animals Moorish and the decoration Armenian in inspiration. It seems unlikely that there should have been any ivory-worker of such a high calibre living in Jerusalem. The plaques were probably a gift from elsewhere.[6]

The slightness of the evidence should not be interpreted to mean

[1] Enlart, *op. cit.* I, pp. 172–201.
[2] *Ibid.* II, pp. 310–11.   [3] *Ibid.* I, pp. 175–9.
[4] See Schlumberger, *Sigillographie de l'Orient Latin*, esp. introduction by Blanchet.   [5] Enlart, *op. cit.* I, pp. 197–8.
[6] Enlart, *op. cit.* I, pp. 199–200; Dalton, *Byzantine Art and Archaeology*, pp. 221–3, and *East Christian Art*, p. 218, points out the Oriental affinities and believes that the carver was local. Boase, *loc. cit.*

that little was done. If architecture flourished, it is likely that the other arts flourished also, and gave the same reflection of life in Outremer. The eclectic architecture of the twelfth century is that of colonists that were ready to fit themselves into the land to which they had come, though they were continually reinforced from the West. But the disasters at the end of the century ended the old balance. In the thirteenth century few of the older great families of Outremer survived. Their place was taken by the Military Orders, who were mainly recruited in the West and had little feeling for local traditions. In the cities the native elements were now set apart. Acre looked westward. Wealth was in the hands of the Italians and power usually in the hands of potentates from the West or their deputies. More and more of the nobility retired to Cyprus, where a new Gothic civilization was arising. A few echoes from Byzantium and the East were still heard, but they were growing faint. Byzantium was in eclipse. The older Arab culture was extinguished by the Mongols, and the newer culture of Mameluk Egypt was aggressively hostile. In Antioch the synthesis may have been continued, but pillage, earthquake and decay have destroyed all the evidence. Further south the attempt of Outremer to build its own characteristic style was ruined on the field of Hattin. The modest, sturdy work of twelfth-century Outremer was a prelude that led to nothing. Thirteenth-century Outremer was only a distant province of the Mediterranean Gothic world.

CHAPTER III

THE FALL OF ACRE

'An end, the end is come upon the four corners of the land.'   EZEKIEL VII, 2

There was rejoicing in Outremer when news came of the death of Baibars. His successor was his eldest son, Baraqa, a weak youth whose time was employed in trying to control the Mameluk emirs. The task was too much for him. In August 1279, the emir of the Syrian troops, Qalawun, revolted and marched on Cairo. Baraqa abdicated in favour of his seventeen-year-old brother; and Qalawun took over the government. Four months later Qalawun displaced the child and proclaimed himself Sultan. The governor of Damascus, Sonqor al-Ashqar, refused to accept his authority and proclaimed himself Sultan there next April. But he was unable to maintain himself against the Egyptians. After a battle close to Damascus in June 1280, he retired to northern Syria and soon made his peace with Qalawun, who thus obtained the whole of Baibars's heritage.[1]

The Franks made no use of the respite. In vain the Ilkhan Abaga and his vassal, Leo III of Armenia, urged an alliance and a Crusade. Their only advocate was the Order of the Hospital. Charles of Anjou, with his hatred of Byzantium and its Genoese allies, ordered his *bailli* at Acre, Roger of San Severino, to keep to an alliance with the Venetians, the Templars and the Mameluk Court. The Pope, who had been promised by the Emperor Michael the submission of the Byzantine Church, encouraged Charles in his Syrian schemes in order to distract him from an attack on Constantinople. King Edward I showed his sympathy with the

[1] Abu'l Feda, pp. 157–8; Maqrisi, *Sultans*, I, ii, p. 171, II, i, 26; d'Ohsson, *Histoire des Mongols*, pp. 519–22.

Mongols; but he was far away in England and had neither the time nor the money for a new Crusade.[1]

In Outremer Bohemond VII might have been willing to co-operate with his Armenian uncle, but he was on bad terms with the Templars; and in 1277 he quarrelled with the most powerful of his vassals, Guy II Embriaco of Jebail. Guy, who was his cousin and close friend, had been promised the hand of a local heiress of the Aleman family for his brother John. But Bishop Bartholomew of Tortosa desired the heritage for his own nephew and won Bohemond's consent. Thereupon Guy kidnapped the girl and married her to John. Then, fearing Bohemond's vengeance, he fled to the Templars. Bohemond responded by destroying the Templars' buildings at Tripoli and cutting down a forest that they owned nearby at Montroque. The Master of the Temple, William of Beaujeu, at once led the knights of the Order against Tripoli, to make a demonstration outside the walls, and when he retired he burned the castle of Botrun; but his attempt to storm Nephin resulted in the capture of a dozen of his knights, whom Bohemond duly imprisoned at Tripoli. When the Templars had moved back to Acre, Bohemond set out to attack Jebail. Guy, with whom William of Beaujeu had left a contingent from the Order, went to meet him. A fierce battle took place a few miles north of Botrun. There were barely two hundred combatants on either side, but the carnage was tremendous. Bohemond was badly defeated. Amongst the knights that he lost was his cousin and Guy's brother-in-law, Balian of Sidon, the last of the great house of Garnier.[2]

After his defeat Bohemond accepted a truce for a year; but in 1278 Guy and the Templars attacked him again. Once again Bohemond was defeated; but twelve Templar galleys which attempted to force the harbour of Tripoli were scattered by a storm. Fifteen galleys that Bohemond then sent against the Templar castle of Sidon succeeded in doing some damage there before the

[1] Hayton, *Flor des Estoires*, pp. 180–1.
[2] *Estoire d'Eracles*, II, p. 481; *Gestes des Chiprois*, pp. 207, 210–13.

Grand Master of the Hospital, Nicholas Lorgne, intervened. He hastened to Tripoli and arranged another truce. But Guy of Jebail was still truculent. He determined to capture Tripoli itself. In January 1282, with his brothers and some friends, he smuggled himself into the Templar quarters at Tripoli. But there had been a misunderstanding and the Templar commander, Reddecœur, was away. Guy suspected treachery and panicked. As he tried to take refuge in the House of the Hospitallers, someone warned Bohemond. The conspirators fled to a tower in the Hospital, where Bohemond's troops besieged them. After a few hours they agreed, at the request of the Hospitallers, to surrender on condition that their lives were spared. Bohemond broke his word. All Guy's companions were blinded, but Guy himself, with his brothers John and Baldwin and his cousin William, was taken to Nephin, and there they were all buried up to their necks in a ditch and left to starve to death.

The rebels' ghastly fate horrified all Bohemond's vassals. Moreover the Embriaco family had always remembered its Genoese origin; and there had been many Genoese amongst the conspirators. As the Genoese were good friends of the Armenians and advocates of a Mongol alliance, Bohemond held aloof from their policy. Meanwhile John of Montfort, who was a devoted ally of the Genoese, planned to move up from Tyre to avenge his friends. But Bohemond reached Jebail before him. Only the Pisans, who hated the Genoese, found unalloyed pleasure in the whole episode.

Politics were not much happier further south. Roger of San Severino's government at Acre was resented by the local nobility. In 1277 William of Beaujeu attempted to bring John of Montfort over to his side and succeeded in reconciling John with the Venetians, who were allowed to return to their former quarters in Tyre. But John kept aloof from the government at Acre. In 1279 King Hugh suddenly landed at Tyre, hoping to rally the nobility round him. John gave him support, but no one else rose in his favour. The four months' period for which he was legally entitled to claim the presence of his Cypriot vassals overseas was passed in inaction. When his knights returned to Cyprus the King had to follow. He blamed the Templars for his failure, with reason, for it was William of Beaujeu who had kept Acre loyal to Roger of San Severino. In revenge the Templars' property in Cyprus was confiscated, including their castle at Gastria. The Order complained to the Pope, who wrote to Hugh to bid him restore the property; but he ignored the Papal command. Though he seems to have approved of the Mongol alliance, chiefly because Roger of San Severino opposed it, he was in no position to take any action on the mainland.[1]

The Ilkhan was eager to strike against the Mameluks before Qalawun should be able to consolidate himself. Sonqor, ex-emir of Damascus, was still defying the Egyptians in northern Syria, when, at the end of September 1280, a Mongol army crossed the Euphrates and occupied Aintab, Baghras and Darbsaq. On 20 October it entered Aleppo, where it pillaged the markets and burned the mosques. The terrified Moslem inhabitants of the districts fled south towards Damascus. At the same time the Hospitallers of Marqab made a highly profitable raid into the Buqaia, penetrating almost to Krak and, as they returned, defeating near Maraclea the Moslem army sent to restrain them. But the Mongols were not in full enough strength to hold Aleppo. When Qalawun assembled his forces at Damascus, they retreated across the Euphrates. The Sultan contented himself with sending a force to punish the Hospitallers, who defeated it in front of Marqab.[2]

About the same time a Mongol ambassador appeared at Acre to tell the Franks that the Ilkhan proposed sending an army of a hundred thousand men to Syria next spring, and to beg them to supplement him with men and munitions. The Hospitallers sent the message on to King Edward; but at Acre itself there was no response. The news of the coming Mongol invasion frightened

[1] *Gestes des Chiprois*, p. 207; *Annales de Terre Sainte*, p. 457; Amadi, p. 214; Mas Latrie, *Documents*, II, p. 109; Raynaldus, 1279, p. 488.
[2] Maqrisi, *Sultans*, II, i, p. 26; Abu'l Feda, p. 158; Bar-Hebraeus, p. 463; *Gestes des Chiprois*, pp. 208–9.

Qalawun. He made peace with Sonqor in June 1281, enfeoffing him with Antioch and Apamea; and he sent to Acre to suggest a ten years' truce with the Military Orders. The truce made with the government at Acre in 1272 still had over a year to run. Some of the emirs in the Egyptian embassy told the Franks not to make terms with Qalawun, as he would soon be overthrown. When Roger of San Severino heard this, he at once wrote to warn the Sultan, who was able to arrest the conspirators in time. Meanwhile the Orders at Acre agreed to the treaty, which was signed on 3 May. On 16 July Bohemond made a similar truce. It was a diplomatic triumph for Qalawun. A united Frankish effort on his flank, even without reinforcements from the West, would have seriously complicated his campaign against the Mongols.[1]

In September 1281, two Mongol armies advanced into Syria. One, commanded by the Ilkhan in person, slowly reduced the Moslem fortresses along the Euphrates frontier, while the second, under his brother Mangu Timur, first made contact with Leo III of Armenia, then marched down through Aintab and Aleppo into the Orontes valley. Qalawun had already gone to Damascus where he assembled his forces, and hurried northward. The Franks held aloof, except for the Hospitallers of Marqab, who refused to consider themselves bound by the truce made by the Order at Acre. A few of their knights rode out to join the King of Armenia. On 30 October the Mongol and Mameluk armies met just outside Homs. Mangu Timur commanded the Mongol centre, with other Mongol princes on his left, and on his right his Georgian auxiliaries, with King Leo and the Hospitallers. The Moslem right was under al-Mansur of Hama; Qalawun himself commanded the Egyptians in the centre, with the army of Damascus, under the emir Lajin, beside him, and on the left the former rebel Sonqor, with the northern Syrians and Turcomans.

When the battle was joined the Christians on the Mongol right soon routed Sonqor, whom they pursued right into his camp at Homs, thus losing touch with their centre. Meanwhile, though

[1] Maqrisi, *Sultans*, II, i, pp. 28–34; Röhricht, *Regesta*, p. 374.

the Mongol left held firm, Mangu Timur himself was wounded in the course of a Mameluk attack on the centre. His nerve left him, and he ordered a precipitate retreat. Leo of Armenia and his comrades found themselves isolated. They had to fight their way back northwards, suffering heavy losses. But Qalawun had lost too many men to follow in pursuit. The Mongol army recrossed the Euphrates without further losses. The great river remained the frontier between the two Empires; and Qalawun did not venture to punish the Armenians.

The Prior of the English Hospitallers, Joseph of Chauncy, who was visiting the East, was present at the battle and wrote afterwards to Edward I to describe it. He said that King Hugh and Prince Bohemond had not been able to join the Mongols in time. He was probably trying to shield them both from the wrath of the English King, who was the only Western monarch still to take an interest in the Holy War, and who strongly favoured the Mongol alliance. But Edward's perspicacity was not copied in the East. King Hugh had done nothing; Bohemond had made a truce with the Moslems; while Roger of San Severino, King Charles's deputy, made a special journey to meet Qalawun and congratulate him on his victory.[1]

On the evening of 30 March 1282, the Sicilians, exasperated by the arrogance of Charles of Anjou and his soldiers, suddenly rose and massacred every Frenchman in the island. The Sicilian Vespers had far wider-flung effects than ever the angry islanders can have suspected. Charles's great Mediterranean empire was shown to be without foundation. For the next decades he and his successors vainly tried to recover Sicily from the Aragonese princes who were elected to its throne. The Angevin kingdom of Naples was no longer a world-power; and the Papacy which had guaranteed to the Angevins their Sicilian kingdom, was humiliated and ruined

---

[1] Maqrisi, *Sultans*, II, i, pp. 35–7; Abu'l Feda, pp. 158–60; Bar-Hebraeus, pp. 464–5; Hayton, *Flor des Estoires*, pp. 182–4; *Gestes des Chiprois*, p. 210; letter of Joseph of Chauncy, and King Edward's reply (ed. Sanders), *P.P.T.S.* vol. v; Röhricht, *Regesta*, p. 375; d'Ohsson, *op. cit.* pp. 525–34.

financially in its attempts to restore its clients. Angevin schemes in the Balkans and further to the east were abandoned. At Constantinople the Emperor sighed with relief. He had no longer to infuriate his people by offering the submission of their Church to Rome if Rome would curb Charles's ambitions.[1] In Outremer Roger of San Severino suddenly found himself without any backing. He was summoned to return to Italy by his master, and left Acre towards the end of the year, confiding his position as *bailli* to his Seneschal, Odo Poilechien.[2]

To the Mameluks of Egypt the collapse of Charles's power came as a shock but also as a relief. Both Baibars and Qalawun had feared and respected him, and therefore had refrained from attacking his new province in Outremer. Now there was no one to restrain the Sultan, as long as the Franks could be kept from alliance with the Mongols. In June 1283, when the truce signed at Caesarea ended, Qalawun offered Odo Poilechien to renew it for another ten years. Odo gladly accepted, but he was unsure of his authority. The treaty was therefore signed on the Frankish side in the name of the Commune of Acre and the Templars of Athlit and Sidon. It guaranteed the Franks in their possession of the territory from the Ladder of Tyre, north of Acre, to Mount Carmel and Athlit, and also of Sidon. But Tyre and Beirut were excluded. The right of free pilgrimage to Nazareth was maintained.[3]

Odo was glad to preserve the peace; for King Hugh was once more about to try to recover his mainland kingdom. The Lady Isabella of Beirut had recently died, and her city had passed to her sister Eschiva, the wife of Humphrey of Montfort, who was the younger brother of the Lord of Tyre. Knowing that he could trust the Montforts, Hugh sailed from Cyprus at the end of July,

---

[1] Amari, *La Guerra del Vespro Siciliano*, remains the best general history for the Vespers and the subsequent war.

[2] *Gestes des Chiprois*, p. 214; Sanudo, *Chronique de Romanie* in Mas Latrie, *Nouvelles Preuves*, I, pp. 39–40. Odo married the widow of Balian Ibelin of Arsuf, Lucia of Gouvain.

[3] Maqrisi, *Sultans*, II, i, pp. 60, 179–85, 224–30. See Hill, *History of Cyprus*, II, p. 176.

with two of his sons, Henry and Bohemond. He had intended to land at Acre, but the wind blew him to Beirut, where he arrived on 1 August and was well received. He sailed on a few days later to Tyre, sending his troops by land down the coast. On the way they were badly mauled by Moslem raiders, incited, so Hugh believed, by the Templars of Sidon. When he landed at Tyre, the omens were unfavourable. His standard fell into the sea. When the clergy came in procession to meet him the great Cross that they carried slipped and broke the skull of the Jewish court-physician. Hugh waited at Tyre; but no one at Acre made any move to welcome him there. The Commune and the Templars preferred the un-obtrusive government of Odo Poilechien. His Cypriot nobles would not stay with him for more than the lawful four months. On 3 November, before the period was over, the most promising of his sons, Bohemond died. Even more serious to him was the death of his friend and brother-in-law, John of Montfort. John left no children; so the King allowed Tyre to pass to his brother and heir, Humphrey, Lord of Beirut; but he added a clause that should he wish he could buy the city back for the crown for a hundred and fifty besants. But Humphrey himself died the fol-lowing February. After a suitable interval his widow was married to Hugh's youngest son, Guy, to whom she brought Beirut. Tyre remained for the time under the rule of John's widow, Margaret.[1]

Even after his nobles left him Hugh remained on at Tyre. There he died himself, on 4 March 1284. He had done his best to restore authority in Outremer. His own qualities had handicapped him; for, with all his good looks and his charm, he was ill-tempered and tactless. But his failure was due far more to the hostility of the merchants of Acre and the Military Orders, who preferred an absentee, distant monarch, who would not interfere with them.[2]

Hugh was succeeded by his eldest son, John, a handsome but delicate boy of about seventeen. He was crowned King of Cyprus at Nicosia on 11 May, and immediately afterwards crossed to

---

[1] *Gestes des Chiprois*, pp. 214–16; Amadi, pp. 214–15.
[2] *Gestes des Chiprois*, pp. 216–17; Amadi, p. 216. See Hill, *op. cit.* p. 178.

Tyre where he was crowned King of Jerusalem. But outside of Tyre and Beirut his authority was unrecognized on the mainland. He reigned only one year, dying at Cyprus on 20 May 1285. His heir was his brother Henry, aged fourteen, who was crowned King of Cyprus on 24 June. He did not venture for the moment to cross into Syria.[1]

There Qalawun was preparing to attack those of the Franks who were not protected by the truce of 1283. The widowed ladies who governed Beirut and Tyre, Eschiva and Margaret, hastened to ask him for a truce, which was granted to them.[2] The Sultan's objective was the great castle of the Hospital at Marqab, whose inmates had too often allied themselves with the Mongols. On 17 April 1285, the Sultan appeared with a great army at the foot of the mountain on which the castle stands, bringing a larger number of mangonels than had ever been seen together before. His men dragged them up the hillside and began to pound at the walls. But the castle was well equipped, and its own mangonels had the advantage of position. Many of the enemy's machines were destroyed. For a month the Moslems could make no progress. At last the Sultan's engineers succeeded in digging a mine under the Tower of Hope which rose at the end of the northern salient, and filling it with inflammable wood. On 23 May the mine was fired, and the tower came crashing down. Its fall interrupted the assault of the Moslems, and they were driven back. But the garrison had discovered that the mine penetrated far further under their defences. They knew that they were lost and capitulated. The twenty-five officers of the Order who were in the castle were allowed to retire with all their portable possessions, on horseback and fully armed. The rest of the garrison could go free but could take nothing with them. They retired to Tortosa and then to Tripoli. Qalawun made his formal entry into the castle on 25 May.[3]

[1] *Gestes des Chiprois*, p. 217; Amadi, *loc. cit.* See Hill, *op. cit.* p. 179 n. 2.
[2] Maqrisi, *Sultans*, II, ii, pp. 212–13.
[3] *Gestes des Chiprois*, pp. 217–18; Amadi, *loc. cit.*; Maqrisi, *Sultans*, II, i, p. 80 (also in p. 86 but dated the following year); Abu'l Feda, p. 161; life of Qalawun in Reinaud, *Bibliothèque des Croisades*, II, pp. 548–52.

The loss of Marqab alarmed the citizens of Acre; and about the same time they learned that Charles of Anjou had died. His son, Charles II of Naples, was too deeply involved in the Sicilian war to trouble himself about Outremer; and the war was gradually embroiling the whole of western Europe. The time had come for a ruler nearer at hand. On the advice of the Hospital, Henry II sent an envoy from Cyprus, called Julian le Jaune, to Acre to negotiate for his recognition as King. The Commune acquiesced. The Hospital and the Teutonic Order sympathized. The Templars, after some hesitation, agreed to give their support; but Odo Poilechien refused to resign his *bailli*-ship. The French regiment, still provided by the King of France, supported Odo.

On 4 June 1286, Henry landed at Acre. The Commune received him with joy, though the Grand Masters of the three Orders thought it more prudent to be absent from his reception, saying that their religious profession obliged them to be neutral. Henry was taken in state to the Church of the Holy Cross. There he announced that he would lodge in the castle, as previous Kings had done. But Odo Poilechien refused to leave the castle, which he had garrisoned with the French. The Bishop of Famagusta and the Abbot of the Templum Domini at Acre went to plead with him and when he would not listen to them drew up a legal protest. The King, who was staying temporarily in the palace of the late Lord of Tyre, proclaimed three times that the Frenchmen could leave the castle in safety with all their belongings and no one must harm them. Meanwhile the citizens were growing exasperated with Odo and prepared to attack him. Thereupon the three Grand Masters, having seen which way the wind was blowing, persuaded Odo to hand the castle over to them, and they gave it to Henry. He made his solemn entry there on 29 June.[1]

Six weeks later, on 15 August, Henry was crowned at Tyre by the Archbishop, Bonnacorso of Gloria, acting as vicar of the Patriarch. After the ceremony the Court returned to Acre, and

[1] *Gestes des Chiprois*, pp. 218–20; Amadi, pp. 216–17; Sanudo, *Liber Secretorum*, p. 229; Machaeras (ed. Dawkins), p. 42; Mas Latrie, *Documents*, III, pp. 671–3.

there they held a fortnight of festivity. There were games and tournaments, and in the great Hall of the Hospital pageants were enacted. There were scenes from the Story of the Round Table, with Lancelot and Tristram and Palamedes; and they played the tale of the Queen of Femenie, from the Romance of Troy. Not for a century had there been so gay and splendid a festival in Outremer. The handsome boy-King charmed everyone; for it was not yet known that he was epileptic. Behind him, to advise him in everything, were his uncles, Philip and Baldwin of Ibelin, who were deeply respected. On their advice, he did not remain long at Acre but returned in a few weeks' time to Cyprus, leaving Baldwin of Ibelin as *bailli*. His uncles knew that a resident King would not be to the liking of the people.[1]

The Sultan at Cairo must have smiled to hear of the frivolous gaieties of the Franks; but to the Mongol Ilkhan at Tabriz it seemed that the time had come for more serious action. Abaga had died on 1 April 1282. His successor was his brother, Tekuder, who in his childhood had been baptized into the Nestorian faith under the name of Nicholas. But his tastes lay towards the Moslems. Hardly was he on the throne before he announced his conversion to Islam and took the name of Ahmed and title of Sultan. At the same time he sent to Cairo to conclude a treaty of friendship with Qalawun. His policy horrified the older Mongols of his Court, who complained at once to the Great Khan Kubilai. With Kubilai's approval, Abaga's son Arghun led a revolt in Khorassan, where he was governor. He was defeated at first. But Ahmed was soon deserted by his generals and was murdered in a palace conspiracy on 10 August 1284. Arghun at once mounted the throne.[2] Like his father, Arghun was religiously eclectic. His own sympathies were for Buddhism, but his vizier, Sa'ad ad-Daulah, was a Jew, and his

---

[1] *Gestes des Chiprois*, p. 221; *Annales de Terre Sainte*, p. 548; Amadi, p. 217.
[2] Howorth, *History of the Mongols*, III, pp. 295–310; Abu'l Feda, p. 160, and other Arab writers refer to Ahmed (see references given by Howorth), but Western writers ignore him. Bar-Hebraeus, pp. 467–71, treats of him at length.

best friend was the Nestorian Catholicus, Mar Yahbhallaha. This remarkable man was Turk in origin, an Ongut born in the Chinese province of Shan-si by the banks of the Hoang-Ho. He had come with his compatriot, Rabban Sauma, westward in the vain hope of making a pilgrimage to Jerusalem. While he was in Iraq in 1281, the Catholicate fell vacant, and he was elected to the office. He had a great influence over the new Ilkhan, who longed to rescue the Holy Places of Christendom from the Moslems, but who always said that he would not do so unless the Christian Kings of the West gave their aid.[1]

In 1285 Arghun wrote to Pope Honorius IV to suggest common action, but he received no answer.[2] Two years later he decided to send an embassy to the West, and he chose as his ambassador Mar Yahbhallaha's friend Rabban Sauma. The ambassador, who wrote a vivid account of his mission, set out early in 1287. Sailing from Trebizond, he reached Constantinople about Easter-time. He was cordially received by the Emperor Andronicus and visited Saint Sophia and the other great shrines of the Imperial city. Andronicus was already on excellent terms with the Mongols and was ready to help them as far as his dwindling resources allowed. From Constantinople Rabban Sauma went to Naples, arriving there at the end of June. While he was there he saw a sea battle in the harbour between the Aragonese and the Neapolitan fleets. It was his first indication that western Europe was preoccupied with its own squabbles. He rode on to Rome. There he found that Pope Honorius had just died, and the conclave to elect his successor had not yet assembled. The twelve Cardinals who were resident in Rome received him, but he found them ignorant and unhelpful. They knew nothing of the spread of Christianity among the Mongols and were shocked that he should serve a heathen master. When he tried to discuss politics, they cross-questioned him about his faith and criticized its divergencies from their own. In the end

[1] See Budge, *The Monks of Kublai Khan*, introduction, pp. 42–61, 72–5.
[2] The text of Arghun's letter is given by Chabot, 'Relations du roi Argoun avec L'Occident', in *Revue de l'Orient Latin*, vol. II, p. 571.

he almost lost his temper. He had come, he said, to pay his respects to the Pope, and to make plans for the future, not to hold a debate on the Creed. After he had worshipped in the chief churches of Rome, he went gladly to Genoa. The Genoese welcomed him with great ceremony. The Mongol alliance was important to them, and they gave due attention to the ambassador's proposals.

At the end of August Rabban Sauma crossed into France, reaching Paris early in September. There his reception was all that he could desire. An escort brought him into the capital, and when he was given an audience by the young King, Philip IV, he was paid sovereign honours. The King rose from his throne to greet him and listened with deep respect to his message. He left the audience with a promise that, if it pleased God, Philip would himself lead an army to the rescue of Jerusalem. The ambassador was delighted by Paris. The University, then at the height of its medieval glory, particularly impressed him. The King himself escorted him round the Sainte-Chapelle to see the sacred relics that Saint Louis had bought from Constantinople. When he moved on from Paris the King nominated an ambassador, Gobert of Helleville, who was to return with him to the Ilkhan's Court and arrange further details of the alliance.

Rabban Sauma's next host was Edward I of England, who was then at Bordeaux, the capital of his French possessions. With Edward, who had fought in the East and had long advocated a Mongol alliance, he found an intelligent and practical response to his proposals. The King struck him as the ablest statesman that he had met in the West; and he was particularly flattered when he was asked to celebrate Mass before the English Court. But when it came to making a time-table Edward prevaricated. Neither he nor Philip of France could say when exactly he would be ready to embark on the Crusade. Rabban Sauma went back to Rome a little uneasy in his mind. Pausing at Genoa for Christmas he happened to meet the Cardinal-Legate John of Tusculum and told him his fears. The Mameluks were preparing at that moment to extinguish the last Christian states in Syria, and no one in the West would take the threat seriously.

In February 1288, Nicholas IV was elected Pope; and one of his first actions was to receive the Mongol ambassador. Their personal relations were excellent. Rabban Sauma addressed the Pope as First Bishop of Christendom, and Nicholas sent his blessing to the Nestorian Catholicus and acknowledged him as Patriarch of the East. In the course of Holy Week the ambassador celebrated Mass before all the Cardinals, and he received Communion from the hands of the Pope himself. He left Rome, together with Gobert of Helleville, in the late spring of 1288, laden with gifts, many of them precious relics, for the Ilkhan and the Catholicus, and with letters for them both and for two Christian princesses at the Court and for the Jacobite Bishop of Tabriz, Denys. But the letters were a little vague. The Pope could not promise definite action on any definite date.[1]

Indeed, as Rabban Sauma came to realize, the Kings of the West had their own distractions. The sinister ghost of Charles of Anjou combined with the old vindictiveness of the Papacy to block any Crusade. The Pope had given Sicily to the Angevins; and now that the Sicilians had turned against the Angevins, both the Papacy and France were obliged by the claims of prestige to fight for the reconquest of the island, against the two great sea-powers of the Mediterranean, Genoa and Aragon. Till the Sicilian question was settled neither Nicholas nor Philip was ready to think of a Crusade. Edward of England saw the danger, and managed in 1286 to arrange a truce between France and Aragon; but it was a precarious truce so long as fighting continued in Italy and on the sea. Moreover, Edward had his own troubles. He might yearn to save the Holy Land, but he found it of more urgent interest to conquer Wales and to attempt the conquest of Scotland. After the death of Alexander III of Scotland in 1286 his eyes were turned northward, as he planned to control the neighbour kingdom

[1] A full translation of Rabban Sauma's account of his travels in Europe is given by Budge, *op. cit.* pp. 164–97.

through the person of its child-heiress, Margaret, the Maid of Norway. The East must wait. Nor was there any force of public opinion to urge the monarchs on. As Pope Gregory X's researches had shown, the Crusading spirit was moribund.[1]

Arghun would not believe that the Christians of the West, with all their pious protestations of devotion to the Holy Land, could show such indifference to its threatened fate. He welcomed Rabban Sauma home with the highest honours, and showed cordiality to Gobert of Helleville. But he wished for greater precision than Gobert could give him. Just after Easter 1289, he sent a second envoy, a Genoese called Buscarel of Gisolf, who had long been settled in his lands, with letters for the Pope and the Kings of France and England. The letter to Philip still survives. It is written in the Mongol tongue, using Uighur script. In the name of the Great Khan Kubilai, Arghun announces to the King of France that, with God's help, he proposes to set out into Syria on the last winter month of the year of the panther, that is to say, in January 1291, and to reach Damascus about the middle of the first month of spring, February. If the King will send auxiliaries and the Mongols capture Jerusalem, it will be given to him. But if he fails to co-operate the campaign will be wasted. Added to the letter is a note by Buscarel, written in French, which pays tactful compliments to the French King and adds that Arghun will bring with him the Christian Kings of Georgia and twenty or even thirty thousand horsemen, and will guarantee that the Westerners shall be amply victualled. A similar letter, now lost, must have been sent to King Edward, to whom the Pope added a note of recommendation and encouragement. Philip's reply has not come down to us, but Edward's can still be read. It congratulates the Ilkhan on his Christian enterprise and pays him friendly compliments. But as to an actual date nothing is said and no promises are given. The Ilkhan is merely referred to the Pope; who could do little

---

[1] For a general picture of the situation see Grousset, *Histoire des Croisades*, III, pp. 711–21, also Lévis-Mirepoix, *Philippe Le Bel*, pp. 22 ff., for the effect of the Sicilian war on general politics. See also above, pp. 338 ff.

without the co-operation of the Kings.[1] Meanwhile another Frank, whose name is unknown, published a treatise showing how easy it would be to land a force of Westerners by Ayas in Armenia, whose King would be most helpful, and from there to make a junction with the Mongols. His advice was unheeded.[2]

In spite of the unpromising answers with which Buscarel returned, Arghun sent him once again, with two Christian Mongols, Andrew Zagan and Sahadin. They went first to Rome, where Pope Nicholas received them, and then set out to visit the King of England, armed with urgent letters from the Pope, who seems to have considered him a likelier Crusader than King Philip. They reached him early in 1291. But the Maid of Norway had died the previous year, and Edward was immersed in Scottish affairs. The envoys returned disconsolate to Rome, there they stayed throughout the summer. By then it was too late. The fate of Outremer had been decided; and the Ilkhan Arghun was dead.[3]

Had the Mongol alliance been achieved and honestly implemented by the West, the existence of Outremer would almost certainly have been prolonged. The Mameluks would have been crippled if not destroyed; and the Ilkhanate of Persia would have survived as a power friendly to the Christians and the West. As it was, the Mameluk Empire survived for nearly three centuries; and within four years of Arghun's death the Mongols of Persia passed into the Moslem camp. It was not only the Franks of Outremer whose cause was lost by the negligence of the West but also the miserable congregations of Eastern Christendom. And this negligence was due primarily to the Sicilian war, itself the outcome of Papal bitterness and French imperialism.

Meanwhile Outremer gave an impression of still more feckless irresponsibility. King Henry had hardly returned to Cyprus from the festivities at Acre before open war started along the Syrian

[1] Chabot, *op. cit.* pp. 593–4, 604–16, giving the texts of the letters.
[2] Kohler, 'Deux Projets de Croisade en Terre Sainte', text and introduction, *Mélanges pour Servir a l'Histoire de l'Orient Latin*, pp. 516 ff.
[3] Chabot, *op. cit.* pp. 617–19.

coast between the Pisans and the Genoese. In the spring of 1287 the Genoese sent a squadron under their admirals Thomas Spinola and Orlando Ascheri to the Levant. While Spinola visited Alexandria to obtain the friendly neutrality of the Sultan, Ascheri sailed up and down the Syrian coast, sinking or capturing any ships that he could find that belonged to Pisans or Franks of Pisan origin. Only the intervention of the Templars prevented the captured sailors from being sold into captivity. Ascheri then retired to Tyre, to plan an attack on the harbour of Acre. The Venetians joined their local fleet to the Pisans to protect the harbour; but Ascheri won a victory off the mole on 31 May 1287, though he could not penetrate into the port. When Spinola sailed up from Alexandria, the Genoese were able to blockade the whole coast. The Grand Masters of the Temple and the Hospital together with representatives of the local nobility at last persuaded them to sail back to Tyre and allow a free passage to shipping.[1]

One seaport had been spared this conflict, having already met a worse fate. For some time past the merchants of Aleppo had been complaining to the Sultan that it was inconvenient to have to send their goods to the Christian port of Lattakieh, the last remnant of the Principality of Antioch. Qalawun's opportunity came that spring. An earthquake on 22 March seriously damaged the walls of the town. Claiming that Lattakieh, as part of the old Principality, was not covered by the truce with Tripoli, he sent his emir, Husam ad-Din Turantai, to take it over. The town fell easily into his hands; but the defenders retired to a fort at the mouth of the harbour, joined to the land by a causeway. Turantai widened the causeway and soon induced the garrison to surrender on 20 April. There had been no attempt to come to its relief.[2]

Its former lord, Bohemond VII, did not long survive its loss. He died, childless, on 19 October 1287. His heir was his sister Lucia, who had married Charles of Anjou's former Grand Admiral,

---

[1] *Gestes des Chiprois*, pp. 220–30; *Annales Januenses*, p. 317.
[2] *Gestes des Chiprois*, p. 230; Abu'l Feda, p. 162; Maqrisi in Reinaud, *op. cit.* pp. 561–2.

Narjot of Toucy, and now lived in Apulia. The nobles and citizens of Tripoli had no particular desire to summon to the East an almost unknown princess who was associated with the discredited Angevins. Instead, they offered the county to the Dowager Princess, Sibylla of Armenia. As soon as she received the offer she wrote to her old friend, Bishop Bartholomew of Tortosa, to invite him to be her *bailli*. But her letter was intercepted, and the nobles of the county came to her and told her that the Bishop was unacceptable. She refused to give way. After an angry scene the nobles withdrew and took counsel with the leading merchants; and together they proclaimed the dethronement of the dynasty and the establishment of a Commune, which would henceforth be the sovereign authority. Its mayor was Bartholomew Embriaco, whose father Bertrand had been the bitter enemy of Bohemond VI and whose brother William had been cruelly done to death, along with his cousin, the lord of Jebail, by Bohemond VII.

The Dowager retired to her brother in Armenia. But early in 1288, Lucia arrived with her husband at Acre, in order to go to Tripoli to take up her inheritance. She was well received by the Hospitallers, old allies of the dynasty, who escorted her as far as Nephin, the frontier town of the county. There she issued a proclamation, declaring her rights. The Commune responded by reciting a long list of grievances and complaints against the cruel and high-handed actions of her brother, her father and her grandfather. They would have no more of the dynasty. Instead, they put themselves under the protection of the Republic of Genoa. A messenger went to Genoa to inform the Genoese Doge, who at once dispatched the admiral Benito Zaccaria, with five galleys, to make terms with the Commune. Meanwhile the Grand Masters of the Three Orders, together with the *bailli* of the Venetians at Acre, had gone to Tripoli to plead the cause of the heiress, the Hospitaller for the old friendship of his Order for her family, the Templar and the Teuton because they backed Venice against Genoa. But they were told that Lucia must recognize the Commune as the government of the county.

When Zaccaria arrived he insisted on a treaty giving the Genoese many more streets in Tripoli and the right to have a podestà to govern their colony, while he guaranteed the liberties and the privileges of the Commune. But the citizens of Tripoli began to wonder whether Genoa would be a disinterested friend. Bartholomew Embriaco, who had secured control of Jebail by marrying his daughter Agnes to his young cousin, Peter, son of Guy II, coveted the county for himself. He sent a message to Cairo to find out whether Qalawun would support him if he proclaimed himself Count. His ambition was suspected; and opinion in Tripoli veered round to Lucia's cause. Without informing the Genoese, the Commune wrote to her at Acre offering to accept her if she would confirm its position. Lucia shrewdly informed Zaccaria, who was at Ayas making a commercial treaty with the King of Armenia. He hurried to Acre to interview her. She agreed to confirm the privileges both of the Commune and of Genoa, and on those terms she was recognized as Countess of Tripoli.[1]

The arrangement pleased neither the Venetians nor Bartholomew Embriaco. He was already in touch with Qalawun; but whether it was he or the Venetians of Acre who now sent two Franks to Cairo to ask the Sultan to intervene cannot now be known. The secretary of the Grand Master of the Temple knew the names of the envoys but preferred not to reveal them. They warned the Sultan that if Genoa controlled Tripoli she would dominate the whole Levant, and the trade of Alexandria would be at her mercy.[2]

The Sultan was delighted to have an invitation to intervene. It justified him in breaking his truce with Tripoli. In February 1289, he moved the whole Egyptian army into Syria, without revealing his objective. But one of his emirs, Badr ad-Din Bektash al-

---

[1] *Gestes des Chiprois*, pp. 231–4; Amadi, pp. 217–18; Sanudo, p. 229; *Annales Januenses*, pp. 322–6.

[2] *Gestes des Chiprois*, p. 234. Abu'l Muhasin in Reinaud, *op. cit.* p. 561, says that Bartholomew warned Qalawun.

2D

Fakhri, was in the pay of the Templars and sent word to the Grand Master, William of Beaujeu, that Qalawun's destination was Tripoli. William hastened to warn the city and bid it unite and see to its defences. No one there would believe him. William was notoriously fond of political intrigue, and it was suspected that he had invented the story for his own profit, in the hope of being invited to mediate. Nothing was done, and the factions continued their quarrels till, towards the end of March, the Sultan's huge army marched down through the Buqaia and assembled before the city walls.[1]

Now, at last, the threat was taken seriously. Inside the city the Countess Lucia was given the supreme authority by the Commune and the nobles alike. The Templars sent up a force under their Marshal, Geoffrey of Vendac, and the Hospitallers under their Marshal, Matthew of Clermont. The French regiment marched up from Acre, under John of Grailly. There were four Genoese and two Venetian galleys in the port, as well as smaller boats, some of them Pisan. From Cyprus King Henry sent his young brother Amalric, whom he had just appointed Constable of Jerusalem, with a company of knights and four galleys. Meanwhile many non-combatant citizens fled across the sea to Cyprus.

Medieval Tripoli lay on the sea, on the blunt peninsula where the modern suburb of al-Mina stands. It was detached from the Castle of Mount Pilgrim, which, it seems, no attempt was made to defend. The city itself was gallantly defended. But, even though the Christians had command of the sea, the vast numerical superiority of the Moslems and their great siege-engines proved irresistible. When the Tower of the Bishop, at the south-east corner of the land walls, and the Tower of the Hospital, between it and the sea, crumbled before the bombardment, the Venetians decided that further defence was impossible. They hastily loaded their ships with all their possessions and sailed out of the harbour. Their defection alarmed the Genoese, whose admiral, Zaccaria,

---

[1] *Gestes des Chiprois*, pp. 234–5. Al-Fakhri had the title of emirsilah, hence the author of the *Gestes* calls him Salah. See Abu'l Feda, p. 159.

suspected them of trying to steal some of his boats. He too called off his men, and they left the city with everything that they could salvage. Their going threw the Christians into disorder; and that morning, 26 April 1289, the Sultan ordered a general assault. Hordes of Mameluks swarmed over the crumbling south-eastern wall into the city.

There the citizens struggled panic-stricken to reach the boats in the harbour. The Countess Lucia, with Amalric of Cyprus and the two Marshals of the Orders, sailed safely away to Cyprus. But the Commander of the Temple, Peter of Moncada, was slain, together with Bartholomew Embriaco. Every man found by the Moslems was at once put to death, and the women and children taken as slaves. A number of refugees managed to cross in rowing-boats to the little island of Saint Thomas, just off the point. But the Mameluk cavalry rode into the shallow water and swam across to it. There followed similar scenes of massacre; and when the historian Abu'l Feda of Hama tried to visit the island a few days later he was driven off by the stench of decaying corpses.[1]

When the massacre and pillage were ended, Qalawun had the city razed to the ground, lest the Franks, with their command of the sea, might try to recapture it. A new city was founded by his orders at the foot of Mount Pilgrim, a few miles inland.[2]

Mameluk troops went on to occupy Botrun and Nephin. There was no attempt to defend them. Peter Embriaco, lord of Jebail, offered his submission to the Sultan, and was allowed to keep his city, under strict surveillance, for about another decade.[3]

The fall of Tripoli came as a bitter shock to the people of Acre. They had persuaded themselves for the last few years that, so long as they were not aggressive, the Sultan really had no objection to the continued existence of the Christian cities along the coast. He

---

[1] *Gestes des Chiprois*, pp. 235–7; Amadi, p. 218; *Annales Januenses, loc. cit.*; Auria, *Annales* in *M.G.H. Scriptores*, vol. XVIII, p. 324; Maqrisi, *Sultans*, II, i, pp. 101–3; Abu'l Feda, pp. 163–4.   [2] *Gestes des Chiprois*, pp. 237–8.
[3] Maqrisi, *Sultans*, II, i, pp. 103–4. Sanudo, p. 230. See Grousset, *op. cit.* p. 745 n. 3.

might attack their castles, which were a potential danger to him. He might resent the Military Orders whose business it was to fight for their faith, even though Moslems as well as Christians employed the Templars as bankers. But the merchants and shop-keepers of the seaports only wanted peace, and the luxury-loving barons of Outremer had clearly no desire for the embarrassment of a Crusade. Acre and her sister-ports were a commercial convenience for the Moslems as well as for the Christians; and their citizens had shown their good-will in refusing the Mongol alliance. The unprovoked attack on Tripoli showed them how false were their calculations. They were forced to realize that a like fate awaited Acre.

Three days after the fall of Tripoli King Henry arrived at Acre. He found there an envoy from Qalawun, bearing a complaint from his master that Henry and the Military Orders had broken their truce with him by going to the aid of Tripoli. Henry replied that the truce only applied to the kingdom of Jerusalem. If Tripoli were covered by it, the Sultan should not have committed aggression there. The excuse was accepted by the Moslems; and the truce was renewed, to cover the kingdoms of Jerusalem and Cyprus for another ten years, ten months and ten days. The King of Armenia and the Lady of Tyre hastened to follow this example.[1] But Henry had little faith now in the Sultan's word. He could not venture to appeal to the Mongols; for the Sultan would certainly have considered that a breach of the truce. But, before he returned to Cyprus in September, leaving his brother as *bailli* at Acre, he sent John of Grailly to Europe, to impress upon the Western potentates how desperate was the situation.[2]

The Western potentates too had been shocked by the fate of Tripoli. But the Sicilian question still filled the minds of all except Edward of England; and his Scottish problem was reaching a crisis. Pope Nicholas IV received John of Grailly with sincere sympathy, and wrote in earnest sorrow to the Kings of the West to beg them

[1] *Gestes des Chiprois*, p. 238; Amadi, *loc. cit.* See Stevenson, *Crusaders in the East*, p. 351 n. 3.   [2] Raynaldus, 1288, p. 43, 1289, p. 72.

to send help. But he himself was entangled in the Sicilian affair; he could do nothing more than write letters and urge his clergy to preach the Crusade. The princes and lords to whom he applied preferred to wait until King Edward made some move. He after all had taken the Cross and had some experience of the East.[1] But Edward made no move. The Genoese republic, which had lost heavily by the loss of Tripoli, had taken reprisals by capturing a large Egyptian merchant ship in the waters off southern Anatolia and by raiding the undefended port of Tineh, in the Delta. But when Qalawun closed Alexandria to them, they hastened to make their peace. When the envoys came to Cairo, they found embassies from both the Greek and the German emperors waiting upon the Sultan.[2]

It was only in northern Italy that the Pope's appeal met with any response; and there it was answered not by any baron but by a rabble of peasants and unemployed petty townsfolk from Lombardy and Tuscany, eager for an adventure that would bring them merit and salvation and probably some loot. The Pope was not quite happy about them, but he accepted their help and put them under the command of the Bishop of Tripoli, who had come as a refugee to Rome. He hoped that under the restraining hand of a prelate that knew the East they would do nothing foolish. The Venetians, who had not wept to see Genoa lose its base at Tripoli but felt differently about Acre where they held the commercial hegemony, provided twenty galleys under the command of the Doge's son, Nicholas Tiepolo, assisted, at the Pope's request, by John of Grailly and Roux of Sully. Each of the three was entrusted with a thousand pieces of gold from the Papal treasury. But there was a lack of munitions. As the fleet sailed eastward it was joined by five galleys sent by King James of Aragon, who, though he was at war with the Papacy and Venice, was anxious to help.[3]

[1] Röhricht, 'Derniers Jours', p. 529. For Edward's attitude, see Powicke, *op. cit.* pp. 729 ff.   [2] Heyd, *op. cit.* 1, pp. 416–18.
[3] *Gestes des Chiprois*, p. 238; Dandolo, p. 402; Sanudo, p. 229; Amadi, pp. 218–19.

The truce between King Henry and the Sultan had restored some confidence at Acre. Trade recommenced. In the summer of 1290 the merchants of Damascus began to send their caravans again to the coast. There was a good harvest that year in Galilee, and the Moslem peasants crowded with their produce to the markets of Acre. Never had the town been so lively and active. In August, in the midst of this prosperity, the Italian Crusaders arrived. From the moment of their landing they proved an embarrassment to the authorities. They were disorderly, drunken and debauched. Their commanders, who were unable to give them their regular pay, had no control over them. They had come, they thought, to fight the infidel, so they began to attack the peaceful Moslem merchants and peasants. One day, towards the end of August, a riot flared up. Some said it began at a drinking bout where Christians and Moslems both were present; others, that a Moslem merchant had seduced a Christian lady, and her husband appealed to his neighbours for vengeance. Suddenly the Crusader rabble rushed through the streets and out into the suburbs, slaying every Moslem that they met; and as they decided that every man wearing a beard was a Moslem, many local Christians also perished. The barons of the city and the knights of the Orders were horrified; but all that they could do was to rescue a few of the Moslems and take them to the safety of the castle, and to arrest a few of the obvious ringleaders.[1]

It was not long before the news of the massacre reached the Sultan. His fury was well justified; and he decided that the time had come to eradicate the Franks from Syrian soil. The government of Acre hastened to send him apologies and excuses; but his envoys came to Acre and insisted that the men guilty of the outrage should be handed over to him for punishment. A council was called by the Constable Amalric. At it the Grand Master of the Temple arose and advised that all the Christian criminals that were then in the gaols of Acre should be delivered to the Sultan's repre-

---

[1] *Gestes des Chiprois, loc. cit.*; Amadi, p. 219; Florio Bustron, p. 118; Maqrisi, *Sultans*, II, i, p. 109.

sentatives as the perpetrators of the crime. But public opinion would not allow the dispatch of Christians to certain death at the hands of the infidel. The Sultan's ambassadors received no satisfaction. Instead, there was a half-hearted attempt to prove that some of the Moslem merchants were guilty of starting the riot and to fix the blame on them.[1]

Qalawun's answer was to resort to arms. A debate between his lawyers satisfied him that he was legally justified in breaking the truce. He kept his plans secret. While he mobilized the Egyptian army, the Syrian army, under Rukn ad-Din Toqsu, Governor of Damascus, was ordered to move to the coast of Palestine, near Caesarea, and to prepare siege-engines. It was given out that the destination of the expedition was in Africa.[2] But once again the emir al-Fakhri warned William of Beaujeu and the Templars of the Sultan's real intentions. William passed on the warning, but, as at Tripoli, no one was willing to believe him. He sent an envoy to Cairo on his own initiative. Qalawun offered to spare the city in return for as many Venetian sequins as there were inhabitants. But when William put this offer before the High Court, it was scornfully rejected. William was accused of being a traitor and was insulted by the crowd as he left the hall.[3]

The complacency of the people of Acre rose higher at the end of the year, when news came from Cairo that Qalawun was dead. He had given up any attempt to hide his intention of marching on Acre. In a letter to the King of Armenia he told of his vow not to leave a single Christian alive in the city. On 4 November 1290, he set out from Cairo at the head of his army. But no sooner had he started than he fell sick. Six days later he died at Marjat at-Tin, only five miles from his capital. On his death-bed he made his son, al-Ashraf Khalil, promise to continue the campaign. He

[1] *Gestes des Chiprois*, pp. 239–40; Amadi, *loc. cit.*
[2] *Gestes des Chiprois*, p. 240; Maqrisi, *Sultans*, II, i, p. 109; Muhi ad-Din, in Reynaud, *op. cit.* pp. 567–8.
[3] *Gestes des Chiprois*, *loc. cit.*; Ludolf of Suchem (trans. Stewart), *P.P.T.S.* vol. XII, p. 56.

had been a great Sultan, as relentless and merciless as Baibars, but with a finer sense of loyalty and honour.[1]

Unlike Baibars, he left a worthy son to succeed him. His death was followed by the usual palace plot. But al-Ashraf was not taken unawares. He was able to arrest the ringleader, the emir Turuntai, and to establish himself firmly on the throne. It was now too late in the year to march against Acre. The campaign was postponed to the spring.[2]

The government at Acre took advantage of the respite to send one more embassy to Cairo. It was led by a notable of Acre, Philip Mainbœuf, who was an accomplished Arabic scholar. With him was a Templar knight, Bartholomew Pizan, a Hospitaller and a secretary called George. The new Sultan refused to see them. They were thrown into prison, where they did not long survive.[3]

The Moslem army began to move in March, 1291. Al-Ashraf's preparations were careful and complete. Siege-engines were collected from all over his dominions. So heavily laden was the army from Hama that it took a month, in the wet, muddy weather, to travel from Krak, where it paused to collect a huge catapult, called the Victorious, down to Acre. Nearly a hundred other machines had been constructed at Damascus and in Egypt. There was a second great catapult, called the Furious, and lighter mangonels of a particularly efficient type, known as the Black Oxen. On 6 March al-Ashraf left Cairo for Damascus, where he deposited his harem. On April 5th he arrived before Acre with all his vast forces. Men spoke of sixty thousand horsemen and a hundred and sixty thousand infantrymen. However exaggerated those numbers may be, his army far exceeded the forces that the Christians could muster.[4]

The news of the Sultan's preparations had at last brought the people of Acre to realize their plight. Earnest appeals had been

[1] Maqrisi, *Sultans*, II, i, pp. 110–12; Abu'l Feda, p. 163; *Gestes des Chiprois*, pp. 240–1; Amadi, p. 219.

[2] Abu'l Feda, *loc. cit.*; *Gestes des Chiprois*, p. 241.

[3] *Gestes des Chiprois*, pp. 241–3; Maqrisi, *Sultans*, II, i, p. 120.

[4] Al-Jazari (ed. Sauvaget), pp. 4–5; Maqrisi, *loc. cit.*; Abu'l Feda, p. 163.

sent to Europe during the course of the winter, but with very little result. A few isolated knights had arrived during the previous autumn. Amongst them was the Swiss Otto of Grandson, with some Englishmen sent by Edward I. The Temple and the Hospital gathered all their available men. The Grand Master of the Teutonic Order, Burchard of Schwanden, made a bad impression by choosing to resign his office at this very moment; but his successor, Conrad of Feuchtwangen, summoned numbers of his fellow-knights from Europe. Henry of Cyprus sent over Cypriot troops and his brother, Amalric, to command the defence, and promised to follow himself with reinforcements. Every able-bodied citizen of Acre was enlisted to play his part.[1] But even so, the numbers were small. The whole civilian population of Acre comprised thirty to forty thousand souls. In addition there were less than a thousand knights or mounted sergeants and about fourteen thousand foot-soldiers, including the Italian pilgrims. The fortifications of the city were good, and they had recently been strengthened by King Henry's orders. There was now a double line of walls to protect the peninsula on which the city and its northern suburb, Montmusart, were placed, and a single wall separated Acre from Montmusart. The castle lay on this latter wall, close to its junction with the double walls. There were twelve towers, set at irregular intervals, along both the outer and the inner walls. Many of them had been erected at the expense of some distinguished pilgrim, such as the English Tower built by Edward I and the Tower of the Countess of Blois next to it. At the angle where the walls turned from running northward from the Bay of Acre to go westward towards the sea, there stood, on the outer wall, a great tower recently rebuilt by King Henry II, opposite to the Accursed Tower on the inner wall. In front of King Henry's Tower was a barbican built by King Hugh.[2] The

---

[1] *Gestes des Chiprois*, p. 241. See also Röhricht, *Geschichte*, pp. 1008 ff.

[2] See above, p. 23, and map on p. 415. Also Rey, *Colonies Franques*, pp. 451 ff. Alice of Brittany, Dowager Countess of Blois, had visited Acre in 1287 and died there (*Annales de Terre Sainte*, pp. 459–60; Sanudo, p. 229).

whole of this angle was considered the most vulnerable part of the defence. It was therefore entrusted to the King's own troops, under his brother, Amalric. On his right were the French and English knights, under John of Grailly and Otto of Grandson, then the troops of the Venetians and the Pisans and those of the Commune of Acre. On his left, covering the walls of Mont-musart, were first the Hospitallers, then the Templars, each com-manded by their Grand Master. The Teutonic Knights supple-mented the royal regiments by the Accursed Tower. On the Moslem side, the army of Hama, with which the historian Abu'l Feda was present in person, was stationed by the sea, opposite to the Templars; the army of Damascus was opposite to the Hospi-tallers, and the Egyptian army stretched from the end of the wall of Montmusart round to the bay of Acre. The Sultan's tent was pitched not far from the shore, opposite to the Tower of the Legate.[1]

Later, when all was over and lost, anger and grief gave rise to recriminations. The Christian chroniclers freely hurled accusa-tions of cowardice at the garrison.[2] But in fact, at this supreme moment of their fate, the defenders of Outremer showed a courage and a loyalty that had been sadly absent in recent years. It may be that when shiploads of women, old men and children were dis-patched to Cyprus at the beginning of the siege, some men of

[1] Abu'l Feda, p. 164; *Gestes des Chiprois*, p. 243.

[2] The main Frankish Chronicles dealing with the fall of Acre are: (1) *Gestes des Chiprois*, written by the so-called 'Templar of Tyre', who was secretary to the Grand Master of the Order. He was an eye-witness and though he admired the Master he was not a Templar himself, and was in general fair-minded (see below, p. 482). (2) Marino Sanudo, the elder, who was not present and bases his account on the *Gestes*. (3) *De Excidio Urbis Acconis* (in Martène and Durand, *Amplissima Collectio*, vol. v), an anonymous work, whose author was a con-temporary but not an eyewitness, and is very free in his accusations of cowardice and treachery. (4) Thaddeus of Naples, *Hystoria de Desolacione Civitatis Acconensis* (ed. Riant), is almost equally abusive. An account by a Greek monk, Arsenius (quoted by Bartholomew of Neocastro, ed. Paladino, in Muratori, *Rerum Italicarum Scriptores*, new edition, XIII, iii, p. 132), accuses the Franks of debauchery and inactivity, but not of cowardice. Nearly all the sources speak well of King Henry.

PLATE XIV

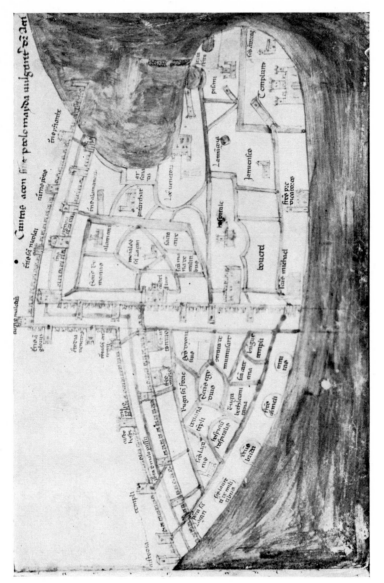

PLAN OF ACRE BY MARINO SANUDO

fighting age fled with them. It may be that some of the Italian merchants showed a selfish anxiety about their own property. Genoa, indeed, took no part in the struggle. She had been

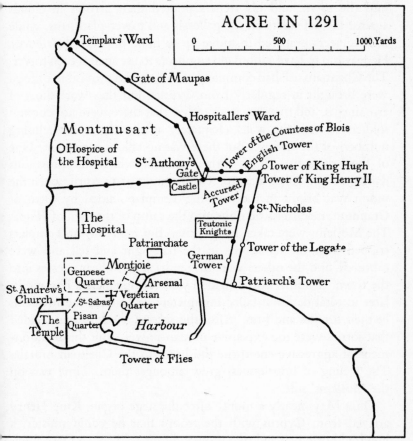

Map. 4. Acre in 1291.

virtually excluded from Acre by the Venetians and had made her own treaty with the Sultan. But the Venetians and Pisans fought valiantly. The latter were responsible for the construction of a great catapult that was the most effective of all the machines of the Christians.

The Fall of Acre

The siege began on 6 April. Day after day the Sultan's mangonels and catapults flung their stone or pottery containers filled with an explosive mixture at the walls of the city or over them into the town, and his archers poured their arrows in clouds against the defenders on the galleries and tower-platforms, while his engineers prepared to move up to mine the crucial defences. He was said to have a thousand engineers to use against each tower. The Christians still had command of the sea, and provisions of food were brought in regularly from Cyprus; but they were short of armaments, and they began to realize that there were not enough soldiers to man the walls adequately against the overwhelming numbers of the enemy. But there was no talk of surrender. One of their ships was fitted with a catapult which did enormous damage in the Sultan's camp. On the night of 15 April, when the moon was bright in the sky, the Templars, aided by Otto of Grandson, made a sortie right into the camp of the men of Hama. The Moslems were taken by surprise. But many of the Templars tripped over the tent-cords in the half-light and fell and were captured, and the others were driven back with heavy losses into the town. Another sortie made by the Hospitallers a few nights later in total darkness failed completely, as at once the Moslems lit their torches and fires. After this second check it was decided that sorties were too expensive in man-power. But the abandonment of aggressive enterprise did harm to the Christian morale. The feeling of hopelessness grew amongst them. Time was on the Moslems' side.

On 4 May, nearly a month after the siege began, King Henry arrived from Cyprus with the troops that he could muster, a hundred horsemen and two thousand foot-soldiers, in forty ships. With him was the Archbishop of Nicosia, John Turco of Ancona. It was probably because of illness that he had not come sooner. He was received with joy. As soon as he landed he took command and put new vigour into the defence. But it was soon clear that these reinforcements were too few to make any difference to the outcome.

In a last attempt to restore peace the King sent two knights, the Templar William of Cafran and William of Villiers, to the Sultan to ask why he had broken the truce and to promise to redress any grievances. Al-Ashraf received them outside his tent, but before they could deliver their message he asked them curtly if they had brought him the keys of the city. On their denial he said that it was the place that he wanted; he was not interested in the fate of its inhabitants, and, as a tribute to the King's courage in coming to fight when he was so young and ill, he would spare their lives if they surrendered to him. The envoys had hardly replied that they would be held as traitors if they promised capitulation when a catapult from the walls hurled a stone into the fringe of the group. Al-Ashraf was furious and drew his sword to slay the ambassadors, but the emir Shujai restrained him, bidding him not to stain it with the blood of pigs. The knights were allowed to return to their King.

The Sultan's engineers were already beginning to mine the towers. On 8 May the King's men decided that the barbican of King Hugh was no longer tenable. They set fire to it and left it to collapse. In the course of the following week the towers of the English and of the Countess of Blois were undermined, and the walls by Saint Anthony's Gate and by the tower of Saint Nicholas began to crumble. The new tower of Henry II held out till 15 May, when part of its outer wall came down. Next morning the Mameluks forced their way into the ruin, and the defence was forced back into the inner line of walls. That same day there was a concentrated attack on Saint Anthony's Gate, and only the gallantry of the Templars and the Hospitallers kept the enemy from passing into the city. The Marshal of the Hospital, Matthew of Clermont, distinguished himself by his bravery.

During the next day the Moslems strengthened their hold on the outer enceinte; and the Sultan ordered the general assault for the morning of Friday, 18 May. The attack was launched on the whole length of the walls from Saint Anthony's Gate to the Patriarch's Tower by the Bay, but the main effort of the Moslems was against the Accursed Tower at the angle of the salient. The Sultan threw all his resources into the battle. His mangonels kept up an unceasing bombardment. The arrows of his archers fell almost in a solid mass into the city; and regiment after regiment rushed at the defences, led by white-turbaned emirs. The noise was appalling. The assailants shouted their battle-cries, and trumpets and cymbals and the drums of three hundred drummers on camel-back urged them on.

It was not long before the Mameluks forced their way into the Accursed Tower. The Syrian and Cypriot knights that were its garrison were pushed back westwards towards Saint Anthony's Gate. There the Templars and Hospitallers came to their assistance, fighting together as if there had never been two centuries of rivalry between them. Matthew of Clermont desperately tried to lead a counter-attack to recover the Tower, but though the two Grand Masters both followed him, they could make no impression. Along the eastern wall of the city John of Grailly and Otto of Grandson held their own for some hours; but after the fall of the Accursed Tower the enemy was able to pass along the crumbling walls and take possession of the Gate of Saint Nicholas. The whole salient was lost, and the Moslems were well established inside the city.

There was fierce fighting in the streets; but nothing now could be done to save Acre. William of Beaujeu, Grand Master of the Temple, was mortally wounded in the fruitless counter-attack against the Accursed Tower. His followers carried him to the Temple building where he died. Matthew of Clermont was with him, but returned to the battle and to his death. The Grand Master of the Hospital, John of Villiers, was wounded, but his men brought him down to the harbour and put him protesting on board a ship. The young King and his brother Amalric had already embarked. King Henry was later accused of cowardice in deserting the city; but there was nothing that he could have done, and it was his duty to his kingdom to avoid capture. On the eastern sector John of Grailly was wounded, but Otto of Grandson took control. He commandeered as many Venetian ships as he could find and placed John of Grailly and all soldiers that he could rescue on board, and himself was the last to join them. There was ghastly confusion on the quays. Soldiers and civilians, women and children amongst them, crowded into rowing boats, seeking to reach the galleys that lay off the shore. The aged Patriarch, Nicholas of Hanape, who had been slightly wounded, was placed by his faithful servants in a small skiff; but out of charity he allowed so many refugees to climb in with him that the boat sank with their weight and they were all drowned. There were some men who had the presence of mind to snatch hold of a boat and charge exorbitant fees from the desperate merchants and ladies on the quay. The Catalan adventurer, Roger Flor, who had fought bravely as a Templar during the siege, took command of a Templar galley and founded his great fortune on the blackmail that he extorted from the noblewomen of Acre.[1]

The ships were far too few to rescue the fugitives. Soon the Moslem soldiers penetrated right through the city, slaying everyone, old men, women and children alike. A few lucky citizens who stayed in their houses were taken alive and sold as slaves, but not many were spared. No one could tell the number of those that perished. The Orders and the great merchant houses later tried to draw up lists of the survivors; but the fate of most of their members was unknown. Subsequent travellers to the East spoke of seeing renegade Templars living squalidly in Cairo and of other Templars working as wood-cutters by the Dead Sea. Some prisoners were freed and returned to Europe after nine or ten years of captivity. The slaves who had been knights and their descendants were said to have been treated with some respect by their masters. Many women and children disappeared for ever into the harems

---

[1] This account is taken from *Gestes des Chiprois*, pp. 43–54; Sanudo, pp. 230–1; Amadi, pp. 220–5; *De Excidio*, cols. 760–82; Thaddeus, pp. 18–23; Ludolf of Suchem (*P.P.T.S.* pp. 54–61); al-Jazari, p. 5; Maqrisi, *Sultans*, II, i, pp. 125–6; Abu'l Feda, pp. 164–5; Abu'l Muhasin in Reinaud, *op. cit.* pp. 569–72. There is a picturesque account (unfortunately without references) in Schlumberger, *Byzance et Croisades*, pp. 207–79. Muntaner, *Cronica* (ed. Coroleu), p. 378, tells of Roger of Flor's conduct.

of Mameluk emirs. Owing to the plentiful supply the price of a girl dropped to a drachma apiece in the slave-market at Damascus. But the number of Christians that were slain was greater still.[1]

By the night of 8 May all Acre was in the Sultan's hands, except for the great building of the Templars jutting out into the sea at the south-west point of the city. The surviving Templars had taken refuge there, together with a number of citizens of both sexes. For several days its huge walls defied the enemy; and ships that had landed refugees in Cyprus came back to its aid. After nearly a week al-Ashraf offered the Marshal of the Order, Peter of Sevrey, to allow him to embark to Cyprus with all the people inside the fortress and with their possessions, if it were given up to him. Peter accepted the terms; and an emir and a hundred Mameluks were admitted into the fortress to supervise the arrangements, while the Sultan's flag was hoisted over the tower. But the Mameluks were out of hand and began to molest and seize hold of the Christian women and boys. Furious at this, the knights fell on the Moslems and slaughtered them, and pulled down the enemy flag, ready to resist to the death. When night fell, Peter of Sevrey sent the treasury of the Order with its Commander, Tibald Gaudin, and a few non-combatants, by boat to the castle at Sidon. Next day al-Ashraf, seeing the strength of the castle and the desperate courage of its garrison, offered the same honourable terms as before. Peter and a few companions went out under a safe-conduct to discuss the surrender. But as soon as they reached the Sultan's tent they were seized and bound and promptly beheaded. When the defenders on the wall saw what had happened, they closed the gate again and fought on. But they could not prevent the Moslem engineers from creeping up to the walls and digging a great mine beneath them. On 18 May the whole landward side of the building begun to crumble. Impatiently al-Ashraf threw two thousand Mameluks into the widening breach. Their

[1] *Gestes des Chiprois*, pp. 254–5; Maqrisi, *op. cit.* p. 126; letter of Sultan al-Ashruf to Hethoum of Armenia in Bartholomew Cotton, p. 221. See Röhricht, *Geschichte*, p. 1021 n. 3.

weight was too much for the sagging foundations. As they fought their way in, the whole edifice came crashing down, killing defenders and assailants alike in its vast ruin.[1]

As soon as Acre was in his power, the Sultan set about its systematic destruction. He was determined that it should never again be a spearhead for Christian aggression in Syria. The houses and bazaars were pillaged, then burned; the buildings of the Orders and the fortified towers and castles were dismantled; the city walls were left to disintegrate. When the German pilgrim, Ludolf of Suchem, passed by some forty years later, only a few wretched peasants lived amongst the ruins of the once splendid capital of Outremer. One or two churches still stood, not wholly destroyed. But the fine doorway of the Church of Saint Andrew had been taken to ornament the mosque built in Cairo to honour the victorious Sultan; and amidst the crumbling walls of the Church of Saint Dominic the tomb of the Dominican Jordan of Saxony was untouched, as the Moslems had peered in and found his body uncorrupted.[2]

The remaining Frankish cities soon shared the fate of Acre. On 19 May, when most of Acre was in his hands, al-Ashraf sent a large contingent of troops to Tyre. It was the strongest city of the coast, impregnable against an enemy that lacked command of the sea. In the past its walls had twice thwarted Saladin himself. A few months earlier the Princess Margaret, to whom it belonged, had handed it over to her nephew, the King's brother Amalric. But its garrison was small; and, as soon as the enemy approached Amalric's *bailli*, Adam of Cafran, lost his nerve and sailed away to Cyprus, abandoning the city without a struggle.[3] At Sidon the

[1] *Gestes des Chiprois*, pp. 255–6; Bartholomew Cotton, p. 432; Ludolf of Suchem, *loc. cit.*; Sanudo, p. 231. The story is also told by Bar-Hebraeus, p. 493 (dated 1292).

[2] Enlart, *Monuments des Croisés*, II, pp. 9–11; Etienne de Lusignan, *Histoire de Chypre*, fol. 90; Ludolf of Suchem (*P.P.T.S.* p. 61).

[3] *Gestes des Chiprois*, p. 254; Sanudo, *loc. cit.*; al-Jazari, p. 6; Abu'l Feda, p. 164; Maqrisi, *Sultans*, II, i, p. 126. Margaret was still Lady of Tyre in 1289 (*Gestes*, p. 237), though the *Gestes* (*ibid.*) talk of Amalric as Lord of Tyre in 1288. See Hill, *op. cit.* p. 182 n. 5.

2E

Templars determined to make a stand. Tibald Gaudin was there, with the treasure of the Order; and the surviving knights had elected him Grand Master, to succeed William of Beaujeu. They were left in quiet for a month. Then a huge Mameluk army came up under the emir Shujai. The knights were too few to hold the town; so they retired, with many of the leading citizens, to the Castle of the Sea, built on an island rock a hundred yards from the shore, and recently refortified. Tibald at once set sail for Cyprus, to raise troops for the castle's assistance. But once that he was there he did nothing, either from cowardice or despair. The Templars in the castle fought bravely, but when the Mameluk engineers began to build a causeway across the sea, they gave up hope and sailed away up the coast to Tortosa. On 14 July Shujai entered the castle and ordered its destruction.[1]

A week later Shujai appeared before Beirut. Its citizens had hoped that the treaty made between the Lady Eschiva and the Sultan would preserve them from attack. When the emir bade the leaders of the garrison to come and pay their respects to him, they therefore anxiously complied, only to find themselves made prisoner. Without its leaders the garrison could not contemplate defence. Its members took to their ships and fled, carrying with them the relics from the Cathedral. The Mameluks entered the city on 31 July. Its walls and the castle of the Ibelins were pulled down, and the Cathedral turned into a mosque.[2]

Soon afterwards the Sultan occupied Haifa without opposition on 30 July, and his men burned the monasteries on Mount Carmel and slew their monks. There still remained the two Templar castles at Tortosa and Athlit, but in neither was the garrison strong enough to face a siege. Tortosa was evacuated on 3 August and Athlit on the 14th. All that now was left to the Templars was the island fortress of Ruad, some two miles off the coast opposite

---

[1] *Gestes des Chiprois*, pp. 256–7; *Annales de Terre Sainte*, p. 460; al-Jazari, p. 7; Maqrisi, *Sultans*, II, i, p. 131; Abu'l Feda, *loc. cit.*

[2] *Gestes des Chiprois*, pp. 257–8; al-Jazari, *loc. cit.*; Maqrisi, *loc. cit.*; Abu'l Feda, *loc. cit.*

Tortosa. There they maintained their hold for twelve more years, only quitting the island in 1303, when the whole future of the Order began to be in doubt.[1]

For some months the Sultan's troops marched up and down the coast-lands, carefully destroying anything that might be of value to the Franks should they ever attempt another landing. Orchards were cut down, irrigation-systems put out of order. The only castles that were left standing were those that were back from the coast, like Mount Pilgrim at Tripoli, and Marqab on its high mountain. Along the sea there was desolation. The peasants of those once rich farms saw their steads destroyed and sought refuge in the mountains. Those of Frankish origin hastened to merge themselves with the natives; and the native Christians were treated little better than slaves. The old easy tolerance of Islam was gone. Embittered by the long religious wars, the victors had no mercy for the infidel.[2]

The lot of the Christians that escaped to Cyprus was not much better. For a generation they lived the miserable lives of unwanted refugees, for whom as the years passed sympathy wore thin. They only served to remind the Cypriots of the terrible disaster. And the Cypriots needed no reminder. For a century to come the great ladies of the island, when they went out of doors, wore cloaks of black that stretched from their heads to their feet. It was a token of mourning for the death of Outremer.[3]

---

[1] *Gestes des Chiprois*, p. 259; *Annales de Terre Sainte, loc. cit.*; al-Jazari, p. 8; Maqrisi, *Sultans*, II, i, p. 126; Abu'l Feda, *loc. cit.*
[2] See below, p. 474.
[3] Sanudo, p. 232; Cobham, *Excerpta Cypria*, pp. 17, 22.

BOOK V

EPILOGUE

CHAPTER I

THE LAST CRUSADES

'And they that understand among the people shall instruct many: yet they shall fall by the sword, and by flame, by captivity, and by spoil.'
DANIEL XI, 33

With the fall of Acre and the expulsion of the Franks from Syria the Crusading movement began to slip out of the sphere of practical politics. After Saladin's reconquests, a century before, the Christians still retained great fortresses on the mainland, Tyre, Tripoli and Antioch. An army of rescue had bases from which it could operate. Now the bases were gone. The little waterless island of Ruad was useless. Expeditions must be organized and provisioned from across the sea, from Cyprus. The only Christian dominion that remained was the kingdom of Armenia, in Cilicia. But the journey from Cilicia into Syria was difficult, and the Armenians could not all be trusted. Again, the loss of Jerusalem in 1187 had come as a terrible shock to Christendom, so sudden was the collapse of the kingdom. But everyone knew in 1291 that Outremer was crumbling. Its disappearance caused grief and indignation, but no surprise. Western Europe now had overriding problems and quarrels at home. There would be no glow of fervour that would drive its potentates eastward, as in the days of the Third Crusade. Still less could a great popular expedition like the First Crusade be launched. The peoples of the West were enjoying new comforts and prosperity. They would never respond now to the apocalyptic preaching of a Peter the Hermit with the simple, ignorant piety of their ancestors two centuries before. They were unconvinced by the promise of indulgences and shocked by the use of the Holy War for political aims. Nor was a great military expedition possible, with the great Empire of Byzantium reduced to a shadow. The end of Outremer was grievous news, but it provoked no violent reaction.

Only the Pope, Nicholas IV, sought to implement his sorrow by deeds; but there was no one to whom he could turn. The prestige of the Papacy had been crippled by the ill-success of the Sicilian war. Kings no longer troubled to carry out the Papal bidding. The Western Emperor, whose oecumenical power the Popes had broken, was fully occupied in Germany. If he emerged, it was only to take a wistful expedition into Italy. King Philip IV of France was able and active, but, having extricated his kingdom from the Sicilian war, he spent his energy in building up the royal authority. Edward of England had his hands full in Scotland. Moreover, England and France were moving into the state of intense rivalry that was soon to produce the Hundred Years War. The monarch with the strongest sea-power in the Mediterranean, James II of Aragon, along with his brother Frederick, claimant of Sicily, was at war with the Pope's client, Charles II of Naples; who was willing enough in theory to help in a Crusade, but had first to eject the Aragonese from Sicily. Further East the Byzantine Emperor was busy enough warding off the Turks on the one hand and the new Balkan monarchies of Bulgaria and Serbia on the other. Besides, the Angevins of Naples were now taking over the claims of the dispossessed Latin Emperors. Their patron, the Pope, could not therefore hope for much sympathy from the Greeks. The merchant-cities of Italy were too busy adjusting their policy to the changed circumstances to make any promises that might embarrass them. The Kings of Cyprus and Armenia were most intimately concerned with the problem; for their kingdoms were in the front line now, and one or other must serve as the base for any new Crusade. But they were desperately anxious not to provoke the Sultan. The King of Armenia had to contend with the Turks as well as with the Egyptians, and the King of Cyprus had to solve the problem of the refugees. Moreover, both royal houses, which were now closely interconnected by marriage, were soon troubled by family quarrels and civil war. The Ilkhan of

Persia remained a potential ally; but the Ilkhan Arghun had been cruelly disappointed by his failure to rouse the West to action before the fall of Acre. He would do no more. In 1295, soon after Arghun's death, the Ilkhan Ghazzan adopted Islam as the state religion of the Ilkhanate, and threw off his allegiance to the Great Khan in the East. Ghazzan was a good friend of the Christians, for he had been brought up by the Despina Khatun, the Ilkhan Abaga's gracious wife, whom all the East revered; and his conversion in no way lessened his hatred of the Egyptians and the Turks. But there were no more Mongol embassies to Rome and no more hope that Persia would become a Christian power. There was, it is true, a Papal envoy in Pekin, Brother John of Monte Corvino; but, though Brother John enjoyed the friendship of Kubilai, the Great Khan had no interest now in the affairs of the Near East.[1]

There remained the Military Orders. They had been founded to fight for Christendom in the Holy Land, and that was still their chief duty. After the fall of Acre the Teutonic Order abandoned the East for its Baltic possessions;[2] but the Templars and the Hospitallers set up their headquarters in Cyprus. There, unable to perform their proper task, they took to meddling in local politics. The Pope could probably count on them to provide help for any actual expedition; for their vast endowments all over Europe aroused jealousy that might have dangerous results unless they were proved to be justified. But the Temple and Hospital unaided could not undertake a Crusade.[3]

Pope Nicholas had failed to rouse the West after the fall of Tripoli. He was equally impotent after the greater disaster at

[1] Baluze, *Vitae Paparum Avenionensium* (ed. Mollat), III, p. 150; Atiya, *The Crusade in the Later Middle Ages*, pp. 34–6; Hill, *History of Cyprus*, II, pp. 193 ff.; Browne, *Literary History of Persia*, III, p. 40. For John of Monte Corvino, see Atiya, *op. cit.* pp. 248–52.

[2] The Teutonic headquarters were moved to Venice in 1291, and on to Marienburg in Prussia in 1309. For the subsequent history of the Order, see the chapter by Boswell in *Cambridge Medieval History*, vol. VII, pp. 248 ff.

[3] See below, pp. 434 ff.

Acre. His advisers gave him no help. Charles II of Naples supported the suggestion, first made some years previously, that to
end their rivalry the Military Orders should be amalgamated; but
he thought that military action in the East was impossible for the
moment. He advocated an economic blockade of Egypt and
Syria. It would be easy to maintain and very damaging to the
Sultan.[1] But that too was in fact impracticable. Neither the
Italian nor the Provençal and Aragonese merchant-cities would
ever co-operate. Their welfare depended on the Eastern trade,
much of which passed through the Sultan's dominions. Indeed,
were it to cease, they would no longer be able to maintain their
fleets, and the Moslems might well dominate the Mediterranean
Sea. It was unfortunate that the chief export with which the
Christians paid for Eastern goods consisted of armaments; but
would it have been worth while to deprive Europe of the benefits
of all this commercial activity? The Church might protest against
this nefarious exchange of goods. But business interests were now
stronger than the Church. Nicholas IV died in 1291 disappointed
in his endeavours.[2]

None of his successors achieved a better result. But, though the
soldiers for a Crusade were lacking, the feeling that Christendom
had been shamed produced a new wave of propaganda. The
propagandists were no longer itinerant preachers, as in the past,
but men of letters who wrote books and pamphlets to show the
need of a holy expedition, for whose conduct each author had his
own special scheme. In 1291 a Franciscan friar, Fidenzio of Padua,
whom the Pope had often used in the past for diplomatic missions
and who had travelled widely in the East, published a treatise,
called the *Liber de Recuperatione Terre Sancte*, which he dedicated
to Nicholas IV. It contains a learned history of the Holy Land,
together with a discussion of the type of army needed for its
recovery and of the alternative routes that this army might follow.
It was informative and well reasoned; but Fidenzio assumed that
an army would be available and considered that the commander

[1] Atiya, *op. cit.* pp. 35–6.   [2] *Ibid.* p. 45.

should make the ultimate choice of the route.[1] Next year, in 1292,
a certain Thaddeus of Naples published an account of the fall of
Acre. It is a vivid narrative, embroidered by lavish accusations
of cowardice against practically everyone who was there. Thaddeus's violent language was intentional. His object was to shame
the West into launching a Crusade; and he ended his book with
a great appeal to the Pope, to the Princes and to the Faithful to
rescue the Holy Land which is the Christians' heritage.[2]

Thaddeus's work certainly influenced the next propagandist,
a Genoese called Galvano of Levanti, a physician at the Papal
Court. His book, which he published about 1294 and dedicated to
King Philip IV of France, was a mixture of analogies taken from
the game of chess and mystical exhortations, and was devoid of
practical sense.[3] A far more important figure was the great
Spanish preacher, Raymond Lull, who was born in Majorca in
1232, and was stoned to death at Bougie in North Africa in 1315.
His fame is highest as a mystic, but he was at the same time a
practical politician. He knew Arabic well and he had travelled
widely in Moslem countries. In about 1295 he presented the Pope
with a memorandum on the action needed to combat Islam, and
in 1305 he published his *Liber de Fine* which elaborated his ideas
and offered a workable programme. Both the Moslems and the
schismatic and heretical Christian Churches must be won over as
far as possible by well-educated preachers, but at the same time
an armed expedition is necessary. Its leader should be a King, the
Rex Bellator, and all the Military Orders should be united under
his command into a new Order which should be the backbone of
the army. He suggests that the Crusade should expel the Moslems
from Spain, then cross into Africa and move along the coast to
Tunis, and so to Egypt. But later he also advocates a naval expedition, suggesting that Malta and Rhodes, with their excellent

---

[1] *Ibid.* pp. 36–43. Fidenzio's Liber (ed. by Golubovitch), is published in
Biblioteca Bio-Bibliografica della Terra Sancta, II, pp. 9 ff.
[2] Atiya, *op. cit.* pp. 31–4; *The Hystoria de Desolacione* is edited by Riant.
[3] Atiya, *op. cit.* pp. 71–2.

harbours should be captured and used as bases. Later still, he seems to prefer that the land expedition should take Constantinople from the Greeks and journey across Anatolia. He is full of concrete advice about the organization of the army and the fleet, and about the supply of food and war materials, as well as about the instruction of the preachers who must accompany the army. The book is prolix and at times contradicts itself, but it is the work of a man of remarkable intelligence and wide experience, though his attitude towards the Eastern Christians is unpleasantly intolerant.[1]

When Raymond Lull wrote it seemed that a Crusade was really in the offing. King Philip of France had announced his wish to launch an expedition, and both at the Papal Court and at Paris plans for its conduct were being drawn up and studied. Philip's true motive, which was to extract money from the Church by this admirable excuse, was not yet apparent. He had recently emerged triumphant from his quarrel with Pope Boniface VIII, who had found that the technique which had ruined the Hohenstaufen was useless against the new monarchies of the West. Pope Clement V, who was elected in 1305, was a Frenchman. He established himself at Avignon, on the border of the French King's dominions, and he showed constant deference to the King. He hastened to collect memoranda for his own and the King's guidance.[2]

The most interesting of these memoranda was destined only for Philip's eyes. A French lawyer, Peter Dubois, submitted to him a pamphlet of which half was to be issued to the princes of Europe, bidding them join the movement under the King of France, and making certain recommendations about the route to be followed and the means for financing the expedition. The Templars should be suppressed and their property annexed, and death-duties should be instituted for the clergy. He added a few general suggestions about the desirability of allowing priests to marry and of turning convents into girls' schools. The second half was private advice

---

[1] Atiya, *op. cit.* pp. 74–94, a full discussion of Lull's life and works in connection with the Crusade.   [2] *Ibid.* p. 48.

to the King telling him how to secure control of the Church by packing the Cardinals' bench, and urging him to set up an Eastern Empire under one of his sons.[1] Soon afterwards in 1310, Philip's chief diplomatic adviser, William Nogaret, sent the Pope a memoir on the Crusade. Its strategic suggestions were slight. Its main emphasis was on finance. The Church was to provide all the money; and the suppression of the Templars was the first item on the programme.[2] At the same time the Pope collected advice. The Armenian Prince Hethoum or Hayton of Corycus, who had retired to France and become the prior of a Praemonstratensian abbey near Poitiers, was asked to send in his views. His book, called *Flos Historiarum Terre Orientis*, was published in 1307 and at once achieved a wide sale. It contained a succinct summary of Levantine history, together with a well-informed discussion of the state of the Mameluk Empire. Hayton recommended a double expedition, to go by sea and be based on Cyprus and on Armenia. He recommended co-operation with the Armenians and a close alliance with the Mongols.[3] Similar views were expressed a little later by the Papal diplomat, William Adam, who travelled widely in the East and subsequently reached India. He added the suggestion that the Christians should maintain a fleet in the Indian Ocean, to cut off Egypt's Oriental trade. He also considered that Constantinople should be recaptured by the Latins.[4] William Durant, Bishop of Mende, sent in a treatise in 1312, recommending the sea-route and laying emphasis on the composition of the expedition, particularly with respect to its morals.[5] The old Genoese admiral, Benito Zaccaria, who had once been podestà of Tripoli, wrote down his views on the naval forces required.[6]

More practical suggestions were laid down by three potentates

[1] *Ibid.* pp. 48–52; Hill, *op. cit.* II, p. 239.

[2] Atiya, *op. cit.* pp. 53–5.

[3] Hayton's *Flos* is published in *Recueil des Historiens des Croisades, Documents Arméniens*, vol. II. See Atiya, *op. cit.* pp. 62–4.

[4] Atiya, *op. cit.* pp. 64–7. Adam's work is published as an appendix to Hayton's in the *Recueil*.   [5] Atiya, *op. cit.* pp. 67–71.

[6] *Ibid.* pp. 60–1. See Mas Latrie, *Documents*, II, p. 129.

who would have to play a leading part in any Crusade. In 1307 the Grand Masters of the Temple and the Hospital were both at Avignon; and Pope Clement asked them for their views. The former, James of Molay, at once sent in a report. He recommended a preliminary clearance of the seas by ten large galleys, to be followed by an army of at least twelve to fifteen thousand horsemen and forty to fifty thousand infantrymen. The Kings of the West should have no difficulty in raising these numbers, and the Italian republics must be induced to provide transport. He disapproved of a landing in Cilicia. The expedition should assemble in Cyprus and land on the Syrian coast.[1] Four years later, at the time of the Council of Vienne, Fulk of Villaret, Grand Master of the Hospital, wrote to King Philip to tell him of the preparations that his Order had made and could make for the Crusade.[2] At the same time King Henry II of Cyprus submitted his views to the Council. He desired an economic blockade of the Mameluk Empire. With good reason he distrusted the Italian republics and urged that the Crusade should not depend on them for its sea transport. He was in favour of an attack on Egypt itself, as the most vulnerable part of the Sultan's dominions.[3]

After all these memoranda and all this enthusiasm it was a surprise and a disappointment to everyone but King Philip that no Crusade was launched. Philip had achieved his object in finding an excuse for raising money from the Church; and he soon showed his true views by an attack on a great organization whose help would have been essential for a Crusade.[4]

The loss of Outremer left the Military Orders in a state of uncertainty. The Teutonic Knights solved their problem by concentrating all their energies in Baltic conquest.[5] But the Temple and the Hospital found themselves restricted and unappreciated in Cyprus. The Hospital, wiser than the Temple, began to look for

---

[1] Baluze, *op. cit.* II, pp. 145 ff.
[2] Delaville le Roulx, *France en Orient*, II, pp. 3–6.
[3] Mas Latrie, *Documents*, II, pp. 118–25; Atiya, *op. cit.* pp. 58–60.
[4] Atiya, *op. cit.* pp. 53, 73.   [5] See above, p. 288.

another home. In 1306 a Genoese pirate, Vignolo dei Vignoli, who had obtained a lease of the islands of Cos and Leros from the Byzantine Emperor Andronicus, came to Cyprus and suggested to the Grand Master of the Hospital, Fulk of Villaret, that he and the Hospital should conquer the whole Dodecanesian archipelago and divide it between them; he would retain one-third himself. While Fulk sailed to Europe to obtain the Pope's confirmation of the scheme, a flotilla of Hospitallers, helped by some Genoese galleys, landed on Rhodes and slowly began the reduction of the island. The Greek garrison fought well. It was only by treachery that the great castle of Philermo fell to the invaders in November 1306, and the city of Rhodes itself held out for two more years. At last, in the summer of 1308, a galley sent from Constantinople with reinforcements for the garrison was driven by storms to Cyprus and was seized at Famagusta by a Cypriot knight, Philip le Jaune, who took it with its passengers to the besiegers. Its commander, who was a Rhodian, agreed, to save his life, to negotiate the surrender of the city; which opened its gates to the Order on 15 August. The Hospital at once set up its headquarters in the island, and made the city, with its fine harbour, the strongest fortress in the Levant. The conquest, achieved at the expense of Christian Greeks, was hailed in the West as a great Crusading triumph; and indeed it gave to the Hospital new vigour and the means to carry on its appointed task. But the wretched Rhodians had to wait for more than six centuries before they recovered their liberty.[1]

The Temple was less enterprising and less fortunate. It had always roused more enmity than the Hospital. It was wealthier. It had long been the chief banker and money-lender in the East, successful at a profession which does not inspire affection. Its policy had always been notoriously selfish and irresponsible. Gallantly though its knights had always fought in times of war, their financial activities had brought them into close contact

[1] *Gestes des Chiprois*, pp. 319–23; Delaville le Roulx, *Hospitaliers en Terre Sainte*, pp. 273–9; Amadi, pp. 254–9.

with the Moslems. Many of them had Moslem friends and took an interest in Moslem religion and learning. There were rumours that behind its castle walls the Order studied a strange esoteric philosophy and indulged in ceremonies that were tainted with heresy. There were said to be initiation rites that were both blasphemous and indecent; and there were whispers of orgies for the practice of unnatural vices. It would be unwise to dismiss these rumours as the unfounded invention of enemies. There was probably just enough substance in them to suggest the line along which the Order could be most convincingly attacked.[1]

When James of Molay went to France in 1306 to discuss with Pope Clement the projected Crusade, he heard that charges were being made there against his Order, and he demanded a public inquiry. The Pope hesitated. He realized that King Philip was determined to suppress the Order, and he did not dare to offend him. In October 1307, Philip suddenly arrested all the members of the Order that were in France and had them tried for heresy on charges laid by two disreputable knights who had been expelled from it. The accused gave their evidence under torture; and though a few firmly denied everything, the majority were glad to make any admission that was required of them. Next spring, at Philip's request, the Pope ordered every ruler in whose dominions the Templars had possessions to arrest them and start similar trials. After some hesitation the various Kings of Europe consented, except for the Portuguese Denys, who would have no truck with the sorry business. Everywhere else Templar property was sequestered, and the knights were haled before the Courts. Torture was not always used; but there was a fixed interrogatory. The

[1] There is a reasoned discussion of the Templars' ill-repute in Martin, *The Trial of the Templars*, pp. 18–24, 46–50. The scandal of their unjust trial has inclined historians to regard them as being entirely blameless, but it is clear that suspicions about their habits were not entirely unfounded. The relevant documents and sources are published by Lizerand, *Le Dossier de l'Affaire des Templiers*. Their most recent historian, Mlle Melvin, is certainly too indulgent towards them (*La Vie des Templiers*, pp. 246 ff.).

ccused knew what they were expected to confess, and many of
them confessed.[1]

It was particularly important for the Pope that the Cypriot
government should co-operate; for the headquarters of the Order
were in the island. But the ruler there was now Henry II's brother
Amalric, who had temporarily ousted the King from power with
the help of the Templars. The Prior Hayton arrived from Avignon
in May 1308 with a letter from the Pope ordering the immediate
arrest of the knights, as they had been found to be unbelievers.
Amalric delayed in carrying out the order; and the knights, under
their Marshal, Aymé of Oselier, had time to prepare to defend
themselves. But after a brief recourse to arms they surrendered on
1 June. Their treasure, apart from a large portion that they hid so
well that it was never recovered, was taken from Limassol to
Amalric's house in Nicosia, and the knights themselves were
placed under guard, first at Khirokhitia and Yourmasoyia, and
later at Lefkara. There they remained for three years. In May 1310,
after King Henry II had been restored to power, the Cypriot
Templars were at last brought to trial at the urgent insistence of
the Pope. In France many of their brotherhood had already been
burned at the stake, and all over Europe the members of the Order
were imprisoned or destitute. King Henry had no love for the
knights, who had betrayed his cause a few years before. But he
gave them a fair trial. Seventy-six of them were accused. All
denied the charges. Distinguished witnesses swore to their innocence, and one of the few hostile witnesses declared that he had only
come to suspect them after receiving the Pope's account of their
crimes. They were entirely acquitted. When news of their acquittal
reached Avignon, the Pope angrily wrote to King Henry to order
a second trial; and he sent a personal delegate, Dominic of
Palestrina, to see that his justice was done. The result of the retrial,
which took place in 1311, is unrecorded. Clement had ordered
that, if there was danger of another acquittal, Dominic was to
secure the help of the Priors of the Dominicans and the Franciscans

[1] Martin, *op. cit.* pp. 28–46; Melvin, *op. cit.* pp. 249–57.

2F

in seeing that torture was applied; and the Papal Legate in the East Peter, Bishop of Rodez, was dispatched to Cyprus to supplement Dominic's efforts. It seems that the King therefore reserved his verdict and kept the accused in prison. They were still there in 1313, when Peter of Rodez read out before all the bishops and higher clergy of the island the Pope's decree of 12 March 1312, suppressing the whole Order and handing over all its wealth and possessions to the Hospitallers, after the civil authorities had recouped themselves for the cost of the various trials. The Kings throughout Europe found that these costs had been remarkably high. The Hospital received little apart from real property. The officers of the Temple in Cyprus were never released. But they were more fortunate than their Grand Master, who after years of imprisonment and torture and many confessions and recantations, was burned to death in Paris in March 1314.[1]

The abolition of the Templars and the migration of the Hospitallers to Rhodes left the Cypriot kingdom as the only Christian government acutely interested in the Holy Land. The King was nominally King of Jerusalem; and for many generations to come the Kings, after their coronation with the Cypriot crown at Nicosia, received the crown of Jerusalem at Famagusta, the city that lay nearest to their lost dominion. The Syrian coast was, moreover, of strategic importance to Cyprus. An aggressive enemy there would endanger her very existence. Fortunately the Sultan was too afraid of a new Crusade himself to make use of the Syrian ports. He preferred that they should lie derelict. Nevertheless Cyprus was in constant danger from Egypt. Believing that to attack was the best defence, King Henry in 1292 had sent fifteen galleys, aided by ten from the Pope, to raid Alexandria. It was a futile effort, and merely determined al-Ashraf to conquer Cyprus. 'Cyprus, Cyprus, Cyprus', he cried, as he ordered a hundred galleys to be built. But he had other grander schemes. The Mongols must first be routed and Baghdad occupied. His ambition alarmed his emirs. They murdered him on 13 December

[1] Hill, *op. cit.* II, pp. 232–6, 270–4.

PLATE XV

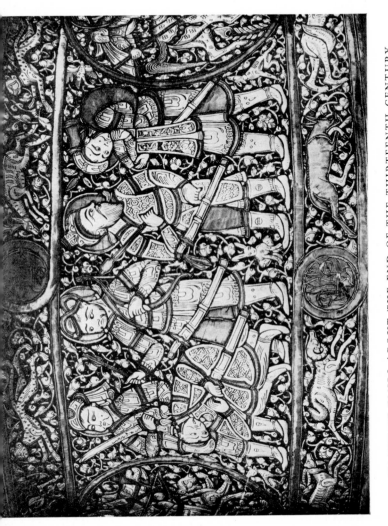

MAMELUK EMIRS ABOUT THE END OF THE THIRTEENTH CENTURY

Metal work from the so-called Font of St Louis. The second figure from the right is probably the Emir Salar, Viceroy of Egypt in 1299. The emirs' costumes were strictly ordained by Sultan Qalawun.

1293. It was a poor reward for the determined young prince who had completed Saladin's work and driven the last remnant of the Franks from Syria.[1]

Al-Ashraf was right to remember the Mongols. In 1299, during the much interrupted reign of the Mameluk Sultan an-Nasir Mohammed, the Mongol ruler Ghazzan, who had changed his title from Ilkhan to Sultan, invaded Syria and routed the Mameluk defence force at Salamia, near Homs, on 23 December. In January 1300, Damascus surrendered to him and admitted his suzerainty. He returned to Persia next month, announcing that he would soon return to conquer Egypt. Moslem though he was, Ghazzan would have welcomed Christian allies. Raymond Lull hastened to Syria on the news of the invasion, but was too late to meet Ghazzan there. He returned to Cyprus to ask the King to help him go on an evangelical mission to the Moslem rulers. King Henry, who did not agree that the friendship of the infidels was best won by pointing out their errors to them, ignored his request. A more diplomatic approach would have been useful, but none was made; and the opportunity ended when the Mongol army was defeated in 1303 at Marj as-Saffar. Five years later, in 1308, Ghazzan again entered Syria and now penetrated as far as Jerusalem itself. It was rumoured that he would have willingly handed over the Holy City to the Christians had any Christian state offered him its alliance. But, though at the time the Pope and King Philip of France were loudly advertising their projected Crusade, no overtures were made to the Mongols from the West, while Cyprus was reduced to impotence by the struggles between King Henry and his brother. In any case Ghazzan, as a good Moslem convert, might have found it difficult to implement such a promise.[2] On

[1] *Gestes des Chiprois*, pp. 61–2; Thaddeus, p. 43; Sanudo, p. 283; Wiet, *L'Egypte Arabe*, p. 461.
[2] *Gestes des Chiprois*, pp. 296–306; Hill, *op. cit.* II, pp. 212–15; Atiya, *op. cit.* pp. 90–1. Felix Fabri, writing nearly two centuries later, gives a legendary account of the good Tartar Emperor 'Casanus', who, he says, was a Christian and offered Jerusalem back to the Christians (trans. Stewart, *P.P.T.S.* vol. x, pp. 372–8).

his death in 1316, the chances of a Mongol alliance with the Christians faded out. His nephew and successor, Abu Said, veered round towards a reconciliation with Egypt. He was the last great Mongol ruler of Persia. After he died in 1335 the former Ilkhanate began to disintegrate.[1]

Despite its apparent isolation, the Kingdom of Cyprus was not yet in immediate danger. The Sultan, even when he was no longer preoccupied with the Mongols, had insufficient sea-power to risk an expedition against the island. He had no wish to offend the Italian republics, for he too derived great benefits from their trade. He captured Ruad from the Templars in 1302, but, unless Cyprus became the base for a new Crusade, he preferred to let it alone. The Cypriot government for its part tried, as far as personal and dynastic idiosyncrasies allowed, to keep on close terms with the Armenian Kings of Cilicia, and with the Kings of Aragon and Sicily, whose fleets commanded respect.[2]

After all the Crusading talk that Philip of France had inspired died down, there was a lull. But about the year 1330 it was revived by Philip VI. His intentions were far more sincere than those of his uncle; and they were encouraged by the Pope, John XXII. Once again memoranda were submitted to the Papal and royal courts. The Queen of France's physician, Guy of Vigevano, wrote a brief account of the armaments required.[3] A longer and more detailed programme was sent to the King by a certain Burcard, an ecclesiastic who had worked in Cilicia to secure the adhesion of the Armenian Church to Rome. Burcard's suggestions were plentiful, but not helpful; for he showed far more animosity against the schismatic and heretic Christians than against the Moslems, and he considered that the conquest of Orthodox Serbia and of Byzantium was an essential part of any Crusade. But his schemes were not to be put to the test. Before any Crusade could

[1] Browne, *op. cit.* III, pp. 51–61.
[2] *Gestes des Chiprois*, p. 309, dating the capture of Ruad 1303; Sanudo, p. 242, dating it 1302. See Hill, *op. cit.* II, pp. 215–16.
[3] Atiya, *op. cit.* p. 96.

be launched the King of France was involved in the outbreak of the Hundred Years War with England.[1]

A more practical programme, which did not require any great military expedition, had meanwhile been published by the historian Marino Sanudo. He was a member of the ducal house of Naxos and had Greek blood in his veins, and he was an acute observer and a pioneer statistician. His *Secreta Fidelium Crucis*, which appeared about 1321, contained a history of the Crusades, somewhat coloured by propagandist aims, but was mainly concerned with a detailed discussion of the economic position of the Levant. He saw that Egypt could best be weakened by means of an economic blockade, but he realized that the Eastern trade could not suddenly be suppressed. Alternative routes and sources of supply must be found. His analysis was profound, and his suggestions were far-sighted and comprehensive. Unfortunately they could only be carried out if all the European powers worked together; and that could never now be achieved.[2]

In fact, there was only one more effort made to rescue the Holy Land from the infidel. In 1359 Peter I ascended the throne of Cyprus. He was the first monarch since Saint Louis of France to have a burning and overwhelming desire to fight the Holy War. As a young man he had founded a new Order of Chivalry, the Knights of the Sword, whose one avowed object was to recover Jerusalem, and he had braved his father King Hugh IV's displeasure by attempting to travel to the West to win recruits for his Crusade. His first wars as King were against the Turks in Anatolia, where he had obtained a foothold by the acquisition of the fortress of Corycus from the Armenians. In 1362 he set out on a general tour of Christendom to further his main object. After visiting Rhodes where he secured promises of help from the Hospital, he sailed to Venice where he stayed over the New Year of 1363. The Venetians were officially sympathetic to his plans.

[1] *Ibid.* pp. 96–113.
[2] *Ibid.* pp. 114–27; Hill, *op. cit.* III, p. 1144. The only edition of Sanudo is in Bongars, *Gesta Dei per Francos*, vol. II.

After calling at Milan, he went to Genoa. There he was busy settling differences between his kingdom and the republic and winning a vague support from the Genoese. He arrived at Avignon on 29 March 1363, a few months after the accession of Pope Urban V. His first task was to defend his right to his throne against his nephew Hugh, Prince of Galilee, son of his late elder brother. Hugh was compensated with an annual pension of fifty thousand besants. While he was at Avignon King John II of France visited the city and promised him his warm co-operation. The two Kings took the Cross together in April, together with many of the French and Cypriot nobility. At the same time the Pope preached the Holy War and appointed Cardinal Talleyrand as its Legate. Peter then made a circuitous tour through Flanders, Brabant and the Rhineland. In August he went to Paris to see King John once more. They decided that the Crusade should be launched the following March. From Paris Peter went to Rouen and Caen, and sailed across to England. He spent about a month in London, where a great tournament was held in his honour at Smithfield. King Edward III presented him with a handsome ship, the *Catherine*, and with money to cover all his recent expenses. Unfortunately he was robbed by highwaymen on his way back to the coast. He returned to Paris for Christmas, then went south to Aquitaine, to interview the Black Prince at Bordeaux. While he was there he learned to his sorrow of the deaths, first of Cardinal Talleyrand, in January 1364, then of King John in May. He went to John's funeral at Saint-Denis and to the coronation of his successor, Charles V, at Rheims, then moved into Germany. The knights and burghers of Esslingen and Erfurt offered to join his Crusade, but the Margrave of Franconia and Rudolph II, Duke of Saxony, though they received him with honour, both said that their decision must depend on the Emperor. He therefore went with Rudolph to Prague, where the Emperor Charles was in residence. Charles professed himself to be enthusiastic and invited Peter to accompany him to Cracow, to a conference that he was about to hold with the Kings of Hungary and Poland. It was there agreed that a circular should be sent to all the princes of the Empire, inviting their collaboration in the Holy War. After visiting Vienna, where Rudolph IV, Duke of Austria, promised further help, Peter returned to Venice in November 1364. As his troops had recently helped the Venetians to suppress a revolt in Crete, he was welcomed there with the highest honours. He remained there till the end of June 1365. While he was there he signed a treaty with Genoa which settled all outstanding differences.[1]

Meanwhile Pope Urban wrote indefatigably to the princes of Europe to urge them to join the expedition; and his efforts were energetically seconded by the new Papal Legate to the East, Peter of Salignac de Thomas, nominal Patriarch of Constantinople, a man of fierce integrity, equally opposed to schismatics, heretics and infidels, but of a devotion that was respected even by those that he persecuted. Working with him was his pupil, Philip of Mézières, a close friend of King Peter, who had appointed him Chancellor of Cyprus. All their united activity did not produce the number of recruits that King Peter had expected and been promised. No Germans came forward, and none of the greater nobles of France or England, or the neighbouring lands, apart from Aymé, Count of Geneva, William Roger, Viscount of Turenne, and the Earl of Hereford. But there were many lesser knights, coming even from so far afield as Scotland; and already before King Peter left Venice, a large and formidable army had gathered there. The Venetian contribution was particularly useful; but the Genoese held back.[2]

It was decided that the Crusade should assemble at Rhodes in August 1365, but its further destination was kept secret. The risk that some Venetian trader would inform the Moslems was too dangerous. King Peter arrived at Rhodes early in the month, and on the 25th the whole Cypriot fleet sailed into the harbour, a hundred and eight vessels in all, galleys, transports, merchant

---

[1] For Peter's journey see Atiya, *op. cit.* pp. 330–7; Hill, *op. cit.* II, pp. 324–7.
[2] Atiya, *op. cit.* pp. 337–41.

ships and light skiffs. With the great galleys of the Venetians and those provided by the Hospital, the armada numbered a hundred and sixty-five ships. They carried a full complement of men, with ample horses, provisions and arms. Not since the Third Crusade had a proportionate expedition set out for the Holy War; and, though there was disappointment that no great potentates from the West were present, there was the counter-advantage that King Peter was the unquestioned leader. In October he wrote to his Queen, Eleanor of Aragon, that everything was ready. At the same time he issued an order warning all his subjects in Syria to return home and forbidding them to trade there. He wished it to be thought that Syria was his objective.[1]

On 4 October the Patriarch Peter preached a stirring sermon to the assembled sailors from the royal galley, and they all cried out: 'Vivat, vivat Petrus, Jerusalem et Cypri Rex, contra Saracenos infideles.' That evening the fleet set sail. When all the ships were at sea it was announced that the destination was Alexandria in Egypt.

Once a decision to attack the Sultan was made, the choice of Alexandria as an objective was intelligent. It would be impracticable to attempt to invade Syria or Palestine without a base on the coast, and the ports there, with the exception of Tripoli, had been deliberately ruined by the Egyptians. But past experience showed that when the ruler of Egypt lost Damietta he had been ready to cede Jerusalem for its recovery. Alexandria was a richer prize than Damietta. Its conquerors could strike a still more profitable bargain. It would also be an excellent base for a further advance; for it was certainly amply provisioned, and the canals made it easy to defend from the land. It was moreover the port for almost all the Sultan's oversea trade. Its loss would subject his dominions to a drastic form of economic blockade. It was also unlikely that he would expect an attack on a city where Christian merchants had such large interests. The moment, too, was well chosen. The reigning Sultan, Sha'ban, was a boy of eleven. Power

[1] Atiya, *op. cit.* pp. 341–4; Hill, *op. cit.* II, pp. 329–31.

was in the hands of the emir Yalbogha, who was disliked by his fellow-emirs and by the people. The governor of Alexandria, Khalil ibn Arram, was away on a pilgrimage to Mecca. His deputy, Janghara, was a junior officer, and had been left with a hopelessly inadequate garrison. On the other hand the walls of Alexandria were notoriously strong. Even if its two harbours and the Pharos peninsula that lay between them were captured, there were still great fortifications along the harbour-front.

The armada arrived off Alexandria during the evening of 9 October. The citizens at first thought that it was a great merchant fleet and prepared to go out to bargain. It was only when next morning the ships entered the western harbour, instead of the eastern which alone was permitted to Christian ships, that their intentions became apparent. The acting-governor, Janghara, hastened to concentrate his men on the foreshore to prevent a landing; but despite the gallantry of some Moghrabi soldiers, the Christian knights forced their way ashore. While native merchants streamed out of the city through the landward gates, Janghara retired behind the walls and collected his small garrison to hold the sector opposite to the landing. King Peter intended to pause in his attack. He wished to land all his men and horses at leisure on to the Pharos peninsula. But when he took counsel of his commanders he found that many of them disapproved of the choice of Alexandria as an objective. They were too few, they said, either to hold so large a fortress or to advance from there to Cairo. They wished to sail away elsewhere, but would stay if the city were at once taken by storm before the Sultan could send a relieving force. Peter was obliged to comply with their wishes; and the assault began at once. It was launched against the west wall, as Janghara had expected; but when they were held there the assailants moved to the section opposite to the eastern harbour. Within the walls access between the two sections ran through the great Customs House; and an officious customs-officer, fearing robberies, had barricaded the doors. Janghara could not move his men in time to face the new attack. Believing that the city was lost they began to desert their posts and flee through the streets to the southern gates and safety. By midday on Friday the 10th the Crusaders were well established within the city. Fighting continued in the streets. During the Friday night there was a fierce Moslem counter-attack through one of the southern gates, which the Christians in their excitement had burned down. It was beaten off; and by the Saturday afternoon all Alexandria was in the Crusaders' hands.

The victory was celebrated with unparalleled savagery. Two and a half centuries of Holy Warfare had taught the Crusaders nothing of humanity . The massacres were only equalled by those of Jerusalem in 1099 and Constantinople in 1204. The Moslems had not been so ferocious at Antioch or at Acre. Alexandria's wealth had been phenomenal; and the victors were maddened at the sight of so much booty. They spared no one. The native Christians and the Jews suffered as much as the Moslems; and even the European merchants settled in the city saw their factories and storehouses ruthlessly looted. Mosques and tombs were raided and their ornaments stolen or destroyed; churches too were sacked, though a gallant crippled Coptic lady managed to save some of the treasures of her sect at the sacrifice of her private fortune. Houses were entered, and householders who did not immediately hand over all their possessions were slaughtered with their families. Some five thousand prisoners, Christians and Jews as well as Moslems, were taken to be sold as slaves. A long line of horses, asses and camels carried the loot to the ships in the harbour and there having performed their task were killed. The whole city stank with the odour of human and animal corpses.

King Peter vainly tried to restore order. He had hoped to hold the city, and, as the Crusaders had burned its gates, he demolished the bridge by which the road to Cairo crossed the great canal. But the Crusaders now only wished to take their plunder home as quickly as possible. An army was coming up from Cairo, and they were unwilling to risk a battle. Even the King's own brother told him that the city was untenable, while the Viscount of

Turenne, with most of the English and French knights, roundly said that they would not remain any longer. Peter and the Legate protested in vain. By Thursday the 16th only a few Cypriot troops remained in the city. The rest of the expedition had returned to the ships, ready to depart. As the Egyptians had already reached the suburbs, Peter himself embarked on his galley and gave the order for evacuation. So heavily laden were the ships that it was necessary to jettison many of the larger pieces of loot. For months to come Egyptian divers salvaged precious objects from the shallow waters off Aboukir.[1]

Peter and the Legate had hoped that, when their gains were safely stored in Cyprus, the Crusaders would start out again with him on a new expedition. But no sooner had they reached Famagusta than they all began to make arrangements to journey home to the West. The Legate prepared to follow them, to win other recruits in their place, but he fell mortally ill before he could leave the island. King Peter held a service of thanksgiving on his return to Nicosia, but his heart was sore. His report to the Pope told of his triumph but also of his bitter disappointment.[2]

The news of the sack of Alexandria had a mixed reception in the West. It was first hailed as a military triumph and a humiliation for Islam. The Pope was delighted, but saw that Peter must have immediate reinforcements to take the place of the deserters. King Charles of France promised to send an army. The most celebrated of his knights, Bertrand du Guesclin, took the Cross; and Amadeus, Count of Savoy, known in romance as the Green Knight, who was preparing a journey to the East, decided to sail for Cyprus. But then the Venetians announced that Peter had made peace with the Sultan. King Charles countermanded his army. Du Guesclin went to fight in Spain and Amadeus to

[1] The Alexandrian expedition is described at length by William of Machaut, in a very prosaic epic (ed. Mas Latrie, esp. pp. 61 ff.). Machaut seems never to have visited the East, but his information, except over the birth and the death of King Peter, is reliable. For a full account of the expedition, see Atiya, *op. cit.* pp. 345–69, also Hill, *op. cit.* II, pp. 331–4.

[2] Atiya, *op. cit.* p. 369.

Constantinople.[1] The Venetians, unlike the Pope, had not been pleased by the outcome of the Crusade. They had hoped to use it to strengthen their commercial hold on the Levant. Instead, their ample property in Alexandria had been destroyed, and their whole Egyptian trade had been interrupted. The sack of Alexandria came near to ruining them as a commercial power, to the delight of the Genoese, whose restraint had been rewarded. Soon the whole of the West experienced the effects of the Crusade. The price of spices and silks and other Eastern goods to which the public was now accustomed rose steeply as the supplies ran out and were not renewed.[2]

Peter had in fact opened negotiations with Egypt, but both sides were too bitter to wish for peace. While the emir Yalbogha, hampered by his unpopularity in Egypt, played for time until he could build a fleet for the invasion of Cyprus, Peter made extravagant demands for the cession of the Holy Land and followed them up with raids on the Syrian coast. But his Crusading mania began to alarm his subjects, who feared lest the resources of the island would be exhausted in a hopeless cause. When a knight with whom Peter had quarrelled planned his murder in 1369, not even his own brothers lifted a finger to save him. The year after his death a treaty was signed with the Sultan. Prisoners were exchanged; and Cyprus and Egypt settled down to an uneasy peace.[3]

The holocaust at Alexandria marks the end of those Crusades whose direct object was the recovery of the Holy Land. Even had all the Crusaders been as devoted as King Peter, it is doubtful whether the expedition could ever have been to the benefit of Christendom. When it took place, Egypt had been at peace with the Franks for over half a century. The Mameluks had begun to lose their earlier fanaticism. Their Christian subjects were receiving kinder treatment. Pilgrims were freely allowed to the Holy Places. Commerce was flourishing between East and West. Now

[1] Atiya, *op. cit.* p. 370; Hill, *op. cit.* II, pp. 335–6.
[2] Machaut, pp. 115–16; Heyd, *Histoire du Commerce du Levant*, II, pp. 52–5.
[3] Atiya, *op. cit.* pp. 371–6; Hill, *op. cit.* II, pp. 345–67; Heyd, *op. cit.* pp. 55–7.

all the bitterness of the Moslems was revived. The native Christians, guiltless though they were, underwent a new period of persecution. Churches were destroyed. Even the Holy Sepulchre was closed for three years. The interruption to commerce did serious damage all round to a world that had not yet recovered from the ravages of the Black Death. The kingdom of Cyprus, whose existence the Mameluks had been ready to tolerate, became an enemy to be deleted. Egypt waited sixty years for her revenge. But the ghastly devastation of the island in 1426 was a direct punishment for the sack of Alexandria.[1]

The only other Christian kingdom in the Levant met with an earlier doom. The Armenians of Cilicia had taken no part in King Peter's Crusade; but their royal house was now Frankish and many of the nobility had close connections with Cyprus. Their Church had admitted the sway of Rome. Throughout the fourteenth century the Egyptians had pressed on them, suspecting them rightly as friends of the Franks and the Mongols and jealous of the wealth that passed through their country by the trade-route that reached the sea at Ayas. The collapse of the Mongol Ilkhanate deprived them of their chief support. Most of their territory was annexed in 1337 by the Turks. In 1375, while the Cypriots were engrossed in a bitter war with Genoa, Moslem invaders, Mameluks and Turks in alliance, completed the subjection of the country. The last Armenian King, Leo VI, fled to the West and died as an exile in Paris; and Armenian independence was ended.[2]

Indeed, a Crusade such as King Peter planned was now an anachronism. Christendom could not afford such luxuries. It had to face too serious a threat further to the north. The planners of the First Crusade had seen clearly that the rescue of the Holy Land depended on the maintenance of Christian power in Anatolia.

---

[1] Atiya, *op. cit.* pp. 377–8.
[2] See Tournebize, *Histoire Politique et Religieuse de l'Arménie*, pp. 644 ff., esp. pp. 654–5, 715–30. The obscure history of the end of the Armenian Kingdom depends chiefly on the chronicle of the Franciscan, John Dardel (published in *R.H.C.*, *Documents Arméniens*, vol. II).

But since Pope Urban II's death no Western statesman had had the wisdom to realize that the maintenance of Anatolia depended upon Byzantium. The Crusading movements of the twelfth century had embarrassed the Byzantine Emperor. They had added to the problems that Byzantium had to face and had never allowed the Emperors the leisure to attend to the subjection of the Turkish invaders. The task may well have been impossible, for the Turkish technique of invasion, with its destruction of agriculture and of communications, made reconquest a difficult task, while the varied ambitions of Emperors such as Manuel and Andronicus Comnenus resulted in a further dispersion of energy. The disaster at Manzikert in 1071 allowed the Turks into Anatolia. The disaster at Myriocephalum in 1176 ensured that they would remain there. But it was the Fourth Crusade and its irreparable destruction of the Byzantine Imperial system that gave them the opportunity to go further. During the thirteenth century Christendom had its last opportunity for dealing with the Turks. Their power in Anatolia had hitherto been dependent on the Seldjuk Sultanate of Konya. The Mongol invasions, which began in 1242, undermined and ultimately destroyed the Seldjuk state. The Byzantine Emperors, living in exile at Nicaea, were aware of their chance, but their European preoccupations and their yearning to recover their Imperial capital against the hostility of the Latin West hampered their efforts, while the Latins lacked the foresight and experience to understand the situation. Once the Byzantines were re-established in Constantinople the occasion was gone. The Emperors of the House of Palaeologus had to contend with young and vigorous kingdoms in the Balkans, with the demands of the Italian republics and with the risk of a Latin reconquest, which was very real till Charles of Anjou was crippled by the Sicilian Vespers. By the end of the thirteenth century it was too late. The Seldjuks were gone, but in their place there were several active and ambitious emirates, strengthened by the immigration of Turkish tribes subject to the Mongols. It would need a long and concerted effort to dislodge them. Chief amongst the emirs was the Grand Karaman, whose dominions stretched along the interior of the country from Philadelphia to the Anti-Taurus. There were other emirs established at Attalia, at Aydin (Tralles) and at Manissa (Magnesia). The north coast was still held by Byzantium and its sister-Empire of Trebizond. But south of Trebizond the country was occupied by the Turcomans; and in the north-west a lively new emirate was arising, under an enterprising prince called Osman.[1]

The Latins were by now growing aware of the importance of Anatolia, though they saw it less as a base for aggression against themselves than as an area in which they needed bases for the control of the Mediterranean. The Hospitallers' occupation of Rhodes was largely the result of chance, but it illustrated a new orientation. The Italian republics had long been interested in the islands of the Aegean. It was natural that their concern, and the concern of the whole Latin world, should spread to the mainland opposite. When the emir Omar of Aydin, who was in possession of the excellent harbour of Smyrna, built a fleet in order to indulge in piracy in Aegean waters, both the Venetians and the knights at Rhodes took action. In 1344 a squadron, to which the Venetians and their dependants contributed about twenty ships, the knights six and the Pope and the King of Cyprus four apiece, set out against Smyrna. The Latin Patriarch of Constantinople, Henry of Asti, was in command. The emir of Aydin was defeated in a sea-battle on Ascension Day, off the entrance to the Gulf. The Christian allies, at the Pope's request, refused an invitation from the Genoese ex-lord of Chios, Martin Zaccaria, who had joined the expedition, to restore him his island which the Byzantines had recaptured, but sailed up to Smyrna. After a short struggle the city fell into their hands on 24 October, though the citadel was untaken. The easy victory was mainly due to the emir Omar's unpreparedness and his jealous fear of his fellow-emirs. He came with his army too late to save the city. But the victors were lured

[1] See Gibbons, *The Foundation of the Ottoman Empire*, pp. 15–34; Köprülü, *Les Origines de l'Empire Ottoman*, pp. 34–79; Wittek, *The Rise of the Ottoman Empire*, pp. 33–51.

to try to invade the interior. They were heavily defeated a few miles from the city, and Henry of Asti and Martin Zaccaria were killed. After the Turks had failed to retake Smyrna, a treaty signed in 1350 entrusted it to the Hospitallers, though the citadel remained in Turkish hands. The knights held Smyrna till 1402, when it was stormed by Timur.[1]

While the fate of Smyrna was still in the balance, a French nobleman, Humbert II, Dauphin of Vienne, announced his desire to go on a Crusade to the East. He was a weak, vain man, but genuinely pious and without personal ambition. After some negotiations with the Pope, it was decided that he should go to supplement the Christian effort at Smyrna. He set out from Marseilles with a company of knights and priests in May 1345, and was joined on his eastward journey by troops from northern Italy. After various ineffectual adventures he reached Smyrna in 1346, and his army defeated the Turks in a battle outside the walls. He did not remain there for long. By the summer of 1347 he was back in France. The whole expedition had been singularly futile. Its importance is that the Church was now ready to regard an expedition to Anatolia as a Crusade.[2]

In 1361 Peter of Cyprus, who had recently acquired Corycus from the Armenians, obtained the help of the Hospitallers in an attack on the Turkish port of Attalia. After a brief struggle it fell into his hands on 24 August. The neighbouring emirs of Alaya, Monovgat and Tekke hastened to offer him allegiance, thinking that his friendship might be useful against their chief enemy the Grand Karaman. They soon withdrew their submission and made various attempts to recover Attalia; which, however, remained in Cypriot hands for sixty years.[3]

But meanwhile the attention of Europe had been forcibly turned further north. The first decades of the fourteenth century saw an extraordinary growth in the power of the Turkish emirate founded by Osman, son of Ertoghrul, and called Osmanli or

---

[1] Atiya, *op. cit.* pp. 290–300.   [2] *Ibid.* pp. 300–18.
[3] *Ibid.* pp. 323–30; Hill, *op. cit.* II, pp. 318–24.

Ottoman after him. In 1300 Osman was a petty chieftain with lands in southern Bithynia. By the time of his death in 1326 he was lord of Brusa and most of the territory between Adramyttium, Dorylaeum and the Marmora. His expansion was due partly to his skilful and supple diplomacy towards his fellow-emirs, and still more to the weakness of Byzantium. In 1302 the Emperor Andronicus II had rashly hired the service of a Catalan company, led by Roger Flor, the ex-Templar who had made his fortune by his disreputable behaviour during the sack of Acre. Roger fought successfully against the Turks but still more actively against his imperial master. He was murdered in 1306, but the Catalan company remained in imperial territory, in hostility to the Empire, till 1315. During its wars it brought a Turkish regiment, formerly employed by the Emperor in Asia, across into Europe.[1] Soon after the Catalan company was gone, there was civil war in the Empire between Andronicus II and his grandson Andronicus III, which only ended on the former's death in 1328. Both sides used the Turks as mercenaries. Meanwhile Osman's son, Orhan, continued his father's work. He established a vague hegemony over the emirs to the south of his lands, and he continued with the conquest of Bithynia. Nicaea was captured in 1329 and Nicomedia in 1337.[2] In the Empire civil war broke out again in 1341, between John V and his father-in-law, John Cantacuzenus, while the growing power of Stephen Dushan of Serbia distracted the attention of all the Balkan peoples.[3]

In 1354 Orhan, who had taken the title of Sultan, sent troops across the Dardanelles to take the town of Gallipoli. Two years later he moved several thousand of his people across the Straits and settled them in Thrace. Next year he was able to advance inland and capture the great fortress of Adrianople, which became his second capital. By the time of his death in 1359 almost all

---

[1] See Vasiliev, *History of the Byzantine Empire*, pp. 605–8. The story of the Catalan company is vividly told by the contemporary chronicler, Muntaner.

[2] Vasiliev, *op. cit.* pp. 608–9; Gibbons, *op. cit.* pp. 54–70.

[3] Vasiliev, *op. cit.* pp. 609–13.

29

Thrace was in his hands, and Constantinople was isolated from its European possessions. His son and successor, Murad I, was well able to carry on his predecessors' work. His first action was to found the corps of Janissaries from forcibly converted Christian slave-children sent to him as tribute.[1]

The expansion of the Ottoman Turks was not unnoticed in the West. There seemed to be little danger as yet for the European continent; for the great Serbian Empire seemed well able to check any advance. But Constantinople itself was obviously threatened, and with it the commercial interests of the Italians. The Greeks, however, were schismatic. The policy of the Western Church was to insist on their submission to Rome before there could be any question of sending them help. This form of moral blackmail was bound to fail. Not only religious conviction but national pride and the memory of past outrages made it impossible for the Greek people to agree to Latin ecclesiastical domination, even if their rulers were ready to comply.[2]

In 1365 Amadeus VI, Count of Savoy, took the Cross. Pope Urban VI had been busily preaching the Crusade on behalf of Peter of Cyprus; and Amadeus had every intention of proceeding to the Holy Land. But he was first cousin to the Byzantine Emperor John V, and he wished to help him. The Pope gave him permission to begin his campaign by fighting against the Turks, on condition that he secured the submission of the Greek Church. The Venetians did their best to check his Crusade, fearing that it might interfere with their commercial policy. They particularly did not wish him to join Peter of Cyprus and were relieved when their rumours of Peter's treaty with Egypt determined him to concentrate on Byzantium. He assembled a distinguished collection of knights, but from the outset he had difficulties over finance. The expedition reached the Dardanelles in August 1366, and at once laid siege to Gallipoli, which fell on 23 August. But instead of landing in Thrace and attempting to clear the province of the Turks, Amadeus sailed on to Constantinople. There he found that

[1] Gibbons, *op. cit.* pp. 100–3, 110–21.   [2] Vasiliev, *op. cit.* pp. 670–2.

the Emperor had been treacherously captured by the Bulgarian King, Shishman III; and all his energy was therefore devoted to the rescue of his cousin, which was only achieved by an attack on Shishman's port of Varna. When John was rescued Amadeus found that he had spent all his own money, as well as all the money that he had extorted locally and borrowed from the Empress. He was obliged to return home. But first he made the Emperor promise to bring his Church under Rome; and when the Patriarch of Constantinople, Philotheus, came with a Greek knight to his galley to tell him that the Greek people would depose the Emperor if he agreed, he kidnapped them and took them with him to Italy. He returned home at the end of 1367. His Crusade had been almost valueless. The Turks recaptured Gallipoli immediately on his departure.[1]

Under Murad the Ottoman Turks rapidly increased their power. He reduced the western Anatolian emirs to subjection, and advanced in Europe. After a victory over the Serbs on the Maritsa in 1371, Bulgaria became a vassal-state and was soon entirely annexed. In 1389 a decisive battle was fought between the Serbs and the Turks at Kossovo. Murad was assassinated by a Serb just before the battle, but his troops, which vastly outnumbered their opponents, were completely triumphant. The Turks were now masters of the Balkans.[2]

Though the Crusading energy of the West was diverted in 1390 by a disastrous expedition led by Louis II, Duke of Bourbon, against al-Mahdiya, near Tunis,[3] it was clear that for the safety of Christian Europe the Ottoman Turks must be checked. When in 1390 the Sultan Bayezit annexed the Bulgarian town of Vidin on the Danube, whose prince had acknowledged the suzerainty of Hungary, the Hungarian King, Sigismund of Luxemburg, the brother of the Emperor Wenzel, appealed to all his fellow-monarchs for help. Both the Roman Pope, Boniface IX, and the Avignonese

[1] Atiya, *op. cit.* pp. 379–97.
[2] Vasiliev, *op. cit.* p. 624; Gibbons, *op. cit.* pp. 174–8.
[3] Louis's expedition is fully described in Atiya, *op. cit.* pp. 398–434.

Pope, Benedict XIII, issued Bulls recommending a Crusade, while the aged propagandist, Philip of Mézières, wrote an open letter to Richard II of England to bid him co-operate with Charles VI of France for the coming Crusade. Sigismund's German connections enabled him to find support in Germany. The princes of Wallachia and Transylvania were sufficiently terrified of the Turkish advance to join him, much as they hated the Hungarians. In the West the Dukes of Burgundy, Orleans and Lancaster all announced their desire to help. In March 1395 a Hungarian embassy, headed by the Archbishop of Gran, Nicholas of Kanizsay, arrived at Venice to secure the promise of transport from the Doge. The ambassadors then proceeded to Lyons, where they were welcomed lavishly by the Duke of Burgundy, Philip the Bold, who promised them his enthusiastic support. After visiting Dijon, to pay their respects to the Duchess, Margaret of Flanders, they went to Bordeaux to meet the King of England's uncle, John of Lancaster, who undertook to arrange for an English contingent. From Bordeaux they journeyed to Paris. The French King, Charles VI, was suffering from a bout of madness, but his regents offered to encourage the French nobility to join the Crusade. A great international army for the rescue of Christendom began to assemble. To finance it, the Burgundian Duke raised special taxes that brought in the huge sum of 700,000 gold francs. Individual French nobles added their own contributions. Guy VI, Count of La Trémouille, provided 24,000 francs. The French and Burgundian lords agreed to accept the leadership of the Duke of Burgundy's eldest son, John, Count of Nevers, a lively young man of twenty-four.[1]

While the Hungarian ambassadors hurried back to Buda to tell King Sigismund of their success and to advise him to continue his preparations, the Duke of Burgundy issued careful ordinances for the organization and behaviour of the Franco-Burgundian troops. They were summoned to assemble at Dijon on 20 April 1396. John of Nevers was to be in command, but in view of his youth an advisory council was formed of Philip, son of the Duke of Bar,

---

[1] Atiya, *Crusade of Nicopolis*, pp. 1–34, a fully referenced account.

Guy of La Trémouille, and his brother William, the Admiral John of Vienne, and Odard, lord of Chasseron. At the end of the month an army of ten thousand men set out to march through Germany to Buda. On its way it was joined by six thousand Germans, headed by the Count Palatine Rupert, son of Rupert III of Wittelsbach, and Eberhard, Count of Katznellenbogen. Close behind there followed a thousand English fighting men, under King Richard's half-brother, John Holland, Earl of Huntingdon.[1]

The Western armies reached Buda about the end of July. There they found King Sigismund waiting with a force of some sixty thousand men. His vassal Mircea, voyevod of Wallachia, had joined him with another ten thousand men; and about thirteen thousand adventurers came in from Poland, Bohemia, Italy and Spain. The united army of close on a hundred thousand soldiers was the largest that had ever yet taken the field against the infidel. Meanwhile a fleet manned by the knights of the Hospital, under the Grand Master, Philibert of Naillac, and by Venetians and Genoese, penetrated into the Black Sea and lay off the mouth of the Danube.

The Ottoman Sultan on his side had not been idle. When news reached him that the Crusade had assembled in Hungary, Bayczit was laying siege to Constantinople. He at once summoned all his available troops and marched northward to the Danube. His army was estimated as numbering rather more than a hundred thousand.

Three centuries of experience had taught the Western knights nothing. When the plan of campaign was discussed at Buda King Sigismund advised a defensive strategy. He knew the strength of the enemy. It would be better, he thought, to lure the Turks into Hungary and attack them there from prepared positions. Like the Byzantine Emperors during the earlier Crusades, Sigismund believed that the safety of Christendom depended on the preservation of his own kingdom; but, like the earlier Crusaders, his allies envisaged a great offensive. The Turks would be overwhelmed and the Christian armies would advance triumphantly

[1] *Ibid.* pp. 41–8, 67–8, 184 nn.

457

through Anatolia to Syria and the Holy City itself. So vehement were they that Sigismund gave way. Early in August the united host set out down the left bank of the Danube, as far as Orsova, by the Iron Gates, and there it crossed into the Sultan's dominions.

Eight days were spent in ferrying the army across the river. It then marched along the south bank to the town of Vidin. The lord of Vidin was a Bulgarian prince, John-Srachimir; but he was vassal to the Sultan, who kept a small Turkish garrison there. On the arrival of the Christians John-Srachimir joined them and opened the gates. The Turks were massacred. The next town down the river was Rahova, a strong fortress with a moat and a double enceinte, and a large Turkish garrison. The more vehement French knights, led by Philip of Artois, Count of Eu, and John le Meingre, better known as Marshal Boucicaut, at once rushed to the attack and would have been annihilated had not Sigismund brought up his Hungarians. The garrison could not hold out for long against the whole Christian army. It was stormed, and the whole population, many of whom were Bulgarian Christians, were put to the sword, except for a thousand wealthier folk who were held for ransom.

From Rahova the army moved on to Nicopolis. This was the chief Turkish stronghold on the Danube, situated where the main road from central Bulgaria came to the river. It was built beside the river on a hill whose steep slopes were crowned with two lines of formidable walls. The Crusaders had come without machines for siege-warfare. The Westerners had not realized the need for them; and Sigismund had prepared only for defensive action. When the ladders hastily erected by the French and the mines dug by Hungarian engineers proved quite inadequate, the army sat down to starve the city into surrender. In this they were aided by the arrival of the Hospitaller fleet, which sailed up the Danube and anchored off the walls on 10 September. But Nicopolis was well stocked with provisions; and the Turkish Governor, Dogan Bey, who had learned of the fate of his compatriots at Vidin and Rahova, had no intention of surrendering.

The delay was fatal to the morale of the Christian army. The Western knights amused themselves in gambling and drinking and all forms of debauchery. The few soldiers who dared to suggest that the Turks were formidable foes had their ears cut off, by order of Marshal Boucicaut, as a punishment for defeatism. There were quarrels between the various contingents, while Sigismund's Transylvanian vassals and Wallachian allies began to talk of desertion.

When the Crusade had passed a fortnight before Nicopolis, news came that the Turks were approaching. The Sultan's army had moved swiftly up from Thrace. It was lightly armed; its cavalry was far more mobile than the Frankish; its archers were superbly trained; and it had the profound advantage of perfect discipline and obedience to the sole command of the Sultan, who was himself a man of exceptional ability. He had sent some troops ahead, which were defeated in one of the Balkan passes by a French contingent led by the Lord of Coucy; but the jealousy of Marshal Boucicaut, who accused Coucy of trying to steal from John of Nevers the honours of victory, prevented any further attempts to stem the Turkish advance. Meanwhile the knights decided to kill the captives taken at Rahova.

On Monday, 25 September 1396, the vanguard of the Turkish army came into sight, and camped in the hills some three miles from the Christians. Next morning before sunrise Sigismund visited all his fellow-commanders and begged them to remain on the defensive. Though he told them frankly that he could not trust his Transylvanians and the Wallachians, only Coucy and John of Vienne supported him. The other leaders were determined to force a battle at once. Sigismund weakly gave way. He drew up his own army in three divisions, with his own Hungarian troops in the centre, the Wallachians on the left and the Transylvanians on the right. The vanguard was composed of all the Westerners, under John of Nevers.

When morning broke, all that could be seen of the Turkish army was a division of light irregular cavalry, just over the slope of the hill. Behind it, protected by a line of stakes, was the Turkish infantry, with the regiment of archers. The main body of *sipahi* cavalry, commanded by the Sultan in person, lay hidden by the crest of the hill. A division of Serbian cavalry, under the Prince Stephen Lazarović, a loyal vassal of the Sultan's, was on his left.

The battle, like the preceding strategy, showed that the Crusaders had learned nothing in all the centuries. The Western knights in the van did not wait to tell Sigismund of their plans. In high, confident enthusiasm they charged up the hill, scattering the light Turkish horsemen before them. While the Turks regrouped behind their own infantry, the knights found themselves held up by the stakes. At once they dismounted and continued the charge on foot, pulling out the stakes as they advanced. Such was their impetus that the Turkish infantry also was scattered. Some of the Turks were able to retire behind the regrouped cavalry, but many more were slain or driven down into the plain. But when the Crusaders, triumphant but exhausted, hastened on and reached the hill-top they found themselves face to face with the Sultan's *sipahis* and the Serbs. The attack of these fresh troops took them by surprise. On foot, tired and thirsty, and weighed down by their heavy armour, they were soon flung into disorder, and their victory was turned into a rout. Few of the knights survived the slaughter. Amongst those that perished were William of La Trémouille and his son, Philip, John of Cadzaud, Admiral of Flanders, and the Grand Prior of the Teutonic Knights. John of Vienne, Grand Admiral of France, fell clutching the great banner of Notre Dame entrusted to his care. John of Nevers only was spared because his attendants cried out who he was and persuaded him to surrender. With him were taken the Counts of Eu and La Marche, Guy of La Trémouille, Enguerrand of Coucy and Marshal Boucicaut.

When the knights had dismounted, their horses rushed riderless back to the camp. The Wallachian and Transylvanian contingents at once decided that the battle was lost and hastened to retire, seizing all the boats that they could find, in order to cross the river.

But Sigismund ordered his troops to advance to the rescue of the Westerners. They slew many of the disordered Turkish infantry as they moved up the hill, but when they approached the battlefield they found that they were too late. The Sultan's cavalry charged down on them and drove them back with heavy loss right to the banks of the river.

When his army was scattered, Sigismund himself was persuaded to abandon the fight. He took refuge on one of the Venetian ships in the river, which carried him to Constantinople and on home through the Aegean and the Adriatic. He feared to journey by land, as he suspected treachery from the Wallachians. His soldiers, together with the few survivors of the Western Crusaders, made their way to their own countries as best they could, harassed by hostile natives and wild beasts and the rigours of an early winter. The Count Palatine reached his father's castle in rags and died a few days later. Few of his fellow-refugees were more fortunate.[1]

Bayezit had won a great victory; but his losses had been very heavy. In his rage, remembering also the massacres committed by the Crusaders, he ordered his prisoners, to the number of three thousand, to be killed in cold blood, only sparing the few noblemen for whom a high ransom could be charged. A French knight, James of Helly, who spoke Turkish, was made to identify them and then was allowed to travel to the West to arrange for the money to be raised. It was not till the following June that a Western embassy reached the Sultan at Brusa and handed over to him the vast sums that he demanded. Many sympathizers throughout Christendom sent contributions, but the greater part was paid by King Sigismund and by the Duke of Burgundy, who provided more than a million francs. The released captives reached their homes towards the end of 1397.[2]

The Crusade of Nicopolis was the largest and the last of the great international Crusades. The pattern of its sorry history followed with melancholy accuracy that of the great disastrous Crusades of the past, with the difference that the battlefield was

[1] Atiya, *Crusade of Nicopolis*, pp. 50–99.   [2] *Ibid.* pp. 102–11.

now in Europe and not in Asia. The faults and follies had been the same. The same enthusiasm had been dissipated in quarrels, jealousy and impatience. All that the West learned from this final failure was that the Holy War was practicable no more.

There would be no more Crusades. But the infidel remained threatening the heart of Christendom. He had reached the Danube and the shores of the Adriatic Sea. Constantinople was Christian still, but isolated, only spared because the Sultan had not yet artillery strong enough to batter its massive walls, nor sufficient ships to interrupt its communications by sea. The Knights Hospitallers at Rhodes and the Italian lords of the Aegean archipelago found themselves on a frontier, and Cyprus was a distant outpost. The King of Hungary, the voyevods of Wallachia and Moldavia and the chieftains of Albania sought help to defend their borders. The Italian republics were kept busy calculating what policy would best preserve their commercial interests. The Pope was deeply conscious of the threat to Christendom. But the powers of the West were no longer interested. Their last experience had been too bitter; and the enthusiasm that prompted it could not be revived after such a disaster. And even the Pope himself continually intrigued in Hungary to replace Sigismund by Ladislas of Naples, regardless of the harm that civil war would do to the defences of central Europe.[1] The French King, who found himself from 1396 to 1409 suzerain of Genoa, was sufficiently worried about the fate of the Genoese colony at Pera, opposite Constantinople, to send Marshal Boucicaut with twelve hundred men to the Bosphorus in 1399. His presence prevented a half-hearted Turkish attempt on the Imperial city; but as no one was ready to pay him or his men, he soon withdrew.[2] The Byzantine Emperor, Manuel II, then journeyed hopefully to the West to seek for help. The Italians were shocked to see how poor the heir of the Caesars had become; the Duke of Milan gave him splendid gifts that his

---

[1] Atiya, *Crusade in the Later Middle Ages*, pp. 463–4; Hefele-Leclercq, *Histoire des Conciles*, VI, 2, pp. 1253–4.
[2] Atiya, *op. cit.* pp. 465–6; Vasiliev, *op. cit.* pp. 632–3.

state might be more suited to his rank. He was magnificently
received at Paris and at London. But no material help was offered.
The Papacy was uninterested, for Manuel was too honest to
promise the submission of his Church to Rome, knowing that his
people would not endure it. But in 1402 he hurried back to his
capital cheered by news that seemed to portend the decline of the
Ottoman Empire.[1]

Timur the Lame was born a petty prince of Turco-Mongol
descent near Samarkand in 1336. By 1369 he was sovereign of all
the lands that had belonged to the Jagatai branch of the Mongols.
Thenceforward he extended his dominions by ruthless warfare,
slowly at first, then with increasing momentum. From 1381 to
1386 he overran the lands of the Mongol Ilkhanate in Persia and
in 1386 conquered Tabriz and Tiflis. For the next four years he
was busy on his northern frontier. In 1392 he captured Baghdad.
During the next years he campaigned in Russia against the
Mongols of the Golden Horde, penetrating as far as Moscow, and
in 1395 he appeared in eastern Anatolia, where Erzinjan and Sivas
fell to him. In 1398 he conquered northern India, in a brilliant
campaign made more efficacious by ghastly massacres. In 1400 he
turned westward again and swept into Syria, defeating the Mameluk armies sent against him first at Aleppo, then at Damascus, and
occupying and sacking all the great cities of the province. In 1401
he punished a revolt in Baghdad by the total destruction of the
city, which was only just recovering from the effect of Hulagu's
conquest a century and a half before. In 1402 he returned to
Anatolia, determined to conquer the Ottoman Sultan, who was the
only potentate left in Islam that he had not humiliated. The decisive
battle took place at Ankara on 20 July. Bayezit was utterly defeated
and taken prisoner, and died in captivity a few months later. Meanwhile the Ottoman cities of Anatolia fell to the conqueror, who in
December 1402, drove the knights of the Hospital out of Smyrna.[2]

[1] Vasiliev, *op. cit.* pp. 631–4.
[2] For Timur's career, see Bouvat, *L'Empire Mongol*, 2me *phase*, *passim*, esp.
pp. 58–63.

The Emperor Manuel had hoped that the disaster to Bayezit might end the Ottoman menace; but he was not strong enough to take action without support. The Italian republics were cautious. The Genoese hastened to make a treaty with Timur to preserve their Asiatic trade but, fearing for their Balkan trade and uncertain of the future, they helped to preserve Ottoman power by ferrying the remnants of Bayezit's army across to Europe. The Venetians held aloof.[1] Their caution was justified. Timur's invasion had in fact prevented an immediate attack on Constantinople by the Sultan, and it preserved Byzantium for another half-century. Had all Europe at once intervened it might have ended the Ottoman Empire. But the Turks were too well established racially in Anatolia and politically in the Balkans to be easily dislodged; nor had Timur the political genius of Jenghiz Khan. On his death in 1405 his empire began at once to disintegrate. The Mameluks quickly recovered Syria. In Azerbaijan the dynasty of the Black Sheep Turcomans arose and established a dominion from eastern Anatolia to Baghdad. There were nationalist stirrings in Persia where soon the great Safawi dynasty appeared. In Transoxiana Timur's descendants lasted on for nearly a century; but it was only in India that they founded an enduring empire, as the Great Moghuls of Delhi.[2]

In Anatolia the only ultimate effect of Timur's invasion was to introduce a new influx of Turks and Turcomans and thus eventually strengthen the roots of Ottoman power. When Timur died the sons of Bayezit took over their father's inheritance. For six years they fought between themselves. The civil wars offered the Christian powers another chance of checking the further growth of Ottoman power, but it was not taken. The Byzantine Emperor won back by his diplomacy a few coastal cities, and the Knights of Rhodes were allowed to build a castle on the mainland opposite their island, at Bodrun, the ancient Halicarnassus. But nothing else was gained. When in 1413 Mohammed I became sole Sultan

[1] Heyd, *op. cit.* ii, pp. 65–7.
[2] Bouvat, *op. cit.* pp. 84 ff.

the Ottoman Empire was intact. Mohammed was a peaceful ruler who avoided aggressive wars but firmly reorganized his dominions. On his death in 1421 the Ottomans were stronger than before.[1]

Mohammed's successor, Murad II, began his reign with an attempt on Constantinople. But he still lacked heavy artillery and ships; and after the Greeks had bravely defended their capital, without outside help, from June to August 1422, he abandoned the siege and concentrated his attention on conquests in the Greek peninsula, in Asia and across the Danube.[2] In 1439 the Emperor John VIII, Manuel's successor, agreed in desperation at the Council of Florence to submit his Church to Rome. His people repudiated the union, and he received little for his pains.[3] In 1440 Pope Eugenius IV preached a new Crusade. Four years later an Albanian chieftain, Skanderbeg, declared war on the Turks and was joined by his suzerain King George of Serbia. The Pope himself and the King of Aragon promised to send ten galleys each to the East. The Hungarian army, under Sigismund's bastard, John Corvinus, surnamed Hunyadi, Voyevod of Transylvania for King Vladislav, prepared to make an incursion across the Danube. But after a few skirmishes the allies lost heart and agreed to a ten years' truce, which was signed at Szegedin in June 1444.[4] Murad then prepared to lead his army away to deal with enemies in Anatolia; whereupon the Papal Legate with the allied army, Cardinal Julian Cesarini, persuaded its leaders that an oath sworn to an infidel was invalid, and urged them to advance. The Orthodox King of Serbia rejected such casuistry and would not allow Skanderbeg to stay with the army. John Hunyadi protested against it, but remained in command. He led the allied army, of some twenty thousand men, to Varna, where they arrived early in November 1444. But Murad, warned of their violation of the truce, hastened to meet them with about three times their numbers. The battle was fought

[1] Hammer, *Histoire de l'Empire Ottoman* (trans. Helbert), II, pp. 120 ff.
[2] *Ibid.* II, pp. 159 ff.   [3] Vasiliev, *op. cit.* pp. 672–4.
[4] Hammer, *op. cit.* II, pp. 288–302.

on 10 November. The Christians resisted gallantly; and at the crisis the Sultan, who had the violated treaty borne into battle with his standard, was heard to cry: 'Christ, if Thou art God as Thy followers say, punish them for their perfidy.' His prayer and his numbers prevailed. The Christian allies were almost annihilated. King Vladislav, who was with his troops, was killed, together with the perfidious Cardinal. Hunyadi himself escaped with a tiny remnant of his army.[1]

Skanderbeg's gallant efforts saved Albanian independence for another twenty years; and John Hunyadi, despite a disastrous defeat in a three days' battle on the ominous field of Kossovo in 1448, kept the Sultan from crossing the Danube as long as he lived.[2] But by the time of his death in 1456 the Turks had achieved the ambition that had dominated Islam since the days of the Prophet. In 1451 Murad II was succeeded by his son, Mohammed II, a youth of twenty-one, of boundless energy, enterprise and ability. He made it his first object to conquer Constantinople. This is not the place to tell of the splendid, tragic story of the last days of Byzantium. The Greeks, divided against their rulers who had sold their Church to Rome, rallied with superb courage to face their last agony. The West sent help that was hopelessly inadequate for all its bravery. The Sultan's vast resources, his careful preparations and his indomitable will were destined to carry him to triumph. Nor was his triumph one only of prestige. Byzantium had been a long time in dying, but its death guaranteed that the Turks would remain in Europe. It was to give them the mastery of the Eastern seas. It sounded the knell of the empires of Genoa and Venice, of the kingdom of Cyprus and of the Hospital at Rhodes; and it left the Sultan free to drive his armies to the gates of Vienna.[3]

All over Europe the fall of Constantinople was recognized as

---

[1] See Halecki, *The Crusade of Varna*, passim.

[2] Hammer, *op. cit.* II, pp. 322–7.

[3] The best history of the fall of Constantinople is still Pears, *The Destruction of the Greek Empire*, pp. 237 ff. See also Vasiliev, *op. cit.* pp. 647–55.

marking the end of an era. The news was not unexpected, but it came as a bitter cause for self-reproach. Yet, except for the princes whose frontiers were immediately threatened, no one cared any longer to take action. Only the Cardinal Nuncio in Germany, the great humanist Aeneas Sylvius, tried to rouse the West to its belated duty. But his speeches to the German Diets bore no result, and his letters to the Pope told of his disillusion. In 1458 he himself became Pope, as Pius II. Throughout his pontificate he laboured to recreate such a Crusade as his great predecessors had sent forth. In 1463 his project seemed near to fruition. A timely discovery of alum mines in the Papal states provided him with unexpected revenues and threatened to break the Turkish monopoly of alum. The new Doge of Venice seemed to favour war. The King of Hungary, at peace at last with the Emperor, was eager for a Christian alliance. John the Good, Duke of Burgundy, showed a welcome interest. The Bull *Ezechielis*, issued in October, mirrored the Papal optimism. But as the months passed, the enthusiasm faded. Only the Hungarians, who were anyhow faced with a Turkish war, offered him material support. The Venetians hesitated. None of the Italian cities was ready to risk the loss of trade that a rupture with the Sultan would bring. John of Burgundy wrote that the plots of the King of France made it impossible for him to leave his lands. Valiantly the Pope determined that he would finance and lead the Crusade himself. On his orders his agents assembled a fleet of galleys at Ancona; and on 18 July 1464, though he was weary and in failing health, he solemnly took the Cross at a ceremony at Saint Peter's.

A few days later he set out for the port of embarkation. His attendants saw that he was a dying man; so they hid the truth from him that not one of the princes of Europe had followed his example and that no armies were marching behind him to embark in his galleys for the East. Instead, as he came near to Ancona, they drew the curtains of his litter across so that he should not see out. For the roads were covered with the crews from his fleet, who had deserted their ships and were hurrying homeward. He reached

Ancona only to die there, on 14 August. He was mercifully spared the knowledge of the utter collapse of his Crusade.[1]

Nearly four centuries before, Pope Urban II by his preaching had sent men in their thousands to risk their lives in the Holy War. Now all that a Pope who took the Cross himself could raise were a few mercenaries who abandoned the cause before ever the campaign was begun. The Crusading spirit was dead.

[1] For Pius II see Atiya, *op. cit.* pp. 227–30; Hefele-Leclercq, *Histoire des Conciles*, VII, 2, pp. 1291–352.

CHAPTER II

THE SUMMING-UP

'He that increaseth knowledge increaseth sorrow.' ECCLESIASTES I, 18

The Crusades were launched to save Eastern Christendom from the Moslems. When they ended the whole of Eastern Christendom was under Moslem rule. When Pope Urban preached his great sermon at Clermont the Turks seemed about to threaten the Bosphorus. When Pope Pius II preached the last Crusade the Turks were crossing the Danube. Of the last fruits of the movement, Rhodes fell to the Turks in 1523, and Cyprus, ruined by its wars with Egypt and Genoa and annexed at last by Venice, passed to them in 1570. All that was left to the conquerors from the West was a handful of Greek islands that Venice continued precariously to hold. The Turkish advance was checked not by any concerted effort of Christendom but by the action of the states most nearly concerned, Venice and the Hapsburg Empire, with France, the old protagonist in the Holy War, persistently supporting the infidel. The Ottoman Empire began to decline through its own failure to maintain an efficient government for its great possessions, till it could no longer oppose the ambition of its neighbours nor crush the nationalist spirit of its Christian subjects, preserved by those Churches whose independence the Crusaders had tried so hard to destroy.

Seen in the perspective of history the whole Crusading movement was a vast fiasco. The almost miraculous success of the First Crusade set up Frankish states in Outremer; and a century later, when all seemed lost, the gallant effort of the Third Crusade preserved them for another hundred years. But the tenuous kingdom of Jerusalem and its sister principalities were a puny outcome from so much energy and enthusiasm. For three centuries there was

2H

hardly a potentate in Europe who did not at some time vow with fervour to go on the Holy War. There was not a country that failed to send soldiers to fight for Christendom in the East. Jerusalem was in the mind of every man and woman. Yet the efforts to hold or to recapture the Holy City were peculiarly capricious and inept. Nor did these efforts have the effect on the general history of the Western Europeans that might have been expected from them. The era of the Crusades is one of the most important in the history of Western civilization. When it began, western Europe was only just emerging from the long period of barbarian invasions that we call the Dark Ages. When it ended, that great burgeoning that we call the Renaissance had just begun. But we cannot assign any direct part in this development to the Crusaders themselves. The Crusades had nothing to do with the new security in the West, which enabled merchants and scholars to travel as they pleased. There was already access to the stored-up learning of the Moslem world through Spain; students, such as Gerbert of Aurillac, had already visited the Spanish centres of education. Throughout the Crusading period itself, it was Sicily rather than the lands of Outremer that provided a meeting-place for Arab, Greek and Western culture. Intellectually, Outremer added next to nothing.[1] It was possible for a man of the calibre of Saint Louis to spend several years there without the slightest effect on his cultural outlook. If the Emperor Frederick II took an interest in Oriental civilization, that was due to his upbringing in Sicily. Nor did Outremer contribute to the progress of Western art, except in the realm of military architecture and, perhaps, in the introduction of the pointed arch. In the art of warfare, apart from castle-building, the West showed again and again that it learned nothing from the Crusades. The same mistakes were made by every expedition from the First Crusade to the Crusade of Nicopolis. The circumstances of warfare in the East differed so greatly from those in Western Europe that it was only the knights resident in Outremer who troubled to remember past experience.

[1] For the intellectual life of Outremer, see below, Appendix II.

It is possible that the general standard of living in the West was raised by the desire of returning soldiers and pilgrims to copy the comforts of Outremer in their homelands. But the commerce between east and west, though it was increased by the Crusades, did not depend on them for its existence.

It was only in some aspects of the political development of western Europe that the Crusades left a mark. One of Pope Urban's expressed aims in preaching the Crusades was to find some useful work for the turbulent and bellicose barons who otherwise spent their energy on civil wars at home; and the removal of large sections of that unruly element to the East undoubtedly helped the rise of monarchical power in the West, to the ultimate detriment of the Papacy. But meanwhile the Papacy itself benefited. The Pope had launched the Crusade as an international Christian movement under his leadership; and its initial success greatly enhanced his power and prestige. The Crusaders all belonged to his flock. Their conquests were his conquests. As, one by one, the ancient Patriarchates of Antioch, Jerusalem and Constantinople fell under his dominion, it seemed that his claim to be the Head of Christendom was justified. In Church affairs his dominion was vastly extended. Congregations in every part of the Christian world acknowledged his spiritual supremacy. His missionaries travelled as far afield as Ethiopia and China. The whole movement stimulated the organization of the Papal Chancery on a far more international basis than before, and it played a great part in the development of Canon Law.[1] Had the Popes been content to reap ecclesiastical benefits alone, they would have had good cause for self-congratulation. But the times were not yet ready for a clear division between ecclesiastical and lay politics; and in lay politics the Papacy overreached itself. The Crusade commanded respect only when it was directed against the infidel. The Fourth Crusade, directed, if not preached, against the Christians of the East, was followed by a Crusade against the heretics of southern France and the nobles that showed them sympathy; and this was succeeded

[1] See Ullmann, *Medieval Papalism*, pp. 120–1, 128–9.

by Crusades preached against the Hohenstaufen; till at last the Crusade came to mean any war against the enemies of Papal policy, and all the spiritual paraphernalia of indulgences and heavenly rewards was used to support the lay ambitions of the Papal See. The triumph of the Popes in ruining the Emperors both of the East and of the West led them on into the humiliations of the Sicilian war and the captivity at Avignon. The Holy War was warped to become a tragic farce.

Apart from the widening of the spiritual dominion of Rome, the chief benefit obtained by Western Christendom from the Crusades was negative. When they began the main seats of civilization were in the East, at Constantinople and at Cairo. When they ended, civilization had moved its headquarters to Italy and the young countries of the West. The Crusades were not the only cause for the decline of the Moslem world. The invasions of the Turks had already undermined the Abbasid Caliphate of Baghdad and even without the Crusade they might have ultimately brought down the Fatimid Caliphate of Egypt. But had it not been for the incessant irritation of the wars against the Franks, the Turks might well have been integrated into the Arab world and provided for it a new vitality and strength without destroying its basic unity. The Mongol invasions were more destructive still to Arab civilization, and their coming cannot be blamed on the Crusades. But had it not been for the Crusades the Arabs would have been far better able to meet the Mongol aggression. The intrusive Frankish State was a festering sore that the Moslems could never forget. So long as it distracted them they could never wholly concentrate on other problems.

But the real harm done to Islam by the Crusades was subtler. The Islamic State was a theocracy whose political welfare depended on the Caliphate, the line of priest-kings to whom custom had given a hereditary succession. The Crusading attack came when the Abbasid Caliphate was unable politically or geographically to lead Islam against it; and the Fatimid Caliphs, as heretics, could not command a wide enough allegiance. The leaders who arose to defeat the Christians, men like Nur ed-Din and Saladin, were heroic figures who were given respect and devotion, but they were adventurers. The Ayubites, for all their ability, could never be accepted as the supreme rulers of Islam, because they were not Caliphs; they were not even descended from the Prophet. They had no proper place in the theocracy of Islam. The Mongol destruction of Baghdad in some way eased the Moslem task. The Mameluks were able to found a durable state in Egypt because there was no longer a lawful Caliphate in Baghdad, but only a shadowy and spurious line that was kept in honourable confinement in Cairo. The Ottoman Sultans eventually solved the problem by assuming the Caliphate themselves. Their immense power made the Moslem world accept them, but never whole-heartedly; for they too were usurpers and not of the prophet's line. Christianity allowed from the outset a distinction between the things that are Caesar's and the things that are God's; and so, when the medieval conception of the undivided political City of God broke down, its vitality was unimpaired. But Islam was conceived as a political and religious unity. This unity had been cracked before the Crusades; but the events of those centuries made the cracks too wide to be mended. The great Ottoman Sultans achieved a superficial repair, but only for a time. The cracks have endured to this day.

Even more harmful was the effect of the Holy War on the spirit of Islam. Any religion that is based on an exclusive Revelation is bound to show some contempt for the unbeliever. But Islam was not intolerant in its early days. Mahomet himself considered that Jews and Christians had received a partial Revelation and were therefore not to be persecuted. Under the early Caliphs the Christians played an honourable part in Arab society. A re-markably large number of the early Arabic thinkers and writers were Christians, who provided a useful intellectual stimulus; for the Moslems, with their reliance on the Word of God, given once and for all time in the Koran, tended to remain static and unenter-prising in their thought. Nor was the rivalry of the Caliphate with

Christian Byzantium entirely unfriendly. Scholars and technicians passed to and fro between the two Empires to their mutual benefit. The Holy War begun by the Franks ruined these good relations. The savage intolerance shown by the Crusaders was answered by growing intolerance amongst the Moslems. The broad humanity of Saladin and his family was soon to be rare amongst their fellow-believers. By the time of the Mameluks, the Moslems were as narrow as the Franks. Their Christian subjects were amongst the first to suffer from it. They never recovered their old easy acquaintanceship with their Moslem neighbours and masters. Their own intellectual life faded away, and with it the widening influence that it had upon Islam. Except in Persia, with its own disquieting heretic traditions, the Moslems enclosed themselves behind the curtain of their faith; and an intolerant faith is incapable of progress.

The harm done by the Crusades to Islam was small in comparison with that done by them to Eastern Christendom. Pope Urban II had bidden the Crusaders go forth that the Christians of the East might be helped and rescued. It was a strange rescue; for when the work was over, Eastern Christendom lay under infidel domination and the Crusaders themselves had done all that they could to prevent its recovery. When they set themselves up in the East they treated their Christian subjects no better than the Caliph had done before them. Indeed, they were sterner, for they interfered in the religious practices of the local churches. When they were ejected they left the local Christians unprotected to bear the wrath of the Moslem conquerors. It is true that the native Christians themselves earned a fuller measure of this wrath by their desperate belief that the Mongols would give them the lasting freedom that they had not obtained from the Franks. Their penalty was severe and complete. Weighed down by cruel restrictions and humiliations they dwindled into unimportance. Even their land was punished. The lovely Syrian coastline was ravaged and left desolate. The Holy City itself sank neglected into a long, untranquil decline.

The tragedy of the Syrian Christians was incidental to the

failure of the Crusades; but the destruction of Byzantium was the result of deliberate malice. The real disaster of the Crusades was the inability of Western Christendom to comprehend Byzantium. Throughout the ages there have always been hopeful politicians who believe that if only the peoples of the world could come together they would love and understand each other. It is a tragic delusion. So long as Byzantium and the West had little to do with each other their relations were friendly. Western pilgrims and soldiers of fortune were welcomed in the imperial city and went home to tell of its splendours; but there were not enough of them to make friction. There were occasional bones of contention between the Byzantine Emperor and the Western Powers; but either the bone was dropped in time or some tactful formula for its division was devised. There were constant religious issues, exacerbated by the claims of the Hildebrandine Papacy. But even there, with good-will on both sides, some working arrangement could have been made. But with the Norman determination to expand into the Eastern Mediterranean a new disquieting era began. Byzantine interests were flung into sharp conflict with those of a Western people. The Normans were checked, and the Crusades were launched as a peace-making move. But there was misunderstanding from the outset. The Emperor thought that it was his Christian duty to restore his frontiers to be a bulwark against the Turks, whom he considered to be the enemy. The Crusaders wished to push on to the Holy Land. They had come to fight the Holy War against the infidels of every race. While their leaders failed to appreciate the Emperor's policy, thousands of soldiers and pilgrims found themselves in a land where the language, the customs and the religion seemed to them strange and incomprehensible and therefore wrong. They expected the peasants and citizens in the territory through which they passed not only to resemble them but also to welcome them. They were doubly disappointed. Quite failing to realize that their thieving and destructive habits could not win them the affection or the respect of their victims, they were hurt, angry and envious. Had it been left to the choice of the ordinary Crusading soldier Constantinople would have been attacked and sacked at a far earlier date. But the leaders of the Crusade were at first too conscious of their Christian duty and restrained their followers. Louis VII refused to accept the advice of some of his nobles and bishops to take arms against the Christian city; and though Frederick Barbarossa toyed with the idea, he controlled his anger and passed by. It was left to the greedy cynics that directed the Fourth Crusade to take advantage of a momentary weakness in the Byzantine state to plot and achieve its destruction.

The Latin Empire of Constantinople, conceived in sin, was a puny child for whose welfare the West eagerly sacrificed the needs of its children in the Holy Land. The Popes themselves were far more anxious to keep the unwilling Greeks under their ecclesiastical rule than to rescue Jerusalem. When the Byzantines recovered their capital Western pontiffs and politicians alike worked hard to restore Western control. The Crusade had become a movement not for the protection of Christendom but for the establishment of the authority of the Roman Church.

The determination of the Westerners to conquer and colonize the lands of Byzantium was disastrous for the interests of Outremer. It was more disastrous still for European civilization. Constantinople was still the centre of the civilized Christian world. In the pages of Villehardouin we see reflected the impression that it made on the knights that had come from France and Italy to conquer it. They could not believe that so superb a city could exist on earth; it was of all cities the sovereign.[1] Like most barbarian invaders, the men of the Fourth Crusade did not intend to destroy what they found. They meant to share in it and dominate it. But their greed and their clumsiness led them to indulge in irreparable destruction. Only the Venetians, with their higher

[1] 'Or poez savoir que mult esgarderent Costantinople cil qui onques mais l'avoient veüe; que il ne pooient mie cuidier que si riche ville peüst estre en tot le monde.... Nuls nel poist croire se il ne le veïst a l'oil le lonc et lé de la ville, qui de totes les autres ere soveraine' (Villehardouin, ed. Faral, I, p. 130).

level of culture, knew what it would be most profitable to save. Italy, indeed, reaped some benefit from the decline and fall of Byzantium. The Frankish settlers in Byzantine lands, though they brought a superficial and romantic vitality to the hills and valleys of Greece, were unfitted to understand the long Greek tradition of culture. But the Italians, whose connections with Greece had never been broken for long, were better able to appreciate the value of what they took; and when the decline of Byzantium meant the dispersal of its scholars, they found a welcome in Italy. The spread of humanism in Italy was an indirect result of the Fourth Crusade.

The Italian Renaissance is a matter of pride for mankind. But it would have been better could it have been achieved without the ruin of Eastern Christendom. Byzantine culture survived the shock of the Fourth Crusade. In the fourteenth and early fifteenth centuries Byzantine art and thought flowered in splendid profusion. But the political basis of the Empire was insecure. Indeed, since 1204 it was no longer an Empire but one state amongst many others as strong or stronger. Faced with the hostility of the West and the rivalry of its Balkan neighbours, it could no longer guard Christendom against the Turks. It was the Crusaders themselves who wilfully broke down the defence of Christendom and thus allowed the infidel to cross the Straits and penetrate into the heart of Europe. The true martyrs of the Crusade were not the gallant knights who fell fighting at the Horns of Hattin or before the towers of Acre, but the innocent Christians of the Balkans, as well as of Anatolia and Syria, who were handed over to persecution and slavery.

To the Crusaders themselves their failures were inexplicable. They were fighting for the cause of the Almighty; and if faith and logic were correct, that cause should have triumphed. In the first flush of success they entitled their chronicles the *Gesta Dei per Francos*, God's work done by the hand of the Franks. But after the First Crusade there followed a long train of disasters; and even the victories of the Third Crusade were incomplete and unsure.

There were evil forces about which thwarted God's work. At first the blame could be laid on Byzantium, on the schismatic Emperor and his ungodly people who refused to recognize the divine mission of the Crusaders. But after the Fourth Crusade that excuse could no longer be maintained; yet things went steadily worse. Moralist preachers might claim that God was angry with His warriors because of their sins. There was some truth in this, but as complete explanation it collapsed when Saint Louis led his army into one of the greatest disasters that the Crusaders ever underwent; for Saint Louis was a man whom the medieval world believed to be without sin. In fact it was not so much wickedness as stupidity that ruined the Holy Wars. Yet such is human nature that a man will admit far more readily to being a sinner than a fool. No one amongst the Crusaders would admit that their real crimes were a wilful and narrow ignorance and an irresponsible lack of foresight.

The chief motive that impelled the Christian armies eastward was faith. But the sincerity and simplicity of their faith led them into pitfalls. It carried them through incredible hardships to victory on the First Crusade, whose success seemed miraculous. The Crusaders therefore expected that miracles would continue to save them when difficulties arose. Their confidence made them foolhardy; and even to the end, at Nicopolis as at Antioch, they were certain that they would receive divine support. Again, their faith by its very simplicity made them intolerant. Their God was a jealous God; they could never conceive it possible that the God of Islam might be the same Power. The colonists settled in Outremer might reach a wider view; but the soldiers from the West came to fight for the Christian God; and to them anyone who showed tolerance to the infidel was a traitor. Even those that worshipped the Christian God in a different ritual were suspect and deplored.

This genuine faith was often combined with unashamed greed. Few Christians have ever thought it incongruous to combine God's work with the acquisition of material advantages. That the soldiers of God should extract territory and wealth from the infidel was right. It was justifiable to rob the heretic and the schismatic also. Worldly ambitions helped to produce the gallant adventurousness on which much of the early success of the movement was based. But greed and the lust for power are dangerous masters. They breed impatience; for man's life is short and he needs quick results. They breed jealousy and disloyalty; for offices and possessions are limited, and it is impossible to satisfy every claimant. There was a constant feud between the Franks already established in the East and those that came out to fight the infidel and to seek their fortune. Each saw the war from a different point of view. In the turmoil of envy, distrust and intrigue, few campaigns had much chance of success. Quarrels and inefficiency were enhanced by ignorance. The colonists slowly adapted themselves to the ways and the climate of the Levant; they began to learn how their enemies fought and how to make friends with them. But the newly-come Crusader found himself in an utterly unfamiliar world, and he was usually too proud to admit his limitations. He disliked his cousins of Outremer and would not listen to them. So expedition after expedition made the same mistakes and reached the same sorry end.

Powerful and intelligent leadership might have saved the movement. But the feudal background from which the Crusaders were drawn made it difficult for a leader to be accepted. The Crusades were the Pope's work; but Papal Legates were seldom good generals. There were many able men amongst the Kings of Jerusalem; but they had little authority over their own subjects and none over their visiting allies. The Military Orders, who provided the finest and most experienced soldiers, were independent and jealous of each other. National armies led by a King seemed at one time to offer a better weapon; but though Richard of England, who was a soldier of genius, was one of the few successful commanders amongst the Crusaders, the other royal expeditions were without exception disastrous. It was difficult for any monarch to go campaigning for long in lands so far from his own. Cœur-de-Lion's and Saint Louis's sojourns in the East were made at the expense of the welfare of England and France. The financial cost, in particular, was appallingly high. The Italian cities could make the Crusades a profitable affair; and independent nobles who hoped to found estates or marry heiresses in Outremer might find their outlay returned. But to send the royal army overseas was a costly undertaking with very little hope of material recompense. Special taxes must be raised throughout the kingdom. It was not surprising that practical-minded kings, such as Philip IV of France, preferred to raise the taxes and then stay at home. The ideal leader, a great soldier and diplomat, with time and money to spend in the East and a wide understanding of Eastern ways, was never to be found. It was indeed less remarkable that the Crusading movement faded away in failure than that it should ever have met with success, and that, with scarcely one victory to its credit after its spectacular foundation, Outremer should have lasted for two hundred years.

The triumphs of the Crusade were the triumphs of faith. But faith without wisdom is a dangerous thing. By the inexorable laws of history the whole world pays for the crimes and follies of each of its citizens. In the long sequence of interaction and fusion between Orient and Occident out of which our civilization has grown, the Crusades were a tragic and destructive episode. The historian as he gazes back across the centuries at their gallant story must find his admiration overcast by sorrow at the witness that it bears to the limitations of human nature. There was so much courage and so little honour, so much devotion and so little understanding. High ideals were besmirched by cruelty and greed, enterprise and endurance by a blind and narrow self-righteousness; and the Holy War itself was nothing more than a long act of intolerance in the name of God, which is the sin against the Holy Ghost.

APPENDIX I

PRINCIPAL SOURCES FOR THE HISTORY OF THE LATER CRUSADES

1. GREEK

Greek sources are only important for the history of the Fourth Crusade. For that story the most important historian is NICETAS CHONIATES.[1] GEORGE ACROPOLITES[2] covers the Fourth Crusade and the period till the Byzantine recapture of the city. For the following period the most important history is that of GEORGE PACHYMER.[3]

The two Cypriot Greek histories of LEONTIUS MAKHAERAS[4] and GEORGE BUSTRON[5] deal very little with the period before the fourteenth century.[6]

2. LATIN AND OLD FRENCH

The most important group of histories dealing with Outremer from the Third Crusade till the fall of Acre is that of the old French continuations of William of Tyre. Up till 1198 the original source seems to have been a lost work by ERNOUL, of which the existing 'ERNOUL' or BERNARD THE TREASURER and the MSS. C and G of the ESTOIRE D'ERACLES are the closest copies and the MSS. A and B, which resemble each other, and D, which slightly deviates from them, are other drafts. From 1198 to 1205 all the versions are practically identical. From 1205

---

[1] See above, vol. II, p. 475.
[2] Edited by Meisenberg in the Teubner series.
[3] Published in the Bonn Corpus.
[4] *Recital concerning the Sweet Land of Cyprus*, edited with a translation by Dawkins.
[5] Χρονικὸν Κύπρου, edited in Sathas, Μεσαιωνικὴ Βιβλιοθήκη, vol. II.
[6] Richard I's conquest of Cyprus is described by Neophytus, *De Calamitatibus Cypri*, edited by Stubbs and published as a preface to the *Itinerarium* (see above, vol. II, bibliography).

onwards 'Ernoul' and C, G, and D of the *Estoire* are identical, till 1229, when 'Ernoul' ends. C, G, and D then follow, with slight variations, A and B of the *Estoire*, which from 1205 has had very little connection with 'Ernoul'. A ends in 1248; B, C and D continue till 1266, 1275 and 1277. Meanwhile another continuation, known as the MS. of ROTHELIN, covers the period from 1229 to 1261; it was certainly edited somewhere in France.[1] The existing ANNALES DE TERRE SAINTE seem to be a shortened compilation of one of the sources of the *Continuations* of William. The MSS. for the period from 1248 onwards are almost identical with it.[2]

The early fourteenth-century compilation known as the GESTES DES CHIPROIS begins with a brief CHRONIQUE DE TERRE SAINTE, from 1131 to 1222, which is based on the *Annales de Terre Sainte*. The second section is a history of the wars between the Ibelins and the Imperialists, composed about 1245, with autobiographical comments, by PHILIP OF NOVARA, an Italian living in Cyprus and writing in French. Philip writes vividly and with a certain grace. He inserts long poems of his own composition into the narrative. They have a pleasant freshness and wit, though no great poetic merit. Philip was passionately devoted to the Ibelins, but, as far as his loyalties allow, he is truthful and accurate. The final section of the *Gestes* is a history of Outremer from 1249 to 1309, written by a man traditionally known as the TEMPLAR OF TYRE. He was certainly not a Templar himself, but seems to have acted for some time as secretary to the Grand Master of the Temple, William of Beaujeu. He apparently knew the source on which the *Continuations* of William of Tyre are based. The *Gestes* was probably put together about 1325 by a certain Gerard of Montreal.[3]

Each of the chief Crusades has its own group of historians. The Third Crusade is covered by various Anglo-Norman chronicles of which the most important are BENEDICT OF PETERBOROUGH, RICHARD OF DEVIZES, RALPH OF DICETO and WILLIAM OF NEWBURGH.[4] These, together with the *Libellus de Expugnatione*, are particularly useful for the earlier part

[1] See above, vol. II, pp. 477–8 and Cahen, *La Syrie du Nord*, pp. 21–5.

[2] See above, vol. II, p. 478 n. 3.

[3] The *Gestes* are published in an edition by Gaston Raynaud. See Cahen, *op. cit.* pp. 25–6, and Hill, *History of Cyprus*, III, p. 1144.

[4] All published in the Rolls Series. See bibliography below, pp. 497–8, and above, vol. II, pp. 493, 495.

of the Crusade before Cœur-de-Lion's arrival in the East. They also contain copies of letters dealing with Near Eastern affairs. For King Richard's own campaigns the two chief sources are the Latin ITINER-ARIUM REGIS RICARDI, apparently written by a Londoner, Richard of Holy Trinity, and the Old French poem by AMBROISE, *L'Estoire de la Guerre Sainte*.[1] The two are very closely related and probably are both derived from a lost journal written by a soldier in the English army, passionately devoted to his King and truthful according to his pre-judiced lights.[2] The French point of view is given in the brief account by RIGORD, *Gesta Philippi Augusti*.[3] German chronicles describing Frederick I's Crusade, such as 'ANSBERT', *Expeditio Friderici*, end with the Emperor's death.[4]

For the Fourth Crusade the main Western source is GEOFFREY OF VILLEHARDOUIN's *Conquête de Constantinople*,[5] written about 1209 by a knight who had himself played a prominent part in the Crusade and was an uncle of the conqueror of the Morea. Villehardouin probably based his story on notes that he took at the time; and, apart from his strong occidental prejudices, he can be regarded as a reliable witness. The *Conquête de Constantinople* of ROBERT OF CLARI is another eye-witness account, but its author was a far simpler and more ignorant man.[6]

For the Fifth Crusade the most important sources, apart from those written in Outremer, are the letters of Cardinal JAMES OF VITRY[7] and the *Historia Damiatana* by OLIVER OF PADERBORN, who was secretary

---

[1] See above vol. II, bibliography, pp. 493–4.

[2] Gaston Paris in his preface to his edition of Ambroise believed that the *Itinerarium* depended on Ambroise. Miss Norgate, 'The *Itinerarium Peregrinorum* and the Song of Ambroise', *English Historical Review*, vol. XXV, suggests that Ambroise depends on the *Itinerarium*. Edwards, 'The Itinerarium Regis Ricardi and the Estoire de la Guerre Sainte' in *Essays in Honour of James Tait* (pp. 59–77), argues convincingly that both are based on a lost common source. His view is followed by Hubert and La Monte in the preface to their translation of Ambroise.   [3] Edited by Delaborde.

[4] Edited by Chroust. See Cahen, *op. cit.* p. 19 n. 3.

[5] The edition (with a modern French translation) by Faral is the most convenient. It has a useful introduction.

[6] Edited by Lauer. The more recent translation into modern French by Charlot (*Poèmes et Récits de la Vieille France*, vol. XVI) is inadequate, especially with regard to its notes.

[7] Edited by Röhricht in the *Zeitschrift für Kirchengeschichte*; see bibliography below.

to Cardinal Pelagius. Despite his loyalty to his master, Oliver's account is vivid and fairly objective.[1]

Frederick II's Crusade did not inspire any specialist writer; but we have for Saint Louis's Crusade the invaluable *Histoire de Saint Louis* by JOHN, Sieur of JOINVILLE. Joinville was present on the Crusade; and his devoted admiration for the King does not prevent him from writing an honest, vivid and very personal narrative.[2]

The final fall of Acre produced a crop of historians, but none of them except the 'Templar of Tyre' was personally present. THADDEUS OF NAPLES and the anonymous writer of DE EXCIDIO URBIS ACCONIS both clearly exaggerated their accounts for propagandist purposes.[3]

Throughout the whole period the Papal correspondence is of the highest importance, together with the letters that have survived from members of the Orders and from the Kings and their ministers.[4]

For constitutional matters the two essential sources are PHILIP OF NOVARA's *Livre de Forme de Plait*, mainly concerned with procedure, and the *Livre de Jean d'Ibelin*, a magnificent work of jurisprudence written by the Count of Jaffa.[5] The *Assises de la Cour des Bourgeois*, compiled between 1240 and 1244, describes commercial procedure.[6] The *Assises d'Antioche* only exists in an Armenian translation made in about 1260 by Sempad, brother of King Hethoum I. It covers briefly the procedure and customs of both the baronial and the bourgeois courts in the Principality.[7]

[1] Edited, with his letters, by Hooeweg. The volumes of the *Scriptores Minores Quinti Belli Sacri*, edited by Röhricht, contain all the lesser authorities covering the Fifth Crusade.

[2] The best edition is that of de Wailly. The other most important historian of Louis IX's Crusade is William of Nangis who wrote some decades later.

[3] See above, p. 414 n. 2. The *De Excidio* is published in Martène and Durand, *Amplissima Collectio*, vol. v. See also Kingsford in *Transactions of Royal Historical Society*, 3rd series, vol. III, p. 142 n. 2.

[4] Innocent III's correspondence is published by Migne, *P.L.* vols. 214–16: Honorius IV's *Regesta* are edited by Pressutti, Gregory IX's *Registres* by Auvray, Innocent IV's *Registres* by Bergen, Alexander IV's by Bourel de la Roncière, Urban IV's by Guiraud, Clement IV's by Jordan, Gregory X's by Guiraud, Nicholas III's by Gay and Vitte, Honorius IV's by Pron and Nicholas IV's by Langlois, all published in the *Bibliothèque des Ecoles Françaises d'Athènes et de Rome*.   [5] Published in the *Recueil des Historiens des Croisades, Lois*, vol. I.

[6] Published in the same volume.

[7] Published with a French translation by the Mekhitarist Fathers at Venice.

Appendix I

There are various important works by contemporary travellers, which are particularly useful in describing Western relations with the Mongols. The fullest of these are the reports on their missions written by JOHN PIAN DEL CARPINE and WILLIAM OF RUBRUCK.[1] The description of the Holy Land by James of Vitry and the later descriptions by LUDOLF OF SUCHEM and FELIX FABRI all provide valuable information.[2]

3. ARABIC

The Arabic chroniclers dealing with Saladin's wars and the earlier decades of the thirteenth century have been mentioned in Appendix I to the second volume of this history. BEHA ED-DIN's valuable work ends with Saladin's death, but IBN AL-ATHIR, ABU SHAMA (who transcribes IMAD ED-DIN), and KEMAL AD-DIN carry us well into the thirteenth century.[3] For the remaining years of that century there are numerous contemporary chroniclers; but many of the most important are as yet unpublished and can only be read in manuscript. IBN WASIL's works, a life of as-Salih which goes down to 1250 and a history of the Ayubites up to 1263, exist in several manuscripts but are only published in a few meagre extracts made by Reinaud in Michaud's *Bibliothèque des Croisades*, vol. IV. Ibn Wasil was, however, freely used by later chroniclers such as Ibn Furad and Maqrisi.[4] IBN SHEDDAD the Geographer's life of Baibars is almost entirely lost; BAIBARS MANSOURI's life of Qalawun is also fragmentary but was used by Ibn Furad.[5] Extracts of IBN ABDAZZAHIR's lives of Baibars and Qalawun are given by Reinaud (*op. cit.*).[6] The chronicle of the Copt IBN AL-AMID provides original information for the period up to 1260;[7] and the anonymous

---

[1] Both translated and edited by Rockhill in *Hakluyt Society Publications*, 2nd series, vol. 137.

[2] All these are published in English translations in the *Palestine Pilgrims Text Society*. The translation is not always faultless, and for Ludolf the Latin text in the *Archives de l'Orient Latin*, vol. II, should be used.

[3] See above, vol. II, pp. 480–2.

[4] See Cahen, *La Syrie du Nord*, pp. 68–70.

[5] See *ibid.* pp. 75, 78–9.   [6] *Ibid.* p. 74.

[7] Edited by Cheikho in *Corpus Scriptorum Christianorum Orientalium*, vol. III. The sixteenth-century translations of Erpennius and Ecchelensius only go as far as A.H. 512 (A.D. 1118).

21

history of the Patriarchs of Alexandria, which breaks off about the same date, gives further information from Coptic sources.[1] ABU'L FEDA's history[2] is entirely a compilation from older authorities till he comes to the events of his own lifetime, from about 1290 onwards.[3] The work of YOUNINI exists only in manuscript. It goes down to 1311, but contains much the same information as the contemporary work of AL-JAZARI.[4]

Of the later historians, apart from IBN KHALDUN and the encyclo-paedist IBN KHALLIKAN,[5] the most considerable literary figure is IBN FURAD, whose history was written at the end of the fourteenth century. It is largely a compilation from earlier works, many of which are lost, but it is composed with a real sense of historiography.[6] His con-temporary MAQRISI lacks his distinction as a writer. Apart from some exclusive information about Egypt his histories of Egypt under the Ayubites and of the Mameluk Sultans are entirely derived from earlier works; but they are full, reliable and easily accessible.[7] The chronicle of AL-AINI, written towards the middle of the fifteenth century, is similarly just a copious compilation, except for the later chapters.[8]

4. ARMENIAN

The Armenian historians of the Cilician kingdom have been mentioned in Appendix I to the second volume of this history. The most useful of them is VARTAN, particularly for Mongol affairs, of which he had an

---

[1] The full text is unpublished. Extracts dealing with the early thirteenth century are given in a French translation by Blochet, *Revue de l'Orient Latin*, vol. XI.

[2] Extracts are published in the Recueil, *Historiens Orientaux*, vol. III.

[3] See above, vol. II, p. 482.

[4] A fragment of al-Jazari, beginning at A.H. 689 (A.D. 1290) is published in a French translation by Sauvaget.

[5] See above, vol. II, p. 482.

[6] The chapters covering the thirteenth century are unpublished. See Cahen, *op. cit.* pp. 85-6.

[7] See above, vol. II, p. 482. Full extracts of Maqrisi's *History of Egypt* are given by Blochet in *Revue de l'Orient Latin*, Vols. VIII, IX and X (cited above as Maqrisi, VIII, IX and X), and his *History of the Mameluk Sultans* is translated by Quatremère (2 vols. cited above as Maqrisi; Sultans I and II).

[8] Extracts are given in the *Recueil, Historiens Orientaux*, vol. II, p. 2.

intimate personal knowledge.[1] Amongst Armenian sources must be included the *Flor des Estoires de la Terre d'Orient* by the Armenian prince HAYTON (Hethoum of Corycus) written in French after his retirement to France early in the fourteenth century. It is a valuable history of his own times. He also wrote annals in Armenian, which are dependent on Armenian sources and the *Annales de Terre Sainte*.[2]

For the thirteenth century the one important historian writing in Syriac is BAR-HEBRAEUS. He died aged 60 in 1286, and, though his account of earlier periods is full of unreliable gossip and legend, when he writes about the events of his own lifetime he provides a large amount of valuable information not to be found elsewhere.[3] RABBAN SAUMA's history of the life of the Nestorian Catholicus Mar Yahbhallaha and of his own career, which was written in Ouighur and translated into Syriac anonymously a few years afterwards, is important for its account of Nestorian life under the Mongols and, still more, for the story of Rabban Sauma's embassy to Western Europe.[4]

5. PERSIAN

IBN BIBI's history of the Seldjuks of Rum, though over-elaborately written, is valuable for Anatolian history during the first half of the thirteenth century.[5] The World-History of RASHID AD-DIN is of extreme importance for the history of the Mongols. It was written in praise of the Ilkhans of Persia, whose point of view it consistently gives.[6]

[1] See above, vol. II, pp. 483–4. The full Armenian text of Vartan, edited by Emin, was published at Moscow in 1861.

[2] The *Flor* is published in the *Recueil, Documents Arméniens*, vol. II. The Armenian annals were published, edited by Aucher, at Venice in 1842. Extracts are given in the *Recueil, Documents Arméniens*, vol. I.

[3] See above, vol. II, p. 484.

[4] Rabban Sauma's work is translated by Budge in *The Monks of Kublâi Khân*. The Syriac text was published by Bedjian.

[5] Turkish translation and Persian résumés published in Houtsma, *Textes Relatifs à l'histoire des Seldjoukides*, vols. III and IV.

[6] The whole work is published in a Russian translation by Berezin. The second part of the history of the Ilkhans is published together with a French translation by Quatremère.

Appendix I

6. Other Sources

The *Georgian Chronicle* continues to be of use for Caucasian affairs.[1] Old Russian chronicles, in particular the versions of the *Novgorod Chronicle*,[2] take an interest in Byzantine affairs and are essential for a study of the Mongols. There are also various useful Mongol sources, of which the most important is the *Yuan Ch'ao Pi Shih*, the official, or secret, history of the Mongols.[3]

[1] See above, vol. II, p. 484.
[2] The best edition of the *Novgorod Chronicle* is by Nasonov (Moscow, 1950).
[3] See above, p. 237 n. 1.

APPENDIX II

INTELLECTUAL LIFE IN OUTREMER[1]

In comparison with the intellectual life of Sicily or of Spain, that of Outremer is disappointing. It might have been expected that, as at Palermo, the contact between Franks and Orientals might have stimulated intellectual activity; but in fact the society of Outremer, which consisted almost entirely of soldiers and merchants, was not fitted to create or maintain a high intellectual standard. Amongst the princes and the nobility there were many men of culture. For example, we are told that King Baldwin III and King Amalric I were both devoted to letters. Reynald of Sidon was notorious for his interest in Islamic learning, while Humphrey IV of Toron had a perfect knowledge of the Arabic language.[2] And Outremer produced one of the greatest of medieval historians in William of Tyre.[3] But we know very little about education in Outremer. As in the West there were undoubtedly schools attached to the chief cathedrals; but it is significant that William of Tyre went as a boy to France to be educated; and, apart from him, all the ecclesiastics who played a prominent part in the history of Outremer were men born and brought up in the West. Many of these prelates, such as the Patriarch Aimery of Antioch, were interested in literature,[4] or like James of Vitry, bishop of Acre in the thirteenth century, in the scientific life going on around him;[5] and the various schemes for the later Crusades encouraged an active interest in oriental

[1] See above, vol. II, pp. 361, 368.
[2] See above, vol. II, pp. 361, 363, 469, and vol. III, p. 59.
[3] See above, vol. II, pp. 476–7.
[4] Aimery of Limoges was almost illiterate himself, but he kept up a correspondence with European men of letters, such as Hugo Aetherianus. The letters are published in Martène and Durand, *Thesaurus Anecdotorum*, vol. I.
[5] James of Vitry's description of the Holy Land shows an interest in local theories about earthquakes (ed. *P.P.T.S.* pp. 91–2). But he disapproved too strongly of Moslems and local Christians to have any direct contact with them.

geography.[1] But on the whole Frankish culture in Outremer remained an occidental importation, with very little contact with native culture, except in the arts. Medicine was left entirely in native hands. The princes seem always to have employed Syrian Christian doctors. When Amalric I rejected his Syrian doctors' advice and consulted a Frank, he died of it; and the examples that Usama gives of Frankish doctoring show it to have been remarkably crude.[2] The Franks seem to have made no attempt, as in southern Italy, to learn from native medicine; though a certain Stephen of Antioch seems to have translated a medical treatise from the Arabic in 1227.[3] There is no record of any effort by the Franks, apart from a few nobles, to study local philosophy or scientific knowledge.

The literary products of Frankish Outremer fall under three headings. First, there are the chronicles and histories. These, with the great exception of William of Tyre's history, and the work of some of his continuators, such as Ernoul, were written by men born in the West and are in the tradition of Western chronicle-writing.[4] Secondly, there is a large crop of legal works. The colonists and their descendants were deeply interested in legal and constitutional matters, and were anxious to have their opinions and findings written down, to an extent unparalleled in the West. But the law that they reproduce is purely Western, though it showed some necessary adjustments.[5] Finally, there was popular and romantic poetry. The colonists in Outremer loved the romantic epics of the time. Several troubadours and minnesingers, such as Rudel or Albert of Johansdorf, went on the Crusades.[6] Ray-

[1] See Rey, *Les Colonies Franques*, pp. 177–8.
[2] See above, vol. II, pp. 318, 399.   [3] Leclerc, *La Médecine Arabe*, II, p. 38.
[4] See above, vol. II, pp. 476–8; vol. III, pp. 482–3.
[5] The various *Assises* and the works of John of Ibelin and Philip of Novara are all based on Occidental law. See La Monte, *Feudal Monarchy*, *passim*.
[6] Rudel seems certainly to have visited the East, as the troubadour Marcabrun dedicates a poem to him with the words, 'to Jaufre Rudel beyond the sea'. But his love-affair with *La Princesse Lointaine*, Melisende of Tripoli, must be regarded as being at least half-legendary (see Chaytor, *The Troubadours*, pp. 44–6). Peter Vidal is said to have gone as far as Cyprus on the Third Crusade, but there he married a Greek girl and decided that she was heiress to Constantinople (*ibid.* p. 7). Raimbald of Vaqueiras went on the Fourth Crusade and died in Bulgaria. Sordello probably went on Louis IX's first expedition (*ibid.* pp. 98–9, 102). Of the minnesingers, Albert of Johansdorf went on the Third Crusade, as did Frederick of Hausen who, however, died before the German army reached Konya.

mond, Prince of Antioch, was the son of the eminent troubadour poet, William IX of Aquitaine. The stirring events of the Crusades were admirably suited to enrich the themes of which the poets sang. Godfrey of Lorraine soon became a legendary hero, whose adventures were incorporated into the cycle of the Chevalier au Cygne; poems about his youth and ancestry were already in circulation in the East when William of Tyre wrote his history.[1] But these poems were composed in the West. Similarly, the two versified accounts of the First Crusade, the *Chanson d'Antioche* and the *Chanson de Jerusalem*, were both almost certainly composed in the West, on information brought back by returning Crusaders.[2] The one epic which originated in Outremer is the *Chanson des Chétifs*, a curious story of Crusaders made captive by 'Corboran' (Kerbogha) in which the stories of the First Crusade and the Crusades of 1101 have become inextricably mixed. This poem was composed by an author whose name is unknown, at the express desire of Prince Raymond of Antioch. It was still unfinished when Raymond died in 1149.[3] The muddled inaccurate historical basis of the story suggests that the author was a newcomer to the East. The Franks found a romantic fascination in the fate of Christian captives in Moslem hands. The theme of the *Chétifs* was one which therefore enjoyed great popularity in Outremer as well as in Europe.[4]

Outremer produced other poetical works; but none of the known authors was born in the East. Philip of Novara, statesman, chronicler and jurist, who was Italian by birth but wrote in French, inserted verse of his own lively if not very poetical composition into his chronicle.[5] Philip of Nanteuil, when captive at Cairo, wrote nostalgic poems about his French homeland.[6] But, though Philip of Novara can be regarded as one of the founders of the provincial Frankish culture of Cyprus, the

---

[1] See Hatem, *Les Poèmes Epiques des Croisades*, pp. 395–400.

[2] See Cahen, *op. cit.* pp. 12–16.

[3] *Ibid.* pp. 569–76; Hatem, *op. cit.* pp. 375 ff.

[4] Cf. the legends of Bohemond's release from captivity (above, vol. II, p. 38 n. 2) and the stories that Ida, Margravine of Austria, was the mother of Zengi (above, vol. II, p. 29) and that Bertrand of Toulouse's sister married Nur ed-Din and was the mother of his heir as-Salih (*ibid.* p. 288 n. 1).

[5] See above, pp. 195, 482, and Hill, *History of Cyprus*, III, pp. 1112–15. William of Machaut, the author of the verse-epic of Peter of Cyprus's expedition to Egypt, seems never to have visited the East (*ibid.* p. 1115).

[6] See above, p. 215.

literature of Outremer is simply a branch of the literature of France. There was no indigenous literature amongst the Franks' native subjects in Syria, though in Cyprus and in Greece itself there grew up under Frankish domination a semi-popular Greek literature strongly affected by Frankish influences.

The intellectual life of Outremer was, in fact, that of a Frankish colony. The Courts of the Kings and Princes had a certain cosmopolitan glamour; but the number of resident scholars in Outremer was small; and wars and financial difficulties prevented the institution of real centres of study where native and neighbouring learning could have been absorbed. It was the absence of these centres that made the cultural contribution of the Crusades to western Europe so disappointingly small.

BIBLIOGRAPHY

(NOTE. This bibliography is supplementary to the bibliographies in vol. I and vol. II of this *History*, and does not include works mentioned there, except when different editions have been used. The same abbreviations are employed; and a few additional abbreviations, used in the footnotes and bibliography of this volume, are given at the end of certain items.)

I. ORIGINAL SOURCES

1. COLLECTIONS OF SOURCES

Acta Imperii Selecta (ed. J. F. Bohmer). Innsbruck, 1870.

Annales Monastici (ed. H. R. Luard), Rolls Series, 5 vols. London, 1864–9.

BALUZIUS, S. *Collectio Veterum Monumentorum*, 6 vols. Paris, 1678–1715.

BALUZIUS, S. *Vitae Paparum Avenionensium* (ed. Mollat), 4 vols. Paris, 1914–27.

BARTHOLOMAEIS, V. DE. *Poesie Provenziale Storiche relative all' Italia*. 2 vols. Istituto Storico Italiano, Rome, 1931.

BONGARS, J. *Gesta Dei per Francos*, 2 vols. Hanover, 1611.

Chronicles: Stephen, Henry II and Richard I (ed. Howlett), Rolls Series, 4 vols. London, 1885–90.

CHROUST, A. *Quellen zur Geschichte des Kreuzzüges Kaiser Friedrichs I, M.G.H.Ss.*, new series. Berlin, 1928.

COBHAM, C. D. *Excerpta Cypria*. Cambridge, 1908.

COTELERIUS, J. B. *Ecclesiae Graecae Monumenta*, 4 vols. Paris, 1677–92.

DELAVILLE LE ROULX, G. *Cartulaire générale de l'Ordre des Hospitaliers de St Jean de Jérusalem*, 4 vols. Paris, 1894–1904.

DU CHESNE, A. *Historiae Francorum Scriptores*, 5 vols. Paris, 1636–49.

GOLUBOVICH, G. *Biblioteca Bio-bibliografica della Terra Santa e dell' Oriente Francescano*, 5 vols. Florence, 1906–27.

HEISENBERG, A. *Neue Quellen zur Geschichte des lateinischen Kaisertums*. Munich, 1923.

Historia Diplomatica Friderici Secundi (ed. J. L. A. Huillard-Bréholles), 6 vols. Paris, 1852–61.

KOHLER, C. *Mélanges pour servir à l'Histoire de l'Orient Latin et des Croisades*. Paris, 1906.

MARTÈNE, E. and DURAND, U. *Thesaurus Novus Anecdotorum*, 5 vols. Paris, 1717.

MARTÈNE, E. and DURAND, U. *Veterum Scriptorum et Monumentorum Amplissima Collectio*, 9 vols. Paris, 1727–33.

Bibliography

MAS LATRIE, L. DE. *Documents*, see Bibliography II.

MAS LATRIE, L. DE. *Nouvelles Preuves de l'Histoire de Chypre*, in *Bibliothèque de l'Ecole des Chartes*, vols. XXXII, XXXIV and XXXV. Paris, 1871–4.

POTTHAST, A. *Regesta Pontificum Romanorum*, 2 vols. Berlin, 1874–5.

RAYNALDUS, O. *Annales Ecclesiastici*, 15 vols. Lucca, 1747–56.

Regesta Honorii Papae III (ed. P. Pressutti), 2 vols. Rome, 1888–95.

Regestum Innocentii Papae super Negotio Romani Imperii (ed. F. Kempf), *Miscellanea Historiae Pontificiae*, vol. XII. Rome, 1947.

Registres des Papes, Bibliothèque des Ecoles Françaises d'Athènes et de Rome. Paris:

Alexander IV (ed. Bourel de la Roncière), 2 vols. 1902, 1917.

Gregory IX (ed. Auvray), 2 vols. 1896, 1907.

Gregory X (ed. Guiraud), 2 vols. 1892, 1906.

Innocent IV (ed. Berger), 4 vols. 1884–1921.

Nicholas III (ed. Gay and Vitte), 2 vols. 1898, 1938.

Nicholas IV (ed. Langlois), 2 vols. 1886, 1905.

Urban IV (ed. Guiraud), 4 vols. 1892–1929.

RIANT, P. *Exuviae Sacrae Constantinopolitanae*, 2 vols. Geneva, 1877–8.

RÖHRICHT, R. *Scriptores Minores Quinti Belli Sacri*, Société de l'Orient Latin. Série Historique, II. Geneva, 1879. (Röhricht, *S.M.Q.B.S.*).

RÖHRICHT, R. *Testimonia Minora de Quinto Bello Sacro, ibid.* III. Geneva, 1882.

RYMER, T. *Foedera, Conventiones, Literae et Acta publica inter Reges Angliae*, 4 vols. in 7. London, 1816–69.

SCHWANDTNER, J. G. *Scriptores Rerum Hungaricarum*, 3 vols. Vienna, 1746–8.

STREHLKE, E. *Tabulae Ordinis Teutonici*. Berlin, 1869.

TAFEL, G. L. and THOMAS, G. M. *Urkunden zur älteren Handels- und Staatsgeschichte der Republik Venedig*, 3 vols. Vienna, 1856–7.

THEINER, A. *Vetera Monumenta Historica Hungariam Sacram Illustrantia*, 2 vols. Rome, 1859–60.

WATTERICH, J. M. *Pontificum Romanorum qui fuerunt inde ab exeunte saeculo IX usque ad finem saeculi XII Vitae*, 2 vols. Leipsic, 1862.

WINKELMANN, E. *Acta Imperii Inedita Saeculi XIII*, 2 vols. Innsbruck, 1880–5.

2. WESTERN SOURCES, LATIN, OLD FRENCH AND GERMAN

Adam, William. *De Modo Saracenos Extirpandi* (ed. Kohler), *R.H.C. Arm.* vol. II.

Alberic of Trois Fontaines. *Chronicon*, in *R.H.F.* vol. XVIII.

Amadi, Francesco. *Chroniques d'Amadi et de Strambaldi*, ed. Mas Latrie. Paris, 1891.

Annales Claustroneoburgenses, in *M.G.H.Ss.* vol. IX.

Annales de Dunstaplia, in *Annales Monastici*, vol. III.

Bibliography

Annales Januenses, in *M.G.H.Ss.* vol. XVIII.

Annales Marbacenses, in *M.G.H.Ss.* vol. XVII.

Annales Romani, in Watterich, *Pontificum Romanorum Vitae*.

Annales Stadenses, in *M.G.H.Ss.* vol. XVI.

Anonymus Halberstadensis. *De Peregrinatione in Greciam*, in Riant, *Exuviae*, vol. I.

Ansbert. *Expeditio Friderici Imperatoris*, in Chroust, *Quellen*.

Assises of Romania (ed. Recoura). Paris, 1930.

Auria, Jacobus. *Annales*, in *M.G.H.Ss.* vol. XVIII.

Bacon, Roger. *Opus Majus* (ed. Bridges), 3 vols. Oxford, 1900.

Baldwin I, Emperor of Constantinople, letter, in *R.H.F.* vol. XVIII.

Bartholomew of Neocastro. *Historia Sicula*, in Muratori, *Rerum Italicarum Scriptores*, new edition, vol. XIII, 3.

Bonomel, Ricaud. Poems, in Bartholemaeis, *Poesie Provenziale*.

Bruno, Bishop of Olmütz, *Bericht* (ed. Höfler), *Abhandlungen der historische Klasse der Bayerische Akademie der Wissenschaft*, series 3, IV, Munich, 1846.

Burcard (Brochard). *Directorium ad Philippum Regem*, in *R.H.C. Arm.* vol. II.

Bustron, Florio, *Chronique de l'Ile de Chypre*, ed. Mas Latrie. Paris, 1886.

Chronica Regia Coloniensis (ed. Waitz), *M.G.H.Ss. in usum scholarum*, 1880.

Chronicle of Mailros (ed. Stevenson). London, 1856.

Collectio de Scandalis Ecclesiae (ed. Stroick), in *Archivum Franciscanum Historicum*, vol. XXIV, Rome, 1931.

Cotton, Bartholomew, *Historia Anglicana* (ed. Luard), Rolls Series. London, 1859.

Dardel, John. *Chronique d'Arménie*, in *R.H.C. Arm.* vol. II.

De Excidio Urbis Acconis, in Martène and Durand, *Amplissima Collectio*, vol. V.

De Itinere Frisonum, in Röhricht, *S.M.Q.B.S.*

Devastatio Constantinopolitana, in *Annales Herpipolenses*, *M.G.H.Ss.*, vol. XVI.

Dubois, Peter. *De Recuperatione Terre Sancte* (ed. Langlois). Paris, 1891.

Durand, William. *Informatio brevis de Passagio futuro* (ed. Viollet), *Histoire Littéraire de la France*, vol. XXXV. Paris, 1921.

Edward I, King of England. Letter to Joseph of Chauncy, in *P.P.T.S.* vol. V.

Epistola de Morte Friderici Imperatoris, in Chroust, *Quellen*.

Epistolae Cantuarenses (ed. Stubbs), Rolls Series. London, 1865.

Fabri, Felix. *Book of the Wanderings*, trans. Stewart, 3 vols. *P.P.T.S.* vols. VII–IX.

Fidenzio of Padua. *Liber Recuperationis Terrae Sanctae*, in Golubovich, *Biblioteca Bio-bibliografica*, vol. II.

Figuera, Guillem. 'Dun Servientes Far', in Bartholomaeis, *Poesie Provenziale*.

Fragmentum de Captione Damiate, Provencialis textus, in Röhricht, *S.M.Q.B.S.*

Frederick II, Emperor. Letter to King Henry, in Bohmer, *Acta Imperii Selecta*.

Galvano. *Liber Sancti Passagii Christocolarum contra Saracenos*, extracts (ed. Kohler), in *Revue de l'Orient Latin*, vol. VI. Paris, 1898.

Gesta Crucigerorum Rhenanorum, in Röhricht, *S.M.Q.B.S.*

Bibliography

Gesta Innocentii III, in *M.P.L.* vol. ccxiv.

Gesta Obsidionis Damiete, in Röhricht, *S.M.Q.B.S.*

Gestes des Chiprois (ed. Raynaud). Geneva, 1887.

Gregory IX, Pope. Letters, in *M.G.H. Epistolae Saeculi*, xiii, vol. i.

Gunther of Pairis. *Historia Constantinopolitana*, in Riant, *Exuviae*, vol. i.

Guyot of Provins, *Œuvres* (ed. Orr). Manchester, 1915.

Haymar Monachus. *De Expugnata Accone* (ed. Riant). Lyons, 1876.

Hayton (Hethoum). *Flos Historiarum Terre Orientis*, in *R.H.C. Arm.* vol. ii.

Hayton (Hethoum). *La Flor des Estoires de la Terre d'Orient*, ibid.

Henry II, King of Cyprus. *Informatio ex parte Nunciorum Regis Cypri*, in Mas Latrie, *Documents*.

Historia Peregrinorum, in Chroust, *Quellen*.

Humbert of Romans. *Opus Tripartitum*, in E. Brown, *Appendix ad fasciculum rerum expetendarum et fugiendarum*. London, 1690.

Innocent III, Pope. *Epistolae*, in *M.P.L.* vols. ccxiv–ccxvii.

John of Ypres. *Chronicon Sythiense Sancti Bertini*, in Martène and Durand, *Thesaurus Anecdotorum*, vol. iii.

John of Tulbia. *De Domino Johanne Rege Jerusalem*, in Röhricht, *S.M.Q.B.S.*

Joinville, John, Sieur of. *Histoire de Saint Louis* (ed. Wailly). Paris, 1874.

Joseph of Chauncy. Letter to Edward I, in *P.P.T.S.* vol. v.

La Broquière, Bertrandon of. *Voyage d'Outremer* (ed. Schefer). Paris, 1892.

Lettre des Chrétiens de Terre Sainte à Charles d'Anjou (ed. Delaborde), in *Revue de l'Orient Latin*, vol. ii. Paris, 1894.

Liber Duellii Christiani in Obsidione Damiate exacti, in Röhricht, *S.M.Q.B.S.*

Louis IX, King of France. Letter in Baluzius, *Collectio*, vol. iv.

Ludolph of Suchem (Sudheim). *Description of the Holy Land* (trans. Stewart), *P.P.T.S.* vol. xii.

Lull, Ramon. *Liber de Fine*, in Gottron, *Ramon Lulls Kreuzzugsideen*, see Bibliography II.

Machaut, William. *La Prise d'Alexandrie* (ed. Mas Latrie). Geneva, 1877.

Manuscrit de Rothelin, in *R.H.C. Occ.* vol. ii.

Matthew Paris. *Chronica Majora* (ed. Luard), Rolls Society, 7 vols. London, 1872–84.

Matthew Paris. *Historia Minora* (ed. Madden), Rolls Society, 3 vols. London, 1866–9.

Matthew of Westminster. *Flores Historiarum* (ed. Luard), Rolls Society, 3 vols. London, 1890.

Memoria Terre Sancte, in Kohler, *Mélanges*, vol. ii.

Molay, James of. Report to Clement V, in Baluzius, *Vitae Paparum*, vol. iii.

Muntaner, Ramon. *Cronica* (ed. Caroleu). Barcelona, 1886.

Narratio Itineris Navalis ad Terram Sanctam (ed. da Silva Lopez). Lisbon, 1844.

Oliver Scholasticus. *Opera*, I. *Historia Damiatana*; II. *Epistolae* (ed. Hooewg), *Bibliothek des Litterarischen Vereins in Stuttgart*, vol. CCII. Tübingen, 1894.

Otto of Saint Blaise. *Chronica* (ed. Hofmeister), *M.G.H.Ss. in usum Scholarum*, 1912.

Philip of Novara. *Le Livre de Forme de Plait*, in *R.H.C. Lois*, vol. I.

Philip of Novara. *Mémoires*, in *Gestes des Chiprois* (English translation by La Monte and Hubert, *The Wars of Frederick II against the Ibelins in Syria and Cyprus*. New York, 1936).

Pian del Carpine, John. *Historia Mongolorum* (ed. Pulle). Florence, 1913.

Richard of Devizes. *De Rebus Gestis Ricardi Primi*, in *Chronicles* (ed. Howlett), vol. III.

Richard of San Germano, *Chronicon* (ed. Pertz), *M.G.H.Ss.* vol. XIX.

Rigord. *Gesta Philippi Augusti* (ed. Delaborde). Paris, 1882.

Robert de Monte (appendix), in *R.H.F.* vol. XVIII.

Robert of Clary. *La Conquête de Constantinople* (ed. Lauer). Paris, 1924.

Roger of Wendover. *Chronica* (ed. Hewlett), Rolls Series, 3 vols. London, 1886–9.

Rutebeuf. *Onze Poèmes concernant la Croisade* (ed. Bastin and Faral). Paris, 1946.

Salimbene de Adam. *Cronica* (ed. Holder-Egger), in *M.G.H.Ss.* vol. XXXII.

Sanudo, Marino. *Chronique de Romanie*, in Mas Latrie, *Nouvelles Preuves*.

Sanudo, Marino. *Liber Secretorum Fidelium Crucis*, in Bongars, *Gesta Dei per Francos*, vol. II.

Sequentia Andegavensis, in Riant, *Exuviae*, vol. II.

Sicard of Cremona. *Cronica* (ed. Holder-Egger), *M.G.H.Ss.* vol. XXXI.

'Templar of Tyre.' *Chronique*, in *Gestes des Chiprois*.

Thaddeus of Naples. *Hystoria de Desolacione et Conculcacione Civitatis Acconensis et tocius terre sancte* (ed. Riant). Geneva, 1873.

Thomas of Spalato. *Historia Salonitana*, in Schwandtner, *Scriptores Rerum Hungaricarum*, vol. III.

Thwrocz, Joannes de. *Illustrissima Hungariae Regum Chronica*, in Schwandtner, *Scriptores Rerum Hungaricarum*, vol. I.

Via ad Terram Sanctam, in Kohler, *Mélanges*, vol. II.

Villaret, Fulk. *Mémoire* (ed. Petit), *Bibliothèque de l'Ecole des Chartes*. Paris, 1889.

Villehardouin, Geoffrey of. *La Conquête de Constantinople* (ed. Faral), 2 vols. Paris, 1938–9.

Vincent of Beauvais. *Speculum Historiale*. Douai, 1624.

Vitry, James of. *Epistolae* (ed. Röhricht), *Zeitschrift für Kirchengeschichte*, vols. XIV–XVI. Gotha, 1894–6.

Vitry, James of. *History of Jerusalem* (trans. Stewart), *P.P.T.S.* vol. XI.

Wilbrand of Oldenburg. *Reise* (ed. Laurent). Hamburg, 1859.

William le Breton. *Gesta Philippi Regis* and *Philippis* (ed. Delaborde), 2 vols. Paris, 1882, 1885.

Bibliography

William of Newburgh. *Historia Rerum Anglicarum,* in *Chronicles* (ed. Howlett), vol. II.

William of Rubruck (Rubruquis). *Itinerarium* (trans. Rockhill), Hakluyt Society, series II, vol. IV. London, 1900.

William of St Pathus. *Vie de Saint Louis* (ed. Delaborde). Paris, 1899.

William of Tripoli. *Tractatus de Statu Saracenorum,* in Prutz, *Kulturgeschichte der Kreuzzüge* (see Bibliography II).

Zaccaria, Benito. *Mémoire,* in Mas Latrie, *Documents.*

3. GREEK SOURCES

Acropolita, George. *Opera* (ed. Heisenberg). Leipsic, 1903.

Bustron, George. Χρονικὸν Κύπρου, in Sathas, Μεσαιωνικὴ Βιβλιοθήκη, vol II.

Germanus, Patriarch of Constantinople. Ἐπιστολαί, in Sathas, Μεσαιωνικὴ Βιβλιοθήκη, vol. II.

Letter of Greek clergy to Innocent III, in Cotelerius, *Ecclesiae Graecae Monumenta,* vol. III.

Makhaeras, Leontius. *Recital concerning the Sweet Land of Cyprus,* entitled *Chronicle* (ed. with translation Dawkins), 2 vols. Oxford, 1932.

Mesarites, Nicholas. *Opera,* in Heisenberg, *Neue Quellen.*

'Narrative of the thirteen holy fathers burnt by the Latins', in Sathas, Μεσαιωνικὴ Βιβλιοθήκη, vol. II.

Pachymer, George. *De Michaele et Andronico Palaeologis,* 2 vols. *C.S.H.B.* Bonn, 1835.

4. ARABIC AND PERSIAN SOURCES

Al-Aini. *Perles d'Histoire,* extracts in *R.H.C.Or.* vol. II, 2.

Dimashki. *Geography* (ed. Mehren). St Petersburg, 1866.

Histoire des Patriarches d'Alexandrie, extracts (trans. Blochet), *Revue de l'Orient Latin,* vol. XI. Paris, 1908.

Ibn al-Amid. *Chronicle* (ed. Cheikho), *Corpus Scriptorum Christianorum Orientalium,* vol. III, I.

Ibn Batuta. *Voyages* (ed. with French translation Defremery and Sanguinetti), 4 vols. Paris, 1879.

Ibn Bibi. *History of the Seldjuks,* Turkish translation (ed. Houtsma), *Textes relatifs à l'histoire des Seldjouqides,* vols. III, IV. Paris, 1902.

Ibn al-Furad. *Chronicle* (part ed. Zouraiq). Beirut, 1935–7.

Ibn Khattikan, Ibn Shedad. *Geography,* extracts (ed. by Cahen), in *Revue des Etudes Islamiques.* Paris, 1936.

Ibn Wasil. *History of the Ayubites,* selections in Reinaud, *Extraits,* in Michaud, *Bibliothèque.*

Idrisi. *Geography,* ed. Gildemeister, *Zeitschrift für Deutsche Palästina Verein,* vol. VIII. Leipsic, 1885.

Bibliography

Al-Jazari. *Chronique de Damas* (trans. Sauvaget). Paris, 1949.

Juwaïni, Sa'd ad-Din Ibn Hamawiya, extracts (trans. Cahen), 'Une Source pour l'Histoire des Croisades', in *Bulletin de la Faculté des Lettres de Strasbourg,* 28e année, no. 7, 1950.

Maqrisi. *Histoire des Sultans Mamelouks* (trans. Quatremère), 2 vols. Paris, 1837–45.

Muhi ad-Din Ibn Abdazzahir. *Lives of Baibars and Qalawun*, selections in Reynaud, *Extraits*, in Michaud, *Bibliothèque*.

Rashid ad-Din. *History of the Mongols* (Russian trans. by Berezin), 4 vols. St Petersburg, 1861–88: Part IV, *History of the Mongols of Persia* (ed. with French translation Quatremère). Paris, 1836.

Yakut. *Alphabetical Dictionary of Geography* (ed. Wustenfeld), 6 vols. Leipsic, 1866–73.

5. ARMENIAN, SYRIAC, SLAVONIC AND MONGOL SOURCES

Ballad on the captivity of Leo, son of King Hethoum I, in *R.H.C.Arm.* vol. I.

Hayton (Hethoum of Corycus). *Chronological Tables*, in *R.H.C.Arm.* vol. I.

Hethoum II, King of Armenia, *Poem*, in *R.H.C.Arm.* vol. I.

Kirakos of Gantzag. *History* (trans. Brosset). St Petersburg, 1870.

Orbelian, Stephen. *History of Siunia*, Armenian text. Moscow, 1861.

Vartan. *History of the World*, Armenian text. Moscow, 1861.

Rabban Sauma. *History of Rabban Sawma and Mar Yahbhallaha* (trans. Budge), in Budge, *The Monks of Khublai Khan*, see Bibliography II.

Novgorod Chronicle (*Novgorodskaya Pervaya Lietopis*, ed. Nasonov), Academy of Sciences of the U.S.S.R. Moscow/Leningrad, 1950.

Histoire Secrète des Mongols (*Yuan Ch'ao Pi Shih*), Mongol text transcribed in Latin letters, with partial French translation and ed. Pelliot. Paris, 1949.

II. MODERN WORKS

ALPHANDERY, P. 'Les Croisades d'Enfants', in *Revue de l'Histoire des Religions,* vol. LXXIII. Paris, 1916.

AMARI, M. *La Guerra del Vespro Siciliano*, 3 vols. Milan, 1886.

ATIYA, A. S. *The Crusade in the Later Middle Ages*. London, 1938.

ATIYA, A. S. *The Crusade of Nicopolis*. London, 1934.

BALTRUŠAITIS, J. *Le Problème de l'Ogive et l'Arménie*. Paris, 1936.

BARTHOLD, W. Articles, 'Cingis Khan' and 'Khwaresm', in *Encyclopaedia of Islam*.

BOASE, T. S. R. 'The Arts in the Latin Kingdom of Jerusalem', in *Journal of the Warburg Institute*, vol. II. London, 1938–9.

BOUVAT, L. *L'Empire Mongol, 2me Phase*, vol. VIII, 3, pt. II of Cavaignac, *Histoire du Monde*. Paris, 1927.

Bibliography

BRATIANU, G. I. *Recherches sur le Commerce Génois dans la Mer Noire au XIIIe Siècle*. Paris, 1929.

BRETSCHNEIDER, E. *Mediaeval Researches from Eastern Asiatic Sources*, 2 vols. London, 1888.

BUCHTHAL, H. 'The Painting of Syrian Jacobites in its relation to Byzantine and Islamic Art', in *Syria*, vol. XX. Beyrouth, 1929.

BUDGE, E. A. W. *The Monks of Kûblâi Khân, Emperor of China*. London, 1928.

CAHEN, C. 'Notes sur l'Histoire des Croisades et de l'Orient Latin, III, Orient Latin et Commerce du Levant', in *Bulletin de la Faculté des Lettres de Strasbourg*, 9e année, no. 8, 1951.

CAHEN, C. 'Turcomans de Roum', in *Byzantion*, vol. XIV. Brussels, 1939.

CARTELLIERI, A. *Philipp II August und der Zusammenbruch des angevinischen Reiches*. Leipsic, 1913.

CHABOT, J. B. 'Relations du Roi Argoun avec l'Occident', in *Revue de l'Orient Latin*, vol. II. Paris, 1894.

CHAYTOR, H. J. *The Troubadours*. Cambridge, 1912.

CLAPHAM, A. W. *Romanesque Architecture in Western Europe*. Oxford, 1936.

COGNASSO, F. *Un Imperatore Bizantino della Decadenza*, in *Bessarione*, vol. XXXI, Rome, 1915.

DALTON, O. M. *Byzantine Art and Archaeology*. Oxford, 1911.

DALTON, O. M. *East Christian Art*. Oxford, 1925.

DELAVILLE LA ROULX, J. *La France en Orient au XIVe Siècle*, Bibliothèque des Ecoles Françaises d'Athènes et de Rome. Paris, 1886.

DER NERSESSIAN, S. *Armenia and the Byzantine Empire*. Cambridge, Mass., 1945.

DESCHAMPS, P. *La Défense du Royaume de Jérusalem*, 2 vols. Paris, 1939.

DESCHAMPS, P. *Le Crac des Chevaliers*, 2 vols. Paris, 1934.

DIEHL, C. *Une République Patricienne, Venise*. Paris, 1915.

D'OHSSON, M. *Histoire des Mongols depuis Tchinguiz Khan jusqu'à Timur Béc.* 2 vols. Amsterdam, 1834–5.

DONOVAN, J. P. *Pelagius and the Fifth Crusade*. Philadelphia, 1950.

DUCKWORTH, H. T. F. *The Church of the Holy Sepulchre*. London, 1922.

EBERSOLT, J. *Monuments d'Architecture Byzantine*. Paris, 1934.

EDWARDS, J. G. 'The *Itinerarium Regis Ricardi* and the *Estoire de la Guerre Sainte*', in *Essays in honour of James Tait*. Manchester, 1933.

ENLART, C. *Les Monuments des Croisés dans le Royaume de Jérusalem*, 4 vols. Paris, 1925.

FEDDEN, R. *Crusader Castles*. London, 1950.

FLICHE, A. *La Chrétienté Romaine*, vol. X of Fliche and Martin, *Histoire de l'Eglise*. Paris, 1950.

FOREVILLE, R. and ROUSSET DE PINA, J. *Du Premier Concile du Latran à l'Avènement d'Innocent III*, vol. IX, 2, of Fliche and Martin, *Histoire de l'Eglise*. Paris, 1952.

Bibliography

GIBBONS, H. A. *The Foundation of the Ottoman Empire.* Oxford, 1916.

GOTTRON, A. 'Ramon Lulls Kreuzzugsideen', in *Abhandlungen zur Mittleren und Neueren Geschichte*, vol. XXXIX. Berlin/Leipsic, 1912.

GREGOIRE, H. 'The Question of the Diversion of the Fourth Crusade', in *Byzantion*, vol. XV. Boston, 1941.

GREKOV, B. and IAKOUBOVSKI, A. *La Horde d'Or* (trans. into French by Thuret). Paris, 1939.

GREVEN, J. 'Frankreich und der Fünfte Kreuzzug', in *Historisches Jahrbuch*, vol. XLII. Munich, 1923.

GROUSSET, R. *L'Empire des Steppes.* Paris, 1941.

GROUSSET, R. *L'Empire Mongol, Ière Phase*, vol. VIII, 3, of Cavaignac, *Histoire du Monde.* Paris, 1941.

HAENISCH, E. 'Die letzten Feldzüge Cingis Hans und sein Tod', in *Asia Major*, vol. IX. Leipsic, 1932.

HALECKI, O. *The Crusade of Varna.* New York, 1943.

HAMMER-PURGSTALL, J. VON. *Histoire de l'Empire Ottoman* (trans. into French by Hellert), 18 vols. Paris, 1843.

HILL, G. *History of Cyprus*, vols. II and III. Cambridge, 1948.

HOPF, K. *Geschichte Griechenlands vom Beginne des Mittelalters bis auf die neuere Zeit.* Leipsic, 1867.

HOWORTH, H. H. *History of the Mongols*, 5 vols. London, 1876–88.

IORGA, N. *Philippe de Mézières et la Croisade au XIVe Siècle.* Paris, 1896.

JORDAN, E. *Les Origines de la Domination Angevine en Italie.* Paris, 1909.

KANTOROWICZ, E. *Frederick the Second.* London, 1931.

KARAMZIN, N. M. *History of the Russian Empire* (in Russian), 3 vols. St Petersburg, 1851.

KINGSFORD, C. L. 'Otho de Grandison', in *Transactions of the Royal Historical Society*, 3rd series, vol. III. London, 1909.

KÖPRÜLÜ, M. F. *Les Origines de l'Empire Ottoman.* Paris, 1935.

LA MONTE, J. L. 'John d'Ibelin', in *Byzantion*, vol. XII. Brussels, 1937.

LANGLOIS, C. V. *La Vie en France au Moyen Age*, 3 vols. Paris, 1927.

LECLERC, L. *La Médecine Arabe.* Paris, 1876.

LEVIS-MIREPOIX, DUC DE. *Philippe le Bel.* Paris, 1936.

LEVY, R. *A Baghdad Chronicle.* Cambridge, 1929.

LIZERAND, G. *Le Dossier de l'Affaire des Templiers.* Paris, 1928.

LONGNON, J. *L'Empire Latin de Constantinople.* Paris, 1949.

LONGNON, J. *Les Français d'Outre-mer au Moyen Age.* Paris, 1929.

LUCHAIRE, A. *Innocent III: La Question d'Orient.* Paris, 1911.

MAKHOULY, N. *Guide to Acre.* Jerusalem, 1941.

MARTIN, E. J. *The Trial of the Templars.* London, 1928.

MARTIN, H. D. *The Rise of Chingis Khan and his Conquest of North China.* Baltimore, 1950.

2K

Bibliography

MAS LATRIE, L. *Histoire de l'Ile de Chypre sous le Règne de la Maison de Lusignan*, vol. I, *Histoire*; vols. II and III, *Documents*. Paris, 1852–61.

MELVIN, M. *La Vie des Templiers*. Paris, 1951.

MUNRO, D. C. 'The Children's Crusade', in *American Historical Review*, vol. XIX. New York, 1914.

NORGATE, K. *Richard the Lion Heart*. London, 1924.

NORGATE, K. 'The *Itinerarium Peregrinorum* and the *Song of Ambroise*', in *English Historical Review*, vol. XXV. London, 1910.

OMONT, H. 'Peintures d'un Evangéliaire Syriaque', in *Monuments et Mémoires publiés par l'Académie des Inscriptions et Belles-Lettres*, vol. XIX. Paris, 1911.

PELLIOT, P. 'Chrétiens d'Asie Centrale et de l'Extrême Orient', in *T'oung Pao*, vol. XI. Leiden, 1914.

PELLIOT, P. 'Les Mongols et la Papauté', in *Revue de l'Orient Chrétien*, vols. XXIII, XXIV, XXVIII. Paris, 1922–32.

PIQUET, J. *Les Banquiers du Moyen Age: Les Templiers*. Paris, 1939.

POWICKE, F. M. *King Henry III and the Lord Edward*, 2 vols. Oxford, 1947.

PRAWER, J. 'Etude de Quelques Problèmes Agraires et Sociaux d'une Seigneurie Croisée au XIIIe Siècle', in *Byzantion*, vol. XXII. Brussels, 1952.

PRAWER, J. 'L'Etablissement des Coutumes du Marché à Saint-Jean d'Acre', in *Revue Historique de Droit Français et Etranger*. Paris, 1951.

PRUTZ, H. G. *Kaiser Friedrich I*, 3 vols. Danzig, 1871–4.

PRUTZ, H. G. *Kulturgeschichte der Kreuzzüge*. Berlin, 1883.

REY, E. G. *Les Monuments de l'Architecture Militaire des Croisés en Syrie et dans l'Ile de Chypre*. Paris, 1871.

RÖHRICHT, R. 'Der Kinderkreuzzug 1212', in *Historische Zeitschrift*, vol. XXXVI. Munich, 1876.

RÖHRICHT, R. *Etudes sur les Derniers Temps du Royaume de Jérusalem, Archives de l'Orient Latin*, vol. II. Paris, 1884.

RÖHRICHT, R. *Studien zur Geschichte des Fünften Kreuzzüges*. Innsbruck, 1891.

SACERDOTEANU, A. *Marea Invazie Tatara şi Sud-estul European*. Bucarest, 1933.

SCHLUMBERGER, G. *Byzance et Croisades: Pages Médiévales*. Paris, 1927.

SMAIL, R. C. 'Crusaders' Castles in the Twelfth Century', in *Cambridge Historical Journal*, vol. X, 2. Cambridge, 1951.

SOBERNHEIM, M. Article 'Baibars', in *Encyclopaedia of Islam*.

STERNFELD, R. *Ludwigs des Heiligen Kreuzzug nach Tunis 1270*. Berlin, 1896.

STRAKOSCH-GROSSMANN, G. *Der Einfall der Mongolen in Mitteleuropa in den Jahren 1241 und 1242*. Innsbruck, 1893.

THROOP, P. A. 'Criticism of Papal Crusade Policy in Old French and Provençal', in *Speculum*, vol. XIII. Cambridge, Mass., 1938.

THROOP, P. A. *Criticism of the Crusades*. Amsterdam, 1940.

VAN ORTROY, F. 'Saint François et son Voyage en Orient', in *Analecta Bollandiana*, vol. XXXI. Brussels, 1912.

Bibliography

VASILIEV, A. A. *History of the Byzantine Empire*, new edition. Madison, 1952,

VASILIEV, A. A. 'The Foundation of the Empire of Trebizond', in *Speculum*, vol. XI. Cambridge, Mass., 1936.

VERNADSKY, G. *Kievan Russia*, vol. II of Vernadsky and Karpovitch, *History of Russia*. Newhaven, 1948.

WINKELMANN, E. *Kaiser Friedrich II*, 2 vols. Leipsic, 1889–97.

WINKELMANN, E. *Philipp von Schwaben und Otto IV von Braunschweig*, 2 vols. Leipsic, 1873–8.

WITTEK, P. *The Rise of the Ottoman Empire*. London, 1838.

YULE, H. *Cathay and the Way Thither*, 2 vols. Hakluyt Society, no. 37. London, 1866–7.

INDEX

Index

Ariqboga, Mongol prince, 293–4, 309
Armand of Périgord, Grand Master of the Temple, 223–7
Arqa, 322
Arsuf, 55–7, 180, 318–19; *see* John of Ibelin
Arthur, Duke of Brittany, 40, 109
Artois, *see* Philip, Robert
Arundel, Earl of, 155
Ascalon, 19, 58–9, 62–4, 67, 69–72, 213–15, 217–19, 222, 226–7, 229
Ascelin of Lombardy, Dominican, 259
Ascheri, Orlando, admiral, 403
Asen family, 127; *see* Ivan, Kaloyan, Peter
Ashmun Tannah, 157, 262, 265
al-Ashraf, Sultan, 82, 150–1, 160, 167, 184–5, 209–10
al-Ashraf Khalil, Sultan, 382, 411–12, 414, 416–18, 420–2, 438–9
al-Ashraf Musa, Prince of Homs, 258, 306, 314–16
al-Ashraf Musa, Sultan, 273, 310
Assassin sect, 64–5, 89, 138, 207, 253, 277–80, 299–301, 332–4, 338
Assir, 71
Asti, *see* Henry
Ata al-Mulk, *see* Juveni
Athens, 120, 126, 328
Athlit, castle, 149, 151, 165, 191, 318, 324, 344, 348, 372, 378 n., 393, 422
Attalia, 451–2
Augustinian Order, 376
Aurillac, *see* Gerbert
Austria, 74; *see* Henry, Leopold
Autoreanus, *see* Michael
Autun, *see* Walter
Avesnes, *see* James
Avignon, 432, 437, 442, 472
Ayas, 322, 359–60, 402, 405, 472
Aydin (Tralles), 451; *see* Omar
Aymar, Archbishop of Caesarea, Patriarch of Jerusalem, 83, 94–5, 107
Aymar, lord of Caesarea, 132
Aymé, Count of Geneva, 443
Aymé of Oselier, Marshal of Tripoli, 437
Ayub, as-Salih, Sultan, 210–11, 216–20, 223–4, 226–9, 258, 261–5, 272
Ayubite dynasty, 29, 82, 101, 154, 170, 184, 186, 209, 211, 216, 224, 228, 249–50, 258–9, 264, 304, 315, 438, 473, 485–6
Azerbaijan, 163, 184, 246–7, 250, 304, 319, 464

al-Aziz, King of Aleppo, 210
al-Aziz, prince of Damascus, 305
al-Aziz, Sultan, 79–82, 92, 97–8
Azov, Sea of, 247

Baalbek, 210, 228, 311
Babylon, 42
Bacon, Roger, 340
Badr ad-Din Lulu, atabeg of Mosul, 305
Badr ad-Din, *see* al-Fakhri
Baghdad, 16, 143, 158, 160, 184, 210, 259, 273, 297, 301–4, 308, 316, 354, 372, 438, 463–4, 472–3
Baghras, 87–8, 100, 135, 138, 208, 322, 326, 390; *see* Adam
Bagnara, 38
Baibars, Rukn ad-Din, Bundukdari, Sultan, early career, 226, 267; murders Sultan Turanshah, 272–3; quarrels with Sultan Aibek, 282; at Ain Jalud, 310–12; murders Sultan Qutuz, 314; becomes Sultan, 314–15; conquests in Palestine, 316–23; conquers Antioch, 324–7; negotiations with Franks, 330–8, 340–2; in Anatolia, 347–8; death, 348. Other references, 382, 387, 393, 412, 485
Baichu, Mongol general, 253, 259, 302, 305
Baidar, Mongol prince, 251–2, 311
Baikal, Lake, 240
Baldwin XI, of Hainault, Count of Flanders, Latin Emperor of Constantinople, 110, 124–5, 127–9, 136
Baldwin II, Latin Emperor of Constantinople, 177, 263, 284
Baldwin I, King of Jerusalem, 356, 376
Baldwin II, King of Jerusalem, 368, 376
Baldwin III, King of Jerusalem, 381, 489
Baldwin IV, King of Jerusalem, 30
Baldwin, Archbishop of Canterbury, 6–8, 29, 31, 36
Baldwin, lord of Beisan, 84
Baldwin Embriaco, 389
Baldwin of Ibelin, lord of Ramleh, 83
Baldwin of Ibelin, Seneschal of Cyprus, 200, 205, 229
Baldwin of Ibelin, Constable of Cyprus, 397
Baldwin, *see* Carew
Balian of Ibelin, lord of Nablus, lord of Caymon, 20, 30–2, 63, 65, 73, 83–4, 86, 104

507

Index

Balian of Ibelin, lord of Arsuf, 278, 317–18, 345–6, 393

Balian of Ibelin, lord of Beirut, 194, 196, 198–201, 205, 220–2, 230

Balian I, Garnier, lord of Sidon, 175, 182, 186, 191, 193, 195–8, 203, 205, 214, 216

Balian II, Garnier, lord of Sidon, 388

Balikesir, 14

Balkans, 12–14, 287, 393, 450, 453, 455, 464, 477

Balkh, 245

Baltic Sea, 245

Bamian, 245

Banyas, 158, 193, 277, 371 n.

Bar, Count of, 25, 212; Duke of, 456; see Philip

Baramun, 265

Baraqa, Sultan, 387

Barbarossa, see Frederick I

Bardt, see Hermann

Bar Hebraeus, historian, 487

Barin, 207

Barlais, Almeric, 180, 183, 192, 194, 196–9, 202, 205

Barlais, Reynald, 93

Bar-sur-Seine, see Milo

Bartholomew, Bishop of Tortosa, 343, 388, 404

Bartholomew of Cremona, Dominican, 280

Bartholomew Embriaco, mayor of Tripoli, 404–5, 407

Bartholomew, lord of Maraclea, 334

Bartholomew Pizan, Templar, 412

Bartholomew, see Tirel

Basil, Englishman, 295 n.

Basil, painter, 380, 384

Basle, 142

Batu, Mongol prince, Khan of the Golden Horde, 249, 251–3, 280, 293–4, 296–7, 300

Bavaria, Bavarians, 168; see Louis, Rupert

Bayezit I, Ottoman Sultan, 455, 457–61, 463

Beatrice of Provence, Queen of Naples and Sicily, 290–1, 335

Beaufort, castle, 22–3, 29, 60, 216–17, 308, 324

Beaujeu, see William

Beauvais, Bishop of, see Philip; see Vincent

Beha ed-Din, biographer, 16, 485

Behesni, castle, 332

Beirut, 27, 47, 51, 60, 63, 69, 77, 92, 96–8, 103, 147, 180–1, 196–8, 205, 220, 329–30, 342–3, 353–4, 361, 381–2, 393–5, 422; Bishop of, see Galeran

Beisan, 148, 185, 318; see Amalric, Baldwin

Beit Nuba, 61, 68–9

Bekaa, 149, 308, 352

Bektimur, lord of Akhlat, 79–80

Bela III, King of Hungary, 11–12, 114–15

Bela IV, King of Hungary, 252

Belgrade, 11

Belmont, abbey, 233

Belus, river, 23

Belvoir, castle, 218, 229, 370–1

Benedict XIII, Pope, 456

Benedict of Peterborough, chronicler, 482

Benevento, battle, 291

Benito, see Zaccaria

Berard of Manupello, 201

Berard, Thomas, Grand Master of the Temple, 344

Berengaria of Navarre, Queen of England, 41–3, 45, 59, 74

Berengaria, princess of Castile, 174

Berengaria, royal mistress, 341

Berke, Mongol prince, Khan of the Golden Horde, 249, 309–10, 316, 320

Bernard the Treasurer, chronicler, 481–2

Berry, 6

Bertrand du Guesclin, 447–8

Bertrand Embriaco, 288, 404

Bertrandon, see La Broquière

Berwick-on-Tweed, 8

Besancon, Archbishop of, 28–9

Bethlehem, 73, 161, 187, 345, 375, 379–80, 384; Bishop of, see Thomas

Bilbeis, 81

Birejik, 305

Bithynia, 124, 453

Blachernae, palace at Constantinople, 120, 122

Black Death, 449

Black Sea, 126, 250, 287, 357, 359, 360

Black Sheep, Turcoman tribe, 464

Blanche of Castile, Queen of France, 256, 274, 279–80

Blanche of Navarre, Countess of Champagne, 132–5

Blanchegarde, castle, 61, 67, 368

Blois, Bishop of, 28; see Alice, Henry, Louis, Tibald

Index

Bodrun (Halicarnassus), 464

Bohemia, 339, 457; see Ottocar

Bohemond III, Prince of Antioch, 17, 20–1, 44, 76–7, 86–9, 99–101, 135

Bohemond IV, Prince of Antioch, Count of Tripoli, 88–9, 99–102, 135–8, 149, 171–3, 179–80, 182–3, 187, 198, 206–7, 328

Bohemond V, Prince of Antioch, Count of Tripoli, 180, 195, 204, 207–8, 221–2, 226, 230–1, 233, 261, 278

Bohemond VI, Prince of Antioch, Count of Tripoli, 278, 283–4, 288, 298–9, 306–7, 316, 319–20, 322–3, 325, 327, 334–5, 404

Bohemond VII, titular Prince of Antioch, Count of Tripoli, 343, 347, 388–9, 391–2, 403–4

Bohemond, prince of Cyprus, 394

Bokhara, 244, 296

Boniface VIII, Pope, 432

Boniface IX, Pope, 455

Boniface, Marquis of Montferrat, King of Thessalonica, 100–12, 114–16, 124–6

Bonnacorso of Gloria, Archbishop of Tyre, 396

Bonomel, Ricaut, Templar poet, 318–19

Bordeaux, 399, 442, 456; Archbishop of, see William

Bosphorus, 13–14, 118, 129–30, 462

Botrun, 197, 388, 407; see John, William

Boucicaut, John Le Meingre, Marshal, 458–60, 462

Bougie, 143, 431

Boulogne, 380 n.; see Eustace

Bourbon, see Louis

Boves, see Enguerrand

Brabant, Brabançons, 96, 442; see Henry

Bremen, 98

Brie, see Anselm

Brienne, Count of (John II), 267; see Andrew, Hugh, John, Maria, Walter

Brindisi, 42, 52, 143, 174–6, 178–9, 192, 212; see Margaritus

Brittany, Bretons, 55, 335: Count of, 292; see Arthur, Peter

Bruno, Bishop of Olmütz, 339

Brusa, 453, 461

Buda, 456–7

Buddhism, Buddhists, 238, 242–3, 294, 296, 299, 397

Buffavento, castle, 45, 198, 200

Bulgaria, Bulgarians, 12–13, 112, 127, 287, 428, 455, 458; see Kama

Buluniyas, 334, 344

Bundukdar, Mameluk emir, 315

Buqaia, 322, 334, 352, 390, 406

Burcard, propagandist, 440

Burchard of Schwanden, Grand Master of the Teutonic Order, 413

Burgundia, princess of Cyprus, 103–4, 134

Burgundy, Duke of (Odo III), 145; see Hugh, John, Philip

Buri, Mongol prince, 252

Burlos, 165

Buscarel of Gisolf, envoy, 401

Bustron, George, chronicler, 481

Buza'a, 150

Cadzaud, see John

Caen, 442

Caesarea, 55, 70–1, 149, 199, 220, 278, 318, 337, 378, 393; Archbishops of, see Aymar, Peter; see Aymar, John

Caesarea-Mazacha, 253, 347

Caffa, 357

Cafran, see Adam, William

Cairo, 80–1, 92, 113, 144, 152, 164, 170, 176, 184, 216, 219, 262, 265, 268–9, 275–6, 282, 301, 314, 316, 324, 327, 380, 382, 387, 397, 405, 409, 411–12, 419, 421, 445–6, 491

Calabria, 38

Calamon, monastery, 381

Calamus, river, 14

Calvary, 381

Calycadnus, river, 14

Camaterus, see John

Camville, see Richard

Cana in Galilee, 148

Canabus, see Nicholas

Cantacuzenus, see Constantine, John

Canterbury, Archbishop of, see Baldwin

Capua, see James, Peter

Carew, Baldwin, 56

Carinthia, 74

Carmel, Mt, 54–5, 70, 86, 149, 318, 337, 393, 422

Carpathian Mountains, 252

Carthage, 292

Casal Imbert, 43, 198–9, 206

Caspian Gates, pass, 247

Caspian Sea, 245–7, 250, 359

Index

Index

Copts, 170, 263, 446
Corazzo, *see* Joachim
Corfu, 74, 117, 126
Corycus, 441, 452; *see* Hayton
Cos, 124, 435
Coucy, Count of (Ralph II), 267; *see* Enguerrand
Courçon, *see* Robert
Courtenay family, 20; *see* Peter
Cracow, 251, 442–3
Cremona, *see* Bartholomew
Crésèques, *see* Robert
Crete, 43, 125–6, 443
Crimea, 247
Croton, 126
Cyprus, 4, 12, 43–7, 49, 58, 66–7, 76, 83–6, 93–5, 103–4, 107, 129–30, 134–5, 137, 147, 166, 172, 179–83, 192, 194–206, 208, 212, 229, 257–61, 278, 280–2, 284–5, 289–90, 319, 321, 330, 334–6, 345–6, 383, 386, 389–90, 393–7, 402, 406–81, 413–14, 416, 419–23, 427–9, 433–5, 437–41, 443–4, 447–9, 451, 466, 469, 481, 490 n., 492

Daimbert, Patriarch of Jerusalem, 356
Dalmatia, 102, 114, 147
Damascus, 21–2, 77–82, 92, 185–7, 207, 209–11, 213, 216–17, 224, 228–9, 261, 269, 275–6, 282, 301, 305, 307–8, 310–11, 314–5, 321, 326, 355, 358–9, 387, 390–1, 401, 410, 412, 414, 420, 439, 463
Damietta, 133, 150, 152–8, 161–9, 171–2, 258, 261–6, 268–74, 292, 444
Dampierre, *see* Reynald, William
Dan, 42
Dandolo, Enrico, Doge of Venice, 114–16, 118–21
Daniel, hermit, 8
Danishmend Turks, 101, 150
Danube, river, 11, 455, 457–8, 460–2, 465–6, 469
Darbsaq, castle, 208, 332, 390
Dardanelles, 13–14, 117, 453, 454
Dardel, John, chronicler, 449 n.
Daron, 67
David, King of Judaea, 118, 385; Tower of, at Jerusalem, 189, 215, 368
David IV, King of Georgia, 250, 319
David, Patriarch of Antioch, 231
David Comnenus, ruler of Pontus, 126

David, Dominican, 346
David, Nestorian, 259–60
Dead Sea, 419
Delhi 245, 295
Demavend, 300
Denmark, Danes, 9, 24, 26, 118
Denys, King of Portugal, 436
Denys, Jacobite Catholicus, 232
Denys, Bishop of Tabriz, 400
Despina Khatun, *see* Maria Palaeologaena
Derby, Earl of, 155
Devizes, *see* Richard
Dhaifa, regent of Aleppo, 210–11, 216, 228
Diarbekir, 269
Diceto, *see* Ralph
Didymotichum, 13
Dietz, *see* Henry
Dieu d'Amour, castle, 182, 194, 198, 200–1; *see* Saint Hilarion
Dijon, 456
Dmitri, prince of Kiev, 251
Dodecanese, 435
Dogan Bey, governor of Nicopolis, 458
Dokuz Khatun, Lady of the Mongols, 299, 303–4, 320, 331
Dome of the Rock, at Jerusalem, 187, 377, 385
Dominic of Palestrina, Papal legate, 437–8
Dominican Order, 232, 260, 280, 340, 437–8
Don, river, 247
Dorylaeum, 453
Dreux, Count of (Robert II), 25
Dubois, Peter, lawyer, 432–3
Ducas, *see* John
Dunbar, *see* Patrick
Durant, William, Bishop of Mende, 433
Durazzo, 117

Eberhard, Count of Katznellenbogen, 457
Ecri-sur-Aisne, 107
Edessa, 5, 79, 210, 224, 305, 380
Edmund of England, Duke of Lancaster, 278 n., 290, 335
Edward I, King of England, 335–8, 341, 346–7, 387–8, 390, 392, 399–402, 408–9, 413, 428
Edward III, King of England, 442
Edward, Prince of Wales, the Black Prince, 442

Index

Index

Fulk of Villaret, Grand Master of the Hospital, 434

Fulk of Neuilly, preacher, 107, 109

Fuwa, 102

Gaeta, 147

Galata, 118, 121

Galeran, Bishop of Beirut, 256

Galich, 251

Galicia, 252

Galilee, 92, 97, 102, 158, 161, 187, 193, 213, 216, 218, 224, 227, 309, 312, 317, 321-2, 410; Sea of, 148, 311

Gallipoli, 14, 125, 453, 454-5

Galvano of Levanti, physician, 431

Garnhi, battle, 250

Garnier family, 20, 388; see Balian, Julian, Reynald

Garnier the German, 191, 193, 195, 198

Gastria, castle, 194, 390

Gaudin, Tibald, Grand Master of the Temple, 420, 422

Gavin of Chenichy, 180, 183, 192, 194

Gaza, 185, 213-16, 218, 225-7, 230, 256, 277, 308, 311, 348

Gelnhausen, 85

Geneva, 142; see Aymé

Genoa, Genoese, 4, 21, 36-7, 49, 62-3, 70, 83-4, 142, 145, 147, 191, 198-201, 220-2, 247, 257, 260-1, 263, 272, 282-7, 307-8, 317, 323-4, 330, 335-7, 360, 387, 389, 399-400, 404-7, 409, 415, 442-3, 449, 457, 462, 464, 466, 469

Geoffrey I, of Villehardouin, Prince of Achaea, 126

Geoffrey, Count of Lusignan, 25, 44, 55, 84

Geoffrey III, Count of Perche, 110

Geoffrey of Sargines, Seneschal, 270, 273, 282, 284, 286, 288-90, 317, 322, 331

Geoffrey of Vendac, Marshal of the Temple, 406-7

Geoffrey, see Le Tor, Villehardouin

George IV, King of Georgia, 163, 247, 249

George, King of Serbia, 465

George, secretary, 412

George, see Acropolites, Bustron, Pachymer

Georgia, Georgians, 101, 163, 246-7, 249, 295 n., 302-3, 305, 312, 347, 401; see David, George, Russudan, Thamar

Gerard, Archbishop of Ravenna, 25

Gerard of Ridfort, Grand Master of the Temple, 26

Gerard of Montreal, chronicler, 482

Gerbert of Aurillac (Pope Sylvester II), 470

Gerold of Lausanne, Patriarch of Jerusalem, 178, 183, 188, 190-1, 195, 197-8, 206, 213

Gervase, Abbot of Prémontré, 145

Gethsemane, 377

Ghazzan, Ilkhan of Persia, 429, 439-40

Gibraltar, Straits of, 9, 101

Gilbert of Hoxton, Templar, 6

Gilbert of Tournay, Franciscan, 339

Giraut, poet, 5 n.

Girdkuh, castle, 300

Gisolf, see Buscarel

Gisors, 6

Giustiniani, Marco, admiral, 283

Gloria, see Bonnacorso

Gobert of Helleville, ambassador, 399-401

Godfrey of Lorraine, ruler of Jerusalem, 356, 376, 391

Godfrey, see Welles

Golden Horde, Khanate, 294, 299, 302, 309, 316, 319-20, 332, 463

Golden Horn, harbour at Constantinople, 118, 122

Golgotha, 375-6

Goliath, Pools of, see Ain Jalud

Grailly, see John

Gran, see Nicholas

Grandson, see Otto

Granicus, river, 14

'Green Knight,' Spanish knight, 19; see Amadeus

Greenland, 338

Gregory VIII, Pope, 4-5, 10, 21

Gregory IX, Pope, 178, 183-4, 195, 203-4, 206, 208, 211-12, 253

Gregory X, Pope (Tedaldo Visconti, Archbishop of Liège), 329, 335, 338-9, 341-2, 387, 401

Gregory Abirad, Armenian Catholicus, 91, 100

Grimaldi, Lucchetto, admiral, 323-4

Guelders, Count of, 25

Guerin of Montaigu, Grand Master of the Hospital, 133

Guienne, 21, 31, 41, 55

Guillem, see Figuera

Gur Khan, ruler of the Kara Khitai, 242-3

Index

Index

Ibn Khaldun, historian, 486
Ibn Khallikan, encyclopaedist, 486
Ibn al-Mashtub, Imad ad-Din Ahmed, 157
Ibn Sheddad, historian, 485
Ibn Wasil, historian, 485
Ibrahim, *see* al-Mansur
Iceland, 338
Ida of Lorraine, Countess of Boulogne, 379
Ignatius of Antioch, Jacobite Catholicus, 232
Imad ed-Din, Zengid prince, 79
Imad ed-Din, historian, 485
India, 294, 359, 433, 463
Indian Ocean, 248, 354, 359, 433
Indus, river, 160, 184, 243
Ingi II, King of Norway, 146
Innocent III, Pope, 94, 95 n., 100, 107–17, 128–9, 131, 133, 136–9, 142, 144–6, 163, 178, 207 n.
Innocent IV, Pope, 231, 256, 259, 279
Innocent V, Pope, 346
Iran, 160, 359, 361
Iraq, 326, 355, 359, 361, 398
Ireland, 145
Irene Angelina, Queen of Germany, 111
Irtysh, river, 244, 246
Isaac II, Angelus, Emperor, 4, 8, 11–14, 43, 74, 111–12, 115, 118–21, 124
Isaac Ducas Comnenus, Emperor of Cyprus, 4, 12, 43–6
Isabella I, Queen of Jerusalem, Queen of Cyprus, 30–2, 45, 51, 64–6, 82 n., 84, 93–5, 102 n., 103, 134, 181, 328
Isabella II, Queen of Jerusalem, *see* Yolanda
Isabella, Queen of Armenia, 164, 171–3, 230
Isabella of Ibelin, Queen of Cyprus, 330
Isabella of Ibelin, lady of Beirut, Queen of Cyprus, 329–30, 342–3, 393
Isabella of Hainault, Queen of France, 9, 34
Isabella of Cyprus, regent of Jerusalem, 206, 289
Ismail, as-Salih, Ayubite prince of Damascus, 210–11, 216, 218, 223, 228, 485
Ivan Asen, Prince of Bulgaria, 13
Izz ed-Din, Zengid prince, 79–80

Jabala 80, 86, 99, 102, 172, 207
Jacobites, 91, 232, 305, 326
Jaffa, 57–9, 62, 69–73, 76, 84, 93, 97–8, 103, 186–7, 190, 213, 220, 225, 277, 282, 324, 358; *see* Hugh, John, Walter

Jagatai, Mongol prince, 249, 251–2, 294, 299, 300, 309, 463
Jamal ad-Din Mohsen, eunuch, 265
James I, King of Aragon, 330–1, 332, 341
James II, King of Aragon, 409, 428
James Pantaleone, Patriarch of Jerusalem, *see* Urban IV
James, Archbishop of Capua, 175
James of Vitry, Bishop of Acre, 146–7, 161–2, 483, 489
James of Molay, Grand Master of the Temple, 434, 436, 438
James of Avesnes, 9, 25, 29, 55, 57
James of Helly, 461
James of Ibelin, 336
James Alaric of Perpignan, envoy, 332
James, *see* Vaseli, Vidal
Janghara, deputy governor of Alexandria, 445–6
al-Jawad, Ayubite prince, 211
Jaxartes, river, 243, 246, 247
al-Jazari, chronicler, 486
Jebail, 47, 92, 96, 98, 99 n., 197, 283, 288, 348, 361 n., 388–9, 405, 407; *see* Embriaco, Rainier
Jebe, Mongol general, 244–7
Jejer Undur, battle, 240
Jelal ad-Din, Khwarismian King, 160, 184, 186, 209–10, 224, 245, 249–50, 253
Jenghiz Khan, Great Khan, 163, 237–49, 299, 464
Jericho, 352
Jerusalem, city of, 3, 17–18, 21, 42, 53–4, 57–9, 61, 63–4, 67–9, 73, 76, 82, 97, 103, 139, 144–5, 158, 160–1, 166, 170, 184–5, 187–9, 193, 195, 215, 218–19, 222–5, 227, 229, 232, 237, 258, 263, 269, 276, 282, 297–8, 308, 332, 354, 357, 368, 375–8, 380, 385, 398–9, 401, 427, 439, 444, 446, 458, 470–1, 474, 476
Jews, 7–8, 353–4, 397, 473
Jezirek, 62, 68, 79–82, 209, 211, 224, 250, 253, 272, 295, 304
Joachim of Corazzo, Abbot of Fiore, 41–2
Joanna of England, Queen of Sicily, 35, 37–8, 40, 42–4, 59–60, 74
Johansdorf, *see* Albert
John V, Palaeologus, Emperor, 453–5
John VI, Cantacuzenus, Emperor, 453
John VIII, Palaeologus, Emperor, 465

Index

John I, King of Cyprus and Jerusalem, 394–5
John, King of England, 8, 63–4, 75, 109
John II, King of France, 442
John of Brienne, King of Jerusalem, Emperor-regent of Constantinople, marries Queen Maria, 132–3; regent for his daughter, 134; marries Armenian princess, 134, 138–71; and Fifth Crusade, 146, 151, 155, 159, 161–2; leaves army, 164–5; returns, 167; end of Fifth Crusade, 168–70; daughter's marriage to Frederick II, 173–5; later career, 176–7, 191
John XXI, Pope, 345
John XXII, Pope, 440, 447
John Camaterus, Patriarch of Constantinople, 127
John of Aleppo, Jacobite Catholicus, 232
John the Good, Count of Nevers, Duke of Burgundy, 456, 459–60, 467
John of Gaunt, Duke of Lancaster, 456
John, prince of Cyprus, 84
John Corvinus Hunyadi, voyevod of Transylvania, 465–6
John, Cardinal of Anagni, 7
John, Cardinal of Tusculum, 399
John Turco, Archbishop of Nicosia, 416
John, Jacobite Bishop of Melitene, 384
John of Villiers, Grand Master of the Hospital, 403, 418
John of Ronay, acting Grand Master of the Hospital, 258, 268
John, Count of Fontigny, 28
John, Count of Sarrebruck, 257
John I of Antioch, lord of Botrun, 226–7
John II of Antioch, lord of Botrun, 288
John of Cadzaud, admiral of Flanders, 460
John, lord of Caesarea, 198–200, 203, 205
John Ducas, Imperial ambassador, 13
John Embriaco, 338–9
John of Grailly, 406, 408–9, 414, 418–19
John of Ham, Constable of Tripoli, 226–7
John of Ibelin, lord of Arsuf, 205, 214, 230, 261, 275, 278, 281, 283, 285, 324, 329, 345
John of Ibelin, 'Old Lord of Beirut', appointed Constable, 84; enfeoffed with Beirut, 96; regent of Jerusalem, 104, 132–3; palace at Beirut, 147, 381–2; leader of baronial party, 180–3, 191–2; war with Imperialists, 194–203; death, 204; family, 205–6

John II of Ibelin, lord of Beirut, 230, 308–9, 317, 329, 342
John of Ibelin, lawyer, later Count of Jaffa, 199, 205, 262, 281–3, 317, 329, 343 n., 484
John of Monte Corvino, Papal envoy, 429
John of Montfort, lord of Tyre, 329, 333, 389, 393–4, 396
John of Nesle, Castellan of Bruges, 101, 102 n., 110
John of Valenciennes, ambassador, 276
John of Vienne, Grand Admiral of France, 457, 459–60
John-Srachimir, Prince of Vidin, 458
John Tristan, prince of France, 271, 292
John, Prester, 163, 240, 254
John, see Boucicaut, Dardel, Holland, Joinville, Parker, Pian del Carpine, Valin, Vaseli
Joigny, Count of, 212
Joinville, John of, biographer, 257, 271, 273–4, 484
Jordan, river, 158, 209, 213, 228, 276, 311–12, 352, 377
Jordan, architect, 377
Jordan of Saxony, Dominican, 421
Joseph of Chauncy, Hospitaller, 392
Josias, Archbishop of Tyre, 4–6, 83
Joveta, princess of Jerusalem, Abbess of Bethany, 383–4
Jubin, see Saint George
Judaea, 80, 368
Juji, Mongol prince, 240, 249, 251, 293
Julian Garnier, lord of Sidon, 308, 324, 342, 343 n.
Julian le Jaune, envoy, 396
Julian, see Cesarini
Justinian I, Emperor, 375
Juveni, Ata al-Mulk, 301

al-Kahf Assassin castle, 89
Kaikaûs I, Seldjuk Sultan, 139, 150
Kaikaûs II, Seldjuk Sultan, 347
Kaikhosrau II, Seldjuk Sultan, 211, 230, 253, 275, 305
Kaikhosrau III, Seldjuk Sultan, 347
Kaikobad, Seldjuk Sultan, 172–3, 209–10
Kalkha, river, battle, 247
Kaloyan Asen, King of Bulgaria, 127
Kama Bulgars, 247

Index

Index

Index

Index

Index

Index

Index

Index

Index

Index

Index

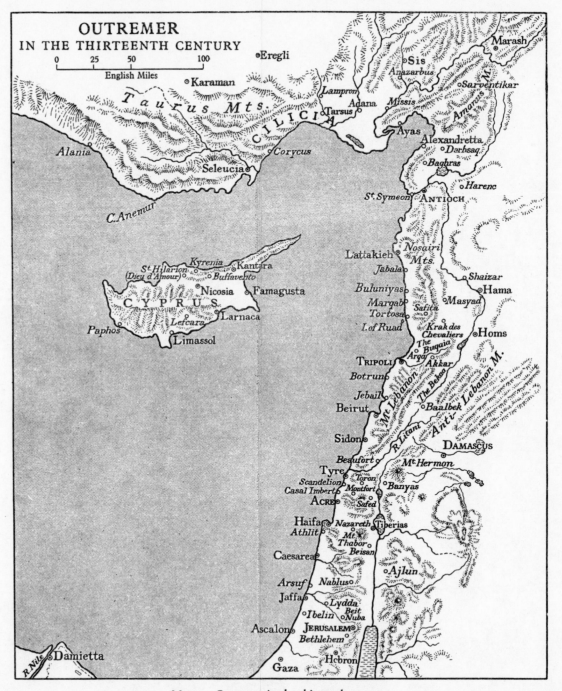

Map 5. Outremer in the thirteenth century.